A GUIDE TO HEREFORDSHIRE
Michael Raven

*Dedicated to
Lady, Foxy and Queenie,
died 27.9.1989*

A GUIDE TO
HEREFORDSHIRE

MICHAEL RAVEN

PUBLISHED BY
MICHAEL RAVEN
1996

CREDITS

Published by
Michael Raven.
First Edition Autumn 1996.
Copyright © Michael Raven 1996.
All rights reserved.
Transcription and typesetting Eve Raven.
Layout and Microsoft Word formatting M.Raven.
Printed and bound in Great Britain
by Halstan of Amersham, Buckinghamshire.
Publisher's address: Michael Raven,
Yew Tree Cottage, Jug Bank, Ashley,
Market Drayton, Shropshire,
TF9 4NJ
Telephone: 01630 672304

*Front cover photograph: King Richard I, the Lion Heart (1115-1199),
from a stained glass window at Dinmore Manor.
M.Raven 1996*

BIOGRAPHICAL NOTE

Michael Raven was born in Cardiff of Lancastrian parents in 1938 and was educated at Towyn Grammar School and Keele University where he studied geology and political philosophy. He completed his National Service with the Cheshire Regiment in Malaya and then did a variety of jobs before going to Spain to learn flamenco. He has always had a keen interest in sport: in 1956 he was the Midlands Decathlon Champion and in the army was a Marksman First Class. For the last 30 years he has earned his living as a classical guitarist, composer and researcher of folk studies. Michael Raven has over 40 albums of recorded music and more than 80 books to his credit. This book is his fourth topographical work. The others are: *Staffordshire and the Black Country, Black Country Towns and Villages*, and *A Shropshire Gazetteer*. Of the latter the *Shropshire Alternative* said "It must be the definitive book on Shropshire", and *Photographers' Britain* proclaimed it "uniquely detailed and splendidly opinionated."

MUSICAL COMPANIONS

Michael Raven has produced two companions to this book, an 80 minute C.D. recording, *Songs and Dances of Herefordshire,* and its sister music book, *The Ross Workhouse Songbook*. "Natural singing and subtly deployed guitar mastery. There's not a trace of studio artifice anywhere...fascinating variants of English folksongs." Nick Beale, *Folk Roots.* The CD (£10.00) and the book (£7.50) are available direct from the publisher.

A FEW STATISTICS AND AN ACKNOWLEDGEMENT

This book contains 227,022 words and 185 illustrations. It took one man and two dogs 13 months (fulltime) to compile with 4 months secretarial assistance, such as typing and proof reading. The final copy was the 9th draft. The number of insertions, and alterations was horrendous but my wife, Eve, battled manfully and without complaint, despite not being in the best of health at the time.

FOREWORD

THERE can be few counties in England that have such a uniformity of general countenance yet such a variety of local detail. It is a gentle, friendly, contented land and its people still have their feet planted firmly in the soil. The wealth of Herefordshire is its pastures grazed by cattle and sheep, its hopyards and orchards, its fields of fodder and its equable climate. The inhabitants are an integral part of this felicitous scene and have a disposition to friendliness that is above the normal; they are half Welsh and half English but have learned to live with the sins of sirehood and they are a notably tolerant breed.

It is impossible to write a book such as this and hope to please everyone. It has to be written from a personal point of view whilst trying to avoid the minefield of self-indulgence. I have no doubt that I have missed much of importance and yet given space to what others may think trivial. At times the writing is perfunctory for there is often a mass of information to be got through as quickly and succinctly as possible.

One theme that recurs plentifully is my passionate dislike of killing animals for pleasure. I make no apology for this. One of the crosses I had to bear whilst writing this book was having to talk to fox hunters and pheasant shooters. I had to take my father's advice and hold candles to devils, but candles shed a flickering light and fail to reach dark corners.

And what of the little personal pleasures given by a misty landscape in the evening light, the turn of phrase of a farmer born and bred, and the cohorts of crows singing in a summer's midnight? There are too few of these and too many listings of things ecclesiastical, too many mansions mentioned in despatches. But these bald, and sometimes boring, facts are to a degree timeless; the others are ephemeral, the stuff of poetry rather than topographical tomes. Similarly, a scene described in Spring as being a heavenly place full of lambs, blossoms and daffodils means nothing to the man who visits in December when it is a cheerless, muddy desert.

As I said at the beginning, to write a book of this kind is an almost impossible task; but at least we went down fighting.

Michael Raven
Ashley, Summer 1996

INDEX TO THE ILLUSTRATIONS
The following abbreviations are used:
PJM Peter J.Manders
HCL Hereford County Library,
 courtesy of Robin Hall
HCM Hereford City Museum,
 courtesy of Anne Sandford
HT Hereford Times
BD Bromyard and District Local
 History Society
NMR National Monuments Record
NLW National Library of Wales
MR Michael Raven
The author has a debt of gratitude to all those whose pictures he has used and which have so enriched this book.

- 11 Bodenham, the Cress Well, J.Sant
  Hops, drawing, BD
  Abbeydore, St. Mary's, PJM
- 15 *Hell in Herefordshire*, poem
- 19 Bosbury village, PJM
  Brampton Bryan, PJM
- 23 Brinsop Court, Cornelius /Parker
  Berrington Hall, R.Winston
- 27 Bronsil Castle, plan, M.Salter
  Brockhampton by Ross, PJM
  Bredwardine church, PJM
  Reverend Francis Kivert, HCL
- 31 Avenbury, hopyard, HCM
  Lady Brilliana, Anon.
  Brockhampton by Bromyard, PJM
  Bridge Sollars, HT
- 35 Colwall, British Camp, Anon.
  Malvern Hills, B. Meadows
- 39 Cloddock, PJM
  Castle Frome, font, NMR
  Downton Castle, Country Life
- 43 Colwall, old village, PJM
  Credenhill, cottage, PJM
- 47 Croft, oak grove, MR
  Croft, church, MR
  Madley, hop-picker, BD
  Clehongar, B.Meadows
- 49 Dorstone, Arthur's Stone, Anon.
  King Arthur's Cave, arrowhead
  Eastnor Castle, Aerofilm
  Eardisley, font, Anon.
- 51 Dilwyn, the village, PJM
  Dinedor Hill over the Wye, PJM
- 53 Eardisland, with swan, PJM
  Bromyard church, PJM
- 57 Eastnor, Sunnyside Cottage, PJM
  Hampton Bishop, PJM
- 61 Fownhope hovels, HCL
  Fownhope, R.Wye, R.Winston
  Fawley, milking a cow, HCM
- 65 Goodrich Castle, Aerofilm
  Goodrich over the Wye, P.Baker
  Longtown Castle, plan, M.Salter
  13th century ladies, Anon.
- 69 Hereford, Eign Street in snow, HCM
  Hereford, Nell Gwynne, HT
  Hereford, *King George V*, Bulmer plc
- 73 Hereford, John Kemble's hand, HCM
  Hereford, Vicars Choral, HT
  Hereford, over the Wye, PJM
- 77 Hereford Races, HT
  Hereford, Church Lane, R.Milne
  Hereford, Gilbert Harding, HT
  Hereford, Jack Sharp, HT
  Hereford, Brian Hatton, HCM
  Hereford, S.A.S. on the Wye, HT
- 81 Holme Lacy, drawing room, HCL
  Tenth Earl of Chesterfield, HT
  Holme Lacy House, A.F.Kirsting
- 85 Kenchester, site of, Anon.
  Kenchester, pavement. Anon.
- 89 Kilpeck, village, Aerophoto
  Olchon Court, PJM
- 93 Kilpeck, south door, PJM
- 97 Leintwardine, by the bridge, PJM
  Ledbury, Back Street, HCM
  Kinnersley Castle, interior, NMR
- 101 Ledbury, St. Katherine's Hosp. PJM
- 105 Leominster, the Grange, PJM
  Leominster Priory, chalice, NMR
  Leominster, Chequers Inn, PJM
- 109 *Why oh Wye?* poem, MR
- 113 Brinsop Court, MR
  Mordiford, Sufton and the Lugg, MR
  Shucknall, over Frome valley, MR
- 114 Hoarwithy, St. Catherine's, MR
  Bircher Common, MR
  Woolhope Dome, MR
  Whitchurch, Wye valley, MR
  Bredwardine Bridge, Anon.
- 115 Eyton Common, travellers, MR
  Abbeydore, the Grey Valley,MR
  Hope-u-Dinmor, Wigwood, MR
- 116 Bromyard Folk Festival, five pictures of dancers and musicians, 1996, MR
- 117 Risbury, landscape, MR
  Pencombe, landscape, MR
  Sutton St. Nicholas, R. Lugg, MR
- 118 Leominster, Church Lane, MR
  Hereford Cathedral grotesques
  Eastnor Castle, intereior, E. Bathurst
- 119 Kinnersley Castle, MR
  Eastnor Castle, red deer, Anon.
  Ganarew, Sellarsbrooke House, MR
  Norton Canon, Garnon's Hill, MR
- 120 Bodenham, Mr. H. Downes, MR
  Hereford, S.A.S. Camp, MR
  Dinmore Manor, Richard I, MR
  Ford, Cook's Folly, Whiston, MR
- 121 Colwall, Old Rectory, M.R.
  Colwall, church and Alehouse, M.R.
  Fred Jordan, traditional singer, M.R.
  Cockyard, dogs and van, M.R.
- 128 Fownhope, tympanum, F. Hornak
  Peterchurch, St. Peter's, NMR
  Llanveynoe, funeral monuments
  Harold Godwinson, Anon.
- 132 Lugwardine, hay-making, HCM
  Hereford man, HCM
  Mowing clover, HCM
- 136 Madley church, PJM
  Mathon in landscape, M.Wright
  Much Marcle, Walter de Helyon
- 140 Moccas, deer park in Winter, PJM
  Moreton on Lugg, tree house, HT
- 144 Much Marcle, Kyrle effigies, Anon.
  Mansell Lacy, Old Post Office, PJM
  Mansell Lacy, cottages, PJM
  Mordiford, B.Meadows
- 148 Owain Glyndwr's Great Seal, NLW
  Henry IV, National Portait Gallery
  Ode to Owain Glyndwr, poem, MR
- 152 *Raven's Nest*, poem,MR
- 156 Pembridge, houses,PJM
  Pembridge, New Inn, PJM
  Putley, Dave Jones, A. Jones
- 160 Hay, Hereford cattle, PJM
  Herfordshire, ploughing match, HT
- 164 *Ross Workhouse*, poem, MR
- 167 *Lilac Tree*, poem, MR
  News at One, poem, MR
  Border Lord, poem, MR
  Robin Hood, poem, MR
- 172 Ross on Wye, PJM
  Ross, Monmouth road, Hammonds
  Ross, Harry Diamond, HT
  Ross, Noele Gordon, HT
  Ross, Dennis Potter, HT
- 176 Stoke Saint Edith, steam engine, BD
  Ralph Vaughan Williams, HT
  Tupsley, Whitehouse Farm, M.Reece
  Rowlestone, capital, R.Winstone
- 180 Stretton Grandison, PJM
  Whitney on Wye, bridge, S.Boulton
  Elzabeth Barrett Browning, HT
- 184 Tyberton church, PJM
  Treago Castle, plan, M.Salter
  Whitchurch, chain ferry, S.Boulton
  Whitchurch, Saint Dubricius, PJM
- 188 Druids in an oak grove, Anon.
  Goodrich, the Queen's Stone, Anon.
- 192 Bromyard area, hop-picking, BD
- 196 Madley, Earth Satellite dish, Anon.
  Llanveynoe, Olchon Beaker, Anon.
  Hereford bull, Anon,
  Wigmore Castle, S,Buck
- 200 Pembridge Castle, K.Freeman
  General Sir Peter de Billiere, HT
  Vowchurch, bridge and church, PJM
- 204 Roman Fort at Buckton, W.Baker
  Plan of fort, S.C.Stanford
  Drawing of gatehouse, S.C.Stanford
- 208 Weobley, Ella Mary Leather, HT
  Weobley, Broad Street, T.Haywood
  Weobley, John Birch, NMR
  Weobley, Unicorn Inn, PJM
  Wormbridge, landscape, J.Topham
- 212 *Lines on Gatley Park*, poem, MR
- 216 Wigmore Abbey, Adforton, PJM
  Wigmore, townscape, MR
- 220 Pembridge church, F.Crossley
  'Lady' and a bullock, MR
  Stoke Edith, pensioners at, HCM
  Cloddock Mill, Sceerboom Coll'n.
  Whitchurch, Wye Rapids Hotel
- 224 Brierley Court, S.Demaus
  Leominster, Broadward, S.Demaus
  Leominster, kingfisher, S.Demaus
  Leominster, Eaton Bridge, S.Demaus
- 230 Hereford, in early 19th century, HCM
  Trow on the River Wye, HCM
  Hereford, Saint Peter's Square, Anon.
- 239 Plan of Hereford, D.Whitehouse
  Hereford, Bye Street Gate, HCM
- 240 *Seven Poems,* M.R.

CONTENTS

The Gazetteer of Places 8

Appendices:
The Lower Lugg Valley 225
Lost Villages 227
Gloucester to Hereford Canal 228
Hereford Cattle 228
Topography and Geology 228
The English Oak 228
Some Social Facilities 229
Deer Parks 229
A Note on Cider 229
Hunting in Herefordshire 231
A Note on Common Land 232
An Affair of Dishonour 231
Sir Thomas Clanvowe 232
Owain Glyndwr's Last Days 232
Roy Palmer, a Brief Biography 232
Border Lords 234
Hereford, a River Port 235
Govilon to Hereford Tramway 235
Stagecoaches and Railways 235
Capel-y-ffin 235
Anglo-Saxon Remains 238
Bits and Bobs 238
Plan of Hereford City 239
Seven Poems 240

Index to the Text 241
Map of Herefordshire 270

ABBEYDORE *9.5m SW of Hereford*
The name means 'abbey by the River Dore'. The settlement stands at the southern end of the Golden Valley and is most easily approached off the Hereford to Abergavenny road at Pontrilas. It is a small village with very few facilities. The former school is now the parish hall, the Old Vicarage is now occupied by an antique furniture restorer, and the grey brick Workhouse has been converted to dwellings. Over the river is the Court with pretty waterside gardens where tea can be partaken. A little to the south is the Neville Arms. The present building is of 1907 but it stands on the site of a much older inn. Lunch is served here every day and there is a camping and caravanning site in the grounds. Grange Farm, 1.1/4m ENE of the village, is a good 16th century, timber-framed farmhouse with prestigious close-set uprights.

People come to the Golden Valley for its tranquil natural beauty but there is no doubt that the Abbey is an attraction in its own right. It was founded in 1147 for Cistercian monks from Morimund in France. The red sandstone building we see today was probably constructed between about 1175 and 1220; there are no definite records. After the Dissolution of the Monasteries in the 1530s the building fell into disrepair. In 1633 Lord Scudamore restored what could be saved, added the tower and so made the parish church we see today. The nave of the present church was the crossing and transepts of the old abbey church (the short spar of a cross). It has cathedral-like proportions with tall walls and tall lancet windows, vaulted roofs, soaring columns and stiff-leaf capitals. Scudamore employed the renowned John Abel, the 'King's Carpenter', to design the acclaimed oak chancel screen and to construct the roof which he decorated with monsters and the heads of men. The 12ft long mediaeval stone altar, complete with consecration crosses, was rescued from a nearby farmyard and is now displayed with a collection of fine carved stones safely stored in the ambulatory and transepts. The monastic buildings, the sacristy, vestibule, chapter house, dormitory, reredorter and infirmary have all but disappeared. The pulpit and pews are Jacobean; there are some 16th and 17th century stained glass fragments and the complete east window of Scudamore's restoration; in the chancel are 13th century tiles, both plain and with heraldic designs; and there are two 13th century effigies of cross-legged knights. The bells of the church are said to chime: "Be good to the poor, Say the bells of Abbeydore". In 1995 the Abbeydore Music Festival was revived after a gap of 30 years. It takes place at the end of June and concerts are held at the Cistercian church, the only one used as a parish church in the whole of Britain.

In 1901 and 1909 sections of a Roman road were discovered under the station of the now disused railway. It has been traced to Bacton, 1.1/4m NNW, and in three short sections to Longtown. The road is 12.1/2ft wide, is constructed of limestone nodules on red marl, and has an unusual design having a flat side and a cambered side. Normally the camber is central. It continued south across the River Wye to King's Caple. (See King's Caple.) At Dunseal Farm on the northern fringe of the hamlet of Kerry's Gate, 2m NNE of Abbeydore, there is a Neolithic/Early Bronze-Age Barrow (SO 391 338) about 6.1/2ft high and oval-shaped, 88ft by 46ft, that does not seem to have been opened. It lies just south of Dunseal Wood and there are good views down the Lower Golden Valley. Would it be too much to ask the archaeologists to leave this religious monument alone and let the occupants rest in peace? At Camp Wood and Minn's Close, 1m NE of Abbeydore, there are earthworks (SO 388 317) on a hillside. A roughly rectangular enclosure with slight, largely natural ramparts might be connected to other natural formations, 650 yards SW, where a hill with a sunken top and steep sides is only approachable by a natural, narrow causeway from the Camp Wood earthworks.

ACONBURY *4m S of Hereford*
The name is Anglo-Saxon and means 'the fort occupied by squirrels'. In Anglo-Saxon place names 'fort' almost always refers to an Iron-Age structure, not one of their own defensive positions. Aconbury Camp is an early Iron-Age hill fort that stands beside the Hereford to Ross road, the A49, and a good 1/2m W of the hamlet of Aconbury. It has a single rampart and outer ditch that follows the contour of the hill and encloses about 17.1/2 acres on the summit and north slope. There are two original entrances at the south-east and south-west corners; the others are probably modern. Trial excavations revealed Iron-Age B and 4th century Romano-British pottery. The fort was occupied during the Civil War and was probably modified at that time. Today it is heavily wooded. In 1820 an account of Twelfth Night ceremonies in Herefordshire in the *Gentleman's Magazine* mentions that 13 fires were lit on Aconbury Hill Camp.

The hamlet is quite charming. We approached from the west and stopped to picnic at King Pitts Wood. Pheasants were everywhere and it was very quiet. The road climbs up to an isolated old stone and half-timber barn. About 300 yards SSE of this, on the other side of the road, is Saint Anne's Well at SO 511 333. The spring emerges into a semi-circular mediaeval stone basin, walled at the back and with a lintel above. The water used to flow to Saint Anne's Pool beside the road and from there to the fish ponds of the priory that stood by the church at Aconbury. The waters of the well were said to cure many ills, especially troubles of the eye. According to local belief the water bubbles and emits a blue smoke at midnight on Twelfth Night. The first bucketful drawn on the 13th day was considered to have greatly enhanced healing qualities. It was bottled and used sparingly for the next 12 months. Above Saint. Anne's Well, at the top of the field in a scrubby piece of woodland, is the Lady Well, sometimes called Saint. Catherine's, at SO 511 332. This holy well is haunted by a young woman who killed her lover here because she suspected him of being unfaithful. She subsequently found that he had proved true and she died of a broken heart.

The hamlet of Aconbury lies 1/4m W of the wells on a kink in the road. The spire of the church just manages to peep over the bland modern sheds of Aconbury Court and the lane runs through the farmyard. Despite this welcome it is a charming little place - stone cottage, stone church, black and white cows, an overgrown graveyard and a pair of modern semi-detached houses - a mediaeval configuration. The church of Saint John the Baptist was originally part of a house of the Sisters of the Order of Saint John of Jerusalem, founded before 1237 by Margery de Lacy and soon after transferred to Canonesses of the Augustinian Order. It was dissolved in 1539. The church is small and always has been, just a 13th century nave and chancel in one with a later bell-turret. The east window is of the typical Herefordshire 'three lancet lights under one arch' type. The church was connected to the nunnery buildings on the south side. The blocked doorways led to the cloister; the little square-headed window probably belonged to a watching chamber. The timber porch is probably 15th century and the single bell is 14th century. The wall paintings of flowers are of the restoration by Sir G.G. Scott in 1863. There are some bits of dark 13th century glass in a north window; a coffin lid with an incised cross, shields and foliage of about 1300; and in the church is a tomb said to be that of Roger de Clifford. There is a legend that the church was haunted by a monk, the spirit of a man buried beneath the Clifford tomb, and that the spirit was laid by being prayed into a bottle and then buried in the wall of the church so that it was 'neither within nor without', and it has been content ever since. So said a former parish clerk.

"A lease dated 24th March 22 Henry VIII, was granted by Thomas Gebons of Hereford, mercer, to Isabella Gardiner, prioress, and to the convent of Aconbury, of a stable situate in the street called Wroughthall, for ninety-nine years under an annual rent of a red rose to be delivered, if lawfully demanded, on the feast of Saint John the Baptist." (Duncombe, *History of Herefordshire*.)

Today the church is redundant but rare herbs such as danewort and elecampane, which were brought here from Europe for the priory garden, have escaped and are now found growing wild hereabouts.

ACTON BEAUCHAMP   *3m SE of Bromyard*
At the time of Domesday Book it was in Worcestershire and was held by the Bishop of Bayeux but by the 12th century it had passed to the Beauchamp family. Acton means 'place by the oak trees'. The church stands alone near a farm and a large orchard. There is no settlement as such; the dwellings and farms are scattered in the hills and along the lanes in this attractive Frome Valley country. It is a hop growing area, though their cultivation is in decline. In 1807 there were 160 acres of hopyards in the parish; in 1985 there were 106, and this is a lot. After Bishop's Frome, with 197 acres, it is the highest acreage in Herefordshire.

The church of Saint Giles has a squat tower with re-set, Late Norman lancets and a pyramid roof, but the chancel and nave were rebuilt in 1819 to a Classical Georgian design with large, airy arched windows. The Late Norman south doorway arch with carved capitals has been retained, but the treasure of Acton is a piece of a 9th century Anglo-Saxon cross-shaft. It has leafy scrolls with a bird, a lion and another creature, all finely wrought, though it was damaged when made to fit as a lintel for the tower doorway. Inside there is a monument tablet to Henry Brace, died 1773, and other members of his family.

A probable Roman road runs from Kenchester to Worcester. It has been traced from Ullingswick eastwards to a point 1m N of Bishop's Frome and then follows the modern road to Acton Beauchamp for about 1/2m. A definite agger (road foundation) with a hard surface about 15ft in width has been located in this area.

Acton Court stands at the crossroads hamlet of Acton Green, 1m ESE of the church, on the Bromyard to Stoney Cross road, the B4220. Acton Mill Farm is 2m E of the church on the road to Suckley. Between Acton Green and Acton Mill a track leads south off the road to Redmarley Farm, at SO 708 500. Near the farm is Hunger Hollow and in it is a spring called Roaring Water. It only flows intermittently and as the water expels the air from underground cavities it makes a roaring sound. Its appearance is said to presage a death or a disaster. Also, at Redmarley Farm, there used to be a Holy Thorn, a cutting from the Glastonbury Thorn, but in the early 19th century it was cut down by the farmer because he was annoyed by the large number of people who came to see it "for it was much venerated by the peasantry of these parts". Shortly after this act of vandalism he broke his arm, then his leg, and finally part of the farm burned down.

In the mid-19th century the Reverend William Copeland, vicar of Acton Beauchamp, enlisted the help of 11 other parsons to lay the troublesome spirit of the first wife of the blacksmith of Acton Cross. They each had a candle and read holy scriptures. First the spirit grew large and snuffed out all the candles except for one, then it grew smaller and smaller until the parsons pushed her into a matchbox and threw it into Amstell Pond. Even today each diocese of the Anglican church has a priest who specialises in exorcisms.

ADFORTON   7m WSW of Ludlow
The name is from the Anglo-Saxon and means 'the settlement of Ealdfrip's people'. At the time of Domesday Book it was one of the manors held by Ralph de Mortimer but lay in Shropshire. Adforton lies on the A4110 between Leintwardine and Wigmore. It is a pretty, stone-built village on the western edge of the Vale of Wigmore.

The small church of Saint Andrew was built by J.P. Seddon in 1875. It has nave, chancel, apse, bellcote and most of the windows have pointed-trefoiled lights. The font is also by Seddon.

Brick House, across the road from the church, has two 13th century carved shafts about 5ft tall, one each side of a fireplace. They undoubtedly came from Wigmore Abbey, which was extensively 'quarried' for domestic building stone by the villagers. Fairfield, about 250 yards WNW of the church, has parts of its 14th century roof in situ.

Wigmore Abbey, 600 yards ENE of the church, shelters beneath a low rise with the Wigmore Rolls to the west and the Downton Hills to the east. It was was founded in 1179 by Hugh Mortimer for Augustinian Canons of Saint Victor of Paris. It was here that many of the great Mortimer family were buried, but their tombs are now lost, gone along with most of their monastery. It was destroyed by the Welsh, rebuilt and then destroyed again by Henry VIII during the Dissolution of the Monasteries. The largest upstanding building is the Abbot's Lodging of the 14th and 15th centuries - the roof trusses and the greystone gateway are 14th century. Of the church, the gable wall and lower parts of the west wall of the south transept are late 12th century; the east parts were remodelled in the late 14th century.

The remains of Wigmore Abbey are now incorporated into Wigmore Grange, a substantial complex of farm buildings. We visited on a misty, muddy-laned Winter's day, so much more evocative, so much more mysterious and redolent of times past than the sun of Summer. This is no dead place, no tarted-up tourist trap; it is alive with sheep, calves, chickens and border collies living contentedly, cared for by human servants. Beside the road is a 14th century stone building with a small doorway, and opposite is the quarry from which the Abbey stone was hewn.

Peytoe, just to the NE of Wigmore Abbey, is a hamlet caught in a similar time warp. Seen from the road the black and white Hall is not beautiful, with its ungainly square framing rising to two and a half storeys; even the duck pond is somewhat woebegone. The house has 16th and 17th century timbers and a barn that incorporates ashlar and worked 12th and 13th century stones brought here from the abbey. It stands just off a major Roman road. This is the southern section of Watling Street that runs from Wroxeter to Caerleon and was constructed about 1179 by Governor Frontinus. For the rest, all there is at Peytoe are a few yew trees, a modern bungalow and a couple of cottages. But stand at the crossroads and listen to the tramp of the legions and the chants of monks at prayer, and wonder what happened to the lavish tombs and dusty bones of the mighty Mortimers and their millions.

Brandon Camp lies 1m N of Adforton church. It is an Iron-Age hill fort covering about 3/4 acre with a pear-shaped enclosure and three entrances. A Roman site of occupation, 3/4m NNW of the church, near Brandon Villa, has been discovered by aerial photography at SO 397 723. In the 17th century an Early Bronze Age bowl-barrow with an urn cremation was excavated at Brandon. Brandon means 'hill clad with broom'.

ALLENSMORE *3.5m SW of Hereford*
In the 13th century Alan de Plontenet of Kilpeck Castle reclaimed marshland south of Haywood Forest. Subsequently, a very large squatter community developed which spread from Allensmore and Goose Pool westwards through the commons of Cobhall, Winnal, Mawfield, and Webtree to Hungerstone. The people were exceeding poor. Their houses were primitive, small and crammed in on the no-man's land verges of the winding lanes. They grew vegetables and kept a few chickens and a pig if they were lucky. They spun flax and hemp, gleaned fields, begged and stole. But they had their pride and their resentfulness burst on to the national scene in the early 17th century when the 'Herefordshire Commotion' was reported countrywide on a broadsheet printed in London. "In May 1605 Alice Wellington, a Catholic, died excommunicate from the Church of England, and was refused burial in the churchyard by the vicar, Richard Heyns. He was woken at dawn the next morning by a funeral procession of around 50 people, and by the time he could reach the churchyard Alice had been laid to rest there. Mr. Heyns' outrage was met with rude responses and threats to his person, so he rushed off to report the scandal to the Bishop. As Allensmore had an absentee Catholic landlord and, like much of south-west Herefordshire, was then a staunchly Catholic area, the Bishop could not have been too surprised. But a stern response was necessary, and the High Constable of Webtree Hundred came that same day with warrants and a posse. They attempted to arrest three ringleaders, who responded so violently that the Constable ended up with one prisoner and several damaged officers. He then lost his solitary captive on the way back to Hereford when he encountered nearly 50 men armed to the teeth with assorted weapons. The Constable sensibly decided to hand back the prisoner. But for the next six weeks there were raids and arrests involving gentry, farmers and villagers over an ever wider area. These punitive expeditions were countered by resistance, attempted ambushes, or empty homes whose occupants had fled to the safety of Wales. By August however the rebels found themselves leaderless and priestless, and the 'Commotion' subsided as swiftly as it had begun." (*Herefordshire Village Book*, 1989.)

The church of Saint Andrew watched with disdain as its vicar and his parishioners squabbled. and it might have reminded the Reverend Heyns that almost every stone in the church's body had been laid by Roman Catholic hands. The doorway is 12th century Late Norman; the 'Y' traceried windows are 13th century; the Decorated chancel east window, the Decorated gabled south window and the timber single-frame roofs are 14th century; the stumpy Perpendicular tower is 15th century; the pulpit is Jacobean; the font is stiff-leaf Victorian; and the stained glass in the tracery of the east window is mediaeval and is thought to have come from Hereford Cathedral. Outside there are the steps, base and broken shaft of a mediaeval preaching cross and inside there is a late 14th century memorial to Sir Andrew Herl and his wife; a tablet to Richard Grumar, died 1702(?); and several painted slate murals of the late 18th century.

The school opened in 1870 but closed in 1957 and is now the village hall. Between them Allensmore and its outlying townships have virtually no other facilities but depend on a flourishing service station-cum-general store-cum-post office at the Tram Inn (p.235) crossroads on the A465(T). Employment is related to the earth, though this is still wet and drainage is still a problem because of a clay barrier below the topsoil. There is a stud farm, the Sun Valley poultry-feed grain mill, two plant nurseries and general farms, though many of the inhabitants commute to office jobs in Hereford. Amongst the humble homes of the squatters are some notable farmhouses. Wood Street, 200 yards NE of the church, is an old timber-framed house which has been eclipsed by an early 18th century, five-bay, brick range with a hipped roof. Cobhall, 1m W of the church, is an early 17th century, timber-framed house with good panelling and a carved overmantel inside. Nearby is Little Cobhall which has a 15th century hall. Mawfield Farm, 1m NW of the church, has a 15th century roof with braces supporting collar beams and wind braces.

ALMELEY *4m SE of Kington*
It lies 400ft above sea level near the borders of Wales. The name is from the Old English elmleah, 'elm wood'. In 1086 it was held by Roger de Lacy from the church of Saint Guthlac in Hereford. It is a nucleated settlement with a goodly number of timber-framed houses and resides happily away from main roads. The church, the manor house and the castle mound make a handsome group. There is a school, a general store, a post office, a recreation hall and the Bell Inn. Within the 3,550 acres of the parish there are pastures and orchards and bees are kept. On the road to Eardisley can be seen the track of the now disused railway that ran from Lyonshall to Almeley and on to Witney-on-Wye.

The church of Saint Mary has a short Norman tower of about 1200 and the rest is of about 1300. The painted ceiling panels with Tudor roses are early 16th century. The manor, or Court House (manors are called courts in Herefordshire), is a handsome timber-framed building with brick infill and a two-storey, jettied porch with a gable. The parlour has prestigious close-set framing. The earthworks of the Norman castle stand adjacent to the church. It has a circular mound, about 35ft in diameter and 20ft high from the bottom of the ditch, and a four-sided bailey enclosure. The Old Castle Twt (Toot) is slightly smaller and stands nearly 1/2m to the NW on the end of a spur. Castle Frome, a half-timbered dwelling 1/2m S of the church, has ancient cruck trusses.

At Almeley Wootton, 3/4m N of Almeley, there is a general stores, a common with dwellings beside, some black and white cottages on the fringes and big arable fields. In 1669 Roger Pritchard bought Summer House Farm. He was a Quaker and at Almeley Wootton, 1/2m N, he built a Friends' Meeting House. It is a simple, well-kept, timber-framed building of one storey with a half-hipped roof. Nieuport House lies 1m NW of the church.

Above left: Bodenham, the Cross Well, c. 1900.
Above right: hops and a vine leaf
Below: Abbeydore, the Cistercian parish church of Saint Mary.

The estate was broken up by 1919 and some of the land is now owned by the County Council and has been split to make tenanted smallholdings. The big house itself became a sanatorium but this closed in 1951. Two years later it became a home for Latvian refugees, and is so today.

Many tales are told hereabouts of Jenkins, a local wizard. One relates to a visit he paid to the Buck Inn at Woonton. He thought he was being overcharged so he put his money down but drew a circle of chalk around it. The landlady reached to pick it up but was taken by a spirit and could only run around the table crying "Four pence to eat, four pence to drink, eight pence in all." Others tried to pick up the money but suffered likewise. As Jenkins left this comical scene of confusion he told an inn servant to pick up the money with a pair of tongs. He did so and normality resumed.

A local saying is: "There will be a witch at Almeley as long as water runs." An old woodman in the village used to make bowls of ivywood. If these were used to feed a child with whooping cough a cure was effected. After a death the church 'passing bell' was tolled 12 times for a man and 13 times for a woman. A delightful local expression for mole hills is 'untytumps'

Almeley's most famous son is Sir John Oldcastle. He was the model for Shakespeare's Sir John Falstaff (King Henry IV part I). As a soldier he took part in the suppression of the Welsh and was made Sheriff of Herefordshire in 1406. However, he was a Lollard, a follower of John de Wycliffe (1330-84) and his Protestant faith. He was found guilty of heresy and in 1417 was hanged in chains and burned as he was hanging.

At Great Oak is the Great Oak Cider company. They produce cider from fruit grown in old orchards near the farm and sell direct to the public.

Woonton, 1.1/4m ENE of Almeley, is known for the tall topiary hedge topped by an aeroplane that dwarfs the cottage of Mr. Miffin, on the A4112 near the Red Lion. The village has a nucleus dominated by the big, modern sheds of Morgan Brothers, agricultural engineers. The old, brick blacksmith's shop where the business began stands opposite. The post office has closed and the Friends' Meeting House of 1888 - red brick with yellow brick dressings - is now a dwelling. The Church of England maintains a presence with a Mission House.

Logaston lies 1/2m SSW of Woonton. There is a charming little village green, some black and white cottages and a red brick livestock farm run by a cheerful Benny Hill look-alike whose premises are, shall we say, in a state of dishevelment. Just to the south-west, down a dead-end lane that leads to the old common area of Little Logaston, is the white painted brick cottage of Alan Johnson who publishes numbers of local books under the Logaston Press imprint. He has a smallholding with a few sheep and pigs, a cat and a cottage garden with a working well. Somewhat intense he has the easy charm of someone who can say 'no' whilst making it sound like 'yes', is on the lanky side, and has the hooded eyes of a gunfighter. Mr. Johnson came up from the south-east and published his first book in 1985.

He now produces three or four new books each year and has some 20 titles in his current catalogue. These include *Owain Glyn Dwr* by the late Geoffrey Hodges, *Walks and More* by Andrew Johnson himself, *Prehistoric Sites of Herefordshire* by George Nash and George Children, *The Folklore of Hereford and Worcester* by Roy Palmer, the rather hypothetical *Arthurian Links with Herefordshire* by Mary Andere, *The Castles of Herefordshire* by Ron Shoesmith, and the somewhat grisly *A View from Hereford's Past* by Richard Stone and Nic Appleton-Fox.

The latter is an interim report on the archaeological investigation carried out prior to the construction of the new Mappa Mundi building in the graveyard of Hereford Cathedral. If you enjoy a good mediaeval skeleton, this is the book for you. The authors, by the way, now have their own private company called Marches Archaeology which currently operates from Cotterell Street, Hereford. At the time of writing they are involved with 'the 'making safe' of the mediaeval ruins of Wigmore Castle on behalf of English Heritage.

Newchurch, 1/2m SSE of Logaston, is a hamlet on a strange right-angled kink in the lane. Here there is a substantial stone and brick farmhouse with twin hop kilns and stone and weather-boarded barns, trees in the fields, a battery chicken shed, a bungalow, a house and an orchard with sheep.

In the Alemeley area a highly polished Neolithic 'prestige' axe has been found. It was made of stone from Cumbria, though that could have been brought here as an erratic by an ice sheet.

AMBERLEY *5.5m NNE of Hereford*

The name is not understood. At the time of Domesday it was a small manor held by Ansfrid de Cormeilles who had been given it by William son of Osbern (died 1071). He was a palatine earl who acted on behalf of King William on the Herefordshire-Welsh border and who built the castles of Clifford, Wigmore, Chepstow and Monmouth and who established the great Marcher lords - the de Lacys, Cliffords and Mortimers - on their lands. Amberley today is not really a settlement; it is the Court and its chapel set in the country by themselves, 2m ENE of Morden.

Amberley Court is a 14th century hall house with solar and buttery wings. (A buttery was a room used to store butts, kegs of wine and ale.) The framing is of simple squares but some of the timbers are exceptionally thick. The roofs are perfectly preserved and have spere trusses, collar beams and wind braces. These are described in great detail in the report of the *Royal Commission on Historic Monuments* which, although published in the 1930s, is still the standard work of reference for the buildings of Herefordshire and is used and quoted from by every scholar and architect who puts pen to paper on the subject. The chapel has a re-modelled Norman entrance porch and a capital in the east wall but the rest is Decorated of the early 14th century. The east window is of the Herefordshire type, three lancet lights under one arch, and there is a two-light bellcote. Amberley, and Sutton Saint Michael to the west, were homes of the Lingen family who have featured prominently in the county's history as sheriffs and soldiers. Sir Harry Lingen of Sutton was their most redoubtable son and played a prominent part in the Civil War, harrying the Parliamentarians with his band of bold cavaliers and famously marching out of Goodrich Castle to surrender but with head held high and the band playing 'Harry Lingen's Fancy'. He died in 1662 and is buried at Stoke Edith.

The damp squatter country of Sutton Lakes and Tumpy Lakes lies 1/2m S of Amberley. They are drained by a stream that runs south to join the River Lugg near Hereford.

ARCHENFIELD (hamlet) *2.5m E of Hay-on-Wye*

A handful of stone-built farms with corrugated iron sheds hide in a fold in the hills east of Hay. There is not necessarily an etymological connection with 'Archenfield the territory'.

Just south of the crescent-shaped wood at Llan-y-coed, 1m ENE of Arkenfield, is a long barrow at SO 277 429. Dry walling can be seen, the lower part having been damaged by excavation. The remains of the burial mound measure about 40ft by 30ft by 6ft high.

ARCHENFIELD (territory)

The name in 918 was Ircingafeld, from the Welsh Ercing, or Erging, which itself is said to be derived from Ariconium (SO 647 233), the Roman iron and pottery manufacturing area, 1/2m S of Bromash. Bury Hill is within the wide area covered by the settlement, but there is no sign of a fort there. Building debris and pottery is found over a wide area. North of Bromash a lot of iron slag and primitive furnaces and working hollows have been found. Ariconium appears to have been an open (undefended) industrial area with service buildings rather than a town as such, but we do not really know. Along with Magnis (Kenchester) it is one of only two named places in Herefordshire included in the Roman *Antonine Itinerary*. Its importance is also reflected in the fact that the Welsh adopted its name for the post-Roman territory they called Irging. This Deanery encompassed the land west of the River Wye and between the Worm Brook and the River Monnow.

After the Norman Conquest it became the Hundred of Archenfield and Welsh custom prevailed here well into mediaeval times, 200 years or more after the Conquest. A man's inheritance went to all his children equally. If he was succeeded by his wife (widow) she had a half but only so long as she remained both unmarried and faithful to his memory (i.e., was chaste). If she failed in this her share went to the children. The men of Archenfield formed the vanguard to the King's army, if attacking, and the rearguard if retreating. Welsh was the language of government. Landowners in the territory who had property adjacent to the River Wye had free fishing rights. If a Welshman killed a Welshman the relatives of the slain man could despoil the killer and his relatives and burn their houses until the body of the dead man was buried the next day about noon. The King had a third share of the plunder, the slain man's relatives the rest. There was no capital punishment. If anyone killed even one of the King's men he paid a fine of 20 shillings to the King and forfeited 100 shillings. Many of the churches in the Deanery of Archenfield are dedicated to Welsh saints and many were established near springs and wells that had been worshipped in pre-Christian times.

Note: King Athelstan, who reigned from 925 to 940, decreed that the border between England and Wales in Herefordshire was the River Wye. (Athelstan compelled the Welsh, Scottish and Danish under-kings to renew the oaths of allegiance they had made to his father, Edward I, and after the battle of Brunanburgh in Lancashire Athelstan was considered to be the most powerful monarch in the whole of Western Europe.)

ASHPERTON *4.5m NW of Ledbury*

The mediaeval name was Aspretonia. It can mean three things: 'ash hill'; 'stream where ash trees grow'; or 'the settlement of Aescbeorg', or a similar personal name. Ashperton straggles along the Dymock to Hope-under-Dinmore road, the A417, in the orchards and hop country of the River Frome (pronounced Froom). There are numbers of black and white cottages such as the 17th century Moorend with its square framing and star-shaped chimneys, and another with an exposed cruck truss, and a mixture of more recent dwellings. There is a stone school and a derelict stone pub, the former Box Bush, and there is a centre of sorts by the War Memorial.

However, the village is spoiled by the fast, busy main road. The vehicles that roar by have the facility of a service station at Blacklands, a crossroads hamlet adjoining the northern fringes of the settlement. The local pub is now the red brick and re-vamped Hopton Arms, also on the main road, opposite Ashperton Park. It was originally called the Royal Oak but was re-named by Mrs. Hopton in the 1930s when she renovated the pub. Nearby there is a cottage with an 8ft wide garden that was once nationally known for its topiary figures, notably a horse and jockey. These were the work of a farm hand, but, alas, they were all but destroyed in the Winter of the early 1980s.

Much of the land hereabouts was owned by the Hopton family of Canon Frome but in the 1950s their estates were sold off to sitting tenants. In the 1970s Sun Valley were allowed to build one of their dreadful factory farms at Woodsend, west of Ashperton Park, much to the disapproval of the local people. Most of the population works outside the area nowadays.

The church of Saint Bartholomew is safely tucked away down a little lane, well off the main road, by the woods of Ashperton Park. It started life as a chapel of ease built by William de Grandison for the benefit of his wife, Sibille, who found the journey from their castle across the marshes to their church at Stretton Grandison both dangerous and inconvenient. Of the church we see today the nave, chancel and transepts are early 14th century; the Early English chancel arch is 13th century; and the tower was rebuilt in the 1840s. The 13th century font has been relegated to the churchyard. The good Gothic organ-case is probably early 19th century and amongst the monuments is a tablet with columns and a pediment to one of the Wilson family.

During the Commonwealth 49 of the 200 parish and cathedral clergy of Herefordshire were deprived of their livings, having been accused of a range of life-styles not fitting for a priest. The vicar of Ashperton was one of those evicted, so, "with other confederate clergy and malignant gentry", he opened an alehouse in Worcester.

In 1292 William de Grandison, who came from Burgundy, obtained permission from Edward I to crenellate (fortify) his manor house. The remains of his castle stand to the west of the church. This was a medium-sized, stone-built fortress but all we have now is the oval-shaped mound surrounded by a wet moat and a rectangular enclosure to the east in which the church is sited. Most of the stone foundations were lost when the planting of trees was begun in the 18th century. The moat is now used for fishing.

Tradition has it that it was Katherine Grandison who lost her garter and had it returned by Edward III, who was so impressed by this small event that he named the Order of the Garter after it. More certain is that her brother, John, was a leading churchman. He was educated in Paris, became chaplain to the Pope and as Bishop of Exeter showed himself to be both a scholar and a philanthropist. A man of refined taste, he oversaw the magnificent Decorated architecture there. Both Katherine and John were born and baptised at Ashperton. He now lies in Exeter Cathedral. The Grandison family died out in 1375.

There are two moated sites in the parish. At Walsopthorne, 3/4m NE of the church, the moat is fragmentary but once surrounded the house, which is of about 1600, and had an enclosure to the north. At Freetown, 1.1/4m NW of the church, the moat formerly encircled the 17th century house and also had an enclosure to the north.

Moorend Farm, 1m E, is black and white gone wrong and is clustered about with derelict outbuildings. It doesn't have a moat but it stands near a clearly defined section of the now abandoned Hereford to Gloucester Canal which was completed in 1845. The canal lurks in deep, wooded cuttings full of dangerous green slime. These lead to and from a 1/4m long tunnel. By the eastern entrance is a tiny, restored canal cottage called Tunnel House (SO 653 418). The mounds of earth that follow the line of the tunnel north-eastwards are spoil heaps from the excavations. The engineer in charge was Stephen Ballard (1804-1891) and he lived here in a temporary home of dry bricks for over a year in 1841-2 whilst overcoming problems such as flooded shafts and landslides on the approach cuttings. Explosives had to be used to remove stone in the tunnel but this was later used for construction purposes. With the opening of the railway in 1861 the canal fell into disuse. The railway line still exists but the Ashperton station was closed in the 1960s.

ASHTON *3.5m NNE of Hereford*
The name means 'settlement by the ash tree'. Ashton is a hamlet on the busy A49 with the usual Herefordshire mix of stone, half-timber and red brick. A lane leads west from here to the main entrance of Berrington Hall. Near the main road there are the sites of two motte and bailey castles. Ashton Castle Tump (SO 514 650) is on a spur on the west side of the road, 350 yards NW of Upper Ashton Farm. It has a roughly circular mound, about 33 yards in diameter at the base, rising to 7ft at the rear of the spur and 19ft above the end of the spur. The earthworks overlook a stream. The Manorial Earthworks (SO 517 643) are just south of Lower Ashton Farm on the east side of the road. Here there is an irregularly shaped 10ft high platform with two low mounds - one round and one rectangular - known locally as The Camp. The base of a round tower has been found indicating the site of an early stone castle with a round shell keep, though documentary evidence has yet to come to light. North of the platforms were a small ditch and a bank. On the east and north sides of the adjoining field are the remains of scarping and a length of dried up moat or pond, probably of mediaeval origin.

The Hundred, 1.1/2m E of Ashton, is a scattered settlement. At Lower Hundred there is a craft workshop run by Paul and Christine d'Albert which has a tea shop and displays of the work of local craftsmen. Items for sale include pottery, enamels, wood-turned goods, hand-painted candles and fabric-covered trinket boxes.

ASTON INGHAM *5m E of Ross-on-Wye*
The name means 'settlement to the east held by Richard Ingan' who was lord of the manor here in 1212. It is not so much a village as a parish of scattered farms and dwellings set in undulating, wooded country hard against the border with Gloucestershire. There is both livestock and arable farming, and in recent times eating-apple orchards, mushrooms and chicory have been cultivated. Even so, most of the people who live here go elsewhere to work. To cater for those who take delight in butchering small animals for pleasure there is a gunsmith. More civilised services include a sports ground, a school and the church.

Saint John the Baptist has a 16th century tower with a Norman doorway but the rest was rebuilt in 1891 by Nicholson & Son, though they kept and re-set the late 12th century chancel arch and the 13th century doorways. There are two 13th century effigies, one each side of the altar. The cylindrical font is quite rare, the only one made of lead in the county; there are only 38 in the whole country. It is dated 1689 and prettily decorated with cherubs and the initials of churchwardens. In the churchyard are the base, steps and shaft of a mediaeval preaching cross. In the tower are six bells, reputedly the lightest ring in the county. Whatleys were vicars here from 1785 to 1964.

The village had three bequests. The best known is that of Richard Garrold who died in 1859 and left money "to buy a loaf of bread for each poor family of the parish to be distributed at Candlemas (February 2nd) forever." The custom continues and the bread is distributed on the Sunday nearest Candlemas.

At Coombe (Cwm) Hill the Romans had what is thought to be a look-out post and in 1855 two chests of 4th century bronze and copper Roman coins were found buried on the hill. It is believed that the church stands on the site of a long barrow. Elsewhere, a Middle Bronze-Age, rapier-like sword has been found.

Some old houses in the parish include: Springfield Grange, with very early parts dated at mid-12th century; Babylon Farm, early 15th century; Upper Coldridge, of the early 16th century with a barn of the 15th century; Warren Farm, mid-16th century; and there are many more, some now derelict.

May Hill, 1.1/2m SSW of the church, belongs to the National Trust. Hill Wakes were held here in the Spring. Such festivities were often, shall we say, high spirited and not the place for your maiden aunt; that is why they were held in comparatively remote places. Little Gorseley, 1m N of Aston Ingham, together with Gorseley Common which adjoins it, is a large, densely populated squatter settlement. Indeed, this squatter community spreads all along the border with Gloucestershire, from the M5 motorway at Linton southwards to Clifford's Mesne and Newent Woods, a distance of three miles. I know these 'townships' are land intensive but they are such an improvement on modern housing estates which really are the human equivalent of rabbit warrens.

ASTON *near Wigmore 4m WSW of Ludlow*
'Settlement to the east'. It lies on the western edge of the lovely Vale of Wigmore and during the Middle Ages was in the domain of the mighty Mortimers. The conifer woods of the extensive Mortimer Forest all but surround the settlement which consists of a handful of cottages, two mounds and the church.

Saint Giles is almost wholly Norman with a good tympanum depicting a lamb with a cross in a medallion held by the winged bull of Saint Luke and the eagle of Saint John. A band of creatures and foliage surrounds them. The posts have dragons and foliage and the outer arch has zigzag. The chancel arch was rebuilt in the late 13th century but was restored faithfully. The roof of the nave is 14th century and has tie-beams, queenposts, collar beams, and wind braces. The cone-shaped stone with a carved dragon, a creature and foliage is thought to be the 12th century stand of the original Norman font. In the nave there is a Norman painting of flowers in red on ashlar.

Aston Castle Tump lies 120 yards NE of the church at SO 462 719. It is almost certainly an Early Norman motte. The mound is roughly circular and about 47 yards in diameter at the base, rising to about 24ft above the bottom of the ditch, and there is some evidence of a stone building

HELL IN HEREFORDSHIRE

The wild white rose is cankered
Along the Vale of Lugg,
There is poison in the tankard,
There's murder in the mug;
Through all the pleasant valleys
Where stand the palefaced kine
Men raise the devil's chalice
And drink his bitter wine.

Unpseakable carouses
That shame the summer sky
Take place in little houses
That look towards the Wye;
And near the Radnor border
And those dark hills of Wales
Beelzebub is warder
And sorcery prevails.

For spite of church or chapel
Ungodly folk there be
Who pluck the cider apple
From the cider apple tree,
And squeeze it in their presses
Until the juice runs out,
At various addresses
That no one knows about.

And, maddened by the orgies
Of that unholy brew
They slit each other's gorges
From one a..m. till two,
Till Ledbury is a shambles
And in the dirt and mud
Where Leominster sits and gambles
The dice are stained with blood.

But still, if strength suffices
Before my day is done,
I'll go and share the vices
Of Clungunford and Clun,
But watch the red sun sinking
Across the March again
And join the secret drinking
Of outlaws at Presteign.

In 1921 the bishop of Hereford complained to the Licensing Commission that there was much 'secret drinking' in his diocese. Subsequently this poem appeared in *Punch*. It is a parody on Charles Kingsley's The Bad Squire.

Another, smaller defensive site lies 350 yards NNE of the church and south of the road to Ludlow at SO 462 721, near the foot of High Vinnals. The mound is circular, about 50 yards in diameter at the base, rising to a maximum of 9ft with traces of a ditch on the south and west and a small outer enclosure on the west.

Bowburnet is the name of an area of land between two streams that lies 1/2m W of the church on the end of the glacial lake that once filled the broad Vale of Wigmore. The name could mean 'the bridge over the stream in the field cleared by burning'. Bow in place names is often derived from the Anglo-Saxon boga, 'a bridge'.

AVENBURY *1m S of Bromyard*
It is thought that the old, local name for the River Frome was Avon, from the Celtic name Abona, meaning 'river'. Hence Avenbury means 'fortified place on the Avon'. In this country of little hills there are a few scattered farms, the rectory, the Court and the church.

Saint Mary's lies romantically in ruins by the river. The 13th century unbuttressed tower with pyramid roof soldiers on but the thick nave walls have collapsed. The chancel windows are Norman and there is an incised slab to a cross-legged knight of the late 13th century. The three bells are now at Saint Andrew-by-the-Wardrobe in the City of London and the chalice is at Hereford Museum. When we visited we could see nothing at first. However, a path leads along the western edge of the buttercup-filled meadows, through a gloomy tunnel of overgrown hedges, to a large yew tree and a macabre jumble of headstones. It was almost as if one had just disturbed grave robbers at work. Tall trees and undergrowth camouflage the ruins of the church. These are real Victorian-Gothic, ivy-clad ruins, so full of atmosphere that here any man could be made to believe in other worldly things.

Avenbury was a major hop growing area, and is one of the few regions that still have some yards. The seasonal labour referred to Saint Mary's as the Haunted Church and refused to pass it during the hours of darkness, even though for some it was on a short cut route from their accommodation to the hopyards.

The church is famous locally for its ghostly organ music. This was first heard in 1896 by several people and some years later the vicar, the Reverend E.M. Archer-Shepherd, also heard it and wrote: "I was on my lawn and the sound of music came up from the church quite clearly. It continued all the time I was walking down the meadow to ascertain the cause. When I got within 10 yards it stopped. The church door was locked and there was no one within. It was like someone improvising a voluntary on a church organ." Local people say that the ghostly organ music began after a man fell out with his brother, an amateur organist, and killed him on the Bromyard road bridge.

Avenbury also had a ghost in mediaeval times. Nicholas Vaughan burnt down one of the Bishop of Hereford's houses. He paid with his life but his spirit returned and had to be laid by 12 priests with 12 candles, who read from the gospels until he was trapped in a silver casket and buried beneath a stone in the River Frome. It has been suggested that this story might have some connection with the concealment of silver plate belonging to a monastery, which once stood on the site of the vicarage meadow at Avenbury at the time of the Dissolution.

For all its ruined church Avenbury has had a long clerical history. In 1066 Spirites, a wealthy priest who had over 80 manors, held Avenbury but by 1086 it had passed to Nigel the Doctor and there was a sizeable population with two priests and a mill.

Morris dancing was a popular seasonal activity at Avenbury from at least the 17th century. The origins of this fertility rite are so old that they are lost in the mists of pre-Celtic time and have their equivalent in almost all primitive cultures worldwide. Stamping the ground to make the crops grow is a universal idea. Because the participants often blacken their faces, soldiers returning from the Holy Crusades saw a likeness with the dark skinned Moors and so developed the absurd idea that our native dances came from the Middle East. Nevertheless, the name stuck. I wonder if anyone has tried using Morris dancers for the exorcism of troubled spirits? Their rituals are millennia older than those of the Anglican church.

AYLTON *3m W of Ledbury*
The names means 'the settlement of Aepelgifu', an Anglo-Saxon woman's name. The hamlet lies just west of the Roman road from Stretton Grandison to Dymock, the A4172, near the woods and orchards of Putley.

The small church does not have a dedication name and all the papers relating to it have disappeared, probably burnt by Colonel Birch during the Civil War. It stands on a mound. The nave walls are Norman and one Norman window survives. The east window is Decorated with ogee-headed lights. The 16th century turret has two bells; the 14th century chancel has a mass dial; the altar table, rails and font are 17th century. The handsome screen is assembled from various parts, mainly of the 15th century. The balusters of the porch were turned in 1645.

Adjacent to the church is Court Farm, once famous for its cider which was popular in Wales, but it is the great 15th century, six-bay, cruck-trussed barn that catches the eye. Aylton Court itself lies a good 1/2m SSW of the church. On the 10th of July 1855, Emma Foulgar, a 14 year old daughter of the Court, was accidentally shot and killed on the staircase by her brother who stumbled and discharged a shotgun at her. She was buried a few days later but shortly after body snatchers stole her corpse, probably to sell to a training hospital for use by students. Emma's ghost is said to haunt the staircase on which she died.

Aylton, and Putley both participate in the local Big Apple festivals which began in 1981. Today the people of the area are actively engaged in reviving old, rural traditions and in the early years of this century Vaughan Williams was at Aylton collecting folksongs. He also visited Ashperton, Dilwyn, Hardwicke, King's Pyon, Madley, Monkland, Monnington-on-Wye, Pembridge, Weobley and Withington.

AYMESTRY *6m NW of Leominster*
The name means 'Aelpelmund's tree' and at the time of Domesday was one of the 16 manors of Leominster. Tree sometimes means 'preaching cross'. The village lies along the busy Roman road from Hereford to Leintwardine, the A4110, in the lovely valley of the River Lugg. It is a most attractive village with an 18th century Court, some black and white cottages, stone-built dwellings, a bridge over the river, a village hall, a post office-cum-general store, a little cream-painted tin chapel, a garden centre, a timber yard, and the Crown Inn. About half the population of the parish is engaged in agriculture, and walkers, attracted by the charms of the wooded limestone hills that surround the village, virtually constitute an industry.

Sand and gravel were quarried at Aymestry from the 1950s and in 1987 a Bronze-Age burial cist (a rectangular stone-sided tomb chamber) containing the skeleton of a child, of about eight years of age, and a beaker were found in 1992 during excavations in the quarry, south of Pyon Wood hill fort, and were removed to Leominster Museum. The workings were closed in 1993 when a new quarry was opened in Pembridge.

There was an Anglo-Saxon mill in the village but the building we see today is of the early 1800s. This was producing flour until the mid-1960s and is still in working order. The old stables have been converted into a flat-bed lithographic art studio which is powered by the old water wheel. The owner has very sensibly installed a water-turbine to produce electricity for heat and light. Why more people in similar old mills don't tap this virtually free source of energy has always puzzled us.

The church of Saint John the Baptist and Saint Alkmund has a much admired 16th century rood and parclose screen decorated with delicately carved friezes of foliage, cresting and linen panels. The pulpit is Jacobean. The tower and its gargoyles are 14th century; the nave has Norman pillars - there was an early Mortimer monastery here for a time before it was moved to Wigmore - and 16th century aisles; the chancel north and south walls are Norman and have one Norman window; the chancel arch and east wall are 15th century. Monuments of note include those to: Sir John Lingen, died 1506, and wife; Robert Weever, died 1728; and members of the Dunne family (see Leinthall Earls) from 1734 to 1786. Outside there is a churchyard cross with a late mediaeval base and shaft and a 17th century top-piece. (The level area behind the Crown Inn is known as the Monks' Bowling Green, a memory of the old monastery.)

The church has six bells, one of which can be rung from the porch. This was reputedly tolled every evening to guide travellers who might be lured off their route by Puck, a sometimes mischievous and sometimes malevolent 'little person' who frequents Poke House Wood. The bell-ringer received the rent from a piece of land donated by one who had been led astray by this woodland spirit. A vicar of the church was the Reverend T.T. Lewis, a geologist and founding father of the Woolhope Club. It was his studies of the rocks of the area that made Aymestry limestone formations internationally known.

Yatton Court, 1/2m NE of the church, is a tall, Georgian, ashlar stone house of four bays with three-bay sides and Venetian lunette windows. Pyon Wood Camp, 3/4m N of the church on the west side of the A4110, is a roughly triangular Iron-Age fort with double ramparts covering an area of about nine acres, with at least one entrance in the north-east corner and presently covered in trees and dense undergrowth. At Camp Wood, nearly 2m W of the church near Upper Lyde, is the site of a substantial motte and bailey castle. The mound has a diameter of about 40 yards at the base and rises to 17ft from the ditch which has an external rampart. It stands on a small, wooded spur above the River Lugg. For something on Croft Ambrey Iron-Age hill fort, 1.1/2m NE of the church, see the article on Croft.

BACTON *10m SW of Hereford*
'The settlement of Bacca', an Anglo-Saxon personal name. Bacton is pleasantly situated on the western slopes of the Golden Valley, a little hamlet of farms and cottages in a scattered parish which had a population of less than 60 souls resident in 1991.

The church of Saint Faith has a squat, late 16th century tower and a rebuilt nave and chancel in one, of the 15th century. However, a window, a doorway and the font have been retained from the 13th century church. The roofs are Tudor, the stalls are late mediaeval and carved with poppy heads, and the chalice and paten are of about 1500. The beautiful altar frontal, embroidered in silk with animals, birds, flowers and insects, is 17th century and believed to be the work of Blanche Parry ap Harry, to whom there is a rustic monument depicting her kneeling before Queen Elizabeth I. The memorial bears a poetic inscription which, rendered into modern spelling (except for a few doubtful words), reads as follows:

I, Parry his daughter, Blanche of New Court borne
That train-ed was in Prince's Courts with gorgeous wights
Where fleeting honour sounds with blast of horn
Each of account to place of world's delights
Am lodg-ed here in this stoney tomb
My harpinger is paid I ought of due
My friends of speech here in do find me dumb
The which in vain they do so greatly rue

For so much as it is but the end of all
This wordly rout of state what do they be
The which unto the rest hereafter shall
Assemble thus each wight in his degree
I would always as handmaid to a queen
In chamber chief my time did to over pass
Uncareful of my wealth there was I seen
Whilst I abhored the running of my glass

Not doubting want whilst that mistress loved
In woman's state whose cradle saw I rocked
Her servant then as when she her crown achieved
And so remained till death my door had knocked
Preferring still the causes of each wight
As far as I doorsee move her grace his ear
For too reward deserts by course of right
As needs recite of service down each year

So that my time I thus did pass away
A maid in court and never no man's wife
Sworn of Queen Elizabeth's bed chamber alway
With maiden Queen a maid did end my life.

Blanche Parry was born at Newcourt Farm in 1508. She was made lady-in-waiting to Elizabeth I when the future Queen was only three years old, and was in her service as Keeper of Her Majesty's Jewels and later as Chief Gentlewoman of the Privy Chamber until she died in 1589. She lived in some style with servants of her own and no-one had been closer to the Queen. Blanche Parry was buried at Saint Margaret's Westminster, but her heart was brought back to be placed beneath the monument at Bacton. In her will she left a bequest of £500 to build an almshouse in the parish and 20 cows to be rented out for two shillings a year, to be paid to the vicar.

Newcourt Farm lies 3/4m N of the church and a little of the house Blanche Parry knew is incorporated in the building we see today. Newcourt Camp, 200 yards SW of Newcourt Farm, is a Norman motte and bailey castle which was probably abandoned in the 14th century. The site forms an irregular triangular enclosure of about one third of an acre protected on two sides by a double natural scarp with a narrow ledge between, and to the west by a ditch and inner rampart. There is a small mound with a sunken top to the east. Bacton Manor Spring is situated

1/4m NE of the church at SO 374 327. It can be approached directly by a footpath that leads off the main road in the Golden Valley. This path follows the course of a stream. The waters of the spring emerge from a round-headed alcove in a stone wall which was probably built when it was tanked to provide a supply to the Bacton Manor Estate. The water is said to cure complaints of the skin.

BAGBURROW *2m E of Great Malvern*
At the time of Domesday Book it was called Bageberge. It belonged to the Canons of Hereford and was a manor of some substance with a population of at least 31 families, including two 'men at arms' and a mill, and had a taxable value much higher than the average. Today it only exists as the name of a wood. Bagburrow Wood is just south-east of Mathon Court in grid square SO 74 45. The name could mean either 'Bacga's barrow' or 'badger's barrow, or hill'. However, it is not certain that this is the location of the lost manor.

BALLINGHAM *6.5m SE of Hereford*
The name is from the Anglo-Saxon and means 'settlement of the people of Badela'. The village stands on a bluff overlooking the River Wye. The old school is now a dwelling and stands beside the village green and the duck pond.

The church was founded by Dubricius, a Celtic saint who died in about 550. It was much restored in 1845 by W.E. Martin, but the oldest part of the building we see today is the 13th century tower and spire and a small 13th century lancet window in the 14th century nave. The Perpendicular vaulted porch is 15th century; the pulpit is Jacobean; there is a black and white tablet monument to William Scudamore, died 1649; the font is 13th century; and in the churchyard there is a good 18th century bronze sundial on the steps of the old cross. In the 1950s a piscina (holy water basin) was found near Buckenhill Farm and could indicate an alternative site for the original chapel founded by Saint Dubricius. Kilforge House, 1m WNW of the church might well have been the site of a much earlier, pre-Roman, Goidelic Celtic hermitage; the prefix 'kill' had that meaning in their language.

Ballingham Hall stands opposite the church. It is a substantial stone-built house of 1642 which originally had mullioned windows and has a two-storey projecting porch. In the gables are blank panels with ovals, fashionable between about 1660 and 1670. It has a handsome red brick barn. Elsewhere there are a few modern bungalows, a bit of red brick and stag-headed oaks in the fields. Ballingham Rifle Club, said to be the oldest in Britain, had to move for safety reasons to Kingsthorne where it operates today.

To the south, near Carey, the Hereford to Ross railway crossed the River Wye. It closed in the 1960s but its cuttings and embankments are still major landscape features. To the north there used to be a ferry for folk heading to Fownhope. The tortuous descent of Ballingham Hill brings one to a hamlet of small stone cottages with splendid views over the Wye and the pastures beyond. The road continues north-west and passes under a bridge to Hollington Farm. On the map it looks as though it ends here, but it does not and carries on north to Holme Lacy.

BARTESTREE *3.5m W of Hereford*
The name is from the Anglo-Saxon 'Beortweald's tree', though tree could mean a preaching cross. Approached from the west, along the A438, one passes the New Inn with its Gothic lancet windows, a derelict service station and Hagley Village Hall, to be rewarded by lovely views from the top of the hill. The road descends into the lush Frome Valley laced with red hopyards, green orchards and fields of golden daffodils. The old village centre of Bartestree lies just off the main road around the church of Saint James. The first chapel here was Norman but what we see today is the third church on the site and is the work of Nicholson & Son. Their church of 1888 has a nave, chancel, apse and bellcote in the style of about 1300. Bartestree Court is a timber-framed house of the 17th century which was enlarged and partly faced with brick in the 19th century. There are no service facilities at Bartestree.

Halfway down the hill, clearly visible from the main road, is the imposing red brick hulk of the Convent of Our Lady of Charity and Refuge. This was paid for by Robert Biddulph Phillips M.P., of Longworth Hall, 3/4m SW, and built in 1863 to a Victorian-Gothic design by Welby Pugin. There were additions in 1881, 1889 and 1895. Phillips had a daughter, Elizabeth, who entered the Order at Caen, Normandy, but who returned home after the death of her mother. The convent was a refuge for the reformation and employment of 'fallen women'. The nuns ran two main businesses: a laundry and the manufacture of underwear. We do not know what conditions were like here but Roman Catholic nuns operated similar convent laundries in other parts of England and Ireland which had fearsome reputations for their harsh regimes, extremely low wages and poor conditions. The scandal was publicly aired just a few years ago in the press and on television but things in Ireland are still no better. In recent times the Bartestree Convent gave a piece of land for the construction of Saint Michael's Hospice for the terminally ill.

The church of the convent is the Chapel of Saint James. This was originally the chapel of Longworth Hall, where it had languished as a barn for many years, but in 1870 it was dismantled, restored and re-erected at the convent. It is of about 1330, built of stone, Perpendicular in style, and has a roof with collar-beams on arched braces and cusped wind braces. Inside there are monuments to Elizabeth Phillips, died 1852, and Mary Anne Phillips, died 1858.

Pomona Farm, 3/4m NNE of the church at Bartestree, lies adjacent to the south side of the Roman road from Kenchester to Stretton Grandison. A hopyard by an old railway bridge marks the position of Godwin's tile works established here, in 1868, to be close to the now abandoned and all but invisible canal and also the railway station.

Five Bridges, 1/2m SE of the church, is where the Hereford to Ledbury road crosses the River Frome. The name seems to infer that the bridge has been rebuilt several times after being destroyed by flood waters. The ruins of an old bridge can be seen just upstream, near Moor Mills.

BELMONT *2m SW of Hereford*
Belmont was the creation of a wealthy Catholic landowner, Mr. F.R. Wegg-Prosser, and it was named after his home, Belmont House. Belmont is from the French 'beautiful hill'. He enlarged the house and built an abbey and these, together with five existing farm cottages, constituted Belmont. However, in the late 20th century, estates of modern houses have been planted to the east of the abbey, on the outskirts of Hereford, and these are also now considered to be a part of Belmont. There are still patches of green and a sand and gravel quarry between the estates and Belmont proper, but not for long, methinks.

The abbey was designed by Pugin and Pugin, successors

Above: Bosbury. **Below**: Brampto Bryan.

to the illustrious A.W.N. Pugin, and given by Mr. Wegg-Prosser to the Benedictine Order. Work started in 1854, it became a provisional cathedral in 1855 and was finally completed in 1882. In 1916 it became a full cathedral but in 1920 it changed to an abbey and has so remained. It has three parts: the monastic buildings; the almshouses by R.C. Carpenter of 1852 which have their own chapel; and the abbey church of Saint Michael. The east parts of the church are the earliest and least lavish; there is a big crossing tower; the nave is in the style of the early 14th century; and there is a striking and brightly coloured west window. The rest is Victorian Gothic with gables and dormers. There are two recumbent effigies: one to the Reverend Thomas Brown, the first bishop, died 1880; and the other to Bishop Hedley, died 1915. The complex has been impaired visually somewhat by the modern 1960s buildings of the former independent school, run by the monks, which was attached to it. The school closed in 1994 and the boarding houses are now used as offices by the Herefordshire Community Health Trust.

The monks are busy and enterprising people. They have a guest house, a souvenir-cum-bookshop, a function room that caters for wedding parties etc., a printing works which undertakes outside commercial work, and they are currently applying for planning permission to replace blocks of the old school with sheltered housing. Sackcloth and ashes are only a part of the job these days.

There are 21 congregations of the Benedictine Order worldwide. The English Congregation is an association of 14 monasteries. Of these three are for nuns and 11 for monks. Three of the men's monasteries are in America, founded by members of the English Congregation. The Order does not have a central organisation; all monasteries are autonomous. Saint Benedict was born in Italy in 480 A.D. and established his Rule in 530 A.D. making the Benedictines the oldest of all the Christian monastic orders. They have a tradition of scholarship and teaching and were largely responsible for preserving the learning of Greece and Rome after the fall of the Roman Empire. Their achievements in the fields of sacred art and music in the liturgy are of the highest order and they set standards for others to follow.

The Webb-Prossers lived at Belmont House, 1/2m NW of the abbey. This is a fine 18th century building virtually surrounded by Victorian Early English Gothic additions and is now the Clubhouse of the Belmont Golf Club. The family also owned the Victorianised Queen Anne house on the other side of the River Wye at Breinton. Mr. Webb-Prosser was probably best known locally, not so much for his abbey, as for his private steam-powered paddle boat which paraded up and down the Wye on hot summer days. It was brought here o a narrow-boat along the Gloucester to Hereford Canal.

BERRINGTON HALL *3m NNE of Leominster*
The name means 'settlement by the castle' There are two castle sites within a mile of Berrington, and there is something on these in the article on Ashton. Berrington Hall and its park lie adjacent to the Leominster to Ludlow road, the busy A49. Now that it is a National Trust property the original 'ceremonial' entrance drives are not used and the paying public is directed to the tradesmen's entrance off a lane from Ashton. Though of modest proportions Berrington Hall is Herefordshire's grandest country house. It sits in an extensive Capability Brown park of 1775 complete with wooded lake and arched entry lodge. The estate used to belong to the Cornewall family of Eye but the present pink sandstone house was built between 1778-81 by the architect, Henry Holland, for Thomas Harley of Brampton Bryan. Harley added to his family's already considerable fortunes in the City of London where he was a banker, a government contractor and became Lord Mayor.

Berrington Hall has a seven-bay front with a tall portico of four unfluted Ionic columns topped by a frieze and a pediment with a segmented window. At the rear is a full set of service rooms - laundry, bakery, kitchen, a beautiful tiled dairy and a servants' hall (now the tea room) set around a courtyard. The Late Victorian service tower was demolished several years ago.

The ground floor rooms are Classical Georgian at its refined best and are all original. The friezes, fireplaces, French furniture, paintings and the decorated ceilings are of the very highest order. The ceilings of the drawing room, with its central medallion of Venus, Cupid and Jupiter, and the library, with silhouettes painted flat but looking like bas-reliefs, are especially admired. The central stairwell rises the full height of the house to a glass-domed lantern. A gallery runs around the hall at first floor level with fine marbled columns, a cast-iron balustrade and statues in niches. The colours throughout the house are the original pastel shades of blue, grey, biscuit, olive green, pink and terra-cotta.

This splendid mansion of the Harleys descended down the female line to George, son of Admiral Lord Rodney and victor of the Battle of the Saints in 1782; many of the paintings in Berrington depict his naval engagements. In 1901 the house was sold to Frederick Cawley, M.P. for Prestwich, Lancashire, and in 1957 it was given to the National Trust, though the dowager Lady Cawley lived there until her death in 1978 at the age of 101. Her room and some of her belongings are preserved, a touching memorial to another age.

BIRCHER *6m SSW of Ludlow*
The name is from the Anglo-Saxon bierce-ofer meaning here 'birch-clad ridge'. Bircher lies on the Ludlow to Presteigne road, the B4361/4362, which hugs the foothills of the lovely wooded country between Ludlow and Presteigne. Much of this is either common land or owned by the Forestry Commission and is highly rated walking country. Bircher itself is a crossroads hamlet with the usual Herefordshire mix of stone, red brick and half-timber farms and houses, both ancient and modern.

Bircher Hall is a modest place of Georgian brick with hipped roofs, a small columned entrance porch and heavily wooded grounds, well-stocked with golden retrievers and a variety of evergreen trees and shrubs.

Hope Farm was a run-down collection of stone barns until John Wick, an ex-SAS officer, bought it and developed the site. Now there are seven comfortable, modern homes in a grouping that is a treat to the eye. Well done, Sir. The red brick dovecote is square with a four-gabled roof topped by a lantern. The Cadwallader family were the previous owners and still farm the land around.

Bircher Common, 3/4m NW of the hamlet, is a wonderful place. One turns north off the B4362 at the War Memorial and travels up a dull little lane to a cattle grid. Here one is confronted with a mediaeval scene. The Common lies on a slope cut through by little valleys and undulations with a ponded stream, stunted trees and clumps of gorse. Stone and half-timber cottages, now mostly rendered, are scattered about the hill connected by unmetalled tracks. Animals are everywhere. We saw goats, chickens, ponies, pigs and ducks. Some cottages have grown into quite smart modern houses; others are virtually smallholdings with make-do-and-mend outbuildings. You could cut the atmosphere with a knife. (See also Yarpole and Croft.)

BIRLEY *4m SW of Leominster*
The name is from the Anglo-Saxon and means 'the forest belonging to the fort'. The Iron-Age fort of Ivington Camp lies 2m NE. Birley is a hamlet on the Honeylake Brook just off the Roman road from Kenchester (Magnis) to Leintwardine (Bravonium), now called the A4110. In 1066 it was held as three manors by Edric, Leofgeat and Ruillic "who could go where they would". Ruillic is thought to be an Old Welsh name. By 1086 it was one of Ralph de Mortimer's many manors.

Much of the settlement of Birley is on the main road at Knapton Green where there are dwellings of stone, half-timber and red brick. The country is undulating with sheep pastures and orchards. Middle Hill, 1.1/4m ENE, retains one bay of its 14th century cruck-trussed hall and the 14th century cross-wing which has exposed square framing on the north side. Lye Court lies 1/2m SSE of the church, Swanstone Court lies 3/4m WSW, and Bucknall Court a good 1/2m NNW.

The red sandstone church of Saint Peter is approached over a narrow stone bridge. It has some Norman windows in the lower tower; a Norman doorway in the nave; a 13th century chancel with lancet windows; a chancel arch of the 14th century enriched with ballflower, beasts and men's heads; a Perpendicular south chapel of the 15th century which is rather good; a splendid Norman font and a pulpit of 1633.

Birley Court is noteworthy for the particular form of the ancient fertility rite called Burning the Bush which was practised here. We quote Mrs. E.M. Leather: "At five o'clock in the morning the workmen fetch the old 'bush'. At Birley Court, near Leominster, the servants, being strangers, objected to the early hour, and suggested that the men should fetch the bush overnight; this plan was evidently not at all acceptable, though the men did not explain what might happen if the kitchen were left a night without a bush. It is carried to the earliest sown wheat field, where a large fire is lighted, of straw and bushes, in which it is burnt. While it is burning, a new one is made; in making it, the ends of the branches are scorched in the fire. An old man, who had lived all his life in the Pembridge district, told me that at Shobdon, in his time, they poured cider over it afterwards, 'to varnish and darken the bush like,' he said; but the practice strongly suggests a survival of primitive ritual. At Birley Court there is a difference I have not heard of elsewhere. They make two globes of bushes, one for the Master, and one for the eldest born'" (child?); sometimes one globe is quite small, and placed inside the other and larger one. One of the men, taking some of the burning straw on a fork, runs with it across twelve ridges, dropping a little on each ridge."

Birley Hill, 1m S of the church, is known locally for its adders. The people of nearby Westhope used to collect the cast-off skins in the Spring and keep them for drawing out thorns. If you have a thorn in your hand place the adder skin on the opposite side and the thorn will loosen and come out. It was from Birley Hill that the Devil took earth with which to dam the River Wye upstream and drown the people of Hereford. (See King's Pyon for the full story.)

BISHOP'S FROME *4m S of Bromyard*
The Anglo-Saxon name was simply Frome (pronounced Froom), from the Celtic river name meaning 'fair, brisk, fine'. After 1066 it was given to the Canons of Hereford, hence Bishop's. At the time of Domesday Book it was a manor of considerable importance with a sizeable population, a reeve, a priest and two mills. Today, it is still a sizeable, nucleated village with a post office, a school, a shop, a neat industrial estate, rows of red brick council houses, a Wesleyan Methodist chapel of 1886 and six pubs - the Holly Bush, The Chase, the Green Dragon, the Major's Arms, the Wheatsheaf, the Five Bridges and the Fir Tree. One explanation for such a remarkably high number of hostelries is that in the height of the hop-picking season the population of the village increased from about 700 to as many as 5,000. A massive range of hop kilns near the village green is a memorial to this trade which is still relatively strong in the parish. By the way, beware of the river; it is entrenched to a depth of 10ft in places with almost vertical banks.

The church of Saint Mary stands on a site of great antiquity, a mound that was probably an Anglo-Saxon religious or defensive position. It has a 14th century tower, a Norman doorway and a Norman chancel arch, both decorated with zig-zag, but was rebuilt by the architect F.R. Kempson in 1847 and 1861. His work is not to everyone's taste. Inside there are mediaeval Italian paintings by Da Messina (1444-93) and Bonfiglio (1420-1500); the effigy of a 13th century knight; and a painted monument to Margery de la Downes, died 1598.

Cheney Court was a handsome Elizabethan moated mansion that burned down in 1888. The present house is 20th century but there are some ruins of the old building and in particular the chapel which adjoined it. Bishop's Frome Court Farm in the centre of the village has been demolished but the name continues in the modern bungalows built nearby. Other notable and existing houses within the parish include Bishop's Frome Manor, a good 1m NE of the church, which is Late Georgian, of three bays and two and a half storeys with a hipped roof and Doric pilasters; Lower Walton Farm, 3/4m SW, a part stone, part timber-framed 14th century house with close-set uprights in the west wing; Lower Vinetree Farm, 3/4m SSE, a mediaeval house with four cruck-trusses; and Woodcroft Farm, 2.1/4m SE, which has a good plaster ceiling that incorporates a wreath of flowers in high relief. New House, a working hop farm, with an extensive acreage, lies 3/4m S of Bishop's Frome on the B4214. The house is set back from the road, almost hidden by a gaunt warehouse, part of which is utilized as a craft shop. The Pudge family have accumulated a wide range of goods from landscapes by local artists, to their own range of cream and green pottery ware, to dried hop bines and a host of 'imported' pieces, including clothing. In the afternoons tea can be taken, and tours of the farm and its machinery can be supplied with advance notice.

BISHOPSTONE *5.5m WNW of Hereford*
The name in 1086 was Malveshille, and it was one of the manors held by the Bishop of Hereford. By 1166 it was Biscopestone, 'the manor of the Bishop'. The dwellings of the modern settlement lie alongside the old Roman road, 1/2m W of Kenchester (Magnis), but the church and the Court are 1/2m NW on the road to Mansel Lacy. In fact, the mediaeval village lay just to the east and south of the church along the lane to Bridge Sollers centred on SO 416 439. The village was referred to in the Nomina Villarum of 1316 and the Lay Subsidy of 1334 and 48 people paid the Poll Tax in 1377. The earthworks have almost been

erased by tree felling and ploughing. There is another deserted settlement, 1/2m WSW of Bishopstone church, on Garnon's Hill. It lies at the back of a flat ledge of level ground about halfway up the hill at SO 408 437 and was probably deserted in the 18th or 19th century. Stone walls can still be seen marking the sites of former dwellings, 10 of which were shown on the Ordnance Survey maps of 1886.

The church of Saint Lawrence is cruciform with a turret and is mostly 13th century. The fabric of the nave walls is Norman and there is at least one genuine Norman window - the one that is blocked. The transepts each have a 'Herefordshire window' (three lancets beneath one arch) of the late 13th century. The 14th century timber porch came from Yazor, and the organ of 1700 was brought here from Eton College in 1884. The roof of the chancel is much admired but its date is problematical: some think it original Jacobean, others that it is excellent work of the restoration of 1842. The pulpit, all agree, is original Jacobean. There are some 16th and 17th century stained glass panels in a chancel window; that of the east window is by W.Warrington of 1843. There are monuments to John Berinton, died 1614, and wife; and Sarah Freer, died 1842, has a sculpture by Peter Hollin. The Court stands just to the north-east of the church. It has a ruined gateway of about 1600 with a well-preserved deep, water-filled moat.

The rectory lies 1/4m SSE of the church at SO 417 434, near the Roman road and the modern settlement. When the foundations were being dug in 1812 the remains of a substantial Roman villa were uncovered. Finds included bricks, Samian ware pottery, coins, and part of a beautiful mosaic pavement (floor) with geometrical patterns, urns and rayed symbols. The foundations of later buildings were also discovered. William Wordsworth, whilst staying at nearby Brinsop, wrote an uninspired sonnet commemorating these finds which was published in 1835. We'll save his blushes by not reprinting any of it here.

BISHOPSWOOD *3.5m S of Ross-on-Wye*
This is a very scattered community in the gorge of the River Wye that lies partly in Gloucestershire. It was formerly part of a hunting forest owned by the Bishop of Hereford, one of whom appointed Alexander Jordan Keeper of the Woods in 1442. Bishopswood is dealt with in the article on Walford-near-Ross.

BLAKEMERE *9m E of Hereford*
'Black mere'. There is, indeed, a pool to the west of the church, sheltering in the lee of the long ridge of Blakemere Hill. It is a small but most attractive village on the B4352. Central to the array is a mature tree. This stands on the village green, complete with a concrete stone on which are written the Rules of the Rural District of Weobley relating to Commons. A large, weary looking Georgian house with a clutch of barns smiles across at a delightful timber-framed cottage. This leans a little to one side as all such venerable places should.

The church of Saint Leonard was rebuilt in 1877 but retains a Norman font, two doorways and a chancel arch of about 1200, and a group of 13th century lancet windows. The pulpit has Jacobean panels. Outside is the shaft of a preaching cross. Churchyard crosses are often so badly damaged and worn that it is impossible to date them. However, most of them are very old indeed and some originate from Anglo-Saxon times.

Half a mile east, on the lane to Preston, is the site of a holy well. Now it is just a small, boggy pool in a roadside paddock. Part of a Celtic cross featuring the ancient four-looped 'endless knot' symbol was found in a field nearby. On the road to Moccas is the round, red brick tower of a windmill, complete with batter (inclined walls). The old ceremony of the Hop-pickers' Feast was performed at Blakemere, see the article on Ullingswick for a description.

BODENHAM *5m SSE of Leominster*
'Boda's water meadow'. Seen from the wooded entrance to Bodenham Manor Restaurant it looks like a lakeland. In fact the pools are flooded sandpits, now well populated with ducks and sailing yachts. The church of this most attractive village is set beside the River Lugg. Saint Michael's is essentially Decorated, of about 1300, though the nave walls were heightened and the east ends of the aisles were widened to form transepts in the 15th century and the chancel was re-built in 1890. It is a tall, striking church rather than a beautiful building.

A variety of old houses surrounds the village green where there is a battered preaching cross and the Cross Well. The well is fed from a petrifying spring nearly a mile away. The handsome Moat House is timber-framed and stands 150 yards NW of the church. By the bridge is a rather strange Georgian house with projecting wings and a central pediment. Opposite is the Blacksmith's Shop, humble and bungalow-like but purpose-built for the Hampton Court Estate. I spoke to the blacksmith, Mr. Downes, who has spent all his working life here. Once there were four smiths. Now that he is about to retire there will soon be none. As we left we heard him singing to himself as metal clanked against metal. Echoes of another age. My dogs swam in the river here. Deveraux Court is a substantial timber-framed house of the 14th century. It was almost certainly the home of the Deveraux family, later Viscounts of Hereford.

To the south is Bodenham Moor. Here there is much modern housing, a pub, a shop and a post office, all safely away from the old settlement.

On the lane that runs west from Bodenham to the A49 at Queenswood there is a waterfall falling from a lime-rich spring (at about SO 515 516) which deposits tufa, a highly sought-after soft rock that is easily worked but which hardens with age and is very smooth and durable. It was quarried here commercially in the 18th century. The ancient woodland on this steep hillside is a site of Special Scientific Interest. It contains stunted, multi-trunked oaks which have grown unchecked from old coppice stools. These were cropped for oak bark to be used for tanning leather at the tannery at Leominster. This building was dismantled and re-erected at the Queenswood centre, 1/2m W of the waterfall.

North of Bodenham, on the A417, is the hamlet of Saffron's Cross. Lurking behind the sheds of a steel-frame building company are the concrete kennels of the North Herefordshire Hunt. Unsuspecting, I blundered into a scene from Hell. A man and woman wielding knives and axes were butchering the bloody carcases of sheep, horses and cattle and were up to their knees in dismembered heads, limbs and lights. Less than one mile further along the lane (to Risbury) is the entrance to Broadfield Court, a rambling mansion begun in the 14th century. Today it is famous for its vineyards. Bottled wine can be purchased at any time but guided tours are by appointment only. A little way down the main road from Saffron's Cross is the England's Gate Inn. Here I popped in for refreshment and met a Scottish soldier just back from training native troops in

Above: Brinsop Court, the handsome, original 14th century open hall roof. So many have been mutilated and had first floors inserted. Here, cambered tie beams support king posts to which are attached foiled principle rafters and foiled struts. Madeleine Carroll, the filmstar, once lived in the house.

Right: Berrington Hall, the principal country house of Herefordshire. The interiors are quite splendid. The park was landscaped by 'Capability' Brown and is considered to be one of best works. Behind the Hall, beyond the car park, is the site of a deserted mediaeval village - house platforms, hollow-ways and a ridge and furrow field system.

Mozambique, a jazz guitarist who makes video films, a member of Lloyds who was embarrassed to the tune of £250,000, a chap who had taught Tim Rice to play squash, and a dog called Nero.

The hamlet of Maund Bryan also lies on the A417, about 1.1/2m SE of Saffron's Cross. In Domesday Book the name was Magena, from the Welsh maen, 'a plain (or a stone)'. The Magonsaetan were the early Anglo-Saxon inhabitants of the area that now constitutes South Shropshire and North Herefordshire. These people were subjects of the kings of Mercia, the first of whom was Credda (583-600). He was followed by the powerful Penda whose son, Peada, was the first of the Mercians to embrace Christianity. The Bryan of Maund Bryan is from Brian de Maghene who lived in the 12th century.

BOLLINGHAM *2.5m S of Kington*
The name is from the Anglo-Saxon and means 'the settlement of Bulla's people'. It lies on the Kington to Hereford road, here called the A4111. It is a tiny hamlet with Bollingham House, a chapel and a few scattered farms. The much Victorianized chapel has nave, chancel and bellcote but the roof is of about 1400 and has tie beams, king posts, collar-beams and foiled braces. Nikolaus Pevsner calls the stone font and the pulpit "horrid". (What a splendid word that is.) English place names beginning with the letter 'Q' are very rare. Half a mile south of Bollingham are two: Quebb and Queest Moor.

BOLSTONE *5m SE of Hereford*

Bolstone, meaning 'Bulla's stone', is well off the beaten track and whilst only a few miles from the county town is quite remote. With a population of only 33 in a parish of only 672 acres it is not surprising that mains water has not yet arrived. Bolstone is most easily approached off the A4399 near Holme Lacy. The lane leads south, following the River Wye for a mile or so, before turning west and climbing uphill to the hidden, wooded, world of Bolstone. The tiny church, built as a chapel of ease, and the adjacent timber-framed farmhouse were both formerly the property of the Knights Hospitallers of Saint John of Jerusalem. The church was rebuilt by W.E. Martin in 1877 but he retained the Norman doorway with its two long monsters' heads, the group of three small lancets with deep displays at the east end, and a lancet window in the nave. The octagonal font incorporates thistle motifs and on this basis is thought to be Jacobean. Today the church is redundant and the parish has been united with that of Bollingham. According to local tradition water from the spring called Monk's Well has curative powers by virtue of having been blessed by monks.

In Trilloes Court Wood, nearly 1/2m SW of the church near The Moors, there languishes a long-abandoned homestead moat.

BOSBURY *3.5m NNW of Ledbury*
The name is from the Anglo-Saxon, Bosanbirig, meaning 'Bosa's fortified place', not necessarily a fortress, perhaps a defended manor house. At the time of Domesday it belonged to the Church of Hereford and was a substantial village with a priest and a mill.

Bosbury stands in the valley of the River Leadon, one of the main hop growing areas of Herefordshire. The red earth of the hopyards (weeds are kept down by chemical sprays, not cultivation) contrasts with the white blossoms of the orchards and yellow fields of corn. The wealth of the land is reflected in the number of dwellings of substance hereabouts: Old Court, a manor of the Bishops of Hereford complete with 14th century gatehouse; Bosbury House, Georgian Italian with seven bays, a balustrade and Tuscan columned porch; Hill House, pretty black and white of about 1600; Nashend Farm, Georgian brick with a pediment; and Temple Court, early 18th century but probably on the site once occupied by the mediaeval Knights Templar. This is in the locality called Upledyn.

As a property of the Knights of Saint John of Dinmore Temple Court any person accused of any crime, however grave, could seek sanctuary there. In 1491 Phillip Baret killed John Berne at Upledyn and went to Temple Court for protection but was arrested there and taken into custody. At his trial the jury confirmed that his right of sanctuary had been violated and ordered the Sheriff to escort him back to Temple Court in safety. Those who obtained sanctuary had the option of standing trial or abjuring the realm. If they chose exile they were escorted to the nearest port.

The Crown Inn was once the home of the Harley family. It used to be much larger but still has an impressive oak panelled room of 1571. There is an abundance of small black and white houses in the main street, all a jumble with others in brick and stucco. Here, too, are those rural boons a post office-cum-general store and a garage.

There used to be a holy well in Bosbury, called Job's Well, famous for curing eye troubles and boils, but no-one knows where it is, or was. Old beliefs do linger though. Roy Palmer was told by some Bosbury nurses in 1991 that coffin-shaped creases in newly laundered sheets were a portent of death. More orthodox beliefs are catered for by the parish church.

Saint Michael's is a large sandstone building with Norman arcades and a splendid Perpendicular chapel paid for by Thomas Morton (died 1511). However, most of the building is of the transition from Norman to Early English - round arches and lancets intermingle. The six-bay arcades, for example, have capitals decorated with Norman trumpet-scallops and pointed Early English arches. The five-columned font is also of that time, circa 1200. But the south door is Norman. The lectern is Jacobean. What strikes the stranger, though, is the detached, fortress-like bell tower. It is unbuttressed and has lancet windows. Inside the church there are two very grand Elizabethan tombs, each complete with sarcophagus, effigy and canopy. The earlier and more finely finished is of John Harford, died 1559. Amongst the decoration is a Green Man with foliage emanating from his mouth. In the churchyard is the Free Grammar School of 1590. It stands next to the jail.

By the south side of the church tower is a two-ton block of stone. This is believed to have been worshipped in 'heathen times'. It was found in 1796 buried beneath a cross in the churchyard. This was presumably an attempt to lay the power of the stone. Another object of probable pagan religious significance is the large, bronze Celtic bell ploughed up in a field near the village in 1890. It is rectangular and was originally carried suspended from a wooden bar. The bell now resides at the Horniman Museum in London.

In Spite of All, a best-selling Victorian novel by Edna Lyall, is thought to have been set in Bosbury. Philip Clisset, a renowned chairmaker and supporter of the Arts & Crafts Movement, lived and worked in the village from 1838 until his death in 1913. Some of his work can be seen at Churchill Gardens, Hereford.

Here are some pieces of Bosbury folklore collected by Mrs. E.M. Leather in the early 20th century. There is a local tale about a Bosbury man who could put curses on people and who was much feared. He had a brick-kiln and the people managed to deprive him of it. He retaliated by cursing it never to fire again. No matter how hard the people tried it would not heat up because a black cat ran backwards and forwards putting out the flames. There is a Gospel Yew at the point where the parishes of Bosbury, Castle Frome and Canon Frome meet. A local saying is "Make your will before going to Bosbury"; more cheerful is the bell jingle "Roast beef and old perry, Say the bells of Bosberry".

At The Slatch, Bosbury, there are large vineyards and gardens with specimen trees, shrubs, ornamental waterfalls and geese. A 16th century timber-framed oasthouse has been converted into a cafe but the owners only take parties of between 20 to 60, and by appointment only.

Catley Southfield, 1m W of Bosbury, is a pleasant linear hamlet of old black and white, stone and red brick Victorian and modern dwellings spaced out along a narrow lane just off the Bromyard to Ledbury road. The name Catley is from the Anglo-Saxon and probably means 'glade in the wood occupied by a wild cat'.

BRAMPTON ABBOTTS 1.5m N of Ross-on-Wye

The name is from the Anglo-Saxon and means 'homestead in the broom belonging to the Abbott'. In mediaeval times it was held by Saint Peter's of Gloucester. This pleasant village lies on high ground only half a mile beyond the northern suburbs of Ross, which have ominously overstepped the 'natural' development barrier of the motorway-like Ross Spur. To the west is the River Wye. The old dwellings have found bungalows and modern houses arising in their midst. Facilities include a nursery school, a sub-post office, and the Traveller's Rest inn and a service station at the junction of the Ross Spur and the M50. The old school of 1857 lies derelict and most of the residents now work in Ross. The outlying townships are mostly the large farms of the area - Netherton, Townsend, Overton and Gatsford.

The church of Saint Michael and All Angels stands on high ground with long views in all directions. Much of it is Norman - the nave and chancel walls, the doorway, the shafts of the chancel arch, an east window and the piscina basin. The roof, the shingled bell-turret and the timber porch are 14th century and the pulpit is partly Jacobean. There is some fresco painting and brasses to William Hulme and Joan Rudhale (wife of John who died in 1507).

Rudhall House lies 1.1/2m SSE of the church on the south side of the M50. It is a most handsome building and beautifully situated. The earliest parts are of the 14th century as evidenced by timbers of the hall-roof and the roof of a cross-wing. But it is the 'L'-shaped entrance facade that is so attractive. There is a happy mixture on one side, of 16th century timber-framing with an overhanging first floor supported by a moulded bressumer and three gables, and on the other side, a Jacobean porch, a Georgian Venetian window, more 16th century framing, gables with carved bargeboards, and a turret-tower. During the Second World War the Chelsea Pensioners were evacuated here, and for several years up to 1996 it was the home of Sir John Harvey Jones, the ex-naval officer and prominent businessman, and who became a household name through a television series called *The Troubleshooter* in which he gave advice on how to turn around ailing businesses. On leaving Rudhall he went to Hay-on-Wye, we are informed; the Herefordshire air agrees with him it seems. Rudhall House stands close by the Rudhall Brook and a series of pools. The prefix rud, in this context, means 'reed'.

BRAMPTON BRYAN 5m E of Knighton (Powys)

'Settlement by the broom now owned by Brian'. Brian is a Norman name of Breton origin. Brian de Brantone was Lord of the Manor here in 1185. We are getting nearer to Wales and the hills are getting higher. The village is a delight. Around the green are black and white cottages, a tea room, the post office-cum-shop and the blacksmith. But what catches the eye is the huge yew hedge, a great green monster with brain-like lobes which slither all over a stone wall. Behind it hide the large, seven-bay Georgian brick Hall and the romantic ruins of its predecessor, the grey stone castle built in 1309 by Robert Harley (of Harley in Shropshire). The gatehouse still stands and behind it is part of the old Hall with an Elizabethan porch and staircase bay.

The Harleys are an illustrious family and count amongst their number Robert, First Earl of Oxford, and Prime Minister to Queen Anne, and the collector of the Harleian Manuscripts now housed at the British Museum. They held extensive properties including Wigmore Castle, and used local names for their London developments. One of these is Harley Street now a centre for medical consultants; another is Wigmore Street, which has the Wigmore Hall, famous as a venue for classical music.

Perhaps the most romantic episode in the family's history was the defence of the castle by Lady Brilliana (1600-43) during the Civil War. Sir Robert Harley, her husband, was in London on Commonwealth business when their home was attacked by a large force of Royalists. Lady Brilliana's household was greatly outnumbered but held out for seven weeks. She caught a chill and died shortly after the siege was lifted. The next year the Royalists returned and the castle fell and was destroyed. The church was also destroyed and was rebuilt by Sir Robert in a rather severe style; he was, after all, an ardent Puritan whose job in London had been to "demolish idolatrous monuments". Later alterations were made by the Victorians. The Harleys still live at the Hall and the castle is not open to the public, though it is occasionally used as a film set.

Brampton Bryan used to be well known for its Bron Horse Fair, attended by gypsies from near and far.

Coxall Knoll, 1/2m over the River Teme, has the earthworks of an Iron-Age fort. By the river the Romans had a marching camp. The site of this is 100 yards E of the church, in fields on both sides of the road from Walford, at SO 373 723. South-west of the village is Brampton Bryan Park, very old, very lovely, and graced by numbers of 300-year-old-chestnut trees. A great storm raged at the time of Cromwell's death and caused much damage to the trees of Brampton Park. Sir Edward Harley, who had fallen out with Cromwell, jested: "I wish the Devil had taken him any other way than through my park, for not content with doing me all the mischief he could when alive, he knocked over some of my finest trees in his progress downwards." Note: Arthur Mee in *The King's England - Herefordshire* devotes nearly two pages to a brief history of the Harley family.

At the foot of the steepest part of the hill, beneath an ancient oak, is Laugh Lady Well. Drop in a pin and if bubbles arise make a wish. Well, you could once but it has been given a beehive cap. 'Laugh' is probably from the Celtic lough (loch) meaning 'water'.

BREDENBURY 3m WNW of Bromyard

The name is from the Anglo-Saxon and means 'the old fort made of boards'. Some Iron-Age Celtic forts had walls of turf sandwiched between board fences, one inside and one outside. Bredenbury lies on the Bromyard to Leominster road, the A44, in attractive hill country. In 1086 it was just one of the 75 manors held by Roger de Lacy in Herefordshire, but the village as we see it today is very much the Victorian creation of W.H. Barneby, a wealthy local landowner. In 1873 he commissioned the architect T.H. Wyatt to build Bredenbury Court, a large, square Italianate mansion built with rock-faced sandstone. His work was extended in 1902 by Sir Guy Dawber and further work was executed in 1924. The old church stood near the Court but in 1877 Barneby had it demolished and Wyatt built him a new one with matching rectory beside the main road. They now have a garagem for company.

Saint Andrew's is small, built of rock-faced stone in the style of 1300, and has a tower with a pyramid roof. Inside there is an alabaster pulpit of 1883 and a silver cup brought here from nearby Wacton church after it was demolished. The old, original Bredenbury font and the Wacton font languish in the churchyard. Mr. Barneby also gave the land for the school and planted most of the roadside trees that greatly to the charm of the village.

Towards the end of the century he sold the Court to the Greswolde-Williams family who had estates in Africa. Their life-style was lavish. To care for their every need they had a butler, a housekeeper, valets, nurses, grooms, three footmen and 14 maids. They had a black and yellow carriage powered by a team of ebony horses, and coal for the house fires was collected each day from the station at Rowden, 1.1/4m E. They provided kennels for the North Herefordshire Hunt and built the Parish Room in a vain attempt to keep the local men away from the temptations of the village pub, the Barneby Arms. The Greswolde-Williams left in the 1920s and the Court is now a private boarding school.

Brockington Grange was built by Mr. Barneby when he left the Court; Brockington House was built later by his son; and in recent times a row of bungalows has appeared on the horizon. Wicton Farm, 1.1/4m ESE, is a handsome timber-framed house of the early 16th century extended probably in the early 17th century. It has close-set verticals, some diagonal bracing and lozenges in the cross-gable. The house lies adjacent to the track of the dismantled Bromyard to Leominster Railway and faces the woods of Rowden Abbey over the upper reaches of the River Frome. There is no record of an abbey at Rowden and when the supposed site was excavated in 1948, nothing was found and a tennis court was subsequently laid over it. There are some earthworks which could be of an old moat but even these are more likely to be landscaping. In all probability the name Rowden Abbey is a Victorian sham designed to impress.

Mundersfield Harold is 1.1/4m SE of the church at Bredenbury. Mundersfield is probably from the Anglo-Saxon Mundel's - feld. A feld was a large area of open country, usually in a recently cleared forest.

BREDWARDINE 11.5m WNW of Hereford

'Homestead on the bank'. It is a delightful place in lovely wooded country with some fascinating historical connections. The area by the river is especially striking and has an air of timelessness. The River Wye has cut a narrow little valley with steep, cliff-like banks. It is crossed by a six-arched 18th century bridge, the earliest and finest brick-built bridge in the whole county. Above it stands the church, approached along a tree-lined avenue.

Saint Andrew's has an unbuttressed Georgian tower of 1790; the rest is Norman with some very early herring-bone masonry on the north side of the nave. Both doorways have very large lintels, on one of which are two grotesque heads, one of a bird, the other of a pig or a monkey. There are tufa quoins in the nave, tufa in the south doorway and two tufa windows. The nave was lengthened and the chancel was rebuilt in about 1300. The large, plain font is Norman also. There are effigies of two knights, one of the late 14th century and another in alabaster of about 1450.

In the churchyard lie the mortal remains of the Reverend Francis Kilvert (1840-1879) who was vicar here for the two years before his death. He is famous for the diaries he kept between 1870 and 1879, in which he gives us a fascinating glimpse of everyday Victorian rural life on the Welsh borders. Some years ago his writings were dramatised for television and the area is now well and truly on the Summer tourist trail. Kilvert came up from Wiltshire to serve as curate at Clyro (just over the border in Wales), from 1865 to 1872, and came to Bredwardine in 1877. In 1879 he married Elizabeth Rowland of Wootton, Oxfordshire, but died of peritonitis scarcely a month after the wedding. He was only 38 years of age. His epitaph reads: "He being dead yet speaketh." The rectory where Kilvert lived still stands near the church.

Also buried here is George Jarvis (died 1793). He was a tramp who wandered the villages of the Bredwardine area. Then he emigrated to America, made a fortune, returned home to die and left all of his money to the people of the places who had treated him well in his days of poverty. Brobury, just over the river, got nothing but Bredwardine did handsomely, so much so that squatters invaded the parish to qualify for his charity. Many of them lived at Crafta Webb, now abandoned and marked only by a few stones.

A third grave to visit is that of Major General Pitman who lived at Brobury House until his death in 1941. His bronze monument is by Madame Sabatini, wife of the author Raphael Sabatini, who once lived at Clock Mill on the road to Hay-on-Wye. Augustus John, the painter, was no stranger to Benfield House.

Most of these worthies would have taken refreshment at the Red Lion, a good 17th century brick house which stands at the crossroads. Just south of the pub is a delightful area of tiny, bright green fields with wooded hedges that wander where they will.

Immediately south of the church, along the west bank of the River Wye, there is a confused Norman castle-cum-17th century mansion site at SO 335 444. The bailey is irregularly shaped with a slightly narrow projection on the south side where the keep stood, probably divided from the bailey by a ditch. A steep scarp to the river along the east side protected the enclosure, whilst on the north and west there were ditches. The south end was protected by a double scarp. There is also a small mound to the west along a trackway to the River Wye. The complex was made confused because Roger Vaughan built a mansion here in about 1640. This later passed to the Cornwall family who dismantled it and took the stone to Moccas Court, 1.1/2m SE, in 1775-81.

In the 1970s a secondary site at the south of the village

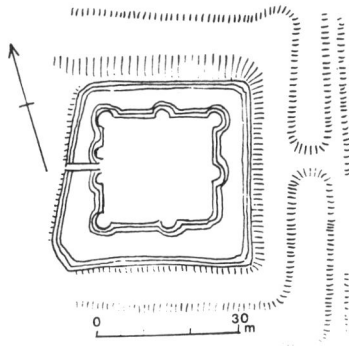

Left: Bronsil Castle, plan of.
Middle: Brockhampton by Ross, All Saints, by W.R. Lethaby.
Bottom: Bredwardine, Saint Andrew's church.
Bottom inset: the Reverend Francis Kilvert.

on the west bank of the Wye at SO 337 440, was excavated. Several periods of occupation were found, the main one being a 14th century farmhouse. An earlier period revealed traces of wooden buildings and the base of a small square stone tower. Coins of Edward I or II were found dating from 1275 to 1327. Some authorities think that this is the mediaeval castle and that the site nearer the church is entirely of Vaughan's mansion; others think there were simply two castles. Between the two sites there are two dams, probably of fish ponds but possibly of mill pools. A castle at Bredwardine was mentioned in 1189 and in the 13th century, but in an inventory of 1374 there is no mention of a castle.

The estate had several owners in the Middle Ages - John de Bredwardine (late 11th century); the Baskervilles (by 1227) who probably built the castle on the secondary site; the Fouleshurst family of Cheshire (from about 1374 to 1439); and back to the Baskervilles when a survey said the site was waste and of no value. By now the Baskervilles were based at Eardisley Castle.

Notable houses in the area include Old Court, 300 yards N of the church, a handsome stone house of the 14th century which has two of the original hall trusses: one has a spere truss with arched braces, collar-beam and traceried spandrels, and the other a tie-beam with collar-beam and cusping. It is now a guest house and in the Summer months a marquee is erected to cater for wedding receptions. This does nothing for the ambience of the area. Nearby is Old Court Mound, a mediaeval moated homestead site, probably the precursor of Old Court. Botterell Farm, 1m SW, has an ancient cruck-truss inside. New Weston Farm, 1m NW, is a good Late Georgian house of brick with three bays, two and a half storeys, segment-headed windows, and a Victorian porch. It has a 150ft barn, originally two separate buildings, and a long tithe barn.

BREINTON *3.5m W of Hereford*
'The settlement of Bryni's people'. Bryni is an Anglo-Saxon personal name. The vast majority of English place names are of Anglo-Saxon origin, either personal names or descriptions of geographical features. Breinton lies along the north bank of the River Wye and is what might be called a rural suburb of Hereford. It stretches from Warham to Lower Breinton, Upper Breinton and Breinton Common, all separated from each other. In the late 19th and early 20th centuries professional people built villas amongst the pastures and orchards overlooking the river. The Victorianised Queen Anne house belonged to the wealthy Wegg-Prosser family who built Belmont Abbey. They had a steam-driven paddle boat and paraded proudly up and down the river to Hereford dressed in their best.

The church of Saint Michael at Lower Breinton stands on a bank amidst yews and a cedar and the trees of adjacent orchards. It is probably an ancient site but the building we see today was raised to a design by F.R. Kempson in 1866-70. All that remains of the Norman church are a re-set Norman window in the west gable of the nave, and the two window heads above. There is a painted tablet to Captain Rudhall Booth, died 1685; a richly carved Elizabethan table; and two mediaeval bells.

Breinton Camp, 60 yards SW of the church at SO 472 398, used to be described as an Iron-Age fort but excavations in the 1920s and between 1959 and 1964 have established that the earthworks are of a fortified domestic dwelling, probably the home of early mediaeval priests. A low, roughly-oval mound with a flat top with traces of an inner rampart is surrounded on three sides by a ditch, the south side being protected by a scarp to the river. It was occupied from about 1150 until sometime in the 13th century, dated by finds of pottery and tiles. The whole enclosure measured 120ft by 80ft and the remains of a wide stone gateway exist on the north side, together with a cobbled surface. Part of the foundations of the main building were found in the south-east corner. A sunken track, a holloway, leads from the earthworks to the site of a ford. The river runs very lazily hereabouts.

The hamlet of Warham, 1/2m ESE of the church, has a pretty black and white house with an early 16th century gable which has narrow-set uprights. Breinton Common, 1.1/4m WNW of the church, has an area built upon by squatters in the 17th and 18th centuries. The little brick and half-timber cottages have been modernised and extended in recent times. Needless to say there has been 20th century infill.

BRIDGE SOLLARS *6m WNW of Hereford*
Simply called Bricge, 'bridge', in Domesday Book. Sollars is a Norman family name, probably derived from Soliers, near Caen. The bridge is constructed of steel, with four spans on three circular steel piers with coursed stone abutments, and was built by public subscription in 1896 to replace the previous ferry. On the southern bank is a tired looking black and white farm with stone barns.

On higher ground to the north of the river is the little church of Saint Andrew, embowered in yew trees. Much of it is Norman, including the thin tower. The south doorway is Decorated with a head that has two dragons emerging from its mouth in the Herefordshire School of Carving style. The chancel was rebuilt about 1300 A.D. and there is good stained glass by Powells in the east window of 1871.

Along the main road, the A438, are a service station, some modern houses, the Lord Nelson pub and fields unbecomingly covered in black plastic. Marsh Court lies all alone and lonely down a dead end track. One mile east of the church is The Weir, famed for its gardens overlooking the Wye with a backdrop of the Welsh hills. It is a National Trust property and open to the public. (See Kenchester.)

BRIDSTOW *1m W of Ross-on-Wye*
Bridstow, 'Saint Bride's holy place' and Wilton, 'settlement by the willows', are now considered as one place. They stand on the opposite bank from Ross on the River Wye and developed first around a ford, and then around the handsome six-arched bridge of 1597 with its massive cutwaters. On the centre parapet is the doom-laden inscription: "Esteem they precious time which pass so swift away; prepare thee for eternity and do not make delay". There used to be a cross by the ford but that has been removed to the gardens of Wilton Court Hotel, a mid-17th century stone-built house with mullioned windows. Other houses that catch the eye near the bridge head are the White Lion of 1779, and two guest houses, the Marian Sykes and The Lockup.

Close by are the splendidly romantic ruins of Wilton Castle. There are signs of the former motte and bailey castle mentioned by Giraldus Cambrensis and in the Pipe Rolls of 1188, but the stonework we see today is of the rebuilding by Roger de Grey at the end of the 13th century. In the late 16th century it was partly replaced with a prestigious new house by the Brydges family. Sir John Brydges remained neutral during the Civil War. Nevertheless the castle was burned by Barnaby Scudamore to prevent it from being garrisoned.

In 1784 the ancient title of Lord Grey of Wilton was revived and granted to Sir Thomas Egerton, and in 1801 the Earldom of Wilton was created. In the 19th century a part of the ruin was made into a house and is occupied to this day. The motte of the first castle probably lay on the south-east corner of the site, commanding the bridge, and close by are the ruins of the Elizabethan mansion. Substantial sections of the curtain walls to the east, west and south and the towers still stand.

The church of Saint Bridget lies 1/2m NE of the bridge in a hollow by a stream with an avenue of Irish yews for company. It has a Norman chancel arch, Early English north chapel, and a 15th century Perpendicular tower but owes much to the restoration of 1868. The stained glass is by C.E. Kempe and there is a small shrine, probably of the late 13th century. The settlement of Poolmill stands by the stream within bow shot of the church; and 2/3 NNW is Asshe Farm which has a cruck-truss and a 'pitch and put' golf course.

On the A49, between the A40(T) and the church, there are new dwellings, a white stone war memorial, a stone-built Voluntary Aided School, a cedar-shack parish hall, a hockey pitch, the four-bay ashlar Old Vicarage with a hipped roof, a sign to the golf course and a Scots pine.

The Ross Spur, the A40T, cuts the settlement in two and Bridstow/Wilton gets all the traffic that its big brother over the water does not want. Those seeking shelter from noise pollution can repair to the sanctuary of Moor Meadows (SO 587 242), a grassy common of 24 acres only a minute's walk from the camping and caravanning park at Wilton, and adjacent to the facilities offered by the Wilton Court Hotel and the Hereford Bull Inn. On the river banks grow the willows of the place name and in Summer the waters are shallow enough to allow children to wade out to the island.

BRIERLEY *2m S of Leominster*
The name is from the Anglo-Saxon and means 'the glade where briers grew'. It lies in the valley of the River Arrow below the conifer-clad Brierley Hill. Until recent times this hill was classified as ancient woodland and there are plans to restore it by planting mixed deciduous trees in the future. At present its coniferous cloak hides the massive earth walls of Ivington Camp. (See Ivington.) At the time of Domesday Book Brierley was called Bretlege, though the identification is not altogether certain. There were eight beadles listed here. A beadle was an under-bailiff to the reeve with minor police duties. Considering that there were only 13 listed in the whole of Herefordshire, this is an unusually high and unexplained concentration.

Brierley is an attractive hamlet of substantial dwellings, some of brick, some of stone and some black and white. The Court is an 18th century sandstone-built house of three bays, two storeys and a hipped roof which has good gate piers to the garden. It is now home to the farm manager who is employed by Carlsberg-Tetley, the international brewing company. Of the 450 acres of the estate 245 are laid as hopyards, the largest single concentration in the whole of Europe. They are, indeed, extensive and virtually fill the valley from the foot of Brierley Hill to the banks of the River Arrow. Another 95 acres are given to a poplar plantation - the wood is used for furniture making - and 40 acres are in an arable rotation which includes barley. Close to the Court are two gigantic, modern, grey and black sheds. One houses the hop-bine stripping plant and the other the drying equipment. These monster machines can be seen in action by the public in the Autumn when they are tended by seasonal labour.

In the Spring of 1996 I collected a song from the traveller Peter Delaney, who was then camped on Eyton Common. He was working in the Brierley Court hopyards at the time. His song describes modern harvesting and stripping processes, though his complaint about wages does not necessarily relate to the Brierley farm.

HOP-PICKING SONG

It's hop-pickers wanted on the minimum pay,
Come feed the hop eater ten hours a day,
No qualifications or union card,
 It's false names only in the Herefordshire hopyards.

At the crack of dawn the great beast awakes
With an almighty roar the whole shed it shakes,
It screams and it rages and roars to be fed,
And the humans out front hang till they feel dead.

Down in the hopyard, come sun or come rain,
The crow's in his nest but he can't fly away;
The tractors keep coming for load after load,
 And the bine cutters sharpen their knives on their stones.

Up in the hop shed the beast's belly so full,
It's spewing out hops into sacks by the ton,
Then carry them into the kilns to be dried,
Where the kiln workers sweat till their brains are all fried.

As dusk comes in the great beast gives a sigh,
And falls down to sleep fast as any man could die.
The pickers go home, they've no thought for next day,
For tonight they'll be drunk on their minimum pay.

Although the harvesting, stripping and drying machines have removed the need for the vast armies of labour once employed, there is still a requirement for considerable numbers of seasonal labourers both in the Spring, to train the young plants to climb the wires, and in the Autumn to bring the harvest home. Several of the footpaths in the Brierley area were established by hop-pickers travelling from their camps to the hopyards. The dried hops are sent from Brierley to Burton-on-Trent in Staffordshire where they are used to flavour beer.

The stone barns adjacent to the Court are rented out to Garden Marquees for storage, and there is an old, disused hop-kiln. We would like to mention that we received every courtesy from the lady farm secretary.

Elms Green, 1/2m NE of Brierley, is a tiny main road hamlet of brick and stone dwellings which now boasts the Arrow Fisheries. This is a complex of water channels with fishing stages all contained within a 9ft high earth embankment. (For Broadward Court see Leominster.)

BRILLEY *4.5m NNE of Hay-on-Wye*
The 13th century name was Brynlegh, from the Old English bryn meaning 'burning', hence 'the place cleared by burning'. The parish of Brilley is bordered by Wales to the west and the River Wye to the south. It is a place of scattered sheep farms and is more Welsh than English. The air is good and the hill views even better.

The parish church and the hamlet of Brilley stand on a steep, winding hill and are most easily approached from the Hay to Hereford road, the A438. Saint Mary's was rebuilt in 1890 but retains its re-cut windows of about 1300, its mediaeval roof and its sturdy Norman font. The tower, with its pyramid roof, was added in 1912. A curiosity is the protective altar canopy, a baldacchino, similar to that at Michaelchurch on Arrow, just over the border in Wales. In the churchyard are two cast-iron slab grave pieces of 1669-70 with sans serif lettering - several hundred years before Eric Gill re-invented the style for public utility purposes. Here, too, is the grave of a barge-owner.

Little doubt he passed more than a few hours at the Rhydspence Inn and Restaurant, 1.1/2m SW, waiting for the water level to rise. The inn is a part stone and timber-framed house of the 16th century with prestigious close-set verticals. It stands at the foot of steep hills close by the river right on the Welsh border. Many a brigand must have drunk here with the comfort of knowing that safety was only a few yards away regardless, of whether it was the Welsh or the English who were after him. It was also used by the drovers on their way to the English markets. While they drank in the pub their cattle drank from the river. Today it is somewhat on the trendy side.

There are several old and interesting farmhouses in the hills. The Cwmma, 1.1/2m NE, is probably the best known because it is open to the public occasionally. It is a handsome Jacobean building with a two-storey porch. In the 1920s the owner 'asset stripped' the house, selling off the panelling, and even the front door, to Americans for the mighty sum of £3,000. He then used it to store animal skins. Subsequently, it was lovingly restored by Mr. Menges who bequeathed Cwmma and nearby Fernhill to the National Trust. Fernhill still has two of its original cruck trusses and other mediaeval parts of the roof circa 1400. Kintley Farm, 1m ENE, and Llanhedry, 1m NE, are both hall houses of about 1400 with parts of their original roofs remaining. Little Merthyr, 1/2m SE, is a hamlet at the foot of the wooded Brilley Hill, and 1m E is Welshwood Farm. Merthyr is Welsh for 'martyr'.

Offa's Dyke circa A.D. 790, runs across the parish 2.1/4m to the east. Close by, at SO 238 486, is Pen Twyn Camp, circa B.C. 500. This is a small Iron-Age hill fort with an internal enclosure of about 1.1/2 acres, which is partly protected by a double rampart and partly by a natural scarp. Early forts were always small. Just north of Cwmma Farm, 1.3/4m NE of the church at SO 276 515, are the earthworks of an early Norman motte and bailey castle. The motte is roughly circular, about 30 yards in diameter at the base and rising to about 18 feet high above the ditch. How effective these small forts were.

The parish of Brilley is essentially a sheep hill farming area, but many of the inhabitants these days are professional people seeking the solitude and sanity of the wilderness with the amenities of the 20th century close to hand.

BRIMFIELD *4m S of Ludlow*
The name is from the Anglo-Saxon bramel-feld, meaning 'bramble field'. Most of the cars whizz by on the busy A49(T) which is just as well because before it was built, all the traffic poured through the main street of Brimfield. The settlement has a certain well matured charm - the red brick and stucco Roebuck, black and white cottages, the cream painted Hall set beside a stream and embowered in tall trees, a boarded barn and the Forge House Gallery.

The church of Saint Michael stands on higher ground away from the village. It retains a 13th century tower with 17th century timber top and a 13th century font but was much restored by the Victorians.

Across the road, 1/2m SW of the church, is Brimfield Common, an area of poorly drained land fringed with squatters' cottages. It is still quite marshy in the centre and wet enough to attract snipe and wild duck. Sheep and cattle graze amongst the tussocks of coarse grass and the commoners, quite properly, jealously guard their rights.

Wyson Common adjoins Brimfield to the west. It has the feeling of fen country with duck ponds and some very good alder woods full of butterflies in the Summer. At the far end of the Common is a strange hummocky landscape of mounds about 18 inches high. These are anthills and have taken 200 years to grow to this size. Brimfield Hall was once home to the Salwey family, local landowners - hence the Salwey Arms opposite the Little Chef at the crossroads.

A member of the Johnny Walker whisky family lived at the big house which now houses the Fabric Workshop south of the village. Brimfield also has a race-horse trainer, a sawmill, a foundry, a baker, Maureen's Fudge factory, and a battery egg farmer. The main line railway is still going strong but Wolferton Junction station and the branch line to Kidderminster fell a victim to Mr. Beeching's Axe in the 1960s. Remnants of the old Leominster to Mamble Colliery (Stourport) Canal and its Wyson Common Tunnel (1796) run parallel with the railway. (See Orleton.) Gone, too, is the cattle market that used to be held in a field adjacent to the Sa'way Arms.

In 1912 there were Morris dancers at Brimfield, the only practitioners of that ancient art in the whole of the county at that time. (For Upton see Little Hereford.)

BRINGSTY COMMON *3m E of Bromyard*
It lies on both sides of the Worcester to Bromyard road, the A44, but mostly to the south. The name is from the Anglo-Saxon, meaning 'Brynca's path', and it is a Regulated Common in the care of Malvern District Council. There are 229 acres of rough pasture, scrub woodland and bracken cut through by rough tracks and dotted with squatters' cottages. At least they were the abode of humble folk once, but they have grown and grown and many are now quite substantial and desirable houses. Much to the discomfort of the birds, lizards and snakes these undulating acres are infested with screaming children and ice-cream vans on sunny Summer days. Not that the landlord of the Live and Let Live really minds, though his pub is not easy to find, tucked away in the wilderness as it is. Ask the way at the service station with attached shop, post office and tea room. A little to the west are the delights of Brockhampton which has its own article.

BRINSOP *5m NW of Hereford*
'Brune's Valley'. The Anglo-Saxon name was simply Hope, meaning 'valley'. By the early 12th century it was Bruneshope, Brun being a French personal name. Brinsop has attractions that have captivated many observers. There is little more than the church and the manor house but both are beautiful and both are beautifully situated. They lie at the foot of Credenhill, the Celtic capital of central Herefordshire, which itself lies just north of the Roman town of Magnis (Kenchester).

The church of Saint George is approached through an orchard field. In the tympanum there is an elegant example of the Herefordshire School of Carving: Saint George slaying the dragon beneath an arched frieze depicting a serpent, a bull, saints, fishes and lions, and an angel. Inside there is a lustrous reredos of alabaster and gold, a wall painting of about 1300, a 14th century rood screen and

Top left: Avenbury, c. 1910. Hops grown on individual poles. Later, frames and wires were used. The doleful nag pulls a load of bagged hops to the drying kilns.
Top right: Lady Brilliana of Brampton Bryan.
Middle: Brockhamton by Bromyard.
Right: Bridge Sollars, sinking the stanchions for the bridge in 1896.

20th century windows commemorating William Wordsworth, his wife Mary and his family. The poet often stayed at Brinsop Court, which was the home of his wife's brother, Mr. Hutchinson. Just north of the church, and west of the rectangular moated site close to it, are the slight earthworks of the now deserted mediaeval village mentioned in Domesday Book and in the Lay Subsidy Roll of 1334 and in the Poll Tax Returns of 1377 when 48 persons were paying taxes here. The large rectangular enclosure defended by a rampart in which the church stands is probably pre-mediaeval.

The Court is a 14th century sandstone house with some timber-framed additions of the 16th and late 17th centuries and some Georgian brick facing. In 1913 it was much restored and the east wing was constructed to enclose the courtyard. It has an extremely impressive hall open to the original roof of combined tie-beams and king posts. The Court lies almost 1m N of the church surrounded by a triumvirate of hills - Credenhill, Merryhill and Badnage - that provide a majestic setting for this superb and well-preserved mansion, which comes complete with a water-filled moat and a reed-fringed pool. It has been home to several families, including the Tirrels, the Daunseys and the Astleys; Madeleine Carroll, the film star, lived here with her husband, Captain Philip Astley.

About 300 yards S of the Court is an abandoned square moat. North of the Court a badly damaged Early Bronze-Age burial chamber, a small cist, has been found. The body lay in a north-south orientation. In such graves males were usually accompanied by weapons and the females by ornaments and domestic items.

At White House Farm, about 200 yards off the main road, a cluster of converted 17th century buildings form the nucleus of a small holiday village. There are nine cottages, a heated swimming pool, saunas, a solarium and a carp lake on the four-acre site.

The Herefordshire Travellers' Support Group give legal aid, moral support and physical assistance (such as digging out council erected barriers in road lay-bys), to both Romany gypsies, Irish tinkers and English travellers. The members are all voluntary and unpaid. They do not have a permanent office but can be contacted through Brian Richardson, Trefoil, Brinsop Common. Brinsop Common is on the south side of the main road, the A480, and faces a short, dead-end lane of old squatters' cottages.

BROBURY *10.5m WNW of Hereford*

The Domesday name was Brocheberie, from broc, 'stream' (it can also mean badger) and burg 'fort', hence 'fort by the stream'. Brobury faces Bredwardine over the River Wye which has a Norman castle. The settlement consists of a few scattered cottages and the abandoned church of Saint Mary Magdalene which now lies in ruins with only the chancel upstanding. Elements of tracery date it at about 1300. The red sandstone cliff 1/2m E is called The Scar. Remains of a prehistoric camp have been found here.

But it is not all ruin and desolation. Brobury House was built in the 1880s in the style of a Scottish hunting lodge and has a characteristic round tower with a conical roof cap. It has splendid gardens with oaks, limes and beeches, specimen shrubs and fish ponds and there is an art gallery which specialises in British prints, maps and water colours. Both gardens and gallery are open to the public and have wheelchair access. Bed and breakfast can be obtained here and there are conference facilities. The views from the gardens of the splendid 18th century Bredwardine Bridge and across the river to Francis Kilvert's rectory are delightful. Brobury House was used as a film set for the television drama *Dandelion Dead*, the true story of a solicitor who poisoned his wife, when it was used as the residence of the character called Major Armstrong. For more on the area see the article on Bredwardine.

BROCKHAMPTON (by Bromyard) *2.5m ENE of Bromyard*

'Settlement by the brook'. As an ensemble the 14th century moated farmhouse and its dainty little gatehouse are one of the most picturesque groups of black and white in the whole of England. Lower Brockhampton Farm lies beside a stream deep in a secluded valley amongst pastures surrounded by woods. The woods are a feature. Although conifer plantations predominate there are stands of mature oak and some fine giant Californian redwoods. Woodcocks and ravens, both very rare in Herefordshire, are frequently seen here. Lower Brockhampton is a mile from the nearest road (the A44) but a metalled track leads to a small car park. From here a path leads through an orchard grazed by sheep, past the duck-filled moat, to the 15th century gatehouse. The farmhouse contains the original hall, open to the roof, with a cross wing to the right; that to the left has disappeared. The central truss of the hall is a base-cruck, a rare construction of which there are only 90 in Britain. The curved crucks do not meet at the apex but they support a collar on which the roof rests. This enables the hall to be a few feet wider.

To the west of the house are the ruins of the Norman chapel which has a 13th century chancel and an early Perpendicular west window. The Norman part is constructed of tufa, a soft, porous limestone.

The estate has been inherited by direct descent for 750 years, albeit twice through the female line. Habbingtons, Barnebys and Lutleys lived here. Then, in about 1750, a Lutley decided to leave his remote little valley and declare his position to the world in the grand manner.

He built Brockhampton Park, a Georgian red brick pile on the top of the hill and nicely in view from the road. It has seven bays and a three-bay pediment and was halfway to being handsome before the windows were butchered in the 1860s. Behind the house is a veritable rabbit warren of outbuildings. Now that these are all converted to dwellings - there are 12 units altogether - it constitutes a village by Herefordshire standards. The Gothic, grey stone New Chapel is of about 1798 and contains monuments to Edmund Higginson (died 1798), Lydia Bulkeley (died 1812) and John Barneby (died 1817). The best view of the house is from the ashlar, temple-like lodge on the main road. It stands proudly in its landscaped parkland with lovely country all around.

The estate is now owned by the National Trust but the house has had several commercial owners. At the time of writing it is about to be renovated and restored as a private house. Constance Sitwell was a visitor on more than one occasion and has recorded her memories of the place in her autobiography *Smile at Time* (1942). James Lee-Milne has a chapter on Brockhampton in his *People and Places*, subtitled Country House Donors and The National Trust (John Murray 1993). He tells of a middle-aged couple he met one lovely Summer's evening at Lower Brockhampton. They came from Bradford in Yorkshire and visited here twice a year. Their son had been a pilot in the RAF and his ashes had been scattered in the park. "After all," they said, "this must be the most beautiful place in England."

BROCKHAMPTON (by Ross on Wye) *4.5m N of Ross*

The old English broc can mean either 'stream' or 'badger'. Here, we favour 'settlement near the badger sett'. Brockhampton is most easily approached off the B4224 at Gurney's Oak pub, Upper Buckenhill. It is situated in romantic country, a land of small hills and little valleys, clumps of trees and pastures like lawns.

The glory of this place is the church of All Saints designed by W. R. Lethaby and built in 1901-2. The venerable Nikolaus Pevsner writes that it is "one of the most convincing and most impressive churches of its date in any country." Lethaby belonged to William Morris's Arts and Crafts Movement. Here he managed to make a mediaeval style church without it being a mere imitation. Stone columns and pointed arches support concrete ceiling vaults; the crossing tower has a stair turret; the roof is thatched and the porch is topped by a pyramid. The creepers were planted deliberately. Inside there is a Burne-Jones' tapestry, 16th century altar pieces and stained glass windows by Christopher Whall.

Opposite the church is the elaborately decorated, Victorian-Jacobean-style black and white lodge of Brockhampton Court. The drive leads past a perfect village cricket ground and through wooded gardens to the impressive castle-like house. The heart of it is the old vicarage which was transformed and extended in 1879. The tower was added in 1893. It faces the setting sun and is perched above a steep valley with rolling blue hills receding to the horizon. With woodsmoke curling lazily on a gentle breeze, the sound of bat and ball, and all the comforts of a country hotel close to hand, well, if there's no room in heaven I'll settle for this. The ruins of the old church are near the Court and most of the village houses lie to the south and east on the lane to Falcon, a hamlet on the B4224.

To the south of Brockhampton is Totnor, lying in a steep-sided valley. The name is probably from Tota-ofer, 'Tota's settlement on the steep bank'. To the north is Capler Hill, a home of prehistoric man. On the lower slopes of the steep bank adjacent to the River Wye is a large quarry (SO 587 328). It is believed that the stone used to build Hereford Cathedral came from here. A lane from Fownhope church leads to the Capler Cottages and from there footpaths lead to the quarry and, further along past a cobbled area, to the remains of the quay. At Brinkley Hill, 3/4m SW of Brockhampton church, is a council maintained Picnic Site beside the River Wye.

BROMYARD *12.5m NE of Hereford*

'Enclosure in the broom'. It stands on high ground above the deep, dark ditch of the River Frome. The country around is hilly and pastoral. Pastoral is a choice word because the town appears to have developed first as an Anglo-Saxon religious centre, a minster from which priests went out to minister to outlying villages. The church was stone-built and some of its fabric was re-used by the Normans. After the Conquest the extensive manor was given to the Bishop of Hereford. He had a residence in the town and ordinations in large numbers were carried out here.

Commercially, Bromyard developed as a market town, one of the most ancient in England it is said. The early borough burgage plots running back from the road can still be traced in High Street and Broad Street. Sales of cattle, sheep and pigs were conducted in the town centre streets. Today there is no market and it lost its borough status in 1968. Nevertheless, it is a flourishing, friendly service town with a good range of individual shops, banks, solicitors, estate agents, pubs, restaurants, a fish and chip shop, assembly rooms, sports facilities, schools and even a theatre. In recent times there has been much fringe residential development and the yards of the disused railway (it came in 1878 and departed in 1964) now house a small industrial estate. Opposite the estate is Quarry Field, flanked by the lugubrious River Frome. This is the venue for an internationally known Festival of Traditional Folk Music that takes place during the third week of September. The festival was founded in 1967 by Dave Jones (1940-1991), a much respected, singer, dancer, musician and collector. Since his untimely death his widow, Annie Jones, and Doug Isles have continued to organize the event. The tented village and giant marquees in the valley are only part of it; the whole town becomes a seething mass of big hairy people banging small Irish drums. Watch out for the women; they wear clogs, drink beer and do fertility dances in the street. Virtually every pub has a session; fiddles, flutes and melodeons pound out jigs and reels and English country dances till the early hours. The Bromyard Gala, famous for its steam engines, is in July.

Here are some notable buildings to look out for. The church has an Anglo-Saxon carved panel of Saint Peter above a doorway, two striking Norman doorways and some Anglo-Saxon masonry. Most of the rest is 14th century, including the eight tomb recesses (an unusually high number). The old market Bushel Measure, dated 1670, is kept in the church. Tower Hill House in Pump Street has close-set timber framing with decorative lozenges and is considered to be the best house in the town. The black and white Falcon Hotel, with its prestigious close-set upright timbers, dominates the mostly brick-built Broad Street. Many of these brick houses are in part timber-framed and only have brick facades.

The stone-built Jackson Almshouses, founded in 1656, are in Cruxwell Street and stand opposite the Georgian Cruxwell House. In the Market Place is the Hop Pole Inn, one of the centres of the folk festival. The brick-built early 18th century Quaker Meeting House has hammer beams, and in Sherford Street is an excellent 18th century Congregational Chapel of 'stone bricks' with Tuscan columns and a pyramid roof. In High Street are the black and white Bay Horse Inn and the King's Arms. Rowberry Street has the council offices, the Tourist Information Office and the Heritage Centre housed in the 18th century stable block of the Rectory. There is a caravan site south of the town by the A44. At the end of Highwell Lane in the southern suburbs is Eye Well, a holy spring. The spring now feeds a garden pond but an old stone well nearby is said to be fed by the same spring.

Less than 1m E of the town are the Bromyard Downs, 132 acres of common land regulated by the Council. The old squatter colony is a village by Herefordshire standards. Beware Summer weekends for the hillside heaves with motor cars and their occupants, mostly day-trippers from Worcester.

On a June day in 1917 Terence McSwiney, an Irish internee and prominent member of the I.R.A., married Muriel Murphy whilst defiantly wearing full uniform. The ceremony was performed at Father Mathieu's Chapel, (now demolished) Frog Lane, Bromyard. Shortly after McSwiney became Lord Mayor of Cork where he was arrested with an incriminating British cipher and imprisoned at Brixton. He went on hunger strike and died 74 days later.

Here are some traditional customs and beliefs collected by Mrs. E.M. Leather in the early 20th century from the

Bromyard area. A mole-tump in the garden is a sign that someone in the family, or a relative, is about to die. Belief in witchcraft and the special powers of wizards such as the famous Jenkins was common in Bromyard. Jenkins was an historical person, known to Mrs. Leather, who lived somewhere between Hereford and Bromyard though that good lady refused to say exactly where. A charm used to cast a spell collected at Bromyard Workhouse was: 'These words was wrote on a marble stone, sinew to sinew, and bone to bone.' On New Year's Eve: "A rush is made at twelve o'clock to the nearest spring of water, and whoever is fortunate enough to bring in the cream of the well, as it is termed, and those first to taste it, have prospect of good luck during the coming year."

At Bromyard the 1st of May was the date of the 'mop', or hiring fair, at which servants and labourers sought employment for the coming year. Sprigs of birch were placed over the door of each house and people wore them in their hats. But traditionally the 29th May was the real May Day hereabouts. It was the custom at burials in Bromyard to throw sprigs of rosemary on to the coffin. Somewhat mysteriously the church bells are said to chime: "Come old man and shave your beard, Say the bells of Bromyard".

A farmhouse near Bromyard was haunted until the tenant took on a servant girl who sat up one night and was visited by two ghostly ladies who took her into the cellar where they showed her a hidden crock of gold. They told her to take it and give some to the farmer. After that the hauntings stopped. It was generally held in these parts that to hide anything made of metal would bring bad luck and, ultimately, death. In speaking to a ghost you should always say "In the name of God, who art thou?" The spirit will then lead you to a hidden hoard.

We cannot conclude without a mention of hops. There is no obvious sign of the industry in the town of Bromyard today but the district around is very much the centre of hop growing in Herefordshire. The greatest concentration of hopyards is south of the town. Until only a generation ago Bromyard was invaded by a cheerful army of poor people from the Black Country and South Wales who came for a working holiday handpicking the hops. Mechanisation has seen an end to that. The Bromyard and District Local History Society have produced a first class book called *A Pocketful of Hops* (1988) packed with information and many evocative photographs. From it one learns that in 1807 the parish of Bromyard had 660 acres of hopyards; in 1985 there were none at all.

BROXWOOD 8.5m WSW of Leominster
The name means 'badger wood'. Most of the dwellings of this hamlet are at Lower Broxwood. In the absence of an Anglican presence the settlement had the Roman Catholic church of the Holy Family of 1863 in dark grey stone to a design by C.F. Hansom. It is now a dwelling-house. The Victorian Broxwood Court that Leonard Stokes built in 1891 has been pulled down and the stone re-used to build a smaller house. The stable block still stands and the whole sits in parkland with woods and a lake.

The village lies 1/2m NE of the Court. It is a pleasant, airy little place with some Victorian red brick houses of 1864, black and white cottages and a stone Independent Chapel of 1844, now occupied by furniture maker Michael Smith. The country around is undulating with small woods. Bolton, 1/2m SW of the Court, has a cruck truss in the south wing.

A cure for rupture practised at Broxwood was to slit an ash sapling, walk between the halves, and then tie the halves together. Wake-like feasts were held in the area before the Victorian Roman Catholic church was built. They might well have been a pre-Christian survival.

Upper Broxwood Farm, 3/4m S of Lower Broxwood, is a late 14th century, timber-framed and stone-built house, now the home of Tom Addyman, an authority on old buildings and an expert 'limer'. Lime mortar has many advantages over modern cement. It is soft and if a building moves lime mortar moves with it and self-heals. Modern cement is hard and cracks. Lime 'breathes' and lets moisture in but dries quickly without perishing. Modern cement traps moisture and delays drying. Mr. Addyman runs courses on the preparation and use of lime as mortar, as plaster, and as a pigmented wash. These are held at Upper Broxwood.

Local builders are beginning to see the merits of lime once more. McNamara & Company of Clyro, near Hay-on-Wye, for example, only use lime mortar now on restorations. They were recently employed to conserve Roman plaster at The Weir. (See Kenchester.) This material had been exposed to the river and the elements for 2,000 years but was still intact. Modern plaster would have perished and fallen off in a fraction of that time.

Lime is made by burning limestone rock in a kiln. The result is quicklime. This can be spread on fields as a 'sweetener'. To prepare it for use as a mortar or plaster it has to be 'slaked', by adding water. This needs to be done whilst wearing goggles and protective clothing to prevent burns.

A layer of limewash was often used to protect timber frames from woodworm, weathering and decay. The traditional Herefordshire pigments are red and pink, obtained from local clays. Pink plaster panels and silver-grey timbers are so much more attractive than the magpie garb adopted in Victorian times and which is still so prevalent. Exposed oak timbers should never be painted. The paint can trap water and so cause rot. Wet timbers are not a problem if they can dry quickly.

BUCKENHILL 1m NNE of Bromyard
The name is from the Anglo-Saxon bocen 'of beech', hence 'hill covered in beech trees'. Here there is an isolated manor house of about 1730, built of brick, with nine bays and Victorian gables. The doorway has a pediment supported by two stone Corinthian columns. Around and about are ancilliary buildings and dwellings all close to a tributary of the River Frome.

BUCKTON 8.5m W of Ludlow
The name means 'Bucca's homestead'. Buckton is a hamlet close to the River Teme 1m NE of Brampton Bryan, and in the past was a place of some strategic importance. One mile west of Buckton is Coxall Knoll Camp, an Iron-Age hill fort with enclosures to the east, west and north, defended by a double ring of ramparts and ditches with an elaborate west entrance. It covers about 8.1/2 acres, is oval in shape and occupies the top of an isolated hill between the Teme and its tributary the Redlake.

Another Iron-Age settlement is situated 1/2m W of Buckton at SO 376 733 but is only discernible from aerial photographs. There are two probable round barrows, 1/4m NE of Buckton Park at SO 392 740. One is oval, about 81 yards x 62 yards and rises to 9.1/2 ft and is surrounded by a ditch. The other is smaller and irregular in shape. For a description of the stone axe and flint implements found at Buckton see the report by L.F.Chitty in the *Transactions*

Above: Colwall, the Iron-Age fort on the Herefordshire Beacon, the Malverns.
Right: the Malverns in Winter.

of the Woolhope Society, 1964, Volume 38, pages 153-5.

Aerial photography has revealed the sites of two 1st century A.D. Roman forts, one 1/2m NE of Buckton at SO 386 735, and another 1/2m E of Buckton at SO 390 733. At the latter excavations have indicated that it was occupied by 500 cavalry housed in wooden barracks, defended by an earth and turf rampart and ditch which were superseded by stone materials at a later date. (For a photograsph and a plan see p. 204.) Just SE of the hamlet at Buckton Farm is Castle Mound, SO 383 733, an early Norman motte and bailey castle. The motte is roughly oval, about 43 yards in diameter at the base, rising to about 14ft above the ditch.

BULLINGHOPE *2m S of Hereford*
The name is from the Anglo-Saxon meaning 'Bulla's valley'. Both before and after the Norman Conquest it was held as three manors. The holders in 1066 were Edwin, Rever and Alnoth. The settlement had two mills and a forested area which was part of the King's Wood. By 1341 the land had been re-arranged as two manors, Bullinghope Superior and Bullinghope Inferior. By 1831 these had become Bullingham and Upper Bullingham and by 1872 as Bullinghope and Lower Bullingham. Talk about confusing! Today Bullinghope is still a separate village, detached from Hereford, but Lower Bullingham, 1m NE, is now a riverside suburb of the county town and has its own article.

Bullinghope is a well-heeled, most pleasant little place that has attracted a development of expensive modern brick houses which in no way detract from the charms of the older black and white.

The Parsonage was built in 1868 but is now a private house called The Cedars. In the garden are the ruins of the old Norman church, a simple rectangular building of about 1150 which had nave, chancel and a later bell-turret. The Norman windows and doorway have been removed and the walls lowered to a safe height.

The new Saint Peter's was completed in 1886 to an Early English design by the local architect F.R. Kempson. It stands on a rise, a neat little red sandstone building with white stone dressings, looking sharp and proud. It looks out over a verdant landscape to Dinedor Hill and Ridge Hill.

The National School of 1886 was paid for by the Misses de Winton and was very much the social centre of the village, being used in the evening for dances and club activities. It is now a private house.

Farming is still the main industry of the area though the population now includes commuters to the county town.

BURGHILL *3.5m NW of Hereford*
'Hill of the fort', but of the prehistoric fortress there is no sign. It might well have occupied the site now taken by the church. Saint Mary's stands on higher ground a little aloof from the village, opposite a boarded barn. It was virtually rebuilt in the 19th century using some Norman and 14th century windows and doors. Inside is a Norman font with applied lead ornament (sketched by Edward Elgar we are told), a beautiful reredos screen, and a monument with effigies to Sir John Milbourne and wife of about 1440. A brass marks the last resting place of Robert Masters (died 1619) who circumnavigated the world with Thomas Cavendish. In the churchyard is a mighty yew tree with a girth of some 25ft; for company it has 12 more, the Twelve Apostles. The village is a charming mix of black and white and brick with the new estates placed out of sight.

Burghill Court is a large, rather gaunt, Georgian brick house of five bays and two and a half storeys with a three-bay pediment and Doric columns to the porch. The barns are now dwellings. It was here, on an Autumn day in 1926, that two rich spinster sisters, Elinor and May Woodhouse, gave their butler his notice. Charles Houghton had served them for more than 20 years but his drinking bouts had been getting worse and this angered the God-fearing sisters. The next day he shot them both dead with a sporting gun. He did not deny killing them but said he did it whilst having an epileptic fit. His defence failed, he was found guilty of murder and was hanged by the public executioner, Albert Pierrepoint, at Gloucester Gaol on 3 December 1926.

Today the village is very quiet. The blacksmith, the wheelwright, the carpenter, the post office and the pub are all gone. However, the village of Tillington 1m NW, has a pub, a Nonconformist chapel of 1857, and a garage; and the hamlet of Portway, 1/2m NE on the A4110, has the Royal Oak Inn. At Portway there are hop kilns, but the Burghill area is now more one of apple and pear orchards, soft fruit, ploughland and pasture. The Manor and Tillington fruit farms are owned by the Co-operative Wholesale Society. Such institutions are taking the place of traditional landowners, like the local Colonel Biddulph.

But what dominates Burghill these days is the County Asylum, 3/4 of a mile SSE of the church. It is almost a village in its own right. It was built to an Italinate design in 1868-1872 and enlarged in 1900. The architect was Robert Griffiths of Stafford. Its red and yellow bricks glow in the sun and from a distance the two towers give the impression of a Saharan fortress. It is now used as a hospital.

Close to the main road at Portway are the remains of a group of three terraces, called lynchets (SO 488 447). Levelling ground like this for agricultural purposes was done in both prehistoric and Anglo-Saxon times. (For something more on the area see the article on Tillington.)

BURRINGTON *5m WSW of Ludlow*
'Beornwynn's homestead' lies on the eastern edge of the serene Vale of Wigmore, the home of the great Marcher Lords of Mortimer. Beornwynn's old homestead might well have been the stone and half-timber Burrington farm, which nestles against a steep bank on the northern fringe of the village below the hill pastures of the common. The settlement consists of a few stone cottages, a most handsome Victorian school (now a private residence) and Lower Farm, a black and white house with a stable barn attached to the right - what is commonly called a Longhouse, man and beast beneath one roof.

But this is not why tourists come to this out-of-the-way little place. They come to see the six cast-iron tomb slabs displayed in the churchyard. These are not unique, but they are very early (from 1619 to the early 18th century) and, what is more, the lettering is most handsome. On several of the slabs it is sans serif, which is quite unusual. Sans serif lettering is plain, that is to say it does not have the little flourishes that were characteristic of most type faces until the mid-20th century. One of the tombstones is for Richard Knight (1659-1745) who set up a forge at Bringewood 1.5m NNE. (See Downton.) The slabs were probably cast at the family's Bridgnorth furnaces. Burrington used to belong to the Downton estate until quite recently. The church of Saint George was re-built in

Victorian times and has lancet windows and a tower that is timber-framed in the upper part and topped by a spire.

However, Burrington's most romantic association is with Wild Edric, the Domesday holder of the manor. Edric Sylvaticus was an Anglo-Saxon nobleman, warrior and rebel whose spirit is said to wander the Welsh borderlands to this day. He also held Staunton and several other Herefordshire manors and had lands in Shropshire. He was a nephew of Edric Streona (died 1017), Ealdorman of the Mercians. Wild Edric acknowledged William the Conqueror as king in 1066 but then joined King Bleddyn of Gwynedd and King Rhiwallon of Powys in raids on Herefordshire that caused great devastation. In 1069 he burnt Shrewsbury but in 1070 finally submitted to King William.

BYFORD *7m WNW of Hereford*
'Ford where trade took place', from the Anglo-Saxon byge, which is related to our word 'buy'. Byford is a little place that stands beside the River Wye, just off the A438. The Court is a handsome 16th century, timber-framed house now largely encased in stone. It has three gables and mullioned and transomed windows. The spacious church of Saint John the Baptist has some Norman work - a window, a door, and three bays of the south arcade. Much of the rest is 13th to 14th century; the tower is of 1717; and there is a tablet to the King family of 1774. In the south transept there are some good stiff leaf capitals.

Fallsbrook Farm, near the church, has a cruck truss. Byford Common is 1/2m NW and has some good examples of both brick and late timber-framed squatters' cottages. Between Byford and Bridge Sollars the road almost touches the Wye. Here there is a high mounded section of Offa's Dyke (SO 407 428) hidden amongst the trees. The hill to the north is Garnon's. (See Mansell Gamage.)

BYTON *8m WNW of Leominster*
'Settlement by the bend'. It stands near the River Lugg which wriggles profusely hereabouts. Presteigne, the old county town of Radnorshire, lies 3m W. The church of Saint Mary is built on a raised mound of glacial moraine and offers good views into the mountains and forests of Wales. It was re-built in 1860 but retains a Norman tympanum with a carved lamb and cross and a Norman font with zig-zag ornament.

Two houses of consequence are: the Woodhouse, 1m SE, which is 17th century but clad in Georgian brick with Venetian windows and a pediment; and Coombe Farm, 1.1/2m WSW which is timber-framed with diagonals in the gable and is mostly of about 1500.

At Lower Kinsham a footpath follows the River Lugg through the dramatic wooded gorge it has cut through the Silurian limestone. By means of an occasional trespass the serious walker can follow the river through splendid country all the way to Aymestrey, some four miles to the east. (See Kinsham for more on Byton.)

CALLOW *3.5m SSW of Hereford*
'Barehill'. The busy A49 now bypasses the small village through cuttings to avoid the steepness of the old road.

In the 19th century Callow Farm used to be a coaching inn. On several occasions passengers who stayed the night there failed to appear the following morning. After some time an inquiry was held and it was discovered that they had been murdered and robbed and the corpses carried across two fields and buried in an isolated house. This house was subsequently left to become ruinous and has now been reduced to a low mound. It is said that the house materializes every now and again - a ghost house in the real sense. Shadowy figures are also sometimes seen stumbling across the fields. People have seen both apparitions in living memory.

Not to be outdone, Callow Farm has its own ghost. A phantom girl dressed in a ball-gown, wearing only one slipper and weeping, was seen entering a particular bedroom. In the 1920s alterations were made and a wall of the bedroom was removed. Behind it was found a small powder closet and a little blue slipper.

From the church there are spectacular, long views over the city of Hereford and the hills beyond. Saint Mary's had connections with the Knights Hospitallers in mediaeval times but was re-built in 1830. It retains only the 15th century font from the old church. The Forge ceased trading in 1944 and became a shop which closed in 1985. The school opened in 1906 and closed in 1953, a familiar pattern in rural villages these days. On Saint Thomas's Day the income from 21 acres of land donated to the Pearle Charity is distributed to the poor and the elderly.

In 1415, Owain Glyndwr, the Welsh national hero, is said to have died of starvation in Haywood Forest, a little to the west. There are still sizeable woods at Callow and Haywood.

At Portway, 3/4m N of Callow on the busy A49, is Callow Filling Station. This is part of a complex which includes two new car dealerships and a cafe. On the first 14 Sundays of Summer, commencing in early June, a huge car boot sale is held on an adjacent field.

CANON FROME *5m NW of Ledbury*
The Anglo-Saxon name was simply Frome, after the river by which it stands. In 1280 it was given to the Canons of Llanthony (in the Black Mountains just over the border in Wales). This is good agricultural country famous for hops.

Coincidentally the notable family name here is Hopton. Michael Hopton came from Shropshire to marry a local heiress in 1591 and the family stayed until 1952 when they sold out to the County Council. Their mansion became a school but in 1978 it was converted to flats and is now under siege from cars and children. In front of the main house there is a pretty lake fringed with specimen trees. During the Civil War the Court was ransacked by Cromwell's men and some 70 Royalists were put to the sword; a field here is called Bloody Acre. The present Court is of 1786. It is built of red brick and has seven bays, two storeys, a pediment, a Tuscan portico and modern additions. Carvings on the entrance gate piers illustrate figures from the Hopton coat of arms - a griffin chewing a human hand, and a Talbot dog resting a paw on Saint Andrew's cross. Inside the Court is a most splendid piece of elaborate carving: a re-set 16th century overmantel with fanciful gatehouses depicted in the blank arches and finely carved female figures, strange animals, fruits and decorative bands. Somewhat on the heavy side but nevertheless something to treasure.

The Swiss Cottage is a curiosity. It is a replica of Queen Victoria's house on the Isle of Wight and stands on the site of the old watermill, once used to generate electricity for the Court. Wargart Engineering developed from the local blacksmith shop, established here in 1868.

The church lies close to the Court, by the river, away from most of the scattered village houses. The tower was re-built in 1680 in red brick using English bond; the rest was re-built in 1860 by G.F. Bodley whose genius had yet to flower. Pevsner describes the rose-window glass as "outstanding".

In 1969 a 1st century Roman fort was discovered in the grounds of the former school at SO 641 433. Finds from within and around the fort include 2nd century pottery and tiles indicating a civilian settlement at the posting house situated near the junction of two Roman roads. (See Stretton Grandison.)

CASTLE FROME 5.5m SSE of Bromyard.
'Settlement by the castle by the River Frome'. This is a scattered community with the pub and most of the houses at Fromes Hill on the A4103. But what the world comes to see resides in the church 3/4m SW, which has its own access lane off the B4214. One is welcomed by the grey cladding and concrete block sheds of Dalgetty Produce who clean and pack potatoes for supermarkets. Ignore this tasteless intrusion; the church stands beyond, on the lower slopes of the hill.

Saint Michael's was restored and given its timber bell turret in 1878 but much early Norman work has survived. Its glory is the font, a late work of the Herefordshire School of Carving dated at about 1170 and a piece of art of international repute. The stem and bowl are large, carved out of one piece, and have scenes depicting the Baptism of Christ. They rest on a plinth of three massive crouching figures; one is a lion but the other two are now unrecognizable. As with all the work of the Herefordshire School there is a perfection of design and sureness of execution that is unrivalled anywhere else in England at this time and which holds its own with the best in Europe.

In the chancel is a small carved bust of a knight holding his heart in his hands. This usually denotes a heart burial. When the body of a deceased person could not be transported, as in the case of a Crusader killed in a far away foreign land., his heart was cut out and sent home. An alternative was to boil the corpse to remove the flesh and send the bones home for burial. There is also a handsome tomb chest of about 1630 with alabaster effigies of a man and his wife with their children kneeling around the base.

The Early Norman motte and bailey castle lies 350 yards E of the church, lost amongst trees. The motte is about 60 yards in diameter at the base rising to about 14ft above the bailey. The scarp to the east and south marks the bailey boundary. A deserted mediaeval village site lay west of Saint Michael's but has now been filled in and the house platforms are badly obscured. A holloway passes the motte to the south-west.

As if all this were not enough for so small a place there is more. In 1840 Wilford Woodruff came to stay at The Hill Farm 1/2m SE of the church. He was an American Mormon missionary, a man of charisma it seems because he baptised some 600 people here in one month. The story goes that the local vicar sent his parish clerk and his church warden to find out what was happening, and they came back converted Mormons! Six months after his arrival at the village 50 local converts set sail for America. During the next 10 years another 1,200 from the Malvern area followed. The pond that Woodruff used for his Baptisms still exists and is visited by large numbers of Mormons from all over the world. It is called the Benbow Pond and is located in the corner of a field near The Hill Farm (SO 674 454). There is a commemorative tablet beside the rather marshy pool which is still used for occasional baptisms.

In the Winter beware of Lock's Hill, (west of Fromes Hill) and Fox Hill (north of the hamlet of Catley Southfield); they are both steep and can be treacherous. To the west is the flat, fertile plain of the Frome. Between Castle Frome and Canon Frome the land is festooned with the poles and wires of the hopyards. At New Birchend, 3/4m S of the church, there is a homestead moat.

CLEHONGER 4m WSW of Hereford.
The name is from the Anglo-Saxon meaning 'clayey slope' and is pronounced locally as Clunger. The old village is quite separate from the new 'dormitory town' that lies 3/4m W. In this century the population of the settlement has increased five-fold, from nearly 500 to 2,500. Such numbers are able to support a school, a pub, a garage, a post office and two shops; but the Methodist chapel is disused, the flour mill is now a house; the cider works closed in 1950; and the corrugated-iron Roman Catholic church has been abandoned to nature.

The parish church of All Saints soldiers on as it has from Norman times. It has a Norman doorway and some re-used zig-zag decorated stones, a 13th century tower and arcades, and a chancel of about 1300. The chantry chapel was founded in 1341 by Sir Richard Pembrugge. It contains a beautiful effigy of Sir Richard in full armour with a dog at his feet; elsewhere there are brasses to Sir John Barre, died 1483, and his wife Eden; and an A.W.N. Pugin window of 1850.

CLIFFORD 2.5m NNE of Hay on Wye
'Ford by a cliff, or a slope'. It lies on the B4350 beside the River Wye, hard on the border with Wales. The river meanders through a broad valley surrounded by hills. The village is dry, drink was outlawed by the local estate and the nearest pubs are at Hardwicke, 1.3/4m SE, and Clock Mills, 2m E. The substantial castle stands on a cliff 150ft above the Wye and covers an area of three and a half acres. The motte is 36ft high and supports a 13th century stone-built, five-sided shell keep with five towers. The outer and inner baileys had a barbican gate between them.
Excavations in the 1960s revealed a Roman sandal buckle and a toga clip. The castle was owned by the Clifford family in the 13th century and it is here that Henry II (King of England from 1154-1189) is said to have met his Fair Rosamund, Jane Clifford (c.1134-76), later immortalised by Tennyson in his *Dream of Fair Women*. Henry's queen, Eleanor, was 11 years his senior and to protect his beautiful young mistress from her wrath he installed Jane, so it is said, in a house surrounded by a guarded maze at Woodstock, near Oxford. However, whilst Henry was away fighting in France Eleanor had Jane taken and forced her to drink poison.

From the Cliffords the castle passed to the de Lacys by marriage and then to the great Mortimers who entertained Richard II and John of Gaunt here in 1381. Owain Glyndwr destroyed the castle in 1402 and by 1485 it had ceased to be of any strategic value.

At the time of Domesday the settlement was a borough and part of the ancient street plan remains. The now disused Hereford to Hay railway (1863) ran along the common (now a nature reserve) below the castle. For much of its route it followed the line of the Brecon to Hay tramway, opened in 1816, which was later extended to Kington and the limestone quarries at Dolyhir.

The church of Saint Mary stands on high ground 1/2m SE of the village. It has a nave and chancel of about 1300, a tower mostly of the 18th century and a north aisle of 1888. Inside is the carved oak effigy of a priest of about 1300; the only other in the county is of Bishop

Top: Cloddock, bridge and church of Saint Cloddock.
Below: Downton Castle, late 18th century.

Above: The font at Castle Frome, an example of the early 11th century Herefordshire School of Carving, probably led by a Spanish or French master craftsman brought here by Oliver de Merlimond, lord of Shobdon, who made a pilgrimage to Santiago de Compostella whilst Shobdon church was being constructed. The pilgrim route is famous for its finely decorated churches. Shobdon had some of the very best work in the whole of Europe before it was vandalised by Richard Bateman in the mid-18th century.

Aquablanca at Hereford. There are also two early 19th century monuments to the Penoyne family.

Priory Farm, 1/4m SSE of the church, stands on the site of a Cluniac Priory, founded in 1130. The house has a stone 14th century range with original roof timbers and an early 18th century range of ashlar with a hipped roof and a re-set 13th century doorway in the basement.

The Romans had a 16-acre fort at Clifford (SO 249 467). The Norman motte and bailey earthworks at Old Castleton, 2m ENE of the church, have extensive crescent-shaped baileys close to the Wye and were probably constructed by William FitzOsbern of Breteuil whom William the Conqueror created Earl of Hereford in 1067. He constructed many early border castles; Old Castleton was held by Ralph de Todini. Between Westbrook and The Bage is Newton Tump, 3m ESE of the church. It is another motte and bailey set in very pleasant pastoral country.

Stone is much used as a building material hereabouts, especially in the barns with arrow-slit windows. A place of sheep and fresh air, as they say. Uphill from the church is Longhouse, a part timber-framed building that once sheltered man and beast under the same roof. Close by, in Priory Wood, is a small, stone-built Calvinistic Methodist Chapel of 1827. The tall dwelling is a converted Malthouse where grain was germinated and dried.

CLODOCK 14m SW of Hereford
'The church of Saint Clydowg'. The hamlet is lost in a green sheltered valley in the foothills of the Black Mountains, most easily approached off the A465 at Pandy. It is a grey stone hamlet that has the Cornewall Arms, a church, a holy well, a mill, a castle mound, trout fishing on the Monnow and a legend.

Prince Clydowg, son of King Clodwyn, a 5th century king of Ewias, was out hunting one day when he was murdered by a rival in love. His body was removed for burial on a cart pulled by two oxen but they refused to cross the Monnow at the ford and then the yoke broke. These were taken to be signs that the prince should be buried here. He had led a godly life, and his murder was considered to have made him a martyr (though the logic of this is not clear). Pilgrims came to visit his tomb, he was sanctified, and a church was built, first in timber, then in stone. A fragment of this early stone church has survived and is set behind the pulpit in the present building. It has a 9th century funerary inscription in Latin: "To the dear wife of Guinndo, a resident of this place". The church we see today is mostly Norman with later windows and a minstrels' gallery used by local musicians. The present day West Gallery singers called Vital Spark, from Malvern, perform here on occasion.

Clodock Mill, somewhat gaunt and grim like Hatterall Hill behind it, is now disused but has a complete set of working machinery and two sets of stones, one for flour and one for animal feed. The water-wheel is unusually large and was made at Leominster in 1868.

Saint Clodock's Well stands on the opposite side of the river from the church, by the side of the footpath leading south from the bridge. Its healing waters are spring-fed and do not come from the stream. It is covered by a slab, like a bench. It is possible that this was a pagan religious site and there is a local tradition that the original church was close by the well. On our visit we met a lovely man with four bonny dogs, all saved from the Birmingham Dogs' Home, who lives in a cottage by the well.

The Mound is a Norman motte and bailey castle. It stands on a spur 1/3m N of the church. The motte is substantial: 150ft in diameter and 30ft high. The bailey is crescent-shaped. The barn of Ty Mawr, 1/2m SSW of the church, is the former hall of the house and retains its original crucks and wind braces.

At Clodock on the local feast day, the first Sunday after November 15, the people had the right to hunt hares on the Black Mountains and kept greyhounds for this purpose. They also bake special cakes on this day.

CODDINGTON 3m NNE of Ledbury
'Coda's homestead' is a tiny hamlet in a land of winding lanes and wooded hills a mile or so from Bosbury. The late Georgian, red brick Court cuts a dash with five bays, two and a half storeys, hipped roof, pediment and Tuscan porch. But what is this, an oil exploration and production company with offices in The Hague and Jakarta whose headquarters are in the depths of Herefordshire? Yes, the powers that be of Clyde Petroleum plc are esconsed at Coddington Court, and have been since 1981. In 1995 the group had a turnover of £140 million and net assets of £227 million. Their most important production areas are the U.K and The Netherlands and they are listed on the Stock Exchange. Their current chairman is Malcolm Gourlay of the Old Vicarage, Bosbury.

The church of All Saints is early 13th century Transitional with rounded Romanesque door arches and pointed early English lancet windows. The tower was built during the restoration of 1865. Outside there is a churchyard cross, complete except for the head.

COLLINGTON 3m N of Bromyard
'The settlement of Cola's people' is a tiny place on the B4214 Bromyard to Tenbury Wells road. Saint Mary's was built in 1856 to a design by A.E. Perkins of Worcester. It was a new church and replaced the old Collington Minor which lay inconveniently on the eastern side of the parish. It has nave, chancel and bellcote with font and silver plate from the old church. Martin's Castle, 300 yards N of the church, is a deserted mediaeval homestead; all that remains is the moat.

Near the pub at Pie Corner, 3/4m N of the church, is the entrance to the long drive that leads to Netherwood, felicitously tucked away amongst woods and orchards on the lower slopes of Wall Hills. The front of the house was rebuilt in brick in about 1780 to provide three big bays, with a one-bay pediment and semi-circular windows in the second storey. At the rear is an early 16th century timber-framed range with closely-set vertical studding. This was the birthplace of Robert Deveraux, Earl of Essex, Queen Elizabeth I's hot-headed paramour who could not hold his tongue and, despite his Errol Flynn life-style and charisma paid the ultimate price for scorning a proud queen. In the gardens there is a circular, mediaeval stone Dovecote and a drooping cedar tree. High on the hill south of Netherwood is the Iron-Age fort of Wall Hills. (See Thornbury.)

COLWALL 3.5m SW of Great Malvern
The Domesday Book name was Colewelle, probably meaning 'cool well, or spring'. We will make a journey starting at West Malvern, a residential area on the west flank of North Hill. The B4232 heads south. Between the trees and houses there are long views to the west. Below the Worcestershire Beacon is a gushing spring (SO 765 450) with off the road parking near a stand of Scots pines. Cars pull up regularly and people collect water in plastic containers. "Very good for making tea", said one old lady. A little further south and a group of buildings on the left

includes a tall, four-storey former brewery of 1905 which now houses the workshops of Malcolm Wycherley, leaded-light specialist. Another spring is inaccessible because it is gridded over. All along the road are villas built to take in the view. At the rock cutting of Upper Wyche the B4232 continues south.

However, we turn east at Upper Colwall passing the Cloud Nine Tea Rooms and two chapels now converted to houses. At the sharp dog-leg bend is the entrance to the long, wooded drive that leads to Linden Manor Restaurant and Conference Centre. It is a substantial three-bay, two-storey stucco mansion of 1860 delightfully situated amongst specimen trees in its own grounds of some 12 acres. It was built for Stephen Ballard, the engineer, who constructed the railway tunnel which passes beneath the Malverns, 1/3m to the north, and who designed the Gloucester to Hereford Canal (begun in 1839). He had travelled the world for much of his life but this is where he settled. He took an active part in local affairs and fought to protect the hills and commons from excessive development. His sons were as enterprising as their father and between them started a vinegar factory (now a plastics works), a gas company (taken over with nationalisation), a brick making business, a garden nursery and a water bottling plant.

We go back to the main road, heading south-west, passing many desirable hillside villas such as Sunfold (stone with a corner turret and elongated battlements), suitably embowered, and emerge at Colwall Stone. This is the modern heart of Colwall. It developed in late Victorian times because the railway station made access to this attractive area so easy. The railway and the station are still open. Colwall has a sufficiency of shops, social services, and houses for the less well-heeled.

The Colwall Park Hotel, near the station, has a place in sporting history because in 1926 Mrs. Scott-Bowden, who owned the hotel, organized a festival of women's cricket. This led to the formation of the National Women's Cricket Association. The annual festival continues. Incidentally, the Horse and Jockey is a reminder that Colwall once had a racecourse. Today it the base of the Silurian Border Morrismen who perform at local festive occasions throughout the year.

The Old Court Nurseries are centred on a large white stucco house and are famous for their Michaelmas Daisies. This is one of the Ballard family enterprises. So, too, is the Malvern Water bottling plant just down the road which now belongs to Coca Cola-Schweppes Beverages Ltd.

The stone of Colwall Stone still exists, a limestone block rolled down the hill by a giant to bring his unfaithful wife and her lover to a sticky end, so the story goes.

We now come to Colwall Green - council houses, bungalows, the Oddfellows, a post office, the cricket ground and the village hall. Through some open country and at the main road junction is the sprawl of Barton Court, hiding behind yellow stone walls. It is a big, Georgian, red brick house of six bays with a hipped roof, pediment and Venetian window and has a farm attached. In the sunken lane by Barton Court the ghost of Sarah Pritchard Lambert is frequently seen. She had married Sir Henry Tempest, a penniless Yorkshire baronet, who threw her out after gaining control of her estate which included Barton Court and Hope End.

But to continue our journey. Turn right and take the lane that leads to Colwall proper, the original settlement on the Cradley Brook. It is a delight. The church, the ale-house, the manor, the old Rectory and a couple of cottages make a superb group. The passing of the years means nothing here. The church of Saint James has a late Norman doorway, an early English arcade, a 14th-15th century tower, chancel of 1865 and north aisle of 1880, a good nave roof, two windows by Kempe and monuments to Elizabeth Harford, died 1590 and John Walweyn, died 1587, and the remains of a churchyard cross.

Park Farm is timber-framed with brick infill and stands on the site of the Bishop of Hereford's mediaeval manor house. The Ale-house is black and white. Beer was brewed here until the building was converted to four tiny cottages. Now it is used as an occasional function room. The Old Rectory is a very large, very handsome, many-gabled Gothic building and has an extraordinary number of chimneys;- we counted 18 and there are probably more. A perfect place in which to set an Agatha Christie whodunnit. From the church take the lane west to Old Colwall, an 18th century, roughcast house of six bays and two and a half storeys with a 17th century staircase.

Now take the lane south to the A449, turn east, across the valley floor, up the hill, (look back, if you can, the view is delightful) to Wynd's Point. To the right is the Herefordshire Beacon, 1,114ft above sea level. On the summit are the considerable earthworks of an Iron-Age fort which covers some 32 acres. Unusually, the outer ditch is inside the earth rampart. Finds include British and Romano-British pottery, flints, whetstones and sling stones. The depressions are probably the sites of huts. At the highest point is The Citadel, a later Norman ringwork - a ditch with an internal earth wall on which a palisade was constructed. Twelfth century pottery has been found here. The Shire Ditch, a low bank with the ditch on the east side follows the ridge from Midsummer Camp in the south, to the Herefordshire Beacon and then north to the Worcestershire Beacon. Beside it, at SO 767 421, are two round barrows both 34ft in diameter and 3ft high. The depressions on their surfaces probably indicate that they were robbed in Victorian times.

Raggedstone Hill, SO 760 364, is one of the Malvern Hills and rises immediately south of the Ledbury to Tewkesbury road, the A438, opposite the quarries of Midsummer Hill. There is a legend that a monk from Little Malvern Priory, 3m N, fell in love with a local girl and as penance for his lustful ways was ordered to climb this exceedingly steep hill on his hands and knees every day. The monk cursed the hill and anyone on whom its shadow should fall. Victims who died shortly after setting foot here include Cardinal Wolsey and George William Huskisson (killed by Stephenson's *Rocket* steam engine).

But to return to Wynd's Point and our journey. From the Malvern Hills Hotel car park take the B4232 north. This is known as Jubilee Drive and was hacked out of the hill in 1887 as a leisure drive for the carriage trade. There are superb views to the west and strategically placed parking areas. On this road is Perrycroft, an early work of the noted architect C.F.A. Voysey which was completed in 1894. With the exception of the outbuildings both the exterior and the interior have remained virtually unaltered. Nikolaus Pevsner describes the house as being amazingly un-Victorian, unpretentious, sensible and graceful.

Several springs emerge on the flanks of the Malverns but the most important of all is Prime's Well, or Pewtress Spring, on the boundary of the old Ledbury Chase at SO 760 403. Together with Waum's Well it was used to supply the Iron-Age fortress of the Herefordshire Beacon. Prime's Well is so abundant that it has been fenced off, tanked, and the water piped away to the bottling plant of

Malvern Water. It was below this well that the hero of William Langland's mediaeval masterpiece, *Piers Plough man*, sat dreaming. It is still an enchanting spot, though spoiled by the noise of the traffic from the main road.

Follow the road north and one is returned to our starting point at West Malvern. (For Hope End see Wellington Heath.)

CRADLEY *3m W of Malvern*

'Creoda's clearing in the wood' lies on the Cradley Brook at the foot of the Malvern Hills, a charming village with some attractive black and white cottages. The church was heavily restored in 1868-1870 but of the earlier work there remain: a piece of Anglo-Saxon frieze decorated with scroll work on the north wall of the tower, a Norman window in the tower, and a Norman south doorway with zig-zag decoration in the arch.

The Parish Hall was once the school. It is a most handsome timber-framed building with an overhanging upper floor resting on moulded support beams. The New Rectory is a modest Late Georgian house. The doorway has Tuscan half columns and a broken pediment. Two other good houses in the parish are Lower Nupend, lm NW at Greenhill, a Georgian house with four bays, two and a half storeys, semi-circular (lunette) windows on the top floor, and a plaster ceiling of about 1600; and Barrow Mill, 1.3/4m N at Bearswood Common, a timber-framed house with a Jacobean porch which has small, decorated, upright columns; and Vinesend, 3/4m ENE, noted for its herringbone work.

A cottage industry prevalent in these parts at one time was glove-making. The pieces were sent out from the Worcester factories, hand stitched in cottage and farm and returned by carrier.

Amisia Daniel, the 'Cradley Witch' lived at Wild Goose Hill, Storridge, between 1397 and 1400. Another woman with strange powers lived on Crampton Hill, 2m NE. Her name was Cofield and hunters whose dogs chased game near her cottage always lost their quarry.

A Cradley man was punished by 'colestaffe riding'. This was not a legal affair but was meted out by local people to those who had committed social misdeeds. The culprit was paraded through the village on poles whilst onlookers jeered and made raucous music by beating on pots and pans. In other places and at other times a straw effigy was used and burned at the end of the proceedings.

Old traditions such as morris dancing and mumming have always been well maintained in Cradley. Dave Jones collected a Boxing Day play here, complete with song, and it is now performed annually by the Old Wonder morris side.

CRASWALL *5m SE of Hay on Wye*

The mediaeval name was Cressewell, and there is, indeed, a well called Cress Well below the gate to the churchyard. The village lies in the foothills of the Black Mountains, close to the Welsh border, in "the highest and wildest parish in Herefordshire".

The church of Saint Mary stands somewhat forlorn on the slopes of a hill, and is in need of a helping hand to save it from further decay. It has nave, chancel and bell turret and retains its original Perpendicular 15th century windows and roof. In the 18th century the west end was walled off and used as a school. Outside, against the north wall is a levelled area once used as a fives court and beyond this is a depression once used as a pit for cock-fighting, so they say. Along the outside of the south and east walls is a stone bench facing the preaching cross.

Past the church the road climbs for a mile and reaches a height of 1,450ft above sea level. Here there is wild moorland, and the views are spectacular, especially towards the twinkling lights of Hay. One hundred yards below (to the right, facing Hay) in Foxes Dingle in the valley of the Monnow are the meagre and uncared for ruins of the Priory of Saint Mary (SO 273 376), founded in 1222 by Walter de Lacy and given to the French contemplative order of Grandmont. (There were only two other Grandmontine houses in the whole of England - at Grosmont in Yorkshire and Alberbury in Shropshire.) Henry VI granted the Priory to Christ's College Cambridge and it was they who abandoned it. Of the church the south wall of the nave and the chancel are still upstanding and the semi-circular apse walls are still evident. The plan of the cloisters and the chapter house are just discernible. A lead casket containing bones was found here, believed to be relics of the martyred virgins of Saint Ursula, massacred by Huns on the lower Rhine in 453 and interred at Cologne. The remains of fish ponds and their dams can be seen south of the Priory down a footpath from Abbey Farm. At the lightly wooded top of a small dingle near the ruins of the Priory is the Pot Well, or Holy Well (SO 2689 3802). There are other springs in the vicinity but the Pot Well can be distinguished by the stone slab with a basin about 28 inches in diameter.

At the top of Cefn Hill, in grid square SO 27 28, 1/2m N of the abbey site, finds were discovered by a ploughman which indicate that there was a New Stone-Age settlement here. The site was surveyed in 1946 by R.S. Gavin Robinson. In a shallow depression, covered by a thin layer of peat, artifacts were unearthed which included leaf-shaped arrowheads, a sandstone mortar, a pebble hammerstone, an axe and spindle whorls.

Two houses with cruck frames are Middle Blackhill Farm, 2.1/4m SSE of the church, and the barn of Court Farm, 1/4m N. 'Many of the farms are Tudor and have no roads and the inhabitants ride on horses as they always did.' (*Shell Guide*, 1955.)

CREDENHILL *4.5m WNW of Hereford*

'Creoda's hill'. It is a flat-topped hill with steep slopes. On the plateau is the largest Iron-Age hill fort in Herefordshire. At about 70 acres it is more than twice as large as the next largest, Sutton Walls. Like the Roman capital, Magnis, and the present county town it lies at the centre of the geographical and political unit we call Herefordshire. It is therefore assumed that Credenhill was the Celtic capital of the area. Recent clearance of the 20th century tree plantation has revealed previously unidentified earthworks. The single rampart follows the contours of the hill and is roughly oval with interned entrances in the east and south-east. Post hole evidence shows that the dwellings of the early 5th century B.C. were oblong wooden huts with four corner posts enclosing an area 6ft by 4ft. (Evidence from other parts of England shows that all early, and some later, dwellings were square.) The huts were arranged in rows 10ft apart along streets 16ft wide and probably had raised wooden floors.

The hill forts of Herefordshire were probably occupied by the Decangi tribe, who were suppressed probably about 50 A.D. by the Romans under Scapula. Their dwellings in the hill forts were burned, or, as at Credenhill, were dismantled. It has been estimated that the population of Credenhill at this time was about 4,000.

Above: Colwall, the church of Saint James and the Brewhouse.
Below: Credenhill, Ye Olde Cottage.

Today, Credenhill once more has a considerable human presence, lowlanders this time living at the southern foot of the hill. They are mostly in the employ of the R.A.F and operate a large storage depot. As we write this camp is in the process of being vacated and will shortly be re-occupied by the S.A.S. who are moving their regimental headquarters here from its previous location in the southern suburbs of Hereford.

Between the R.A.F camp and the Iron-Age fort are the church and the Court. The embowered grey stone church is mostly 13th to 14th century with a late Norman doorway, a palm tree beside the porch, and two lovely stained glass figures of about 1310 representing Thomas, Archbishop of Canterbury, and Thomas Cantelupe, Bishop of Hereford.

Another Thomas, Thomas Traherne, was vicar here from 1661-1670. He is a highly-acclaimed metaphysical poet whose reputation has grown in recent years. A contemporary described him as "one of the most infectiously happy men this earth has ever known". Born a shoemaker's son in Hereford about 1638 he studied at Oxford and then came to Credenhill where, amongst other things, he wrote three books of *Meditations*.

The red brick Court lies just to the NW of the church and is now a nursing home. To the front there is a ha-ha and a battered cedar. The house was built in 1760 and has five bays, three storeys, a Venetian window, a parapet and giant angle pilasters.

On the main road is Ye Olde Cottage, a thatched timber-framed dwelling with one gable wall clad in ship-lap. Amongst the security netting, huts, houses and offices of the R.A.F. complex, a modern Voluntary Controlled School lurks behind the old stone school of 1885, and there are some farms with stone barns. By the suburban semis there is a post office-cum-general store and on the fringe of the village is the National Snail Farming Centre, or rather a heap of breeze blocks, sheds with asbestos roofs and a Portakabin proclaiming itself as such. They do guided tours.

CROFT *5m NW of Leominster*
The name is Old English and means 'the enclosure'. The entrance to the estate is off the B4362 at Cock Gate. There are many good and interesting things here: an ancient stone castle and its church, lovely grounds with the biggest oak tree in England, a large prehistoric fort, mediaeval charcoal burning terraces, lime kilns and the delights of the Fishpool Valley.

The castle is large, not quite square in plan, with round towers at each corner. It dates from about 1400; the windows are Elizabethan and Georgian. The entrance side was added in Gothic style in about 1755; the porch, parapet and gables are of 1913.

Domesday Book has Bernard (de Croft) holding the manor and his descendants kept it until 1746 when debt forced its sale to the Knight family of Downton. They sold it to the Davies family of Wigmore about 1785 and they sold it back to the Croft family in 1923. The Crofts live there today but the castle and the estate are now in the hands of the National Trust.

The Croft family has been lucky in both love and war. They married into the Mortimers and were duly rewarded with many high Offices of State for supporting them in the Wars of the Roses, at the end of which Edward Mortimer became Edward IV, King of England from 1461 to 1483. They have been Sheriffs of Herefordshire on numerous occasions and had Members of Parliament from 1296 to 1727. One of them married, Janet, a daughter of the great Welsh national hero Owain Glyndwr (c.1355-c.1415) and there is a tradition that a Welshman can always get a night's lodging at Croft Castle with a palliase of straw in the attic. The Croft family suggest that this could have originated from the time of Owain Glyndwr who might have sought refuge here between battles with the English and in his old age.

The church of Saint Michael has a nave and chancel of about 1300 and a 17th century bell-turret. Inside is an impressive monument with effigies and canopy to Sir Richard Croft, died 1509, and his wife Eleanor (Cornewall).

The castle grounds have lawns and specimen trees separated from the deer park by a ha-ha. There is a sense of tranquility. Two splendid avenues lead to the castle, one of oaks (planted in 1590) and one of beeches. However, the star of this arboreal show hides away in a disused limestone quarry, situated in a remnant of mediaeval woodland pasture. It is the Croft Oak (SJ 448 653) which, at 42.1/2ft around its girth, beats the previous British record by 1ft. It is thought to be about 700 years old and is completely hollow but very much alive. On the bluff above are several more ancient and majestic trees.

The 5th century B.C. Iron-Age hill fort of Croft Ambrey lies 3/4m N of the castle. It has massive defences with ramparts that are still almost 16ft. above ground level. There were three main phases of building and the site covers 24 acres. Excavations have unearthed a wealth of material including iron tools and weapons, pottery, the bones of sheep, cattle and pigs and the post holes of some 300 wooden hut dwellings. These were burned by the Roman troops of Scapula about 50 A.D. and the site was never properly occupied again. Findings from Croft Ambrey can be seen at Hereford Museum.

Below Croft Ambrey, to the north, along the Aymestrey limestone escarpment of Leinthall Common, is a complex of small, mediaeval limestone quarries, tracks and charcoal burning terraces. They are probably related to the making of burnt lime for agricultural purposes. Later production was on a bigger scale. In the Fishpool Valley there is a large quarry and the remains of stone-built lime kilns. The Fishpool Valley lies adjacent to Bircher Common but is most easily accessed from the main drive to the castle. It is a steep-sided valley, heavily wooded with a series of fishpools and is a Site of Special Scientific Interest. The path continues up to the Iron-Age fort. The author has fond memories of Croft. It was one of his last days out with his mother before she died of cancer in 1992.

Cock Gate is a crossroads hamlet of stone and timber-framed dwellings at the entrance to the Croft estate. Here are the workshops of Four Seasons Products who make bird-feeding tables, nesting boxes and rustic garden furniture.

(For Bircher Common see Bircher and Yarpole.)

CUSOP *1m SE of Hay-on-Wye*
The first element of the name might well be from the Welsh cyw, meaning 'the young of birds', which was probably the original stream name. Cusop lies in Cusop Dingle on the Dulas Brook which here forms the border between England and Wales. The stream rushes down a delightful wooded valley, narrow and steep, singing as it goes. The Welsh borders are full of such charming watery dells but they are rarely as accessible as Cusop Dingle. In places like this one begins to understand why the Celts worshipped trees and streams in preference to the graven images so clumsily worked by man.

The church stands on high ground in a large churchyard with four ancient yew trees. Saint Mary's is essentially Norman with nave, chancel and bellcote much restored by J.P. Saint Aubin. The chancel arch, blocked north doorway, and part of a nave window are Norman; two lancet windows in the chancel are 13th century; the tub-shaped font with saltire crosses and lozenges is Norman but has been 'freshened up' by re-tooling, thus spoiling its aura of age; the roofs and some of the pulpit panels are 17th century. In the churchyard is the grave of William Seward, a Nonconformist preacher who was killed by a mob incensed at the content of his sermons.

Cusop Castle, 150 yards SE of the church, is the site of an early motte and bailey. It consists of an irregular, oval-shaped enclosure with the remains of outer earthworks which were destroyed when the road was constructed.

Just down the hill from the church is the London Borough of Barking and Dagenham Trewern Outdoor Education Centre. Snappy title, that. It is housed in an irregular Victorian, pebble-dashed building with a steeply hipped roof, dormers and an elegant stand of pines.

For the rest, Cusop is a Victorian suburb of Hay-on-Wye with modern infill, playing fields, a veterinary surgeon and the Conygra horse stud. But this is not what Cusop is about. Head on up the hill, past the spaced out Victorian villas - Redwing, Lower House and Brynmelin - through the plantain shrubs, past the orchard, the specimen trees and yews, following the laughing waters dancing over the weir, past Duffryn and old stone cottages, past Paper Mill House and its lovely water gardens, waterfalls and hidden mill pond, past Llanwathan, to a bridge and high meadows and mossy banks.

"Fairies have been seen dancing under foxgloves in Cusop Dingle within the memory of some now living there." (Henderson, *Folklore of the Northern Counties*, 1879.) An old lady from Cusop said that a bend or a crook in the iron bar that supported kettles and pots over the fire was the 'Brownie sway', Brownie being the Herefordshire name for a hobgoblin. (E.M. Leather, *The Folklore of Herefordshire*.) A farmer near Cusop named his daughter Chloe, after his favourite mare, despite local belief that to name a child after an animal was to court disaster. The child was burnt to death in a rickyard fire at the age of three and the mare fell and broke her back at the same spot shortly afterwards. (Ibid.)

In 1955 David Verey in his *Shell Guide* wrote: ".....this place ought to be in Wales; people cannot understand English, still less the Oxford accent." Snobbery at its most splendidly flamboyant, methinks.

Mouse Castle, 3/4m NE of the church, is probably an Iron-Age hill fort site which was later developed by the Normans. What we see now are the earthworks of an early motte and bailey castle. The motte has been damaged by the removal of soil and is no longer circular. The Broad Ditch was probably a small bailey enclosure and has fragmentary ramparts. At 800ft above sea level there are good views. Best of all, though, are the oak woods which cover the hill. These are in the care of the Woodland Trust and the trees are allowed to grow completely naturally. The birds sing their praises all and every day.

The Obelisk, 1/4m NNW of Mouse Castle on the edge of Mouse Castle Wood, was erected by Anna Maria Broadbelt Stallard-Penoyre who inherited the now ruinous Moor Mansion and its estate in 1827. The work was commissioned to relieve local unemployment and can be seen on the skyline from the Hay-on-Wye to Hereford road, the B4348.

Hay Bluff, 3m S of Cusop, stands 2,219ft above sea level and is a convenient point for walkers wishing to join the Offa's Dyke Path and gain access to the Black Mountains. To get there take the minor road out of Hay-on-Wye that runs parallel with Cusop Dingle, forking west just past New Forest, passing the prehistoric monument of Twyn y Beddau, to the stone circle at SO 239 373 where there is a marked parking place and long views into the Welsh hills. Tracks leads up the steep face of Hay Bluff. If one chooses one can continue south and follow the road, past Lord Hereford's Knob, through Gospel Pass and down the Vale of Ewyas to Llanthony Priory, an area very dear to the late Bruce Chatwin; for a detailed description of a journey down this road from Hay to Crucorney see the article on Capel-y-ffin.

DEWSALL *4.5m SSW of Hereford*
The mediaeval name was Dewyes Welle, 'St. David's Spring'. Dewi is Welsh for David. Dewsall is a scattered hamlet down a dead-end track from Callow, off the A49. The church of Saint Michael and All Angels was consecrated in 1340 but was much restored in 1868. It has a nave, chancel and bell-tower with shingled spire and the remains of a preaching cross in the churchyard.

The Court, south of the church, is a 17th century stone-built 'H'-shaped house with a hipped roof. Inside is a Jacobean overmantle (ornamental shelves over a mantlepiece). It was built for the Pearle family. In 1674 James Brydges was born here. He became Paymaster-General to Queen Anne, flourished financially and becane Duke of Chanders. Handel wrote the *Chanders Anthem* for him. However, easy come, easy go, and the family's extravagance forced the sale of the Dewsall estate in 1731. Their property went to Guy's Hospital and remained with them until sold to Sir Charles Clore in the 1950s. He in turn sold the land to the Prudential Assurance Company.

On the lane between the Old Rectory (now called Farmore) and the church is The Ark cottage which was once an alehouse. An agricultural holding here is evocatively called Cold Nose Farm. Monkhall Court is now divorced from its land. The Rhydd stands all alone and lonely 3/4m SW of the church. The name is Welsh, meaning 'free, liberty'.

DILWYN *5.5m SW of Leominster*
Anglo-Saxon etymologies suggest the name means 'secret, shady or lovely place'; but Dilwyn is also a Welsh Christian name. At the time of the Norman Conquest it was held by Raven Knell. It lies just off the A4112 which in 1973 was moved slightly to the west through expensive cuttings to bypass the village. It is a complete place, an archetypal village, with its own school, post office, shop, pub and village hall. The village green has a magnificent spreading chestnut tree which faces the great Tithe Barns, now converted to dwellings, 19 in all.

The handsome church of Saint Mary stands on a rise flanked by gardens and orchards and a disused graveyard. It has a tower of about 1200, topped by an 18th century spire; the nave, aisles and chancel are of about 1300;but the clerestory windows were later replaced in the Perpendicular style. The tomb of a knight in mail armour in the chancel is thought to be that of a Talbot, of the family that founded Wormsley Priory (1216). In the chancel windows are the coats of arms of Talbot and Delabere. The key to the south porch is 17 inches long.

260 yards south of the church is the site of the mediaeval manor, now built on. The earthworks might originally

have been a part of an early Norman motte and bailey castle. The mound of this stands in the garden of a modern house at SO 416 544. It measures about 54 yards in diameter and rises slightly above ground level. In 1981 there were other earthworks nearby which appeared to be house platforms indicating a deserted mediaeval village but new estate roads were already cutting through the site. There is another, almost square, isolated, moated site 1/2m SSE of the church, near Field's Place.

Some notable houses include: Great House, Early Georgian with good wrought-iron gates; Bidney Farm, 1m N, with decorated square framing and a most attractive 17th century black and white dovecote; Luntley Court, 1.1/2m WNW, felicitous Jacobean timber-framed with gables, many good outbuildings and a black and white dovecote in pretty flat country by Tippet's Brook; Middleton House and Yew Tree Cottage, both 1m NE, have cruck frames (big curved beams that support both the wall and the roof, a very early form of construction): and Swanstone Court, 2m ESE, which has an 18th century centre block with a 14th century cross wing.

Vaughan Williams collected some folksongs at Dilwyn early in the 20th century and the village has a tradition of morris dancing. On Oak Apple Day (29th May) the children of Dilwyn still wear a sprig of oak to commemorate the escape of Charles II in 1651 when he hid in an oak tree at Boscobel, Shropshire. He was restored to the throne on 29th May, 1660. At Hay's Head, Luntley, 1.1/2m WNW, is Dunkerton's, a small, independent producer of cider.

At Little Dilwyn, 1.1/2m ESE of the church, is a probable deserted mediaeval village with a moated site situated by a stream just south of Little Dilwyn Farm at SO 438 539. The earthworks include some later soil quarrying.

Pigmore Common, 1.1/2m NNE of Dilwyn church, on the Lower Hardwick to Lower Burton road at SO 417 565, is a five-acre Regulated Private Common. The land is wet but wild flowers grow in abundance, especially marsh marigolds, irises and the increasingly rare cowslip. Ducks also live here.

If on leaving Dilwyn the traveller takes the main road south-west in the direction of Hay-on-Wye he is treated to wide-ranging views over peaceful, gentle pastures, wooded hedgerows and rolling arable fields. The verges are bedecked with wild flowers and in the distance are the dark hills of Wales. Indeed, these lands once belonged to the Welsh; you can see why the Anglo-Saxons and the Normans were so keen to steal them.

Bagley Head, 1m W of Dilwyn, is a scattered hamlet of cottages and farms, holly in the thick hedges, honey for sale, old orchards and Hereford cattle. At Headland there is a black and white farm with a brand new red brick and weather-boarded barn with a rusty-red corrgated iron roof. That is class. Stockmoor Cottage has a timber barn with wattle panels.

DINEDOR 2.5m SSE of Hereford
The Domesday Book name was Dunre, from the Welsh din, 'fort', and either bre 'hill', or tre, 'a village'. So, the name means either 'hill with a fort', or 'village by a hill'. Dinedor lies at the foot of Dinedor Hill, a favourite weekend resort for the people of Hereford. On the summit is Dinedor Camp, an Iron-Age hill fort. It is approximately rectangular with a high single rampart to the north and east and a lower rampart to the west and south where the ground falls away steeply. The entrance is on the east. The fort covers 9.1/2 acres and excavations have shown it was densely populated both before and after the Roman Conquest. Finds include animal bones, pottery, coins and iron fragments, now in Hereford Museum. The hill is well organised for visitors with car parking, toilets and picnic benches. The mature beech trees are an added attraction. Access is most easily gained from Dinedor Cross which is off the Hereford to Hoarwithy road just south of Green Crize.

At Dinedor Cross there is a holy well but the spring now only feeds a garden pond at Holywell Farm. The first water to be drawn on New Year's Day was called 'the cream of the well' and there was much competition to get it for those that drank of it or washed in it would have good fortune, health and beauty.

Another pre-Christian custom celebrated at Dinedor until recently was the Twelfth Night wassail. Twelve fires in a ring with a larger fire at the centre burned whilst the people ate, sang and drank to promote the growth of the next season's crops. The village of Dinedor has a rural aspect, the hill protecting it from Hereford and its suburbs. It has houses old and new, set amongst ploughland and pasture. Access is off the B4399.

The church of Saint Andrew was re-built in 1868 by F.R. Kempson but retains 14th century masonry in the tower. There is a monument to Francis Brickenden, died 1799, and a brass to Bertie Davies who drowned in the River Wye attempting to save two men. In the field just south of the church are the holloways and house platforms of the deserted mediaeval village.

Rotherwas Chapel, 1m N, now ingloriously resides in the water meadows of the Wye next to a large sewage works. The nave and chancel are 14th century; the roof is 17th century; the tower is of about 1800 and the spire is 'strange Victorian'. The chapel belonged to Rotherwas House, a large eleven-bay mansion built in 1732 around an earlier core. It was the house of the Bodenham family, local landowners, until 1912 when the estate was sold. In 1924 the house was demolished. The chimney piece of 1611 and the dining room are now at Amhurst College, Massachusetts. All that remains are some garden walls, a pool and the parkland trees. During the war there was a munitions factory and store here. The unsightly mess that was left when they departed is in the process of being removed and replaced with an industrial estate - out of the frying pan...... The Hereford City Pistol Club has meetings in premises here every Monday and Wednesday evening.

DINMORE 5.5m S of Leominster
The name is from the Welsh din - mawr, 'great hill'. Anyone who travels the busy A49 will know Dinmore Hill with its swooping bends and crawler lanes cutting through Queenswood. Dinmore is really one house, the village is Hope under Dinmore which has its own article.

Dinmore Manor lies 1m to the west of the main road, but can be seen from it, perched high up at the end of the valley pastures flanked by deciduous woods. It is a delightful place, a little mediaeval domain. The settlement was founded in 1189 when the Knights of Saint John of Jerusalem built a preceptory here. (See the note below.) What little of this remains is incorporated in the house and the chapel. The house was much restored and extended between 1929 and 1936 when the great, Gothic, grey stone west wing was added. It contains a magnificent baronial hall and cloisters which overlook a delightful rock garden with a grotto. Inside there are numerous examples of modern craftmanship at its very best.

The new building work was commissioned by Richard Hollins Murray who bought the house in 1927. Three

Top: Croft, the author and his mother in the ancient oak grove.
Left centre: Madley, a hop bagger, 1901.
Right centre: Croft, Church of Saint Michael adjacent to the castle.
Left: Clehonger, church of All Saints.

years earlier he had patented his invention of reflecting lenses, later developed by others as the cats' eyes which have been such a great aid to road safety. The Murray family still occupies the house.

A range of about 1700 links the new work to the east wing of about 1600 which stands on foundations of about 1300 - see the basement windows and doorway. The chapel was once connected to the house, and the north-east buttresses are, in fact, remnants of the connecting walls. The doorway between the buttresses is of the original preceptory. The somewhat austere chapel was originally much longer and extended another 16ft at the west end. The tower and the rest of the chapel are 14th century. Close by is an ancient yew, expertly assessed to be over 1,000 years of age. Dinmore Manor is a peculiar, or extra parochial parish. The church is a parish church but as the parish church is not a part of any diocese neither the Bishop nor the ecclesiastical authorities have any jurisdiction. The old stone barn and the free range chickens add greatly to the ambience;: the modern bungalow decidedly does not. The gardens are protected from the deer park by a ha ha, but there are only sheep; the park palings were left in disrepair in the 1940s and the fallow deer escaped to live in the broad acres of Queenswood where they can still be seen.

West of the church is the well-head of the stream (SO 482 502) that carved the lovely valley below. It is covered by a beehive-shaped stone structure that supplies a more recent reservoir disguised as a folly.

The present access drive was constructed in 1830; that used by the knights and pilgrims followed the south side of the stream along the edge of Wellington Wood, marked by a clearly defined holloway.

On leaving the manor we followed the track through the woods and high pastures to Kipper Knowle, a stone farm with a brick cottage, and on down into a secluded valley. Pheasants scuttled by and there was the sound of shooting. The prospect before us resembled a mercenary training camp: a scaffolding tower, sheds and Portakabin offices, a tree house and shooting shelters all clustered around an old, and rather ugly, stone cider mill in the woods of Friars Grove. We left the Herefordshire Shooting School (SO 488 514) in sombre mood. The people who harmlessly shoot clay pigeons today are often the same callous and cold-hearted people who shoot small birds and animals for pleasure tomorrow. It would not be quite so bad if they used proper guns that require some element of skill, but shotguns are the weapons of butchers, not sportsmen. The shotgun was a favourite with the SAS in Malaya because it was so murderously effective and easy to use at close range. But that only proves my point; it is a weapon of butchery.

Lawton's Hope Hill lies 1/2m W of Dinmore Manor. It is on this hill that Owain Glyndwr is said, by an early authority, to have died of starvation whilst wandering as an exile dressed in shepherd's garb. Incidentally, Glyndwr for all his powers of leadership and national acclaim was notorious in his day as a soldier who showed no mercy and who delighted in killing. Mind you, he was a quarter English and brought up as an English gentleman.

Note. The Order of Saint John was founded in 1113 after the First Crusade. In peacetime Knights tended the sick and wore a black habit with an eight-pointed star on the left shoulder; in wartime they wore a red surcoat with a white cross but they only took up arms to defend the Christian faith and were not supposed to take part in wars between Christian powers. They were based in Jerusalem but when that fell in 1187 they moved to the port of Acre, then to Cyprus, then to Rhodes for 200 years, and finally to Malta. An English branch was formed in 1130. This was based at Clerkenwell, London and lasted until 1540 when it fell victim to Henry VIII's Dissolution.

In Herefordshire the Order's prime possession was Dinmore Manor and was founded some time before 1170. It was used as a conventual, giving help and lodging to travellers and the needy and as a retreat for Knights going to or coming from the Holy Land. Dinmore had dependant cells at Garway (which formerly belonged to the Templars), Harewood, Rowlstone, Sutton, Upleadon (Bosbury) and Wormbridge. There was also a cell, not dependant on Dinmore, in Hereford on the site of the present Coningsby Hospital. Anyone could seek sanctuary at a house of the Knights of Saint John although we only know of two cases in Herefordshire, in 1485 (see Wormbridge) and 1491 (see Bosbury). The most eminent of Dinmore's commanders was Sir Thomas Docwra (died 1527). He had survived the siege of Rhodes in 1480 and was appointed Prior in 1486. In 1501 he became Grand Prior at Clerkenwell and was a favourite of Henry VIII. Indeed, he sat as the king's First Baron of the Realm and was present at the Field of the Cloth of Gold (1520) when he rode with the king of England to his meeting with Francis I, King of France.

In 1831 the Order was re-established in England and the Saint John's Ambulance Association was formed in 1877, receiving its Charter from Queen Victoria in 1888.

DOCKLOW *4.5m E of Leominster*
The 'hill where docks grow' is a main road hamlet strung along and around the A44, Leominster to Bromyard road. Originally the churches of Stoke Prior and Docklow were chapels of ease for the church at Leominster. In payment for conducting services at these chapels the Vicar of Leominster received payment in the form of Trug Corn. A trug was a twelfth of a one horse-drawn load. When the chapels became one parish, about 1650, the Trug corn was paid to the new vicar. Docklow church was mostly re-built in the late 19th century by Thomas Nicholson, who was quite busy in Herefordshire. The tower is original.

Uphampton Farm, 1/3m NE, is an early 17th century stone-built house of three storeys with gables. Behind the farm are the earthworks of Uphampton Camp, at SO 570 585, a small Iron-Age hill fort that housed a village community and which continued to be occupied after the Roman Conquest. Shards of Roman pottery have been found here.

Just beyond the fort are more earthworks, the cuttings of the now dismantled railway that ran from Bromyard to Leominster. At West End Farm are a series of pools. Grumpy old David Verey says in the 1955 *Shell Guide*, that at Docklow there are 'several scattered 17th century farms approached by gated or very bad roads, or no roads at all as in the case of Lower Buckland, where one has to walk through the final orchard filled as usual with sheep'. He didn't like walking; indeed, he didn't seem to like Herefordshire very much.

Hampton Wafre Farm, 3/4m ESE, derives its name from hamm-tun meaning 'settlement in a meadow', and Wafre, probably from Simon le Wafre. In Old French Wafre means 'wafer'; but it could be a corruption of wafrer, 'wayfarer'.

DONNINGTON *2m S of Ledbury*
'The settlement of Dunna's people' lies off the B4216 close to the Gloucestershire border. There is no village as

Top left: Dorstone, Arthur's Stone, burial chamber, originally covered with earth. Many New Stone-Age and Bronze-Age flints have been found in the area.
Top right: Flint arrowhead found at Arthur's Cave, Whitchurch.
Middle: Crasswall, from the old Bull's head; Black Mountains in background, c.1950
Bottom left: Eastnor Castle, 1812 and after.
Bottom right: Eardisley, Romanesque font c.1150.

such and hardly anything is near to anything else. The grey stone church of Saint Mary stands amongst yew trees in a field at the end of a track guarded by a sheep-dog who lives at the adjacent red brick farm. Arthur Mee described the churchyard as "trim" in 1938 and trim it still is. The nave and chancel are of about 1300 but were much restored by the Victorians who added the north aisle and the wood bell-tower. Inside is a monument to E.H. Webb, died 1655, and some colourful modern glass, one scene depicting Queen Bertha and the beggar.

In the early 19th century some Roman remains were found hereabouts - a kiln, a dome-shaped building and some fragments of pottery and tiles. There is nothing left to see now. An abandoned moated site lies a stone's throw south of the church. It stands beside a stream that flows down to the River Leadon, 1/4m W. The river marks the county boundary here for a mile or more.

Donnington Hall stands on a wooded rise in parkland 1/2m S of the church. It is constructed of rendered brick and has nine bays with a recessed centre, a one-bay pediment and a stone porch with half pillars, hipped roofs with stone-clad chimneys and Georgian windows. In the 1950s a part to the left was removed. The old house was remodelled in 1909 for Admiral Fanshaw by Gilbert Ogilvey, son of Sir Reginald Ogilvey of Baldoven. Correspondence between the architect and the Fanshaws (they left in 1915) is kept at the house by the current owner, Roger Gouldstone, who has retired from manufacturing. Just to the north of the house is a substantial half-timbered 17th century barn with red brick infill. There is a local tradition that Donnington Hall was a Bishop's retreat. It still has 200 acres of the estate attached.

Broom's Green lies 3/4m SSE of the church. Most of the hamlet is actually in Gloucestershire, but it shares its meagre social facilities - The Horseshoe Inn, telephone box and the Memorial Hall - with Donnington. There are cottages of stone, brick and render, mistletoe in an old tree, and a brick barn with 'arrow-slit' windows.

The Vineyard Farm lies 1/4m NE of Broom's Green on the lower, south-east facing flanks of a hill. There are records of 35 ancient vineyards in Herefordshire. The land at The Vineyard was formerly terraced. In 1289 the Bishop's vineyard 'south of Wall Hills' yielded seven pipes of good white wine. The fortress we call Wall Hills today lies 3/4m W of Ledbury, but this is a common name for Iron-Age earthworks and there is a small oval-shaped univallate fort 1/4m NE of The Vineyard.

The white painted house called Haffield stands just below this fort. It has seven bays and two storeys and a most unfortunate porch of six ugly little Doric columns. Sir Robert Smirke designed the house; surely the porch was not his idea. Opposite the disused avenue drive is a stone chapel, now a dwelling.

A little further west is Bromsberrow Heath, a red brick hamlet with a post office-shop overlooked by a grassy bluff. The Ledbury Hunt has its kennels here, at Egg Tump. We turned north and came to Grove House opposite which we photographed a grubbed-out orchard with bush trees lying with their roots in the air, a forlorn sight. On the other side of the lane was a more fortunate tree in full blossom. There were more grubbed out orchards higher up the hill beside Dyke House Farm. However, it seems we have strayed into Gloucestershire - these Philistines are not of our domain - and with a sense of relief we cross the border to a more civilised place. We emerged on to the Gloucester to Ledbury road, and headed north to Parkway, a strung-out hamlet in undulating pasture and ploughland country, past Dingwood Park - five bays, brick, of about 1700 - and on to Ledbury.

DORMINGTON *4.5m E of Hereford*
'The settlement of Dearmod's (or Deormund's) people'. Just off the A438, Hereford to Ledbury road in the valley of the Frome at the foot of the Woolhope Dome. It is a land of hopyards and high wind-brake hedges and fields of daffodils in the season. Court Mills furniture factory used to dominate the settlement until 1996 when it was replaced by a development of red brick, four-bedroomed detached houses with plastic window frames. At the other end of the village is a crescent of council houses. In between are the Court and the church. The Court has Elizabethan two-storey side wings of three bays each, with a taller three-bay Georgian centre and a central dormer. It is no longer a hotel but operates as a private house that does bed and breakfast. To the right of the church is a tall, white rendered, two and a half storey house with one-storey wings and sloping roofs.

Saint Peter's has been very much restored, though the windows and chancel arch are of the 13th century. The door-knocker is Norman, a sculpted, grimacing feline face which some think represents the Devil. It was quite probably a sanctuary ring: any outlaw who put his hand on it was entitled to sanctuary in the church. The original is very valuable and was once stolen. It has been removed for safe-keeping. And a copy has been substituted. Inside the church there are monuments to Margaret Carpender, died 1666; and John Brydges, died 1669.

In September 1911, the child of some gypsies working in the hopyards at Dormington was accidentally burned to death. The family ritually burned their caravan home because it was their belief that the child's spirit would not be able to rest and would haunt them if this sacrifice was not made - a common belief amongst travelling people.

Backbury Hill Camp, sometimes called Ethelbert's Camp, is 1m SSE of Dormington. It is a small Iron-Age hill fort of nearly five acres. Substantial ramparts survive to the north and the west with a south-west entrance, altered to accomodate a modern track, and an original north-east entrance.

DORSTONE *5.5m E of Hay-on-Wye*
The name is not properly understood but probably means 'the settlement of Deorsige's people'. It lies on the B4348 at the head of the Golden Valley close to the source of the River Dore. Between the Norman castle and the church there is a triangular market place, complete with market cross. Around the village green there is a post office-cum-general store, village hall (founded in 1643, closed in 1965) and the Pandy Inn.

The church of Saint Faith has fragments of about 1300 but was virtually re-built in 1889. Inside there is a handsome double piscina (hand basin), and a pewter chalice and paten of the early 13th century found in the coffin in the south chancel recess. Richard de Brito founded a chapel here. He was one of the four knights who murdered Thomas a Becket in 1171 and took sanctuary in Dorstone after completing 15 years' penance in the Holy Land.

The mediaeval lords of the manor were the Fitzponz and in 1404 Owain Glyndwr attacked the settlement. In more recent times Dorstone was the terminus of the Golden Valley railway which was begun in Pontrilas in 1881 and reached Hay-on-Wye in 1889. It closed in 1957. The old platform stands in a field beside the main road. The Golden Valley Cricket Club has its ground at Dorstone.

Herefordshire 'Black and White' Dilwyn

River Wye and Dinedor Hill - Hereford

In Mill Lane is a house with sandstone cladding fastened to the timber frame with iron pins. This is a traditional building technique in this area where stone flags are readily available. Bodcott Farm, 1.3/4m N of the church, is a good 16th century house with gables, a porch and close-set uprights.

The substantial earthworks of Dorstone Castle lie 1/4m SW of the church. The oval motte has a diameter of 61 by 67 yards and rises to 28 feet above the ditch. Together with its bailey it covers 2.1/2 acres. In the 13th and 14th centuries the castle was held by the Solaris family, knights who served the Mortimers. No stone buildings remain, if indeed there ever were any. At Mynydd Brydd, isolated in the hills 2m W, is another smaller motte and bailey.

The well known and much visited Arthur's Stone, 1m NNE of Dorstone church, is a cromlech, a New Stone-Age (2000-3000 B.C.) tomb and territorial marker. It lies high on Merbach Hill, and the approach lanes from both directions are very steep indeed. The earth mound that originally covered it has disappeared. What remains are the side slabs of the entrance passage and the burial chamber. The massive chamber roof stone measures 20 feet by 11 feet and is estimated to weight 25 tons. In a field near Arthur's Stone there is said to be buried a village engulfed in an earthquake landslip. The spire of the church can be seen in the bottom of the pool, it is said.

At Cross Lodge Farm, 1m E of Dorstone, is a similar but undisturbed oval long barrow (SO 333 416), 20 yards long. Let's hope the archaeologists can leave it in peace; there is too much grave robbing in the name of science.

The Golden Well (SO 308 422), the traditional source of the River Dore, is 1/2m NW of the church, and 1/4m E of a Bronze-Age standing stone (SO 306 422), now used as a gate post. It is in this pool, now fed by drainage ditches and land drains, that Saint Peter, by way of a blessing, placed a holy fish with a golden chain around its neck. It was to live there forever but man's avarice got the better of him. It was speared but escaped down river to Peterchurch. Alas, it was seen again and killed. They say you can still see her blood on the stones at the Golden Well, and above the south door in the church at Peterchurch is a sculpture of this holy fish.

An Iron-Age promontory hill fort lies in the woods on Dorstone Hill, 3/4m ENE of the church at SO 327 422. It occupies a very small one-acre triangular site with steep slopes on two sides. The third side has a rampart and ditch with a narrow causeway to the entrance.

Just to the west of the fort, and stretching westwards from SO 36 423 to SO 322 422, is an 18-acre site occupied during the New Stone-Age. It was enclosed by a low wall on the west side. Amongst the finds were some 4,000 flint chippings (including arrowheads), pottery and fragment of about 50 polished stone axes, together with food storage pits, and floors bounded by stones. The flint and axe stones came from the Cotswolds and South Wales and the settlement was occupied into Roman times. The site was first discovered by field walkers - people deliberately searching for ancient sites and artefacts - and was excavated by C. Houlder and W.R. Pye between 1965 and 1970. Their work was funded by Birmingham University but, much to the annoyance of other archaeologists, does not seem to have been properly written up and published, and the finds have not been made available to other researchers. (For Dorstone near Leominster see Stretford.)

DOWNTON *5.5m WSW of Ludlow*
The name is from the Anglo-Saxon and means 'settlement on a slope'. Downton lies hidden in the dramatic wooded gorge of the River Teme and is most easily approached off the A4113. Downton Castle was built by English ironmasters but has since passed to a Greek millionaire and the estate thas been acquired by the French Perrier Water heiress. The valley was once a wild garden, a haven for wildlife. In recent times the woodland has been brutally 'managed' and the gamekeepers kill pet cats to protect their pheasants. We have spoken to four people who lost pets to their guns and poisons, and there are more.

The old village of Downton on the Rock lies at the southern entrance of the gorge. It consists of a few dwellings, the earthworks of an early Norman castle, the ruins of the Norman church, the Bow Bridge, and the Hotel Cottage, which has a mediaeval stone panel featuring a lion passant. The bridge used to carry the Ludlow to Leintwardine road before it was diverted to avoid the landscaped grounds of Downton Castle.

The house was built between 1772 and 1778 by Richard Payne Knight. He was the grandson of Richard Knight (1659-1745) of Madeley, one of the early Shropshire ironmasters who had lived at nearby Bringewood Hall before buying the Downton estate. The family had an iron-working forge at what is now called Bringewood Forge, 1.1/2m up river from the old village. The site has not been properly investigated but there are some remains - a fine horseshoe weir, parts of the wharf and a tin-plating works. The Teme powered the water-wheels of the forge and charcoal for the furnace fires came from local forests. As early as the 16th century woods at Deerfold, 6.1/2m SW, were being stripped to supply the works at Bringewood. Note that it was a forge, not a smelting furnace. The crude iron was brought here to be beaten by big hammers to drive out the impurities that made the iron spongy and brittle. The resulting wrought-iron was much more valuable and had a greater range of uses.

Richard Payne Knight took good advantage of his family's wealth. He was educated and erudite, with a vast range of interests - the arts, archaeology, anthropology and architecture - and was a prolific writer.

But to get back to Downton Castle. Richard Payne Knight designed and built a most picturesque Gothic castle-cum-mansion, one of the first of its kind in Britain. In his *Analytical Inquiry into the Principles of Taste* Knight extols the virtues of "uniting the different improvements of different ages in the same building", very much the philosophy adopted by the Victorians 50 or 60 years later. Indeed, between 1860 and 1870 the Victorians extended the house a little and altered the windows. Downton Castle really is a grand, Romantic pile in a splendid location. To see it to its best advantage one has to cross the river on the Forge Bridge (SO 453 750) and head south towards Deepwood. Inside, the house is totally Classical and most beautifully done. The principal room is in the larger of the south towers. It imitates the Pantheon with a dome, columns, niches and statues, all colourfully painted.

A magnificent house needs a comparable setting. Nature had been bountiful and Payne Knight, a Romantic in landscaping as well as architecture, was wise enough to leave well alone. Unlike Capability Brown, Payne Knight liked the wild and rugged and here he had it for nothing. All he did was a little planting and cutting of paths to some small oddities such as the cave, approached by a path that passes through a tunnel, and the Roman Baths with vaulted chambers, which stand beneath the cliffs 1m W of the house on the north side of the river. The two bridges, Forge Bridge (with battlements) and Castle Bridge

Above: Eardisland, on the River Arrow.
Right: Bromyard, church of Saint Peter. In September the Folk Festival Morning Service should not be missed.

(without battlements) are both sturdy and elegant. There are public footpaths through the estate, much to the chagrin of the new owners.

When we first saw the gorge it was wild and overrun - a magical place and just how Knight would have liked it. Now that the Perrier woman has descended upon it - literally, she arrives by helicopter - and ordered the undergrowth to be cleared and for 'no right of way' signs to be posted on public footpaths it is not quite what it once was.

The new mansion became the centre of the new village of Downton. This consists of a a few estate workers' cottages, the school and the new church. New Saint Giles was built in 1861 to an Early English (13th century) design by Pountney Smith. It stands 1/2m SW of the house at the end of a long Victorian parkland vista. The pre-historic settlement of Downton Camp at SO 429 732 lies about 1/4m SSE of the ruins of the 12th century Old Saint Giles, at SO 428 734, near Bow Bridge. The camp covers half an acre and is defended by an earth wall, except on the river side where there is a scarp. A track leads down to the site of the old ford.

The history of the Downton-Bringewood gorge needs further investigation - a nice little Ph.D thesis in the offing for someone.

DULAS *11m SW of Hereford*
The name is from the Welsh, du-glais, which means 'black stream'. The settlement stands beside the Dulas Brook in the wooded foothills of the Black Mountains, close to the Welsh border, and is most easily approached off the A465(T) Hereford-Abergavenny road at Pontrilas. The Dulas valley is a delightful, hidden place and it is fitting that for many years the Court was a home for retired musicians. They left in about 1994 and the mansion is now being set up as a general retirement home by the new owners, Kathleen Keene and her husband. The grey stone Victorian house has a six-bay block to the right and a four-bay block to the left with a central tower and coach porch. It was built in about 1860 to replace the 16th century manor house. The beautiful grounds abound with rhododendrons, wild flowers and specimen trees watered by the Dulas Brook. The Old Norman church stood in the lawned area facing the house. All that remains of this is an arched doorway in the garden gate and some woodwork that was incorporated into the new house.

The new Saint Michael's stands by the road and was built in 1865 by the architect G.C. Haddon in the style of about 1300. Inside there is some good 17th century woodwork - the pulpit, lectern, desk and 14 carved chairs (one dated 1640) and no two alike.

At Walk Mill cloth was fulled. The material was soaked in urine and literally walked on to remove oils and greases. The house and farm buildings are timber-framed and some of the infill between the posts consists of stone slabs. Plash Farm, 1/2m S of the church, gets its name from the nearby pool; plasch is Middle Dutch and means 'a shallow pool'.

Local tradition has it that at Twyn-y-beddan, 'the mound of graves', a great battle was fought and that so many men died the Dulas Brook ran red for three days. It is also said to mark the spot where the Welsh made a gallant last stand against the armies of Edward I. The mound itself is a pre-historic tumulas in which burnt human bones have been found.

EARDISLAND *4.5m W of Leominster*
The early mediaeval name was Erleslen, from the Anglo-Saxon eorl, 'earl'; and the Welsh llion, 'floods'. It lies astride the River Arrow and is a very pretty place, one of the villages on the Black and White Trail and much photographed. The land around was once a marshy moor and the river frequently flooded until drainage works were carried out. The Anglo-Saxons often used marshes as defences; the county town of Stafford is a classic example. At Eardisland there are two mounds, thought to be Saxon defensive lookout points. The larger stands beside the church and is 16 feet high from the bottom of the ditch, and about 50 yards in diameter at the base; and the other, at Monk's Court, 1/4m NNW, on the north bank of the river, is about 30 yards in diameter rising to 4 feet. The church of Saint Mary is of the 13th and 14th centuries but was much renewed in 1864. It has a highly-regarded peal of bells which has admirers nationwide. The village has a number of good black and white houses, lawns by the river, a post office, a craft-shop-cum tea room, a village hall (once the school), and on the main road there are two pubs, the White Swan and the Cross Inn. The area by the bridge has great character. The river widens and here stands Staick House. The name is from 'stank', to dam water. It is a splendid timber-framed building: hall range of the late 14th century, west cross-wing of the 16th, addition to the east wing of the 17th, and a sandstone roof with swept valleys. On the south side of the river is the old Grammar School which became reading rooms in 1936. At its north end are the iron rings of the whipping post. The 17th century Old Manor House is timber-framed but has a considerable Queen Anne brick extension of three bays topped by a parapet. In the grounds is a handsome, tall, square, brick-built dovecote with four gables.

The mill-leat took water from the river to power the water-wheel of the Eardisland Mill and continues down to Arrow Mill, 1m W at Arrow Green. This still has all its machinery, and three sets of grinding stones in working order, and was functioning as late as the 1960s. It is part of a complex which includes a clover bossing mill in a tall timber-framed building, a cider-press and mill and the remains of a hop-kiln. The ruins of a longhouse - cottage and cowshed under one roof - can be seen between the mill and the road.

Burton Court lies 3/4m SSE of the village, adjacent to one of the orchards that the area is noted for. It is an 18th century house but retains an open 14th century hall, and has a Tudor front of 1912 designed by the young Clough Williams Ellis, famous for his fantasy village of Portmeirion near Port Madoc. The house stands on a mound and has a pleasing aspect. Inside there is a large collection of period costumes and curios from all over the world.

It used to be the custom in Eardisland to bless orchard trees on Saint Peter's Day; not to do so would result in a poor crop. A glass of cider was poured on the trunk of each tree, which was then tapped three times and a blessing said.

EARDISLEY *4.5m S of Kington*
Eardisley lies on the A4111, 2m N of the River Wye. The name is Anglo-Saxon, from Aegheard's leah. It is an attractive main road village, famous for the magnificently carved circular font in the parish church of Saint Mary Magdalene. There are two scenes: two knights fighting, one with a spear, the other with a sword, and the Harrowing of Hell which shows Jesus pulling a man free from a web of twisted knots. They are separated by a figure with a halo and book, and the picture is completed by a large lion. The sculpture is dramatic and fluent, characteristics

of the Herefordshire School of Carving. It is dated at c.1150 (see Kilpeck and Castle Frome and page 39).

The Harrowing of Hell is a common mediaeval motif. As to the fighting men it has been suggested that they represent a duel fought between two local land holders, Lord Clifford and Sir Ralph de Baskerville. This combat at arms took place at Whitecross in the reign of Henry I (1100-1135) and resulted in the death of Lord Clifford.

The Baskervilles played a large part in local history for over 500 years. They came from Bacqueville, near Rouen. At the time of the Domesday Book Robert Baskerville held Eardisley. He lived in "a fortified house in the middle of a wood with two slaves and a Welshman". The family also had control of estates in Yazor, Stretton Sugwas, Cusop, Arcop, Bredwardine and Willersley. Today there are no more Baskervilles at Eardisley. (See Kington for the Black Dog of Hergest and Sir Arthur Conan Doyle.)

Robert Baskerville's 'fortified house' was on the 14ft high castle mound west of the church. It was here, in 1263 during the Barons' War, that Peter Aquablanca, Bishop of Hereford, was kept prisoner after being arrested at the altar of his cathedral and his treasure looted. He was a close associate of the king, rarely visited his Diocese and 'fundraising' for Henry III made him immensely unpopular. On his release from Eardisley he retired to France where his mercenary ways made him equally unpopular.

Opposite the church is the brick-built Victorian school and in the vicinity are some good black and white houses. The main street has a variety of buildings in stone, brick and half-timber. The village hall was provided by the vicar, Canon Palmer, and the Curzon Herrick Institute (1877) was given to the parish by the family of that name, the current lords of the manor. The New Inn of 1902 replaces its timber-framed predecessor which was burned down.

The Tram Inn takes its name from the old tramway that ran between Brecon and Kington. Trams, trains of tubs carrying coal from Brecon, were hauled by horses until 1864 when the railways came and utilised much of the track. The railway closed in 1962. The goods wharf and station were near the church and have subsequently been developed as a small trading estate. The embankment of the old tramway can be seen alongside the road to Almeley. Near the Tram Inn is the Old Pump House and a cruck cottage. On this northern fringe of the village is Upper House Farm with its handsome, close-set, upright timbers and two projecting mullioned windows. The former great hall lies behind a 17th century addition and is not visible from the road.

In 1974 George H. Haines could report that: "Once a year the people of Eardisley let their hair down and stetson-hatted cowboys canter along the street on the occasion of the annual 'Stampede' which includes riding the bucking bullock and other events which are usually associated with the Wild West rather than with a quiet Midland County."

Eardisley Wootton House lies 1m NNW of the church. It has square framing with central crucks (the former open hall) and crucks also in a barn. Eardisley Park, 1/4m W, is an early 18th century, five-bay rendered house with a dovecote and cider house amongst the outbuildings. Parton, 2/3m SE has a Jacobean core of square framing with brick infill.

To the north of the village is Hurstway Common on which stands a mighty oak, a remnant of the Hurstway Forest. It has a girth of 30ft and is 100ft tall. North again, at Quebb, 1.1/2m N of the village, are two cruck-framed farmhouses which face the mounded remains of earlier buildings. One mile WNW of Quebb is Apostles Farm which also has two cruck-framed houses. Lower Welson, 1m WNW of Eardisley, is an attractive scattered 'township'. Holywell Dingle, a wood fringed stream, lies 1/2m N of Eardisley. At the end of the Dingle is Lemore Farm which has a circular moated site just north of the house. The Camp Earthwork, 2.1/4m NW of Eardisley church, is a circular enclosure, about 45 yards in diameter surrounded by a ditch.

EASTNOR *1.5m SE of Ledbury*
At the time of Domesday Book it was called Astenofre which means 'settlement east of the ridge'. The ridge is Eastnor Hill.

Eastnor lies on the A438 Hereford to Tewkesbury road amongst gentle, wooded hills at the southern foot of the Malverns. It is an attractive village and comes complete with: church, woodyard, cricket pitch, thatched post office, clusters of stone and half-timbered cottages, village green, Victorian well with pyramid roof and terra cotta reliefs, school, rectory, and a magnificent neo-Norman castle which is frequently used as a film-set.

The castle was commissioned by Charles Cocks (who paid for it with his wife's money) and designed by Sir Robert Smirke. Building began in 1812 with stone brought here by mule trains from the Forest of Dean. It is approached along a drive lined with splendid, mature speciment trees, and through a gatehouse with round towers. In the courtyard we saw dead pheasants and expended cartridge cases. The castle is symmetrical with corner towers and a raised centre. The great hall is 60ft long and 65ft high. The fan-vaulted dining room was designed and furnished by Pugin; the library by G.E. Fox is in Italian Renaissance style and utilizes 17th century woodwork brought from Sienna. The roof trusses are made of iron, an unusually early use. The whole Romantic edifice is richly furnished with all manner of expensive works of art and looks over the castellated terrace to the tree-fringed lake and the caravan site in the 500-acre deer park beyond. The animals kept here are red deer. The obelisque in Eastnor Park was erected in 1812 to the memory of Charles Cock's son who died during the Siege of Burgos by Wellington.

The church of Saint John was re-built in 1852 to a design by Sir G.G. Scott. Only a late Norman doorway and the 14th century tower survive from the old church. The font is unusually deep, designed for total immersion. There are numerous monuments to members of the Cocks family ranging from Joseph Cocks, 1778; to Charles Cocks (First Lord Somers), died 1855. Scott also designed the rectory of 1850. Today the castle and the estate are occupied as a private house by James and the Honourable Sarah Bathurst, the 6th earl's daughter, the freehold having descended through the female line. The castle is open to the public, but is closed on Saturdays for private wedding receptions.

Way End Street is a hamlet on the A438, about 3/4m ESE of Eastnor. Here is the famous and much photographed timber-framed cottage and garden called Sunnyside, the home of Maurice Martindale and his late wife since 1962. Mid-morning in late May or early June is the best time to view this delight.

The meagre remains of Bronsil Castle lie 1m E, just beyond the boundary of the deer park. Robert Beauchamp, Lord Treasurer to Henry VI, obtained permission to crenellate in 1460. It was once a substantial rectangular building with polygonal corner towers and a gatehouse.

All that remains is part of one tower and the moat. (See Lugwardine for the ghost and Beauchamps' bones.)

On Midsummer and Holybush Hills, 1.1/3m E of Eastnor, are the double rampart and ditch earthworks of an Iron-Age hill fort, though an undisturbed Neolithic tumulus, a massive 150ft long, and bronze pottery shards and a bronze palstave indicate earlier occupation of the site. The ditch was originally drystone walled. The entrances at the south and north-west corners are original. At the north end is another bank and ditch, the Red Earl's Dyke. This was made at 1287 by Gilbert de Clare, Earl of Gloucester, to mark the boundary between his land and that of the Bishop of Hereford. Today it marks the boundary with Worcestershire.

EATON BISHOP *4m E of Hereford*
The Domesday Book name was Etune, from the Anglo-Saxon meaning 'settlement by the river'. By 1316 it was Eton Episcopi. It lies close to Hereford and was once a weekend resort but is well and truly lost amongst the lanes. Eaton Bishop lies close to the River Wye, though that waterway is rarely visible. Steep hills and winding lanes make it a secret place, and it comes as a small surprise to see a sign directing one to the home-cum-office of John Williams, a dirctor of Sydney Phillips, the estate agents who market hotels and inns nationwide.

We approached Eaton Bishop off the A465 out of Hereford, forking right at Belmont, and passing through Cleonger. An unfenced lane to the right leads through the scrub woodland and rough pastures of the water-logged Honeymoor Common, grazed by sheep but only in the summer. At one time they had the company of donkeys, working animals that could be hired for the day for a shilling to pull carts to market for personal transport and even for ploughing. They had names that reflected the trade of their village owners - Beer Barrel (innkeeper), Pig Iron (blacksmith) and Letter Bag (postman).

The land about is the typical Herefordshire mix of ploughland and pasture. The village comes into view straggling down the lane, the cottages mostly of brick or render, some council houses and a red telephone kiosk. Opposite the church is a group of larger houses: Martin's Croft, a simple red brick house with five bays; the White House and the 'Manor House', five bays also, but lower. The village is very quiet, too quiet. Once it had a full compliment of tradesmen - butcher, baker, tailor, wheelwright, grocer, blacksmith, shoemaker and a post office.

The church of Saint Michael was restored in 1885 but retains its strong Norman tower, early 13th century arcades and several windows of about 1300. But it is for its stained glass of about 1330 that the church is famous. The best of its date in the county it has the typical Decorated style colour scheme in which browns, greens and yellows predominate and fine, animated designs typical of illuminated manuscripts of the period. (Note: in the 15th century blues and reds became more prominent.) The glass was probably the gift of Adam de Murimonth, Canon of Hereford, and later cantor of Exeter in 1328. There is a touching memorial tablet to Richard and Margaret Snead who died within a few months of each other in 1678. The inscription reads: "One bed we shared; one tomb now holds us, and our bones, mingled with dust now lie together. One death was ours; one year took us away, one day saved us and gave us back to God."

Downhill, south-east of the church, is Ruckhall Mill, a charming group of white painted buildings in the wooded valley of the Cage Brook. All the buildings are now dwellings. The stream is crossed by a stone bridge. A limestone track leads through the woods to Tuck Mill, also now a residence and also painted white. A big, black goat glares at strangers. Just beyond the end of the track the Cage Brook joins the Wye. What a desirable location this is. On the heights of the steep northern side of the valley is an Iron-Age fort. It covers a triangular promontory, with a single rampart on the western boundary. (Elsewhere in the parish an Early Bronze-Age flat axe-head has been found.)

Back at Ruckhall Mill we proceed uphill, past Hill Fort House, an orchard, and a handkerchief-sized common to the Ancient Camp Inn. From the narrow car park one has long views over the River Wye. It is very shallow here and one mile north is the site of the crossing of the Roman road from Kenchester (Magnis) to Abergavenny.

We now head northwards past Lanehead Farm, a striking ensemble of tall stone walls, stone and brick barns and a red brick house of six bays with hipped roof and wood mullioned lights all set amongst orchards and parkland. From the entrance to Shepherd's Meadow Farm a track leads down to the Wye and the house of the aforementioned, John Williams, estate agent. The tall, stone and render house is partly ivy-clad and boasts a large, plate-glass viewing window, designed to take in the delightful setting. About 200 yards south-west is Lower Eaton, a late 18th century Georgian house of which Nikolaus Pevsner writes: "but sadly re-modelled in the High Victorian years to make a Georgian house Gothic without spending too much". The old Squire, Sir Joseph Pulley (died 1901), will be turning in his grave.

We leave by heading south-west down the old Roman road past Warlow Farm, black and white cows, ploughland and pasture and sheep, turn left at the crossroads and return to our starting point at Honeymoor Common. Just down the road is Cagebrook House, of about 1700, built of brick with seven bays and two and a half storeys and a Georgian addition to the left, all in English bond.

EDVIN LOACH *2.5m NNE of Bromyard*
The Anglo-Saxon name was Gedeuen, meaning 'Gedda's fen' (wet ground). In 1212 it was held by John de Loges. There are several Loges in France.

The church of Saint Mary stands embowered on a lovely hilltop and serves a scattered farming community. It was built about 1860 to an Early English design by Sir George Gilbert Scott. A little to the east are the overgrown ruins of the old 11th century Norman church. This is noted for the Anglo-Saxon herring-bone masonry which underpins the 'new' Norman work. The tower and west wall were rebuilt in the 16th century, but little is left standing. Just outside the churchyard there is an earthwork, possibly a castle ringwork. Edvin Loach is sometimes quoted as an example of a village in the process of becoming deserted.

Hope Farm, 2/3m N, has a 17th century timber-framed gable porch, a first floor supported by scroll decorated brackets and a Georgian front, partly of brick. Saltemarshe Castle, 1/2m SE, was a Victorian pile, demolished about 1955. The castellated east and west lodges still stand.

EDVIN (EDWYN) RALPH *2.5m NNW of Bromyard.*
The name is from the Anglo-Saxon meaning 'Gedda's fen'; Ralph held the land in 1176. The village hall and most of the modern developments stand alongside the B4214 Bromyard to Tenbury Wells road in a tributary valley of the River Frome. It is sheltered and fertile and produces high yields of potatoes, oats, barley and wheat. There are hopyards and orchards, cattle for milking and

Above: Eastnor Sunnyside Cottage, Way End Street. England Personified.
Left: Hampton Bishop, near Hereford.

cattle and sheep for slaughter. Country to kill for and, indeed, local tradition tells of a ferocious fight that took place close to the bridge on the road to Buckenhill.

The mediaeval lords of Edvin Ralph and Edvin Loach fell out over the love of a lady. The lady tried to intervene during the ensuing duel and was accidentally killed. The knights fought on and both died of their wounds.

The home of the lord of Edvin Ralph would have been on the moated site by the church, 1/4m east of the main road. The moat encircles an island about 40 yards in diameter and there are traces of an outer enclosure to the north and north-west. The village people drifted away in the years after the Black Death (1348). and only a few farms remain here, notably Brickhouse Farm and Townsend Farm.

The church of Saint Michael (a dedication that often indicates a pre-Norman religious site) retains a Norman doorway in the nave, though the original round arch was made pointed in the 13th century, and the unbuttressed 13th century tower. The north doorway was rebuilt in the 14th century using Norman fabric.

The church is well known for its mediaeval effigies, all members of the Edefen family. There are three groups: a cross-legged knight with wife of the late 13th century; a cross-legged knight with two wives of the early 14th century; a miniature lady with a dog at her feet of the early 14th century; and an incised stone to Matil de Edefen of about 1325. The latter is a rare example of a pardon monument. The inscription tells us that those who say a pater and an ave for the soul of Matil will be granted 30 days' pardon by the Bishop of Worcester and 60 days' pardon by the Bishop of Hereford. The effigies used to be in the tomb recesses of the chancel, but were moved, irreverently, to their present position beneath the bell tower.

ELTON 4.5m SW of Ludlow
It lies in the lovely Vale of Wigmore, the domain of the mediaeval Mortimer family. Behind it, to the east, are the wooded slopes of the High Vinnals; before it are the gentle pastures laid down by the meandering River Teme. The name is from the Anglo-Saxon and could mean either 'Ella's homestead' or 'the place where eels are caught'. The settlement consists of little more than the Hall, the church, a farm and a couple of cottages.

As the traveller approaches the Hall he is greeted by the sight of a flock of black Galloway sheep, complete with curly horns, and a folly shelter. This construction has latticed windows and ogee-shaped gables topped with ball finials. The culprit is antiques dealer James Hepworth who owns the Hall, and who has other follys about his grounds.

We pulled in and parked at the entrance to the Hall. The fore-garden was all a-bustle. Four immaculate milking cows were being preened and posed for David Platt, a freelance livestock photographer, who had been commissioned by the Milk Marketing Board to take pictures to illlustrate a magazine article.

He posed the cows with their front legs raised on a small mound camouflaged with grass. This is done to make it appear that their backs are parallel to the ground, not sloping forwards as they actually do. What a peculiar deceipt! Yet Mr. Platt was only following the established convention.

As to Elton Hall, it is brick, 18th century, has six bays, a hipped roof with dormers, a doorway with Tuscan pillars, and windows with ogee heads. The range to the left of the Hall, the stables and kitchen wing, are 17th century. A previous occupant of the Hall was Thomas Andrew Knight (1758-1838), of the family who made a fortune out of iron. He was an eminent Victorian botanist and in 1829 was elected President of the Horticultural Society. He developed techniques for the improvement of vegetables and fruit, especially cherries, apples and plums. It was his brother, Richard Payne Knight (1750-1824) who designed and built the spectacular Downton Castle.

The little stone church of Saint Mary is Norman but was much restored in 1876. It hides amongst trees within yards of the Hall. Inside there is an early 17th century pulpit and the arms of Elizabeth I carved in wood. A little further down the road is Elton Farm, a timber-framed, 'H'-shaped house of about 1600. This is from whence the cows came to be photographed. We continued on following the road south-west to Leinthall Starkes.

A highly polished Neolithic 'prestige' axe fashioned from Penzance Greenstone has been found in the parish. Such axes could not be used for serious work - they shattered - but were symbols of power and authority.

EVESBATCH 4.5m SE of Bromyard
In 1200 the name was Esbec, from the Anglo-Saxon, meaning 'Esa's valley'. Evesbatch is lost in the lanes, but then is not half of Herefordshire? There is little more than a handful of cottages, a church and a mildly Continental-looking place of agriculture imaginatively called The Farm. But the landscape is glorious, especially in Spring when the old orchards and the hawthorn hedges are in pink and white blossom and rabbits scuttle in the pastures between the sheep. It is a steeply rolling land, a place of contentment and picture book views.

The small church of Saint Andrew was much restored in 1877. It has a nave, chancel, and timber bell-turret with a Decorated south window saved from the old church. The Norman tub font has a pleasing carved Jacobean cover. There are monuments to Mrs. Dobyns, died 1658, and to Catherine Dobyns died 1710. The latter is graced by two putti. A putto is a small, naked boy.

One mile north-east of Evesbatch is Frome Manor complete with hop kiln. It stands at the end of Wards Hill where the lane begins a steep descent to the River Frome. The view is wonderful.

EWYAS HAROLD 10.5m SW of Hereford
It lies on the Dulas Brook near the entrance to the Golden Valley, just off the fast A465 Hereford to Abergavenny road. The name is probably from the Welsh ewig-dinas meaning 'deer town'. Harold was the son of Earl Ralph, a nephew of Edward the Confessor (ruled 1042-1066). Historically the town was more Welsh than English and was in the parish of Saint David until 1852. It had one of the very few pre-Conquest castles in England and was one of only five boroughs in Domesday Herefordshire.

The early Norman castle was built by Fitz Osbern in the late 11th century on the site of the pre-Conquest fortress. It was one of the most important in the Marches. Fitz Osbern had supplied Duke William with 60 ships for the invasion of England and was duly rewarded with the Earldom of Herefordshire. When William went to visit France Fitz Osbern was left as co-ruler of England. Only the earthworks of his Ewyas Harold castle remain, the mound measuring 75 yards in diameter at the base and 42ft from the bottom of the ditch with a kidney-shaped bailey to the east. To the south-east is the probable site of a Benedictine Priory, founded about 1100. The castle stands on a spur about 300 yards W of the church.

Saint Michael's has a sturdy 13th century fortress tower with walls over 7ft thick which was originally detached from the church, and a chancel of about 1300, kept when the nave was re-built in 1868 by G.C.Haddon. There is a Jacobean pulpit, and in the carved reredos there are some mid-16th century Dutch figures and mid-17th century German scenes from the Passion. In the tomb recess is the effigy of a lady holding her heart in her hand, said to be Lady Clarissa, daughter of John Tregoz, Lord of Ewyas, who died in 1290.

The modern village has spread down the hillside towards the confluence of the Dulas Brook and the River Dore at Pontrilas. It is a thriving, cheerful little place with a school, two grey stone pubs - the Temple Bar and the Dog Inn - a post office, general store, butcher, doctor, dentist, Memorial Hall, petrol service station, Methodist and Baptist chapels and the modern brick-built Roman Catholic Church dedicated to John Kemble.

Saint Martin's Well, 3/4m NNE of the church at SO 380 298, is a well known local boundary marker. Its waters were reputed to cure complaints of the eye. The commoners have the right to take water but in the 1940s it was tanked and fenced off. The commoners repeatedly broke the fences and won the day. Now, however, all there is to see is a concrete reservoir with some stone walling. Squatter cottages are dotted over this high hill common; some have the very thin timber-framing, all that the very poor could afford.

EYE *3m N of Leominster*

It lies in a shallow valley between two streams to the west of the A49. The name is from the Anglo-Saxon and means 'an island, or place beside water'. To the west is the main line railway and to the east is a well-defined stretch of the disused Leominster to Mamble canal. The settlement stands on a low rise and consists of little more than the embowered Manor and attached farm, and the church.

The Manor was re-built in 1680 by Ferdinando Gorges, a Barbados sugar and slave-trader. To his contemporaries he was known as King of the Black Market. The Manor is of red brick with five bays, two storeys and dormers. The original stone mullioned and transomed windows were replaced in the late 18th century. Inside are some note worthy ceilings richly decorated with flowers, fruits, foliage, animals and mythological Greek heroes, and in the Great Parlour is a floor of Spanish chestnut. The house holds collections of corn dollies and the finely printed and bound books of the Golden Cockerel Press.

The red sandstone church of Saint Peter and Saint Paul stands beside the Manor, but is separated from it by a tall yew tree hedge. The south arcades are of about 1190 and the north arcades of about 1215, and there are two blocked doorways of the period. Most of the rest is 13th and 14th centuries except for the tower and turret which are of 1874 by W. Chick. Inside there are two alabaster effigy monuments: Sir Richard Cornewall (probably) of Berrington Hall, died about 1520; Sir Richard Cornewall and wife, of about 1540; and a memorial pilaster, designed by Sir Reginald Blomfield, to three sons of Lord Cawley who died between 1914-18 during the Great War. A wall monument commemorates Thomas Harley, son of the third Earl of Oxford and Lord Mayor of London. He was MP for Herefordshire for some 25 years and towards the end of life he lived at the Manor and died there.

To the east of Eye by half a mile is Moreton ('settlement by a fen, a marshy place'), a pleasant hamlet that stands beside the boundary of the park of Berrington Hall. It has cottages of half-timber, red brick and stone, tiny green, a school that closed some 20 years ago, a handful of new houses, cows in the pastures and a Dedicated Referral Practice Veterinary Clinic.

EYTON *2m NW of Leominster*

The name is from the Anglo-Saxon meaning 'settlement by a river or a marshy place'. The River Lugg meanders by 1/2m S but marsh is probably the real meaning. There is rough common land on the lane to Coxall.

The Marsh is the 'big house' of this extremely pleasant little hamlet. The Marsh (or Marsh House) was recently renovated and is now a superior country hotel. The hop kiln has been converted to a Baronial Dining Hall. The nucleus of the house is a 14th century hall with tie-beam and foiled wind-braces. Opposite is the quaint, black and white of Eyton Court. The west range has close-set timber framing of the early 16th century and an oriel window. The living room has moulded beams and a panelled ceiling. In size it is a modest building, more like a cottage than a Court. Nearby is another black and white house called Pondside Cottage. The grounds are surrounded by a high wire fence that runs through a wet pool adjacent to Eyton Common and provides protection for wild water birds.

At Eyton Hall, 1/4m NE, is Dale's Nursery. The Dale family are, to all intents and purposes, the local squires, having built workers' houses named after their racehorses. The hamlet lost its school in the 1960s and the buildings have been converted to a house. Opposite the old school is a wall-gate which is the entrance to a passage that leads to the cellar of Eyton House. Here there was a cider press.

On the wooded slopes of the hill is the church of All Saints. It has been much restored but retains one Norman window in the chancel and some tall, thin 14th century windows with ogee heads. Inside there is a monument to Joseph Coates, died 1793, a pre-Reformation rood loft, and a good late 15th century rood screen. Eyton Old Hall, 1/4m NW of the church, is a mature Georgian brick mansion of two and a half storeys with a wide, five-bay front, a canted bay window and a gable. It stands well off the road on a rise in wooded grounds. When we visited it was in the process of being tastefully renovated with not a plastic replacement window in sight. The Old Hall was the house of Richard Hakluyt (1553-1616), whom many consider to be the father of modern geography. He wrote extensively on the voyages of discovery by explorers of many nationalities and his works were known and admired all over Europe. The family was prominent in Herefordshire for several generations. Sir Leonard Hakluyt was with Henry V at Agincourt and they count sheriffs and members of Parliament among their numbers. When Barry Freeman, the author of the excellent *Shire County Guide Herefordshire*, visited the house in the mid-1980s he was shown two priceless Elizabethan globes.

We passed through Eyton several times whilst compiling this book and on one occasion, in May 1996, we chanced upon Peter Delaney who was camped on the common. He was working on a farm at Brierley, near Leominster, training and tying the young hop vines. He came from a Birmingham council housing estate and left school in 1979 at the age of 16. After three years working in vineyards in France and Italy he returned to England and has been 'on the road' ever since. He does seasonal work on farms, handyman jobs and he busks. He has three children, all born in bender tents (large domes consisting of a framework of bent poles covered with heavy tarpaulins), two ponies, a traditional style gipsy caravan that he made himself from an old apple cart, several chickens, an almost-human pullet, three dogs and a wife, Rachel. He is more gipsy than some Romanies, too many of whom now live in council flats. I recorded two songs from Peter, The Hop-Picking Song, and Burning the Bread, both of which he had written himself, and interviewed him about his way of life. He had worked for an eletrical retailer for several years before taking to the road. I should emphasize that his family are true travellers, not Rainbow Circle people and not Beatniks. The travellers have the same gentle and caring attitude but they belong to a different cultural tribe altogether and are more akin to true gypsies. Peter has told his children that if they ever get lost they must seek out a gipsy camp, not the police. Within hours they would be reunited with their family via the 'bush telegraph'. Incidentally, the headmaster of the Dame Elizabeth Cadbury School, which Peter Delaney attended, was Roy Palmer, the author and folklorist, with whom I had just been communicating. Small world.

Bicton, 1.3/4m NNW of Eyton, has battery-farm sheds at The Lowe, sheep in the water meadows, a group of half-a-dozen dwellings, a farm and Hitrees Plant Nursery. They lie in a shallow valley. Opposite Oaklee Farm is a dense, mixed woodland called Oaker Wood, wherein lurks a lake. Hidden here is an ash tree growing out of the stump of an old oak. Local people used to place locks of their children's hair in notches of the bark believing it to be a cure for whooping cough. Incidentally, another Herefordshire cure for whooping cough is to hold a live spider over the child's open mouth and chant: "Spider as you pine away, whooping cough no longer stay". The cough then enters the spider which is released taking the ailment with it.

Enmore Field, 1/2m NW of Bicton, is a hamlet of brick cottages with bonny black border collies, a stream that runs across the road, coppiced woodland, croaking pheasants and a roadside pool in unremarkable, undulating country.

Aston, 1m NW of Eyton, is a picturesque hamlet consisting largely of three black and white farmhouses and their outbuildings. The Knapp is most attractive. It has four bays, square framing and a gable to the left. There is holly in the hedges and deep ditches by the road. Basker's Gate, just to the north-west, is a scattered hamlet of mostly brick cottages.

FAWLEY 8m SE of Hereford

The name is not properly understood but is probably derived from the Anglo-Saxon meaning 'forest where fallow deer are found'. It lies hidden away on a great loop of the River Wye. If approaching from King's Caple one passes over the track of the disused railway and through unfenced pastureland to the striking Fawley Court, home of the Kyrle family. The front is of red sandstone, of about 1630, and not quite symmetrical, with canted bays and transomed windows. At the back the house is half-timbered, of the early 16th century with narrowly spaced uprights. The modern water gardens complete a felicitous picture. One continues east to Fawley Cross then south through a farm to the hamlet by the river. The church of Saint John has a plain Norman chancel arch and Norman tub font with large scallop decoration. Much Fawley, a house just south of the church, has two 14th century stone doorways and foil decorated wind braces in the roof.

This is as convenient a place as any to say something about the River Wye. It is already a site of Special Scientific Interest along its entire length and is thus protected from development, but this is now in the process of being redesignated by English Nature to safeguard the natural vegetation of its banks, shoals and waterbed habitat. The river is famous for its fishing and carries stocks of stoneloach, gudgeon, dace, roach, chub, perch, tench and, of course, salmon.

Salmon was once so plentiful that in the 18th century servants and apprentices had it written into their contracts that they should not be fed on it more than twice a week. However, netting and the construction of weirs so diminished their numbers that controls had to be established. However, these have proved inadequate and salmon numbers have, in recent years, seen an alarming decline. Mature salmon return to their spawning grounds between November and December. The eggs hatch three to four months later. These alvin become small fish called parrs, feed in the Wye for two years then head for the sea in the Spring.

FELTON 6.5m NE of Hereford

The name is from felde-tun, meaning 'settlement in open land'. The hamlet lies down a lane off the A417. The church stands on a bank. It was re-built in the Decorated style in 1853 and the spire was added in 1891. The plays of Shakespeare used to be enacted by local people on the embowered Vicarage lawn on pre-war Summer evenings. Small woods and orchards and wind-wells dot the rich ploughland and pastures of the surrounding countryside.

Felton Court lies 1/4m SW of the church, but today it is Rosemaund Farm, 1m WSW, that is the centre of attention. It was purchased by the Ministry of Agriculture shortly after the end of the Second World War to be used as an Experimental Husbandry Farm. The work is of a practical nature and covers both livestock and arable crops; including hops. In recent times trials have been conducted on the rearing of deer as a lowland farm animal.

FORD 2.5m SSE of Leominster

On the banks of the River Lugg are a handful of dwellings, an orchard and a small chapel with nave and apse rebuilt in Norman style in 1851. The foundations might be Norman. Just to the south is the golf course at Marlbrook. The tall, gaunt Jacobean house 1/2m N, on the opposite bank, beside the A49, is the 17th century Wharton Court. It has three and a half storeys, three bays, mullioned and transomed windows, a two storeyed porch (of 1659) with pilasters and blank ovals, a hipped roof and four chimneys. About 90 yards east of the house is a pool with a small rectangular island. It could be a moated site but is more likely to be the remains of a duck decoy pond.

The hamlet of Wharton itself lies on the other side of the A49 on the old road from Leominster to Hope-under-Dinmore, the B4361. It is a place of new bungalows but not all is lost, for some years ago Mr. Ian Norris bought Cook's Folly. He stripped off the render and renovated the four-bay, Grade II listed, 15th century farm cottage that lurked beneath. In its new brown and cream livery it looks most attractive. Together with the matching timber-framed garage block of 1988 to the left and the weeping willow water gardens to the front they make a fine group.

Local tradition has it that the left-hand side of the old building was used as a Nonconformist Chapel at one time. The new block, by the way, was constructed under the supervision of Rod Dovaston who lives nearby at Ford Farm. He recommends that oak timbers be treated with Rustin, made from oil obtained from timber from the Far East. Whilst photographing the cottage I kept waiting for a

Right: Fownhope, primitive plaster and thatch cottages, homes of the very poor. Such hovels were hardly ever photographed and now none are left anywhere in the county.
Middle: Fownhope, the River Wye.
Bottom: Fawley, farmer milking in 1932.

little white cloud to move from behind the roof. Silly me. It was the white painted dome of one of the two redundant silos belonging to Wharton Bank. These are a landmark used by low flying fighter aircraft who zoom in and turn at this point. In the land around there are orchards, sheep pastures and arable fields.

FOWNHOPE 5.5m SW of Hereford
It is a substantial village located along the B4224, sandwiched between the meandering River Wye to the west and the limestone hulk of the Woolhope Dome to the east. It was substantial even in 1086 when its new Norman lord was Hugh the Donkey. Then it was simply called Hope, meaning 'valley'. By 1242 it was Fagehope, fage meaning 'coloured'.

From the higher ground to the east there are splendid views over the Wye - lush, alluvial pastures grazed by sheep, ploughed fields, pebble beaches and the sun glinting on the gentle, running water. To the north are steep, wooded slopes, graced with wild cherry blossom in the Spring. These give their name to Cherry Hill, at the top of which are the earthworks of an overgrown five acre Iron-Age hill fort defended by natural scarps and ramparts. The village itself is not unhandsome with its church and the usual Herefordshire mix of half-timber, stone, and red brick dwellings. Amongst these are a service station, two pubs, two shops and a fountain. The charm of the array is somewhat dulled by modern intrusions, especially the group of flat-roofed bungalows. How could the Council allow them? The answer, of course, is that the Council built them.

The church of Saint Mary has a 12th century Norman tower and of the same period are some windows, but best of all is the beautiful tympanum, wisely reset inside the church. It is an example of the Herefordshire School of Carving whose craftsmen were unmatched in the whole of England. It depicts the Virgin Mary and Child, both with their hands raised in blessing, accompanied by a lion and a bird. Most of the rest of the church is 13th and 14th centuries. Inside there are monuments to the Lechmere family, dating from 1692 to 1829, and John Kidley and wife, after 1718. The village stocks are in the churchyard..

The 22,000 oak shingles of the church spire are a reminder that Fownhope was once a collection point for oak bark, used for tanning leather. It was stored on land now occupied by Fownhope Motors whilst awaiting shipment down the Wye, hence the name Bark Cottage. There is another Bark Cottage, formerly The Warehouse, 1.1/2m NNW, near the Holme Lacy Bridge. The tenant kept three barges. A mooring ring and some remains of the old quay can still be seen.

There was a lime burning industry in the area during the 17th and 18th centuries and in the 19th century there was a brewery at what is now called Rock House. There were also two corn mills, at Pentaloe and Nupend. One of these may have been the silk mill known to have existed here. This history of industry, and the freedom it gave owners and workers from the Establishment, led to Fownhope developing a nucleus of religious dissenters who had a Meeting House for Plymouth Brethren and a Baptist Chapel. The local part-time ferry trade was not insignificant with boats being kept at Lechmere's Ley, Leabrink, Mill Farm, Ferry Lane, Mancell's Ferry and Alford's Ferry (below Capler Wood). On the top of Capler Wood Hill, by the way, is Capler Camp, another Iron-Age hill fort, 228 yards above sea level. On the hills around Fownhope, Neolithic finds of flint flakes and arrowheads have been found in some numbers.

The Green Man - the green man was a pagan fertility symbol - is a pub of some renown. It has a vainglorious fabric. The original half-timbered front was given a cosmetic brick face, probably about 1800 when brick was fashionable, and now that black and white is chic it has been re-timbered (1965). This architectural sandwich can be seen from the entrance to the courtyard. At one time it was also used as the Court House for the local petty sessions. It is to the Green Man that the Hearts of Oak Society process on Oak Apple Day (29th May). Each man carries a stick highly decorated with flowers. And there is more; Tom Spring was once the landlord here.

Tom Spring was born Thomas Winter at Rudge End, 1m NE of Fownhope. His father was a butcher. The story goes that he was dancing at a village wake when the local bully insulted his girlfriend. Young Tom won the ensuing fight and thus began his pugilistic career. In 1821 he became the Champion of All England. In 1824 he fought the Irish champion, Jack Langan, at Worcester. The contest went to 84 rounds (a round ended with a knockdown) and lasted for two and a half hours. Some 40,000 spectators watched this epic battle and a 12 verse ballad describing the fight was published in Gateshead. This is printed in full in *The Folklore of Hereford and Worcester* (1992) by Roy Palmer. Tom Spring was also landlord of the Booth Hall Inn at Hereford. Here he thrashed six Irish troublemakers and threw them into the street. He died in London, whilst keeping the Castle Tavern in Holborn, and is buried in West Norwood cemetery. On the road between Fownhope and Woolhope there is a cider mill memorial to Tom Spring (SO 588 351).

Barns with cruck trusses can be found at the Vicarage and at Capler Farm, 1m SE of the church. Fownhope Court, the old home of the Lechmere family, is Jacobean and it has the base of a mediaeval semi-circular turret. Nash Farm, 1/2m E, is Georgian brick with three bays, two and a half storeys, tripartite windows and a one-bay pediment.

FOY *9m SE of Hereford*
The pre-Conquest name was Lanntimoi, meaning 'the church of Saint Moi or Mwy'. Later it was called Eton Tregoz. A handful of dwellings stand around the church of Saint Mary, isolated on a tongue of land formed by a long, narrow meander of the lovely River Wye. This peninsula is locally known as Welsh, or West Foy. Only one vehicular road leads to the hamlet.

The church has a nave and chancel of the 13th century, a tower, porch and south door of the 14th century and a Jacobean pulpit. There are two 13th century effigies and monuments to George Abrahall, died 1675 and John Abrahall (of Eton), died 1702. The Old Vicarage is early 18th century, stone with five bays and two storeys.

The farms of Underhill, Inglestone and Hill of Eaton were once described as townships. The large Jacobean mansion at Inglestone burned down in 1785 and was replaced by the present Georgian style house in the late 1830s.

A charming suspended footbridge of 1876 (re-built in 1920) with iron columns crosses the Wye 1/2m E of the church. This leads to the wooded high ground of English, or West Foy. It is said that the local lord had a stone castle at Hole-in-the-Wall. There is no sign of it now.

Opposite Perrystone Court on the south side of Yatton Wood there is a substantial 500 yard long earthwork with double ditches at its east end. It runs from the Hereford-Ross road (B4224) westwards to the River Wye (SO 627 295 to 631 294). There are indications that it continued to the east and the south-east. Its age is not known; it is quite possibly Anglo-Saxon, some think earlier than King Offa.

GANAREW *6.5m SW of Ross-on-Wye*
The name is from the Welsh genau - rhiw, meaning 'pass of the hill', and it does, indeed, lie in the pass now followed by the motorway-like A40T. The road runs through a cutting which has access lanes and a stone bridge with a concrete arch linking the hamlet of Ganarew to the high, wooded hills of Little Doward, Great Doward and Symonds Yat.

Approaching from the south-west one leaves the main road and the rather splendid Sellarsbrook House comes into view. It lies across a little valley in which there is a lake and a folly temple. The house is painted white from top to toe, a modest Classical Georgian mansion, elegant and well-proportioned, of five bays and two storeys with a giant portico of four Ionic columns supporting a plain pediment. A lawned promenade leads from the right of the house to another Greek temple. The hamlet of Lewstone lies 1/4m NW, but we re-trace our steps 1/4m southwards to the nucleated settlement of Ganarew itself.

The grey stone church of Saint Swithin was re-built by J. Pritchard in 1850. It has a nave, a chancel and a bell-turret with a little spire, and a monument to John Bannerman, died 1870.

The cream-painted, ashlar Manor House has five bays and an extension to the right. Ganarew House is a rambling stone-built building now used as a retirement home. For the rest there is a Scots pine, a bungalow, a stone cottage and sheep pastures.

We now cross the bridge over the A40 and come to a war memorial and the red sandstone lodge of Wyastone Leys. The name Wyastone is from Wye Stone, a pre-historic megalith; leys are pastures. The entrance drive passes through a wooded park recently stocked with a herd of 65 to 70 deer. These are kept as a visual attraction, not as a source of venison. The drive descends towards the water meadows that flank the River Wye. The modern grey, blue and pale green sheds in the valley belong to Nimbus. One of them housed the first Compact Disc manufacturing plant in England.

The mansion of Wyastone Leys was built in 1818 and extensively remodelled for John Bannerman by William Burn in 1862. It stands on the foot of Little Doward, on an elevated platform with fine views to the south, over the river to the broad pastures and the dark outlines of the High Meadow Woods, to the hills of Monmouth. On the entrance side it has six bays of three storeys with a Tuscan-columned porch set to the right. To the left is a clock-tower with an ogee cap and a lower extension. The house is rendered with stone dressings and decorated with shaped, Jacobean gables, and strap-work heads to the windows. The river-view side has eight bays, if you count the two ogee-capped towerlets, and two canted bay windows.

The once extensive estate is now reduced to 43 acres of delightful woods and meadows, free, we are glad to report, of any 'sporting' activities.

Wyastone Leys is now the home of Nimbus, the music recording company. The founding partners were Michael and Gerald Reynolds and Count Numa Labinsky, a Franco-Russian Jew who died in 1994. They used the profits from their Birmingham property development company to fund their first recording studio in 1970, and moved to a very run-down Wyastone Leys in 1975. Here they revived the old way of recording, where musicians played as if performing a live concert. Today, the recording world has become one of many short takes, multi-tracking, extensive editing and artificial effects, even in Classical music. Reynolds and Labinsky wanted to put back some reality, integrity and life back into recording.

Today the company has a catalogue of nearly 600 Classical titles and two subsidiary labels, one for 'world music' and the other, Prima Voce, to present archive material from early recordings.

To the right of the river-view side of the house is a modern brick and steel-frame concert hall-cum-recording studio. This has a low stage and fans out to the rear of the auditorium to provide an ideal acoustic for solists and small ensembles.

In the sheds adjacent to the approach drive the company manufactures and assembles C.D. mastering equipment which is sold to other companies. Nimbus's own C.Ds are now pressed by Nimbus Manufacturing in Cwmbran, South Wales. The group as a whole has a turnover of £30 million and employs 700 people. In 1995 the company commissioned John Griffiths to write *Nimbus*, the story of the company and its 20-year rise to success..

The big, heavily-wooded, dome-shaped hill above Wyastone Leys is Little Doward. There are three pre-historic sites here.

Little Doward Camp (SO 540 160) is an Iron-Age fort defended by double ramparts. The earth walls are between 8ft and 10ft high and enclose an area of 19.1/2 acres. There are four entrances but one or more might be modern. A further area of 2.1/2 acres, defended by a single rampart, adjoins the main fort. Here there are the mounds of at least three Bronze-Age barrows.

King Arthur's Cave (SO 546 156) is in Lord's Wood, most easily approached down a lane from Crocker's Ash, 1m SW of Whitchurch. The cave has a double entrance with a large internal chamber. This has been extensively excavated by archaeologists. Finds include Mesolithic, Neolithic and Bronze-Age remains of men, and animals such as bears, rhinoceroses and mammoths. These can be seen in museums at Monmouth, Hereford, Gloucester and the British Museum.

Merlin's Cave (SO 548 152) lies to the south-east of King Arthur's Cave. The single entrance is in an outcrop of rock. Beware, there is a sheer drop halfway along. Excavations have unearthed a flint implement and pottery of possibly Neolithic-Age, and a Bronze-Age razor. At various times iron ore has been mined in both the cave and the immediate vicinity.

To conclude this article it must be mentioned that the views of the Wye Valley from the A40(T), looking south from a point in line with Wyastone Leys, are spectacular - one of the great landscapes of Britain to be enjoyed from the comfort of your car. Seen on a misty Winter's evening you could believe that giants and wild boar still roam there, that knights are busy rescuing maidens and slaying dragons, that Owain Glyndwr really is not dead and is out there gathering his men to free Wales from the English yoke.

GARWAY *8.5m WSW of Ross-on-Wye*
The settlement is most easily approached off the A4521 at Broad Oak. Broad Oak itself is a crossroads hamlet with a venerable oak, a 12ft grey stump but one that has flowering shoots in profusion - there's life in the old dog yet. It stands in the fore-garden of the former inn, now a house.

There was once a toll gate at Broad Oak; today there are new developments of pleasant four-bedroomed dwellings that have good views to the Welsh hills. Just south of the crossroads is a cedarwood hut which provides accommodation for Saint Mary's Catholic Church; and just north of the crossroads is a Primitive Methodist chapel of red brick with pointed windows dated 1896(?)

Following the lane to Garway for a mile one first comes to Garway Common. Here there is a post office, and the Garway Inn. This, fittingly, faces the cricket pitch, which has been hacked out of the scrub woodland of the very large and very attractive Common. This wild and windy place has attracted some small developments of private bungalows and cottages with dormer windows to complement its handsome, stone farms and desultory council houses. The old stone school is now a transport yard and the village hall is a turquoise painted corrugated-iron hut (Mothers and Toddlers meet Thursday evenings). Nevertheless, this is a fine, proper village with real character, the centre of a scattered agricultural parish.

The settlement lies on the south facing slope of the River Monnow valley, which here marks the border with Wales. The country around is handsome, though somewhat remote. Indeed, mains water did not arrive until the 1930s, and electricity not until the 1950s.

Down the road from the common, at what is locally called The Turning, is the church of Saint Michael. This dedication often indicates an ancient religious site. In fact the name Garway is from Lann Guoruoe, 'the church of Guoruoe', a personal name. The church is very interesting. What we see today is this: a square, unbuttressed 13th century fortress tower joined by a 17th century corridor (made of re-used Norman tufa blocks) to a 13th century nave. The tower was designed to be free-standing and the original church of 1180 had a round nave with a chancel. The original chancel arch remains complete, decorated with Norman water-leaf, and a grotesque head with streams issuing from its mouth. Outside, part of the foundations of the excavated round nave have been exposed.

Round churches were favoured by the Knights Templar because the Holy Sepulchre in Jerusalem was round. The Knights Templar were at Garway from 1170 to 1312, when they were dispossessed (nationally) and their holdings passed to the Knights Hospitallers. It was the Hospitallers who re-built the church.

They also built the adjacent, and well preserved, Dovecote of 1326. It is round with a domed ceiling beneath a conical roof. The walls are 4ft thick and there are 666 resting places. (In English folklore buildings are built round so that there are no corners in which the Devil can hide; similarly, the 'triple six' is the Devil's number and an ill omen.)

A 'return' to the Bishop of Hereford in 1394 declares that the people of Garway only spoke Welsh, and that the curate only spoke English. By 1690 things were even more uncomfortable. The churchwardens complained to the Bishop that the Vicar, Jeremiah Jackson, was setting his neighbours against each other and refused to wear his surplice on Sundays. The vicar counter-complained that the wardens were bringing their children up as Papists and that they invited their friends into the church where they got roaring drunk and rang the bells all day. What a wonderful picture that conjures up.

In the area by the church there were once shops and a forge. These have long gone but the Baptist Chapel has survived and there is a new school, built in the 1960s, and a sub-post office. These serve a scattered, agricultural parish.

On the slopes of Garway Hill (1200ft above sea level) is the hamlet of White Rocks, 1.1/2m NW of the church. The farms and cottages are scattered around the Garway Hill Common, on which the occupants have grazing rights. Beware: a local saying is that there will always be nine witches from the bottom of Orcop, 2m N of Garway, to the end of Garway Hill as long as water runs.

One poor soul who had cause to think that perhaps he was a subject of one of their curses was the wrestler, Gritton of Garway. A broadside ballad, printed at Ross on Wye in the early 19th century, tells how, despite a sense of foreboding, he accepted a match at "Garway's Cruel Feast". After the contest had been under way for some time the men of Arcop grabbed him and beat him to death.

Just south of the White Rocks are the Little Corras Woods. The Garway to Kentchurch road passes through a neck of these at Ramping House (SO 438 231). How handsome they are, these broadleaved woods with their array of oak, rowan, silver birch, yew, beech, chestnut and their kind. They form a green, vaulted roof over the fern-fringed road. Does such a fine show have something to do with Kentchurch Court, 1.1/2m NE? (Kentchurch has its own article.)

GOODRICH *4m SSW of Ross-on-Wye*

The name was castellum Godric, 'Godric's castle'. Nothing remains of his castle, first mentioned in 1101. The oldest part of the new fortress is the late 12th century grey stone keep. The red sandstone curtain walling is early 13th century.

Much of this fabric remains, perched dramatically above the River Wye, guarding two ancient crossing places, and is everyone's idea of a mediaeval, ruined castle. It is entered through a large Barbican. A causeway leads to the Gatehouse, the left tower of which houses the Chapel. Around the square courtyard are various apartments. The Great Hall is in the west range and adjoins the south-west tower, the largest of the castle, which houses the Buttery (a store for wine and beer butts) and the pantry. To the other side of the Great Hall are the main living quarters, the Vestibule and Solar. The Garderobe (lavatory) Block has three cubicles and a chute into an impressively large moat. Fragments of the outer bailey to the west and north sides remain. The views are splendid indeed.

During the Civil War Sir Henry Lingen held the castle for the Royalists, but it fell after a siege by Colonel John Birch. Meg, a giant mortar, was used during bombardment and is now displayed in the Churchill Gardens, Hereford.

During the siege of 1646 Colonel Birch's niece was in the castle' having eloped with her beloved, Charles Clifford. They attempted to escape but were drowned in the river. Their ghosts are said to haunt the castle and whenever there is a storm their shrieking can be heard on the Wye.

There is a picnic site at Coppet Hill Common and at the castle there is an information centre and other facilities.

The church of Saint Giles lies at the south end of the village. The round arcade piers are 13th century; much of the rest is 14th century Decorated. Of the windows, the chancel east is Perpendicular; but most of the rest are Victorian. The north aisle east window has some good, 15th century, yellow and white stained glass and there is a late 13th century shrine.

The village lies on the slope leading to the castle and developed to service it. There are stone and render cottages, a post office-cum-general store, a village hall, and a

Above: Goodrich Castle, early 12th to 14th century.
Right: Plan of Longtown Castle, drawn by Mike Salter.
Bottom left: Goodrich Castle seen over the River Wye.
Bottom right: Ladies' costume of the 13th century.

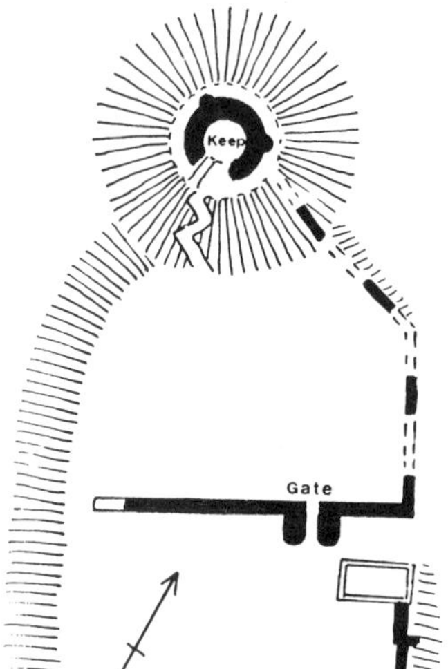

playing field. The buildings which catch the eye are Y Crwys, stone with a slit window and steps; and Ye Olde Hostelrie, Gothic with tall, chapel-like window and numerous pinnacles of about 1830.

Goodrich Court, 1/2m from the castle, was a vast, Romantic mansion with towers and battlements, begun in 1828 to a design by Edward Blore but sadly demolished about 1960. Only the red sandstone east gatehouse on the main road to Ross survives. It has round gate towers with conical roofs and projecting battlements, giving one some idea of the "fantasy that floats on the Wye" which was an important feature in the Victorian landscape - this Rhineland of England.

Follow the sign to the youth hostel and Welsh Bicknor and you will cross a tall, rare, dry-arch bridge, a road over a road.

Flanesford Priory lies 1/2m NE of the castle on the lowland beside the Wye. The Priory of Saint John the Baptist, as it is properly called, was founded by Sir Richard Talbot for Canons of the Augustinian Order in 1346, but all that remains is a refectory range. This has been developed in recent times as a pottery, and further schemes are afoot.

Newhouse Farm, 2/3m WNW of Goodrich, was built as a parsonage for the Reverend Thomas Smith in 1636. It has three, three-storey blocks with mullioned windows arranged radially, presumably to represent the Holy Trinity.

Huntsham Court, 1.1/4m SSW of Goodrich on the Wye flood plain, is a Jacobean house with mullioned windows and a columned porch and is now called Huntsham Farm Park. Here they have stocks of rare and endangered animals - cattle, pigs, poultry, ducks and geese. North of Huntsham Court is the site of a Roman villa (SO 565 175). Tiles found during ploughing led to an excavation being commenced in 1961. The site extends to some 21 acres. Foundations have been found of a very large aisled barn together with a corn drier, a washing tank, a main dwelling, a separate small house and a boundary wall. It was occupied from the 2nd to the late 4th centuries.

Huntsham Bridge (SO 568 182) was built by the Courtfield Estate in 1885. Before that a ferry operated here. The ferryman's cottage still stands. The bridge is of metal construction and is supported on four iron pillars. There is a weight limit of five tons. Just to the east of the bridge is Rocklands, a castellated house of about 1820 that does, indeed, stand below a line of rocky outcrops.

In a meadow in the loop of the river west of Huntsham Bridge, at SO 562 182, is the enigmatic Queen's Stone. The name is from the Anglo-Saxon Cwen stan, 'woman's stone'. It is a pre-historic monolith of local sandstone conglomerate, thought by Alfred Watkins to be Bronze-Age of about B.C.2000, and contemporaneous with Stonehenge. It has deep grooves, about 2 inches wide and up to 7 inches deep, on each of its four sides, and a single cup mark depression on the eastern face. These grooves stop at the old ground level; the present ground level has been raised by ploughing. The stone projects downwards some 8ft below the old ground level.

Watkins, a pioneer photographer and member of the Woolhope Club, excavated the area and found fragments of burnt bone, worked flints and large amounts of charcoal. He proposed that the stone had been used as a sacrificial altar, that the grooves held wooden rods which formed a cage in which humans and/or animals were confined and burnt to death. Others think that the grooves are symbols of the earth goddess. For Watkins the stone had special significance because it was a marker on three ley lines, the theory of which he propounded in his book *The Old Straight Track*.

GRAFTON *2m SSW of Hereford*
The suburbs of Hereford have all but reached here. The name is from the Anglo-Saxon meaning 'settlement in, or by, a grove'. It is approached off the A49 alongside which stands the Grafton Inn. The hamlet proper lies west of the main road, beside the railway.

The church of Saint Peter is of 1880 by F.R. Kempson. It has a nave, a chancel and a tower with a spire in early mediaeval style. Inside there is a monument to John Daubeney, died 1741. In the vicarage garden are the ruins of the old church. This has indications of a Norman doorway and two Norman windows. Close by there is an hotel and an attractive black and white house which has lozenge-trellis bracing in the gable.

At the junction of the main line railway and the lane from Grafton to Merryhill Farm (SO 491 371), there is part of the old Hereford to Abergavenny Tramroad. This was built in the early 19th century and used to transport coal by horse-drawn tubs from the South Wales coalfield via the Newport to Brecon canal. The tramway was at its busiest in the 1840s but was soon superseded by the steam railway.

GRENDON BISHOP *6.5m ESE of Leominster*
In Domesday Book it was Grenedene, meaning 'green valley', and it was held by the Bishop of Hereford. Grendon Bishop and Grendon Green together barely constitute a hamlet, more a scatter of houses along the A44, Leominster to Bromyard road. The church of Saint John the Baptist lies isolated in fields, 300 yards from Grendon Farm. The old Norman church collapsed and all that remains is a small window (now in the tower) and the round, tapering font. The red sandstone building we see today was begun in 1787 and then much restored by the Victorians.

Grendon Court lies on the slopes of a little valley 1m S of the church and Westington Court lies 1/2m NW. Near the latter is Westington Camp (SO 580 566), a small hill fort covering about one acre. The rampart has been ploughed and the ditch is only visible as darker soil. Slopes of the spur, especially on the north-west side appear to have been steepened. Neolithic flints and axe heads have been found on the site.

HAMNISH CLIFFORD *2.5m E of Leominster*
In 1123 it was Hamenessce, meaning 'Hamma's ashtree'. It is a scattered little place surrounded by orchards that hides amongst lanes between the A44 and A4112. The small church of Saint Dubricius was built in 1910 to a design by W.J. Weatherley and has a stained glass window by Kempe & Tower, made in 1924. The old church, a corrugated iron building of 1897, is now the Church Hall.

Hennor House lies 1/2m SE, adjacent to a small wood. The front, with its Adam-style porch, is of about 1775, but at the back are two stone wings, one dated at 1679. Inside there are two good fireplaces. Nearby is Brock Hall, the name probably referring to an Anglo-Saxon badger sett. A Roman road from Risbury, in the south, passes through Stretford and up Widgeon Hill to Stockton in the north.

Upper Hamnish and Brockmanton lie to the east of the church and are equally scattered and rural. Bach Camp (SO 546 603), is 300 yards north of Brockmanton on a rise between two streams. It is an irregularly shaped pre-historic enclosure of about 6.1/2 acres surrounded by a double rampart with three entrances.

HAMPTON BISHOP *3m SE of Hereford*

The name is from the Anglo-Saxon meaning 'settlement by a water-meadow'. The village is so much in a water-meadow that it is surrounded by high earth banks to keep out the flood waters of the River Lugg and the River Wye which all but surround it. In December 1960 the stank, as the earth walls are called, gave way and the village was badly flooded by the deluge. Troops of the 22nd SAS Regiment helped evacuate the residents by boat and helicopter. Subsequently, the walls were raised by 15 inches and strengthened with internal steel plates. The same flood waters have, however, made the surrounding cattle pastures very fertile. This stretch of the Wye is famous for its salmon fishing and Hampton Bishop is on the Wye River Valley Walk. The village inn, The Bunch of Carrots, has a well-known sign - a friar dangling a bunch of carrots in front of a donkey to make him move more quickly. However, there are two other local explanations of the name. The gillie on the adjacent Carrots Fishery says it is named after the fact that a fisherman ran out of bait, used a carrot and caught a salmon; the other is that at low water an outcrop of rocks is exposed that resembles a bunch of carrots. Down the lane leading south from the inn is one of the last timber-framed houses to have been built in Herefordshire (not counting modern revivals).

Along the main road, the B4399, are a few scattered cottages and The Lawns, a good Georgian brick house which has five bays, three storeys and a Tuscan-columned doorway. However, the village proper lies 200 yards to the north, around the embowered church of Saint Andrew. It is a somewhat unusual building with the tower placed midway along the north side of the nave with an aisle running east along the chancel thus leaving the nave with an arcade at one end only. The tower and nave walls are Norman and the modern porch protects a Norman doorway, which is decorated with saltire crosses, scales, zig-zag and the head of a man. The chancel is 14th century but has a Norman arch leading to a 15th century chapel with a damaged stone reredos. Inside there is a Norman font and monuments to the James family, of about 1837, and Colonel Thomas Weare, died 1850; outside is a 14th century churchyard cross with steps, base, shaft and modern head. The upper part of the tower is timber-framed under a steep conical roof; there are six bells, five of which were cast in the 17th century.

Near the church are several black and white cottages, notably Church Farm with two gabled cross wings and a 17th century side porch. There are 12 properties in the village that still have commons rights of grazing and mowing on the Hampton Meadow, Big and Little Million and Swan Bed pastures. The owners of Lower House used to charge a toll to let cattle cross the river at the Ox Ford. Basket weaving was an important craft industry hereabouts but along with the blacksmith and the wheelwright it is no more.

In the manor of Hampton Bishop the custom of Borough English prevailed, that is the youngest son inherits his father's estate. Today we normally follow the Norman-French custom of passing to the eldest son. Should someone die without leaving a will in Hampton Bishop it would be for the lawyers to decide how the inheritance should be divided. Three other manors in Herefordshire have Borough English, namely Holmer and Shelwick, Barton and Tupsley and Ledbury. All once belonged to the Bishop of Hereford.

HAMPTON COURT *4m SSE of Leominster*

Hampton means 'settlement on a river bank', the river here being the Lugg. River names, by the way, are usually very ancient, at least Celtic Iron-Age and most probably much earlier than that.

Hampton Court consists of an impressive red sandstone castle and a few service dwellings set in parkland off the A417, less than a mile east of Hope-under-Dinmore. Licence to crenellate (that is permission to build a fortified house or fortify an existing building) was granted in 1434 to Sir Rowland Lenthall. He had made a fortune from the hostage money paid for prisoners he took at the Battle of Agincourt. Of the original structure the Gatehouse (but not its arches or bay window) and the chapel (chiefly the walls) constitute most of what remains. The majority of the rest was re-modelled for Lord Coningsby in about 1700 and later by the architect Sir Jeffrey Wyatville in the early 19th century for R. Arkwright, of the famous cotton spinning family. Amongst other things Wyatville Gothicized all the windows and built the cloister corridors around the courtyard.

When we visited in 1995, further extensive modernisation work was in progress under the care of a man with a transatlantic accent and an abrupt manner. The estate had recently been purchased by a wealthy American, a Mr. Van Kempen. I hope he has not removed the picture of hounds hanging in the house; local tradition has it that to do so will bring the speedy death of either the perpetrator or someone close to him. Why tempt providence, that's what we say.

The north transept of the chapel was built as a memorial to John Arkwright and in it is a brass to his son Henry who died in an avalanche whilst climbing Mont Blanc. His body was found 30 years later and was buried at Chamonix in 1897.

On a more cheerful note the Archaeological Research Section of the Woolhope Club have made a comprehensive study of the water gardens at Hampton Court. These waterworks consist of a system of pools, fountains, leats, bridge, mill and dam sites and were made for Lord Coningsby. These may have been inspired by the grand scheme of irrigation works constructed by Rowland Vaughan in the Golden Valley towards the end of the 16th century.

Two hundred yards downstream of the single-arched bridge of 1826, that carries the A417 over the River Lugg, is the weir (SO 515 526). This was used to lift the level of the river and allow water to be diverted to the Hampton Court Old Mill. The mill was later replaced by a new one on the other side of the valley, but the leat waters were used to feed Lord Coningsby's elaborate water gardens. These waterworks were abandoned in the 19th century but the weir was kept and refurbished because the leat was used to power a sawmill used for cutting both stone and timber for the restoration of the Court by the Arkwright family. Hampton Court is a former home of Lord Hereford who moved here from Trecoyd, near Hay-on-Wye.

The park at Hampton Court once had a herd of deer. It is a deer park no longer but some animals escaped and their descendants live to this day in the Queenswood, which adjoins the park, just over the river.

HARDWICKE *2.5m ENE of Hay on Wye*

The name is from the Anglo-Saxon leord-wic, 'flock-farm', meaning a sheep farm. And sheep there are in this friendly, green hill country. The farms are built of stone, likewise the barns, many of which have arrow-slit windows. It is a scattered community, but boasts a pub, the Royal Oak, long and low and painted white; a hotel, The Haven; a Hall; and a small church, Holy Trinity, built in 1851 in a style of about 1300 with stained glass windows by John Bell of Bristol. To the east is Westbrook where the track of the disused Hay to Golden Valley railway can be seen. To the north is Windle Park.

Pen, found in several place names hereabouts - such as Pen-y-Park, Pen-y-lan, Pentwyn Farm and Pen-y-moor Farm - is Welsh meaning 'head', 'top', 'end', usually of a geographical feature such as a valley or a hill.

HAREWOOD *4.5m WNW of Ross on Wye*

The name is from the Anglo-Saxon and could mean either 'grey wood' or 'hare's wood'. It straggles along the A49, Hereford to Ross road, from Harewood End in the south, where there is an inn, to Harewood Park in the north. As to buildings of note, sad news we bring. Harewood Park has been demolished and only a gate lodge with pediment and two pairs of Tuscan columns has survived.

The church of Saint Dennis, built in 1864 to a mixed Early English and Norman style is now disused, which is not surprising bearing in mind the close proximity of the churches at Llandinabo, Hentland, Michaelchurch and Pencoyd.

HATFIELD *6m E of Leominster*

The Domesday Book name was Hetfelde, meaning 'open land where heather (or similar shrubs) grow'. Approaching from Leominster, one leaves the A44 at Stretford and travels down a lane through an agreeable landscape of gentle hills, woods and watery valleys. Before reaching the nucleus of the settlement one passes fields dotted with ancient oak trees and Hatfield Court, set on rising land.

The Court has two gables with a recessed centre and porch set to the left. It is constructed of grey stone under a slate roof with brick chimneys and hooded windows. At present it is in the process of being engulfed in ivy. The hall behind the porch is large and has a panelled ceiling. In the garden are several gipsy caravans. The present occupant is Jeremy Sandford, the playwright who wrote the television dramas *Cathy Come Home* and *Edna, the Inebriate Woman*. He has an interest in gypsies and in 1995 he published *Songs from the Roadside*, subtitled 100 years of Gipsy Music. Amongst the 34 titles are some little known traditional pieces, carols, and newly composed songs, complete with melodies, collected by Sandford in Herefordshire and neighbouring counties. A feature of the book is the excellent artwork of Peter Upton.

At the back of Hatfield Court is a later range of brick dwellings. The stable block has also been converted into several freehold domestic units and behind this are some cattle farm buildings, a Victorian walled garden and a mobile caravan site.

The church of Saint Leonard lies 1/2m further east along the valley, which is here followed by the disused track of the Leominster to Bromyard railway. The church has been restored but retains its Norman nave and north doorway with diamond-patterned stones, and some very early Norman herringbone masonry. The square font is also Norman, brought here from Chardstock in Dorset. The timbered porch is 14th century, and the two bells are 13th century. In the churchyard are monuments to the Colles family. They were the local landlords and lived in the original Hatfield Court from the 16th to the later 17th centuries.

Opposite the church is the modern Court Farm, built behind the remains of the Elizabethan Hatfield Court. This was constructed in about 1560 and was the earliest brick house in Herefordshire. When it was demolished the staircase and other parts of the fabric were incorporated in the present Hatfield Court. In the orchard of Court Farm can be seen the foundations of the mediaeval village.

In the modern village there is a post office but the school of 1852 is now a private house. The Old Hall is 16th century, a yeoman farmer's house. Rough Cast Farm now houses the Coltsfoot Gallery, purveyors of paintings. The Fencote Railway Station, in the valley south of the road, was sold for housing development shortly after the line closed in 1952.

For an anecdote relating to a Hatfield 'wise man' see Little Cowarne. The ceremony of the Hop-pickers' Feast, which concluded the harvest, was a custom at Hatfield. For a description of this see Ullingswick.

HAYWOOD *3.5m SW of Hereford*

The name means 'enclosed wood', but that is long gone. It is a tiny place that lies between the A465 and the A49, overlooking the railway from Hereford to Abergavenny.

Haywood Lodge is a substantial brick house of about 1710. It has seven bays, two storeys, a hipped roof and a doorway with pilasters and pediment. Within is a good staircase; without are good wrought-iron front gates. Haywood (Farm) lies a mile to the south, beyond Wellington Coppice. It is of 1740, stone-built, and crouches low beside Blakemore Hill, as though to cheat the wind. The dovecote has been demolished.

Owain Glyndwr is said to have wandered the woods here in 1414, a broken man in shepherd's garb begging for food before he died of starvation, and that his body taken was taken to Monnington-on-Wye to be buried.

HENTLAND *4m WNW of Ross-on-Wye*

The name is from the Welsh hen-llan, meaning 'old church'. It is approached down lanes off the A49 and consists of a few cottages by a substantial church. The chancel, nave and north aisle are of the early 13th century and there are many period windows. The tower is 14th century and still has its original bell. However, the whole church was much restored in 1853 by J.P. Seddon. Inside is a fine Jacobean chair with grotesque figures and a carved font. The church is dedicated to Saint Dubricius (or Dyfrig) a 6th century Welsh missionary scholar who founded a college, or monastery, at Hentland, and taught 2,000 clergy over a period of seven years. (For a short biography of Dubricius see Madley). Until recently the only clue to the site of Saint Dubricius' college was a farm near Hoarwithy called Llanfrother, from Llanfrodyr, Welsh for 'the church of the brothers'. However, in recent times extensive excavations in the field on the south side of the churchyard (SO 543 263) alongside a possible Roman road have revealed the foundations of a large, previously unknown, mediaeval building with 13th to 16th century pottery ware and tiles. Also, most interestingly, Romano-British shards were found indicating occupation of the site at a time close enough to that of the Saint to excite the imagination.

On Palm Sunday pax (peace) cakes are distributed after the morning service at Hentland and nearby King's Caple and Sellack. The cakes have now been diminished to wafers stamped with the words 'Peace and Good Neighbourhood', a phrase often inscribed on church bells in Here-

Above left: Hereford. Eign Street, c.1900
Above right: Nell Gwynne.
Right: Hereford, the King George V GWR 6000, now at the Bulmer Railway Museum.

fordshire. The custom is believed to have been started in 1570 by Lady Scudamore who made a bequest for its continuance.

Gillow Manor, 1m SSW of the church, is an appealing red sandstone house. The Gatehouse, which constitutes the south-west front, is of the late 14th century. It has four-centred arches, a Perpendicular window with a transom, tunnel vaulting and leads to the courtyard. In the basement there is a statue of about 1430, the function of which is a mystery. It has been suggested that it was one of several dummy watchmen that might have been placed on walls and at windows to warn off persons with hostile intentions. (The Beau Geste ploy.) A few yards north of Gillow Manor on both sides of the A4137 are the much ploughed-out earthworks of Gaer Cop (SO 537 253), a prehistoric fort. A single rampart surrounds an oval enclosure of 17 acres on a gentle rise.

Just south of the crossroads settlement of Saint Owen's Cross is Great Treaddow, a house with ancient crucks in the west front. Cruck construction is the earliest form of timber building.

Pengethley Manor Hotel, 1/2m S of Hentland and just off the A49, is a white rendered Georgian house that has a seven-bay front (three of which form a central canted bay), two storeys and a hipped roof. It is beautifully sited in 15 acres of grounds and has a high reputation. Well-known people who have stayed here include Anthony Hopkins (whilst filming *Shadowlands*), Barbara Windsor, Status Quo and the Tottenham Hotspurs football team. The hotel has its own nine-hole golf course.

The country around Hentland is most pleasantly littered with orchards and small woods.

HEREFORD *capital town of the county*

INTRODUCTION
Hereford is a comfortable, unpretentious place, with some good river views, some buildings of character and all the services offered by a county town. The old centre is well preserved but externally the cathedral is, by common consensus, something of a disappointment. Geographically the county is saucer-shaped and Hereford lies near the centre on flat land beside the River Wye. This flatness is convenient for pedestrians but does little for the prospect of the town. It has a population of about 50,000 and a shopping catchment of about 150,000, not large for a county capital. This all sounds rather glum, but you will find that Hereford is a friendly place which gets its fair share of tourists in the summer.

A BRIEF HISTORY
A number of Late Bronze-Age socketed axe-heads and a bronze sword have been found at Fairoaks, Hereford, but discounting isolated finds such as this and a Middle Bronze-Age dagger found elsewhere, the earliest settlement in the area was the Iron-Age hill fort on Credenhill 4.1/2m NW of the centre of Hereford. This was superseded by the Roman town of Magnis (Kenchester) which is situated at the foot of Credenhill. There is no evidence of a settlement at Hereford until the 7th century - most major English towns had been established long before that. It developed on a gravel terrace that commanded two fords across the River Wye. The name Hereford is not altogether properly understood but probably means 'army ford', a crossing place where soldiers could keep close order. The Bishopric was established in A.D. 676. In A.D. 760 there was a battle at Hereford between the Welsh and the Anglo-Saxons.

By the 9th century the town occupied the north bank of the Wye from the present day Greyfriars Bridge on the west to the Victoria suspension bridge on the east, and northwards to the line of West and East Streets. The town walls consisted of a clay rampart faced with timber built on top of an earlier gravel bank and ditch. A reconstruction of a section of this can be seen behind the modern flats at the junction of Mill Street and Saint Owen Street. The cathedral was almost certainly built of timber.

In the 10th century the town defences were re-faced in stone. Border towns at that time had two enemies - the Welsh and marauding Danes. A commercial area developed beyond the northern town walls and in about 1046 Edward the Confessor appointed his Norman nephew, Ralph, as Earl of Hereford. Ralph built a castle, probably on the rise now called Hogg's Mount, but his army was defeated by Llewelyn ap Gruffydd in 1055. The Welsh sacked the city, destroyed the castle and pillaged the cathedral. Enter Harold Godwinson, who became King of England in 1066. He assumed the title Earl of Hereford and drove the Welsh back into the mountains.

After the Norman Conquest King William gave the Earldom of Hereford to William Fitz Osbern. He rebuilt the castle and established a market place and two new churches, All Saints and Saint Peter, centred on the present day High Town. The relative peace of the late 11th and early 12th centuries was broken by the bitter feuding between Stephen and Matilda, rivals for the English throne. Hereford was sieged and changed hands several times.

By now civic authority was challenging that of the clergy. In 1224 the town's defences were greatly strengthened with the construction of a 12ft high wall with 17 semi-circular bastion towers and six gateways. The last of the gates was demolished in 1798, but substantial sections of the wall can still be seen. The defences survived a siege by Roger de Mortimer in 1265. By 1300 a flourishing cloth trade had developed - cappers, hosiers, dyers, fullers and weavers.

Hereford's only involvement in the Wars of the Roses seems to have been that it was in High Town that Owen Tudor was beheaded after the battle of Mortimer's Cross. In the early 16th century Leland wrote of Hereford Castle that it was "one of the fayrest, largest and strongest castels in England". With the Reformation the town became impoverished. Saint Guthlac's Priory and the houses of the Greyfriars and the Blackfriars were suppressed. Worse, a royal charter to demolish the fulling mills on the Wye ruined the city's cloth trade. (Saint Guthlac's was a pre-Conquest church that was originally housed within the castle grounds but which was united with Saint Peter's and re-located outside the city walls in the mid-12th century. The ruins of Blackfriars and its well preserved preaching cross can be seen behind Coningsby Hospital.)

In 1597 the guilds obtained a new royal charter and helped pay for a new Town Hall. This was a magnificent construction, one of the finest timber-framed buildings in England. Alas it was demolished in the 1860s. Its position is marked in High Town with coloured paving slabs on the site of its 27 oak support piers.

In the 17th century charitable institutions flourished with the foundation of hospitals - Kenning's, Coningsby's, the Weavers' - and some 20 Almshouses, many of which survive, notably the long, timber-built terrace of Aubrey's in Berrington Street, and the stone-built range of Saint Ethelbert in Castle Street. During the Civil War the town was under a royal governor but twice fell to the Parliamentarians. The defences were strengthened after the second invasion and it withstood two long sieges in 1645. It finally fell after a ruse by Colonel Birch enabled the Parliamentarians to rush the main gates and it remained in their hands thereafter. By the 18th century Hereford was freshly established as a regional centre of trade and the Wye was exploited as a trade route. (See p.235.) The gloving trade was a major industry and the town's prosperity can be seen in the number of public buildings that were constructed in the newly fashionable brick - Bluecoat School (1710); Mary Shelley's Hospital (1710); Congregational Church (1740); Guildhall (1759); Infirmary (1793); County Gaol (1793); Lunatic Asylum (1794); Countess of Huntingdon's Chapel (1796); and the Wesleyan Chapel (1796). Half-timber gave way to brick in domestic buildings also, though often only to the facade.

In the 19th century the Hereford to Abergavenny tramroad (1829) was constructed. This was a railway but the wagons were hauled by horses. (See p.235.) The railway proper came in 1854, substantially following the same route. Of the extensive rail network that developed only the Crewe-Newport and Ledbury-Worcester lines have survived to the present day. The canal from Gloucester reached Hereford in 1845. This had a short life but remnants can be seen in the northern suburbs of Hereford and elsewhere in the county. Until the 1850s there were twice as many houses within the walls as there were without. Then the suburbs grew apace and now stretch for one and a half miles in every direction from the old centre. This outward development has enabled the ancient core to be substantially preserved. As everywhere in England unsympathetic modern shop fronts have marred the townscape but behind them lurk ancient fabrics. And there are secrets. Many have extensive and elegant mediaeval cellars beneath their timber frames, for example, but those you must seek for yourself in the pages that follow.

CIVIC AUTHORITY

The Bishop had been granted a fair in 1121 by Henry I, but the earliest secular charter is of 1189 by Richard I. This granted relief from the 'intrusion' of the county sheriff in return for the citizens maintaining the town's fortifications. King John gifted a Merchant's Gild and Henry III gave the right to hold a three-day fair on the 9-11 October. Edward I gave a murage grant to pay for the upkeep of the walls and Richard II permitted Sir John Burley, the Hereford Bailiff, to adopt the title of Mayor in 1382 and gave the burgesses a site for their Courthouse.

In 1597 Elizabeth I granted incorporation of the town "as a body politic". This Great Charter made the town a fully fledged borough with many rights and privileges. The charter of 1690 has attached the finest example of the William and Mary seal in England. In 1974 Queen Elizabeth II granted a charter reconstituting the City Council. The city charters are kept at the Town Hall and can be seen by appointment with the Mayor's secretary.

Today Hereford is run by a City Council. The offices of the Chief Executive and the Town Clerk are in the Town Hall, Owen Street, HR1 2PJ, and the Housing, Works & Environment Directorates are in Garrick House, Widemarsh Street, HR4 9EU.

The Coat of Arms of the city of Hereford consist of a shield charged with the three lions of England belonging to Richard I surrounded by a blue border bearing 10 Saint Andrew's crosses supported by two silver lions rampant gardant each having a collar with three gold buckles. The Crest is a lion passant gardant holding in his dexter paw a sword and the motto is Invictae Fidelitates Praemium.

HEREFORD CATHEDRAL

The cathedral is dedicated to Mary and Saint Ethelbert. Saint Ethelbert was murdered about 1794 and his relics were the prize possessions of the Cathedral. The foundations of the building we see today were laid in 1080 and substantial parts of the Norman fabric remain, particularly the south transept. In the 13th century the east end was altered to include an ambulatory and a new Lady Chapel (1220) was built above a crypt. This chapel is remarkable in that it was completed in purely Early English Gothic style, the first in England and many think the most beautiful. Also in the 13th century the north transept was built by Bishop Peter Aquablanca, a close friend of Henry III. It houses the stone shrine of Saint Thomas Cantilupe, Bishop of Hereford from 1275-1282, who was canonised in 1320 and became a great attraction to pilgrims.

In the 14th century the central tower was constructed in Decorated style. It used to have a spire but this collapsed in 1726. Ballflower motifs of the Decorated period are prominent. The belfry houses a ring of ten bells.

The delightful Bishop Stanbury Chantry Chapel was built in 1480-96. It has an intricate, Perpendicular style fan- vault and an original oak door with open ironwork, and the glass-stained windows of 1923 are quite excellent.

The cathedral houses a number of treasures and works of art. Foremost is the Chained Library, a collection of 1,500 books, some dating back to the 8th century, complete with reading desks and book presses made in 1611. It is the largest chained library in the world. There are also 227 manuscripts and some very valuable incunabula, i.e. books printed before 1500.

The Mappa Mundi received much publicity in the mid-1990s when the authorities tried to sell it to a foreign buyer. Decency prevailed and it is still here. The map was drawn on vellum (64 inches x 54 inches) in about 1290 and shows how mediaeval scholars viewed the world: flat and centred on Jerusalem. It is unique. In 1996 a new building was opened in the Cathedral grounds. It had been substantially financed by John Paul Getty Junior and was specially designed to house the Chained Library and the Mappa Mundi. The site was examined by archaeologists and some 1,100 human skeletons were exhumed. It was a deplorable thing to do. Many of the bones were crushed by heavy machinery. This was desecration on a grand scale and how the church could countenance such a scheme is beyond belief. After all, they only needed the building for commercial purposes.

In the sanctuary near the high altar is King Stephen's Chair, said to have been used by King Stephen when he attended mass here in 1138, and more recently by the present Queen in 1957 and 1976.

Modern objects of art include the three Tree of Life tapestries designed by John Piper, in the south transept, and the yellow metal candlelit Corona suspended over the central altar, the work of Simon Beer, installed in 1992. The Vicars Choral library is also held in the cathedral (This by no means consists only of music).

Note: This description of the cathedral has, for reasons of space, been brief. For a full architectural description see *The Buildings of England:Herefordshire* by Nikolaus Pevsner.

Cathedral Precinct
The cathedral does not have a proper precinct. There are ranges to the south, but otherwise the lawn that surrounds the other three sides is enclosed by streets and secular

buildings though some of these are owned by the church.

Bishop's Cloister The Bishop's Cloister is early 15th century, but utilizes a much earlier Norman buttress in the wall of the east walk and parts are of the 1360s. All the arcading is 15th century except that below the Lady's Arbour. The south walk has been separated and now forms the Lower Library. The west range was rebuilt as the Library by Sir Arthur Blomfield in 1897.

Chapter House
All that remains of the ten-sided mediaeval Chapter House are some cloister entrance mouldings and the lower parts of three sides. The lead was stripped from the roof during the Civil War and it was pulled down in 1769. Recently it has been realized that the Chapter House had the earliest historically documented fan-vaults in the whole of England. Thomas de Cantebrugge was contracted to complete the work within seven years from 1364.

College of Vicars' Choral
The college was founded in 1396. It consisted of a custos and 26 vicars. These were men in orders, or minor orders, who acted for absent prebendaries, i.e., honorary canons. Their original hall was in Castle Street but they complained of the dangers and discomforts of journeying at night and were given the present site in 1473. Here they built four ranges around a quadrangle. Each vicar had two-roomed accommodation. They shared a Hall, much worked on by the Georgians; a Chapel, part stone and part timber-framed; and a first-floor Library, made Gothic in 1830 and now the Dean's private study.

Bishop's Palace
It stands behind the cathedral to the south west. The Perpendicular Gatehouse has a timber-framed gable above the entrance arch which leads to the courtyard and a Victorian, stone stable block. Much of the Palace is timber-framed but has Georgian and Victorian brick facades. It is singularly unimpressive from the outside. However, inside there is a late 12th century Great Hall. It is 55ft wide and was 75ft long and much of the huge timber arcading remains. With the Great Hall of Leicester Castle it vies for the title of 'oldest secular building in England'. The excellent panelling of the Chapel was originally in the dining room.

Bishop's Chapel
It was the oldest building in Hereford before it was demolished, some time after 1737, when it was illustrated by Stukey. Properly called the Chapel of Saint Katherine and Mary Magdalene it was built before 1095 by Bishop Losinga. All that remains is the wall against the south range of the cloister which has some low, unmoulded arches on the ground floor and segmented arches on the first floor. All the arches are now blocked with tufa (lightweight, spongy limestone) almost certainly came from the original chapel.

The Boy Bishop
The mediaeval custom of electing a Boy Bishop is still enacted at Hereford Cathedral. This is akin to the 'officers serving the men' common in the British Army. It is a token act of servitude and humility by the high and mighty to appease the lower ranks; a token, but nevertheless charming. The Boy Bishop is chosen by the real Bishop and ordained at a special service on the Saturday nearest to the Day of Saint Nicholas, 6 December. (St. Nicholas is the saint of children, merchants, pawnbrokers, apothecaries, performers and unmarried women - make of that what you will). The Boy Bishop replaces the bishop on the episcopal throne, and until the day commemorating the Slaughter of the Innocents' by Herod, he takes his place in all services except those requiring the presence of an ordained priest.

Cathedral Ghosts
The Cathedral has had at least two ghosts. In 1786 a Mr. Hoskins was seen on numerous occasions in the cathedral. His spirit was summoned at midnight by 12 priests each carrying a candle. At first Mr. Hoskins said he was in Ireland (!) but then appeared. He asked to be laid to rest in the Red Sea but the priests decided, more prosaically, to banish his spirit to the bed of the Wye, beneath the now demolished Bye Street Gate Bridge which stood near the Kerry Arms. In 1934 a policeman saw a cowled figure in the cathedral close. More sightings followed and up to 200 people gathered at night hoping to see the ghost. The apparition is still seen from time to time.

CHURCHES

All Saints, High Street, has some early 13th century survivals but was much rebuilt in the 13th and 14th centuries. The stalls are 14th century and the seats have misericords - carvings of bearded faces, mermaids, birds, mice, bears and a lion. In the daytime coffee is served inside and buskers perform outside. We saw a very good accordion player here. All Saints is the main centre of Anglican workship in Hereford and the subject of a million-pound development scheme as a community centre for concerts, plays and craft workshops.

Saint Peter, Saint Peter Street, has a strong, late 13th century stone tower with buttresses. The form of the present church is of about 1300 but it was much restored in 1880-5 by Thomas Nicholson, who was also busy elsewhere in the county. Saint Peter's Church also has a ghost, again a cowled figure, that has been seen walking through solid oak doors. Witnesses include a former organist and, in 1926, a policeman. The spirit has been variously attributed to a mediaeval monk murdered by marauding Welshmen, and Walter de Lacy who fell to his death from the tower of the church in the 13th century.

Saint James, Green Street, by Thomas Nicholson 1869, in 'Geometrical style'. Restored internally in 1902 after a fire.

Saint Martin, Ross Road. What we see is of 1845, in lancet style (tall, thin, pointed arches to the windows). In mediaeval times this was the mother church to All Saints which was then but a chapel.

Saint Nicholas, Friars Street. Of 1842 to a design by Thomas Duckham in stone, lancet windows.

Saint Paul, Church Road, Tupsley. By F.R. Kempson;

Saint Francis Xavier, Broad Street. Of 1838 by Charles Day. An ill-proportioned copy of the Treasury of the Athaenians at Delphi the facade dominated by two giant stuccoed, Doric columns. Roman Catholic and up for sale at the time of writing.

Holy Trinity, 1883 by F.R. Kempson in Early English style with chancel of 1907.

Baptist Church, Commercial Road, 1880, Italianate yellow brick and stone.

Eignbrook Congregational Church, Eign Street (Gate). Of 1872 by Haddon Brothers. "A perverse little Gothic job," says Mr. Pevsner. Iron pillars from Coalbrookdale.

Friends Meeting House, King Street. Of 1882, red brick. Built in the backyard of the attached house.

Church of Our Lady of the Universe, Roman Catholic c.1975.

Other churches: include *First Church of Christ* (Scientist); *Apostolic Church* (Jehovah's Witnesses); *Church of Latter Day Saints, Christian Life Centre, Christadelphian Church*; *Barton Hall* (Salvation Army); *Society of Friends; Hall of the Church of Our Lady, Belmont Road*

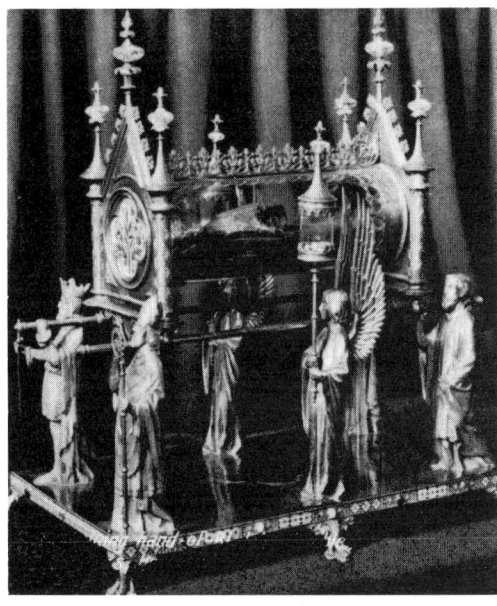

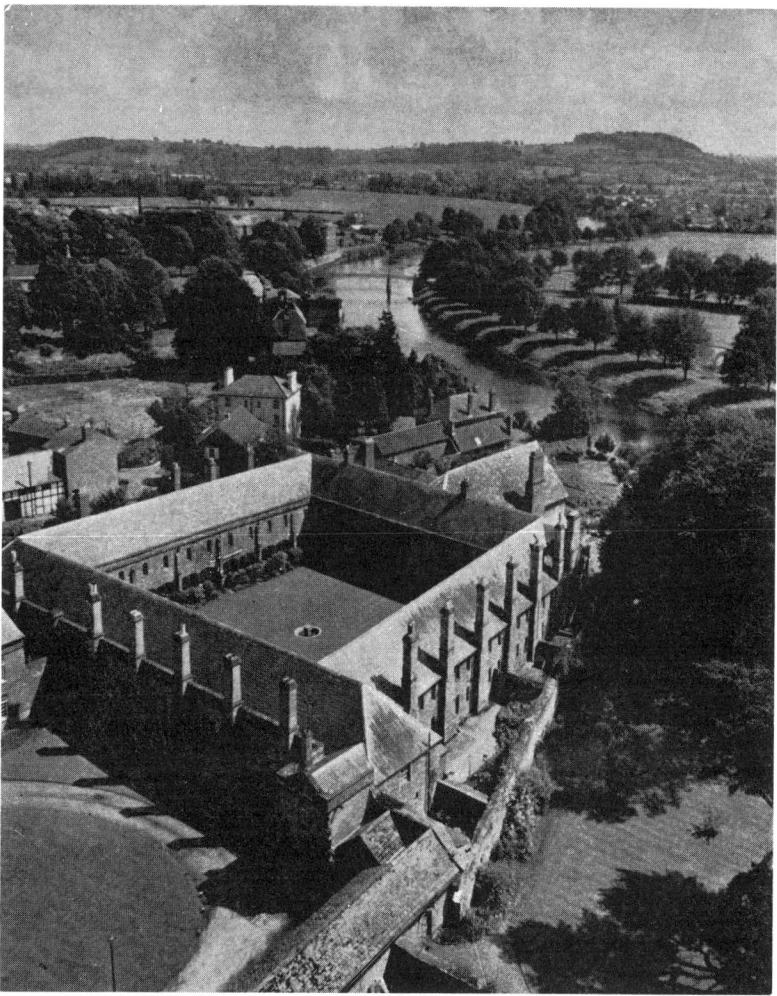

Above:
Reliquary at Saint Francis Xaviers, Hereford, which contains the left hand of the martyr John Kemble (1599?-1679) hanged at Hereford for saying mass at Pembridge Castle.
Right:
Hereford, the Vicars Choral and the Wye beyond.
Below:
Hereford seen over the Wye.

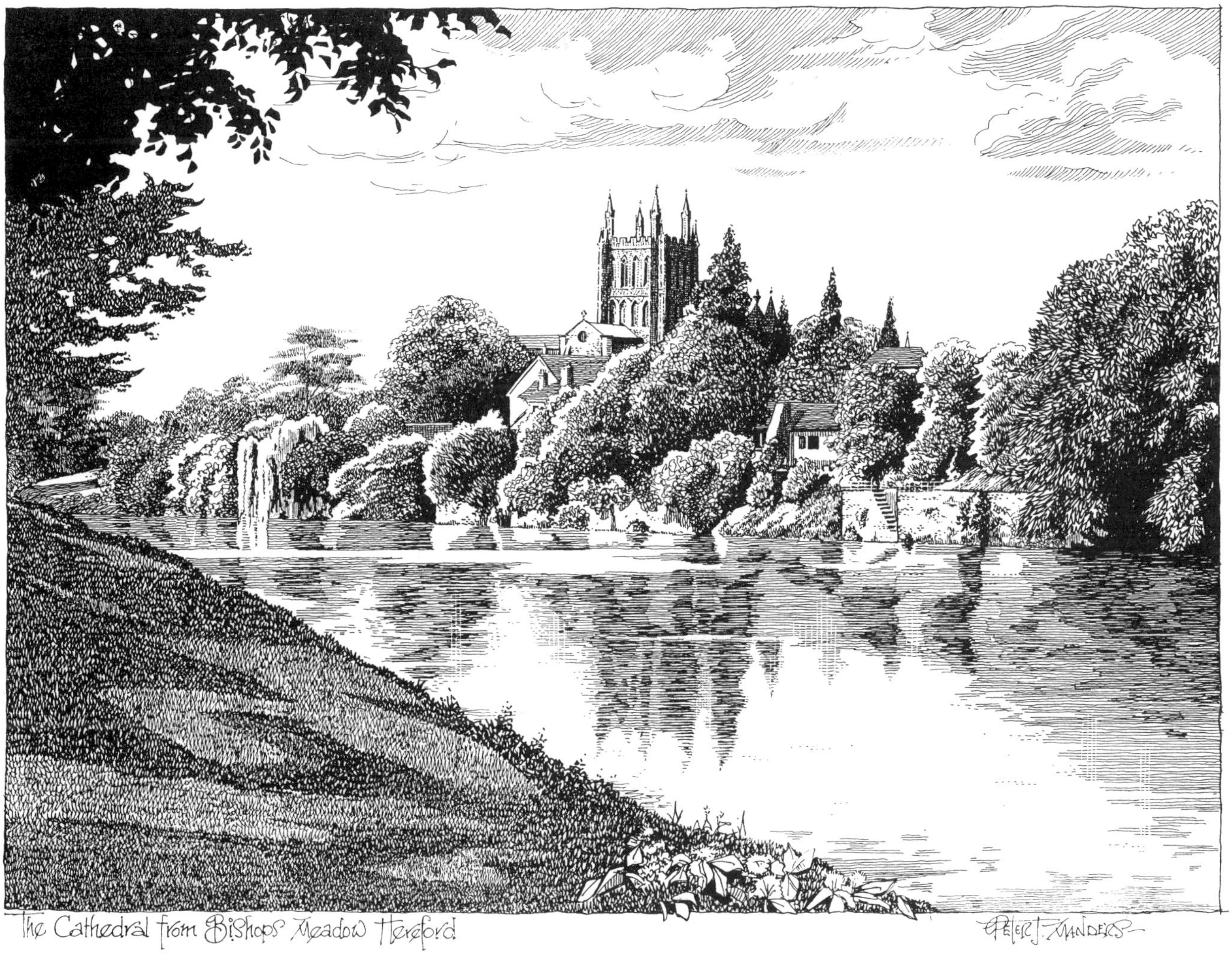
The Cathedral from Bishops Meadow Hereford
Peter J. Manders

(Jewish). There are Methodist Chapels in Saint Owen Street and Chandos Street and there is also a Bahai group. A list of church services appears in the *Herefordshire Times* (weekly).

MUSEUMS AND LIBRARIES

Hereford City Library, Museum and Art Gallery, Broad Street. The museum has displays of local historical artifacts. Pride of place goes to the Roman Kenchester Mosaic. The art gallery has exhibitions of local artists and travelling national displays. The library has the usual stocks of general books and a good local collection. All three amenities are housed in the tall Gothic building of 1874 designed by F.R. Kempson that stands opposite the cathedral. It was the gift of James Rankin to the Woolhope Naturalists' Field Club and provided a museum for their collections, a library and a meeting room. This illustrious club was founded in 1851 for the practical study, in all its branches, of the natural history and archaeology of Herefordshire. It has a membership of nearly 1,000 and its scholarly papers are taken by universities and libraries all over the world. A complete set of its *Transactions* is held in the library.

The Old House, High Town. This fine half-timbered house of 1621, has narrow set uprights and carved bargeboards, and is all that remain of the old Butchers' Row. It has three floors furnished with period pieces - furniture, kitchen utensils, paintings, embroideries and rare 17th century baby-walkers in the nursery. The Coat of Arms over the front door belonged to the Butchers' Guild.

Saint John Mediaeval Museum, Widemarsh Street. It is housed in the Coningsby Hospital, founded by Sir Thomas Coningsby in about 1614. He incorporated the remaining parts of the 13th-14th century house of the Order of Saint John of Jerusalem. The stone-built hospital is ranged around a courtyard. Today it houses displays of armour and information on the Crusades and there are models in period dress of the Coningsby Pensioners. Local tradition has it that the famous Chelsea Pensioners were modelled by Charles II on those of Coningsby at the suggestion of Nell Gwynne. The charming 13th century chapel of the Order of Saint John is still used as a place of worship.

Herefordshire Regimental Museum, Harold Street. Housed in the Territorial Army Centre is a collection of memorabilia, weapons, uniforms, regimental silver and the flag and pennant of Admiral Doenitz, the last Fuhrer of the Third Reich.

Herefordshire County Record Office, Harold Street. Hidden in a back street, south-west of the town centre, is a treasury of old documents including family papers, the Parish Registers and Census returns.

Churchill Gardens Museum, Aylestone Hill. Set amongst lawns, the museum contains costumes, furniture and painting of the late 18th and 19th centuries in period rooms. There is also a costume gallery and displays of locally made clocks, barometers, corn dollies and straw work. The Hatton Gallery is dedicated to the local work of the Edwardian landscape artist Brian Hatton who was killed by Turks near the Suez Canal in World War One.

Hereford Cider Museum, east of the town centre off the road to Brecon (A438). It tells the history of cider, for which Herefordshire is world renowned. Displays include examples of the huge beam presses used to crush the apples, a farm cider house, travelling cider-makers' tack, a pressing house and bottling line of the 1920s, and a champagne cider cellar. Cider brandy is actually produced on the premises. They might even be persuaded to sell you some. (See the article on cider.)

Bulmer Railway Centre, Whitecross Road. This was established in 1968 to give a home to the magnificent 'King George V', the former Great Western Railway's locomotive number 6000 which was renovated at the cost of H.P. Bulmer. There are several other engines and rolling stock. Open weekends only and steamings are advertised.

Herefordshire Waterworks Museum, Broomy Hill, west of the town centre. The building is of 1882 and has an Italianate tower of red and yellow brick. It houses the giant Broomy Hill pumping engine and its Lancashire boiler. There is also a collection of pumps garnered from all over England. Steamings are held on some weekends in the Summer.

NOTABLE BUILDINGS

Brief notes on buildings of importance or interest not already mentioned in other sections of this article.

Shire Hall, St. Peter Street. Of 1819 by Sir Robert Smirke. Greek Doric portico of six columns. The statue in the forecourt is of Sir George Cornewall by Baron Marochetti, 1864.

Town Hall, St. Owen Street. Brown terra cotta of 1904 by H.A. Cheers, with domed polygonal towers. City Regalia kept here including 15th-17th century swords, porters' badges, seals, maces and 14th century silver Bailiff's Seal.

Police Station, Gaol Street. Originally the city gaol of 1842 by Trehard & Duckham. Rock-faced with pediment.

Hereford Training College (Former), Venus Lane. Of 1881 by Kempson. Gothic. Boarding school until 1904.

Bluecoat School, Widemarsh Street. Of 1915 by G.H. Jack. Red brick and brown stone. Was originally the Girls' High School.

High School for Boys, Widemarsh Street. Of 1912 by G.H. Jack. Elaborate turret and semi-circular gables.

General Hospital, Nelson Street. Big and bleak and built of brick. Faces the Wye. Nine bays and three storeys with five bay pediment. Old part 1779-83 with several later additions.

Market Hall (Former), High Town. Of 1861 by John Clayton.

Barr's Court Station, off Commercial Road, north-east of the city centre. Of 1855 to a Tudor design by Johnson of Birkenhead.

Wye Bridge. Mostly original fabric of 1490 though frequently repaired. Widened in 1826. Of the six arches and double ended cutwaters four are original. One arch was deliberately destroyed in 1645 to hinder the sieging army. Re-built segmented.

Mediaeval City Walls. Substantial sections remain standing, especially in Victoria Street and New Market Street.

Alban House, High Town. Giant pilasters, pedimented first floor windows and balustrade of about 1865.

Number 20, High Town. Has a tunnel-vaulted cellar of about 1500.

Market Hall, High Town. Of 1861 by John Clayton.

Number 3, High Street. Ornate half-timber with concave lozenges and carved bargeboards.

Number 2, Eign Street. Has a rib-vaulted cellar with round and pointed arch recesses.

Moorfield Terrace, Edgar Street. Brick, with pediment of about 1823.

Number 3, Widemarsh Street. Two tunnel-vaulted cellars.

Mansion House, Widemarsh Street. Of about 1700 with five bays, two storeys, hipped roof on carved brackets and dormers.

Number 42, Widemarsh Street. Early 17th century timber-framed house. Ground floor faced with stone in 18th century. Carved Jacobean brackets to former doorway.

Blackfriars, Widemarsh Street. Behind the Coningsby Hospital are the small remains of the House of the Blackfriars (Dominicans) - the west range and the Preaching Cross - begun in 1322. After the Dissolution it went to the Scudamores and then to the Coningsbys. Sir Thomas Coningsby, who founded the hospital, lived here and the windows, stair turret and fireplaces were inserted by him. The hexagonal, stone, pulpit-like Preaching Cross is 14th century and is the only friars' preaching cross to have survived in the whole of England.

County Gaol, Commercial Road, opposite the bus station. Of 1792-7 by John Nash but all that remains of his work is the rusticated three bay Governor's House with arched doorway.

Workhouse, Union Road. Red brick of 1839. Now part of the County Hospital.

Kerry Almshouses, Commercial Street. Two low ranges, brick with pointed windows of 1821.

Owen Street. Noted for its Georgian houses.

Williams Almshouses, Saint Owen Street. Present building is of 1893; ignore the 1675 plaque. Re-set Norman carved capital probably of The Good Shepherd.

Saint Giles' Hospital, Saint Owen Street. The present single storey building is of 1770 but the foundations are 12th century. When the chapel of 1682 was re-built in 1927 the foundations of a rare circular chapel typical of the chancel of a Knights Templar or Hospitallers' church were uncovered. In the north wall of the hospital is a reset, badly worn Norman tympanum.

Constitutional Club, East Street. Dull exterior but has a good plaster ceiling of about 1670 and wood panelling.

Booth Hall Hotel, East Street. Two storeyed with cellars. On the first floor is a handsome hall thought to have been used by the Merchants' Guild. It was first mentioned in 1392 but was much restored in 1921. The roof has shortened tie-beams, hammer beams with carved figures, king posts, tracery and wind braces which form trefoils top and bottom with quatre-foils between them. Also a good fireplace with pilasters and blank arches with shields. The hall is sometimes used as a concert venue.

Aubrey's Almshouses, Berrington Street. Timber-framed of 1630, three gables and concave lozenges below gable windows.

Black Lion, Bridge Street. Has an intact 17th century room on the first floor with stuccoed ceiling and primitive wall paintings of some of the Ten Commandments.

Drybridge House, St. Martin Street. Of about 1700, five bays, two storeys, gable pediment and moon window.

Corn Exchange (later the Kemble Theatre), Broad Street. Of 1857 by William Stanton. Has portico and pediment.

Green Dragon Hotel, Broad Street. Of 1857. Impressive, 13 bays, giant pilasters, painted white with good, big, green dragon sculpture on top. Inside is an original, in situ, Jcobean room. Was one of the town's coaching inns.

City Arms Hotel, Broad Street. Built as the Duke of Norfolk's town house in 1790. Stucco and brick.

Harley Court, Cathedral Close. Of 1730, five bays and a pediment. Built of stone taken from the Cathedral Chapter House when that was demolished.

Hall of the Vicars Choral, Castle Street. Stone with a good roof of collar beams and queen posts, probably built in the 14th century. The Vicars Choral were employed to sing at services in the place of the regular Cathedral clergy who were often engaged in other duties. Over the years their humble position improved to the point where they were allowed to possess freehold property. They also had a library which is now a prize possession of the Cathedral. Near Vicars Choral are some good red brick Georgian houses with cast-iron balconies.

Saint Ethelbert's Hospital, Castle Street. Of 1805, sandstone, one storey, pointed windows with 'Y' tracery.

The Nelson Column, Castle Street. Tuscan column of with urn (no statue) of 1806-9 by Thomas Hardwicke.

Castle Pool Hotel, Castle Street. Converted from a pair of Late Georgian houses. Has two pediments on giant pilasters. Classic lines.

Cathedral School and Tuck Shop (restored), Quay Street.

Castle Green Bailey, Castle Street. The ramparts vary in height from 20ft. to 30ft. Excavations south of the Nelson Column have revealed the nave and chancel foundations of a small 12th century church.

Castle Cliffe, Castle Street. White, with Doric pilasters. Now the School of Arts & Crafts; it lies within the castle bailey. Most of what we see now is early 19th century but there is some 14th century stone on the west side.

Ethelbert's Well, Castle Hill. (51123969). The site of the well is marked by a newly constructed fountain in a wall and by a garden stone. The original water supply was disrupted by building works after the Second World War and it was ignominiously connected to the mains. Water still does not flow! Legend has it that the original well sprung up on the spot where Ethelbert's body was rested when being brought here from King Offa's palace at Sutton Walls. Those who offered a pin to the waters and then used them to cure sores or ulcers were granted relief. Nearby are two square, brick, 17th century summerhouses.

Bride Well, Redcliffe Gardens (51143959). Named after the former gaol, or bridewell, that once stood above it.

Price's Almshouses, Whitecross Road. Of 1665. Brick on stone base, central gable with lantern and a chapel.

Lingen's Hospital, Whitecross Road. Of 1609. Brick, one storey, with Tudor-style extension of 1849.

The White Cross, Whitecross Road. Sandstone. Erected by Bishop Charlton (1361-70), reputedly in thanksgiving for the passing of the plague. The base and eight steps are original but the whole was much restored in 1864 when it was given a new shaft and head. A folk tale related by Mike Rust tells of an entrance to the underworld beneath the White Cross.

The Moor, Moor Park Lane. 17th century timber-framed farmhouse with star chimneys now engulfed by suburbia.

Three Counties Hotel, Aylestone Road. Built in about 1850 for the founder of the *Hereford Times*. Italianate stucco with giant pilasters.

Causeway Farm, Belmont Road. 17th century black and white.

Pool Farm, Belmont Road. 15th century black and white and a porch dated 1624.

Putson Manor House, Hinton Road. 'L'-shaped timber-framed farmhouse of the early 16th century with closely set uprights. Situated near the River Wye.

SHOPPING

The town has a population catchment of some 150,000, enough to entice all the national chain stores. There is a first-class array of small, specialist shops and all the usual services such as banks and estate agents. Many of the streets are pedestrianised and the city centre is also very flat, a blessing to the aged or infirm. The new Maylord Orchard development is a precinct of some 80 shops, and in Commercial Street is a rare, independently-run department store. Church Street is a delight - a lane crammed with boutiques, a bookshop, a map shop, a classical CD store, tea rooms and the like. It leads from the High Town, the centre of the city, to the Cathedral Close. It is interesting to note that many of the town centre shops are timber-framed behind their brick and plate-glass facades. Some were mediaeval merchants' houses and have extensive stone-vaulted cellars which were used as store rooms and places of refuge in times of peril. An example, open to the public, is that of the ale-house on the corner of Bewell and Widemarsh Street.

The council run a shopmobility scheme. Persons with a disability or an infirmity can have the free use of a choice of scooters and wheelchairs from the underground car park at the Maylord Orchard shopping centre. Buskers can be seen about the town most days of the week, a welcome sight in these days of 'canned music'.

Markets

The county is rich in agriculture and the local markets were, and still are, an important part of the area's economy. Until 1856 the Hereford City livestock markets were held in the roads around Broad Street. In 1856 a purpose-built New Market complex was built adjacent to Newmarket Street, now part of the ring road. A century later this was modernised and the present stock market with its auction ring and ancilliary facilities is one of the most up-to-date in England. Sheep and cattle worth several millions of pounds pass through here every year. The ordinary, general market is on the same site. Wednesday and Saturday are market days. Within the wall is the Butter Market (Market Hall), a covered market in High Town which operates six days a week.

Wife Selling

It was a not uncommon practice for a man to sell his wife, usually at market. Until the middle of the 19th century an Act of Parliament had to be obtained to authorise an official divorce. Common folk found an alternative. A well-documented case was recounted by a 90 year old lady to the *Hereford Times* in 1876. She witnessed a smartly dressed woman with a rope around her neck being offered for sale at the Hereford pig market. Her husband auctioned her off. The best offer was a shilling and the woman agreed to be led off by the purchaser and to be his wife. Apparently, the new husband tamed her - she was something of a shrew - and she helped in his trade as a weaver. They had a son and lived happily ever after. The old lady recounted other instances of wife selling that were not so felicitous where the women were distraught at being put up for sale.

The May Fair

The right to hold this fair, locally called Saint Ethelbert's Fair, was granted to the Bishop of Hereford by Henry I in 1121. An Act of Parliament in 1838 empowered the Corporation of Hereford to buy out the Bishop's rights to the revenues from the May Fair for 12.1/2 bushels of wheat or its monetary equivalent. The ceremony is enacted each year as part of the festivities. The fair is a major event in the Hereford calender and the Showmen's Guild of Great Britain sets up attractions throughout High Town and adjacent main streets. In 1988 the old custom of singing madrigals from the cathedral tower during the May Fair was revived.

ARTS AND ENTERTAINMENT

No one would accuse Hereford of being a centre of culture, but it is not entirely without comfort from the muses. Before we launch into listings let us mention a rather wonderful thing called The Hereford Lore Group. This collects the oral history and reminiscences of its members and publishes a bi-monthly newsletter. Good luck, and God go with you.

Age to Age deals with the problems of the old but also encourages the creative use of leisure time. Live in High Town organise professional street entertainment in the town centre each August. Hereford Arts in Action organise workshops, art classes, special projects and art festivals such as the Summer Festival held in July, which features both national and local performers. The City Art Gallery in Broad Street features both traditional and contemporary art and changes its exhibitions every 4 to 6 weeks. The Hatton Gallery at the Churchill Gardens Museum displays the work of Brian Hatton, a local artist of international standing, who was cut off in his prime during the First World War.

The Canon Cinema shows the latest commercial releases, the Hereford Film Club shows a more eclectic choice and The West Midland Rural Media Company, based in Hereford, specialises in community film, video and photography. The Hereford Photography Festival runs through September showing the work of both local and amateur photographers. The Hereford Theatre presents a range of drama and is the venue for the Herefordshire Drama Festival, a competitive event held each February. There are also theatres at the College of Art and the Cathedral School and several amateur and community drama groups.

Nightjar Music organise a series of traditional folk music concerts in several venues in the town and the Hereford Concert Society bring classical musicians to the city. Choral groups include the Hereford Choral Society, the Britten Singers, the Hereford Savoy Singers, the Hereford Gilbert & Sullivan Society and the Hereford Amateur Operatic Society. There is a Silver Band and the Hereford Big Band. Popular artists such as Status Quo, the Hollies, Gene Pitney and the like appear at the Leisure Centre which can hold 2,200 seated. Jazz evenings, organised by the artist and caricaturist, Peter Manders, are held at the Green Dragon Hotel, and the Netherwood at Tapley, and several other pubs have 'live' entertainment.

Every year the choral societies and cathedral choirs of Hereford, Worcester and Gloucester meet in Hereford. This Three Choirs Festival rotates annually around the three cities. It was founded in the early 18th century and is said to be the oldest music festival in Europe (as distinct from festivals that involve music, many of which are much older). Orchestras and chamber groups also perform and the music is both old and new. The formal concerts are complemented by a range of fringe activities. Major English composers such as Edward Elgar and Ralph Vaughan-Williams have been closely connected with the Three Choirs. Hereford. The city council organises a programme of Autumn Music events every 2 years. This features local amateur musicians and leading professionals.

Morris Dancing, under one name or another, has probably been practised in England since pagan times. Herefordshire has an especially strong tradition and in 1609 a local pamphleteer wrote: "Lancashire for Horne-pypes: Worcestershire for Bag-pypes: but Herefordshire for a Morris-dance puts down not only Kent but verie near.......three quarters of Christendome". The pamphlet was published on the occasion of a remarkable gathering of 12 morris men whose ages totalled 1,200 years. They danced on Widemarsh Moor, just north of the town centre, for the entertainment of the crowd that had gathered for

Top left: Hereford races.
Top right: Hereford, Church Lane.
Middle left: Gilbert Harding, born Hereford Workhouse.
Centre oval: Jack Sharp, played for England at both cricket and football. Born Hereford.
Above: Brian Hatton, artist, born Hereford
Opposite: SAS training on the Wye at Hereford.

a horse-race meeting. The 12 dancers were:

> James Tomkins, gentleman of Llangarron,
>   the foreman, 106
> John Willis, bonesetter of Dormington, 97
> Dick Phillips of Middleton, 102
> William Waiton, fisher and fowler
>   of Marden, 102
> William Mosse, 106
> Thomas Winney of Holmer, 100
> John Lace, tailor of Madley, 97
> John Carlesse of Holme Lacy 96
> William Maio, an old Soldier and now
>   a lusty labourer of Egelton, 97
> John Hunt, the Hobby Horse 97
> John Mando of Cradley, 100
> Meg Goodwin of Eardisland,
>   Maid Marian 120

They danced to the music of a fiddle and a fife and tabor. Morris dancers from Herefordshire, Shropshire and Worcestershire perform in multiples of four, often making a group of 12, though in 1609 the 12 Widemarsh dancers performed in two groups of six, as in the Cotswold Tradition. There is currently a revival of morris dancing in the county, largely due to the work of Dave Jones (1940-91) of Putley.

Maypole dancing was long practised on May Day at Broom Hill, Hereford, and on the same day the town's chimney sweeps made merry on Sweeps' Green, Broom Hill.

Mumming is closely related to morris dancing. Though the themes of death and resurrection are pagan in origin these short folk plays in the form we have them now owe much to the mediaeval pageant plays staged in the streets by members of city craft guilds. In 1503 there were 25 such pageants in Hereford.

INDUSTRY

There is not a lot. Until the early 1950s manufacturing industry in Hereford was mostly related to agricultural equipment, though there were 19th century shipyards on the Wye from which a brig of 170 tons was launched in 1823 and at which the steam-ship Paul Pry was constructed in 1827. (See page 235.)

Today there is a handful of major producers. Foremost is Inco-Alloys International (formerly Henry Wiggins). This is an international company which specialises in nickel based alloys. Its European headquarters and research centre are in its extensive factory which dominates the northern entrance to the town on the A49.

H.P. Bulmer plc is the largest cider-maker in the world. They have been in Hereford since 1887. (See the article on cider.) Sun Valley Poultry Ltd., is the largest producer of fresh poultry products in Britain. The company was formed in 1960 by a group of Herefordshire farmers. It has its own farms, factories, feedmill and cooking plant. McDonald's Chicken McNuggets are supplied from Hereford and it is the town's largest employer.

Denco, now a part of AMEC, are manufacturers of air conditioning and compressed air drying equipment. Thorn Lighting produce road, industrial and floodlighting equipment at their Rotherwas factory. Opella manufacture bathroom fittings in moulded thermo-plastics and Gelpack Excelsior manufacture polythene refuse sacks, bin liners and carrier bags. Other firms include DRG Plastics, Dowty Seals & Precision Rubber Products, Hereford Galvanisers, Luk (tractor clutches). Viking Packaging and Baugh & Weedon (electronic instruments).

HEALTH

The city has three hospitals: Hereford County Hospital, Union Walk; Hereford General Hospital, Nelson Street; and the Victoria Eye Hospital, Eign Street. Community health services are organised by the Herefordshire Community Health NHS Trust whose headquarters are at St. Mary's Hospital, Burghill.

SPORT

Swimming. The Hereford Leisure Pool was built in 1976. It has a 25 metre, international short course main pool, squash courts, meeting room and sauna. In 1991 a leisure pool with wave-making machine and various other popular attractions, including a 'fitness suite', were added at a cost of £1,500,000.

Athletics. The Hereford Leisure Centre in Holmer Road was built in 1985. A wide variety of sports, both indoor and outdoor, are catered for. There is an all-weather athletic track, a floodlit, synthetic turf, sports pitch for hockey and soccer, squash courts, and a hi-tech Gym'n"Tonic fitness room. Arena concerts are also held here by international stars.

Golf. The Municipal Golf Course, 9 hole 4 par, is situated alongside the Leisure Centre.

Bowling. The Castle Green Bowling Club is open from May to September. There is also a green behind the Bowling Green Inn, Bewell Street, which has been here since at least 1697 (some say since 1484).

American Football. Yes, folks, Hereford has an American football team, the Hereford Chargers.

Soccer. Third Division Hereford United has a modern floodlit ground in Edgar Street. The team had a long-remembered moment of glory in 1972 when it beat first division Newcastle United 2-1 in the FA cup competition. The ground holds 12,000.

Rugby. Hereford Rugby Club was born more than 120 years ago. At present its home is at Wyeside, on the banks of the River Wye, where five teams have two pitches and all modern conveniences including floodlighting.

Rowing. Hereford Rowing Club is nationally known. It has a modern club house on the sylvan banks of the Wye just upstream of Greyfriars Bridge. They even have an indoor tank for training. The club holds its own regatta on Spring Bank Holiday Monday.

Cricket. Herefordshire has a very strong county team which was admitted to the Minor Counties Championship in 1992. The foremost club in Hereford itself is Hereford City Sports Club which has a ground on Hereford Racecourse. In W.G. Grace's time the town pitch was on Widemarsh Common.

Racing. National Hunt (hurdles and steeplechasing) race meetings are held on the 1.1/2 mile racecourse, situated on the northern fringe of the city. The grandstands are on high ground overlooking the gorse-clad course but public facilities are minimal. There are 15 meetings per year.

Rafting. A new sport developed on the River Wye in the 1970s. It is a fun thing designed to raise funds for charity but is taken very seriously by the competitors. Rafts can be sophisticated constructions and have a controlling organisation - the Committee for Herefordshire Amateur Rafting, CHAR for short. The main meeting is held over three days in May and attracts more than 80 crews. A crew consists of 12 men and they compete over a 100 mile course from Hay-on-Wye to Chepstow. A women's race over 40 miles is held later in the year.

Angling. This is not a true sport. It is causing pain for pleasure and involves little more exertion than a short walk and a long wait. The Wye is a clean river, a river frequented by salmon but trout and coarse fish are also to be found in abundance. Visitors' permits can be obtained from local shops and the disabled angler (you would have thought he might have had an insight into the suffering of fish) has a special platform at the King George Playing Fields, near the Victoria Footbridge.

Canoeing. Rarely a day goes by when canoes cannot be seen from the bridges over the Wye.

Boxing. Not a sport that has any great following in the town, but Tom Spring, the champion of All England in 1823-4 kept the Booth Hall tavern for a time.

PARKS

There are no public parks in Hereford but there are playing fields and open spaces, such as the lawns around the cathedral.

The Castle Green is situated south-east of the cathedral, high above the Wye, on the site of the castle bailey. The Redcliffe Gardens are on the site of the Norman keep itself and Castle Pool is part of the moat. Here one can promenade between the flower-beds and admire the ducks and the Nelson Monument.

From Castle Green steps lead down to the Victoria Suspension Bridge (1898) which provides access to Bishop's Meadow and the King George Playing Fields. Here there are tennis courts, a putting green, paddling pool, children's playground and tree-lined river walks.

The Churchill Gardens are on Aylestone Hill, to the north-west of the town centre. Next to the Churchill Gardens Museum there is a Fragrant Garden, open all year round. In 1975 the once widespread custom of rolling decorated hard-boiled eggs on Good Friday was begun at Churchill Gardens and has become an annual event.

EDUCATION

As well as a full complement of Primary and Secondary Schools there are Colleges of Further Education which include the Herefordshire College of Technology, the Hereford Sixth Form College, the Herefordshire College of Art & Design and the Royal National College (for the blind). The oldest school in the town is the Hereford Cathedral School. The earliest reference to it is in 1381, but it was almost certainly founded shortly after the cathedral in A.D. 676.

NOTABLE PEOPLE

Saint Ethelbert (died A.D.792). Ethelbert was a godly man and King of the East Angles. On the night before his marriage to Elfrida, daughter of King Offa of the Mercians, he was murdered at the command of the jealous Queen Quendreda (Elfrida's mother) at Offa's palace (situated on what we now call Sutton Walls Hill Fort). Ethelbert's body was buried privately at Marden but later transferred to the church at Hereford (now the cathedral). There are healing wells dedicated to him at both Marden and Hereford.

Miles Smith (died 1624). One of the translators of the Authorised Version of the Bible. Son of a Hereford butcher.

Thomas Traherne (1636-1674). Metaphysical poet, son of a Hereford shoemaker.

David Garrick (1717-1779). Actor-manager, born at the Angel Inn in Widemarsh Street.

Brian Hatton (1887-1916), landscape and portrait painter, born Carlton Villas, Whitecross, Hereford.

Roger Kemble (1721-1802). Actor-manager. Lived in Church Street.

James Wathen (1751-1828). Traveller, writer and artist.

David Cox (1783-1859). Water colourist, taught at Hereford Grammar School.

Tom Spring (1795-1851). Bare-fist boxer. Real name Thomas Winter. Champion of All England 1823-4; he kept the Booth Hall Tavern.

Alfred Watkins (1855-1935). Pioneer photographer. Invented the first light meter, the Bee Meter, and expounded the theory of ley lines in his book, The Old Straight Track.

Vice-Admiral Thomas Bennett (1785-1870) Born Hereford, enlisted at the age of 12, served under Nelson, survived numerous battles and adventures around the world, loved birds, died at West Bank, Broomy Hill, aged 86.

Edward William Elgar (1857-1934). Celebrated composer. Lived at Plas Gwyn in Hampton Park Road from 1904 to 1911 where he wrote many of his major works including the two symphonies, The Kingdom and the violin concerto. Before moving to Plas Gwyn Elgar was a frequent visitor to the Church Street home of his good friend George Robertson Sinclair, the cathedral organist, where he wrote much of The Apostles. His association with the Three Choirs Festival began in 1878 and ended in 1933.

Gilbert Harding (1907-1960), the celebrated cantankerous radio and television personality, was born in Hereford Workhouse where his father and mother were master and matron. He was a school teacher and a policeman before becoming a broadcaster in such programmes as Round Britain Quiz, The Brains Trust, Twenty Questions and We Beg to Differ. When he died television programmes were interrupted to bring the news. Harding was very fond of Hereford and was a frequent visitor here whilst his mother was alive. She lived in Three Elms Road and died in 1954.

Jack Sharp (1878-1938) was one of the very few people to have played for England at both football and cricket. He was the son of an Eign Street butcher who also kept the Grapes Tavern in East Street. Sharp played league football for Aston Villa and Everton and as an all round cricketer played for Lancashire, often as captain, between 1899 and 1925. On a personal note, this means that my father, Leonard Raven (1908-74) who came from Salford and was a cricket enthusiast, almost certainly saw him play. Sharp was short and stocky and was nicknamed 'the pocket Hercules'.

Eleanor M. Brent-Dyer (1894-1969) Author. Wrote the well-known Chalet schoolchildren's books and was headmistress of Margaret Roper School in Bodenham Road, Hereford.

Nell Gwynne (1650-87). The town of her birth is not known for certain but there is a strong local tradition that she was born in a cottage in Pipewell Lane, Hereford. This is now called Gwynne Street (a change of which we disapprove); it leads, downhill, off the Cathedral Close. Nell Gwynne was an actress of some renown but it is as the mistress of Charles II that she is best remembered. One of her sons was made the Duke of Saint Albans and Lord James Beau Clerk, a grandson, became Bishop of Hereford in 1746, an office he held for 41 years.

SPECIAL AIR SERVICE

The headquarters camp (SO 512 379) of the 22nd Special Air Service is called Stirling Lines. It is tucked away in the southern suburbs of Hereford, between the A49 and B4399 public roads, and the rear gardens of domestic houses encircle the outer perimeter security fence. Beyond this is a few feet of 'killing ground', then another fence. On the south side the camp is flanked by the embankment of the main line railway, from which almost aerial views into this top security establishment are afforded. Endurance and navigational exercises are carried out on the Brecon Beacons to the west. However, fit young men can be seen regularly running along a course from the camp, through Green Crize up Ridge Hill and down to the A49 where they risk life and limb by running back to the camp against the flow of traffic on this very busy road. Survive this and the rest of the world can offer little in the way of terror.

The origins of the S.A.S. lie in the Second World War when Long Range Desert Groups were formed by Colonel David Stirling to make hit-and-run raids behind enemy lines in North Africa. Since then the S.A.S. has gained a reputation as the elite special force in the world. The breaking of the siege of the Iranian Embassy, broadcast live on national television, made the S.A.S. a household name. Normally they shun publicity and much of their work is covert. Your author was in the army when an S.A.S. trooper could proudly parade in the streets of Kuala Lumpur, Malaya, wearing his sand-coloured beret and winged-dagger cap badge. No more. Anti-terrorist and undercover duties (not to mention the occasional immoral act) make them prime targets for men with revenge in mind. Incidentally, the Hereford bridges over the Wye are used in S.A.S. exercises. Men on demolition courses study them and write reports on where best to place explosive charges to cause the maximum damage. The camp church is dedicated to Saint Christopher. As we write it has been made public that the regiment is moving to a recently vacated RAF camp at Credenhill, 3.1/2m NE of Hereford.

HOARWITHY *7m SSE of Hereford*

Hoarwithy is an old name for the small tree we now call the Whitebeam. This was commonly used as a boundary marker, so in a place name it means 'boundary willow'.

We approached Hoarwithy from Little Dewchurch. Heading south in the evening light through most attractive hill country we began the gentle descent to the village when we had a sudden shock: the mass baa-ing of enormous numbers of sheep even alarmed my dogs. As the settlement comes into view the descent becomes very steep and one passes scattered stone cottages and some large stone houses, such as Apple Orchard, to arrive at the New Harp Inn, most pleasantly situated by a tributary stream of the River Wye.

There is a post office and a Reading Room but the shops are gone, the two schools are gone, four inns and three water-mills are gone, and the chapel is disused. But they do have a striking Italianate church standing proudly and prominently on the hillside.

Saint Catherine's was built in the 1880s by J.P. Seddon who enlarged a small chapel of ease of 1843. It is constructed of red sandstone which has weathered badly and restoration work was carried out in the 1970s and 1980s. The style is South Italian Romanesque. One approaches up steps to the bell-tower. This is open on the ground floor and reveals a delightful array of arches. At the east end is a Byzantine-style cupola supported on four giant monolithic columns of grey marble with tunnel vaults to the north and south. The stained glass in the apse, as elsewhere, is of the highest order but the artists are unrecorded. There is room for 'out of place' and 'out of time' buildings such as this so long as they are well done, and Saint Catherine's is certainly that.

The man who oversaw the rebuilding of the church was the Reverend William Poole who was vicar of Hentland and Hoarwithy from 1854 to 1901. He is fondly remembered in the village for his generosity in meeting the cost of this and other works such as the school, the reading room and the restoration of cottages.

The village stretches out from its nucleus on the hillside and there are groups of cottages scattered along the Wye, from Red Rail in the south to Altborough in the north. The river attracts tourists, water sportsmen, fishermen and retired professional people. Tressack, 'the settlement built on drained land', lies in a pretty tributary valley of the Wye.

Llanfrother, 1/2m SW of the church (but much further by road), is from the Welsh Llanfrodyr, meaning 'the church of the friars' (brothers). It has long been thought that this was the site of Saint Dubricius's 6th century college but a more likely site has recently been discovered close to the church at Hentland. (See Hentland.) Llanfrother is 'L'-shaped, partly built of half-timber and sandstone, and has two storeys. The cellars are 16th century, the rest was rebuilt in the 17th century with subsequent modifications. The mounds of buildings mentioned in 1633 can be seen in the grounds.

The River Wye was originally crossed at Hoarwithy by a ford and a ferry. In 1856 a timber toll-bridge was constructed. Some 20 years later this was replaced with the present metal bridge, which is constructed as a single pair of continuous Warren girders supported by two intermediate stone piers to give three equal spans of 85ft. The tollhouse at the west end is of coursed stone. The County Council assumed responsibility for the bridge in 1935 and it is now free of toll charges.

There is a time-honoured right, owned by people having land or a house built beside the 'free water' of the Wye, to take fish provided they display, and offer for sale, their catch on a table on the old turnpike road between Llanfrother and Hoarwithy. Any poor person could then claim a small piece. Over time this display became a token obeyed for only one day in the year and had ceased altogether by the late 1790s. In mediaeval times fishing rights were a valuable commodity (they are today) and this rare concession reflected the fact that the county was largely populated by turbulent Welshmen. It was a sop.

Bromley, 3/4m NW of Hoarwithy, is a delightful hamlet of terraced stone cottages by a bridge over a brook in a steep-sided, well-wooded valley. Promither Mill is a rambling white rendered cottage in pretty grounds. Nearby are small fields with donkeys and sheep. Bromley Court lies 1/4m SW of the hamlet on higher ground. It is a cattle and cider-apple farm with a square, stone-built three-bay, two-storey house with a featured round-headed window. The flat-roofed wooden building is a day nursery for children.

To conclude, I called in at the New Harp Inn one sunny June lunchtime and ordered fish and chips. As I ate an old ex-butcher of the village described how they slaughtered animals in his shop, how a live sheep was stabbed in the neck with a knife and how the butcher then put his hand into the wound and snapped the spinal column with his fingers. He was apologetic and acknowledged the cruelty involved but, well, those were the days. Also at the table was an ex-Royal Navy diver who had trained the SAS to blow the hatches off sea-going ships and clear mines off the coast of Vietnam.

Left: Holme Lacy House, the Yellow Dining Room, c.1905
Above: the 10th Earl of Chesterfield who sold Holme Lacy in 1910
Below: Holme Lacy House, south front.

We then took the river road to Carey, past a fleet of 13 swans on the sparkling Wye, a gentle place of flat, wood-fringed meadows and footpaths enjoyed by cows and walkers. A short arboreal tunnel brings one to Carey, a rather super little hamlet of stone cottages, a red telephone kiosk, a small bridge, mature trees and a shady bench. But now we are in the domain of Ballingham which has its own article.

HOLME LACY *4m SE of Hereford*

The name in Domesday Book is Hamme, Anglo-Saxon meaning 'low-lying meadow', and the Norman landlord at that time was Roger de Laci. It lies on the west bank of the meandering Wye above the broad flood plain. The land is mixed arable and pasture. Its close proximity to Hereford has brought it more than its fair share of bungalows, council houses and modern developments. Amongst the facilities are a post-office-cum general store, a school (a luxury, indeed, these days) a Tudor-style village hall and a large playing field. Bower Farm is the nucleus of the Herefordshire College of Agriculture but it is for its big house that the village is best known.

Holme Lacy House is the largest dwelling in the county. It was built for the second Viscount Scudamore after he got married in 1672. Originally, it had four facades of red stone ashlar but one was removed in 1910 and a ballroom built in its place. The exterior is dignified but unspectacular. Inside, however, is some impressive decoration, especially the magnificent plaster ceilings of 1680-90 in nine of the rooms. These are regarded as being some of the best in the whole of England. The collection of carved wood overmantles, garlands and trophies, thought to be the work of the master, Grinling Gibbons, have been removed and are now at Kentchurch Court (another Scudamore house) and in the Metropolitan Museum, New York.

Outside there is a brick orangery with arched windows. To the south is an extensive parkland with two lakes and beyond that are pastures fringed with woods. The gardens were once very splendid with wide lawns, yew hedges, topiary and a maze. The house has changed hands several times in this century and for 50 years was a hospital. It is now empty but there are plans to develop it as a hotel.

The church of Saint Cuthbert lies 3/4m SE of the house, isolated in water meadows by the river. It has an unusual plan, there being no division between the nave (and south aisle) and the chancel (and south chapel). Most of what we see today is of the 13th and 14th centuries. The stone font is late 17th century and the stalls of about 1400 have misericords: a lion, a bird, human and grotesque faces and an angel. The monuments are almost all to the Scudamores.

The Holme Lacy branch of the family took over the estate from the de Lacys in the 14th century and lived here until 1820 when it died out. Amongst the Scudamores buried in the church are: Sir John, died 1571, High Sheriff of Hereford and Gentleman Usher to Henry VIII; his son, also Sir John, MP and Gentleman Usher to Queen Elizabeth I and benefactor of the Bodleian Library; his son, Sir James, knighted for bravery at the siege of Cadiz and immortalised by Edmund Spenser in *The Faerie Queen* (1596) as "Sir Scudamore, pattern of chivalry", and his son John, first viscount, Ambassador to France, Royalist during the Civil War, and philanthropist.

The first viscount brought back French varieties of apples, including the famous Redstreak, to improve his orchards. Talking of orchards, an 18th century vicar, who lived in the 17th century rectory, now a private house, developed a pear orchard from a single tree by bending boughs to tip root. This remarkable arched orchard produced 14 hogsheads (a 50 gallon cask) of perry in 1776.

The old school lay 3/4m SSE of the village on the road to Ballingham. It is a two-storey building with four bays and round-headed windows. The stone is said to come from the old, original Holme Lacy House and has now been coverted to a dwelling, well protected by three springer spaniels and two Jack Russells. (See Hoarwithy for a note on ancient fishing rights on the River Wye.)

HOLMER *1.5m N of Hereford*

The name was Holemere in Domesday Book, meaning 'mere in a hollow'. It is a northern suburb of Hereford, centred on the crossing of the A49 and the A4103. Part of the parish was given to the city in 1884 and this is called Holmer Within; the part that remains outside is called Holmer Without. South of the old Roman road, the A4103, is Hereford racecourse which comes complete with the town cricket pitch and golf course. There is a shop, and at the crossroads is the Starting Gate Inn which faces the giant works of Inco Alloys (formerly Henry Wiggins). This has been joined by a sizeable commercial and retail estate. Modern domestic dwellings fill the spaces in between and provide fodder for the local primary school. North of the Roman road is what one thinks of as Holmer today.

The church of Saint Bartholomew has nave and chancel in one, of about 1300 when Norman Romanesque was changing to Early English, and is almost entirely of its period except for the roof. The nave roof is 14th century and that of the chancel is a 15th century hammerbeam with carved figures: a serpent, a griffin, angels, women and a 'pelican in piety' A 17th century oak panel to the memory of Jane Howorth has an inscription which reads: "Here Age and Virtue lie, and who would have Two fairer partners buried in one grave?" The elaborate organ case is Victorian and was probably made for an international exhibition. Outside there is a churchyard cross with ball-flower decoration on the base.

Just north of the church is Holmer House, the bulk of which is of 1739. It has five bays, three storeys and a hipped roof. Burcott Farm, 1.1/2m ESE of Holmer church, now lies in ruins. It was a beef and arable farm but from the mid-18th century on it has been cut through and had bits cut off. First came the Hereford to Gloucester Canal. Then, even before the canal was finished, came the railway within yards of the back door and then came the North Sea Gas pipeline. Subsequently, much of the land was sold for housing development, and there is worse to come because the proposed Hereford by-pass is destined to become a neighbour in the near future. Poor old Burcott; it just gave up and died.

And yet another grim tale. There are local rumours that the 19th century owner of Turvey Hall, a Mr. Oliver, murdered his wife and buried her in the garden. Certainly, she disappeared without explanation.

Munstone, 1/2m NE of the church at Holmer, is a residential area on a small rise surrounded by ploughland and pasture. Near a stream with pollarded trees stands Munstone House Country Hotel, a rendered, Georgian house under a hipped roof. The small Evangelical Free Church is of red brick. There are some old stone cottages but it also has its fair share of mundane 20th century dwellings.

Proceeding eastwards one comes to Shelwick. The name is from the Old English, scild, meaning 'a shield', and wic which can be several things but often means 'dairy farm'. 'The defended dairy farm' is a likely meaning. Shelwick

Court is a timber-framed house. It was a crumbling ruin but has recently been most handsomely restored. We do not have a date but it has a six-bay, open timber-framed roof. The great timbers are cusped and chamfered and it is likely the hall is mediaeval. The previous owner told tales of witch burnings in the grounds but these have gone unrecorded and he is now dead. Beyond the railway is Shelwick Green on the banks of the River Lugg. To the north is Wergin's Stone. (See Sutton St. Nicholas.)

HOPE MANSELL *3.5m SSE of Ross-on-Wye*
Hop is Anglo-Saxon for 'valley' and the Mansell family were lords of the manor. Mansell is from Maloisel, a nickname meaning 'ill bird' (bird of ill omen?). The hamlet lies in a lovely, wooded valley, one of those quiet, secret places so typical of this part of Herefordshire which is really a northernmost reach of the Forest of Dean. The cottages are mostly of stone and there are some very substantial houses and farms amongst the cattle pastures and potato fields. Social life centres on the Village Hall and the church.

Saint Michael's has an undecorated Norman doorway, an early 14th century chancel, and 18th century nave windows. The nave and chancel have mediaeval, single-framed, scissor-braced roof timbers.

The scattered settlement of Dancing Green lies 3/4m NNE on Lea Bailey Hill. The name refers to Maypole dancing. There is a tradition of open air religious meetings in the area, and an annual open air service is still held on the green. Parkfields, 1.1/2m N of the church, is on the Penyard Park estate. It is a Late Georgian house built of red sandstone with a five-bay front and a two-bay side with one-storey bow windows.

Puddlebrook, near Drybrook, is 1m SE of the church, just over the border in Gloucestershire. In 1921 Cecil Sharp collected several songs from Mrs. Kathleen Williams at Puddlebrook, including a fine version of The Trees They Do Grow High. Near Great Howle Farm, 1m NW of Hope Mansell church, is a prehistoric earthwork.

Near the scattered hamlet of Lane End, 1m ENE of Hope Mansell, are the spoil mounds of a gold mine. The actual mine entrance is just over the border in Gloucestershire at SO 645 196. In 1906 the Chastan Syndicate was formed to prospect for gold in the Old Red Sandstone rocks here. An exploratory Bailey Level was driven into the steep western slope of Wigpool Common but only six grains of gold per ton of rock was found. This was not a commercial proposition, so in 1921 the level was extended in an attempt to find iron ore. The site is most easily approached from the Ross to Gloucester road, the A40, and by taking the lane south in the direction of Drybrook. After passing through Lane End you enter woodland, turn left at the junction and after about 300 yards you will see the spoil mounds on the right amongst the trees. A short track leads to the mine entrance.

HOPE-UNDER-DINMORE *4m S of Leominster*
'The settlement in the valley below Dinmore Hill'. The village lies just to the west of the busy A49 Hereford to Leominster road which climbs and descends the hill in long, sweeping curves. The main line railway passes close by before disappearing into a 3/4-mile long tunnel. During the Second World War soldiers were stationed in temporary huts to guard the tunnel. Council houses now stand on the site. The old village hall was built at the expense of John Arkwright as a rest room for the workmen who dug the tunnel. Today it has been superseded by a new hall built in 1970.

The Cadbury factory lies 3/4m N alongside the main road at Newton, its pale green towers and pale blue chimneys making it a landmark of some consequence. It came here in the 1930s and is the major local employer. In about 1961 the plant changed over from milk processing to the manufacture of chocolate crumb, the basic material from which all Cadbury's products are made. Some 550,000 litres of milk are delivered each day. About 50% of this comes from local dairy herds, and 50% from Whitland, Carmarthen. This is blended with 150 tons of sugar and 40 tons of cocoa in liquid form (which is processed at Chirk). Marlbrook is the only Cadbury's chocolate crumb factory in England, though there is another in Rothmore, County Kerry, Ireland. In very recent times a Little Chef and a service station arrived to keep the factory company.

The church is isolated from the village by the main road. Saint Mary's was rebuilt by F.R. Kempson in 1879 and 1896. The circular font is of about 1275 and is decorated with seated figures of Jesus, Saint John the Baptist, Saint Peter and Saint Paul and the Evangelists under five foiled arches. There are monuments to Humfry Conyngsby, died 1559; and to the Earl and Countess Conyngsby and their baby son who choked to death on a cherry in 1708. The north transept was built as a memorial to John Arkwright (see Hampton Court.) The vicarage is now an Outdoor Activities Centre, but the Victorian primary school still serves its original purpose.

Motor sport 'scrambles' commenced in the 1940s and meetings are still held at Dinmore.

Winsley House, 1.3/4m W of the church, has some 14th century roof timbers with cusped wind braces and a Jacobean timbered porch at the rear. The front is Georgian and has five bays with a five-bay pediment.

Wigwood Manor, 1/2m NW of the church, is a traditional timber-framed house of Elizabethan style but was erected on a virgin site in 1996. It is located at SO 516 531 and can be seen from the A417, peeping over an arable field. It has two storeys and two gables, an offset porch, a mixture of square and close vertical framing, cream and brown livery and is charmingly irregular. It was built at the expense of Mr. Mercer, a local landowner, and it really is a most splendid piece of work. The house is named after Wig Wood which shields it from the Cadbury factory to the west.

However, the dominant feature at Dinmore is the extensive woodland of Queen's Wood County Park. The services provided include car parks, refreshments, toilets, and a County Rangers' Office. The Visitor Centre and Cafe are housed in rescued and newly restored timber-framed buildings. The cafe was the Essex Arms, a 17th century inn formerly in Widemarsh Street, Hereford' and the Visitor Centre was a tannery at Leominster. The woods look somewhat nondescript from the main road but the walker is rewarded with a host of specimen trees. The arboretum was established in 1945 by Sir Richard Cotterell and now has a national reputation. All the trees are numbered and a catalogue is available. Among the many species are Handkerchief trees, Japanese Maples, a Lime Avenue and a grove of Californian Redwoods. If you are lucky you might also spot one of the wild deer that escaped from the nearby deer parks of Hampton Court and Dinmore Manor.

Dinmore Camp is a large Iron-Age hill fort with a single rampart and ditch still visible at the north end but all the rest is badly eroded. It covers about 24 acres and uses steep hillside as a defence to the north and south sides.

The name Dinmore is from the Welsh din mawr, meaning 'great fort'. The hill was named after the fort, which is situated about 1/2m E of the memorial on the main road, and can be approached down a bridle way. (Hampton Court and Dinmore Manor have their own articles.)

HOW CAPLE *8.5m SE of Hereford*
The name means 'Hugh's Chapel' and once there was a Hugh's holy well. The hamlet lies in a pretty, secretive, little valley where a tributary stream joins the River Wye, and is most easily approached off the B4224. There are sheep in the meadows, chickens in the road, flowers in the verges, a mill and a handful of cottages, two of which have chinoiserie summerhouses. The Court and the church lie at a landlordly distance of 1/2m N of the dwellings of the common folk. The country hereabouts really is pretty with woods and hills and an air of friendliness.

How Caple Court is a modest three-bay, two and a half storey house with a hipped roof but it is the gardens that are the attraction today. Set high above the Wye there are 11 acres of Edwardian landscaping with pools, cascades, yew hedges, a Florentine sunken garden, shrubs and woodland. These were the work of Lennox Bertram Lee, a Manchester textiles magnate who bought the house in the early 20th century. They became overgrown but were restored by Peter Lee (died 1996) who held opera and jazz concerts in a magnificent natural auditorium fringed by oak, chestnut and beech to help pay for the work. Facilities include a tea room, a plant nursery and a fabric shop. The Wye Valley Walk runs nearby. This commences at Hay-on-Wye and finishes at Chepstow.

The ashlar faced church of Saint Andrew and Saint Mary has a 14th century chancel but most of the rest was rebuilt in 1695. Inside there is a priceless German diptych of eight panels depicting the martyrdom of Saint Clare and Saint Francis, and Mary Magdalene washing the feet of Christ. The font is Norman and was found buried in the nave; the pulpit is Jacobean; the carved arms are of William III; the stained glass is of about 1920 and was designed by L.B. Lee and made by A.J. Davies; and the monuments are mostly to the Gregory and Lee families. The Lees are latterday occupants of the Court and their crest, a chained bear, is not conspicuous by its absence.

How Caple Grange, at Crossway, 1/2m NE, is a substantial gabled and mullioned stone-built house of 1730 constructed for the then Speaker, Sir William Gregory. It was later extended in Victorian and modern times and is now a hotel complete with sauna, solarium and jacuzzi. There are some Victorian and modern houses and a post office. Just to the south is Stocking. The name Stocking usually refers to a piece of woodland newly cleared in mediaeval times. Old Gore (a small, crammed-in field), 1.1/2m SSE of Crossway on the B4224, has a big stone house, a war memorial and a handful of cottages.

HUMBER *3m SE of Leominster*
Humber was a common Celtic name for streams, probably derived from hu - amber meaning 'good river'. Our Humber lies beside the Humber Brook, a tributary of the River Lugg.

The settlement is most easily approached by turning south off the A44 Leominster to Bromyard road at The Drum. The lane is very straight and does, indeed, follow the route of the Roman road from Ashton (near Berrington) to Ariconium (Bromash, near Ross on Wye). The track of the now dismantled railway from Leominster to Bromyard crosses the road at SO 531 566. In 1881, when the railway was under construction, workmen found quantities of Roman coins, a gold ring and bracelet, pottery fragments, a kiln (or hypocaust) and skeletons. These relate to a Roman Villa site at SO 534 565, a little to the east. The defended area is just south of the now disused railway cutting. It covers about 20 acres and represents a sizeable settlement occupied from the late 2nd century to the late 4th century.

Humber is a hilltop hamlet, consisting of little more than the rectory, a farm and the church. Saint Mary's has a chancel of about 1200 with a 14th century roof; a priests' doorway and piscina; Jacobean panels in the pulpit; a 14th century porch with traceried barge boards; a Norman font with original rope moulding; and a 14th century tower with shingled spire. All were much restored by T.H. Wyatt in 1876-8.

The Roman road continues south, but between The Witsetts and Bowley Town its track has to be followed across country, the modern lane diverting to the east for 1.1/2 miles. For the walker here is a guide: leave the road south of Witsetts. Follow hedge. Embankment (agger) can be seen. Enter a green lane. Holloway, enter overgrown green lane, enter large field, down ravine to Humber Brook, out of ravine, broken pier of bridge arch over tributary stream, field with hedgerow aligned to route, back to road at Bowley Town.

The modern lane takes one to Risbury, 1m SE of the church. Here are the houses, the pub and the post office and Risbury Camp, a pre-historic hill fort. The Camp occupies about 28 acres; the actual enclosure is only 8.1/2 acres, the rest being occupied by extensive defences. There are three lines of ramparts on the west and four on the east each with an entrance. The oval-shaped fort stands on a long promontory between the valleys of the Humber Brook and the Holly Brook. It is now planted as an orchard.

Humber Marsh Nature Reserve is 1/2m N of the church, on the lane to Steen's Bridge, just off the A44. There are 13 acres of woodland, wild flower meadows, ponds and marshland with boarded walkways. Wild flowers, herbs and pond plants can be bought and there is a tea-room, a gift shop, and a picnic site. Educational and guided tours are available.

HUNTINGTON (near Hereford) *2m NW Hereford*
The name means 'settlement of the huntsmen', but they are the quarry now as the suburbs of Hereford reach out. A glance at the map shows it to be a prime target for developers, encircled as it is by four major roads. Westfields and Moor Park have already fallen.

Meadows still surround the hamlet and trees still stand by the church and the Court. Saint Mary's all but gets its feet wet in the brook. What we see today is a nave, chancel and apse in Norman style to a design by B. Cranstown of 1850. Inside there are memorials to the Tulley family, breeders of high fat content Hereford cattle. Huntington Court is painted white, has four bays, two storeys, a hipped roof and an attractive cast-iron porch. Huntington House is black and white and stands near the Yazor Brook; it was formerly called Pool House.

To the north is the Roman road to Stretton Sugwas and Magnis, to the south is King's Acre on the A438. All about are the extensive nurseries of Swainshill Garden Centre. The track of an old road from Huntington to Tillington and Burghill is still followed by public footpaths. The road was diverted north of the Court and the church in 1802 when changes were made to the water system. A

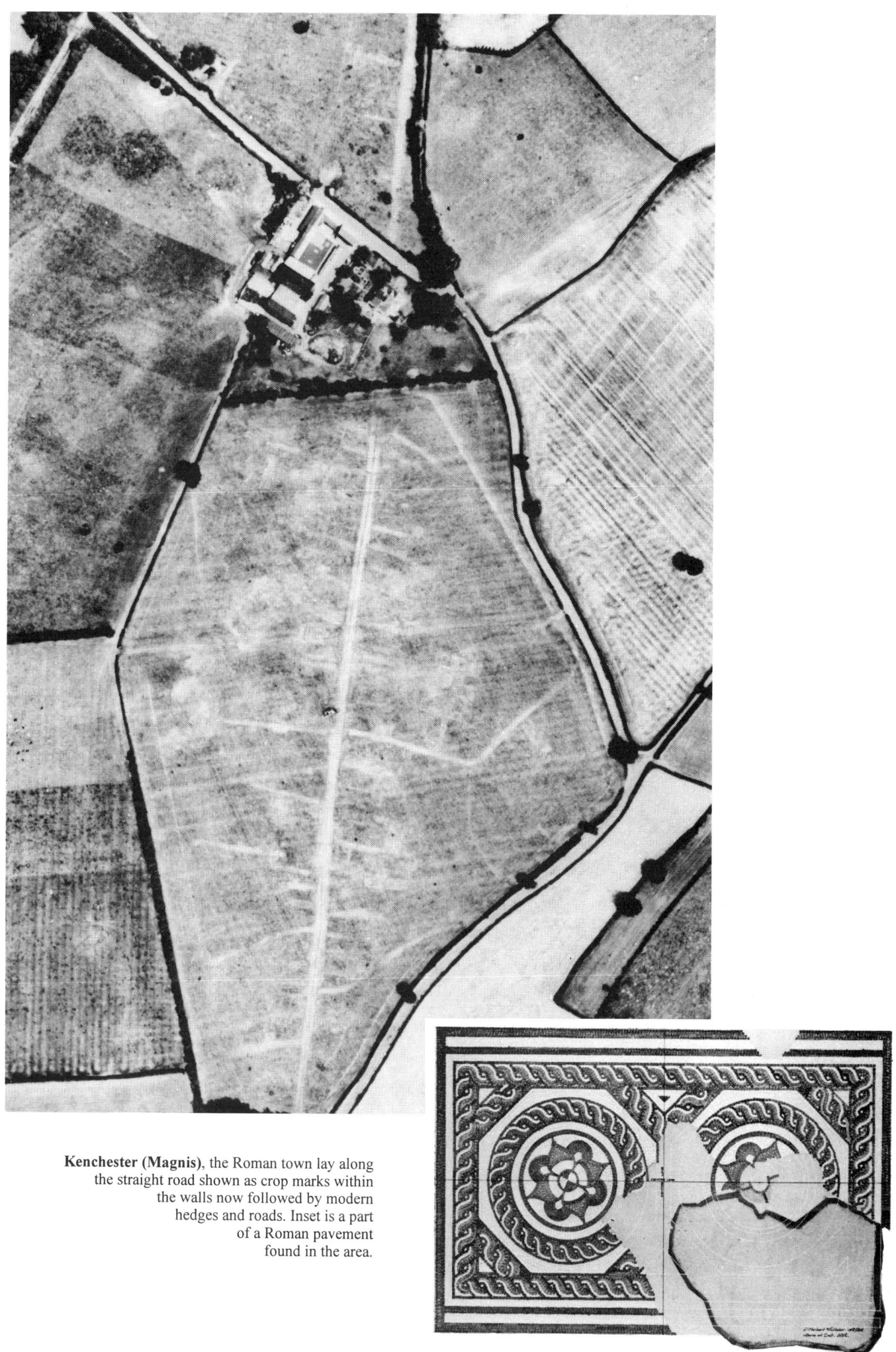

Kenchester (Magnis), the Roman town lay along the straight road shown as crop marks within the walls now followed by modern hedges and roads. Inset is a part of a Roman pavement found in the area.

holloway runs east of the church to the main road and cobbles are visible where the Yazor Brook has washed away the bank. Earthworks can be seen in the orchard and large stones in adjacent fields. Huntington is a pre-Conquest settlement. Much later, during the Barons' War of 1264-5, the township and the adjacent Moor were burned.

HUNTINGTON (near Kington) *4m SW of Kington*

The name means 'the settlement of the hunters'. It touches the Welsh border and lies on high ground between Gladestry Brook to the north and the River Arrow to the south. The old manor, which belonged to King Harold before the Conquest, was much larger and more extensive than the modern parish. Today ther are less than 80 persons on the electoral roll. It is a scattered farming community, mostly livestock with only one dairy farm. It has seen its share of troubles and has four castles to prove it. There are two mottes at Hengoed, 1m SSW of Huntington: Turret Castle, a 50-yard motte and bailey on a spur of Hell Wood, 1/2m SE of Huntington; and the extensive earthworks of Huntington Castle, which lie in the village itself.

The motte of Huntington Castle is about 30ft high with an oval-shaped inner north-east bailey and traces of the outer bailey and a 13th century tower. The ruined stone keep we see today was built in 1228 and owned by the Braose, Bohun and Stafford families in the Middle Ages. In the early 1400s it was captured by Owain Glyndwr and by 1460 had been abandoned. However, the tower was still being used as a prison in 1521. Close by are the traces of the abortive mediaeval borough.

The village stands on high, windswept ground. We visited when there was a snowstorm and the roads were icy. How we made it up the hill from Gladestry I do not know. There is a big stone farm, a few scattered dwellings, a red telephone kiosk, a post office and a pub. The Swan Inn is known as a meeting place for gypsies.

A fair was held at Huntington from 1403 until 1956. Originally a sale of general livestock, it became famous as a horse fair and was held twice a year. The mountain ponies, known as 'munts', were rounded up and brought down to be auctioned. The animal that gained the highest price was ceremoniously ridden through the pub.

The fair was associated with Saint Thomas a Becket because the church was re-built and dedicated to him by Richard de Brito, one of the Archbishop's murderers, as an act of penance. It has a nave and chancel in one and the windows are of about 1300. The timber bell turret is of the 17th century. Inside are oak benches with huge, somewhat crude, threfoiled ends. It stands in a circular churchyard, often a sign of a pre-Christian temple or defended place.

At Hengoed there is a Congregational Chapel of 1805 and Edward Goff's Endowed Day School of 1791, a three-bay two-storeyed stone house. Goff was a local lad who made good in London as a coal merchant.

Huntington Park, 1m ENE of the church, is a Late Georgian red brick house with five bays and two storeys extended by the Victorians, and stands in woodland near the River Arrow.

There are timber-framed buildings with ancient cruck trusses at the following: (distances from the church) Penllan 1/2m SSE; Burnt Hengoed 1.1/4m SE; Great Penllan 1.1/2m SE; and Little Penllan 1.3/4m SE. Pen can mean either 'head of' or 'top of'; llan can mean either 'church' or 'village'.

The Offa's Dyke Path passes by 1m E of the church.

IVINGTON *2.25m SW of Leominster*

The name means 'settlement of Ilfa's people'. Ivington, and Ivington Green to the west, combine to form a small village on the flood plain of the River Arrow. There is a brick-built Primitive Methodist Chapel of 1907 with yellow brick dressings and pointed-arch windows; concrete tile-hung council houses; the church of Saint John which has, pointed windows and nave and chancel in one of 1842, a modern, brick-built Church of England primary school; stone walls; two bridges; deep drainage ditches; a primrose yellow bus to Leominster; sheep, orchards, and black and white cows.

The substantial village farm called Ivingtonbury has a most handsome, castle-like Jacobean gatehouse with close-set timber-framing, above stone lower parts and slated square windows

Knoak's Court, 1.1/2m SW of Ivington, is early 18th century brick. At Upper Wintercott, 1.1/4m SSW of Ivington, on a tributary of the Honeylake Brook, is one of many-moated homestead sites in these western reaches of Herefordshire.

But the king of constructions hereabouts is Ivington Camp, 1.1/4m SSE of the village, on the heavily wooded Brierley Hill. This majestic Iron-Age hill fort stands at the end of a ridge. The massive double ramparts of the 37 acre site follow the natural contours of the hill. It has been damaged by ploughing and quarrying but one of the inner ramparts still rises to 20ft above the enclosure. There are elaborate entrances in the ramparts in the south-east and north-east; to the north-west, west and south-east the camp is protected by precipitous natural slopes of the Old Red Sandstone bed-rock. The smaller enclosure of about 13 acres in the north-west corner of the camp, which has a crescent-shaped earthwork, is probably the original settlement. The grand extensions were the work of the second invasion La Tene Celts who arrived about 390 B.C. The whole site awaits thorough investigation but one doubts whether the tunnel said to link the camp to the priory church at Leominster will ever be found.

Local tradition has it that Ivington Camp was occupied by Owain Glyndwr during the early years of his rebellio, though it is doubtful if he held it for more than a few days, or weeks, at the most.

KENCHESTER (MAGNIS) *4.5m WNW of Hereford*

The name is Anglo-Saxon and means 'Cena's Roman fort'. The centre of the Roman town of Magnis lies 1/3m SSE (at SO 440 428) of the nucleus of the modern settlement of Kenchester. It lies on both sides of the line of the Roman road from Gloucester to Brecon. Much of this is followed by modern roads, which are plain to see on the map. On the ground, however, all that is visible is the hexagonal outline of the town's boundaries preserved in hedges and the modern road to the south. The 22 acre site itself is flat grassland.

Magnis was not an important Roman town but served as a staging post for troops engaged in subjugating the Welsh. It probably began as a lightly defended fort but in the 2nd century high, 7ft thick walls were constructed with gates to the east and west. The main street was built of successive layers of sand gravel and cobbles and was 22ft wide. A drainage channel ran down the centre and it was edged with stone culverts. The houses were timber-framed and had wooden verandahs, mosaic floors and hypocausts for heating. The town was occupied to a late date, large quantities of Roman coins being circulated into the 5th century. Other finds include Samian pottery, a small bronze axe head and an occulist's stamp. When it was abandoned is unknown but there is an ominous layer of charcoal beneath the topsoil. The sites of numerous buildings have been excavated and plotted 'within the walls' and there are several related sites in the vicinity. The Roman road from Caerleon to Watling Street and Wroxeter brushes the eastern gate and east of this is the site of a roadside temple.

At New Weir (SO 439 418) 1/2m S of Magnis, are the remains of a Roman wall where flue tiles and tessellated paving have been found. Excavations have exposed a complex of rooms and surrounding buttresses. About 50 yards SE is another complex and debris found between them suggests they were connected. They are close to the River Wye and a Holy Well, and could be a temple with associated residential buildings. A local legend has it that a Celtic girl suspected her Roman soldier lover of being unfaithful. Distraught, she flung herself into the river. Her lover tried to save her but both drowned. Now, on New Year's Day, the well fills up with their tears. The stone-lined well stands within the Weir Gardens which are open to the public all year round. The house was built in 1784 and has an attractive semi-circular porch. It is now a nursing home.

The restored church of Saint Michael has two Norman windows in the chancel and a Norman south doorway. The bellcote and chancel east window (three stepped lights under one arch) are 13th century. The roof is Jacobean. The font is thought to have been carved out of a Roman column. Also a rarity is the wide timber chancel arch decorated with vine carving. Lady Southampton's Chapel, 1/3m SE of the church, was built in red brick under a pyramid roof for the Countess of Huntingdon's Connexion. The Methodist preacher's accommodation forms a part of the whole.

Just east of the Roman town and south of the track of the Roman road at SO 446 426 is the site of an Iron-Age, lowland farm settlement, one of only two to have survived and been located in the county.

Finally, tales of ghostly Romans are legion in the area. One old lady was adamant that she saw a troop march through her house on the night of every full moon; another that they camped in her garden. And that is not all. A king of the Fairies has been seen dancing with his cohorts since the time of Henry VIII. Part of the ruins, now gone, was said to be his chair. However, Camden reports that the chair belonged to the spirit of Thomas a Becket who often materialised out of 'a pool in this parish by the roadside abounding with fine trout'.

KENDERCHURCH 10m SW of Hereford
The early 12th century name was Lanncinitir from llan-cynidr, 'the church of Saint Cynidr'. It stands on a rise near the confluence of the Worm Brook with the River Dore. What with the roar of the busy main road, the clatter of the main line railway, the squeals from the timber yard and the hum of the electric grid cables, it knows little peace these days.

Saint Mary's was much restored in 1871. It consists of nave, chancel with a Tudor waggon roof, and a Victorian bellcote. The pulpit is Jacobean, the screen is Perpendicular and the font is Norman with zig-zag ornament around the rim. There are two Norman, or possibly Anglo-Saxon, stone coffin lids with incised crosses, and in the churchyard there is a cross with a mediaeval base.

To the north-west there are views up the Golden Valley. At Howton, 1m NE of the church, between the road and the railway is a mound about 45 yards in diameter and about 7ft high with traces of a ditch around the base. It could be a motte and bailey castle site. (See Pontrilas.)

KENTCHURCH *11m SW of Hereford*
In the early 12th century the name was Lan Cein, from the Welsh meaning 'the church of Saint Ceina'. St. Ceina was female and her name is from the Welsh cain meaning 'bright and beautiful'. (Ceinwen is a current Welsh first name.) Kentchurch is most easily approached off the A465 at Pontrilas. A broad, undulating valley with pastures and arable fields and oak trees galore narrows as the River Monnow approaches the hamlet. By the bridge is the Bridge Inn and a couple of cottages along the road is Cupid's Inn, a cider and tobacco store. But now we are in Wales.

The entrance to Kentchurch Court is 1/2m E of the bridge. Beyond the battlemented grey stone lodge a long avenue of elms leads to the Court. These days, however, this ceremonial entrance has been abandoned. The gates are locked and blocked by parked cars and the entrance is now opposite the church on the road to Garway. Some of the original 14th century castle has survived but it was enlarged and partly rebuilt in the 17th century and remodelled extensively by John Nash in the early 19th century. This was an early job for Nash who went on to be a leading architect of his day and who designed Buckingham Palace.

The original 14th century castle consisted of a moated manor with a strong stone tower at one corner and a large stone gateway. The tower and gateway survive and would have been familiar to Owain Glyndwr (died 1415?), the great Welsh national hero, for whom it might well have been a place of retreat during his rebellions against the English. He had three daughters and one of them, Alice, married Sir John Scudamore, the squire of Kentchurch. Glyndwr had many victories but ultimately failed in his attempt to free Wales. However, he was not captured and the date and place of his death in unrecorded. He simply disappeared. Some think that he ended his days at either Kentchurch or Monnington Straddel, which was also owned by Sir John, but no one really knows.

Years later, in 1461, Lady Alice lost her husband and three sons after the battle of Mortimer's Cross. They had fought for the losing Lancastrians, were captured and subsequently executed. Members of the Scudamore family still own and occupy Kentchurch Court.

Amongst the the furnishings of the house are some highly ornate carved garlands of birds and fruit from overmantles brought here from Holme Lacy, another Scudamore Herefordshire house. They are attributed to Grinling Gibbons.

The beautiful deer park is still stocked with fallow deer and is one of only four left in Herefordshire out of the original 35. It lies on steeply rising ground to the east of the Court and is surrounded by most handsome broad-leaved woods.

The church of Saint Mary stands near a stream opposite the entrance to the Court. It was rebuilt in 1859 and has a nave, chancel and tower in Decorated style. Inside are some small pieces of 17th century sculpture and a monument to John Scudamore, died 1616, and family. He lies in full armour surrounded by his wife, nine children and an infant in a cradle.

John Kent was a vicar here in the late 14th century and he is one of several historical persons who might have been the legendary Jack of Kent - Sir John Oldcastle, Doctor John Gwent (a Welsh Franciscan who died in 1348), and even Glyndwr himself are other contenders. A striking picture of a wild-eyed man dressed like a priest is held at the Court and if he is not Jack of Kent he certainly ought to be!

For Jack was fearsome: "As great as the devil and Jack o' Kent". Stories about him are legion, not only in Herefordshire but also in Gloucestershire and Monmouthshire. Most of the tales involve Jack either outwitting the devil or performing Herculean tasks. One that has both elements is this:

Jack made a pact with the Devil. In return for the strength to build a bridge over the Monnow at Kentchurch in a single night the Devil could have the soul of the first being to cross it. Jack built the bridge and then threw a bone over it for a dog to chase. So, the first being had no soul and the Devil was cheated. Truth be known all manner of widespread folk tales have become attached to Jack's name. Most are fanciful and none that we know of have any historical documentation. Still, better be safe than sorry; don't be too scornful, you might be his next victim. All right, Jack?

An elaborate earthwork (SO 421 270) lies 1m NNE of the church in an isolated hillside position. A roughly oval mound has three platforms on top, approximately 50ft, 43ft and 12ft high, surrounded by a dry ditch, except on the south-west where there is a natural slope to a stream. There are more earthworks to the south and traces of a causeway linking them to the motte. There is no stonework. Its age has not been determined.

In the garden of Twyn-y-Corras, 1/2m south of the church at Kentchurch, is a 12ft high mound with a 12ft flat top. Its age and purpose are unknown. In the mid-1990s an excavation carried out by Ruth Richardson, in the orchard adjacent to Twyn-y-Corras, revealed the walls and a doorway of a chapel. The orchard belongs to the substantial Great Corras Farm, a grey rendered house with stone barns which stands on the opposite side of the road.

Close by, a short, stony track leads to a ford across the River Monnow which utilises a natural rock shelf. This is a delightful spot. Just downstream there is a skimpy concrete footbridge on strong piers, built to allow access to the farmland on the west bank and for the benefit of men from White Rocks who worked at Garway. In times of flood the waters can rise dramatically here and have even been known to submerge the bridge. The little wooden hut beside the road houses a river-level recording mechanism. The view from the bridge is truly splendid. The Monnow is a pretty river anyway; here it excels itself. The rocks lie a-tumble and in Summer it is a delight.

A little further south is Little Corras Farm. In the woods is the Monnow Valley Shooting School. Parked by the road is their large and very smart travelling-show truck. Both Great and Little Corras Farms belong to the Kentchurch Estate.

KILPECK *7m SW of Hereford*

Kilpeck is most easily approached down lanes off the A465 Hereford to Abergavenny road. The name probably means 'the refuge of Pedic'.

The church of Mary and Saint David is famous throughout England. It is sumptuously decorated with stone carvings made by 12th century craftsmen who were the equal in skill of any in the land. What is more, even the external work has weathered incredibly well. Quite literally it could have been completed but yesterday, so crisp and clean are its lines. The artists were probably Anglo-Saxons who had been trained and were led by a French or Spanish master craftsman. They are now collectively called the Herefordshire School of Carving and worked on several other churches in the county and beyond. Their work was always of the highest order but that of their master is quite exceptional, in both detail and overall design.

Such a masterpiece is the wonderful south door. On one jamb, fat Viking Ringerike dragons entwine behind a pair of lean, leather-clad warriors. On the other are two birds in flowing interlacing. The jamb shafts support an arch with patterns of beaks, fish, a phoenix, birds' heads and a flying angel which in turn enclose a tympanum with a stylized 'Tree of Life' resting on vertical zig-zags.

Below the roof are some 70 carved corbels. These include a bear, a dog, a deer, a rabbit, a falcon, two wrestlers, a grotesque man with a rebec (fiddle), two lovers kissing, a man dancing, and a sheila na gig (a woman flagrantly exposing herself). Some were defaced or removed by Victorian ladies because of their sexually explicit nature. Inside there are more carvings - the chancel arch is especially noteworthy - and a huge Norman font.

The church is small, built of glowing red sandstone, and has nave, chancel and apse. It was built in the early 12th century to replace the previous Anglo-Saxon church. The large stones in the north-east corner of the nave are from this pre-Conquest building. The chancel windows and doorway are of about 1300 and the bellcote of 1864. The rest is pure Norman. The church was restored in 1848 but the architect, Lewis Cottingham, used admirable restraint.

Adjacent to the church are the tree-clad remains of the castle built by William FitzNorman shortly after the Conquest. The substantial mound is 54 yards in diameter at its base rising to 27ft from the bottom of the ditch. Some 12th century masonry remains from the polygonal shell-keep. There is a kidney-shaped bailey and beyond this three other enclosures.

To the north-east is the rectangular enclosure that held the mediaeval village and the church. The house platforms lie close together alongside a street, typical of farming communities using the open field system of agriculture. This enclosure measures about 200 yards by 300 yards. An earthwork consisting of a platform and one or two small banks about, 70 yards SW of the Priory House, probably marks the site of the Benedictine Priory founded by Hugh, son of William FitzNorman, in 1134. It was a daughter cell of Gloucester. The church was probably built shortly after the Priory was established.

As to the present village, it looks much as it did at the beginning of this century - a few cottages and a farm surrounded by fields. Until, that is, you go up to the pub, the Red Lion. Here electric pylons lead the way to a modern village hall and a considerable estate of bland, modern brick houses. Why couldn't the builders and planners have followed the example of the old house opposite the church, which has a cosy mixture of stone, red brick, and black and white. Elsewhere in the county they are doing this today and they look a treat.

A narrow, winding, undulating lane leads to Marlas. Here is a gaunt two and a half storey stone-built mill and a great raft of farm sheds with skylights glinting in the sun. A black and white cottage with pretty gardens struggles to redress the architectural balance. The forbiddingly named Gallows Knapp lies 1/2m NE of the churchyard; 1m ENE

Above: Kilpeck. From the top: the Norman castle mound and moat, then the 12th century church, and below this the village house platforms and holloways enclosed by their own earth ramparts.
The farm below the church is of about 1600. The church was built for a Benedictine priory, the site of which is out of the picture to the left.
Right: Olchon Court, at the north end of the Olchon Valley, north of Longtown. The last hiding place of Sir John Oldcastle.

of that is Crac o' Hill. This name probably means 'the hill frequented by crakes'. Dippersmoor Manor has two old crucks incorporated into a later 15th century part of the house.

Incidentally, we saw our first wild mistletoe in a little orchard alongside the lane between Kilpeck and the main road. Mistletoe needs old, established trees and very clean air. Herefordshire and south Shropshire are first in the whole country for the quantity and quality of their mistletoe. At the winter auctions buyers come from all over England. Farmers complain of mistletoe rustling and gypsies are accused of using shotguns to bring the mistletoe clumps to the ground. Typically, mistletoe grows in loose balls about two or three feet in diameter.

KIMBOLTON *2.5m NE of Leominster*

The name is Anglo-Saxon and means 'Cynebald's homestead'. It stands astride the A4112, Leominster to Tenbury Wells road, but the area immediately south of the road belongs mostly to Stockton. To all intents and purposes they are now one village, somewhat spread about but with a pleasant mixture of old and new dwellings. We approached from the north past Pateshill Farm, a 16th century stone-built farmhouse with five gables. each having a blocked window, past an orchard and fields of sheep, and down a sunken lane with wooded hedges to the black and white Stockton Cross Inn. This stands at the crossroads in the heart of the village. In the fields immediately south of the pub, by the Cogwell Brook, are the earthworks of the deserted mediaeval settlement.

On the opposite side of the lane (SO 522 611) is the care-worn Brook House. It is an irregular 16th century timber-framed building with red brick infill and big stone chimney stacks. It is derelict but must have once been quite splendid - a yeoman farmer's house to be proud of. The owner now lives in a modern bungalow on the other side of what is now the Kimbolton Transport yard. South of Brook House are Rowley Fields, Sweet Apple Tree Field and Grantsfield, of the mediaeval three-field system. The house called Grantsfield, 1m SSE of the pub, was the home of the Hutchinson family.

The Reverend Thomas Hutchinson was vicar of the parish for 62 years. I bet he could tell a few tales. He was the nephew of Mary Hutchinson, who became the wife of William Wordsworth. His church stands on high ground, 1/2m NE of the pub, approached up sunken lanes. Saint James has two Norman windows. Of the 13th century are the short buttressed tower (with a later shingled brooch spire), the south side of the nave and its door, the north pointed and trefoiled windows, and the south transept with its lancets. The back panels of the stalls have good Tudor linenfold.

Kimbolton Court lies beside a stream 1/2m NE of the church. At Lower Stockton, or Stockton Bottom, is the 19th century Old Workhouse, with blocks from the 15th, 17th and 18th centuries, now converted to four cottages. The Victorian school is on the main road. It was built in 1856 and modernised and extended in 1972.

Stockton Bury, 3/4m SW of the church, was an 18th century Georgian brick house with a pediment but in 1970 it was replaced by a modern building. The charming old, circular stone dovecote with conical roof and lantern still stands, along with a tithe barn and the depression of a large fishpool to the south-west of the house. In the surrounding pastures a famous Hereford bull once grazed. Anxiety IV was bred here by Thomas Carwardine in the late 19th century and it is claimed that over 90% of American Herefords are descended from him.

Between Stockton Bury and the Cogwell Brook is the site of the deserted mediaeval Domesday village, centred on SO 516 609. The earthworks are quite substantial - level house platforms and scarped terracing bounded by a holloway to the west and by a terraced approach road to the south.

The Lea on the A4112, 1.1/4m NE of Kimbolton, was farmed in the late 16th century by the Quaker Lloyd family, who founded Lloyds Bank. Like much of the large Kimbolton parish it was formerly a part of the Berrington estate and has a 'Berrington Barn' to prove it. These are typified by arched, window-like decorations and open brickwork.

At Upper Bach Farm, 3/4m SE of the pub, is a square, 18th century dovecote. On a ridge south-east of the farm is Bach Camp, a small oval-shaped Iron-Age hill fort of about six acres. It has a single ditch and rampart with an entrance to the west and another to the east. The latter is slightly interned.

On the A49, on the parish boundary 1m NE of Leominster, is a wharf on the disused Stourport Canal. Coal was unloaded and stored here. Further north the canal track can be seen for long stretches as it skirts the western boundaries of Berrington Hall Park.

KING'S CAPLE *8m SSE of Hereford*

Caple is from the Norman-French capele, 'a chapel'. It is a delightful little village that stands near the end of a tongue of land made by a great, looping, horse-shoe meander of the River Wye.

The main lane, called Caple Street, runs between the church and the castle to the old ford crossing marked on the 'mainland' bank by Red Rail. This road passes Pennoxstone Farm and is almost certainly Roman. Its construction is unusual and identical to the Roman road (part of Fine Street) discovered under the railway station at Abbeydore. The crown of the road is offset leaving the other half flat. This indicates either a widening of the highway or that it was designed so that heavier traffic used the crown (which is rutted), leaving the flat half for pedestrians. Iron nails, like those from the Abbeydore road, have been found by the river. The name Red Rail is from the Welsh rhy-yr-heol, meaning 'ford on the street'.

We approached from Hoarwithy, over the cast iron bridge of 1876. This replaced the stone and timber bridge of 1856 which in turn had replaced the ferry last operated by one William Fido. Incidentally, there was another ferry 1.1/2m SW, from Sellack Boat to Sellack. This was discontinued when the suspension footbridge of 1895 was constructed. The last ferryman here was George Harris. He exercised the ancient rights of free fishing that belonged to river bank dwellers in the district of Archenfield (see Holme Lacy).

However, in 1909, the owners of the fishing (riparian) rights on the Wye took legal action to get this ancient charter written off. They were lead by the arrogant Lord Chesterfield and a mercenary Mrs. Foster whose money bought them a judgement in their favour from the House of Lords.

After crossing the bridge we turned right (south) into Ruxton, past horses, a bed and breakfast farm, a stone barn with arrow slits and boarded uppers, a stone cottage in ruins, a black and white cottage, and through a farmyard. Pennoxstone, once the home of a local squire and magistrate, is now owned by a farmer. The lane leads past sheep and orchards up to the church on higher ground.

The church of Saint John the Baptist has a delightful setting. It stands opposite The Tump which was probably the site of a timber-framed Norman castle, but could be older. It was a traditional meeting place and until about 1930 the Caple Feast was held here on Whit-Tuesday - a time of dancing and frivolity. The church is not small. The oldest existing fabric is in the nave south wall where there is a 13th century window with geometrical tracery and a tomb recess. The tower is Decorated (1290-1350) with ballflower ornament, and the Aramstone Chapel is 14th century Perpendicular and has some 15th century stained glass. The pulpit is Jacobean, tall, and with a tester (soundboard). The West Gallery is probably 18th century. Monuments include one to Mrs. Holcombe Ferguson, died 1814, by John Flaxman; and one to Eliza Woodhouse, died 1833, by Richard Westmacott.

The lane continues on, eastwards, past modern orchards with 4ft high modern trees with their little branches, past a Georgian brick house with five bays and two and a half storeys, a roofless barn and the remains of a tower, past a 'fish pond' by the crossroads, on past cottages and modern houses and a primary school defended by high wire fencing to the British Lion, which stands near the cutting made for the disused railway. The pub, the school of 1899 and the Parish Room (which was a National School of 1840) are all that remain of the services that the village once possessed. The butcher, the post office, the grocer, the smithy, the basket maker, the thatcher and the dairyman have all gone. Mains electricity only came here in 1952 and mains water after that.

King's Caple is one of three parishes where Pax Cakes, peace cakes, are distributed on Palm Sunday. These are paid for by a bequest of the 16th century Scudamores. (See Hentland.)

There was once a splendid house at King's Caple. It was called Aramstone, a mansion of 1730, and was of national importance. Alas, in 1959, whilst a preservation order was being considered, the owners had it demolished. Greed had again reared its ugly head. The quarry pool at Aramstone is noted for the large salmon that have been caught there.

KINGSLAND *3.5m NE of Leominster*
In Domesday Book it is Lene, an ancient name for the district in which it lies. This was the part held by the king for himself, a part rich in the resources of the river, the woods and the good farmland now dotted with orchards. It lies on the old Roman road from Mortimer's Cross to Leominster, now called the B4360.

The village is long and linear, and stretches for 1.1/4 miles. At the eastern end the modern road makes an abrupt, right hand turn before assuming its original direction 1/2m further on at Cobnash. The probable route of the original road is marked by a lane from Holgate Farm to Mousenatch. Such sharp deviations in old roads are usually the result of a local landlord wishing to keep the public away from his land. The obvious contender here is an owner of Pinsley Park.

Kingland stands on flat land between the dark and brooding River Lugg and its tributary the Pinsley Brook. The Lugg is peppered with weirs, built to deepen and control the flow of the water both for fishing and to drive mills. In the area there were mills designed for processing corn, apples, bones and timber. There was once an aerial 'railway', 3.1/2 miles long, that brought timber down to the local sawmills.

The village has many black and white houses and, in fact, many more are timber-framed behind a brick facade which became fashionable in the 18th century. Here the process was spurred on by a master mason, John Gethin (1757-1831), who owned the local brickworks and became the County Surveyor and Inspector of Bridges. The somewhat bleak aspect of the main street is enhanced by the gap in the houses that looks like a bomb-damaged site. This is the outlook for The Angel Inn, which has a sign depicting an angel skewering a grovelling dragon with a lance. Over this rough and overgrown patch one can see the church.

Saint Michael's is a spacious place built about 1300 and is unusual in still being all of one style. It has a notable crown-post roof and some stained glass in the chancel, all of the time of the building. The south porch is 15th century. Some mystery attaches to the Volka (Vaukel) chapel attached to the north porch. It was probably built as a chantry, where a priest was paid to pray for the person who once occupied the now empty tomb, but it might have been a hermit's cell. No one knows when or for whom it was built but it could have been for a Mortimer. The Mortimers paid for the first priest here in 1285. The name Volka could be derived from Volk Ley, from Folk Ley, 'the water-meadow of the people'. There is a Volka Meadow at the confluence of the Arrow and the Lugg near Leominster that has this proven etymology.

Until the outbreak of the Second World War it was the custom to toll a bell to announce a death: four times for a man, five for a woman, and then the age of the deceased.

The substantial earthworks of an early Norman castle stand behind (to the west of) the church. The mound is about 60 yards in diameter and about 17ft high. It has two baileys, separated by a ditch, and the depression of a possible fishpond to the south.

As to services in the village, there are a couple of pubs, a post office, a fire station, a rugby club shack, a Coronation Hall, and a stone-built school of 1846. There used to be a station on the Leominster to Radnor line, which opened in 1856, but that closed in the 1960s. Gone, too, is the annual fair, begun in 1305 and held on the 11th of October on a field east of the church; likewise its successor, the Foal Show, which was held on the same date at Boarfields.

There are several notable houses in Kingsland. Foremost of these is Kingsland House, the former rectory, a dignified 18th century mansion of five bays and two storeys with a hipped roof and a pilastered porch. Local tradition has it that Merewald, a 7th century king of Mercia, lies buried in a tumulus in the rectory garden. The Angel House is the most outstanding black and white building in the main street. Must Mill, at Brook Bridge, 1m W of the church, has close-set timber-framing of about 1500. Black Hall, at Aston, 1.1/4m NE of the church, has a surprise at the back: a 14th century window of four lights with pointed trefoiled heads set between two thick diagonal braces. Close to Kingsland is a humble abode, Waterloo Cottage, which had crossing gates on the old railway. The famous flat race jockey, Freddie Fox, was born here.

Beyond the northern, bungalow-land end of the main street, at its junction with the A4110 Kington to Hereford road, is a white pedestal monument commemorating the Battle of Mortimer's Cross of 1461. The site of the battle is actually on the Great West Field, one of the three mediaeval fields of Kingsland, and crossed by the road to Mortimer's Cross, 1.1/2m NW of Kingsland. This was a decisive battle in the Wars of the Roses. Edward Mortimer, son of Richard, Earl of March and a descendant of Edward III, defeated a force of Lancastrians led by the Earl of Pembroke. He left the field with 4,000 dead and slaughtered fleeing remnants in the gorge at Kinsham, before going on to London where he was unopposed and at the age of 19 became king of England as Edward IV. He incorporated into his coat of arms the triple sun he had seen before the battle. One of the dead he left at Kingsland was Owen Tudor whose descendants were to become kings themselves in later times.

The following are notes on some customs associated with Kingsland. Dancing around the Maypole on May Day was still practised in Kingsland in 1912. The pole was a birch tree bedecked with ribbons. On May 29th, Oak Apple Day, a great bough from an oak tree was put on the church tower. A children's counting out game rhyme from Kingsland went: Ena, mena, mona, mi, Startle, story, story, sti, Ef, wef, rose knee, E, tot, P and P. Sometimes such rhymes are purely modern fancy; but sometimes they are folk memories of ancient counting systems handed down through many generations, even from as far back as Celtic times. As late as 1912 a heriot was collected by the Lord of the Manor on the death of a tenant. The heriot used to be the tenant's two best beasts; later money was accepted.

KING'S PYON *6m SW of Leominster*

Pyon is from the Old English peona-eg, which means 'gnat infested island'. In 1066 it belonged to King Edward the Confessor.

The settlement lies on the Wellington Brook, approached down lanes off the A4110 in a landscape dominated by the twin peaks of Robin Hood's Butts. There are several related folk tales regarding their origin, but the gist of them all is that the Devil was travelling to Hereford with two sacks of earth intending to bury this good and Christian city. However, on the way he met a holy man who persuaded the Devil not to bother because the people of Hereford were, in fact, sinful and corrupt. So the Devil dumped his sacks of earth and that's how the hills came to be. They are called Robin Hood's Butts because Robin Hood stood on one and shot an arrow into a tree on the other, they say.

Belief in witchcraft seems to have been strong in the area. If someone was thought to have been made ill by a spell, the cure was to burn a lock of hair (or broom according to others) on a fire at midnight. The witch would be drawn to the fire and having become known the spell would be lifted. Other superstitious beliefs relating to death, birth and a cure for whooping cough have been collected in the village. In the late 19th century it was still the custom to deck every nook and cranny of the church on Whit-Sunday with greenery, a relic of pagan homage to the Green Man, the spirit of Spring.

Saint Mary's church has a Norman nave and chancel, a 13th century south transept and a 14th century tower. The handsome black and white roofs are of the 14th century. The north transept is of 1872 and is dedicated to John Webb-Peploe, who was vicar here for 40 years. In the south transept there is an alabaster effigy of a knight with a lion at his feet and the stone effigy of a lady, both from the late 14th century. The modern font is made from oak; wooden fonts are a rarity.

Brookhouse, just north of the church, has a dour 19th century facade, but in the grounds is a cheerful black and white dovecote with a glazed lantern.

Benjamin Tomkins the Younger was an important improver of Hereford cattle. When his father, Richard Tomkins of King's Pyon, died in 1723, he left his cattle to be divided amongst his sons. Benjamin inherited Silver, a cow which became the founder of the pedigree Hereford we have today.

Butthouse, 1m S of the church, is a charming early 17th century, timber-framed house with brick infill and tall chimneys. The east side has two gables and below them are two gabled bays. The very pretty Gatehouse is of 1632. It has an overhanging upper storey, and the support beam (bressumer) and bargeboards are carved with dragons and scrolls. The current owner is Major Philip Verdin, who owns extensive estates hereabouts.

Just north of the Butthouse is a roadside tumulus at SO 442 489. It is thought to be a communal burial mound and measures 30 yards in diameter at the base, and rises to 9ft. It has been scheduled for protection and has not been excavated. There is a possibility that it was also used as a motte by the Normans.

The Hill, 1/2m N of the church, is a timber-framed house with narrow uprights and a gable with diagonal bracing of about 1600. Blackhall, to the SW, has a cruck-trussed mediaeval barn.

The crossroads settlement of Bush Bank lies 1m NE of King's Pyon, at the junction of the the Roman road from Kenchester to Leintwardine and the old road from Weobley to Leominster. The hamlet has cottages in red brick, stone, render and black and white, a service station and a painted brick pub, the Bush Inn. The presence of prehistoric man is marked by a monolith (SO 449 515). Sheep and orchard country.

KING'S THORN *5m S of Hereford*

It lies off the A49 Hereford to Ross road and is a 'dormitory village' to Hereford. Modern houses predominate and it is now virtually joined with Little Birch to the east.

The name is the subject of a local story to the effect that it was the custom to send to the king each year a cutting from the Glastonbury Thorn. One year King Charles I was staying at Much Birch, 1m S, and received his cutting there. He commanded that it be planted at what we now call King.'s Thorn. The settlement has a flat-roofed school by a clump of pine trees, a post office-cum-general store, the King's Thorn Rifle Club which has its own 15 yard range, a garage, and long and lovely views to the west. The woods of Aconbury Hill are close by to the east. Just to the north, beyond a modern orchard with tiny waist high trees, the lane rejoins the fast main road, the A49.

KINGSTONE *6m SW of Hereford*

The 'stone' in the name is a corruption of 'tun'; the name means 'settlement held by the king', a royal manor. In 1066 it was held by King Edward.

It is a proper, nucleated village with a Norman church, two pubs, three doctors, a three-school complex, a shop, a post office-cum-general store, some light industry, and a pleasant enough mixture of old black and white and modern houses. During the last war there was an airfield here and the hutted encampment to the north was built to service it. The site is now host to a galaxy of gleaming radio satellite communication dishes.

The church of Saint Michael (a dedication that often denotes an Anglo-Saxon site) is embowered in cypress trees. The original aisle-less Norman church, with its plain south doorway, was given a north aisle in about 1200.

Kilpeck, the wonderful west doorway of the church of Saint Mary, c. 1145. It was protected by a porch into the 19th century and perhaps ought to be again, if only in the Winter.

Shortly after, the chancel was rebuilt and the north chapel added. About 1315 the north aisle was widened and the tower was constructed. The much admired font bowl is Norman, carved out of dark coloured breccia stone and left undecorated. The reredos has Jacobean panels and there is an 8.1/2ft long, wooden chest carved out of one piece. There is a memorial to Robert Jones, a Kingstone man, who won the Victoria Cross at the famous siege of Rorke's Drift (1879) during the Zulu wars, and lived to tell the tale.

Notable houses in the area include: Arkstone Court, 1/2m NE, and Bridge Court, 1/2m NNE, both 18th century Georgian brick with a feature lunette window; Whitfield, 1.3/4m SSW, near Cockyard, Georgian brick with big bay windows and a stable range decorated with arches and a pediment, sitting rather grandly in its own wood-fringed parkland; and Kingstone Grange, 3/4m S, a gabled, timber-framed house of about 1600.

At Blackmoor Farm, 1.3/4m SW of Kingstone, at the north end of the lovely Grey Valley by a stream, there are enclosures protected by well-defined steep banks. In the field between these and the farmhouse, 1/4m SE, the ground has been much disturbed. The age and purpose of these earthworks are unknown.

Here are some old customs and superstitions associated with Kingstone. At Kingstone and Thruxton (1m SE) on the evening before May Day people would put trays of moss outside their doors for the fairies to dance on. To ease the pain of a baby cutting its teeth 21 live woodlice were sewn up in black ribbon and hung around the child's neck. The pain would then pass from the child to the lice, it was believed.

Similarly, to cure whooping cough the folk cure at Kingstone and Thruxton was to recite the Lord's Prayer whilst passing the child beneath an arch of bramble briar. During this procedure the child must be eating bread and butter. This is then fed to a bird or an animal, transferring the cough by so doing.

On Twelfth Night there was merry-making around a circle of 12 fires built around a central fire of straw tied to a pole. Indeed, for many country people Twelfth Night was the 'real Christmas'; this was the night when the holy thorns blossomed and when oxen went on their knees at midnight. At Kingsland, the vicar was told, only seven-year old cattle made obeisance - the cattle in the stall at Bethlehem were seven years old. Even in this century a farmer at Kingstone Grange kept the 'real Christmas', and for the 12 days from the church Christmas would not borrow fire for it brought bad luck. (People would often borrow burning coals from a neighbour to start their own fire). The same farmer kept the practice of the Yule Log; a tree was drawn into the kitchen by two carthorses and when it was burned a small piece was kept for lighting the next year's Yule Log. He also ceremonially bled his ploughing oxen and carthorses on St. Stephen's Day and they were not worked at all until after the Twelfth Day.

In Domesday Book it is recorded that the pre-Conquest tenants of the manor of Kingstone held their land in return for carrying the game killed in the Treville Wood to Hereford, and did no other service. Treville Wood covered 2,014 acres and stretched from Kingstone south and west to the River Dore. After the Conquest William kept the manor for himself. His rent was "20 shillings of blanched pence and one hawk".

Treville is actually a parish, though no place bearing that name appears on the Ordnance Survey Landranger map. It is bounded to the north by the parishes of Kingstone and Thruxton, to the west by Abbeydore, to the south by Wormbridge, and to the south and east by Saint Deveraux. It does not appear to have its own parish church.

KINGSWOOD *1.75m S of Kington*

In the 13th century a great wood extended between Kington and Eardisley. When Walter de Baskerville acquired the Eardisley manor in 1252 the northern part of the wood was called Kingswood and belonged to Kington. Parts of this wood, adjacent to the common, existed well into the 19th century and were managed as traditional 'standard and coppice'. Squatters' cottages are dotted around in the area and we were struck by the smallness of the fields and the number of ponies.

The Kingswood estate was broken up in 1868 and the wood was cleared for farming. Very little woodland now remains, but place names perpetuate its memory - Woodbrook, Ashmoor, The Woodlands, Coppice House, The Birches and Chickward. Chickward could mean 'lookout place in the wood'; it stands at the head of a valley.

Most of the village common has also been enclosed and used for agriculture. Close by the common are the earthworks of a small Norman motte and bailey castle (SO 304 544), about 25 yards in diameter and 5ft high. The ditch had an outer rampart on the west and south and bailey enclosures on the north and west sides. The Wesleyan chapel, of 1863 was built on the common. It is now used as a private house.

In 1795 the vicar of the parish church at Kington forbade his congregation to celebrate the church's Saint's Day (Assumption of the Virgin Mary on 15th August) in the grounds of the church, but permitted its transferral to Kingswood Common. Here the people sported, drank, fought and participated in lewd acts to their hearts' content. The present August Fete is a continuance of this festival. It is just as well it is held in the Summer, for a local rhyme goes: "Kingswood Common and Moseley Mere, the two coldest places in Herefordsheer".

Kingswood is a scattered community but has a sense of identity. Without a church or a school the village hall, of 1960, is the centre of things and plays host to all manner of social gatherings, from religious services to the August fete.

An important local industry was brick-making, the local clay being eminently suitable for the purpose, but the brickyard closed and was demolished in about 1970.

Kingswood Hall is now a nursing home, and Kingswood House (near Kington) was formerly the Workhouse. It was built of stone in 1857 to a radial plan.

There are several good, old farmhouses in the area but pride of place goes to Apostles, 1.1/4m SW of Kingswood. It is a characterful mediaeval house, part stone, part timber-framed with cruck trusses. The lane from Apostles runs to the main road, and at the junction now called Crossway there is a cross. Local tradition has it that there used to be a gallows here. Today there is a Council maintained Picnic Site.

The Oaklands Small Breeds Farm has a collection of owls, rabbits (including a giant one), mice, tortoise, chinchillas, guinea pigs, black swans, Hotentot teal and 28 other water-fowl species, not to mention miniature horses, pigs, five breeds of goats, sheep, cows, a peacock and more. Educational and guided tours are available.

Kingswood is on the Black and White Village Trail, a signed, circular, motorists' route that starts and ends at Leominster. The other villages on the trail are Dilwyn,

Weobley, Almeley, Eardisley, Kington, Lyonshall, Pembridge and Eardisland.

KINGTON *18 NW of Hereford*

It was known as Kington from at least 1055, in the reign of Edward the Confessor (1042-1066), when the land of the area was re-divided after an attack by the Welsh on Hereford. It was called Chingtune in Domesday Book where it is described as 'waste'. The settlement lies near the Welsh border, at the confluence of the River Arrow and the Gilwern, below the heights of Bradnor Hill to the north and Hergest Ridge to the west.

The early history of Kington was closely connected with that of Huntington, 4.1/2m SW, and several of the mediaeval lords held both manors. The castle lies west of the town, below the church, guarding the Gilwern valley. It is mentioned once in mediaeval documents - in 1186, with a reference to the repair of its timber palisade - and it seems to have had little importance. Its time-ravaged ruins now consist of a mound, about 50 yards in diameter which rises to 15feet above the moat. The causeway, which crossed the moat to the north, has been removed.

The church of Saint Mary is altogether more impressive. It stands on high grounds to the south, a large, grey stone building with a tower of about 1200. The tower walls are battered - that is, they have a buttress-like slope in their lower parts - and are topped by a brooch spire of 1794. An impressive arch with continuous roll moulding leads to the beautiful 13th century chancel, which has lancet windows. The nave was re-built about 1300, when it was given aisles, and the south chapel is 14th century Decorated. Most of the rest, including the north aisles of 1874, is Victorian. The font is Norman with rope moulding to the base and zig-zag to the top. A rarity is the immersion pit, quite probably dating from the Baptist boom of the 17th century. Of monuments, the chief is that of Thomas Vaughan, a knight in full armour, and his wife Ellen. Both had fearsome reputations, about which more is said later in this article. Here they lie in alabaster effigy surrounded by angels. William Mathews, died 1633, is remembered by a tablet with columns and putti (small, naked boys). In the churchyard there is the stump of a preaching cross.

The town is a friendly place with a good selection of small, traditional shops ranged along its narrow main street. It is a proper, small town though its borough status (pre 1267) seems to have withered away so long ago that nobody seems to know when its demise occurred. Kington has never had a Parliamentary representative.

A charter granted by Edward I gave the town six fairs but by 1845 it was described thus: "If you passed through at any time other than on Market Day you would have seen the shops open, and the houses open, and a few persons walking about the streets with their eyes open; but all the shops and the houses and the people therein were all asleep. Whenever a coach came the indolent, gaping, staring and yawning population came out to look and when it left the town became so quiet that the quacking of a duck could be heard from one end to the other." (Abbreviated from R. Parry's *History of Kington,* 1845).

Connecting the town to the church is Church Road. Here is the Lady Margaret Hawkins Grammar School. Something of what the illustrious John Abel designed in 1625 remains - a five-light mullioned and transomed window in the north, and the division into school room and headmaster's house - but it has been much altered and added to. Lady Margaret was the wife of the infamous Sir John Hawkins (1532-95), slave trader, privateer, and third in command of the English navy which defeated the Spanish Armada in 1588. She was of the Vaughan family and lived at Hergest Court. Today, the school still flourishes as such and is also an important social centre, with adult evening classes and performances by the local Operatic Society being held in the hall.

Opposite the school there used to be a tollhouse, the home of one Tommy Wormington, a local Chaplin-esque character of this century, who is still fondly remembered for his all-black attire and umbrella and his courteousness and concern for the health of everyone he met.

Towards the town is The Terrace, a handsome 19th century building of seven bays with a Tuscan-columned doorway. At the crossroads is the red brick Market Hall of 1885 to a design by F.R. Kempson. The tower was added in Queen Victoria's Jubilee year, 1897. The signpost in front of it is a former Victorian cast-iron water pump.

Other buildings of note in the town include: Burton House Hotel, red brick of 1851 with assembly rooms; the Chained Swan Inn, 18th century with a little pediment; the former Town Hall of 1845 by Benjamin Wishlade, giant pilasters, five-bay centre with lower wings; the Albion House Hotel, Georgian; the Oxford Arms, 17th century timber-framed with a Victorian stucco front and an assembly room, named after the Harleys, Earls of Oxford; the Corn Mill, big, four storeys, stone, brick and boarding, and the miller's house with a moon-shaped window and broken pediment; the former Iron Foundry, now a laundry, in Victoria Street; the former Workhouse of 1857, now Kingswood House, also by Wishlade, is 1/2m SSE of the town centre.

It was largely to service the iron foundry and the limestone quarries at Burlinjobb and Dolyhir, 3m WNW of Kington, that in 1820 the Brecon to Hay-on-Wye to Eardisley tramway was extended to Kington. (Brecon was linked to the South Wales coalfields by canal.). The 3ft 6" gauge lines carried tubs with a capacity of about 1.3/4 tons and they were hauled in trains by horses. Coal was brought up from South Wales and lime, foundry-ware and grain made the return trip. However, the railway came in 1857, stole the trade, and the tramway was sold to the Hereford, Hay and Brecon Railway Company in 1860. The bridge by the castle used to carry the tramroad over the Gilwern and can still be seen. The track is discernible as a raised bank in some sections and as a line of trees in others. C.R. Clinker has written a history of this tramroad.

Kington also had a considerable road-carried trade. It is on a main route into mid-Wales and in the early 19th century the tollhouse by the bridge over the River Arrow did brisk trade. So brisk that in the 1830s it attracted the attention of the Rebecca rioters. Aggrieved at having to pay to use the roads men, with blackened faces and often dressed as women, publicly protested and attacked the gates. Many drovers simply by-passed the roads and the gates, making their own trackways. The great commons (in 1845 a quarter of the parish was common land) on the surrounding hills would have been welcome overnight grazing grounds for their herds.

Livestock still feature in the local economy and in September the Kington Show attracts entries of cattle, sheep, horses, goats, dogs, vegetables and flowers of the highest standard and has a national reputation. In June the town has several attractions including an Eisteddfod, the Kington Festival and the Vale of Arrow Trotting Races.

On market days, Tuesdays, Thursdays and Saturdays, the town bustles, especially if the local football team is playing at home. During the Summer it also has a thriving tourist trade and is well known to walkers following the Offa's Dyke Path which passes through the town. A good section of the Dyke can be seen on Rushock Hill, 2m N of Kington.

The town used to have clothing, glove-making and tanning industries; now it depends largely on agricultural suppliers, some light industry, the market and tourism.

Hergest Croft lies 1/2m W of the town on the lower slopes of Hergest Ridge in the valley of the Gilwern. It has a large collection of different species of rhododendron and is home to the National Collection of Maples and Birches.

Hergest Court, and its phalanx of barns, stand close to the River Arrow, 1.1/4m SW of Kington, between Bredward and Lower Hergest. The 'L'-shaped, somewhat forbidding, house was once much larger. The oldest part is the stone range with a two-centred-head doorway, the old home of the Vaughan family; the closely set timbered range is probably of the 15th century.

The 15th century lord, Thomas Vaughan, was killed at the Battle of Banbury in 1469, during the Wars of the Roses. He became known as Black Vaughan. Why, is something of a mystery. There are no historical documents relating to any of the wickedness attributed to him; indeed there are virtually no specific stories of his misdeeds. But, as far as tradition is concerned, he was an evil man. So bad, they say, that after his death his ghostly spirit returned and caused all manner of mishaps in the area - causing a farmer's hay wagon to overturn, becoming a fly and tormenting horses, entering the church as a bull, and other minor mischiefs. The spirit was laid by parsons with 12 candles who prayed and talked it down to a small size, put it in a snuff box and buried it beneath a large stone in Hergest Pool.

In the early 1990s Roy Palmer was told by the wife of the present owner that her husband planned to fill in the pool, which lies between the road and the house. However, on the day that the JCBs arrived the water began to bubble ominously and the owner changed his mind and left well alone.

Another tale relates to Vaughan's Oak Tree. Here he stood to admire the deer in his park. Where he stood the grass refused to grow long after his death and the man who cut down the tree went mad and ended his life in a lunatic asylum.

Thomas Vaughan's wife was called Ellen the Terrible. This is rather unfair because she was, it seems, a good and honourable woman. She did have her moment though. Her brother, David, was murdered at Llanbister and his assailant, John Hir, evaded punishment. To exact retribution Ellen attended an archery contest in disguise and shot the culprit at point blank range. Accidents do happen, don't they?

Now, as if all this were not enough, the wretched Vaughans had to tolerate the baying of a great black hound, a Cwn Annwn, a 'Hound of Hell'. This jet-black dog is said to have belonged to Black Vaughan and to have been his faithful companion, ever at his side. He had his own room at the top of the house and he is often heard clanking his chain there at the dead of night. Whenever he appears to the sight of man it is a portent that a member of the family is about to die. His favourite watering place was a pond on the high road from Kington, a dreaded spot and best avoided.

Sir Arthur Conan Doyle, the author of the Sherlock Holmes stories, stayed at Hergest Croft and knew of the Black Dog of Hergest. He would also have heard of the Baskerville family, lords of nearby Eardisley, hence, everyone presumes, The *Hound of the Baskervilles.*

Another, and much more important, literary work has associations with Hergest Court, for it was here that Charlotte Guest discovered a red book which contained the manuscripts of a number of mediaeval Welsh mythological stories. This is now called *The Red Book of Hergest* and is held at Jesus College, Oxford. The manuscripts were written in the period 1375-1425 but the stories have their roots in very ancient Celtic times. *The Red Book of Hergest,* together with *The White Book of Rhydderch* (1300-25), constitute what in modern times has been called *The Mabinogeon.*

"The eleven stories of *The Mabinogeon* are amongst the finest flowerings of the Celtic genius and are a masterpiece of our mediaeval European literature," so wrote Gwyn Jones and Thomas Jones in the introduction to their translation of *The Mabinogeon,* published in the Everyman's Library series by Dent.

To this day there must be many literary, musical, ethnological and artistic gems lurking unkown or forgotten in the libraries of old border country houses. Some kind of investigative survey by a panel of travelling experts ought to be undertaken, funded perhaps by National Lottery money. Your author will never forget that, whilst working on his *Staffordshire and the Black Country* gazetteer, he learned that the departing squire of Swythamley Hall burned all the family's ancient estate records. He did this unthinkingly, not realising their historical value. Recent research has shown that another great mediaeval poem - *Sir Gawain and the Green Knight* - was set on the lands of the Swythamley estate. What a loss.

Across the road from Hergest Court there is a series of watercourses, controlled by a sluice gate up river. These were used to irrigate the land and, also, at times, to flood the fields turning them into nutrient rich water-meadows. The Vaughan family were pioneers of such agricultural-cum-industrial waterworks and in the early 17th century Roland Vaughan designed and operated a complex system in the Golden Valley. (See Peterchurch.)

On the hillside at Lower Hergest, 200 yards W of the Court, is Castle Twts (SO 277 555), a small Norman motte and bailey castle. It stands on an irregularly-shaped hillock of which the sides were probably steepened, and measures about 8ft in height and 57ft in diameter at the base. The south part of the top was roughly levelled to form a bailey. The total defended area does not exceed half an acre.

A track leads past the castle and The Bage up to the top of Hergest Ridge and the area called Whetstone. Here there is a large rock. Local lore has it that this rock goes down to the Hindwell Brook to drink, every morning that it hears the cock crow. It is also believed that during the great plague of 1366 a weekly market was held in this high place. To avoid the infection farmers would place wheat (hence whet) near the stone and retire. The townspeople would then take the goods and leave coins on the stone in payment.

In modern times the slopes of Bradnor Hill, north of Kington, were home to Mike Oldfield, the musician whose composition *Tubular Bells* made him a small fortune and started the home studio boom, which is now so much a part of the popular music business He also wrote a piece called *Hergest Ridge,* which dominates the view from his old home. This is now called the Beacon Country House Hotel. It adjoins the Kington Golf Club, established in 1924.

Above: Leintwardine, the River Teme, the bridge and the Lion Hotel.
Left: Ledbury, houses in Back Lane c.1900, demolished in the 1960s.
Below: Kinnersley Castle, the drawing room with ceiling and fireplace of the 1590s

Another artiste with Kington connections is Stephen Kemble, brother of the more famous John Kemble, who was born here and worked at a chemist's shop before joining a travelling company of actors. He is buried at Durham Cathedral.

Being situated in relatively remote border country it is not surprising that old customs, traditions and superstitions lingered long in the Kington district. Here is a kaleidoscope: Stanmer Rocks, the Devil has a garden here where nothing will grow; a Kington tailor made a suit for a man with cloven feet (the Devil) but was saved from selling his soul by refusing to accept payment.

Fairies inhabit the area, playing tricks, being quarrelsome and often frisking and dancing in companies; a girl coming home late from a ball passed the Dancing Gates at Kington where she heard beautiful music, was caught up in a fairy ring and disappeared; Jack with a Lantern is seen in marshy places and draws travellers to their doom; if you had misfortune through being bewitched you took the heart of an animal, stuck pins in it and burned it on a wood fire, whereupon the witch would be compelled to make herself known.

Into this century the custom of Burning the Bush was practised whereby a globe of hawthorn was hung up for a year, burned on New Year's morning and replaced by a new one. On Shrove Tuesday and Easter Monday cockfights were held in the afternoon and in the evening there was much drinking.

Well into the 19th century it was believed by both gentry and peasantry that a corpse candle, a glow of ghostly light, precedes a death and marks a trail from the house of the person to the place they are to be buried; to keep away evil spirits a bucket of earth should be placed beneath the bed of a dead person until they are buried; the funeral procession would take a roundabout route to the churchyard and rest the coffin on the ground for a few moments at every crossroads.

Bull-baiting and bear-baiting were great attractions on feast days, the meat of the slaughtered bulls being sold cheaply to the poor. The last bull to be baited was chained to a tree near the Crooked Well footbridge.

Talking of animals, there is a Working Horse Centre just out of Kington on the A4111 to Eardisley. We passed three cartloads of people having rather a jolly time.

There are two healing springs at Kington. The Crooked Well, SO 294 570, is on the north side of the Kington bypass. It has been covered by a wooden shed and has been tanked as a water supply since 1831. The water was used for curing ulcers and eye complaints. Holy Well is 1.1/2m NNE of Kington on the northern slopes of Bradnor Hill at SO 283 590, near the ruins of Holy Well Farm. It lies at the end of a sunken track and is a wishing well.

At Old Radnor, 3.1/2m WNW of Kington, just over the border in Wales, are the extensive Dolyhir limestone quarries. These are sometimes referred to as the Burlingjob Quarries. They are now operated by Nash Rocks Stone and Lime Company Limited, a major supplier of limestone products. They also have offices on the Rotherwas Industrial Estate, Hereford. Lime for use as a mortar, plaster and colourwash is making a comeback, especially on restoration projects. It has so many advantages over modern cement mortars and plasters that one wonders why it was ever superseded. (See Broxwood)

Mahollan Bridge, 2m SW of Kington in the Arrow valley near Hergest Court, has numerous derelict asbestos, breeze-block and brick sheds, a woe-begone horse and a tall, broad red brick water tower of four bays. It was an army camp and is now the grim home of broiler chickens. A transport yard and council houses complete the idyll. There are still wood-fringed water meadows but nature is fighting a losing battle here.

At Rushock, 1m NNE of Kington, there is a plant nursery on the main road but the settlement lies up a lane that leads to Rushock Hill. It has a good, stone-built, four-gabled house, a few old cottages, a collection of rotting motor cars, council houses and a lone dog barking but receiving no answer. Below the pastures of the hill there is a stand of pines, bent in the wind. Footpaths leads up to a good section of Offa's Dyke, built in about 784, probably as a border marker rather than a true defensive work. Between the summit of Rushock Hill and Kennel Wood there is a well-preserved section almost one mile long. In one part it has a rounded bank 26ft wide with a west ditch 13ft wide. The stretch of the dyke that faces west has a south facing dich, and that to the east, at Kennel Wood, has a north facing ditch. There does not seem to be any good strategic reason for this. It could simply be an embarrassing error on the part of one of the local landowners, each of whom had to complete a section.

KINNERSLEY *5m SE of Kington*

In 1038 it was called Cyrdes leah, from Cyneheard's leah, meaning 'Cyneheard's glade, or clearing in the woodland'. Kinnersley is a hamlet beside the A4112 and is the focal point of a rural area which includes the small settlements of Newton, Hurstley and Ailey.

They were once served by the Midland Railway that ran from Hereford to Hay-on-Wye. This opened in 1864 and closed one hundred years later. It was to Kinnersley station that Francis Kilvert travelled from Bredwardine, 3m S, where he was the vicar. He delighted in rail travel. Alas, the station now lies derelict, a forlorn monument to another, more gracious, era.

On the main road is Upper Newton, a 17th century black and white house with square framing and a gable. It now serves as a bed and breakfast establishment.

Kinnersley Castle is a mediaeval tower-house, a fortified manor, which was remodelled and extended in late Elizabethan times. It is a striking building, with a battlemented, five-storey tower surmounted by stepped brick gables. The gables were an early 17th century fashion, imported from the Low Countries. Even the gables of the stone part of the house have a veneer of brick.

The Elizabethan work was probably carried out on behalf of Roger Vaughan, who bought the estate in about 1588. In an upstairs room there is some notable plasterwork with cornucopias (goats' horns overflowing with fruit, flowers and corn) and sea serpents, and a chimney breast with the Vaughan arms and a splendid oak branch that spreads across the whole overmantle. Elsewhere in the house there is more good plasterwork.

Kinnersley Castle lost its park and woods when it became an old persons' home. But to the south-east are place names that speak of a late woodland area: Norton Wood, The Parks, Woodmanton Farm, and Ailey, 'the clearing in the wood of Ali', an Old Scandinavian name.

When we called in 1996 the castle was owned by Martin and Kate Henning. They are folk musicians and are host to a variety of musical events from French Early Music to Blowzabella reunions and local Scottish pipe band rehearsals. Nimbus, the Classical music recording company, sometimes use the Ballroom, or Great Hall, for acoustic recording sessions. The Hennings can offer accommodation and catering facilities and there really is a mediaeval atmosphere in the castle. Best of all, it is slightly in need of refurbishment; long may it remain so.

Local tradition has it that Hitler stayed here as a guest of the former owner, Lord Brockett, who was a notorious Nazi sympathizer. The good lord even had the village houses painted white so that German bombers would know to avoid his estate. He paid for new bells in the church, to the great chagrin of the villagers because every time they rang they reminded them of their errant lord of the manor. There is no doubt at all that Herr Ribbentrop stayed here. On a more congenial note the poet Elizabeth Barrett-Browning had associations with the castle.

The church of Saint James stands embowered opposite the castle. It too has a strong mediaeval stone tower attached by only one corner to the body of the church. It is probably of about 1350 and has a sturdy saddle-back roof. The oldest parts are a blocked Norman west doorway, the string course with rope moulding above this, and the string course of the north wall which is now inside the north aisle. About 1300 the Norman church acquired aisles and was much renewed. The timber porch, with its traceried bargeboards, is probably 14th century; the chancel arch is of 1868. The decoration of the nave and chancel was designed by G.F. Bodley. The reredos and the stalls have some Jacobean panels and there are monuments to William Leviot, died 1421; Francis Smalman, 1635; Lady Morgan, died 1764; and John Parkinson, died 1804.

Ailey, 1m SSW of the castle, has the local pub, The Masons' Arms. The walls are decorated with painted prayers, not the commonest of features to be found in a public house. Close to the railway station there were some mediaeval strips of land still held in the ancient way, but in the 1970s these were, alas, consolidated. South and east of Ailey is a watery plain drained by the Letton Lake, so called because an area of several square miles was, and still is to some degree, liable to flooding. No roads cross it and the farms that stand on its 'shores' have evocative names such as World's End, Waterloo and Darkley.

For a folk tale concerning a local farm worker and the Lady of Deveraux Wooton see the article on Norton Canon. A Kinnersley charm used to mend a beast that was lame is as follows:

> Our Saviour Jesus Christ trod on a marble stone.
> He said, "Flesh to flesh and bone to bone,
> Sinew to Sinew and skin to skin,
> Blood to blood, air to air,
> Each one in your place."
> In the name of the Father,
> Son and Holy Ghost,
> Amen.

It was also the custom for a widow to set a place at mealtimes for her departed husband for as long as she lived.

KINSHAM *4m E of Presteigne*
The name is probably from Cynehelm's ham. Ham(m) is Anglo-Saxon and can mean several things, most commonly either 'village' or 'settlement' or 'low lying flatland by a stream'. As the hamlet of Lower Kinsham lies at the foot of Coles Hill, formerly called Cow's Hill, on low ground beside the River Lugg, the second meaning fits rather well. In fact Kinsham, Byton and Coombe Moor stand along the eastern shore of a former glacial lake, the remains of which are a bog at Byton. As the ice sheet melted the waters were dammed by the Silurian limestone hills to the east. Finally, they burst through and formed the picturesque gorge now followed by the River Lugg.

Kinsham Court, in Upper Kinsham, stands above this wooded gorge on a site believed to have been formerly occupied by a priory. In the 15th century the estate was held by the Blaneys, but it passed to the Harleys, Earls of Oxford. and was occupied by members of that notable family. In 1812-13 Lord Byron rented the house from Lady Oxford and local tradition has it that he wrote *Childe Harold* here. His favourite place of contemplation was beneath the tree known as Byron's Cedar. Another famous tenant was the father of Florence Nightingale and she spent some of her childhood at Kinsham.

In 1910 the estate was purchased by the Arkwright family. Their fortune had been made by Sir Richard (1732-1792), the barber from Bolton, who had developed the spinning frame (not the Spinning Jenny) which made mass production of cotton goods possible. Sir John Arkwright, the poet whose Hymn of Sacrifice was sung at the burial of America's Unknown Warrior, had two sons by Lady Stephanie. One died when his submarine went down in 1942 and the other died a bachelor in 1984. The present occupant of the house is a cousin, Mrs. Susan Wood, and her family.

The church of All Saints is approached down a lovely road lined with pine, giant silver fir and larch. It is a simple building, mostly of about 1300, with no division between nave and chancel. The three-light windows are of a later date. In the floor is an ancient stone altar with crosses; the east window has some fragments of re-assembled 14th century glass; and there is a tablet to Thomas Harley, died 1738.

Lower Court stands by the river and was formerly surrounded by a moat. The stout timber-framing of the gable, the projecting upper storey, and the ogee-headed doorway are part of the 14th century house. The rest of the stone building is 17th century. The quiet waters of the Lugg in the gorge, called here Kinsham Dingle, once ran red with the blood of Lancastrian soldiers who had fled the field of the Battle of Mortimer's Cross (1461). Here, some of them were captured and slaughtered. A sharp rise on the road to Lye, 2m E, is known as Slaughterhouse Pitch where another massacre of the Lancastrians is said to have taken place.

Byton, a good 1/2m SSE of Lower Kinsham, is a hamlet at the foot of the steep slopes of Shobdon Hill. A footpath leads up to Byton Common. The slopes have been colonised by bracken but this is increasingly giving way to naturally regenerating woodland: first briar, then elder, then hazel and lastly oaks. If left alone the steeper slopes will be a natural woodland within 30 years. The tracks are made by a herd of hardy hill ponies who wander wild. From the summit there are long views. Note the swampy areas of Coombe Moor Common below, to the south-west, which was a spot favoured by prehistoric people.

The area around the confluence of the River Lugg and the Hindwell Brook had some special significance to early man. We know of three Bronze-Age round barrow burial mounds and two standing stones, and there were quite probably more now destroyed by ploughing and flooding. In the corner of a field between Lower Kinsham and the River Lugg is the Devil Stone, at SO 538 643. It has now fallen but is 9ft long and has seven probable cup marks on what were the upper and northern faces. Near the Devil Stone are two round barrows, at SO 358 641. One is about 42 yards in diameter, rises to 6ft, and is surrounded by a ditch, 9 yards wide, with an outer bank about 1.1/2 feet high; the other is very similar but only 35 yards in diameter.

At Combe, 1m SW of Lower Kinsham, is a round barrow at SO 348 635, close to the south bank of the Hindwell Brook. The mound is circular, about 40 yards in diameter and rises about 8ft above the ditch, which is 6ft deep. It might have been used as a Norman motte and bailey castle, and is marked as such on the Ordnance Survey map. A fallen Standing Stone lies in the water meadows south of the River Lugg between Combe and Combe Manor, about 300 yards north of the B4362 at SO 357 635. It is nearly 5ft long and 2.1/2ft wide.

The B4362, by the way, was part of the main route from London to Aberystwyth. This partly explains why the big houses of the area often had well-known guests taking advantage of their hospitality - Byron at Kinsham, and Wordsworth and Shelley at Eywood, near Titley, 2m S of Coombe.

(Byton has its own article.)

KNILL *3m SW of Presteigne*
The name is from the Old English cynlle, derived from cnoll, meaning 'a knoll'. It lies beside the Hindwell Brook below a steep wooded hill, on the summit of which is a large Iron-Age fortress.

Just over the border in Wales, is an area full of the marks of ancient man with at least one Roman fort, 10 tumuli, 7 standing stones and 5 Norman castles - a veritable and venerable battleground it seems. Little wonder that a particularly good section of the great earthen dyke constructed by King Offa (757-796) is to be seen here.

The hamlet of Knill has a few dwellings, a bridge over the river, an avenue of chestnut and beech trees, a sawmill, a burnt-out Elizabethan mansion and a church surrounded by tall pines. Saint Michael's has nave and chancel in one, a Norman window in the chancel, and a stubby tower. The octagonal font is of about 1200 and in the churchyard there is a preaching cross with a short, tapering shaft and a square head. There are memorials to the Walsham and Knill families, lords of Knill in mediaeval times. They lived at Knill Court, the burnt-out mansion close to the church.

It was here that Anne Garbett was born. She became the wife of Sir Samuel Romilly, the noted humanitarian reformer. He was born in London in 1757, the son of a wealthy jeweller, and was a brilliant Classical scholar. He became a lawyer, and entered Parliament where he fought for many causes including the humane slaughter of animals, the emancipation of slaves, the repeal of the death penalty for trivial offences such as pocket-picking, the repeal of the Game Laws, and the cessation of military flogging. One of the Bills he supported would have enabled a creditor to claim off the estate of a deceased debtor. Common sense, one would have thought, but the aristocracy were outraged: "Why, estates may have to be broken up". So the Bill that was finally passed only applied to the landed estates of men in commerce! Times have not changed. The common man's blood sports of cockfighting and bull-baiting are rightly banned, but the 'noble' art of fox-hunting is protected, even the baiting with terriers of animals which have gone to earth.

Sir Samuel was an erudite man, a man who could list amongst his friends the likes of Benjamin Franklin, Mira(beau and Diderot. However, the love of his life was his wife. In 1818 she became ill and died. He was so full of grief that he killed himself. Her funeral was held up and they were buried together in Knill church. A sad but lovely end to such a good and honest life.

LAYSTERS *5m NW of Leominster*
The name is spelled Leysters on the Ordnance Survey map, but whichever way it is spelt it is not understood. Two possibilites that we would like to suggest are Beacon Hill from leg, Old English meaning 'fire'; and untilled ground, from Old English laeg, meaning 'fallow'. Both leg and laeg are often corrupted to 'lay' in place names. Layster stands on a high point, hence the presence of a turf-clad reservoir tank, and the soil is dry, hence the presence of a wind-driven well.

The hamlet stands at the crossing of a minor road to Pudleston and the A4112 Leominster to Tenbury Wells road, a ridge road with streams running northwards on one side and southwards on the other. Ridge roads are almost always of prehistoric origin for early man chose the safer high ground for his trackways. Indeed Portway, the name of a cluster of dwellings 1/2m SW of Laysters, is a name often associated with ancient highways. The road traverses a land of small woods, orchards, pastures and farms dotted around the little hills.

Most of the dwellings of Layster lie along the main road. They consist of a mixture of old stone cottages and more recent red brick houses. Here, too, are the post office, the wooden but well-used village hall, and the Duke of York. The latter ought to be listed and the landlady, Clarice Coates, given divine permission to live for eternity. The stone fabric is some 400 years old and the warehouse-like bit on the right hand side once housed the pub's own brewery. The public bar is smoke-stained and has a proper coal fire, and the lounge is how lounges should be, with easy chairs and settees, brown and faded and lived in and definitely not all 'tarted up'.

The church lies 3/4m SE, next to Castle Mound, a small moated motte which measures 25ft in diameter at the base, and rises to 9ft above the ditch. Saint Andrews is "a small church below a big cedar tree. Wonderfully poetic in its peaceful, remote setting", wrote Nikolaus Pevsner. The porch protects a Norman doorway and the stone slates protect a splendid 14th century black and white roof with quatrefoils, arched braces and collar beams. The squat tower is 13th century. Other Norman remnants are a blocked window in the nave, the blocked south door, and the tub font.

A path across a field leads to the Wordsworth Stone, set in a clearing in the woods on a hillside. It marks the spot where William Wordsworth came with local friends to admire the idyllic view towards Tenbury. Paths lead down from the stone to a little dingle with a waterfall.

Hills Farm, on the main road, is a 15th century stone house which is now a bed and breakfast establishment. Cinders, 1.1/2m NE of the church, is set in this picturesque vale. It is a 14th century stone house with a two-centred arch doorway, and a chimney breast topped by a brick ,star-shaped chimney stack of about 1600. The rusticated main stack is of about 1720. Great Heath, 1m WSW of the church, near Woonton, has a cider house with a press dated at 1771. Whitehouse, 1.1/2m WSW, has a cider press thought to be from the 17th century. Moor Abbey, 1.1/2m W of the church, has a mediaeval fish pond.

The name Raddle Bank, a steep incline on the main road 2/3m NE of the crossroads at Laysters, probably means 'red bank'. To the north side of the main road there are a significant number of place names relating to woodland:

St. Katherine's Hospital
The Almshouse
Ledbury Herefordshire

Ash Farm, Wood Sutton, Redwood, Five Ashes, Hayes Farm (from the Old English haes, meaning 'a wood'), and Berrington Green (a green was a clearing in a wood). Such a cluster of names usually means that the woodland was only cleared in late mediaeval times. Robin Hood would have been quite at home here.

THE LEA *3.75m ESE of Ross-on-Wye*

The old name was The Lake, from the Old English leacc, or lec, meaning 'a stream'. It stands on the Rudhall Brook, at its junction with the A40(T) Ross to Gloucester road.

Entering from the hamlet of Ryeford, on the main road, one crosses the track of the abandoned railway and passes Castle End, a house of seven bays and two storeys with a hipped roof. The facade is probably early 18th century and it has a 17th century dovecote. For the rest there is a stand of Scots pines, a double row of electric power pylons, a young orchard, a smart new Village Hall of brick with a clock and a weather vane, the village school, the parish church, a post office, a general store, two garages and a pub.

Because of its main road position several of the older houses in the village have been taverns in the past. Today only The Crown remains. But be warned; as you sup your ale, partake of a meal, or lie in a bed at night, watch out for the phantom coach and horses that regularly passes the portals. Opposite the pub is a mediaeval hospital with a five-bay, 18th century, Queen Anne facade.

Historically, The Lea was a part of the Forest of Dean, which borders it to the south-east. Iron ore was mined in the Forest and smelted at the extensive Roman iron-working site of Ariconium, centred on Bromash, 1.1/2m NNW on the road to Hereford. Today, Lea has attracted developments of modern housing and more are planned.

The incomers will find a delightful surprise in the pink sandstone church of Saint John the Baptist. It has a 13th century tower with a 14th century spire; a 15th century north chapel and north arcade; and a massive oak chest hollowed out of one piece, with zig-zag ornament on the metalwork, and which is probably 13th century.

But the jewel in the crown here is the unique Italian white marble font, or stoup. The shallow bowl is supported by a shaft carried on the back of an elephant. The whole is wonderfully carved with saints, rams heads, curious animals engaged in combat, a mermaid and a fish, a merman, a man sailing and a border of coloured mosaic. This masterpiece was bought from a dealer by the daughter of Sarah Decima Bradney who gave it to the church in 1907 in commemoration of her mother.

Whilst compiling this guide the author had many and varied sources of information. One of the most quirky, but delightful, was the *Herefordshire Village Book* in which articles are written by members of the Women's Institute. They often come up with touches of local colour that are quite beguiling. What happened, I wonder, to the donkey man who came for a week once a year to entertain the children of The Lea. He camped with his cart in a lane and charged 3d for a donkey ride and 1d to watch his flea circus, and his dog performed tricks for free. Then he was off to the next village. Who was he, where did he come from and what happened to him and his little dog?

We left The Lea in the direction of Gloucester, through Knightshill which is really a part of The Lea, to Lea Line, a handful of cottages, yew trees and a nice Georgian house, then north up to Crews Hill. The view north is almost aerial and exposes The Lea council house estate and mobile caravan park. As we passed under the double row of electric pylons for a second time we waved farewell.

The road leads to Aston Crews, a place where six roads meet. It is a red brick and stone-built village with two hostelries: the White Hart (now called The Ha'Penny), and the Penny Farthing freehouse restaurant. Both are now owned by Marston's. At the corner of Warran Lane, 75 yards NW of the pink rendered Ha'Penny, is a good, three-bay, red brick, Georgian house of two and a half storeys with wrought iron gates. This is the home of the retired General, Sir Peter de la Billiere, ex-Director of the SAS and Commander of the British forces during the Gulf War. His autobiography, published in 1994, is entitled *Looking for Trouble*. (See An Affair of Dishonour in the Appendices.)

The road north from Aston to Linton provides lovely, long views.

LEDBURY *12m E of Hereford*

It is a complete small market town, a regional centre with a good range of traditional shops and other services such as banks, solicitors, fire brigade, police, library and medical facilities. It is a cheerful town with a wide, light High Street with two fish and chip shops, two bookshops, and some twelve ale houses. It has a poet - John Masefield was born here - and that even more scarce commodity, a railway station.

This is privately run by transport consultant Gareth Davies by agreement with British Rail. He re-opened the station in 1988. From the platforms can be seen the eastern entrance of the mile long tunnel that carries the track beneath the Silurian limestone ridge of Bradlow Hill.

The traveller who approaches by road from either the west or south is greeted by the the horrid new ring road. It follows the line of the marshy River Leadon, where bits of abandoned land alternate with dour industrial sheds. At the northern, New Mills, roundabout there is a brash outcrop of bright red brick dwellings. Here you are advised to avert your eyes and admire instead the impressive Victorian viaduct of 1861, as it strides disdainfully above the agglomerations below carrying the main line to Worcester.

Ledbury is still very much a market town, with well attended cattle and produce markets held off Bye Street every Wednesday and Saturday. On Tuesday and Saturday there are stalls under the Market House selling fresh produce. Half-day closing is on Wednesday.

The name Ledbury means 'the fort by the River Leadon'. When the Anglo-Saxons used the term 'bury' it usually related to either a prehistoric or a Roman-Age fort. The substantial earthworks of Wall Hills, an Iron-Age hill fort, stand 1.1/2m W of Ledbury town centre, and the Leadon runs closer to this camp than it does the modern town. Alternatively, the bury could be a Celtic fortified religious site now occupied by Saint Michael's church.

The church was founded about 720 AD at an important road junction, where the road from Gloucester to Bromyard crossed the Hereford to Worcester and Droitwich salt road. This junction was moved in the 1740s, when the Worcester road was rebuilt and the gradient lessened. The site is irregular, and the church stands in one corner. What is more, a stream had to be diverted. There had to be a good reason for these abnormalities. The most likely is that the first missionary church was built next to a pagan temple. Saint Augustine had recommended this 'insinuation' to his missionary priests.

Hereford was the mother church of Saint Michael's. The

Norman church was constructed in the 1100s and largely rebuilt between 1230 and 1350. The detached belfry, tall with a massive base, dates from this rebuilding period. Altogether, Saint Michael's is Herefordshire's premier parish church and has cathedral-like proportions. It has a peal of eight bells and a carillon that plays hymn tunes at certain times of the day. The long nave has aisles with tall piers and the north chapel is airy, elegant and arrayed with beautiful ballflower ornament. Monuments to the notable deceased proliferate and are of the highest quality. Of particular interest is that of Edward Moulton Barrett, died 1857, the harsh father of the poet Elizabeth Barrett Browning. (See Wallington Heath.)

Overlooking the churchyard are Upper Hall and Lower Hall, once the homes of 'portioners', lay vicars who owned a portion of the church's income. Ledbury, like Ross and Bromyard, was a large manorial parish belonging to the Bishop of Hereford and needed a team of priests to service it. This Anglo-Saxon system lingered on in Ledbury. The Upper Hall has all but become part of the Grammar School; Lower Hall has a five-bay Georgian front, a pediment with lunette windows and a segment-headed window.

A settlement had grown up by the church in Anglo-Saxon times and a market was held on the village green at Church Lane. In 1138 King Stephen granted a Charter and the market was moved to the triangle between Upper and Lower Crosses.

In 1232 Hugh Foliat, Bishop of Hereford, founded Saint Katherine's Hospital to care for the needs of the sick and aged, and travellers and pilgrims. It occupied the site of the Bishop's Palace and consisted of one large hall with beds along two walls and a chapel at one end. Farm and service buildings were attached. The Katherine of the dedication was Saint Katherine of Alexandria, not the local Saint Katherine of Audley, who was, in fact, never canonised. Only the old sandstone part of the building that we see today is of the 14th century; the left front is by Sir Robert Smirke of 1822 and the right front is of 1866. The old part lies at right angles to the front.

The town was developed by the bishops and 12ft wide burgage plots were laid out in Homend, along the High Street sides of the Market Square. These burgage plots were often up to 100 yards in depth. An alley between two shops on the east side of the High Street leads to Worcester Street and follows the line of the burgage plots. Later, many of the plots were developed and small slum-like houses were crammed in. Witness a door plate in Homend that reads Nos. 41-67; access to these were gained down Smoke Alley.

During the 13th century the settlement grew steadily. After the deprivations of the plague it flourished, and after the Reformation it did especially well, when church lands were sold and civic affairs were run by men of commerce.

The later 16th century saw a revival in the cloth and leather working trades and the townspeople built some of the finest ranges of Jacobean timber-framed houses in Herefordshire. Of this time are The Talbot Hotel; the famous 'house on stilts' in New Street, the most romantic building in the town; the pretty Steppes; Ledbury Park, of about 1600, a large, handsome, black and white town house with close set uprights and at the rear a substantial range of brick outbuildings that back on to open land and woods; the Feathers Hotel, of about 1570 extended in the 17th century, which plays host to the Ledbury Hunt on Boxing Day; the impressive Market House, c.1620-c.1660, attributed, without documentary evidence, to John Abel, which stands on 16 tall pillars of Spanish chestnut; and Church House, of about 1600.

Church House is at the top of Church Street, one of the most attractive and best preserved mediaeval lanes in England. A cobbled path curves up a gentle slope and passes between jettied black and white buildings on both sides. These include the 15th century former council offices and the Ledbury Heritage Centre located in a meeting house-cum-market hall of about 1500, which was later used as the Grammar School. Here, too, is the re-erected 16th century Butcher's Row house, now used as a folk museum. The lane frames to perfection the tall, elegant spire of Saint Michael. The whole is architecturally exquisite and is frequently used as a film set.

On the first floor of No. 1 Church Lane there is a painted room. The murals and 'uplifting texts' are painted on the plaster between the oak framing and date from about 1560. They were discovered in 1988 beneath many layers of old plaster, paint and wallpaper.

The town has had its moments of high drama. During the Civil War there were skirmishes between Prince Rupert and Colonel Massey, in 1644, and between Scudamore and his Royalists and Major Hopton. In 1735 most of the Ledbury turnpike gates were destroyed by mobs angered at the high tolls charged. The problem in Ledbury was exacerbated because all the roads into the town had toll-gates. Three of the rioters were caught and hanged.

In the 1730s the wool trade went into decline, partly because of imports from the east, but also because the production and processing of agricultural produce, such as grain, cider apples and hops, was more commercially rewarding.

By 1798 the canal linking Ledbury to the River Severn at Gloucester had been constructed, though it suffered from a shortage of water until linked to the River Frome in 1830. The canal was superseded by the railway which arrived here from Gloucester in 1885 and in places actually used the track of the by then disused canal.

In the early 19th century the two lines of infill shops that had developed in the centre of the mediaeval market place (now the High Street) were demolished. The major part of this development was called Butcher's Row. It was not a pleasant place, for here pigs were butchered - their terrified screams causing distress to the townspeople - and the fires, used to singe the hair from their skins, were a danger to passers-by.

It is nice to see the old brick-built Workhouse of 1836 preserved. In plan it has the shape of a cross and was constructed to a Late Classical design with a gable pediment. The Union Workhouses were loathed. The regime was harsh and the inmates felt totally disgraced. Many years ago I remember talking to an old man in Shropshire who could not bear to enter the local hospital to see his ill wife because the premises used to be the Workhouse. "Nothing in this world, nor in heaven, nor in hell, would get me to set foot in that place." Today, Ledbury Workhouse is called Bell Orchard House.

The local saint, Saint Katherine, has been mentioned but here is her story in more detail. Her proper title and name is Blessed Katherine of Audley. Despite the legends that are attached to her name she was an historical person. She was born in 1272 to the wife of Sir John Giffard of Brimpsfield in Gloucestershire. At the age of 15 she married Sir Nicholas Audley of Audley, Staffordshire, but in 1299 both her husband and her father died leaving her with substantial estates in Staffordshire, Cheshire and Shropshire and the castle and town of Llandovery. (Your author once recorded an L.P. of solo guitar music in the church hall there.) In 1308 she gave these to her son in return for an annuity of £100.

She then went to live at Much Marcle, either at Hellens or Audley Cottage and it was there that she had the revelation that she should only make her home in a place where she heard bells ringing, without them being rung by man. She set off on her wanderings with her maid, Mabel, and arrived at Ledbury. It was evening and they sat on a stone to rest. This stone was later called Cattern's Stone and stood in Cattern's Meadow, next to Mabel's Furlong (now a street name).

Whilst resting they heard the bells of Saint Michael's ringing. Mabel could find no bellringers, probably because she did not realize that they would have been in the detached belfry. Katherine's revelation fulfilled she and Mabel spent the rest of their days in two hermitages at Hazel Farm living on herbs and milk. It is said that Katherine was a cousin of King Edward II. Whether for this reason or as a reward for her piety he granted Katherine an income of £30 a year.

It is said that Katherine had a mare and colt stolen from her. The thief, a girl, led the horses down several brooks to avoid leaving tracks, but Katherine prayed that their hooves would leave marks wherever they trod and her prayer was answered. The tracks were followed and the horses were found at Ledbury. This tale is offered as an explanation for the 'whirl-holes' created by pebbles spinning around and wearing circular depressions in the beds of local streams, in particular the Sapey Brook.

John Edmund Masefield (1875-1967) was born at Ledbury and spent an idyllic childhood at The Knapp, in which a relative still lives. After a short spell as a mercantile seaman and factory worker in America he published *Salt Water Ballads* in 1902. It was an instant success and from 1906 he was able to earn his living as a writer. In 1911 he published the first of his long narrative ballads, *The Everlasting Mercy*, which told of the conversion of a village drunkard. He also wrote novels and plays and in 1930 he followed Robert Bridges as Poet Laureate. Memories of his early life in Ledbury and the surrounding countryside pervade many of his works. He was not just born here; he was made here. Even so, he managed to keep a sense of compassion not commonly found in country people. This is the last verse of *The Towerer*, the story of a shoot:

"I think of the towering bird with its choking lung,
  Its bursting heart, its struggle to scale the sky,
  And wonder when we shall all be tried and hung
  For the blue September crime when we made it die".

William Wordsworth (1770-1850) made frequent visits to Herefordshire. (See Brinsop, Laysters and Kimbolton). He undoubtedly knew Ledbury and wrote a poem about Katherine of Audley.

William Langland (c.1330-c.1386), the author of *Piers Ploughman*, has been claimed to be a son of several places in Herefordshire and south Shropshire. No one knows where he was born but one claimant is Ledbury, largely because of a farm called Langlands.

The custom of lighting 13 fires on Twelfth Night was practised at Ledbury. The 13th fire was called Old Meg; elsewhere the 12 fires represented the disciples and the 13th Judas Iscariot. As the Ledbury revellers drank good cheer they sang a song that concluded:

"The leaves they are green, and the nuts they are brown,
  They all hang so high they cannot come down.
  They cannot come down until the next year,
  So thee eat thy oats and we'll drink our beer."

Traditional arts lingered long at Ledbury. Street ballad singing was commented on by John Masefield and Vaughan Williams in the early 20th century, and in Thomas Ward the town had a leading regional broadside printer. Mumming plays were familiar to Masefield who makes allusion to them in his poems, and recollections of Morris dancing in the town were recorded in the 1960s by Dave Jones of Putley, who also noted several songs from old singers. Today, the Silurian Border Morrismen are no strangers to the streets of Ledbury, and the August Bank Holiday Carnival has been revived.

At the Ledbury Easter Folk Fair of 1989 the ancient custom of heaving was re-enacted. A woman is placed in a chair and lifted, or heaved, into the air by a gang of men - and vice versa. The ceremony was probably originally connected to the raising of Christ from the dead (or the Green Man or earlier days), but has long been a fun thing, though not without a touch of lewdity being involved.

A more ancient fair is the Ledbury Mop held in October. This is now a pleasure fair but was originally the annual Hiring Fair, where servants and farm workers came to be hired. Flush with pay and a new year's contract signed, the evening was one in which "the very devils in hell would delight and be satisfied with the orgies and revels that follow", wrote the Reverend E. Jackson in 1860.

Mind you, his brother-in-trade, the Reverend John Jackson, the vicar of Ledbury in 1869, might have had more sympathy. He was charged with fathering illegitimate children and suspended for two years. He was finally officially exonerated, but not in the eyes of some of his parishioners who set up a new 'tin church' in New Street. They even refused to be buried in his church, and made arrangements at Eastnor, until the Reverend died in 1891. He has two memorials: a pulpit carved by his own hand in the church, and a ribald ballad which has some currency amongst revivalist folk singers and is performed by Roy Palmer on the C.D. *Songs & Dance Tunes of Herefordshire*, MR 76, published by your author.

Wall Hills Camp is an Iron-Age hill fort that stands 1.1/2m W of Ledbury and can be approached along a farm track from the road east of Flights Farm. It is defended to the south and west by steep scarps. The inner enclosure of 9 acres is defended by double ramparts and a ditch partly filled with water with east and west entrances. A further area of 16 acres to the north is defended by a less clearly defined single rampart and ditch. This outer enclosure has two in-turned entrances.

South of the fort by half a mile is the large, gleaming Just Juice factory. The air is heavy with fruity flavours. Adjoining it to the west are large, flat, arable fields and pastures with low hedges. North of the town, at Beggars Ash, there is another fruit factory, Wye Fruit Limited, packers, close to the European Aviation works.

LEINTHALL EARLS *6.5m W of Ludlow*
The settlement is most easily approached off the A4110, south of Wigmore. The name means 'the halh on the Lent held by the Earl'. A halh is Old English for 'a secret, hidden place', and Lent is presumed to be the old name of the stream beside which it stands, derived from the Welsh lliant meaning 'a torrent, a stream'. The Earl would have been Roger Mortimer, Earl of March, whose family caput

Above: Leominster, the old Market Hall, moved and now called the Grange.
Right: Leominster Priory church, the late 13th century silver chalice, stolen in 1996.
Below: Leominster, the Chequers Inn, Etnam Street.

was at nearby Wigmore Castle, and who owned vast etates.

We approached from Yatton, a somewhat marshy little place with a few cottages hugging the laneside and a Bronze-Age round barrow on the lower slopes of Yatton Hill, at SO 437 669.

We were greeted at Leinthall Earls by a handsome, heavy, timber-framed farmhouse with pink-washed infill, and a good stone barn that stands aghast at the array of modern black sheds it has been given for company by the owner of Gatley Farms.

The village has a charming, small Norman church, a restored 17th century almshouse, and, amongst other timber-framed buildings, the old school which closed in 1962. They lie in a secluded valley with the wooded heights of Leinthall Common and Croft Ambrey hill fort to the south, and the steep slopes of Gatley Park to the north. Both hills have been extensively quarried for limestone. Two small, conical hills between Croft Ambrey and Bolstone are said to have been formed by the Devil, who was walking in the valley when it was very muddy and kicked the mud from his heels.

The humble and time-worn church of Saint Andrew has a nave and chancel in one, and an octagonal timber bellcote with a conical roof. The chancel has two Norman windows and the nave has an undecorated Norman doorway. The west gable is timber-framed and the roof is tie-beamed with queenposts. The pulpit is Jacobean. Simple country churches always seem to be more in tune with the spirit of Christianity than ornate cathedrals.

Gatley Park stands a landlordly 1/2m NE of the church in an idyllic setting sheltered by woods. It was an old timber-framed hunting lodge which was bricked around and extended by Sir Sampson Eure, a wealthy London merchant, in 1634-37. It is a square house with a porch to which additions were made in 1894 and later. The windows are mullioned and transomed, and it has two storeys. Gatley Park is the home of Thomas and Henrietta Dunne. Captain Dunne is the Lord Lieutenant of the County of Hereford and Worcester and his family has been here for many generations. Members of the royal family sometimes stay at Gatley Park where the Princes of Edinburgh and Wales can participate in a variety of country pursiuts.

The entrance drive from the village passes through an avenue of the most magnificently gnarled trees and winds up through lovely woods, home to a multitude of game birds. It was not so long ago that I thought people cultivated pheasants for their ornamental beauty, innocent that I was.

The Dunnes own the big limestone quarry that dusts the hedges white, and attracts large lorries which deposit white mud on the lanes. It is, of course, sited close to the village houses and not their own. The rock is broken up for use as roadstone and the quarry has been operating for about 35 years. Today it is worked by Johnsons of Kingsland who pay a tonnage royalty to the Dunnes.

On leaving the village we took the lane that heads northeast and passes up a valley. At the head of this is a round, stone-built tower house (SO 457 688) with low side wings and a domed cap. This is at Wylde, which consists of nothing more than two cottages and Dion's Court. This Round House is also called The Folly and was built in 1963. We arrived on a cold January evening just as the sun was setting beyond the misty, western hills. The long view down the valley was magical. It was stunning. Little wonder that the royals are said to stay here.

If one then proceeds over the ridge, and down into the valley on the other side, one passes through meadows unencumbered by fences or hedges and flanked by sporting woods, typically graceful estate land, almost park-like. However, it was in these serene surroundings that a very rare Red Kite was killed by a gamekeeper some years ago. This magnificent bird of prey had taken bait laced with an illegal poison and the case was widely reported both in the newspapers and on television. The authorities were especially shocked at this callous act because conservation groups had been trying to re-establish this once common bird, which had been hunted to the point of extinction in Britain. The Red Kite was down to five breeding pairs in Wales but by 1990 had been brought up to 50 pairs through the efforts of the R.S.P.B. The society says that, at worst, the owners of sporting estates encourage the use of poison and, at best, turn a blind eye. It is pressure from them that causes gamekeepers to act so barbarously to protect their pheasants for the Winter shoots.

Endrin, the poison used by John Noble, Captain Dunne's gamekeeper, is lethal in even very small amounts and causes a lingering and agonising death. Noble pleaded guilty and was fined £600 with £300 costs. That was for the killing of the red kite which had eaten a dead pheasant laced with Endrin. It did not cover the four dogs known to have been poisoned by him - two of his own, one of a policeman, and the 1988 champion gun dog of the Midlands - or the several cats that had gone mysteriously missing.

All this had been going on under the eyes of Captain Dunne who was then, and still is, the president of the Herefordshire Nature Trust. John Noble, the gamekeeper, had obtained his poison from Michael Baker, a gamekeeper of Mill Lane, Much Cowarne. The prosecutions were brought by the Ministry of Agriculture and Fisheries. What, with the Dunne's servants poisoning Red Kites, and the Perrier woman of Downton shooting domestic cats, the pheasant breeders of Herefordshire have something to answer for.

But to continue our journey. Just as the lane starts to climb uphill is Oldfield Farm, a half-timbered yeoman's house, that was in the last stages of being restored to a very high standard when we saw it. The owner is Lady Vestey of London who intends to use Oldfield as a weekend cottage.

The country here really is picturesque. We travelled on past a patch of blasted heath with brown bracken and spiky trees, and the conifers of High Collis. At the Goggin we turned right, past the scrubland of Brightall Common to the substantial black and white Woodhouse Farm engulfed in red brick barns and big modern sheds. The road levels out and there are long views over the Herefordshire plain; and so to Richard's Castle and the main road to Ludlow.

However, if at the Goggin you park at the track that commences at SO 471 700, there is a good walk in lovely country up to Hanway Common. This is a high meadow where locals will tell you that The Colonel, winner of the 1886 Grand National, was trained. Altitude training in 1886! There are superb views from up here. Tracks lead north-east through Haye Park Wood to Climbing Jack Common. The name is from Climber's Oak; oak is traditionally pronounced ake, from the Anglo-Saxon ac.

LEINTHALL STARKES *6m WSW of Ludlow*
The name Leinthall has been explained with Leinthall Earls. This is part of the land held by a mediaeval tenant

called Stercher, a personal name. It stands on the southern edge of the Vale of Wigmore.

As the ice melted at the end of the last Ice Age, flood waters formed a lake stretching from Leinthall Starkes and Wigmore, in the south, to Adbaston, in the north-west, and Burrington, in the north-east. The waters finally escaped by eroding a gorge through the limestone hills at Downton in the north. The old shore line can be seen from a lane running southwards from Leinthall Starkes. The village straggles along the road: cottages and farms of stone, some timber-framing, including a pair of crucks, and a few red brick houses.

The church of Saint Mary Magdalene stands isolated on lower ground in a field, 1/4m ENE of the settlement. There are some mounds near the church that could be the remains of an abandoned village. Saint Mary's has four tall yew trees for company, two at each end. The only other building in sight is the Round House tower on the wooded ridge of Gatley Long Coppice just to the south. (See Leinthal Earls.) By Norman hands are the nave, the lower chancel and its windows, and the wide plain south doorway. The other windows are 13th century but have been restored. The 17th century bellcote houses a 14th century bell. The rood screen and the nave roof are 15th century.

The village, often called Long Leinthall by local people, once had: a school, founded in 1704, which closed in 1946 and is now a house; a pub, the Fox Inn, now a house; a corrugated iron Methodist Chapel, removed elsewhere; a blacksmith and a wheelwright. In 1841 there were 147 inhabitantsin the parish; in 1971 this had declined to 70.

LEINTWARDINE *7m E of Ludlow*

Leintwardine is a most attractive village situated just to the east of the confluence of the rivers Teme and Clun. The name is Celtic and means 'the homestead by the fast-flowing river'. The Teme is crossed by a handsome stone bridge and adjacent to this is the village green. Otters and kingfishers have been seen hereabouts, providing competition for the human anglers - pity the poor fish.

The Roman settlement of Bravinium lay within a rectangular, 10-acre enclosure. Most of this has been built over but parts of the north-west banks survive and the site of a bath house has been located near to Griffiths' Garage. Finds include coarse pottery, Samian ware, roof tiles, coins and a bronze ring.

The village lies on a slope and is centred on the area between Watling Street and High Street. Its present configuration is that of a planned Norman town. Indeed, Leintwardine could almost be called a town. It has a bank, a post office, a new primary school, a number of shops, a social centre (in the stone-built school of 1845), streets of good-looking houses, the Lion Hotel, a village green, a fish and chip shop, a fire station, a tiny Methodist Hall of 1992, a small industrial estate (in Paytoe Lane), and a large, handsome church.

Saint Mary Magdalene stands on the site of an Anglo-Saxon chapel. It has been much restored but amongst the older parts are: the 12th century, blocked, west wall doorway; the 13th century south arcade and doorway; and the 14th century north arcade. The font is of about 1350, and the choir stalls probably came from Wigmore Abbey after the Dissolution.

Sir Banastre Tarleton has a wall monument. He was a curious mixture. Strong, handsome, an expert cavalryman, courageous and daring, he fought in the American War of Independence and achieved considerable fame for his exploits. He became an M.P. for Liverpool, held military commands in Portugal and Ireland and then made himself a laughing stock by writing a book which claimed that had he been properly supported by Lord Cornwallis, he could have kept the United States as a British colony.

On the northern fringe of the settlement, beside the A4113, is The Plough, a 16th century, timber-framed and thatched farmhouse that was formerly an inn. Leintwardine Manor, a good 1/2m N of the church, is an irregular, Victorian-looking, stone-built house with a slate roof and incongruous plastic-framed windows. Opposite, in Dark Lane, is the hulk of Wheatstone, a run-down Victorian, villa, and across the road is a small lake with swans.

Stormer Hall, 1.1/4m N of the church, is a modest Victorian stone-built house of four bays with two bay windows, a gable over the porch and a slate roof, which stands amongst conifers and specimen trees. Behind it there are very substantial stone farm buildings with red brick dressings. The complex has been built over the line of the Roman Watling Street.

Marlow, 2m NNW of Leintwardine church, consists of a derelict roadside cottage with a stag plaque in the gable, a couple of cottages and a stone-built farm with red brick dressings and modern extensions. It looks very old at the back. There are beef cattle in the sheds and sheep in the fields.

Kinton, 1/2m NNE, and Whitton, 1/2m E of the church, are unspoilt hamlets of stone farms and timber-framed and thatched cottages amongst sheep pastures at the foot of the Downton hills. Much of the land around here is part of the Downton Castle estate, now owned by the French Perrier Water family.

Heath House, 2m NW, is a mid-17th century mansion built of brick using the English bond, that is, alternating layers of headers and stretchers. It has eight bays, two storeys, a hipped roof with dormers, a doorway with tapering pilasters, and two projecting wings to the north.

The Leintwardine Fishery, 1m SSE, is a commercial enterprise that utilises the gentle waters of the River Teme for a considerable stretch.

LEOMINSTER *11m N of Hereford*

The first element of the name is from the Old English Leon, the old name of the district on the Rivers Arrow and Lugg. This is also preserved in other names in the area where it has become 'land', such as Eardisland, Kingsland, Monkland;and as Lyon in Lyonshall and The Leen, a farm near Pembridge. The Old English leon is from the Celtic-Welsh lei, 'to flow', hence stream or river.

Leominster, pronounced Lemster, lies just north of the confluence of the Arrow and the Lugg. It is Herefordshire's second town and could easily have been its first. "Rather quiet and rather a lot of antique shops" is often the visitor's first impression, though many tourists will have been diverted from its venerable charms by the by-passes. It is a proper town with all the usual services - including three supermarkets which have caused many shops to close - and was, indeed, the only surviving borough in the county until the re-organisation of local government in 1974.

The settlement is Anglo-Saxon in origin. These invaders from the Lowlands were at home in marshy places and utilised them as town defences. In 660 A.D. King Merewald of Mercia founded a minster here, a place which missionary priests used as a base. It stood close to the marshes on the northern fringe of the town. This was destroyed by the Danes, re-established in the 9th century and suppressed in 1046 after a notorious scandal involving the Abbess and Earl Swein, They had a protracted dalliance after he had returned from a sortie into Wales.

In 1052 Gruffydd ap Llewellyn, king of most of Wales, attacked Herefordshire to regain stolen lands and took the county. He had his headquarters at Leominster, improved the town's defences and crushed the army of Ralph, the Earl of Hereford, at Battle Bridge, now the site of the Friends' Meeting House in South Street. Gruffydd went on to capture Hereford where he killed the bishop and seven canons and plundered and destroyed the cathedral. However, the new Earl, Harold Godwinson, the future king of England, drove the Welshmen back into Wales where they turned upon their leader and assassinated him. After the Norman Conquest the church lost most of its extensive estates. In 1125 Henry I established a priory, a cell of the Benedictine Abbey at Reading, and much of the fine,if somewhat austere, church we see today dates from then. The Priory governed and controlled the town which at that time was west of the present site, by Vicarage Street, with a defensive bank and ditch along School Lane.

Leominster was a wealthy town at an important communications crossroads and constantly came under attack from both the Welsh and the Normans. Its wealth lay in the excellence of its wool, the famous Lemster Ore, renowned for its fineness. It came from a native Herefordshire breed, the Ryeland, and was highly sought after not only in England but on the Continent as well. It was lauded by poets and Queen Elizabeth I wore stockings made from Lemster Ore. The sheep is small of stature, so what are 20th century breeders doing?

By 1235 Leominster market challenged those of Hereford and Worcester. Edward I granted the town fairs and gave it two representatives in his Parliament. In the early 15th century Owain Glyndwr invaded north Herefordshire. He defeated Edward Mortimer, and it is likely that he captured Leominster and occupied the hill fort at Ivington, 2.1/2m S, near Brierley.

During the Wars of the Roses Leominster took the side of the Yorkists. In the reign of Henry VIII there was a flourishing textile industry in the town - cordwainers, glovers, mercers, tailors, tanners and fullers. In 1539 the priory was dissolved and the abbott hanged at Reading.

In 1554 Queen Elizabeth I gave Leominster its prestigious Charter of incorporation and the citizens were a municipality in their own right. However, the wool trade was in decline and despite attempts to establish a cotton industry - Daniel Bowne had built a factory but it burned down - and several other ventures, such as French hat-making, the town was described in 1830 as appearing more in a state of decay than improvement.

In 1714 the Lugg was made navigable between Leominster and Lugwardine. A basin was built at Eaton Bridge and, though flooding made navigation difficult and sometimes dangerous, it was considered safe enough to transport the priory bells to Chepstow and back for re-casting in 1750.

The short-lived Leominster-Stourport Canal of 1796, designed to link Leominster to the navigable River Severn, only got as far as the Mambles Collieries. The small remains of the Leominster terminus are about 1m N on the road to Ludlow.

In 1853 the Shrewsbury to Hereford railway line, which passed through Leominster, was opened. This was followed by the Worcester to Bromyard line which reached Leominster in 1897. Coal for the hop kilns was a major item of freight. Leominster is still the proud possessor of a railway station on the Shrewsbury to Hereford line.

The Priory church of Saint Peter and Saint Paul is built of pale, red stone, and is surrounded by the churchyard and lawns. Notable features are the Norman west door and its twin naves, one Norman with massive columns, the other of the 13th century, which was built as a parish church and has a large, richly traceried west window. In the early 14th century the south aisle was added, though some call it a third nave. The windows are lavishly decorated with ballflower ornament reflecting the wealth brought to the church by its own extensive flocks of Ryeland sheep.

All that remains of the monastic buildings are an early 14th century doorway with ball-flower which led from the north aisle to the former cloister, now half buried; and the Priory House, which could have been either the infirmary or the lavatory block. A stream runs beneath it. The west part was probably rebuilt after the Dissolution but the first floor, with small windows and a good doorway, is of the 15th century. The Priory House lies at the east end of the Old People's Home, formerly Leominster Workhouse.

A curiosity kept in the church is the town ducking stool, nearly 12 yards long when extended, and one of only a handful of working machines in England. It was last used in 1809 for a scolding wife called Sarah Secke. Most of the ancient furnishings were destroyed in a fire of 1699, and in 1996 a priceless silver chalice was stolen from its diplay case. On the north wall of the nave is a painting of the Wheel of Life, of about 1275. The handsome churchyard gates are cast-iron, made at Stourport in 1788. The gates from the Grange side are wrought-iron of 1791.

The Grange is a good point to start a tour of the town. Use the Etnam Street car park and walk to the playing fields. The raised walk on the south boundary was part of the town's mediaeval defences. Continue on to Grange Court, which now houses the offices of the local council. This exceptionally handsome building was built as the Market House by John Abel in 1633. The ground floor was originally open and it used to stand at the junction of High Street and Broad Street. In 1855 it was sold to the Arkwright family who re-erected it as a house in its present position. The Town Hall that replaced it was designed in an Italian style by James Cranston.

Pass the Priory churchyard and from the churchyard the main gate leads to Church Street, This has some excellent Georgian houses and the Forbury Chapel, the plain 13th century Chapel of Saint Thomas a Becket, now used as an auction hall. It is also used as a rehearsal room by the Forbury Consort, a recorder-harpsichord based early music group. Their director, Alan Crumpler, is a maker of musical instruments with an international reputation. He is based at Capriole Crafts, a shop in the High Street.

At the end of Church Street turn into the mediaeval Drapers Lane with its 16th century timber-framed houses and alleys running to the High Street. One arrives at Corn Square, where a market is held every Friday. The Corn Exchange is New Gothic by Cranston. Then cross to Old School Lane past more mediaeval houses and charming small shops to the Tourist Information Centre. Close by is the Folk Museum in Etnam Street. This is a voluntary enterprise and has a collection relating to the archaeology and the agriculture of the area. It is housed in a mission hall of 1855, built as a hostel for navvies working on the railway. Also in Etnam Street are the black and white Chequers Inn, the early 16th century White Lion, Dutton House, neo-Gothic of about 1850 but with a 16th century

Why Oh Wye?

I'm flowingly Wye,
I'm knowingly Wye,
I'm hurrying, scurrying,
Floodingly Wye.

What have I done?
Oh! Where is the sun
That guided my soul
To the sea?

From out of the hills,
By runnels and rills,
My waters they meet;
The earth they defeat

Like men with barbed arrows,
Like chattering sparrows,
Like rooks in the trees,
I do as I please.

Through gorges and valleys,
So steep and so flat,
I wander first this way
Then change it to that.

I curtsey to ladies,
And then doff my hat
To men in canoes
With waterproof shoes.

I gurgle and splurgle,
I cough and I sneeze
At bridges and midges,
I do as I please.

I laugh at the rain,
The winds I disdain,
For I'm homeward bound
To my burying ground.

But then I go back,
To the high mountain track,
And do it all over again.

Michael Raven 1996

core; and the Royal Oak, a late 18th century hotel with a two-storey assembly room running the length of the building.

The Apolostic church in Gateway Lane was built in 1938. The Apostolics believe that the second coming of Jesus is imminent, that they have the 'gift of tongues', and that the prophecies of Daniel and the Apocolypse will be fulfilled. Otherwise, their creed is orthodox.

There are many examples in the town of houses with some blocked windows. The Window Tax of 1747, devised by Pitt, taxed owners of houses according to the number of windows they contained, similar to the Hearth Tax of Charles II. A Leominster clergyman writing in the late 18th century said: "Our dwellings have gone into mourning and the sun cannot fully shine into their apartments." The tax was abolished in 1851.

Here are brief details of some notable houses south and west of Leominster: Broadward Hall, 1.1/2m S, is a handsome Georgian brick house of five bays and two storeys with pediment, Venetian window, Tuscan pilasters to the door and a square dovecote of 1652. (There is another Broadward Hall in Shropshire where a hoard of Iron-Age bronze swords and barbed spearheads was found. This has given its name to a military tradition which extends from south-west Wales, through Herefordshire and eastward to East Anglia.)

Stagbatch, 2.1/2m WSW of Leominster, has a 14th century cruck-truss in the north wing and a mediaeval cruck barn. Brierley Court, 2m S, is a sandstone house of the 18th century with three bays, two storeys, and a hipped roof. (See Brierley.) Cholstrey Court, 2m W, has a cruck barn.

Eaton Hall, 1m SSE, is a mid-14th century house with a hall roof of collar beams on arched braces with trefoils above. South-east of the house is a bridge across the River Lugg. It has two spans and is at least 17th century. Eaton Hall was a home to the Hakluyt family, who count amongst their numbers several Sheriffs of Herefordshire, a knight who fought for Henry V at Agincourt, and Richard, the author of *Hakluyt's Voyages*. (See Eyton.) On Eaton Hill, which stretches from Eaton Hall for a mile northwards to Ridgeway, there are some unexplained earthworks known as Castle Comfort. The name could be a corruption of Cwmffordd, Welsh for 'valley-road'.

Whilst on the subject of buildings it should be mentioned that John Scarlett Davies, the painter noted for his large scale pictures of the interiors of public buildings, was born at Leominster in 1804.

At the junction of the Lugg and the Arrow, 1.1/2m SSE of Leominster, there is an ancient common-land water meadow called the Volca, or Vokey Meadow, which is surrounded on three sides by water. The name was originally Folk Ley, 'the people's meadow'. West of Wheelbarrow Castle by 300 yards is the Volca Bridge, SO 513 573. This was built of brick in about 1750, under the Navigation Scheme, probably to replace a ford drowned by the construction of a lock lower downstream. Just north-west of the bridge is a good specimen of the rare English Black Poplar, with its characteristic down-reaching branches and gnarled bosses.

Dishley Court, 3/4m SW of Leominster centre, just beyond Ryelands, is an attractive 'barn development'. Half-timbered outbuildings have been converted into dwellings and with the four-bay, brick-built farmhouse and its friendly yew tree, form a quadrangle with lawns and small trees. This felicitous scene is only marred by the litter of cars. Newtown, 1/2m further south-west from Dishley is a hamlet, home to Classic Jaguars, which is housed in a Victorian villa with wooded grounds. In the plain below are the lush, cattle-grazed water meadows of the River Arrow, divided by wooded hedgerows.

Cursneh Hill near Cholstrey, 1.1/2m W of Leominster town centre, rises above the Pinsley Brook. According to local tradition this is the site of a battle fought in 1554 between the forces of the Duke of Northumberland, which included several local squires who championed the Protestant pretender, Lady Jane Grey, and the supporters of the newly installed Catholic Queen Mary. Northumberland was entrenched on the hill, encircled by the Catholics, and tried to break out but was defeated. The Battle of Cursneh Hill was of some small importance, though it is doubtful if it was the 'bloody massacre' of popular belief. (For a full discussion of this event, and much more besides, see *The Town in the Marches*, a most excellent history of Leominster and its environs by Norman C. Reeves.)

Here are some customs, legends and folk practices connected with Leominster. In the Bargates there are four small almshouses founded by a widow, Hester Clark, in 1736. As well as the 'official inscription' there is the roughly carved figure of a man with an axe in his hand and the words: "He that gives away all before he is dead let them take this hatchet and knock him on ye head". Local tradition has it that Hester Clark was ruined financially in building the almshouses and had to occupy one herself. The significance of the axe-man is that he is a folk memory of the pre-Celtic mallet-man. The old, infirm or anyone unable to support themselves were despatched by a blow to the head with a wooden mallet while they slept. There are examples of the carved mallet-man with similar inscriptions to ours in Germany. These have been researched by Sir Lawrence Gomme.

On a May morning on Eaton Hill "the people of Leominster and thereabouts came once a year to sport and playe", we are told by John Leland, in the mid-16th century. In Leominster as late as the 1890s the custom known elsewhere as 'riding the stang' was followed. An effigy of straw was made of an unfaithful husband or wife, placed astride a long pole and carried to the house of the offender, accompanied by a crowd banging pots and pans. A bonfire was made and the effigy burned. It seems likely that originally the real person rode the stang and only the effigy was burned (one hopes).

There is a very dubious late legend that appears to be a rather naive attempt to explain the name Leominster and at the same time show King Merewald as a gentle lion. We have no time for it.

"Trip a trap a trencher, Say the bells of Lemster", so goes an old bell rhyme.

(For Wharton see the article on Ford; and also see the appendix article on the Lower Lugg.)

LETTON (near Staunton-on-Wye) *11m WNW of Hereford*

It lies on the Hereford to Hay-on-Wye road, the A438. The name is from lece-tun, 'the settlement by the stream' and it stands beside the Letton Lake, a stream named after the extensive lowland to the north which often flooded. The pool to the south of the road is actually a truncated meander of the Wye.

Letton consists of a few dwellings, a pretty black and white cottage, a pub, the big house and the church. The treasure of Saint John the Baptist is the door. It is a handsome piece from the 12th century and still hangs on its original, elaborately worked iron hinges. It fills a narrow

Norman doorway, the large sandstone lintel of which is decorated with circles, heads and stars The jambs have zig-zag ornament. The doorway in the west wall is also Norman, with a tufa frieze and a tympanum, and there is some herringbone masonry on the north side. The Norman chancel was rebuilt and extended in about 1300. The Herefordshire style thee-light east window and the chancel tomb recess are of this date.

The transepts were added in the 14th century making the church cruciform. The lower part of the tower is also 14th century; the boarded belfry is 17th century. There are three more tomb recesses, one with ballflower decoration in the east wall, and two in the south wall The pulpit, complete with tester, and reader's desk, are 18th century and of the highest quality. The benches are Jacobean.

Mick Saunders, of Waterloo Lane, makes Celtic harps in the £400 to £1,000 range, distributed by Hobgoblin.

LETTON (near Brampton Bryan) *9m WSW of Ludlow*
The Domesday name was Lectune, from leoht, Anglo-Saxon for 'light', hence 'settlement in a light place'. It is a tiny hamlet in a broad valley on the road between Walford and Lingen. To the west are the wooded hills of Brampton Bryan Park. To the east are the conifer-clad slopes of the Wigmore Rolls, beyond which lie the romantic ruins of the mediaeval Mortimer's castle at Wigmore.

The stone gate posts of a house in the settlement contain pieces of 12th and 13th century sculpture taken from Wigmore Castle. They include friezes decorated with lozenges and an excellent stiff-leaf capital of about 1235. Lodge Farm, 1m SSE, is a timber-framed house with close-set framing of about 1700. A track from Letton ends unceremoniously at a mound 200 yards NE of Lodge Farm.

Britley, 1m SW of Letton, is a place name with a similar meaning to Letton; it is from beorhte-leah, meaning 'bright field'.

At Pedwardine, a red brick farmhouse 2/3m WNW of Letton, are the mounds of two Norman motte and bailey castles. Pedwardine probably means 'Peoda's dairy farm', an important one it seems, judging by the defensive attention it received. The fields are undulating, some arable, some sheep pastures, with oaks in the hedgerows and little wooded knolls on the slopes above. There are some very small fields and the road is of the 'enclosure type' with grass verges and hawthorn hedges. Indeed, the whole area is known for its well-preserved, late enclosure features dating from the 1820s.

LIMEBROOK *4m ENE of Presteigne*
In 1221 it was called Lingebrok. It stands on the Lingen Brook. Lingen is from the Welsh llyn-gain, meaning 'water-beautiful', hence 'stream with clear water'.

Limebrook lies hidden in lovely, wooded, hill country, 1/2m N of the gorge of the River Lugg. (See Kinsham.) The hamlet consists of little more than a ramshackle stone farm with chickens running wild, and Limebrook Cottage. This is a 16th century timber-framed dwelling with some moulded beams, and a handsomely carved length of barge-boarding on the stairway. These doubtless came from the small, stone-built priory a few yards away. The priory now lies in ruins, just two small sections of upstanding walls and a doorway, and grass covered mounds.

Augustinian canonesses came here in 1190 when Ralph of Lingen founded the house and granted them land. They were further endowed by the Mortimers of nearby Wigmore and, by the Dissolution in 1539, had a goodly estate with some rich farmland. They might well have been the builders of the stone bridge over the River Lugg, 3/4m SE, mentioned by Leland, and Upper Limebrook Farm, 1/2m N, was almost certainly one of their farms. It has three cruck trusses. A very rare herb, the asarabacca, used for medicinal purposes, has been found growing wild near the priory. Coincidentally, the present occupant of Limebrook Cottage is a herbalist.

Chapel Farm, 2m NE, is said to be the first home of the Limebrook nuns. The house we see today has a 15th century hall, which was later divided by inserting a first floor. The original roof of tie-beams, cusped brackets and wind braces remains. There are also traces of an original four-light window on the north side, and a doorway on the west side. The house is said to have been used as a refuge by the Lollard, John Oldcastle, in the early 15th century.

LINGEN *3.75m ENE of Presteigne*
It lies in sheep and cattle country in the valley of the Lingen Brook. The meaning of the name is as given for Limebrook, 1m SSE.

Lingen is a most pleasant village of black and white cottages, and weather-boarded barns. It has the Royal George; a post office-cum-general store; a yellow brick Methodist church, opened in 1877 with a grand tea party for 400; an alpine plant nursery; a Norman castle; and the parish church of Saint Michael. The castle stands by the church. The motte rises to 22ft and there is a square bailey with remains of an inner rampart. At the time of Domesday Book the manor lay in Shropshire.

The Lingen family, formerly retainers of the Mortimers of Wigmore, held the land from 1256 to 1583 when the Crown dispossessed them. They were reinstated by James I but in 1685 they sold up and the family left the area. Their house was probably the 17th century Court, close by the church. It was Ralph of Lingen who founded the priory at Limebrook, and it is Constantia, the daughter of Sir John, who features in the grim little tale related in the Much Cowarne article in this book.

The church has an old tower, thought to be 16th century, but was burnt down in 1891 and re-built shortly after to a design by H. Curzon. The nave, chancel, bell-stage and spire are of that date. The piscina in the chancel is of 1300. The pews are early 16th century with heavy roll-moulding, and are reputed to have come from the priory church at Limebrook after the Dissolution. They survived the fire of 1891, but still have scorch marks. In 1877 the churchyard was ringed with horse chestnut trees and the total ensemble really is as pretty as a picture.

The oldest house in the village is Turn Farm, 15th century black and white. The field opposite is believed to have been the pound field where stray animals were kept until claimed and the fee paid. Lingen Hall was home to the Gisborne family, the local squires from the mid-19th century until the 1940s when the estate was dispersed. There used to be a wheelwright, a cobbler, a carter, and next to the church there used to be a blacksmith's shop. The school is now a house.

At Archer's Ford, 1/3m SW of the church, is a house once occupied by stone knappers who dressed stone for buildings and roads. On the hillside above their house are six well-preserved lynchets, small terraces over 100 yards long, constructed by prehistoric farmers. Upstream is the site of a corn mill, of which no trace is left. The Church-yard, 2/3m NNE of the church, is a defensive mound, about 12ft high from the bottom of the ditch and about 40 yards in diameter at the top.

Birtley, 1.1/2m N of Lingen, is a scattered hamlet of brick houses, stone cottages, rendered dwellings and some black and white buildings. The name means 'bright field'.

From here we will take a five-mile circular trip into the hills to the west following the valley of Lingen Brook for half the journey. These are my travel notes.

"Curious brick house with a remarkable concrete and stone porch topped by reindeer antlers, somewhat dilapidated and reminding one of Miss Havisham. Past an orchard; holly in the hedges (in times past used as cattle fodder in winter); a picturesque stone and thatch cottage; a backwoods feel to the area; sheep; into the steep, wooded valley of the Lingen Brook; a quarry of shallow white stone and a conifer plantation, ran the dogs here; ancient woodland coppice of oaks and beeches; Boresford Farm, stone-built and substantial, little orchard, lambs and daffodils; head SW to Hicks Farm on right, red brick; narrow valley; to Willey Lodge, stone topped with half-timber, prominent chimney stacks, a feeling of remoteness up here; steep hill, opens out to high pastures, hill to the left, to the east is Harley's Mountain (Brampton Bryan, home of the Harley family is only 2.1/2m NNE); to a crossroads; carry straight on and you will come to Willey Hall, where there is an ancient oak with a 26ft girth, but we turn left; past a little brick primitive Methodist chapel of 1869 with lancet windows in the process of being converted to a house; high ground, long views southwards, black and white cows (you do not see many Herefords in Herefordshire); marker hollies in the hedges, to show the road line in deep snow, lovely, long views; downhill and back to Lingen.

The ruins of Willey Old Court have a tale to tell. The house was occupied by the Legge family at the time of the Civil War. One day the menfolk were in the fields bringing in the harvest. Midday came and lunch had not arrived so Mr. Legge went to the house to see what the delay was. He found that Cromwell's soldiers had come searching for the king. They had sacked his house and violated his women. Mr. Legge gathered his men, pursued the perpetrators, caught them and killed their leader with a pitchfork. The pitchfork was a Legge family heirloom for centuries after.

The hills between Lingen and Wigmore to the east are called Deerfold. From here wood was taken to fuel the iron-works at Bringewood Forge in the 16th century. The late enclosures of the 1820s have left many features: straight enclosure roads with grass verges and quickset hedges, and some very small fields. There are some charming names, too: Deepmore Farm, Cross of the Tree, Mistletoe Oak, Woodhampton Wood and Ongar Street. Ongar is from the Anglo-Saxon angr, meaning 'grazing land'.

The southern lanes from Lingen lead to Aymestry. On the way one passes through Upper Lye, a tiny hamlet with a stone-built farm, a red telephone kiosk and lovely views at every twist and turn. The lane continues past the regimented conifers of Shed Wood, through Lower Lye, which has a big black and white house with five bays and two gables, to Nether Lye, a scattered hamlet, surrounded by woods, to Ballsgate Cottage and the meandering River Lugg. A leat from the river follows the road to a rough-stone mill with a small water-wheel in an old orchard garden. But now we are in Aymestry.

LINTON-BY-ROSS *4m ENE of Ross*

The name is from the Anglo-Saxon and could mean either 'the settlement by the lime tree', or 'settlement by the flax field'. Somewhat lost in the lanes it is most easily approached off the A4221 Ross to Gloucester road. Linton stands on high ground and has long views over lovely countryside, spoiled only by the M50 which ploughs a great furrow through cuttings 200 yards north of the church. Orchards fringe the village to the east, and to the west are the lakes of Rudhall Brook and the golf course at The Fordings.

Village facilities include a post-office-cum general store, and some years ago the postmaster was also the local undertaker. Apparently it was not unusual for him to park his motorcycle and sidecar, complete with attached coffin, outside The Alma while he popped in for a quick one. The Victorian school closed its doors to pupils in 1959 and is now used as the village hall.

Linton is a long, very pleasant village of old cottages and houses with some Victorian and 20th century infill. It was in Bromash Hundred and before 1066 it belonged to King Edward the Confessor. By 1086 King William held it for himself and it was a prosperous and well populated manor.

In mediaeval times the abbey of Corneilles, in Normandy, held the church. Saint Mary's has retained some Norman fabric: a fragment of roll moulding in the south doorway; two unmoulded arches and a pier with a scrolled capital in the north arcade; and the solid wall west of the arcade which belonged to the Norman tower. The chancel, the south arcade and the south aisle are 13th century and the present tower is 14th century Perpendicular. The good, vaulted roof springs from corbels decorated with figures including a beast and a hooded man. On the tower doorway are two dragons, one scratching his ear, the other his leg. There are several coffin lids, one particularly good piece is of the 13th century with an elaborately carved cross. There are monuments to: John Elmehurst, died 1662; the Reverend Peter Senhouse, died 1760, and the Reverend Arthur Mathews, died 1841. The latter met his end by his jumping from a moving stagecoach, the horse having taken fright. Near the church is a cottage with cruck framing, the oldest dwelling in the village.

Linton is still very much a country place. Mains water and electricity did not arrive until the 1960s and 'cows and corn' are the staple local industry. The orchards are in decline but Revell's Farm has a sound fruit juice business based on the apples and blackcurrants they produce here.

Strange to think that in the 17th and 18th centuries there were iron furnaces powered by water wheels at Linton. The ore came from the Wyre Forest to the south and had been previously exploited by the Romans at their extensive iron working site centred on Bromash, 1m SW of Linton. (See Arkenfield and Bromash.)

There is an undated 130-yard-long bank and ditch located 250 yards NW of the church at Linton. In the area around this numerous finds of flint cores, scrapers and other implements have been found, indicating a Neolithic or Early Bronze-Age working floor. Linton Hill stretches for 3/4m SE of the church. It is traversed by two parallel roads alongside both of which agricultural labourers and tradesmen have built squatter cottages. In recent years many of these have been improved and extended.

To the east lies the extensive squatter development of Gorsley Common, Little Gorsley and Beavon's Hill. Northwards from Linton the road passes over the M50, past nursery gardens, whose owners disfigure the fields by covering them with plastic sheets, past windbrakes and loggers working in the woods, to Crow Hill. (See Upton Bishop.)

Opposite: Brinsop Court with Credenhill beyond.
Centre: Mordiford, Sufton Hall, home of the Hereford family, over the River Lugg.
Bottom: Shucknall and West Hide Wood over the Frome valley from Stoke Edith.

Top left: Hoarwithy, church of Saint Catherine from the road to Bromley,
Top right: Whitchurch, the Wye valley from Symonds Yat.
Centre: Bircher Common near Croft.
Bottom left: Woolhope, view on the lane to Checkley.
Bottom right: Bredwardine:, bridge over the River Wye.

Top: Eyton Common, Peter Delaney's Camp, 1996.
Centre: Abbeydore, the Grey Valley from Cockyard.
Opposite: Hope under Dinmore, Wigwood Manor under construction in 1996.

Bromyard Folk Festival, organized annually by Annie Jones and Doug Isles. Photographs: September, 1996
Top left: Jockey Morris Men dancing in the church of Saint Peter as part of the Festival Sunday morning service.
Top right: Morris musicians outside the church share a joke.
Centre: A 'session' in the bar of the Hop Pole Hotel.
Bottom left: Social dance in a marquee.
Bottom right: Saddleworth Morris Men, who wear clogs on their feet and fresh flowers on their hats.

Risbury, view east of the village looking north.

Pencombe, Westfields Farm, two miles south-west of the village.

Sutton Saint Nicholas, the River Lugg south-east of Wergin's Bridge.

Opposite: Ledbury, Church Lane, often used as a film set.
Bottom left: Hereford Cathedral grotesques.
Bottom right: Eastnor Castle, the Great Hall.

Opposite:
Kinnersley Castle.
Above:
Eastnor, a red deer.
Below:
Ganerew, Sellarsbrooke House, built 1800.
Bottom:
Norton Canon, Garnon's Hill from Upperton.

Opposite: Bodenham, Mr. H. Downes, a working blacksmith, 1995
Below: Hereford, the S.A.S Camp, 'Stirling Lines', in 1995.
Bottom left: Dinmore Manor, Richard the Lionheart, in stained glass.
Bottom right: Ford, Cook's Folly at Wharton and Mr. Ian Norris.

Top left: Colwall, the Old Rectory.
Top right: Colwall, the church of Saint James and the Alehouse.
Centre left: Fred Jordan (rear of picture), traditional singer and a regular at Bromyard Folk Festival.
Below: Pirate and Bruno and their mobile dog kennel.

The Ross-on-Wye Golf Club course is situated on this same northern side of the motorway, 1/2m NNE of Linton. It lies adjacent to Linton Wood, part of the extensive Queenswood.

Burton Court, 1m S of the church, is the local 'big house'. It is a stone building faced with an 18th century brick facade, five bays, two storeys and a pediment with lunette windows. It has large gardens in which charity events are sometimes held. Nearby is the 17th century Burton Mill on the Rudhall Brook. This was working into the 1920s but now the water wheel is overgrown and the millpond has been drained and turned to pasture.

Eccleswall Castle, 1.1/4m SSW of the church, was a Norman motte and bailey castle with four fish ponds situated to the east of the present Eccleswall Court, but today virtually nothing is left. The earthworks are barely discernible and a few fragments of stone can be hunted down in later buildings, such as the man's head above the entrance to the dovecote.

Eccleswall was the original home of the great Talbot family, scourge of the French and premier Earls of England to this day. From here they moved to Goodrich Castle. In the 18th century a junior branch of the Talbots acquired Ingestre Hall in Staffordshire by marriage. The title of Earl of Shrewsbury came to them in 1846 but some years ago the family sold up and the present premier earl, now a Black Country businessman, lives in a modest farmhouse near Uttoxeter. In the early 1990s Lord Shrewsbury spoke in the House of Lords against the introduction of the National Contaminated Land Register.

Hay Wood, 2m NE of Linton, was once part of Queen's Wood before the M50 separated them. Here there is a stand of oak trees that has been licensed by the ECC as a 'seed stand'. In the Autumn local people are employed to collect the acorns which are used for commercial propagation. Only the best and strongest trees with a proven record of resistance to pests and diseases, are licensed. The main entrance to Hay Wood is at Shaw Common, though finding your way through the tangle of lanes at Gorsley can take a bit of doing.

LITTLE BIRCH 5m S of Hereford

The name is from the Anglo-Saxon, birce, meaning 'birch', hence, 'birch wood'. Little Birch lies to the east of the A49, adjacent to King's Thorn, and is contained on the other three sides by broadleaved woodland - Aconbury Hill, Wellbrook Wood, Rough Hill Wood and Athelstan's Wood. The cutting from the Glastonbury Thorn, that gave its name to King's Thorn, is actually in a lane in Little Birch.

However, the spread of modern houses has effectively made these two places a single settlement. Between them they have two post office-cum-general stores, three garages, a village hall and community centre, a pub, a doctor's surgery, and a former Primitive Methodist.

The church of Saint Mary, at Little Birch, is of 1869 to a Geometric design by W. Chick. It has a five-sided apse; a bellcote; a Norman, cup-shaped font with rope moulding on the base of the bowl; a wrought-iron screen of about 1870; and an Elizabethan silver cup dated at 1576.

A track from the church leads down to Higgins' Well (SO 511 314). The stonework is early 19th century and it was enlarged to commemorate Queen Victoria's diamond jubilee, when the large outer pool was made for the convenience of bathers. The story goes that the well was originally higher up the hill but the owner, Mr. Higgins, had it filled in to stop villagers coming over his land for water. So, the waters broke through the floor of his house. To compromise with the water spirit Mr. Higgins dug a hole lower down the hill from which the water now flows, and everyone was happy.

The agriculture of the area is mixed cattle and sheep pastures with arable crops such as maize, barley, wheat and potatoes. There is a fruit farm and a mushroom farm but the orchards are in decline.

The Primitive Methodist Chapel lies 1m NW. It is of 1858 with arched windows and bargeboards.

LITTLE COWARNE 4m SW of Bromyard

The name Cowarne is from the Anglo-Saxon Cu-aern, 'cow-house'. The village lies by a tributary stream of the Leddon in lovely hill country west of Bromyard, and is most easily approached off the A465. Like so many country places it has lost its blacksmith, carpenter, mason, wheelwright, dressmaker, shop and cider house. Still, it does have a church and a pub, The Three Horseshoes, and a mile up the road at Pencombe there are most of the other facilities that Little Cowarne lacks. There are some modern houses, and at Bernando there is a Caravan Club Site.

At the time of the Norman Conquest the manor was held by Spirtes, a priest at the court of King Edward the Confessor, and it is thought that the base of the church tower dates from his Anglo-Saxon times. However, in the mid-19th century the roof collapsed and in 1870 the church was virtually re-built by F.R. Kempson. He retained the Norman font and a Norman window in the chancel, and a 13th century lancet in the nave, and gave it a new saddleback roof.

The court of justice of the Norman Broxash Hundred was held at Little Cowarne. Broxash was the name of a wood and the Hundred encompassed the area between Upper Sapey, Withington, Much Cowarne and Bodenham.

A 17th century occupant of Cowarne Court - the manor house, not the place of jurisdiction - was Humphrey Smith, one of the first Quakers. He travelled the country preaching and writing and gained something of a reputation as a soothsayer, the Prophet of Herefordshire. Amongst his predictions were The Great Fire of London and that the Thames would freeze over. He died of fever in Winchester Prison in 1663.

Belief in the special powers of chosen people lingers long in the country. In this century Mrs. E.M. Leather was told by an old farmer from Little Cowarne that he had a mare who had dislocated a shoulder and no one could help her. So he went to a 'charmer', a butcher who lived at Hatfield, 5.1/2m N. The man asked the mare's name and said he thought he could cure her without seeing her and within three days she was as right as rain.

In the early 19th century the large common fields were enclosed and there was a time of prosperity. The population was twice the 90 souls who live here today. Most of them were engaged in agriculture. This is orchard and hopyard country and at Little Cowarne in 1841 a third of all the farms and smallholdings had a hopyard. Little Cowarne Court has an interesting stone outbuilding of about 1600 known as The Mill, after the cider mill contained in one corner. It appears to have begun life as the original farmhouse but over the years was adapted for drying hops, with brick cone kilns being added about 1880. The bricks were made on site. The kilns were in use until 1959 and the whole building is fully described and illustrated in *A Pocketful of Hops* (1980).

Farmers these days have to be imaginative to make

ends meet. At Shortwood, 1/2m WSW of the church, there is a working dairy farm which opens its doors to the public, and has extra attractions which include rare breed farm animals and cider making demonstrations. (Note that access is from a lane that leads off the Pencombe to Bodenham Moor road, a 2.3/4m journey from Little Cowarne itself.)

The White House and Meadow Court are notable timber-framed houses.

LITTLE DEWCHURCH *5.5m SSE of Hereford*

Dewchurch means 'the church of Dewi', Dewi being Welsh for David. There are four churches named after David in Herefordshire; the others are Kilpeck, Much Dewchurch and Dewsall. It was the practice to name a church after its founder, in this case probably a local saint rather than the patron saint of Wales.

The church stands in a hollow. Of the building we see today the tower is 14th century, with gargoyles and a tunnel-vault in the bell chamber, and some 13th and 14th century materials have been used in the rebuilding of 1869-71 by F. Preedy. In the churchyard there is a preaching cross with steps, base and a truncated shaft.

The nucleated settlement stands on high ground, midst fields mostly laid to pasture for cattle and sheep with some arable, and has commanding views in all directions. It lies on the road to Hoarwithy, less than 6 miles from Hereford, yet mains water and electricity did not arrive until the 1960s. Since then there have been developments of new houses. Facilities include a brand new village hall, opened in 1996, a bus shelter, the Plough Inn, a shop, a Gothic primary school of 1867, and an over 60s club. Court Farmhouse is 16th century with a 17th century wing.

Recent pipe laying operations in the district have revealed quantities of Roman pottery.

LITTLE HEREFORD *3m W of Tenbury Wells*

At the time of Domesday Book it was held by the Church of Hereford. In those days it was of some importance with a sizeable population and five mills. The village stood much closer to the River Teme than it does now and was probably driven on to higher ground by flooding. There was a mill within living memory near the Station House and in the same area there is evidence of other old buildings.

Between the church and the river there are some grassed-over mounds in a roughly triangular enclosure (SO 355 679). These have been variously explained but are most probably the remains of the fortified manor house of the Delamere family. This was abandoned in the early 16th century when later occupants, the Danseys, built Bleathwood Manor, well away from the river.

The church remains close to the Teme, and has suffered from flooding as a consequence. Indeed, this is probably the reason for the unusual rood altar set above the arch of the stone screen which separates the nave from the chancel. Here may have been stored the Sacrament, safe from flood waters. Saint Mary Magdalene has a massive 13th century tower that springs from an equally impressive internal arch; the nave is mostly 13th century but has one Norman window; the chancel is 14th century and has priests' seats (sedilia), hand basin (piscina) and rood loft stairway. There are three early 14th century tomb recesses, in one of which is the effigy of Sibel Dansey, at her feet a lion. There is also a monument to Joseph Bailey, a 19th century incumbent of Easton Court.

Easton Court, 1/3m NE of the church, stands pleasantly sited in its park but is not a happy sight. Of the old house only the 18th century stables remain. The present ugly, ashlar and brick pile started life in the early 19th century as a modest but pretty Georgian house, home to the Dansey family. They sold it to Sir Joseph Bailey in 1837 and it was his family that added the ungainly extensions. In 1911 it went to the present owners, the Cardiff family. They now live in the Laundry and the Garden Cottage because in the 1950s the Court was badly damaged by fire and now lies derelict. Easton Court is not signed from the main road, the A456, but has a lodge with a green verandah.

The A456 is the main road from Brimfield to Tenbury Wells. It uses the valley pass of the River Teme, as did the 18th century canal and later the railway, both now disused. The Leominster to Stourport Canal embankment remains and there is a lock-keeper's cottage on the road to Bleathwood. It crossed the river by means of a stone aquaduct, blown up by the army during the Second World War. The canal was short-lived and was taken over by the railway company who used some of its course for their rail tracks. This met its demise in the 1960s. The station is now a house, and the platform has been preserved and incorporated into the garden.

The village has a centre of sorts at the crossroads near the Temeside Inn. Here are brick houses, old and new, council houses and some good black and white. The old bridge of 1761 was replaced by a new, not unattractive, concrete construction in 1924. At nearby Pulpits Farm there is a caravan site.

Middleton, 2/3m N, is a hamlet of orchards, sheep and Charolais/Hereford cross bullocks being fattened for slaughter. Temple Farm has a section constructed using a unique herringbone pattern of timber-framing and a tall, thin window of about 1580. Upper House, Middleton is timber-framed and has an Elizabethan barn. The red brick Nonconformist chapel of 1868 closed in 1972 and is now a house, spoiled by modern windows.

The lane leads east, skirting Bleathwood Common and numerous black and white cottages and barn conversions, past the Wragg Transport yard to Bleathwood Manor Court. The house is late-17th century, brick laid to Flemish bond - alternating headers and stretchers in each course - with semi-circular gables and dentil friezes.

From here the lane heads south to Broadfields on the main road. By the old railway embakments is Franklin's Farmhouse (The Cliff), a neat, brick-built house with neat, well-kept orchards that produce cider, perry and honey for sale to the general public. The Franklin family has orchards with some 2,000 trees which include traditional varieties such as Dabinetts, Michelin, Vilberie and Kingstone Black. Their perry is made from pears brought in from local farms. Pear trees are not suitable for growing in orchards because they are prone to a disease called fire blight. Furthermore, pear trees can take up to 40 years before they bear fruit - hence the expression 'pears for heirs'. Little wonder that in these impatient times the pear is in fast decline.

Other small businesses in Little Hereford include turkey rearing, cabinet-making, agricultural engineering, and a tree nursery that has world-wide exports.

Little Hereford's most illustrious son is Robert Hughes, born in about 1553. He went to Brazenose College, Oxford, as a servitor, and then to Magdalene College as a student of mathematics. He wrote several books including *Tractus de Globis*, 1593, in which he describes his circumnavigation of the world with Thomas Cavendish.

(1560-1592) Hughes did not marry and died in 1632. He is buried at Christchurch Cathedral, Oxford.

Upton Court, 1.1/4m S of the church, is a most attractive timber-framed house with a low, wide front, two gables, porch with a gable, diagonal bracing and brick, star-shaped chimneys. It stands on high ground in pleasant, rolling sheep country and has a range of big red brick barns. The land is let and the house is empty, the owner now living in a converted barn. The Court is divided by a large, stone chimney range; the left half is the oldest, believed to be of the 14th century. It used to house a large collection of armour, swords and spears which were donated to Hereford Museum. When the current owner enquired of them he was told that the collection had been dispersed to other museums and individuals and that no records had been kept of their whereabouts.

Lower Upton is a hamlet of red brick cottages and stone barns with yews in the hedges and sheep in the fields.

Nun Upton, 1m SW of the church, stands below Brimfield Hill, near the red brick hamlet of Stony Cross. It is one of the manor houses that was owned by the nuns of Limebrook Priory, near Wigmore, and a very fine one at that. A black and white centre with close-set uprights is flanked by brick extensions in English bond of about 1630. It has large, shaped gables, moulded window hoods, dog-tooth friezes, a porch with a half circle gable, a star-shaped chimney and a rusticated brick chimney of about 1700. The long approach drive is flanked by rows of daffodils in the Spring.

At the time of the Norman Conquest Upton and the adjacent manor of Laysters to the south were held jointly by the Anglo-Saxons, Arketel and Arngrim. (Their holdings in Shropshire were also held jointly.) By 1086 Upton and Laysters had passed to Roger de Mussgros, a native of Mussegros in the Department of Eure in France. The surname Musgrove, as in the traditional English ballad, *Little Musgrove and Lady Barnard* (Child No. 81), is derived from Mussgros.

LITTLE MARCLE *2.5m WSW of Ledbury*
The name Marcle is from the Anglo-Saxon mearc-leah, meaning 'boundary wood'. It is a little settlement on the A4172, part of the old Roman road from Stretton Grandison to Dymock. It has Lilands, Old Lily Hall, Laddin and Little Marcle Hall - Anglo-Saxon places are often grouped alliteratively, as were their family names.

The church of Saint Michael, a common Anglo-Saxon dedication, was rebuilt in 1870 by J.W. Hugall. The venerable Pevsner writes, with a chuckle, that Mr. Hugall was one of "the naughtier High Victorians". His sandstone church has unexpected features: the bell-turret with spire stands on a shaft which rests on a buttress; the vestry chimney is prominent and there are crosses on the nave, chancel and porch. The silver cup and cover paten are late-17th century. The churchyard is inhabited by a venerable yew and a monster bunny rabbit.

At the crossroads there is a post office, a line of modern brick houses and the white rendered Old Rectory. Brook Farm is a substantial red brick building with orchards, hopyards and a pair of silver, cone-topped hop kilns. Half a mile up the main road is Newbridge Farm Park, a children's tourist trap complete with play area, donkeys, exotic birds, sheep and all manner of other little feathered and furry things.

Further along the road, 1m N of Little Marcle, is Prior's Court. This is a charming farmhouse with a Tudor core and a delightfully irregular stone, brick and half-timber countenance. Here there are ducks and dogs, a stream and buttercup meadows and bed and breakfast at very reasonable rates.

Pleasant though the country is hereabouts, watch out for the main road. It is very straight for a very long way and almost everyone goes horribly fast, making it both noisy and dangerous.

LLANCILLO *2.5m SW of Pontrilas which is 11m SW of Hereford on the A465*
The name in about 1150 was Lann Sulbiu, 'Sulbiu's church'. It overlooks the valley of the River Monnow, which is here followed by the road and the railway from Hereford to Abergavenny. Do not miss the turn off the main road to the access track, which lies between Maerdy Farm and Great Goytre, it is the only way in to this secret little place.

The Court, the parish church and the Norman castle huddle together in a little tributary valley. The church of Saint Peter has a nave and a chancel. The chancel has one altered Norman window and tufa (spongey limestone) quoins. The pulpit is of 1632; the silverware is early-19th century. The motte and bailey castle stands at the side of a footpath, 100 yards E of the church. It has a circular mound, 40 yards in diameter, and the scant remains of a round stone shell-keep, about 50ft in diameter. Llancillo Hall is 1/2m SW, in its own little wooded valley.

There was a 17th century iron forge at Llancillo. Here the metal was heated white hot by a charcoal fire, blown by water-driven bellows, and then beaten by water-driven hammers to drive out the impurities.

LLANDINABO *7m S of Hereford*
'The church of Iunopui', a Celtic Christian dedication showing that the influence of the ancient Britons lingered on through the Roman occupation, through the Dark Ages and well into the Norman period. For Celtic company it has Llanwarne to the west and Llanfrother to the east.

Llandinabo is now too close for comfort to the busy A49. Picturesque, but smaller than this you do not get for there is little more than a part timber-framed, part stone-built 17th century house of five bays attached to the church. Saint Dinabo is the only church in England with this dedication. It was rebuilt in 1881 by A. Lloyd Oswell of Shrewsbury and has nave, chancel and bell-turret. However, the very beautiful early-16th century rood screen was retained. It has a memorable frieze of dolphins, angels and a mermaid. In the east window is stained glass, by C.E. Kemp, of 1893, and there is a sad little brass monument in the chancel to Thomas Tompkins, who died in 1629 from drowning.

Llandinabo Court is a good five-bay Georgian brick house with dormers in the hipped roof. It is the home of Major Symonds who has has a well known pedigree herd of Hereford cattle. In recent times Continental and North American animals have been imported into Britain. These have debased our native stock to such an extent that the pure bred Hereford is now on the official Rare Breeds Survival Trust list of British endangered breeds. Major Symonds is a champion of the pure breed; good for you, Sir.

LLANGARREN *4.5m WSW of Ross*
'Church in the valley of the Nant Garren'. Sometimes spelled Llangarron it lies in the district of Arkenfield, a kind of Welsh-England no-man's land which had its own laws and customs, detailed at the beginning of the Here-

fordshire Domesday Book in 1086. The settlement is most easily approached off the A4137 which links the A40 to the A49. But watch out for witches.

A doctor from Llangarren was returning home late one night after visiting a patient near Monmouth and over Llanlodi Pitch he met three witches. He knew them well as local women but that night one rode a grindstone, another a besom and the third a hurdle. A man from Ross stayed at an inn near Llangarren and somebody stole his watch. He went to a Llangarren witch and she saw to it that it was returned the next day. A local rhyme runs: "Llangarren for riches, Arcop for poor, Buckle for witches, the Kymin for more."

The village has a post office-cum-general store, a garage, an agricultural repair shop, a chain-saw specialist and a village hall. The school and the pub are both now houses but the vicar has a new vicarage from which he administers several parishes. His stone-built church at Llangarren is dedicated to Saint Deinst. It stands at the centre of the village, in a large churchyard. The tower, spire and the chancel are 14th century, the porch is 15th century, and the pulpit early 17th century Jacobean. The church was enlarged in 1841 and the whole was restored in 1900. The mediaeval altar stone with consecration crosses is now incorporated in the floor. In the nave wall is a relief carving of a man in early mediaeval dress. There are monuments to: an unknown person in effigy; Rowland Scudamore, died 1697; Johan Philpott de Sonke, died 1689; William Gwyllyn, died 1698; and Mrs. Audley, nee Gwyllyn, died 1715.

In the mid-19th century Llangarren had 4 mills, 10 shoemakers and 12 carpenters, enough to constitute cottage industries. There are said to be two holy wells in the parish, but no one seems to know their location. Likewise, a farmhouse is said to stand on the site once occupied by the Celtic kings of Arkenfield; but which one? Seven lanes meet at the village and in the countryside around there is a goodly number of handsome farmhouses. There are rich cattle and sheep pastures, fields of soft fruit, and arable land.

Langstone Court, 1/2m NNE of the village centre, is considered to be one of the most handsome late-17th century medium-sized country houses in Herefordshire. It is of brick and has five bays, two storeys, quoins, hipped roof, gabled dormers, pediment and blank arches in the chimneys. Inside there is a good staircase of about 1675 and fine plaster ceilings. The rear of the house is Jacobean and there are good gate piers with 18th century iron gates. South-east of the house is a moated site (SO 532 219).

Bernithian Court, 3/4m ENE, is a twin to Langstone Court but it retains the original wooden cross windows which have been removed at Langstone. A barn has the date 1695. When Bernithian Court was restored in the early 1930s a small room under the stairs was discovered in which were a table and two chairs. On the table was a pack of playing cards and on one chair there was the skeleton of a man with a bullet hole in his head. The impressive wrought iron gates and crested pillars were found in the duck pond, and in another pond nearby the two largest carp ever caught in Britain were taken - one weighed 34lbs, the other 44lbs.

Ruxton Court, 1.1/4m SE, is part stone with mullioned windows and part timber-framed with a porch. Trerible, 1.1/4m NW, is a rendered house of five bays, and three storeys. It has a doorway with pediment-hood, and two three-bay brick ranges with hipped roofs to the left and right fronts. The Grove, 1m S, has a plaster ceiling dated at 1594. Trereece Mill, 1/2m SSW, lies deep in the valley downstream and it still has its water wheel. Nearby is the pumphouse for the Llangarren water supply of 1906 which supplemented the earlier system of 1888. Incidentally, there are many place names beginning with the prefix Tre hereabouts - Tredunnock, Tre Essey, Trewaugh, Trehumphry, Treverven, Trebandy. Tre is the Welsh equivalent of the English suffix 'ton' and simply means 'settlement, homestead or hamlet'.

An Early Bronze-Age burial has been uncovered in the parish. It contained a crouching skeleton in a flag stone-lined cist-grave which was not mounded above.

Kilreague Farm, 1m W of Llangarren, might well have been the site of a pre-Roman Goidelic Celtic hermitage; the prefix 'kil' had that meaning in their language.

LLANGROVE 5.5m SW of Ross

The best thing that ever happened to Llangrove was Mrs. Agnes Lawrence. Hers is a small but touching story; how she was made a widow in her mid-20s, how she scrimped and saved to raise five small children without any state benefits, how she kept a daytime job, delivered papers and the post to a scattered community and never missed a day through the snow and storms of the dreadful winters of 1940 and 1946, how she cleaned the church and rang the bell and was the school caretaker. A life of toil and dedication acknowledged by the British Empire Medal she received from Colonel J.F. McLean, the Lord Lieutenant of the county, in 1969.

Although Llangrove is in Arkenfield, and thus more Welsh than English, the name is deceptive. Until the mid-19th century it was Long Grove, and often simply The Grove. This is no picture book place, and modern development is no stranger, but it has the basic facilities of school, shops, post office, public telephone box, village hall, garage-cum-blacksmith's shop and a pub, The Royal Arms. It stands on high ground and commands long views from the Malverns to the Brecon Hills.

There were formerly three churches here. The Congregational and the Wesleyan chapels closed in 1968 but the Church of England soldiers on. Christ Church was built in 1856 by that illustrious architect, G.F. Bodley. It is one of his earliest, if not the first, of his ecclesiastical works. It has nave, chancel and bellcote in Early English style of about 1300. Simplicity rules; piers with no capitals and plain roofs, but it does have a colourful stained glass east window. The Church of England School was built shortly after the church and extended in the 1960s to accommodate the children of the neighbouring villages of Llangarren, Llanrothal and Welsh Newtown Common.

To conclude, one has to ask the obvious: does the name The Grove perhaps have a Druidic association? Could the site of an ancient oak grove be located near The Grove homestead north of the village?

LLANROTHAL 4m NW of Monmouth

It hides at the end of a dead-end track in meadows deep in the valley of the River Monnow, and is most easily approached from Welsh Newton on the A466 north of Monmouth. The name is not fully understood. Llan means 'church' and Rothal is presumed to be a personal name.

The church is dedicated is to Saint John the Baptist. It has a Norman nave with two Norman windows. The south nave windows and doors, and the chancel arch east window, are of about 1300. The large four-light window is Perpendicular (c.1330-c.1530, a style rather than period).

The altar is a massive stone, 90 inches long by 8 inches in depth; the porch is Tudor; the pulpit is Jacobean; the brass chandelier decorated with the Virgin Mother is part 15th century and part 19th century and came from Thrumpton Hall, Nottinghamshire; the cross and candlesticks are Italian silvered wood, probably of the 17th century. Services are infrequent and only the east end is in use today.

The hamlet lies 200 yards NW of the church. Llanrothal Court is built around a 14th century stone great hall. The doorway is single-chamfered and two recently discovered windows have two cusped lights.

The Cwm, 1.1/4m SE of the church, is a large, irregular house of 1830 with a Doric columned-porch. It stands on the site of a house of about 1600 which became the secret Jesuit missionary centre for South Wales. In 1622 it became the official residence of the head of the new Jesuit province, but in 1678 this illegal Catholic enclave was attacked and pillaged by men in the pay of the Bishop of Hereford.

In the valley below the Cwm - cwm means 'valley' - beside Tregate Farm is a Norman motte and bailey castle. The mound is about 60 yards in diameter at the top and rises to 12ft above the bailey. There are traces of the foundations of a stone shell keep and to the south-west are a series of terraces which probably formed two or three enclosed rectangular courts. To the north-east are traces of a ditch. This was obviously a fortress of some consequence. However, there are several other castles in the immediate vicinity and not all of them could be maintained. The Welsh were obviously a bit of a handful hereabouts - and why not? It was their land.

Skenfrith, 1.1/4m E, is over the border in Wales and the castle is most impressive, its great walls looming over the little village, which has a pub and a motel for the convenience of travellers. The motel is called The Priory and stands on the site of a hermitage. To get there from Llanrothal use the bridge at Tregate, to cross the Monnow, and turn north at Maughan's Green.

LLANVEYNOE *8m SE of Hay-on-Wye*
It lies on the northern slopes of the remote Olchon Valley, a mile from the Welsh border. The name is more probably Llanbeuno, 'the church of Beuno', a 6th century saint. The lands of Ewyas were granted to Saint Beuno by King Ynyr of Gwent and here, at Llanveynoe, he founded his first church. The king left his royal duties and became a disciple of the saint. However, on hearing that his father was ill Beuno left for Powys to attend to him. He never returned to Llanveynoe but went to Flintshire where he is closely associated with the legend of Saint Winifred. He settled at Clynnog in Carmarthenshire where he founded another church and there he died in about 648 A.D. There are many legends about Saint Beuno and he is said to have performed miracles, such as raising six people from the dead. His shrine at Clynnog became a place of pilgrimage for several hundred years. For a full biography of Saint Bueno see Baring Gould's *Lives of the Welsh Saints*.

The village is a scattered little place centred on the church. Saint Peter's has a nave, chancel and bellcote, mostly of the 19th and 20th centuries, but it does have two interesting 10th or 11th century sculptures: a worn 4ft high panel with a crudely inscribed crucifixion scene; and a broken smaller panel with an incised cross and initials and the inscription HAEFDUR FECIT CRUCEM. Feast days, Saints Days and Sundays in the Summer were important social occasions with celebrations held in the churchyard. At Llanveynoe, as at Crasswall and Garway, there is a stone shelf running around the outside of the church that was used as seating by spectators of the sports and games.

We took a trip around the Olchon Valley commencing at the north end of Longtown where a lane leaves the Longtown to Hay road (at SO 317 300) and heads south-west, signed to Turnant. The lane wends its way steeply downhill. Facing the traveller across the valley is the hulk of the Black Mountain. The small, dull green, irregularly-shaped fields give way to dull red moorland about two-thirds of the way up the slope. Continuing downhill we passed a caravan-dweller by a ruined stone cottage. At the bottom of the descent is the bridge over the Olchon Brook. Look right, up the valley, and note the volcano-like hill. This is the end view of the Cat's Back, about which more later. Cross the bridge, pass the modern bungalow on the corner and start to climb the hill. The first dwelling on the left, down a short drive, was called Sneyd's Barn and was the home of the actor Robert Newton, star of films such as *Treasure Island*. He lived here after serving on Russian convoys during the Second World War. His house is now called Olchon Cottage.

We continue uphill, past a modern bungalow, through the dull green, hedged-about fields. The lane is steep and there are piles of grit beside the road for use during inclement weather. We pass a derelict stone farm and a little higher up come to another, Great Turnant. This large farm is virtually derelict but is guarded by a husky-like dog, who lies in the sun, drinks in the stream that runs through the yard, and lazily watches the little waterfall. Someone lives here, it seems, presumably in the cruck-framed part. They keep a few cows. Cattle were common here once, but now the valley is alive with sheep.

The basic history of farming in the valley is that in the 17th century there were a few large farms with large heads of cattle. Then, in the 18th and 19th centuries a number of small-holdings were created that ran sheep. In the early 20th century cattle came into favour again and the small-holdings were largely abandoned. In more recent times sheep have come back in favour - with a vengeance.

Just above Great Turnant one passes over a cattle grid and now the sheep really take over. They are everywhere. The road follows a hillside contour which is more or less level. The old hedges have been let go and are now gapped, with bleached, gnarled bushes.

At the Red Darren Picnic Place there is a wide platform which has been made by levelling the scree that has fallen from the rocky outcrops above. The ragged cliffs of both Red Darren and the adjacent Black Darren were created by the Old Red Sandstone rocks slipping on layers of wet clay. There are long views to the west over the whole of Herefordshire to the Malverns. A tiny stream chatters through the litter of little rocks and alongside are the bleached bones of sheep that succumbed to illness or exposure. Overnight parking is allowed up here; it is not often you see an official sign making this declaration.

The lane continues northwards, past the dwarf hedgerow trees and over tumbling brooks, to the entrance to Charity Farm. Beyond this is another cattle grid and the lane enters a tunnel of overhanging trees. Turn left at the junction, past a modern dormer bungalow with beehives and trimmed hedges, and one arrives at Olchon Court, a substantial stone farmhouse with stone outbuildings. It is a good 16th and 17th century building and is thought to be one of the houses in which Sir John Oldcastle, the Lollard, sought refuge. Olchon Court was orignally constructed as a longhouse - man and beast under one roof, often sharing the same front door.

However, we have just passed what the Olchon Valley is most famous for: the site of the Early Bronze-Age burials discovered here in 1930 by a ploughman. Two tombs were discovered at SO 280 323, about 200 yards south of Olchon Court, opposite the bungalow just mentioned. The full excavation report was published in the *Transactions of the Woolhope Society* in 1932, page 147, but here are a few details. The tombs were cists, rectangular enclosures consisting of stone slab walls with a heavy cap stone. They were small, the first to be found measured 2ft 8ins by 1ft 4ins and was 1ft 3ins deep. The other had similar dimensions and was found only 3ft 3ins away from the first. They were both arranged exactly magnetic north-south, the skulls to the north, lying on their left sides. The bones were laid in a crouching position. The flesh would probably have been removed by allowing birds of prey and carrion crows to feed on the corpses before the bones were buried. The incumbents were probably young noblemen. In earlier times they would have been laid to rest in a communal tomb. Amongst the grave goods were a beaker, dated at 17-1600 B.C., and a beautifully made tongued and barbed arrowhead. Both tombs were removed from the site and the best preserved of them has been reconstructed and is on display at Hereford Museum. One must question the ethics of archaeologists who despoil religious sites for no very good reason.

It has been suggested that there is a socio-religious connection between these cist tombs and the cairn and stone circle on the top of the Black Mountain, 2.3/4m SSE at SO 300 283, almost on the Welsh border at a height of 612ft. The cairn is doughnut-shaped, the result of an unrecorded excavation, and the stone circle is about 30ft away covered in undergrowth. They probably served as both territorial boundary markers and religious sites.

But to continue our journey. Beyond Olchon Court the tunnel of trees returns. The lane curls round and starts to head westwards, past several ruined, stone smallholdings. At the Little Black Hill a signed track leads to another Picnic Place, at SO 288 328. From here the intrepid explorer can climb to the top of the Cat's Back, a ridge walk that puts you on the tracks followed by prehistoric man.

The main lane now descends through view-obscuring hedges to Tir Bill Farm. Below this one can turn right to reach the Olchon Brook. North of the bridge by a quarter of a mile is the Cae Thomas Well, at SO 284 320. This is quite famous because it is one of the few healing wells whose waters have been tested by 'eminent scientists' and found to be efficacious for the treatment of rheumatism and weak eyes. There was a scheme to bottle it as Glen Olchon Water. The water emerges from a rock spring and flows into a natural pool and is given a helping hand by means of man-made concrete. Ancient holly trees grow from above and overhang the spring. It is more than likely that our Bronze-Age noblemen drank here.

It is not surprising to find that old customs and superstitions have lingered long in this remote, mountainous place. Here are some collected by Mrs. E.M. Leather in the early years of the 20th century.

As protection from the Evil Eye and witchcraft in general, a cross was made by placing a piece of withy (rowan, mountain ash) at right angles to a piece of birch. These crosses were placed anywhere it was important to protect - the garden, the front door of the cottage, the pigsty, etc.

On the night of the day of a death no one in the household went to bed. Everyone stayed awake to keep the departed spirit company. People at Llanveynoe remember being terrified by a phantom dog, a Hound of Hell, that regularly appeared at a certain cottage half a mile below Clodock church and would run beside vehicles and horses before suddenly vanishing. (I've met many of these; they are bored Border Collies; in fact I used to own one.)

LLANWARNE 7.5m S of Hereford

It is a nucleated, rural hamlet situated between the A49 and the A466 Hereford to Ross road but has a felicitous disposition for all that. The name is from llan-gwerne, Welsh for 'church by the swamp (or alder grove)'. The settlement is in Arkenfield where Celtic Christianity took root long before it did amongst the border English to the east.

It is likely that the church at Llanwarne is therefore very ancient - 6th century perhaps. The old church of Saint John the Baptist, formerly dedicated to Saint Dubricius, now stands in ruins, abandoned in 1864 because of the waterlogged ground and the flooding of the Gamber Brook. The floor had been raised progressively to more than 3ft above the original level and burials were only possible if the coffins were weighted with stones. The building we see today is of the 13th century, but was re-built with a tower in the 14th century. The churchyard cross is also 14th century, the lych gate is probably 15th century, and there is a monument with four shields of 1608-9. The new Christ Church was built on higher ground in 1864 in the modern Geometrical style. Features include a polygonal bell-stage to the tower, transepts and a polygonal apse. The font is 17th century; the stained glass medallions are 16th and 17th century and were made by craftsmen in the Netherlands.

The settlement has little in the way of facilities. The school of 1854 closed in 1957 and became the village hall. That, a war memorial and the church, is all they have. Mains water and electricity only arrived in the 1960s.

Llanwarne lies in the old Wormelow Hundred. Wormelow Tump lies 1.1/2m NW. This was where the Hundred Court was held. Tump means 'a pronounced little hillock', but this has disappeared. In its place is a most pleasant little crossroads settlement with a petrol station, a stand of Scots pines, and a pub. The sign of the cream-painted Tump Inn has a king with sword and axe in hand. (See Much Dewchurch.) In Tump Lane, opposite a group of council houses, there is a tree with a large clump of mistletoe which we photographed for posterity.

Turkey Tump, 1/2m NNE of the church, has an Ordnance Survey Trigonometrical Point. Lyston Court, 3/4m NW of the church, has a 16th century core, was re-built in the early 18th century and altered considerably in 1870 and 1928. Today it appears as a Regency house of about 1820. It was used as a dower house to Bryngwyn. (See Much Dewchurch.)

Blewhenstone, 2m NE, has ancient cruck trusses only visible from inside.

LLANWONNOG 0.5m NE of Longtown

Llanwonnog is a tiny hamlet by a bridge over the River Monnow. Two houses of near equal status are built adjacent to each other. This is unusual in England but quite common in Arkenfield where the Welsh custom of Gavelkind, the equal sharing of an estate between a deceased's offspring, was common until recent times. Here, both houses have cruck framing and stone fabric, one being of about 1420 and the other of about 1520. The name means 'the church of St. Gwenog'; there was a chapel here with that dedication until 1733. Legend has it that in very early

Top:
Fownhope church, the Anglo-Saxon/Norman tympanum of the Virgin and Child.
Opposite:
Church of Saint Peter, Peterschurch, a Norman rebuilding of the Anglo-Saxon church with the three 'chancel arches' typical of Italian 8th century style.
Below left:
Anglo-Saxon funeral monuments at Llanveynoe church; 10th or 11th century.
Bottom right:
Harold Godwinson, Anglo-Saxon Earl of Hereford, later King of England. From the Bayeux Tapestry.

times a church was begun at Llanwonnog but each night the new work collapsed, a sign that a new site must be found.

LONGTOWN *10m SE of Hay-on-Wye*
The name describes it well. It is over one mile long and, as an ancient borough, it could be called a town. It is still something of a local centre in this remote corner of the Welsh borderlands. Between the old cottages and modern bungalows there are two castles, a village hall, a post office-cum-general store, a separate shop, a church, a school, an outdoor education centre and a stone-built Ebenezer Methodist chapel.

However, the overriding memory we have of this place are the lovely, small fields, enclosed by hedges and mature trees, to be seen from the road to Hay, 1.1/2m out of the village, near Cwm Farms. They crowd along the crest of the eastern section of the valley of the River Monnow; fields as fields should be, friendly and protective, as much living things as the animals they succour and shelter.

But back to the village. It runs up the ridge that divides the valley of the Olchon Brook from that of the River Monnow. These two rivers join at the southern end of the village. What is more, the Escley Brook/Monnow confluence is only half a mile upstream, making this an important local 'meeting of the waters'. Indeed, the Normans built a motte and bailey castle at Ponthendre, by the bridge over the Olchon Brook, close to its confluence with the Monnow. The motte is 51 yards in diameter and about 35ft high, and has a crescent-shaped bailey protected by a scarp.

This, "the old castle of Ewyas Lacy", was superseded by the new castle, 3/4m NNE, at the northern end of the present village. This stands on a spur overlooking the Monnow and was probably built by Gilbert de Lacy in about 1145. The motte stood at the northern end of a three-acre, rectangular bailey by high earth ramparts. This was possibly the site of a Roman fort. Later, the timber tower and palisades were replaced by a round stone keep and a stone wall with gateway that divided the enclosure into inner and outer baileys. This work was probably carried out by Walter de Lacy between 1216 and 1231 when he was Sheriff of Herefordshire. Henry III was at Longtown in 1233.

The ruins we see today are very substantial and are every man's idea of a romantic border castle. The keep has three floors, a basement, a hall and a bedroom. Only the hall had windows, just two narrow slits. Spaced evenly around it were three semi-circular buttresses. Two remain. The third had a spiral stairway and the entrance to the keep was next to it. Another had a latrine opening off the top floor bedroom; the other backs on to the fireplace in the hall. The bailey dividing wall is 10ft thick where it flanks the gateway passage. They look like towers, but in fact are solid stone. Part of the eastern wall that joins the gateway to the keep remains but there is nothing left of the west wall.

The castle changed hands many times, often to absentee landlords, and fell into disrepair. However, in 1403 Henry IV ordered it to be re-fortified against the Welsh. Shortly after the new castle was built the borough of Ewyas Lacy was established. The manor court, the Court Leet, used to meet at the castle but in the 19th century it moved to the adjacent New Inn, which then became Court House and is now the nucleus of the Outdoor Education Centre. The innkeeper was also the stray-animal-pound keeper.

Saint Peter's church stands by the Market Square. It was probably founded by the Normans but was rebuilt in 1868 by T. Nicholson. It has nave, chancel and bellcote. The chancel east window is Decorated, of about 1300, and the roof is dated at 1640. The piscina is a re-worked Norman capital.

The old main street ran south from the Market Square. The village green has been the scene of at least two gibbetings. In 1808 a man poisoned his wife, was hanged at Hereford and left to rot in a cage on a pole until the flesh fell off his bones. In 1811 John Gwillin, a murderer, suffered the same fate. The smell of his rotting carcass so offended the villagers that they appealed for its removal.

The population of Longtown was formerly much greater than it is now. Well, they do seem to have homicidal tendencies, which reminds one of the case of the shepherd and the crows. In the mid-19th century a newly hired shepherd came to the area. The sheep of different farmers ran wild on the Black Mountains and there were constant disputes as to ownership.

Anyway, two shepherd brothers took a violent dislike to the new shepherd. One day they cornered him on the mountain and threatened to kill him. "If you kill me", he said, "the very crows will cry out and speak it." Subsequently, they did kill him and buried the body. This was discovered but there was no evidence as to the identity of the culprits. Not long after, the shepherds were bothered by flocks of crows following them and croaking all the time. It drove them to distraction. One day one of them called out, "brother, do you remember that when we killed the poor shepherd on the mountain top there, he said the very crows would cry out against us?" He was overheard by a man working in the next field who reported it and the brothers were tried and hanged. The tale is almost certainly apocryphal, but is a good example of the kind of folk morality story that calls upon nature rather than organised religion as the ultimate sanction.

A related tale is told of a Longtown farmer. A white crow perched on his plough and followed him home and hovered over his house. He told his wife that this was a sign and he was going to die. The next night he was poisoned by a lodger in his house who was afterwards hanged for the murder. Likewise, it is a brave man who continues on his journey if a hare or a stoat crosses his path shortly after setting out. Misfortune awaits those who dare.

A Longtown man related how to lay the spirit of a dead hurdle maker; they dug up his body and turned it over. Unfortunately, "he came back seven times worse tap, tap, tap all over the place where he used to work". Another spirit is the helpful ghost of a local man attired in a wide-brimmed hat and a cloak, who guides strangers lost on the Black Mountains to safety. However, he has a competitor, for the Devil, in the form of a big black crow, also wanders the mountain at night. He causes a traveller's light to go fail and leads him astray.

And they have fairies in the village: "Little people that comes into folk's houses and steal things; they can fly anywhere". Avoid fairy rings at all costs. Enter one and you may disappear forever. If you hear lovely music, ignore it. Do not be tempted to dance with fairies.

Having avoided the little people you must now avoid the witches. A man of the Black Mountain near Longtown bred greyhounds for gentlemen. Before they went he had a day's sport with them hunting hares. One day they found a hare beneath a bush and a little boy on the hill cried: "Run, granny, run, the hounds be after thee". The hounds chased the hare and ripped a back leg as it flew through a hole in the cottage door. When the huntsman went into the cottage he found the old lady nursing a bite mark on her leg. That's how he knew she was a witch. Witches could be helpful. A Longtown man once went all the way to Llandovery to see a "celebrated conjurer", a wizard, to arrange for the return of a stolen ram. Within three days he had it back at exactly the place and time promised by the wizard. Before funerals at Longtown, as all over the Welsh border, it was the custom to drink red wine in the presence of the body in his own house, "to kill the sins" of the deceased.

Still on the subject of death - they really are a doom-laden lot at Longtown - here is a Reprieve Riddle. A young Longtown man sentenced to be hanged was told by the magistrates that he could go free if he could make a riddle that confounded them. His mother, who was suckling a young child at the time, made a suggestion and this was his riddle:

> "A riddle, a riddle to you I'll tell
> I drank out of a needful well.
> Through a gold ring the stream did run,
> If you tell me the riddle I'll be hung."

The solution was that he went into the garden with his mother and she told him to suck milk from her breast through her wedding ring. These are legend-ridden hills. One, to the east of the castle, is called Mynydd Fyrddyn, which can mean either 'sloping mountain', or 'Merlin's Mountain', and is the reputed burial place of Merlin, King Arthur's magician. Beneath the keep of Longtown Castle there is said to be a chest containing a thousand gold guineas, but if anyone should dig it up a terrible curse will fall upon them. There is also said to be a tunnel from the castle, under the Black Mountain, to the Llanthony Abbey. Somewhere on the Cat's Back is Saint Martin's Well, whose waters are a cure for rheumatism and weak eyes.

The Royal Commission on Ancient Monuments lists over 40 houses having a date of 1714 or earlier in the parish of Longtown. Anywhere else in England and any one of them would have justified a paragraph. All we have space to mention is Old Court Farm, 1.1/4m NE of the church. It has a 14th centure core with cruck trusses surviving in the roof, a two-light trefoiled window at the back and an inside doorway with a two-centred arch. Adjoining the house at right angles is another, built about 200 years later, now used as an outbuilding. This juxtaposition of two houses, each sharing the same yard, is not unusual on the Welsh border because of the custom of gavelkind, the equal sharing of an estate between sons.

To conclude, here is yet another tale of doom and despond, but this one is true. It is called The Case of the Longtown Harriers and the year is 1893. Six local thugs spent a Winter's evening at the Cornewall Arms drinking beer laced with rum, to the music of a melodeon and the wooden whistle of William Prosser, a slightly-built and sickly labourer. On leaving the pub the high-spirited gang dragged out an itinerant stonemason from his bed in a barn and threw him into the snow, rolling him over and over. He escaped so they broke into the wheelwright's house and took him to the River Monnow where they repeatedly ducked him in the freezing water.

Then it was poor Prosser's turn. The gang went to his house, Hunthouse Cottage, and started to smash their way in. Prosser tried to escape but they caught him and rolled him in the snow. Absolutely terrified he made a run for it but the 'harriers' chased him. They hunted him as far as The Garn but shortly after gave up. Poor Prosser, however, did not know that. He ran, and ran, and ran. The next morning he was found dead of exposure and exhaustion. His shirt and waistcoat had caught on a cottage gate and he had been too weak to free himself. One of his hands was clasped to the back of his head and his eyes were staring at a tree in Cloddock Churchyard, beneath which he was later buried.

The 'harriers' were found guilty of 'technical manslaughter' and the two ringleaders were sentenced to 12 months with hard labour.

LOWER BULLINGHAM *1.5m SE of Hereford*

For an explanation of the name and its manorial roots see the article on Bullinghope.

As one drives out from Hereford on the Holme Lacy road, the B4399, things do not look promising. This is suburbia at its blandest. But this was once a separate settlement, in later times the estate village of the Bodenham family of Rotherwas. The site of the deserted mediaeval village adjoins the main road and the railway in fields off Watery Lane, south of the River Wye, around SO 522 382. When it is excavated historians expect to learn much about the mediaeval trade and economy of the area.

The Manor House is early 17th century brick. The Sisters of Charity fell into the hands of property developers, were bankrupted in about 1993 and took refuge at Bartestree. Their convent, latterly occupied by the Marian Fathers, has been demolished and the site developed. Likewise, the convent of the Poor Clares was sold in 1996 and also developed. The 15 nuns moved to Much Birch.

The Wye Inn has played an important part in the social life of the community. It once served as the village hall and as the coroner's meeting place. People who had committed suicide by drowning in the River Wye tended to be washed up here, and the stables were used as a mortuary. Boxing Day lunches were served in several sittings and the Sheepskins, a dance that involved prancing around four spitoons laid on the floor, was performed to the music of the local fiddler, nick-named The Marquis, who kept his fiddle at the inn and performed on all festive occasions. (For something on Rotherwas, 1m W, see the article on Dinedor.)

LUCTON *8.5m SW of Ludlow*

It lies just off the B4362/B4361 Mortimer's Cross to Ludlow Road. The name in early mediaeval times was Lugton, 'the homestead on the River Lugg'. It must have moved for the Lugg is 3/4m SW now.

A most pleasant atmosphere pervades the village. There is an old farmhouse of grey stone with a hipped roof and boarded barns, a stream that crosses the road, 16th and 17th century black and white cottages, a black and white collie, orchards and sheep, a kiln converted to a house, honey for sale, cosy curling lanes and the church.

Saint Peter's is of 1850 with lancet windows and a bellcote, to a design by James Cranston, built to replace the earlier Norman church. Gravestones form a macabre wall. Inside there is a stained glass window by Charles Westcope, R.A. and a monument to John Pierrepont, died 1711.

John Pierrepont was a local lad who made good in London as a wine merchant and founded Lucton School in 1708. This considerable establishment stands north of the village near the main road. The original school is the north range. This is built of brick with seven bays, two storeys, a hipped roof and a bell-turret to the front, and eight bays to one side and five to the other. Above the doorway is a good, white painted wooden statue of the founder. The rest are modern additions.

Stocking Farm lies near Lucton Hall. Stocking is a name usually derived from late mediaeval woodland clearance; stocks were tree stumps. The Gospel Oak stands at the point where the parishes of Lucton, Kingsland, Aymestry and Shobon meet. At Rogationtide the bounds were beaten, that is they were walked around and prayers said at important boundary markers such as large stones, trees, wells or crossroads.

The Wigmore family held the lands of Lucton in Anglo-Saxon times and consolidated their position when one of them married a daughter to Sir Jasper Croft soon after the Norman Conquest. A great oak post stood beside the gateway to their homestead, Lucton House. Tradition had it that the Wigmores would keep their estate for so long as this stood. In August 1670 it fell and three days later their lands went to one William Hooper for non-payment of the mortgage. The family had spent all their inheritance fighting for the king during the Civil War.

The country to the north-east and south-west of Lucton is characterised by numerous, low, elongated hillocks called drumlins. These are formed of glacial boulder clay which has been scraped off the ground and re-deposited by an ice sheet. This was moving in an easterly direction; ascertained by the alignment of scratched stones in the boulder clay. It is sometimes called 'a basket of eggs' landscape. (For Lucton Mill see Mortimer's Cross.)

LUGWARDINE *2.5m ENE of Hereford*

It lies on the A438, the Hereford to Ledbury road, in the valley of the wriggling River Lugg. The name of that river means 'enclosure (or settlement) by the Lugg', and it does, indeed, stand on a low bluff above the flood plain. The bridge is mediaeval. It has three arches with cut-waters; the west arch is 14th century, the middle arch was rebuilt with 14th century materials and the east arch is 15th century. The water meadows are most interesting. They cover several hundred acres on both sides of the main road and are called the Lammas Lands. These are held by several owners 'in common', as distinct from the land being 'a common'. From Lammas Day (2nd August) to Candlemas (2nd February) the holders graze their horses and cattle in common, i.e., they wander freely over the area as a whole. During the rest of the year the grass is allowed to grow for hay 'in severalty', i.e., they each have their own strips marked by boundary stones. A meeting is held each year at the Crown and Anchor Inn to sort out any problems or disputes. How marvellous that such an old tenure system has survived from mediaeval, or even earlier, times to this day. Over 60 species of grassland plants have been found in these ancient water meadows, including the snake's head fritilleries and the even rarer narrow-leaved water dropwort. The pastures are lush because of the nutrients deposited during periods of flooding. (See the Appendix article on the Lower Lugg.)

The river was harnessed to three power mills, Longworth, Tidnor and Lugg Mill, none of which now operate. Lugg Mill stands 1m NW of the village on the A4103 Worcester road. It is large and ugly, even forbidding. The old stone part is derelict but part of the red brick extensions of the 18th and 19th centuries have been converted to a house. There is a big, overgrown and dangerous looking pond-leat. Downstream, 1m SE of the village, is Tidnor Mill, once used to power an iron working forge as well as for grinding corn. Traces of the barge moorings can be found.

A journey through the village starts at the bridge on the A438, heading east. The road goes uphill. On the left is the dusty drive that leads through parkland to New Court. What we see now is a Georgian house made Gothic in 1810 by the architect H.H. Seward. It has five bays, a recessed centre, a porch and two turrets. all with battlements. It was the home of the Reed family. William Reed mentions "my mansion of Newcourt" in a deed of 1579. The family came here from Bronsil Castle, near Eastnor. William's father, Gabriel, was troubled by a restless spirit. To exorcise it he was told to obtain bones from the tomb of the first Lord Beauchamp, an earlier owner of Bronsil. Once the bones were back in the castle the spirit left Mr. Reed in peace. When the Reeds came to Lugwardine they brought the bones with them but these have since been mislaid.

The farm adjacent to the New Court has a fine herd of pedigree Hereford cattle, a comparatively rare sight in the county these days. Further up the main road, past the old village water pump, a thatched black and white cottage and the Crown and Anchor, is Lugwardine Court. From 1865 it was the home of Sir Herbert George Denman Croft, M.P., a county worthy and noted cricketer of Croft Castle. Now it is an old persons' home. The flat-roofed modern school is Saint Mary's RCVA High School and belongs to the Archdiocese of Cardiff. Next comes Saint Peter's Church which stands by a group of trees with cedars amongst them. It retains a Norman window, a 15th century tower with gargoyles, a 13th century chancel with lancet windows and 13th century transepts in the east half of the aisles. However, much of it is the work of F.R. Kempson in 1872. There are monuments to William Reed, died 1634, Sheriff; William Reed, died 1634; and John Best, died 1637.

Rose Cottage and Sweet Briar Cottage were built as the offices of a tile and brick works set up by William Godwin in 1849. He used the local red clay. His kilns and works have been demolished but many of his mediaeval style encaustic tiles can still be seen in more than 300 churches, including Hereford and seven other cathedrals. Old Court Farm, Hemhill, was the original manor house of Lugwardine and part of the moat survives. Close by is an early thatched house called The Steppes. In the grounds of Wilcroft there is a new housing estate, mostly occupied by commuters, and near the crossroads is the village hall. The impressive stone lodges with hipped roofs, quoins, pediments and Tuscan columned windows guard the entrance to Longworth, 1.1/4m SE of the church. This was built in about 1788 by the architect Anthony Keck. It has six bays and two storeys with feature bow windows, and has recently been used as an hotel.

This new house was built on the site of the Old Longworth Hall and some of the old materials appear to have been re-used. A moat formerly encircled the site and a private chapel, part of which was 14th century, was dismantled and re-erected at Bartestree Convent in 1869. (See Bartestree.)

Some 200 yards north of the Hall, beneath a tree, is an urn which commemorates a racehorse. Approximately 50 yards west of this, at SO 562 400, is the probable site of a Roman civil settlement of the 2nd century. Pottery and tile fragments have been found, but not Samian ware.

Longworth Hall can also be approached from the bridge end of the village where there is a good, five-sided thatched cottage.

This all sounds rather grand, but we approached the Hall from Tidnor, and here I quote from my travel notes: "Tidnor, flat pastures, tan coloured cows. Tidnor House Farm, three bays, two storeys, stone-built, hipped roof.

Above:
Lugwardine, Edwardian
haymaking in the Lugg Meadows.
Opposite:
a Herefordshire man,
probably late Victorian,
place unknown.
Below:
mowing clover
with an Albion type mower.

Buttercup meadows, old orchards with trees of a proper size, tall wind-brake hedges and poplar trees all in a-row. To Longworth Hall (West), stone stable-block with arch, red brick Hall with out-of-character modern extension. Company called Fine Furniture in an abominable shack at the back. Beautiful grey mare with a black mane in a buttercup meadow. Walled garden, partly collapsed. Rundown estate, glory days long gone. Back on to lane. Stone, canal-like bridge over stream, nasty black tunnels of a plant nursery. Stile Cottage Cattery. To Larport."

LUSTON 2.5m NNW of Leominster
The meaning of the name is unknown. It is a long village and straggles along the busy B4361, a happy mixture of old black and white and modern brick with hedges and stone walls, a school, post office-cum-general store, village hall and The Balance Inn. Next to the pub is the Tudor House, an early 17th century timber-framed building with concave-sided lozenges beneath the gable. On the other side of the road is a Methodist chapel and next to that is a cottage with an internal cruck. Orchard House is black and white of about 1500 with square and close vertical framings and in its garden, beside the road, is the close-boarded Old Blacksmith's Shop. Lady Meadow Farm is Georgian red brick and now doubles as a guest house with camping and caravanning facilities.

The village water used to come from the Holy Well (SO 486 634) at the northern end of the settlement, but this has been tanked and is not accessible any more. Mains water did not arrive until the 1950s. Riggall's Motorway is a little-used but attractive bye-way that leads from Luston to Croft, 4m NW. It had fallen into disrepair until Mr. Riggall of Lydiatts Farm insisted that the council re-metal and maintain it. It joins the main road 1/2m S of Nordar Hall, an ashlar, stone four-bay house with a hipped roof.

One of the oldest houses in the area is Bury Farm, at the southern end of the village at the junction of the road to Eyton. It is a striking 17th century, timber-framed house and until about 1850 the manor court was held here. Luston Court is a house of some character tucked away on the road to Eye. It has square framing, odd-looking leaded windows, a cider mill and climbing plants in the garden and a red brick barn. A local rhyme runs:

> "Luston short and Luston long,
> At every house a tump of dung;
> Some two, some three,
> Dirtiest place you ever did see."

At the time of the Norman Conquest, Luston was a named member of the Leominster manor held by Queen Edith, sister of Earl Harold, King of England from January to October 1066. At the time of the Domesday Book William the Conqueror held it.

LYONSHALL 2.5m ESE of Kington
The name means 'settlement in the valley in the territory of Leon', the Anglo-Saxon name for the territory between the rivers Arrow and Lugg. Leon is from the Old Welsh lion meaning 'a stream'. The castle, church and deserted mediaeval village site stand on the A44 Kington to Leominster road. Some time after the Black Death in the 14th century, the village moved 1/2m SE, along the A480.

It is a place of some charm with a pub, the 16th century Royal George, a shop, the Old Forge, Church House known for its Edwardian teas, cottages of stone, timber-framing and red brick and a Baptist chapel.

The old station, on the Titley Junction to Eardisley Railway (GWR), now forms part of a private house, which is situated between the village and the church. The railway opened in the 1860s but was not commercially viable and finally closed in 1940. The eye-catching stand of Wellingtonias opposite the old station are a local landmark. The village is primarily residential but there is a wool grader, a flower nursery, a marquee supply company, some country craftsmen, a developing bed and breakfast trade and two long established ghosts. One is an old lady smelling of lavender who haunts an old house, and the other can be heard clattering up the steps to the old railway station.

At the other centre of the village, to the north along the A44, is a row of old cottages called The Wharf. The east wing has the remains of two cruck frames. The Wharf once faced a loading place on the horse-drawn tramway that ran from Kington to Eardisley. (See Kington.) This opened in 1820 but fell into disuse some 40 years later and was taken over by the railway who utilised much of the tramway route.

Opposite The Wharf is the church, screened from the road by oaks and pines. Saint Michael's has a Norman tower and two Norman windows; the north arcade is of about 1250; the south arcade is Decorated (1290-1350) and most of the windows are of about 1300. The font bowl, decorated with leaves and a headless man, is 13th century, but rests on a 19th century stem. The headless man in effigy is also 13th century.

The castle stands just to the north-east of the church. To the north is a small, rectangular, moated bailey. South of this is the main, moated, rectangular enclosure. In the south-western corner of this is a circular moated inner bailey. On the north side of this is a polygonal plinth on which stand the substantial remains of a round, stone-built shell keep which has walls 10ft thick. The circular, inner bailey was originally defended by a stone wall above the moat, but very little of this is upstanding. This moat is water-filled but the other rectangular moats are only partly filled with water and are overgrown with trees.

Lyonshall Castle was probably founded very soon after the Norman Conquest by the de Lacy family. There was almost certainly an existing settlement here and in 1090 they obtained a Charter which granted them a weekly market and a Michaelmas Fayre. It was probably Stephen d'Ebroicis who built the round, stone keep in about 1220-7 in imitation of that built by his overlord, Walter de Lacy, at Longtown. It passed through several hands and in 1403 Walter, 5th Baron Fitz-Walter, was ordered by Henry IV to garrison the castle against the Welsh. It then passed in turn to the Devereaux, Thynne and Cheese families and became a neglected ruin.

Offa's Dyke runs parallel with the A480 for about 1.1/4 miles from Holme Marsh to the A44. A particularly good section can be seen in fields 1/4m SW of the church. Here the bank stands high and the flat-bottomed ditch is about 13ft wide. Penrhos Court, 1m W of the church, is a good 14th century house with four cruck beams.

The Yeld, 1.1/4m E of the church, has a moated site just north of the farmhouse. The 6ft deep ditch was filled and the site levelled in 1971. There were some structural remains and sherds of 13th and 14th century pottery were found. The Yeld was mentioned in the Lay Subsidy Rolls of 1334. A holloway connects the site to the farm.

Lyonshall Hall, formerly called Lynhales, lies down a long access track 2/3m SSW of the church. This is also a public footpath and provides access to the good section of

Offa's Dyke already mentioned. The hall is a Victorian-looking pile now used as a nursing home. Here I met Jack Gore, a lovely old man with a twinkle in his eye, a straight back and a grip of iron. He was a farmer and a singer of "old songs that no one else had heard of, like The Flowers of the Meadows", I had been told at the Angel Inn in Grosmont. Alas Jack's memory had gone and he could not even recall the Angel itself, where he had passed many an hour with friends and where his photograph hangs on the wall.

New Street, 1/4m NE of Lyonshall, lies in a charmng wooded dell. There is a dinky little stone cottage with a picture book flower garden, a red brick Primitive Methodist Chapel of 1864, lots of old, derelict cars, birds singing, cottages being renovated and the embankment of the disused railway.

Next End, 1/2m N of New Street, is set in a landscape of little green knolls, charming country graced by the park-like wooded grounds of The Whittern, a modest, rendered country house with cross mullioned and transomed windows and a hipped roof. There is a pool and marshy ground, holly in the hedges, stones cottages being improved and ditches running like streams.

Holme Marsh, 1m SSE of Lyonshall, has The Holme, a gabled yellow-brick, Victorian farmhouse and a scatter of cottages and farms, some of which are black and white. It is a squatter community in origin and still has that flavour with a graveyard of Volkswagen caravanettes rubbing shoulders with smart new houses and tiny un-modernised cottages. Woonton Ash, 1/2m SE, is a hamlet of stone cottages.

MADLEY *5.5m W of Hereford*
The name Madley is from the Old Welsh matle, 'good place'. The village stands at 87 yards above sea level on flattish land in the broad valley of the River Wye. The drainage ditches alongside the roads indicate wet land and the fields are mostly laid to pasture. It is an unprepossessing place with some half-timbered cottages, a shop, a garage, a modern school with a paper-aeroplane-style roof, the cream painted Red Lion, a large Parish Hall, and several pleasant estates of modern houses.

The cross at the centre of the village has taken a beating from motor cars over the years and the shaft looks decidedly 20th century. This is a pity because it is reputed to mark the birthplace of the Anglo-Saxon saint, Dubricius, about whom more later. The church of the Nativity of the Virgin was formerly dedicated to Saint Dubricius. It is a light, airy place, both large and handsome. By the early 13th century the original Norman church had been given a massive new tower, nave and aisles. In the 14th century it received a north chapel and a new chancel, complete with a rare polygonal apse and crypt below. Of the Norman work all that remains are two small windows by the north porch and the undecorated font, said to be the second largest in England.

In the 14th century the church contained a statue of the Virgin Mary which attracted pilgrims in great numbers. The wealth they brought accounts for the rather grand proportions of the building. Today it is the stained glass that people come to see, in particular the 13th century roundels of the east window. There are monuments to Richard Willison (died 1575) and wife, and Peter Garnons (of about 1626) and family. In the churchyard is a badly worn preaching cross with crucifixes, shaded by a venerable yew tree. The church is the centre of the Madley Music Festival, held each June. A curiosity: in 1821 Arnold Rogers wrote in the fly-leaf of his Bible an account of the last public penance performed in Madley church. A woman called N. Gardiner had committed slander. "She had a white sheet placed upon her head and she walked up and down the aisles of the church and recanted all that she had said."

In March 1942 Lieutenant-Commander Stephen Beattie, son of the Rector of Madley, won the Victoria Cross for commanding the destroyer HMS Campbeltown as it ran the gauntlet of enemy fire to ram the dock gates at St. Nazaire. His ship was packed with high explosives which detonated and sealed the entrance to the docks. He survived but was captured, though when it was announced that he had won the Victoria Cross his German Camp Commandant held a special parade and saluted him.

The Roman road from Kenchester to Abergavenny passes close by the village; the Madley Arms stands at its junction with the B4352. Alongside the Roman road, on the site of an old war-time aerodrome, 1m S of Madley, is a Satellite Earth Station. Its big white dishes are a monument to modern technology. They are focussed on satellites, and all manner of electronic, television and radio signals are received and transmitted worldwide. The first dish was installed in 1978.

Things of another age, and infinitely more beautiful, can be found at Brampton, a tiny hamlet 1/2m to the west of the Satellite Earth Station. Here is Great Brampton House in Regency Italianate stucco of 1806 with two storeys (a third was removed in the 1930s) and five bays. It is owned by Lady Pamela Pidgeon and is an Aladdin's cave of very expensive antiques. She started the business from scratch and on the proverbial shoestring. Today, she has a multi-million pound turnover and wealthy clients from all over the world are whisked to her door in a chauffeur-driven Rolls Royce. In April 1995 Adam Faith, the popular singer and financial journalist, interviewed her on the television programme *Working Lunch*. He was quite taken by her enthusiasm and integrity.

Madley's most famous son is the 5th century saint, Dubricius (Dyfrig). Tradition has it that he was born here, the son of Pabiali and grandson of Brychan, King of Brecon. His mother was Eurddil, daughter of Peibau, King of Erging (Archenfield). Dubricius founded a monastery at Hentland near Ross-on-Wye where he stayed for seven years before moving to Moccas. He founded some 24 churches though only four are still dedicated to him - Hentland, Saint Devereux, Ballingham and Whitchurch. According to Geoffrey of Monmouth, Dubricius officiated at the coronation of King Arthur at Cirencester. He spent his last days on Bardsey Island and was buried there about 550. In 1120 his remains were removed to Llandaff Cathedral on the instruction of Bishop Urban.

There are very few examples of the classic Anglo-Saxon three-field system of agriculture in Herefordshire. Indeed, before the Enclosures there were 30 'open fields' in the parish of Madley. A group of five Bronze-Age burial mounds lies 1.1/2m WNW of the church: a disc barrow 64ft in diameter; a bell barrow 33ft in diameter; and three small round barrows surrounded by a low bank and ditch. A local belief is that a Scottish Queen was hidden from her enemies on top of the small hill called The Bacho (from the Welsh bach, 'little'). There is no historical record of this but a Scottish prince did rule the nearby kingdom of Brecon in the early 6th century. He was defeated in battle and forced to flee.

The custom of dancing round the Maypole was once practised in Madley. At Upper Chilstone, 3/4m NW of the church, a tall, thin, freshly-cut birch tree was used as the pole. In 1924 one was photographed, stored against the wall of a farm building. At Castle Farm, 3/4m WSW of the church, a crock of gold was unearthed in the cellar. There is also a ghost here and, it is said, a tunnel to the church.

See the article on Turnastone for a description of the Corn Showing fertility rite performed at Lulham, in Madley parish.

MANSELL GAMAGE 8m WSW of Hereford
The name Mansell is probably from the Anglo-Saxon malwes-hyll, meaning 'gravelly hill'. In 1194 the manor was held by Matthew de Gamagis. Gamagis is from Gamaches in Normandy. A hundred years earlier, at the time of Domesday Book, Mansell Gamage had 13 families and 10 ploughs, and was held by Roger de Lacy, one of the leading marcher lords. The hamlet lies off the A438, Hereford to Hay road, on the lower slopes of the wooded Garnon's Hill. The settlement consists mostly of black and white cottages with stone lower parts, a few farms, and the 17th century Scut Mill. To the west there are long views to the Welsh mountains.

The church of Saint Giles lies against the hillside. A timber porch of about 1400 shields a simple Norman doorway. Several windows are of about 1300; the tower is of 1824; the chancel roof is mediaeval but most of the interior and the east window are of 1877 by L. Powell. Monuments include an 8ft long, 13th century coffin lid with a finely engraved foliated cross, and an urn on a pedestal to Frances Isabella Evans, died 1813, decorated with a mourning young man

A good stretch of King Offa's 8th century Dyke runs north-west to south-east over the crest of the heavily wooded Garnon's Hill, sometimes called Mansell Hill. Here are some magnificent oak trees, one grove having several trees that rise in excess of 120ft. Between the woods and the main road is Garnon's Park which is also dotted with fine old oaks. The park was landscaped by the illustrious Humphrey Repton in 1791 and the most recent incumbent of the big house, Sir Richard Cotterell, maintains an interest in trees and donated an arboretum at Queenswood. (See Hope-under-Dinmore.)

The name Garnon is possibly from the Welsh garan, 'a crane'. The original gabled Elizabethan mansion was extended in 1815 to a scheme by William Atkinson. This has a big, tall tower of which only the ground floor remains as the present loggia, and a three-bay range to the right that is now the conservatory. The Elizabethan house was demolished and replaced in about 1860 by the ashlar-faced, castellated, seven-bay range that forms the greater part of the house today. This range was decorated internally in Georgian style by Sir Reginald Blomfield in about 1907. Garnon's is splendidly set against the lower slopes of the hill and can be seen quite clearly from the road. It has good views over the orchards of Monnington and the valley of the Wye to Moccas and the Welsh hills beyond. The line of the Roman road from Kenchester to Hay-on-Wye passes through Garnon's Park from Home Farm in the east to Portway in the west.

MANSELL LACY 6m WNW of Hereford
The name means 'settlement by the gravelly hill owned by de Lacy'. It lies off the A480, Hereford to Kington road, an old Anglo-Saxon manor and very much an estate village to this day. The original manor house was probably sited on the oval island that rises 4ft above the moat situated at Court House Farm, 100 yards SE of the church.

At the time of the Norman Conquest the land was held by the Anglo-Saxon Godric. By 1086, the time of Domesday Book, it had passed to Grufydd ap Mareddudd. His father, Maredudd ap Owain ab Edwin, of the house of Hywel ab Edwin, was the Welsh King of Deheubarth about 1063. He allied himself with Earl William and was rewarded with estates in England. He was killed in 1071, on the banks of the River Rhymney, by Caradoc ap Gruffydd ap Rhydderch with the assistance of the Normans. A fitting end for a traitor, methinks. His son, Gruffydd, lived in exile on the old king's English estates and was killed in 1091 trying to recover his father's lands in Wales. A sorry tale. (Ap and ab both mean 'son of'.)

Later, Mansell Lacy was acquired by the powerful de Lacy family and their name became attached to it to distinguish it from Mansell Gamage. Domesday Book also mentions that the settlement had three radmen, or rad-knights. They were common on the Welsh border but not this far east. Their duties were to act as escorts and messengers, but as civilians, not military men.

The present village has some delightful mediaeval timber-framed and stone cottages, the old school of 1889, and a venerable and memorable black and white post office which has a dovecote in the forward-facing gable. The church of Saint Michael has a Norman nave, Norman south and north doorways, 13th century south aisle and chancel arch, and several 14th century windows, including the east chancel window with exterior ballflower decoration. Both the chancel and nave have barrel roofs. There is a peephole under the arch at the end of the south arcade and another in the surround of a 13th century lancet window in the chancel. In the churchyard there is a preaching cross on a mediaeval base.

With a stream, pools, and lovely wooded hills as a backdrop this is a place to be savoured. Mind you, the woods are no accident. The whole landscape hereabouts owes much to Sir Uvedale Price (1747-1829), the leading theorist of the English Picturesque school of landscaping. He lived at a now demolished house at Foxley, 1m NW of the village. This was a tall, square, red brick mansion with giant pilasters and arched windows of 1717. He incorporated distant landmarks such as Sugar Loaf and Skirrid Mountain, near Abergavenny, into his vistas.

After he died his widow had to sell the estate to pay off his enormous debts. It was purchased by the Davenports, from the Midlands, in 1855. The estate was virtually self-sufficient with its own farms, laundry, gas-house, water supply, school, church and tradesmen. In the Second World War it was used first by French-Canadian forces and then the Americans who had their 123rd American General Hospital here.

After the war it housed a Polish re-settlement camp and, subsequently, the mansion was demolished. It was followed in later years by the demise of the post office and the shop. The woods, however, still pay their way as cover for sporting birds bred for those prepared to pay handsomely to exercise their bloodlust.

MARDEN 4.5m N of Hereford
The name is said to be from the old Anglo-Saxon district name of Magonsetum (AD 811), derived from the Welsh, maen, meaning 'stone, plain or field'. Plain is probably what is meant here. Marden stands close to the east bank of the River Lugg 1.1/4m E of the A49, Hereford to Leominster road, and is probably most easily approached from Moreton on Lugg. It is a large and well-populated parish and has had more than its fair share of new houses

Above: Madley, the church of the Nativity of the Virgin which has much admired stained glass.
Right: Much Marcle, wooden effigy of Walter de Helyon, a wealthy freeholder (a franklin), in civil costume of about 1360.
Below: Mathon, with the Malverns in the background.

in recent times.

Approached from the south, things look promising. One passes the low hill on which is situated the Iron-Age camp of Sutton Walls (see Sutton Saint Nicholas) and comes to a crossroads where stands Marden Old School House. This is an attractive black and white and brick cottage with a thatched roof and a plaque on the chimney that reads:"The Old School House founded 1610 by Jane Shelley widow of William Shelley who suffered for a plot in favour of Mary, Queen of Scots 1583."

Averting one's eyes from the council houses and the ugly modern barns of Church House one comes to an orchard grazed by sheep. Beyond this are the rectory and numbers of mature trees that watch over the large, striking church of Saint Mary. It stands within a few feet of the dark, forbidding waters of the Lugg. The large car park is to cope with the curious who come to see the famous well that lies within the walls of the church near the font. If ever there was a relic of pagan water-worship this must be it. The early Christians often either built their churches alongside Celtic temples or brought the pagan altar into their own church.

Here, the presence of the well is explained by a legend which has some elements of fact and which was elaborated on by the early missionaries. In 1792 Saint Ethelbert, King of the East Angles, had been murdered at the palace of the King of Mercia, on Sutton Hill 2/3m to the SE. His body was buried at Marden and the church built over the grave. Later, about 1030, the bones were exhumed and prepared for re-burial at Hereford Cathedral. As they left the ground water gushed in and formed the well. Alas,Today it runs dry.

Not content with one story, Marden church has another to the effect that as a bell was being raised to the belfry it fell into the river and was dragged into the depths by a mermaid. A wise man told the villagers how to recover it. Twelve white free martins (heifers) were harnessed by yokes made of yew and mountain ash and the bell was drawn out in complete silence so as not to wake the mermaid. It was almost safe on the bank when the oxen driver made a boastful cry. The mermaid awoke and dragged the bell back into the river where it lies to this day. Occasionally it can be heard ringing.

It should be remembered that in mediaeval times bells were valuable and prized possessions carted from distant foundries at great cost. They were also an integral part of everyday life, telling the time of day, the curfew, and warning of danger, as well as calling the faithful to prayer.

However, the plot thickens for in 1848 a muddy pond situated a few yards from the church was cleaned out and at a depth of 18 feet a pre-historic Celtic bronze bell was discovered. It is rectangular in shape, the plates being riveted together on each side. The clapper is lost but the loop from which it was suspended remains. It is now in Hereford Museum.

You can't escape bells at Marden. The bellringers have a curious Forfeit Song which commences: "O green grow the leaves of the ackorn tree......and ends with counting backwards from 20 to 1". Anyone who misses a number has to drink a tot of cider. They're not daft in Marden.

The church has grey stone Early English arcades of about 1230, though the nave and aisles were otherwise rebuilt by T. Nicholson in 1858. A rare feature is the way the 14th century chancel continues unbroken into the polygonal apse. The ashlar-faced tower has a parapet and a recessed stone spire. It adjoins the church but is not connected to it internally. The 10-sided font is probably of about 1300. The well beside it has already been mentioned. Dame Margaret Chute is commemorated by a beautifully engraved brass of 1614. She died in childbirth, together with her new born daughter, Anne, and lived at Wisteston Court which is now derelict.

The village lies a good 1/2 mile to the north-east of the church. There is a desultory group of shops which constitute a small centre - a general store, butcher, the Blue Bee Sewing Service, and a petrol service station. Elsewhere there is a primary school of 1874, a modern, pantiled community centre, a riding school, a cricket club, the New Inn, the Volunteer Inn, a Plymouth Brethren chapel, a hairdresser, tennis club, children's playground, post office, and a real, traditional blacksmith still working in the family forge. Every year there is a local Eisteddfod, held on St. Ethelbert's Day. It is, however, very much modern bungalow-land.

Laystone Bridge, just east of Marden at SO 518 477, has four spans and is 17th century with a Georgian central arch and cutwaters both up and down stream. Venwood, 1.3/4m ENE at Venn's Green, is a neat little country house set in parkland. The Vauld, 1.1/2m NE of the village, is a handsome, early 16th century, black and white house with a centre and two cross gables. Anglo-Saxon place names are often clustered in groups alliteratively.

To go with Vauld and Venwood - names beginning with 'V' are quite rare - we have The Vern, 2m N of Marden, near Bodenham. This is an ancient settlement and stands close to an important ford over the River Lugg. Parts of the stone track can still be seen under the water. The big farm from which the area takes its name was well known for its herd of Hereford cattle. Between 1850 and 1873 John Hewer played a large part in developing the colour markings of the breed, especially the characteristic white face which came from a white-faced bull born in 1797. Between 1922 and 1965 Captain de Q. Quincy was instrumental in changing the shape of the cattle. He bred the smaller, quicker maturing animals that we see today. However, regarding agriculture in general in the area, there has been a decline in the breeding of cattle for slaughter and in dairy farming, and an increase in the cultivation of arable crops, particularly wheat and potatoes.

To the east of the village are some evocative names: Hawkersland Cross, Framington, Paradise Green, and Pikestye. A little further out is Amberley Court, which has its own article.

A curiosity is that in the reigns of Edward III (1327-1377) and Richard II (1377-1399) there were 17 acres of land at Marden the rent of which went to the person who had the duty of carrying a cord to measure the site of any castle which the Crown might think proper to build in the Marches of Wales.

MARSTON *4m E of Kington*
The name is from the Anglo-Saxon mersc-tun, meaning 'settlement by a marsh'. It lies just north of the A44 Kington to Leominster road, 1.3/4m WSW of Pembridge, in flat wet land. It is an attractive and atmospheric hamlet of timber-framed houses, and most interesting because it has seen little change since the early 16th century when it belonged to the nuns of Limebrook. (See Limebrook.)

At the time of the Dissolution of the Monasteries those anchorite nuns had eight tenements here. The rents they received ranged from 16 shillings and three pence and a hen to fourpence and a hen. There were two large farms and six small farms. Today they are two large timber-framed houses and six smaller timber-framed houses.

Doctor Who would have been confused. His time-machine would not know what to do next. No doubt some of the houses have been adapted and even rebuilt, but the pattern is still of the 16th century.

The church of Saint Matthew has nave, chancel and gabled bellcote and was built in 1855 to a design by T. Nicholson, an architect who did much work in Herefordshire - too much, some would say.

Grange House is now a School for Dyslexic Boys and Girls and has a wind-bent orchard with mistletoe. The large, mature commercial orchard belongs to Bulmer plc.

Rowe Dyke, sometimes called Rowe Ditch, crosses the road to Pembridge 1m E of Marston. This 8th century defensive earthwork is about 2.1/2 miles long and has been interpreted as a barrier across the woodland-cleared-valley of the Arrow, closing the gap between dense forests to the south and the hills to the north. It consists of a single bank, up to 19 yards wide, thrown up from a ditch dug on its western side. It also provided a causeway to be used by troops over the often flooded valley.

Upper Marston, 3/4m NW of Marston, has three spaced out cottages, neat hedges, ducks and geese on a pond, the modern farm buildings of The Rhyse, and the cuttings and embankments of the disused railway from Kington to Leominster.

MARY KNOLL VALLEY *2m SW of Ludlow*
This is not a settlement. It is a valley in the extensive Mortimer Forest, part of the woodland area that stretches from Ludlow south-east to Presteigne, much of which belongs to the Forestry Commission. The area has some of the best walking country in England with a surprise or a delight at every turn and with varied wildlife including some 500 fallow deer.

Access to Mary Knoll Valley is off the B4361 at Overton, Shropshire, at SO 495 742. Park under the trees at the bend. The path leads up a steep-sided valley beside a small stream which, for a short distance, marks the boundary between Herefordshire and Shropshire. The path leads to many others and one can wander at will. Mary Knoll itself is 1.1/4m NW of the access point.

MATHON *4.5m NNE of Ledbury & 3m E of Malvern*
The name is thought to derive from the Anglo-Saxon mapm, meaning 'treasure, or gift'. It lies by the Cradley Brook in the foothills of the Malverns, most easily approached off the B4220 north of Bosbury. In 1086 it was held by Aethelhelm who held it from Drago son of Poyntz. They don't make names like that anymore.

It is an attractive little village with some black and white houses; the old school, now a dwelling; a pub; a bridge over the river; a ghost that can be heard walking down the lane outside Little Southend Farm; its own variety of hops, Mathon Hops, which were developed at Church Farm; a stinking weed with a daisy-like flower called Mathon Weed, or Metheurum; a large plant nursery; and the church of Saint John the Baptist.

This is a Norman church and retains three Norman doorways and the Norman walls of the nave and chancel; there is some herringbone work on the outside. Of the 14th century are the tower, the much admired nave roof, and some fragments of glass in a nave window. The timber porch is of about 1440. There is a fine 17th century French painting of the Flight into Egypt, and the tomb chest of Jane Walweyn, died 1617.

At Ham Green there is a moated site. The wooded Cockshot Hill stands 1/2m NE of the village. The name could well be from Cock-shutt, meaning a place where wild birds were caught in funnel-shaped nets.

In a field immediately north of Southend Farm, at SO 737 448, the only Bronze-Age urn burials ever found in Herefordshire were discovered in 1910, during sand quarrying excavations. The two collared urns, which contained bones, and two bronze spearheads are now at Malvern Museum. The remains of 13 cremations were found altogether. Some were partly surrounded and covered by flat stones, a Continental practice. A later stone battle-axe, beakers, traces of burials and three urns, found east of the original site, are in Hereford Museum. This Middle Bronze-Age cemetery was occupied from about 2,000 B.C., through the Iron-Age and into the Roman period.

MICHAELCHURCH *5m W of Ross*
In about 1150 it was called by its Welsh name, Lann mihacgel cil lwch, 'the church of Saint Michael, the retreat by the pool'. It is a tiny hamlet in the valley of a tributary of The Gamber, most easily approached from the A49 at Harewood End.

The church has a prize possession, a Roman altar stone dedicated by one Beccicus to the God of the Three Ways. It was altered at a later date to make a roughly shaped capital with a bowl-like depression was used as a vessel for holding holy water, a stoup. The original Welsh name rings true because the church was founded in 1056 by Bishop Herwald of Llandaff, though there may well have been a religious site here long before that. Nothing of the Celtic church remains but there are several Norman windows, a fragment of the Norman north doorway tympanum with a lattice decoration, and a Norman tub font with zig-zag, interlaced arches and saltire crosses. The painting of the walls in imitation ashlar with a flower in the middle of each 'stone', some chequerwork and two crosses with circles, are 13th century. The screen has Tudor panels and the panelling of the pulpit and on the chancel walls is 17th century. The church itself is very small and has a nave, a chancel and a wooden bell-turret.

Harewood End, 3/4m NE, is a linear settlement on the busy A49. It has the Harewood End Inn, a lodge to Harewood Park, a ring of pines, dwellings old and new and polythene-covered fields.

MICHAELCHURCH ESCLEY *7.25m SE of Hay-on-Wye*
It was originally Michaelchurch. The name of the stream, the Escley Brook, on which it stands was added to differentiate it from the other Michaelchurch near Ross. It is a very large parish of scattered farms that reflect the ancient Celtic land-holding systems of planting your house in the middle of your holding. A glance at the Ordnance Survey map shows how distinctive this pattern is. Compare it to the nucleated settlements, with wide open spaces in between, typical of the Anglo-Saxon period in the Wye Valley to the north, between Peterchurch and Monnington. Barns with mediaeval cruck framing are found at Quaker's Farm, 2m NW; Lower House Farm, 2.1/4m NW; and Upper Pen-y-Park 2.1/4m N.

Several folk superstitions have lingered on into the 20th century in these remote Welsh borders. An old lady explained that the little wooden cross above her front door was to counteract the influence of a malicious neighbour who had the 'evil eye', the ability to cast spells. Several people remembered the terror caused by a phantom dog of hell that appeared in a lane near Clodock church. The name Pwcha Farm is from the Welsh name for the sometimes helpful, sometimes mischievous and sometimes malevolent spirit of the woods called elsewhere puck.

The small village has a pub, two bridges over the Escley Brook, a Court and, of course, the church. Saint Michael's has a 14th century nave and chancel in one with an open wagon roof; a sturdy, unbuttressed tower with pyramid roof of 1897; and a large, rare wall painting depicting Christ of the Trades, in which Jesus is surrounded by a collection of mediaeval craftsmen's tools such as shears, a wool comb, a jug, scissors, a flail, a plough, an axe and a gridiron. Of the 17th century there is a panelled chest and a chair with twisted legs and a carved back.

Michaelchurch Court lies 1/2m WNW of the church at the end of a long avenue, with a backdrop of woodland befitting a grand house. It is 'L'-shaped; the left wing is of about 1870; the majority of the right wing is 17th century, timber-framed above a stone ground floor. It has three gables decorated with narrow uprights and concave lozenges, and the porch of 1602 has good plasterwork.

Ancient sites in the parish include: at Wern Derris, 2m NNW down a bridle track off Urishay Common, a standing stone about 7ft 6ins tall; and nearby, at The Glibes, an oval burial mound 21ft by 15ft by 3ft high with the scant remains of two more possible burial mounds at the upper end of the field. At Nant-y-Bar, 4.1/2m NW of the village - it really is a big parish - are the earthworks of an early motte rising above the surrounding ditch, with traces of a rampart round the top, and a small causeway across the ditch on the north-east side. The Camp, south of Camp Wood about 1.1/2m NW at SO 296 357, is an oval-shaped enclosure surrounded by a rampart with a flat top at the east end which was probably an Iron-Age defensive post rather than a fort.

MIDDLETON-ON-THE-HILL *4.5m NE of Leominster*
The meaning of the name seems obvious, but it is not. The Domesday Book name was Miceltune, from the Anglo-Saxon Micla-tun, meaning 'large settlement'. Size is comparative; today it is a small hamlet lost in the lanes and the little hills to the north-west of Laysters, on the Leominster to Tenbury road.

We visited on a Spring evening as the sun set behind the church causing a glare that rendered the village all but invisible. The effect was quite magical. It appeared as a storybook vision, a place that knew not of anger or grief; a veritable land of lost content. The lane ran through a corn field, unencumbered with hedges, and down a little dip.

It took courage to continue for the vision would doubtless vanish as one came closer. And it did, though it need not have. It is all down to those damnable farmers who litter 'our' countryside with 'their' awful sheds. The planning laws allow them licence and they take full advantage. Two charming cottages, one of stone the other black and white, are confronted by a large, derelict corrugated asbestos thing, and the church does its best to ignore a monster shed that, though sturdy and well kept, is still an eyesore and totally out of character with the rest of this little place.

The grey stone parish church is dedicated to Saint Mary. The nave and chancel are Norman; the strong, gaunt tower and the east window (which was brought here from Pudleston church) are 13th century and the roof of the nave is 15th century. The double piscina and the font are both Norman, the latter with characteristic zig-zag ornament. Just to the north of the church is Middleton Farm, a pleasant brick house of 1692 with sandstone quoins, four bays, two storeys and a hipped roof. In the grounds there is a square, brick-built gazebo.

At Five Ashes, 1/4m SE of the church, is Lower Wither Farm, a modest two-and-a-half-storey Georgian house of three bays, nicely set with woods to the rear, and bleached shipboard barns romantically collapsing to the front.

Easton, 1/2m ESE of the church, is just one farm, properly called Lower Easton. Much of what we see is handsome Victorian stone, though parts of the house are timber-framed. The owner intends to restore the barns, not develop them into dwellings. Good for him. A feature of the outbuildings is the triangular vents in many of the walls, a feature also to be found in a barn at the crossroads in nearby Laysters. An estate owner's foible, no doubt.

Nurton Court, 1/4m N of the church, is an irregular two-and-a-half-storey, red brick Georgian house approached along a daffodil-lined drive. It has a stabling range, very much in its proper use, and a large development of superior terraced houses based on the farm outbuildings.

Ford Farm, 1/2m NE of the church, is a friendly stone house with three gables, gambolling lambs and a stream. The kind of place where the sun always shines.

Moor Abbey, 1m SSE, just off the A4112, is a 16th and 17th century house that once belonged to the Priory at Leominster. The dovecote is 17th century; the fishpond is probably mediaeval. A public footpath from the main road leads around the very side of the house and on up to Middleton-on-the-Hill. I bet that pleases the occupants.

Some customs, quaint and curious. At Easter, tenants holding land from the church paid six eggs every three years as ground rent. A lady dressed all in white can be seen sitting on Gravenor's Bridge on moonlit nights. Dick Phillips of Middleton danced the morris on Widemarsh Moor in 1609 at the age of 102. He had 11 fellow dancers from other parts of the county whose combined ages were 1,200 years. It must be the good air, or the cider.

MOCCAS *10m WNW of Hereford*
An early tale has it that Dubricius, or Dyfrig, a 6th century Celtic Christian saint, had a vision and was told by an angel to search for a place that had a white sow and a litter of pigs, and to found a monastery there. He found such a place and named it moch-rhos, 'pig-moor', which in time has become Moccas. The saint lived in this place "well wooded and abounding in fish" for several years. His monastery was destroyed by Anglo-Saxon raiders and the yellow plague. It is a very scattered settlement, without a nucleus, on the B4352 in the valley of the River Wye.

We approached from Preston-on-Wye, along the river road, through Bycross which consists of a farm, a couple of cottages and an orchard full of sheep guarded by a black and white border collie. There are craggy oaks in the grey-brown fields and hedgerows, and the roadside ditch runs like a stream. The abutments of a now dismantled bridge to Monnington look very forlorn. The river runs placidly. A stone lodge stands at the entrance to the dusty drive that leads into the grounds of Moccas Court. It passes the walled garden now packed with a plantation of conifers - the old Victorian gardeners must be turning in their graves - a herd of Hereford cattle and suicidal pheasants, and delivers one to the church.

Saint Michael's is a delightful little Norman building. Except for the belfry, some enlarged Decorated windows of about 1300, and a restoration by G.G. Scott (Junior) in 1870, it is very much in its original state. It has a nave, chancel and apse all built of tufa, a spongy fine textured limestone, soft to work with when newly quarried, but

Above: Moccas, the deer park in Winter.
Right: Moreton on Lugg, an old hollow oak tree used as a house, a station master's office and a donkey stable.

very durable. The sandstone tympana were richly carved but have worn badly. That on the south side had a Tree of Life and men being attacked by animals.

The de Fresnes family, who built this church, are commemorated in the early 14th century stained glass windows. One depicts a castle turret with two figures dressed in yellow holding the red, white and blue standard of the de Fresnes; another has their shield with two green birds. One of their knights lies in stone effigy on his 14th century tomb-chest, his legs crossed. The de Fresnes castle stood 3/4m SW of the church, but more on that later.

Moccas Court as we see it today was built in 1775-81 by Anthony Keck to plans drawn up by Robert Adam. We found it empty and somewhat forbidding. It is of brick, two and a half storeys high, with five bays by seven bays, a Venetian window and a one-storey bow to the front (added in 1792), and a larger bay to the rear overlooking the River Wye. The interior is very fine with a flying staircase, a circular viewing room, an oval hall that rises the full height of the house to a glass dome, good fireplaces and expensive wall coverings. The grounds were landscaped by Capability Brown in 1778 and after. Humphrey Repton also did some work here. The lodges are early 19th century by G.S. Repton who was working for John Nash at the time. There is a cricket pitch within the grounds.

Edward Cornewall of Berrington married Frances, the widow of Henry Vaughan, in 1650. We know nothing of his house but it was his descendants who ordered the new mansion of 1781. Sir George Cornewall was rector of the church for 40 years and he is mentioned frequently in Francis Kilvert's diaries. In 1839 Mary Jane Cornewall, aged 17, was drowned in the River Wye. It is said to be her ghost, a lady dressed in grey, that has often been seen walking the grounds. The Cornewalls played a major part in the social life of the county and the first Sir George was a friend of Handel; indeed, he was an executor of his estate. It is said that music could always be heard in the house.

However, in 1916 Sir William Cornewall moved to a smaller house in the grounds and in 1946 he sold the furniture and the contents, including some 3,000 books. He died unmarried and childless and the estate was inherited by the Chestermaster family. They are the present owners and are slowly refurnishing, sometimes with the original pieces. At the time of writing the Court is only open on Thursday afternoons in the summer months. The gardens are well cared for and are still a feature of the property.

The sole facility the villagers have is a village hall. Their dwellings have arranged themselves into several little clusters. One is by the main entrance drive to the Court which had the school, which became the post office, which is now a house; one is on the main road which has the War Memorial, telephone box, a few black and white cottages, the old blacksmith's shop (now run as a gun shop), and a man with a Caterham car; and another is to the north-west at Cross End Farm. Some 300 yards N of Cross End, on the banks of the Wye at SO 345 434, is a petrifying spring. The water emerges from the gravel and deposits lime to form a slope of travertine, or tufa, the material used for the church. It is initially very soft but hardens with age. Depple is probably from Drip Well.

On the dark hill to the west are the 300 acres of the mediaeval Moccas Deer Park, still well stocked with fallow deer who come down to drink at the stream in the evening. There is a deer fence between the park and the road which has a deer leap. This is so designed that a stray deer can jump in over the lowered fence, but because of the deep ditch on the inside cannot jump out. Every lord worth his salt had a deer park and there were some 35 in Herefordshire at one time. Now there are only four. The woods are ancient and have an ancient ecological system making them a Site of Special Scientific Interest. "Mosses and lichens are particularly notable and the beetles include three species known only from this site in Britain." *The Macmillan Guide to Britain's Nature Reserves*. The oak trees, some of which have girths exceeding 25ft., have been made famous by the Reverend Francis Kilvert's description of them: "I fear these grey old men of Moccas, those grey, gnarled, low-browed, knock-kneed, bowed, bent, huge, strange, long-armed, deformed, hunchbacked misshapen oak men that stand waiting and watching century after century biding God's time with both feet in the grave and yet tiring down and seeing out generation after generation, with such tales to tell, as when they whisper them to each other in the midsummer nights, make the silver birches weep and the poplars and aspens shiver and the long ears of the hares and rabbits stand on end. They look as if they had been at the beginning and making of the world, and they will probably see its end."

Just beyond the eastern boundary of the wooded area of the deer park is a pool, 100 yards or so south of the main road. To the west of the pool is the site (SO 384 425) of the early Norman motte and bailey castle. It has all but disappeared but once it had a roughly oval bailey enclosed by a ditch, with a subsidiary scarp within it, and enclosed about 2.1/4 acres. At the east end was a small motte with a ditch between it and the bailey, but this is now totally ploughed out.

Licence to crenellate this castle was granted to Sir Hugh de Freyne in 1293 but there were restrictions: the walls were not to exceed 10ft in height beneath the battlements and there were to be no towers or turrets. The Freynes, later Frene, lived here at least until the death of Richard Frene in the 1370s. By the mid-15th century the estate had passed to Edward ap Meredith and from the mid-16th century the Vaughan family were in possession. From the Vaughans it went to the Cornewalls as already detailed.

The Round House, 3/4m SW, on the main road, is a dwelling made from the battered tower of a red brick windmill. Battered means it has a batter, a slope to the walls as in a cone.

MOCKTREE *5.5m E of Ludlow*

The name is from the Welsh, moch - tref, 'pig-homestead', meaning 'pig farm'. It lies to the north of the Ludlow to Leintwardine road, the A4113, near Leintwardine. The original 'horse road' passed right through the handful of farms and cottages that now lie marooned on a dead-end track. The route of the old road can be seen quite clearly on the Ordnance Survey map. It leaves the modern road at the bend called Fiddler's Elbow (SO 426 758) as a public footpath, passes through Mocktree and joins up with a lane north of Todding Cottage at SO 412 754.

It seems that this old road with its gentle gradients and airy views was abandoned when the large limestone quarries were developed south of the hamlet. The new road provides access to these cliff-faces by following a rather tortuous route along a steep, wooded valley. It is undoubtedly scenic, with a precipitous drop to one side and the quarry faces and batteries of limestone kilns to the other. The produce of the kilns, the burnt lime, was primarily used for agricultural purposes.

A dead straight lane now joins Mocktree to the new main road. The landscape up on the hill is a little strange.

The hedgerows have not been cut back and trimmed for many years and are now full of gaps and small trees. Many of the pasture fields are small, grazed by sheep. What is obviously another old, abandoned road leads north. It passes through a tunnel of overhanging trees and for all the world is everyman's idea of what an 18th century coaching road should look like. It ends at some barns but continues as a footpath down to a point just east of Far Barn, where six paths and tracks meet in the middle of nowhere at SO 426 760. Intriguing. The people are suspicious of strangers up here in the high pastures close to the Shropshire border.

At Todding, on the main road 3/4m WSW of Mocktree, there are a few cottages and the aptly named Cottagers' Comfort, a white rendered freehouse. Mine host is an amiable ex-miner, who remembers the pick and shovel days. He it was who gave us the information about the old road. In the cellars there is a well, a baking oven and a boiler, once used for brewing beer and cider in the days when it was a cider house. Much of the land hereabouts still belongs to the Downton Castle estate, now owned by the French Perrier Water heiress. Her gamekeepers have been shooting, snaring and poisoning the local cats for several years now. There was a local outcry and it stopped for a while. Now, we learn, it has started again. Four-wheel drive vehicles are seen roaming the country at night 'lamping'. Anything whose eyes shine in the light is shot.

MONKHIDE *7m ENE of Hereford*

Monkhide is a spread-about village 2/3m S of the crossing of the A4103 and the A417 at Newtown, which is now considered to be a part of the settlement. The name presumably means what it says 'the hide belonging to the monks'. At the time of Domesday Book the one hide of the manor was simply called Hide and was held by Tesselin from Roger de Lacy. Presumably, it later passed to a monastery. A hide is a unit of land, but it can vary greatly in size from one area to another. What is more, it does not always mean a physical dimension, rather a unit of value for the purpose of taxation. However, in Herefordshire a hide can be taken to be about 120 acres.

Today you are never very far from an orchard at Monkhide. The River Lodon skirts the settlement to the east and less than a mile downstream joins the River Frome.

The dominant feature, though, is a well preserved stretch of the now disused Hereford to Gloucester canal of 1839. It is crossed by three bridges. The most elegant is the Skew Bridge (SO 612 440) which has fine brickwork on the underside of the arch. It was designed by the engineer, Stephen Ballard (1804-1891). The canal meets the road at a very oblique angle, but rather than put a dog-leg in either the road or the canal to make the crossing at right angles, Ballard took up the challenge and produced a little bit of engineering art. Standing underneath is rather like being in a gigantic rifle barrel with bricks spiralling from one corner to the other. Anyone interested in canals, and there are a lot of us around these days, is recommended to *The Hereford and Gloucester Canal* by David Bick.

The Wharf House stands beside the old wharf, which was mostly used for unloading coal. The stables have been converted into two houses but in recent years a canal society has been clearing the canal and restoring the towpath. Monksbury Court stands near the canal.

Newtown has grown up around the crossroads to the north of Windmill Hill. There used to be a tollgate here. Now it has a garage, a post office-cum-general store, a retailer of motor cars, a carpenter's shop and a public house, The Newtown, which has accommodation.

MONKLAND *2.5m ESE of Leominster*

It stands in the valley of the River Arrow, just off the A4112 Hereford to Hay road which acts as a by-pass. The name means 'the part of the Lene district belonging to the monks'. The Lene was the Celtic name for the land between the rivers Arrow and Lugg. It is from lleoni, 'easily flooded'. In the reign of William II, 1087-1110, there was a small cell of Benedictine monks on the manor. They were subordinate to Saint Peter's Abbey at Conches in Normandy, and to the Priory at Wootton Wawen in Warwickshire.

Monkland is situated in 'big country' - large expanses of fields without any human habitations. The farms are mixed beef and arable with some hops. The village is nucleated but has been by-passed by the new road. It has a post office, village shop, a modern village hall and a pub, the Traveller's Rest, which backs on to the 11-acre common. Only a few of the black and white cottages remain. In 1966 a cafe and farm shop was opened at Pleck Farm, just off the main road. The owners are specialists in cheese and manufacture Little Hereford, as made by Ellen Yeld about 1900. Visitors can see a demonstration of the process and purchase a variety of other English and Welsh farmhouse cheeses.

The church of All Saints was rebuilt in 1866 by G.E. Street who took great care to be as accurate to the original as possible. There are four Norman windows in tufa surrounds. Of the late 13th century are several windows, the south doorway and the tower. The new shingled spire curiously overhangs the tower. The font is Norman and the stained glass in the east window is by Hardman, to a design by G.E. Street. Sir Henry W. Baker (1821-77) was vicar here from 1851 until his death. He was the chief compiler of the monumental *Hymns Ancient & Modern* and was himself the author of the words of many hymns. Perhaps his best known work was Praise, O praise our Lord and King. He was also the author of the quaintly titled *Daily Prayers for the Use of Those who have to Work Hard*. Sir Henry is buried near the lych-gate, which he paid for and which was erected by Street at the time of the rebuilding.

In the autumn of 1912 Vaughan Williams accompanied the folklorist Mrs. E..M. Leather to a hopyard near Monkland to collect traditional songs. The great composer said later that it was his most memorable musical impression of that year. This is Mrs. Leather's description of that evening: "After some trouble Dr. and Mrs. Vaughan Williams and I found their camp in a little round field at dusk, on a fine September evening. There were several caravans, each with its wood fire burning, the Stephens and other families being there, besides Alfred Price Jones, whom we were seeking. His wife was very ill, and we found him with her under an awning near one of the fires. He agreed to sing, so we all sat down on upturned buckets, kindly provided for us by the gypsies, and while Dr. Vaughan Williams noted the tune his wife and I took down alternate lines of the words. It is difficult to convey to those who have never known it the joy of hearing folk-songs as we heard that pathetic ballad (Cold Blows the Wind); the difference between hearing it there and in a drawing room or concert hall is just that between discovering a wild flower growing in its native habitat and admiring it when transplanted to a botanic garden". Jones and his wife, Harriet, ended their days at Clun Workhouse.

Some bits and pieces. In the Monkland area it is considered very bad luck to point at the rainbow. It is also bad luck to put a horse to work on New Year's Day. The Domesday Book mentions a mill at Monkland. In 1861 it was still on the same site.

Wall End, 1/2m W of the village, is really one large farm. An unbelievably rough track leads to an agglomeration of stone and timber-framed barns, big modern sheds, a ruined cider-mill and Hereford cattle. As we drove away we passed a party of city slickers in smart four-wheel drive vehicles out to butcher a few birds.

At Arrow Green, 1m NW, is the square-framed Arrow Mill with a tall, grey house beside and a three-arched stone bridge over the river. Golden Cross has a pair of red brick cottages at the crossing of the A44 and the B4457, 2m WSW of Monkland, in undulating sheep and cow country. Golden Cross sounds like a pub name.

MONNINGTON-ON-WYE *8.5m ENE of Hereford*
It lies in the valley of the meandering River Wye, off the ancient Celtic Portway, now the A438 Hereford to Hay road. The name Monnington is Anglo-Saxon and means 'settlement of Manna's people'. Orchards line the access lane to the hamlet which consists of a few cottages, some black and white, the Court and the church. Monnington Court is a 17th century stone house but has a 'great hall'. This is now divided by a first floor, but the panelled ceiling of the hall, of about 1600, and part of the finely worked screen dated at 1656 (though it might be an assembly of earlier work) have survived. The screen divided the living area of the great hall from the buttery (where butts of beer and wine were kept) and the kitchen. Over the wide front door, which leads to the screens passage, is a carved headpiece depicting two monsters.

An avenue of Scots firs, called Monnington Walk, runs north-west from the Court towards the river cliffs of The Scar at Brobury. It was probably planted in 1679 by Ulvedall Tomkyns to celebrate his election to the House of Commons for the Weobley Division. The Walk heads south-west after about 1/2m and leads to the old river crossing. From 1868 to 1962 there was a Gothic, cast-iron bridge to Moccas but it suffered flood damage and was demolished. The abutments remain.

The church of Saint Mary stands hard by the Court. It has a 15th century Perpendicular tower but the rest was replaced in 1679 by Ulvedall Tomkyns. The new church is remarkably complete and of its time. The windows are mullioned and transomed and have round arches. The furniture is noted for the profusion of columns with twists and there is a good, carved coat of arms of Charles II. The font is dated 1680. Ulvedall Tomkyns has a black stone monument and Robert Perrott, died 1667, is commemorated by a bust. Just outside the porch is a stone slab reputed to mark the last resting place of Owain Glyndwr, (1349-c.1416) the Welsh national hero. One of his daughters, Margaret, married Roger Monnington, the early 15th century squire.

Recent restoration work on the church was carried out by the Hereford architects Peter Cripwell and Associates on behalf of English Heritage. They used lime mortar because this traditional material has many advantages over modern cement which is brittle and cracks easily. Lime mortar is flexible. If movement takes place it self-heals. What is more, the lime 'weathers'; it gets wet because it is porous but dries without trapping moisture in the fabric. Old buildings of both stone and timber are 'soft'; new buildings are 'hard' and it is wrong to mix building methods when restoring. One of the county's experts on old buildings and a confirmed 'limer' is Tom Addyman of Upper Broxwood Farm, near Weobley.

It was a custom of the people in Monnington to nail crosses of birch and rowan (mountain ash) to their houses and barns to protect them from evil and the spells of witches. These crosses were renewed each New Year's Day. Vaughan Williams collected some folksongs at Monnington in the early 20th century.

MONNINGTON STRADDEL *8m WSW of Hereford*
It lies off the B4348 near Vowchurch in the Golden Valley. The tiny hamlet is overlooked by the high ground of Vowchurch Common to the west, and Timberline Wood to the east. When Owain Glyndwr vanished from history in 1415 it is thought by some that he came to live in Herefordshire with one or, at different times all, of his three surviving daughters: Janet at Croft, Alice at Kentchurch and Margaret at Monnington-on-Wye. It has been suggested that as he lay dying Glyndwr wished to see his three daughters for the last time. On the journey he died and was buried at either Monnington-on-Wye or Monnington Straddel. Alice had married John Scudamore who owned both Kentchurch Court and Monnington Straddel. The most impressive aspect of Glyndwr's powers of leadership was this: there is no record that any of his men either betrayed him or tried to usurp him, and he lived in treacherous times.

Close by the Court are the remains of either a castle or a moated manor house. An oval mound stands on a broad natural terrace surrounded by a ditch. A stream runs through part of the ditch, which was probably the outer defence of a crescent-shaped bailey. In the deciduous woods of Timberline Hill there is a prehistoric fortress, 1/4m ESE of the castle. It guards a gap into the Golden Valley and its rich pastures. As to the name, Monnington Straddel, Monnington means 'settlement of Manna's people'; Straddel is the old name for the Golden Valley and is derived from the Welsh ystrad, meaning 'valley'.

MORDIFORD *4m SE of Hereford*
The first element of the name could be from the Welsh mawr-ty, 'great house'. The settlement stands on the River Lugg which is normally quite sluggish here and easily fordable. The crossing is important because it is on one of the main roads out of Hereford. Less than 1/2m downstream the Lugg joins the River Wye which presents a much more formidable barrier to the traveller heading east. The hills that loom to the east belong to the Woolhope Dome, an area of woods and limestone hills and beautiful, unexpected vistas. It is justifiably most famous and a paradise for walkers.

The river is crossed at Mordiford by a long, sturdy stone bridge with nine arches. Two arches cross the river; the west, pointed arch is of the 14th century; and the east, rounded arch is 16th century, as are the two flood arches on the west. The causeway has a further five arches. There are central pedestrian refuges and cutwaters.

On occasion the river runs very high indeed and before the earth walls were built around the road, and the village of Hampton Bishop to the west, flooding was a major problem. From the lay-by at the west (Hereford) end of the bridge there is a signed walk to the confluence of the River Wye and the River Lugg.

The Battle of Mordiford Bridge took place during the Civil War. Barnabas Scudamore held the bridge for the king against the Scots but when the Earl of Leven began a

Top left: Much Marcle, Sir John (died 1650) and Lady Kyrle, in the church of Saint Bartholomew.
Top right: Mansel Lacy, the Old Post Office.
Centre: Mansel Lacy, once the estate village of Foxley.
Left: Mordiford, the River Lugg and the church of Holy Rood.

flanking movement Scudamore retreated to Hereford, which he held until relieved by the king's army.

The area adjacent to the south side of the bridge, where the Pentaloe Brook joins the Lugg, is a scrubby, watery wilderness; to the north it is gentle with meadows, meanders and sandy beaches. On summer weekends and evenings it has the air of a resort with dogs chasing balls and children splashing in the shallows.

In the mid-18th century a series of some 12 locks were constructed. These made the Lugg navigable by small, commercial boats as far as Leominster to the north. At Mordiford Bridge the Navigation Channel passed under the left bank arch and led to a stone-built lock. This is the best preserved lock on the river was in use until the early years of the 20th century. It was a pound lock with double gates and the remains are clearly visible where the Navigation Channel rejoins the main river. There was another lock a little further south at the confluence of the Lugg and the Wye but nothing can now be seen. At the bridgehead is the village.

The church, rectory, bridge and dwellings make a delightful group. The rectory is a handsome, Early Georgian, brick house of two and a half storeys, five bays with a projecting central bay, quoins, tall chimneys and steps to the front door. There has been a mill at Mordiford since Anglo-Saxon times. The present building was milling corn and animal feedstuffs until about 1935. During the Second World War it was given firing slits so that riflemen could defend the bridge over the Pentaloe. The original power source was a stream south of the Woolhope road but later a leat drew water off the Pentaloe. The mill is in the process of being restored and it is hoped to be used for milling wheat once again. The village has a post office-cum-general store, the Half Moon pub, and cottages of various shapes, sizes and ages, ranged close to the curling main road. They huddle together and an air of slightly austere mediaevalism pervades. In the mid-19th century, however, this was a thriving, bustling little regional centre with several shops, tailors, shoemakers and other tradesmen.

Before mains water came The Spout was used as a water supply. It has been tested and found to be of excellent quality, but water caused a tragedy here once. In 1811 the Pentaloe Brook became a raging torrent after a tremendous thunderstorm. The swirling waters brought down hundreds of tons of rock and mud and carried away a cider-mill, a barn and a cottage in which four people were drowned.

Sufton Court, a Palladian mansion, 1/2m N of the village, can be seen from the bridge. Humphrey Repton landscaped the grounds and it has a wooded park. The house is built of bath stone and has five bays, two and a half storeys, a one bay pediment with Venetian window below, a hipped roof and a porch of Ionic columns. It is undated but was standing in 1790. Sufton Court is the home of the Hereford family, who have held the estate since Norman times, and it is open to the public occasionally in the summer.

Old Sufton lies 500 yards to the north of Sufton Court. It has been reconstructed but has features of several periods, from a single-storeyed manor house to a 19th century farmhouse. There is something left of a painted room of about 1450, and a coffin lid variously described as Celtic and 13th century is located in the chimney breast. Outside there is a good 18th century, circular, brick dovecote crowned with a large lantern. Close by Old Sufton there are impressive quarry exposures of the Silurian limestone for which the Woolhope Dome is famous in geological circles.

The Hereford family held their Sufton manor on the condition that whenever the king rode across Mordiford Bridge they present him with a pair of gold spurs. In 1304 this became a pair of gilt spurs annually to the value of sixpence, and by 1387 to half a mark, three shillings and fourpence.

Mordiford is the estate village of Sufton. Agriculture is the main industry - cattle, sheep, arable, some orchards and hops, and timber. There are large areas of old woodland on this north-eastern quarter of the Woolhope Dome and oak bark, used for tanning, was quite an important crop at one time. The Mordiford Corn Dolly, originally an offering to the Celtic goddess of fertility, is quite famous. They are still made and are sought after by collectors. Modern ones incorporate hops. It is very likely that there has been a religious site at Mordiford from prehistoric times. The present church of Holy Rood has a Norman south doorway with carved capitals and an arch decorated with zig-zag; and in the vestry there is another, re-set, Norman doorway. The present tower was built in about 1811 but the two 13th century arches of the previous tower remain inside. Also of the 13th century there is a small inscribed coffin lid. All the windows are of the Victorian re-building. There are monuments to: Mary Vaughan, died 1635; Francis Woodhouse, died 1710; Francis Woodhouse, died 1726; and James Hereford, died 1823.

Until 1811 there was a 12ft long, green dragon with a red mouth and tongue painted on the tower of the church, which Professor Tristram says was probably of the 14th century. Now, big green dragons on church towers are not all that common in England and a number of folk tales developed to explain this unusual feature - or did they? Folk memories are exceeding long. They are often provably Celtic and even earlier. We must always remember that man was around when the most enormous and savage creatures inhabited this country. Actual events become mythologized and apparently absurd to modern people.

Anyway, here is Roy Palmer's synopsis of the Green Dragon of Mordiford tales. "Until 1811 a large green dragon could be seen painted on the west wall of Mordiford Church. Although the beast shown was in fact probably a wyvern from the arms of the priory of St. Guthlac (which held the living of Mordiford) it gave rise to a clutch of dragon stories. A girl called Maud found a dragon 'no bigger than a cucumber' wandering in the woods. Ignoring warnings she insisted on treating it as a pet. It soon moved from milk to meat, and started hunting first poultry, then sheep, then cattle. Finally it became a man-eater, living in Haugh Wood and following a path still known as Serpent Lane down to the confluence of the Lugg and the Wye. The dragon's end came in one of several ways. A condemned criminal, after being offered his life as a reward, hacked it to pieces while it slept; or hid in a cider barrel by the river and killed it by firing a gun through the bunghole. Alternatively the dragon impaled itself on a knife-studded barrel from which the man emerged to administer the coup-de-grace. The three stories unite in saying that the criminal failed to enjoy his triumph because he died from the after-effects of the dragon's noxious breath. A further twist is provided by the notion that the unfortunate hero was no outlaw, but a member of the respected Garston family. Yet another suggestion is that the villagers of Mordiford combined to hack the dragon to death as it slept off the effects of gorging itself on a drowned ox washed down the river. As late as 1875 the rector found two old women trying to drown a couple of newts in the font lest they grow up to renew the scourge. In 1973, to celebrate the centenary of their school, local children staged a pageant showing a battle between green and red dragons which ended when the red dragon went to the west to become the symbol of Wales while the green dragon became the picture on the church."

The domain of Mordiford extends to Checkley 1.3/4m ENE. I made a journey from Larport, in the flat valley of the River Frome, and here is a quote from my unedited notes:

"Larport, Georgian house, three bays, two storeys, dormers, hipped roof, hopkiln with cone and wind vane, stone walls. A single lonesome pine at crossroads. Straight over, uphill then fork left. Fir Tree pub at Priors Frome. Busy, many cars. Bank Holiday Monday (May 1995). Full of colourful salt of the earth locals and a few from foreign shores. Couple of pints. Talked to a farmer. About £180 a year rent to have an electric pylon on your land. Long views over plain of Frome valley marred by the pylons. Cottages of stone, black and white and some modern.

Uphill to Swordon Quarry Picnic Place. Sufton Estate sign. Beautiful wooded views, meadows, hills, super country. Farm, black and white and stone; such lovely country. Down into a bowl. Two orchards. Cottage with skinny timber framing, poor people, not afford to buy thick beams, stone outbuildings. Now in Checkley. Stilebridge over stream to buttercup field. Telephone kiosk, new. Open grassland, common land, like village green but uncut; grass fringed with woods. Delightful. Thatched cottage with stables; black and white, render, red brick, scattered squatters cottages.

Spoke to old man snoozing beneath a tree with flagon of cider beside him. Problems with water supply up here. Apparently some cottages have own wells, others abandoned. Had some cider and a sleep. Orchards, conifer plantations, gentle landscape. Heaven. Photographed country near Oxwood Farm. Crossroads, right. Such lovely country. On to Woolhope."

MORETON JEFFRIES *5m SW of Bromyard*
Moreton is from the Anglo-Saxon mor-tun, 'settlement by the fen, or marsh'. Jeffries, or Jeffreys, was presumably a mediaeval holder of the manor. It lies down a dead-end track off the Bromyard to Hereford road, the A465. At the time of the Norman Conquest it was a flourishing manor worth 100 shillings a year and was worth the same 22 years later, at the time of Domesday Book, when it was part of the estates of the church at Hereford. The manor also owned a salt-house in Droitwich.

At that time it was simply called Mortune, and was in Radlow Hundred. Radlow is from the Anglo-Saxon readhlaw, meaning 'red hill' and lingers on as the name of a wood just north of the former railway station (SO 611 416) at Stoke Edith.

Today, Moreton Jeffries is a small hamlet on the southwestern slopes of Windmill Hill, which is crowned with an Ordnance Survey Trigonometrical Point. The church is tiny and lurks amongst farm buildings and tall trees. It has a plain 14th century door; nave and chancel in one; a timber bell-turret and a Jacobean pulpit with sounding board, and dragons in the carvings.

Around Court Farm there are slight earthworks, the remains of the Domesday settlement also mentioned in the Lay Subsidy Roll of 1334. The line of a holloway is visible in a field east of the farm and there were remains of three fishponds south-west of the farmhouse, but these have been ploughed-out recently.

MORETON-ON-LUGG *3.5m N of Hereford*
'The settlement near a marsh on the River Lugg'. It lies on the A49 on which there is, indeed, a Marsh House, In Domesday Book it is recorded that there was a mill here and that it was worth £3 a year to the king, making it a manor of some substance. Moreton stands on flat land but above the flood plain of the river. Its proximity to Hereford and its position on a main road has meant that in the second half of the 20th century it has become that bland creature a 'dormitory town'.

The big house, Moreton Court, was very much the centre of things once upon a time, but was demolished in the 1950s, a reckless period when so many English mansions disappeared. But Church Farm soldiers on. This was the original moated manor and has seen the upstart come and go.

The bridge over the River Lugg was an important crossing point. The three-arched structure we see today is probably of the 16th century. It is a grand old man of a bridge so positioned that it crosses two waterways. The east bank arch is higher than the other two. This was the Navigation arch, raised in height to allow ships passage under the Act of 1697. The water flowing under the west bank arch runs in a separate channel from the river. This was the tail-race from the King's Mills that stood just upstream of the bridge. The site of this once very important mill is marked by pollarded willows. There was a mill here from at least Domesday and it belonged to the crown. In the 19th century floodgates were fixed to the arches of the bridge, probably to 'drown' the water meadows upstream to warm them and to enrich them with nutrients.

Moreton once possessed a feature probably unique in the whole of England, namely a station house and ticket office housed in a hollow oak tree. This was known locally as Eve. It had a circumference of 62ft and 15 people could take tea within it at one time. When the Hereford & Shrewsbury Railway was constructed a navvy made his home here. He thatched it, built a brick chimney and fitted a front door. It later became a store and lamp room and in 1862, when the line was leased to the Great Western Railway, it became the station house and ticket office. The railway still operates and runs hard by the river bridge.

The church of Saint Andrew is a Norman foundation but was rebuilt in 1867 by W.H. Knight. The cost was largely borne by Thomas Evans of Moreton Court. It is in the Geometrical style with a tower and stone spire. A solitary Norman window has been re-used in the chancel and the roof of the nave is 13th century. The mosaics are of 1887 and 1899. The first time the bells of the newly restored church were rung was to welcome their patron, Thomas Evans, to his last place of repose.

MORTIMER'S CROSS *5m NW of Leominster*
Mortimer's Cross is strategically placed in the valley of the River Lugg, at the crossing of the Roman Watling Street from Hereford to Leominster, the A4110, and the Presteigne to Ludlow road, the A4362. It consists of a few cottages, a wayside cider mill, a toll-house, an inn and a water-mill. The battle of Mortimer's Cross (Candlemass Day 1461) was actually fought on the Great West Field on the northern outskirts of Kingsland, 1.1/4m SE of Mortimer's Cross. There is something in the article on Kingsland about Edward Mortimer's bloody victory over the Lancastrians which concluded the War of the Roses. Seen from a position opposite the lay-by, on the B4362 immediately east of the crossroads, with the Lugg bridge to his left, the battlefield lies in front of the observer.

The hostelry at the crossroads is called Mortimer's Cross Inn. It is a stone and brick, colour-washed Georgian house of four bays with a hipped roof and dormers. At the time of writing it is up for sale and looking somewhat sorry for itself. The sign depicts the Yorkist emblems of the sun and the rose, united in the colours blue and purple.

Lucton Mill faces the pub across the river. It is a handsome stone-built building and the running gear, last used commercially in the 1940s, is in good order. It is now in the care of the Department of the Environment and can be seen grinding corn on selected days in the summer. The mill is gravity fed and has an undershot wheel, i.e., the water hits the wheel at the bottom, not the top.

Beside the main road is the timber yard of Good Brothers, established in 1946. They specialise in English hardwoods. At the time of writing the retail prices per cubic foot of the most important timbers are: oak, £14; elm, £16; yew, £25; and walnut, £45.

The lane between Mortimer's Cross and Upper Lye, 2m NW, follows the Covenhope Valley. This was the original course of the River Lugg before it was altered by glaciation. Grain is a traditional crop here and wheat and barley are sometimes grown together as 'muncorn'. The hamlet of Covenhope lies below the wooded upper slopes of Shobdon Hill to the west and Mere Hill to the east.

MUCH BIRCH *6m SSW of Hereford*
For its sins it stands on the A49, the Hereford to Ross road. At the time of Domesday Book it was called Mainavre and was held by Roger de Lacy who sub-let it to Costelin for six sesters of honey. Costelin is from the Old German Costila. Much Birch shares the social facilities of Little Birch and King's Thorn which lie one mile north. At Much Birch there is the Pilgrim Hotel, and at the hamlet called The Cleaver, 1/4m SE, is the Axe and Cleaver Inn. The Old School of 1865 is now a guest house run by Captain Hulland formerly of the Merchant Navy, and Dock Harbour Master at Boston, Lincolnshire. A cedar tree beside the road acts as a marker to the settlement.

The church of Saint Mary and Saint Thomas of Canterbury was rebuilt in 1837 by Thomas Foster. It has a nave, a chancel, a tower with battlements on corbels and steeply gabled buttresses, and lancet windows. Cherubs and clouds are painted on the vaulted chancel ceiling and the stained glass is High Victorian. In the little valley, 400 yards to the east, the Wrigglebrook flows past Strickstenning Hall and New Mills on its way to join the River Wye.

In 1996 the Poor Clares moved from Lower Bullingham to a brand new 'all mod cons' monastery at Little Birch. The 15 nuns were criticized by journalists who seem to have confused vows of poverty with abject poverty.

MUCH COWARNE *5m SSW of Bromyard*
In 1086 it was Cuure, from the Old English cu-aern, 'cowhouse', and was a sizeable manor, with a priest, a reeve, 26 villagers, eight smallholders, four slaves and a blacksmith and its value was correspondingly great at £25. It had been a part of King Harold's holdings, but by the time of Domesday it had passed to Alfred of Marlborough whose castle at Ewyas Harold was only worth £10. In mediaeval times it had a Charter to hold a weekly market and an annual fair.

Much Cowarne is most easily approached from Burleygate on the A465 Bromyard to Hereford road, and lies in the valley of the River Lodon, an ancient British name meaning 'muddy water'. The farms and cottages are scattered over the 3,535 acres of the parish. Only a handful stand by the church. This is hops and orchard country, though both these crops are making way for cereals and pasture these days.

The last of the land-owning local squires, the Bournes, moved away in 1921. Today most of the farmland belongs to the Royal Assurance company, though some old farming families remain - the Orgys, Buftons, Boulcotts and Pudges. A farmer Pudge is mentioned in the poem Cider Annie recorded by Pat Palmer on the CD *Songs and Dances of Herefordshire* (1996). In the lanes are old cottages and farms of stone and half timber. Many of the farms turn their backs to the highway, their fronts to the fields.

Parsonage Farm, 1/4m N of the village, is a good timber-framed farmhouse. At Cowarne Court, 1/2m SSW, there is a circular dovecote, thought to be mediaeval, and a mighty oak tree. The village itself has a notable Gothic style school of 1858, paid for by the squire of the day but which closed its doors in 1969. It then served as a Straw Craft Centre, but has subsequently been converted to holiday cottages. The rock-faced, ivy-clad, sandstone buildings, the wooded gardens - home to four tame pigeon-doves - make a most charming ensemble.

Paunceford Court is a stone and brick farmhouse which stands hidden behind several large, derelict stone and brick barns. They also obscure the church which stands on a rise just to the west.

The church of Saint Mary has a tower, Norman in its lower part, Early English in the upper; a 14th century aisle, and a Victorian porch. The rest, including the graceful arcade, is mostly 13th century. There are four piscinas altogether. Amongst the monuments are memorials to: Edmund Fox, died 1617, and wife; Sybil Reed, died 1624; the battered stone effigy of a 13th century knight with crossed legs that might be Grimbald Pauncefot; and another stone effigy in the chancel.

In the 17th century Silas Taylor, a captain in the Parliamentary army, writes of having seen the stone effigies of Grimbald Pauncefot of Cowarne and Constantia, daughter of Sir John de Lingen. They had been married in 1253. Grimbald was cross-legged and Constantia had her left arm partly raised but the hand was missing and apparently deliberately sculpted in this way. The story goes that Grimbald was captured by the Moors whilst on a Holy Crusade. As ransom Saladin sadistically asked for "a joint of his wyffe". Constantia sent for a surgeon from Gloucester Priory and had her left hand cut off above the wrist. It was sent to Saladin and Grimbald was released. Part of the moat at Pauncefoot Court, just east of the church, still exists but there is little here now that Grimbald would recognise.

In the 17th century the inhabitants of Much Cowarne believed that the church was originally intended to be built on a hill to the north-east of its present position but every night the materials were mysteriously removed to where the church now stands.

It was Michael Baker, a gamekeeper of Mill Lane, Much Cowarne, who supplied the Lord Lieutenant of the County's gamekeeper with the illegal poison called Endrin which was used to kill a rare Red Kite and four dogs at Gatley Park, Leinthall Earls, in 1990. The case was covered by the national press and television. Vast stocks of the chemical were discovered locally at Much Cowarne and Whitbourne. The poison is not only lethal in very small doses, it causes lingering and agonising death.

Today, Burleygate, 1.1/2m NW, is considered to be part of the 'settlement at large'. Here, clustered along the main

Ode to Owain Glyndwr

Those rainy nights in the mountains.
That's what I remember most.
Old bones beginning to ache,
Wondering if this madcap
Scheme should continue;
Counting the dead
Glistening in glory,
But tomorrow the men must be fed.
My need is for bread,
Not songs in metres
Known only to bards.
Yesterday we saw the plumes
Of Henry's fires.
The smoke whirled round
Their funeral pyres.
Go home Englishmen,
Leave our mountains
And our streams,
Leave us to our Celtic dreams.

Those rainy nights in the mountains,
That's what I remember most.
Not the clamorous din
Of Henry's mighty host.
Not the woods on fire,
Not the cohorts,
Not the brave,
Just those rainy nights,
And those oh so aching bones.
Henry, I beg thee stay your hand,
Leave us to our restless land,
Leave us to our mountain streams,
Leave us to our Celtic dreams.

Michael Raven

Top: Owain Glyndwr's Great Seal. The only known contemporary likeness we have.
Centre: Glyndwr's Great Seal, the reverse.
Opposite: King Henry IV of England, Glyndwr's opponent for ten bitter years. He died in 1413, two years before Glyndwr disappeared in 1415.

road are a post office-cum-general store, a new school, a pub, the police station and the village hall. Together with modern houses they form a rather bleak prospect. It is always a surprise when travelling by night to come across the floodlit road island at the junction of the A465 and the A417.

MUCH DEWCHURCH *5.5m SSW of Hereford*
It stands by the Worm Brook on the B4348, about 3/4m west of the Hereford to Monmouth road, the A466. The name Dewchurch means 'the church of Dewi', Welsh for David. It was probably founded by a local patron called David and in the Celtic tradition was named after him. Later, this dedication became confused with Saint David, the patron saint of Wales. Until the mid-17th century Welsh was the first tongue of the people of Much Dewchurch. Just to the south is the blessed hill of Bryngwyn, a strong clue that there was a pagan religious site here in pre-Roman times.

The village lies amongst gentle, wooded hills. There are several old buildings. Church Farm House has a 13th century core; the vicarage is 14th to 15th century; the Church House is Elizabethan and was once the village school; the village school is now a private school; the Black Swan is timber-framed and has a 14th century core.

The church of Saint David is mostly Norman with a 13th century tower, some windows of about 1300 and a 14th century porch. The font is Norman, the pulpit Jacobean. There are many handsome monuments to members of the Pye and Symons families who lived at The Mynde. Amongst their numbers was Walter Pye, Attorney General to James I, died 1625.

The Camp, in a field 350 yards east of the church, is probably an early Norman motte and bailey timber-stockaded castle. It stands on a small hill. The earthwork is a roughly oval-shaped mound surrounded by a ditch with slight traces of an inner bank and a further bank beyond. Traces of two outer enclosures also remain.

The Mynde, 1.1/4m SW of the church, is the capital house of the parish. The name is from the Welsh mynydd, 'mountain'. It lies on a spur by the ponded source of the Worm Brook and is approached down a very long access track that passes through the old deer park. The house we see from outside is Georgian. The east front has nine bays, and two and a half storeys, all rendered, and a Tuscan columned porch. Two long wings extend behind, to the west. The original house had a great hall in the east front with two short cross wings which may have been towers. The space between was later infilled and the wings extended. The house was then given its present facade and the great hall was made resplendent, the finest Early Georgian room in Herefordshire. It is five bays long and two storeys high with a coved ceiling and giant Corinthian pilasters between which are panels decorated with still life representations of the arts - painting, music, sculpture and architecture. Above the doors are medallions with profiles of early English kings. The door surrounds and friezes are richly decorated with a variety of traditional plaster motifs, and in the room behind the hall there are two Jacobean fireplaces.

The Woodlands, 200 yards S of The Mynde, was once home to Gwen McBryde. She was the widow of a friend of the much admired ghost story writer Montagne Rhodes James. Mr. James was a regular visitor to The Woodlands and sometimes used local people and places in his stories. *The Stalls of Barchester Cathedral* and *A View from a Hill* partly used the setting of Hereford Cathedral, and *The Five Jars* was written for Gwen's daughter in 1916. Several of his tales have been broadcast as television dramas in recent years. These include *The Mezzotint, Lost Hearts* and *Oh Whistle and I'll Come to You, My Lad. The Ghost Stories of M.R. James* was published in 1931.

At Hill Farm, Much Dewchurch, Major Haig has 120 acres of dessert apple orchards and 40 acres of cider trees. He makes 1,500 gallons of cider a year, the limit that avoids excise duty, and sells the unused apples to Bulmers.

A mile or so south of The Mynde is the Devil's Wood. It stands on the north side of Orcop Hill and is also known locally as the Fairy Ring or Poor Man's Wood. It is said to have been a sacred grove of the Silurian Celts and that human sacrifices were made here. It is also said that if the wood is felled the owner of The Mynde will die within a year. Another belief is that the wychelm on the Witches' Tump, in the grounds of the house, marks the spot where a witch was burned alive.

Bryngwyn, 3/4m SE of the church, lies close to the hamlet of Wormelow Tump. The name is Welsh and is from bryn 'hill', and gwyn 'blessed', hence 'blessed hill'. The present house was built in 1868 and is mock-Tudor stone with gables and an irregular front. The previous house which stood on the square, moated site lies 1/4m NW. In 1681 this was the scene of a murder. Robert Pye, of The Mynde, was a Protestant magistrate. He attempted to serve a summons on his Catholic neighbour at Bryngwyn. A struggle took place and Robert Pye was killed. On several occasions since then the spirits of two men have been seen reliving the struggle beneath a big walnut tree in the grounds of Bryngwyn. The moat itself is haunted by a black cat. The new house at Bryngwyn was the home of Sir James Rankin, M.P. who gave the Free Library to Hereford City in 1872 and founded the Hereford County College in 1880. He had 15 gardeners. Today the house suffers in silence as a place in multiple occupation. Flats and holiday accommodation are bad enough but an engineering works in the ballroom!?

At the entrance to Bryngwyn there used to be a prehistoric burial mound, the Wormelow Tump. This was the reputed grave of Mordred, nephew of King Arthur, who was murdered by Arthur at Gamber Head, 3/4m S on the A466. Alas, the mound was removed for road widening in the 19th century. At Gamber Head there is a clump of trees beside a stone barn at SO 494 296. Amongst the trees is a spring-fed pool called The Eye of Amr, the source of the Gamber Brook. Amr is an alternative name of Mordred.

MUCH MARCLE *4.5m SW of Ledbury*
It lies on the A49 Ledbury to Ross road. The name Marcle is from the Old English mearc-leah, 'boundary wood'. It is a handsome, mature village which exudes an air of landlordly confidence. And well it might because from Anglo-Saxon times it has been an important regional centre, not a town but influential nevertheless.

At the time of Domesday Book Much Marcle was held by the king and had a considerable population. Its wealth was reflected in a tax value of £30. Fuel timber from its woods was exchanged for salt from Droitwich and before 1066 the outlier of Turlestane (probably Perrystone Hill area) paid a rent of 50 lumps of iron and six salmon. There was a mill, a reeve, a Frenchman and a radknight (a civilian messenger-cum-escort); and the church of Saint Mary Cormeilles, Normandy, held the land, the tithe, a priest and the church.

Today the village has a post office-cum-general store, three pubs, a Memorial Hall of 1921, a garage, a Church of England primary school of 1833, and a goodly variety of dwellings. These include the elegant Queen Anne rectory of 1703, which has quoins, five bays, two storeys, dormers and a hipped roof, and is now called Phillips House; and at the other extreme is the Bower, just south of the church, which is a tiny, single cell, 16th century house of cruck construction with a thatched roof. Originally it was one room with a platform, like a minstrels' gallery, used for sleeping.

The church entrance leads off a 'close of cottages'. The lychgate is a topiary yew hedge arch. By it stands a huge and ancient yew tree now thought to be some 1,500 years old. That means that it has lived through all history from the time that the Romans left Britain. Stand beside that tree and things take on a new perspective. It has for company an old preaching cross which has steps, base and the stump of a broken shaft.

In 1616 Joanna Nurden came to Saint Bartholomew's and whilst kneeling in the churchyard placed a curse upon John Sargeant and his wife. Not an uncommon practice. In more recent times the ashes of the body of the serial-killer Frederick West, who hanged himself in 1994 whilst awaiting trial, were scattered in the graveyard. His family came from Much Marcle and his parents are buried here.

The tall, grey stone church of Saint Bartholomew has a central red stone tower. This is 15th century but most of the rest is 13th century including the typical Herefordshire east window of three stepped-lancet lights. Below the graceful arcades and arches is a fine collection of grotesque carvings, including a pagan Green Man with foliage emanating from his mouth and a Christian cross hanging from his neck. Someone was hedging his bets. There is stained glass by C.E. Kempe of 1877 and a Musica Celestis relief by Lady Feodora Gleichan of about 1928.

However, it is the effigies that take pride of place. Lady Grandison, nee Blanche Mortimer, died 1347, was the wife of Sir Peter who died in 1352 and lies in Hereford Cathedral. Her effigy is strikingly beautiful and realistic; the slightly parted lips, closed eyes, and elegant hands command one's attention. She lies on an elaborate altar-tomb with close-fitting head-dress, long veil, tight-sleeved gown, her rosary in her hand and a long-eared dog at her feet. In the Kyrle Chapel are two stone effigies of about 1400, a knight with pointed helmet and moustache, and a lady with angels at her head and puppies playing in the folds of her skirt. Here, too, is Sir John Kyrle, died 1650, of the family that spawned the Man of Ross. Best of all, though, is the oaken effigy of a franklin, a wealthy freeman of about 1360. He is probably Walter de Helyon and lies here not dressed in lavish finery or battle armour but in simple civilian costume: a close-fitting, buttoned jerkin, a tipper (like a very short cape) with rolled collar, a hip belt, a short sword and a wallet. Until 1878 he used to head funeral processions at the church, a survival of the ancient custom of leading the cortege with an effigy of the deceased person. It was more convenient to use a ready-made stand-in. Wooden effigies are quite rare, and those of the lower orders even rarer.

The de Helyon's house was on the site now occupied by Hellens which stands 1/2m NE of the church at the end of a very long and very dusty, bumpy track. There has been a dwelling here since at least 1290. From that date it has been owned and lived in by descendants of a branch of the Mortimer family, though not in direct line. In 1326 Roger Mortimer (IV) became enamoured of Isabella, the French queen of Edward II, and he installed her at Hellens, protected by a small private army. Edward II was subsequently murdered at Berkeley Castle but it did not do Roger Mortimer a lot of good for he was hanged for treason by Edward's son and successor. But to return to Walter de Helyon. Walter was succeeded by his son-in-law, Richard Walwyn, and it was this family who built the early 17th century Jacobean brick house with mullioned and transomed windows that we see today. Some parts of the preceding house were incorporated into the new, in particular the tower containing a stone staircase at the rear of the property. The new Jacobean house was subsequently much reduced in size. Inside there are some good ceilings and fireplaces, and one overmantel refers to Mary Tudor (1553-58). Thomas Walwyn, died 1532, owned Hellens but also held messuages (houses with land) in Ledbury from the Bishop of Hereford by fealty (allegiance) and by the delivery of a red rose at the nativity of Saint John the Baptist. Later the estate passed to the Kennys. In the grounds there is an octagonal brick dovecote erected by Fulke Walwyn in 1641 which bears both his initials and those of Margaret Pye.

The house is embowered but the park is given over to agriculture. The main entrance gate piers stare forlornly on to a field. In the front garden there are some deer sculptures. Inside there are a number of rooms furnished with tapestries, armour and family possessions, and in an outbuilding there is a cider press and cider mill in situ. Hellens is open to the public but opening times are very restricted.

A local story tells how a daughter of the 16th century Walwyn family eloped with her lover and returned many years later with only the diamond ring he had given her. The family only took her back on the condition that she remain confined to her room for the rest of her life so that no one would know of the shame she had brought upon them. Her room with its barred windows and the bell she used to call for attention can still be seen.

Hellens also has three ghosts: a lunatic dressed in a long, hooded gown; a nun, regularly seen in this century; and a monk, killed here by Parliamentary troops during the Civil War, whose room has indelible bloodstains and a chilly atmosphere.

Saint Katherine of Audley, born 1272, is thought to have been staying at either Hellens or Audley Cottage (in Much Marcle) when she had the revelation that led her to Ledbury to live as a hermit. (See Ledbury.)

Mortimer's Castle, an early Norman fortress, stands just to the north of the church. The motte is about 50 yards in diameter and stands some 20ft above the bottom of the ditch. There is an inner bailey to the east defended by a semi-circular ditch; an outer bailey to the north and east, and beyond this another enclosure.

Between the castle earthworks and the church are the gate piers of the entrance to the long drive down to Homme House, nearly 3/4m SSW of the church. It is essentially an 'L'-shaped building. The south front is early Tudor Gothic of about 1500 and has a low tower with battlements on a canted oriel window. The adjacent gateway and turret are 19th century. The east front is Late Georgian and has six bays, two storeys and a Tuscan-columned porch. Inside there is a good flying staircase, heraldic glass of 1623, late Jacobean panelling and a wooden chimneypiece. Behind the Tudor wing is a Queen Anne range of brick with mullioned and transomed windows. In the garden there is an octagonal, stone-built summerhouse with a staircase and oval windows of about 1670.

Hall Place was a home of the Fell family. One of their number, Doctor John Fell, Bishop of Oxford in 1685-6, has been immortalised in the popular children's rhyme:

"I do not love thee, Doctor Fell:
The reason why I cannot tell.
But this I know, and know full well,
I do not love thee, Doctor Fell."

The countryside around Much Marcle is rich farmland, and substantial timber-framed houses dot the landscape. Until recently labour intensive hops, Hereford beef cattle and dairy herds were predominant but today arable rules and machinery takes the place of manpower. One of the saddest sights is the rapid decline of the old perry pear trees, so wonderful to see when in full blossom.

Cider has fared better and Much Marcle has its own commercial producer. About 100 years ago Henry Weston bought The Bounds and founded his cider company which is now a flourishing concern. In 1987 Weston's Cider revived the ancient custom of wassailing the orchard trees on Twelfth Night. Cider is poured on the roots of the trees, guns are fired three times through the branches and toast songs are sung. The first year they had the best crop in living memory! The event has now re-entered the tradition and is attended by several hundred people who process by flaring torches in the company of the Leominster morris men. Cider is consumed copiously, courtesy of Weston's. A related custom was the baking of small loaves on Good Friday. Crumbs from these could be eaten to cure minor ailments throughout the year,

On the 17th of February 1571, during the reign of Elizabeth I, The Wonder occurred. This was a dramatic landslip on Marcle Hill, 3m NW of Much Marcle church. About 20 acres of land broke away with a roar and slipped down a layer of clay. It continued moving for three days carrying with it Kynaston Chapel, sheepfolds, hedges and trees. The chapel bell was unearthed by a plough some 250 years later and is now at Homme House. The Wonder caught the attention of the nation and was alluded to by Samuel Butler (1612-80) in *Hudibras*. There is a pictorial representation of the slip on the signboard of The Slip Tavern. The actual location of The Wonder is marked under that name on the Ordnance Survey map; it is halfway along a line between Woolhope and Putley at SO 634 365. What one sees today is a south facing rock face about 15ft high.

Nearby, at the crossroads hamlet of Rushall, is Hall Court, 1.3/4m NW of Much Marcle. It is a good black and white house of 1608 and on the opposite side of the road is the site of its predecessor, an oval platform surrounded by the remains of a ditch and bank. The north part has been destroyed. In 1974 the County Archaeological Field officer investigated the site and confirmed that there had been a late mediaeval structure here and that there was also evidence of an earlier 13th century property. The house was partially dismantled in 1608 but the fishponds seem to have remained in use. During the exploratory dig several artefacts were uncovered including a beautiful pendant which is now at Hartlebury Museum. The site is to be further investigated.

The Iron-Age hill fort of Oldbury Camp, 1.1/2m W of the church at Much Marcle, stands at the southern end of Ridge Hill and covers about 17 acres. An oval enclosure is defended by a single bank and ditch with a secondary line of defences to the north-west. The earthworks have been much reduced by ploughing and cultivation and have been all but destroyed on the south. Nevertheless, there are ramparts that still stand between 10ft and 12ft high.

In one of the valley farms, namely Gamage Farm, grid square SO 64 31, numbers of flints have been found indicating a Stone-Age flint factory in the area. Elsewhere in the parish a Middle Bronze-Age palstave has been found. A palstave is a chisel-like tool designed to fit into a split-wood handle.

At Bodenham Bank, on the A49 south of Much Marcle, there are stone barns with black painted window shutters and doors. Opposite them is the main entrance to Homme House, hiding behind a screen of woodland. South by another 3/4m, up the valley of the Preston Brook, is Lyne Down, a hamlet of cream painted houses in sheep pastures. At Lyne Down Farm they make their own traditional cider for sale to the public. Lyne is an ancient British river name probably related to the Welsh lliant, 'a stream'; but our Lyne could also be from lind 'lime tree', or lin, old Scandinavian for 'flax'. Linen is cloth woven from flax fibres. A little further south again and a sign advertises Rock's Place Hotel, a timber-framed house with a converted 16th century barn. The restaurant is Three Crown recommended.

MUNDERFIELD *2.5m S of Bromyard*

The name is probably from Mundel's-feld. A feld was usually a large area cleared of forest, rather than a field as we understand it. Munderfield is an unremarkable village that straggles along the Bromyard to Ledbury road, the A465, and consists of Munderfield Stocks to the south, and Munderfield Row to the north. There are farms and cottages of brick and stone with some modern infill. The Victorian red brick school is now a house and there is a substantial stone-built farm with three bays and a hipped roof that hides anonymously behind an unsightly array of modern sheds. The settlement lies on high ground with cattle and sheep in the pastures, orchards and a disused hop kiln. To the east is the lovely country of the Upper Frome Valley.

Goodships, 1/4m N of the north end of Munderfield Row, is a Relaxation Farm, a Seventh Wonder Clinic with a swimming pool. I passed by early in May, on my way back from the Upton-on-Severn Folk Festival. In the field adjoining Goodships was a large and motley collection of caravans. It was a camp organised by the Rainbow Circle who hold seven such meetings each year. It turned out that Gareth, the lanky, black-bearded gatekeeper at this event, had an L.P. that I had made 30 years ago and he invited me in for tea. His 'office' was a very large dome-tent heated by a wood-burning stove. There were no chairs; we sat on mats on the floor. Some of the clientele were New Age Travellers but many were people who otherwise lived perfectly ordinary lives such as schoolteachers and civil servants. What they all have in common is an interest in spirituality, a gentleness of nature and an integrity from which the world can do nothing but profit. This particular gathering had been called to celebrate the Celtic fire ritual of Beltane and lasted for 11 days from 26th April to 6th May. At the end of May there is a Family Fun Camp followed in July by a meeting to study Earth Mysteries and Astrology, in early August by a Music and Dance Camp, in late August by the Healing and Wholeness Camp, in September by an exploration of the Nine Insights (of the Celestine Prophecy) and in the same month there is a Celebration of Life. The venues vary. Details can be obtained from: Sampson's Cottage, Seven Leaze Lane, Edge,

Raven's Nest

Few men see the Raven's Nest,
He hides it well, his place of rest,
Betwixt the twigs and mossy down,
Between old bones he lays him down.
His evil, black, unwinking eye
Makes the sleepless night to cry:
"Here, take my every secret thing,
My gift unto your gilded king."
"Thank you well", the Raven croaked,
But smiling to his mate, evoked
The dancing dawn with daggers bright
To put poor feeble night to flight.
Now, his great black wings unfurled,
He flew once more around the world
To spy and store all that he saw
Blind Odin's servant evermore
So, when the Raven's in his nest,
Tiptoe by, best let him rest.

Michael Raven

near Stroud, Gloucester GL16 6NL. You do not have to be into herbal teas, the smoking of exotic substances and tribal drumming at midnight, but it does, as they say, help. Most of the people who attend these camps think of themselves as belonging to an extended family, a tribe, with all the traditional benefits which that bestows.

MUNSLEY *3.5m NW of Ledbury*
It lies in the shallow valley of the Stony Brook, a tributary of the River Leadon, 1m E of the A417 Roman road near Ashperton. The name is from the Old English Mundel's-leah, 'Mundel's glade'. In Domesday Book four manors are listed as being at Munsley, held by four different people. Today the Norman church has little more than a farm, a wind-driven well and a yew tree for company. There is also an unexplained 6ft high mound with the remains of a moated enclosure that could be the earthworks of an early Norman castle.

The church of Saint Bartholomew has some herringbone masonry above the tiny east window. This might well have been laid by an Anglo-Saxon hand. Early Norman features include other tiny windows in the nave and chancel and the unmoulded chancel arch. A stone slab in the south wall of the nave has an inscription in Anglo-Saxon which has been deciphered by the Reverend C.G. Hunt and Professor L.A. Waddell to read HAMLET XHETI AD 362, 'Hamlet the Jute AD 362' and it has been suggested that it is a fragment of the sarcophagus of the Hamlet, Prince of Denmark, immortalised by William Shakespeare. When the church was being restored in 1863 some gravestones were found inscribed with pre-Christian crosses. There are fragments of mediaeval glass in black and gold, a 13th century chest hewn out of a solid piece of oak, and a 15th century font.

At Swinmore Common, 1m NE, there are a few scattered squatters' cottages. The name is probably from 'swine-moor'. A footpath leads eastwards through the orchards to the public house at Staplow on the Ledbury to Bromyard road. The name Staplow could mean 'the burial mound marked by a pillar'; stapol is Old English for pillar, or post.

Half a mile south of Munsley is the main line railway from Hereford to Ledbury; 1/2m to the north is a deeply entrenched and overgrown section of the short-lived Hereford to Gloucester Canal of 1845. (See Ashperton.) At Quatsford, a good mile ESE of the church at SO 680 404, a moat surrounds an extensive enclosure on which is a mainly 18th century house. Parts of the present dwelling are 16th century and early 17th century. The moat is fed by Stores Brook. (For Mainstone and Verzons see Pixley.)

MYNYDD BRITH *2m W of Dorstone*
Today, Mynydd Brith is a wooded hill slope, part of New House Wood. The name is from the Welsh meaning 'speckled hill'. It was a Domesday Manor with a priest, a smith and a mill and was held by Drago, son of Poyntz. The area is marked on Bryant's map of 1835 as The Township of Vowmine. The Norman castle motte of Nant-y-Bar is 1/2m N, and 1/4m N of that is the motte and bailey at the hamlet of Mynyddbrydd.

NEWTON (near Saint Margaret's) *9m SE of Hay-on-Wye*
Just listen to the sounds of some farm names; within a mile of the settlement to the south-west are Yatt: Wainherbert, Quarrelly, and Gworlodith. That is a five-word poem. Here ancient Britons, upstart Celts and Anglicized Normans share a platonic bed in the foothills of the Black Mountains.

Newton is a scattered crossroads hamlet that lies in the valley of the Dulas Brook, hidden in the hills 2.1/2m NW of Abbeydore and five miles from the border with Wales. In areas like this it is not the villages that matter, not that there are many anyway, but the houses of the men and the fields and high pastures that surround them.

The population of Newton parish is 108, at the last count, but procreation is a popular pastime in these parts. The church of Saint John the Baptist was built in 1844 by a man who was, in that quaint but meaningful phrase, a 'yeoman farmer'. John Powell was his name and a booklet available at the church tells his story. The church has a nave, a chancel with lancet windows, and a small tower. The pulpit is of about 1660 and there is a silver bowl decorated with leaves dated at 1682.

Close by the church is a small schoolroom with an adjoining stable for the horses of visiting vicars. Today, of course, the reverend arrives by car, and the schoolroom is mostly used as a meeting place by the local Women's Institute, a worthy organisation if ever there was one.

The Methodist Chapel stands on the lane to Middle Maes-Coed. It was built in 1832 and has regular services and a Sunday School. Amongst the outbuildings of the main farm in Newton is a good malt-kiln. In high, damp country such as this the grain needed to be dried and most farms in the area have, or had, a malt-kiln, often in the kitchen. The locality has several sandstone quarries from which were taken good roofing stone and the slabs which were pinned to timber-framed dwellings as infill panels. Quarrelly, or Quarelau, 1m SSW of Newton has exposed 15th century cruck trusses in one wing.

Tonly person in this parish to receive Maundy Money from the Queen at Hereford Cathedral in 1976 was Mrs. Mary Shaw of The Oaks, Newton.

NOTE: the Newton of this article should not be confused with: Newton or Newton Camp, 2m NW of Dorstone; or, the Domesday manor of Newton Court, 1m NW of Weobley; or the Domesday manor of Newton, 3m S of Leominster; or Newton Tump, 2.3/4m ESE of Clifford, near Bredwardine; or Newton Farm, 1/2m SE of Orcop, or Newton near Kinnersley. The name is from the Anglo-Saxon neowa tun, and most Newtons are very old. The later form was Newtown.

NORTON CANON *9m WNW of Hereford*
It lies just south of the A480, part of the Hereford to Kington road, and 2.1/2m SSW of Weobley. The name means 'the settlement to the north owned by the dean and chapter of Hereford Cathedral'. The cruciform church of Saint Nicholas was rebuilt in brick in 1716 but retains its 13th century tower and windows of about 1300. In the porch there is a fragment of a Norman capital. The interior was restored 'and brought up to date' by the Victorians. The grey monochrome stained glass is of about 1300, the pulpit is Jacobean and the communion rail is early 17th century. Brick churches are not common in Herefordshire.

The following ghost story is told about Deveraux Wootton, a farm 1/2m NE of Norton Canon. One day a man was walking to work when he saw a woman sitting on a stile. He asked her to make way for him and she said that she had been waiting two years for someone to speak to her. She said she was Lady Berrington and asked him to follow her. She led him to the farmhouse at Deveraux Wootton where she took some papers from a chest and asked him to throw them into a nearby pool. If he then heard sweet music she would have gone to 'the other place'. He did as she asked and heard sweet music but he talked about his adventure to others and went mad because of it.

Talk of magic reminds one of the old man at Norton Canon who had been ill-treated by his children. He was thinking of cursing them, but with great reluctance because he knew that, as a dying man, he had the power to make his curse or blessing work, especially on his children. Old traditions die hard and well into the early years of this 20th century it was the practice in these parts to be beneficent on Saint Thomas' Day, December 21st. On this 'gooding day' alms were distributed at Norton Canon.

Eccles Green, a brick and render hamlet 3/4m NW of the church, is really a part of Norton. Here, on the main road, the A480, is an establishment that sells bedding plants, a petrol filling station, a village stores and the Three Horseshoes. The big apple orchard of Bunn's Lane Farm belongs to Bulmers who are proud to proclaim their establishments, unlike many big concerns who do their best to remain anonymous. The farmhouse has an extension to the left that exhibits some of the skinniest timber framing we have seen. The heavily wooded rise to the east is Burton Hill, part of the landscaped Foxley estate.

Moorhampton, 3/4m SE of the church is also a part of Norton. The two blocks of four brick houses with round-headed windows and small lights of roundels and squares were built in 1864 by Charles Davenport. The Davenports are still major landlords hereabouts and own the Foxley estate one mile to the east. Whilst talking to a local lady the quiet was shattered by a low flying fighter aeroplane. This lady's mother used to drive wounded officers from the station at Moorhampton up to the hospital at Sarnesfield run, by Mrs. E.M. Leather, the folklorist, during the First World War. The railway cuttings and the old station area are now a carefully tended and popular Caravan Club of Great Britain site. It can be clearly viewed from the rust-red riveted bridge.

Opposite the entrance drive to the station is the red brick Moorhampton Farm rapidly being submerged by climbing plants. For a time it was a hotel. It is said that the first Hereford bulls to be exported to Russia came from here. That was in the early years of this century.

Upperton, 1/4m E of Moorhampton, is in lovely rolling country with views south to the Welsh hills. The farm is directly on the line of Offa's Dyke and slight earthworks can be discerned running due south. We photographed Garnon's Hill from near here and were rewarded with one of our most pretty pictures. To the west of Norton church are the outlying hamlets of Pig Street, Calver Hill and Norton Wood, all close to the track of the old railway.

Ladylift, a high hill 1m E of the church, is topped by a distinctive clump of trees, a local landmark. When this is obscured by cloud or mist locals take it as a sign that heavy rain is forthcoming, a portent which gave rise to this pleasant, but not very traditional sounding little rhyme:

"When Ladylift puts on her shift
She fears a downright rain;
But when she doffs it you will find
The rain is o'er, and still the wynde
And Phoebus shines again."

NUNSLAND *2m NE of Weobley*
All there is here is an isolated farm at the end of a long access track, set in a land of pastures and small orchards. The big moat formerly surrounded the farmhouse and its outbuildings, and was square-shaped. The name suggests a monastic grange but to which establishment it was connected is not known.

OCLE PYCHARD *6.5m NE of Hereford*
At the time of Domesday it was called Acle and was held by Roger de Lacy. Acle is from the Old English ac-leah, 'grove or clearing in the oak wood'. Pychard is from Roger Pichard who held the manor in 1242. Pichard is Old French for 'green woodpecker'. A later medieval holder of the manor was Sir Thomas Clanvowe, one of the knights who fought against Owain Glyndwr at the Battle of Pilleth in 1402.

The settlement stands on a little hill, 3/4m S of Burleygate, which lies on the Hereford to Bromyard road. It is a most attractive village that straggles along a peaceful lane amongst sheep meadows and stands of mature trees. Approaching from the west one comes first to Ocle Court, which has seven narrow bays, two storeys, a four columned porch, a parapet and a hipped roof of slate. It has Tudor-age timber-framing to the rear but was given a stone front in Georgian times, since rendered. The pond between the back of the house and the churchyard could have formed part of a moat. It is said to be haunted.

A little further up the hill is the church of Saint James. The new, green, copper-covered brooch spire looks somewhat brash compared to the mellow grey stone of the short, small tower beneath. The nave, chancel and vestry are 13th century Early English; the east window is Perpendicular in style. The font is thought to be Anglo-Saxon. They have a custom here of 'ringing home' the dead. As a funeral procession approaches all the church bells are rung. There are three bells, all very old: the tenor is a mediaeval head group bell cast in Worcester about 1410; the treble is of 1600; and the second is of 1639, cast by John Finch of Hereford.

Ravenham House is nicely sited on top of the hill and has long views over peaceful country to the Welsh hills. The present house is of Victorian red brick with stone dressings, a round arch over front door, a window with three-leaded lights above, and a chimney stack made as an integral part of the front design. It is now used as commercial offices. Downhill, to the east, is a pleasant mixture of old cottages and desirable modern houses. Here is the White House, late 16th century grey sandstone with a mullioned window and a re-used 14th century door head. It has a slightly austere countenance, as if scowling at the timber-framed barn across the yard which, if not given assistance fairly soon, will be lucky to see the century out.

It is with constant surprise that we learn how late mains services came to country areas in Herefordshire. Ocle Pychard is hardly remote but electricity did not arrive here until 1956, and mains water not until 1965. Before that many people had boreholes and wind operated pumps. Farming in the area is mixed - sheep and cattle grazing, grain, hops and cider orchards. The land is good and there are many sturdy, timber-framed yeoman farmers' houses along the lanes.

Castleton, 1/2m S, has the feel of a deserted mediaeval village. A good Georgian red brick house of three bays, two storeys with a hipped roof, dormers and quoins, it has an attached stone barn, partly timber-framed, which has two round hop kilns with conical slate roofs adjacent. Together they make a very solid, strong ensemble. On the opposite side of the road, beside a stream, is an area of disturbed ground which could have been a moated site.

Kymin lies 1/2m SW of Castleton, beyond a big orchard with small trees and a few spaced out cottages. A little group of dwellings stands close to the destroyed bridge over the Hereford to Gloucester Canal of 1845. The channel is now overgrown and a line of trees marks its route.

Half a mile NW of Ocle Pychard there is an un-named township that has all the hallmarks of an ill-conceived council development. An enclave of modern terraced houses is watched over by a pink brick, three-storey block of flats. A collection of old cars and a high wooden fence complete the dismal scene.

Lyvers Ocle lies 1.1/4m W of Ocle Pychard. It hides behind a screen of trees just to the north of the Hereford to Bromyard road. It consists of one large house. An outbuilding is known as the chapel. The name Lyvers is from Lyre. It was a gift to FitzOsbern's monastery at Lyre, in Normandy, and a Benedictine cell was established here in 1100.

Burley Gate, on the main road 3/4m N of Ocle Pychard, has a few basic facilities shared by several of the surrounding villages. Here is a large village store, post office, police station, village hall (old school of 1892) and a service station. This development was very much the work of Mrs. Higgins of Thinghill Court, 2.1/2m SW of Burley Gate. The Burley Gate Inn is a half-timbered house, formerly called Griffith Farm, which had its own commercial cider house.

ORCOP *8m SSW of Hereford*

Orcop is a scattered village lost in the lanes and wooded hills in the south of the county close to the Welsh border. The name is from the Old English ora-cop, meaning 'ridge-top', a reference to the hill on the slopes of which most of the dwellings are located. The distinctive clump of trees on top of the hill is a well-known local landmark.

The church lies 1.1/4m S in the valley of the Garren Brook. Saint Mary's stands on a low hill ringed around by higher hills. It has a 13th century Early English north aisle, 14th century chancel walls, Tudor roofs, and a tower with a weather-boarded upper storey and a spire. The whole was much restored in 1860 by T. Nicholson who added the polygonal vestry. In the chancel there is the top of a scalloped Norman pillar piscina and in the churchyard stands a cross with steps, base and the stump of a shaft. There is a local expression, 'Orcop, God Help Us!' which could be a corruption of Ora pro nobis which is inscribed on the bells.

At Moat Farm, about 300 yards north of the church in the valley bottom, are the substantial earthwork remains of a Norman motte and bailey castle. The site covers two acres. The motte is 74 yards in diameter and 2lft high from the bottom of the ditch. To the north is a kidney-shaped bailey, probably entered originally from the north. At one time the village had five public houses; now there is one, The Fountain, and that, with the village hall, is all they have in the way of facilities.

In the early years of this century Mrs. E.M. Leather collected several folk beliefs and customs in the Orcop area. Here are some examples: To protect children from having fits, tie rue around their wrists and ankles. To cure whooping cough give a child a piece of bread and butter that has been placed in the hand of a dead man(!) It is unlucky not to have closed the lid of a teapot properly. To find an adder on the doorstep means that someone is about to die in the house. A giant on his way to build a dam to turn Orcop valley into a lake dropped the stones accidentally on Garway Hill, 1.1/2m SW, and that is how Garway White Rocks came to be there.

Belief in fairies was quite common. One concerns the old Celtic tale of the Fairy Changelings. A woman came home one evening and found that her two young children treated her as a stranger and would not speak. She went to a wizard and he told her to brew some beer in an egg shell and make sure they saw her do it. Still following the wizard's instructions she took the two half-egg shells and dropped them into the river, one from each side of the bridge. The next thing she saw was two children walking down the stream saying: "We are old, ever so old, but never saw beer brewed in an egg shell before". They walked off into the distance, and the woman returned home to find her two children smiling at the door and as chatty as ever they had been.

The Holy Thorn of Orcop was quite famous once. It was reputed to be a cutting descended from the original Glastonbury Thorn which grew from the staff of Joseph of Aramathea. The Orcop Thorn grew beside a ruined forge near The Malsters Inn, now called The Stars, at Little Mill, 1/2m NNE of the church. Large numbers of people came to see it on Old Christmas Eve, Twelfth Night, when traditionally itshould burst into blossom. Alas, the Holy Thorn blew down in the winter gales of January 1980.

From the high road on Orcop Hill there are splendid long views, a place to watch summer sunsets from and think things spiritual. You would not be the first. On the north side of Orcop Hill is the Devil's Wood in which local tradition has it that the priests of the Silurian Celts had a grove in which human sacrifices were made. The Celtic name for the hill was Bryngwyn, 'blessed hill'. For more on this see the article on Much Dewchurch.

Newton Farm, 3/4m SE of the church, stands on the Garren Brook. Most Newtons are either Norman or early mediaeval foundations; that is, they are usually quite old, though it must be remembered that all but a handful of English settlements are at least of Anglo-Saxon origin.

ORLETON *5m SSW of Ludlow*

The name in Domesday Book is Alretune, from the Anglo-Saxon alor-tun, meaning 'settlement among the alders'. It lies on the old Portway, the B4361, which was the main road from Ludlow to Leominster until superseded by the up-rated A49 trunk road. Orleton is a quiet, mature and attractive village in country which can be similarly described. On the eastern fringes it has a water-pumping station and some modern houses but the old centre retains its charm.

Facilities are few - a post office, a pub, an architectural consultant and a flat-roofed modern school. There are some good houses along the winding main street, including the pretty black and white Lower House and the substantial stone and timber-framed Orleton House. The Old Vicarage is now an old persons' home. On the southern fringe of the village is the handsome Orleton Court (sometimes called the Manor House) which has close-set vertical framing, a gabled porch and a large, five-sided oriel window. Charles Stuart was a guest at Orleton Court and to this house came Alexander Pope in search of the hand of the squire's daughter, Miss Martha Blount.

At the other end of the settlement is the sturdy, stone church. Saint George's stands well above street level opposite some big, stone-built barns. Of Norman hands are a blocked nave window, a doorway to the vestry and part of a shaft with a carved dragon. The chancel is early 13th century with lancet windows and the tower is mid-13th

Left: Pembridge, the New Inn and the Market House.
Below: Dave Jones of Putley, folklore collector.

century with a shingled brooch spire. The nave windows are early 14th century. The font is late 12th century and an example of the work of the Herefordshire School of Carvers. Their nine apostles standing beneath arcaded arches are much admired. In the vestry are two 13th century oak chests each hewn out of a single piece. In the east window are some mediaeval stained glass fragments, and in the churchyard is a cross with steps, base and shaft of about 1400. The church was much restored in 1865 and it is said that the remains of a gigantic race of men were unearthed, but there are no records of this discovery. It is also said that people used to come from far and near to be buried at Orleton because they believed that the resurrection would begin here, and those who were buried first would be the first to rise.

Adam of Orleton was born in the village in 1285. He became Bishop of Hereford, Worcester and Winchester, a clever man but as much a political schemer as a cleric. He connived with Roger Mortimer and played a major part in forcing Edward II to abdicate and in his subsequent murder. Orleton's other, less grand, but much more worthy son is Sir Arthur Keysall Yapp who devoted the best part of his life to the Y.M.C.A. During the First World War he raised £3,000,000 to bring comfort to the troops.

The black and white 16th century Boot Inn shelters beneath a yew tree in the main street. In recent years a phantom pianist has been heard playing here. An unlikely explanation is that he is a former barman who was painted out of a picture in the pub after an argument with a previous owner. Each October a barbecue and blessing is held at the Inn to celebrate the bringing-in of the hop harvest, and to wish for success in the following year. Methinks that the landlord here has one eye on tradition and the other on the till. No doubt he awaits, with eager anticipation, the arrival of St. George's Day, 23rd April, when the annual Orleton Fair is held. On this day the cuckoo first sings in these parts and came to the fair to buy a new horse, they say.

At the top of the hill, on Orleton Common, 1.1/4m NW of the village, is a cleft in the rock called Palmer's Churn. A 6ft deep hole leads to a 12ft long passage that rises to the surface. Young people would crawl through the hole. If they got stuck or turned back they would not get married. A goose once entered the hole and re-emerged four miles away. As it came out it cried, "Goose out!" and that, they say, is how Gauset got its name. Oh, yes.

Half a mile north-east of the church, close to Comberton Farm, is a house with a gable decorated with curved diagonal struts and cusped, concave-sided lozenges. On the sill-post of the window below is a carving of a man with an axe. Could this be another of the pre-Celtic 'mallet man', a folk memory of the dark days when the aged and infirm were despatched with a blow on the head? (See the Hester Clarke Almshouses, in the Leominster article.)

At the western end of the village is a crossroads marked by the War Memorial. Millbrook Way leads north but head south, down Tunnel Lane, past the red brick Methodist church, an orchard, a plant nursery and the many-coloured cattle of Line Farm and one comes to a stone bridge over the Ludlow-Leominster railway, 3/4m SE of Orleton. The line of trees to the right (the south-west) marks the cutting of the disused but water-filled Leominster to Stourport Canal of 1796. About 50 yards from the bridge is the entrance to the Putnall tunnel (SO 503 666), which has a stone head above the brick arch. It is a grim, spooky, but nevertheless romantic little spot. Before the land was drained this broad valley was an inhospitable, marshy place. Note the names of Marsh Hall and Inchmoor, and even the stream is now called Main Ditch. Between Orleton and Leominster, a distance of 5 miles, only two little lanes cross this wetland.

The tall masts and attendant buildings that stand beside the B4362, a good 1m NE of Orleton, belong to the B.B.C. and are used for transmitting their World Service and British Overseas Forces programmes. This is a secure complex and callers are discouraged.

The wooded limestone hills to the west, fringed by Orleton Common and Bircher's Common, are home to foxes, squirrels, rare birds and wild deer. This walkers' paradise stretches for 14 miles between Ludlow and Presteigne.

PAUNTON *3m SSE of Bromyard*

It lies in the lovely valley of the River Frome, near Acton Beauchamp. The name could be derived from the Welsh, pant, meaning 'valley', hence 'settlement in the valley', which is exactly what it is. Paunton is an unspoilt, stone-built hamlet. The Court is a three-bay, two-storeyed house with irregular windows and a timber porch. It is by no means handsome but looks most interesting, especially when seen through the gateway which is flanked by stone and ship-boarded barns. It has a hop kiln and alongside the river is a very large hopyard. Paunton Mill has three stone-built storeys and is now a house. Paunton is a place of daffodil fields and barking dogs, and is a delight.

A good half-mile to the west is Instone Court. It looks somewhat gaunt, and again there is some erratic fenestration.

PEMBRIDGE *6.5m W of Leominster*

The Domesday Book name is Penebruge. The first element could be either pen, 'an enclosure', or from Paegna, an Anglo-Saxon personal name. It stands on the A44, the London to Aberystwyth coaching road. The village lay in the domain of the mighty Mortimer family and was once a very flourishing market town with a borough Charter. It has large numbers of picturesque black and white buildings which are quite understandably a magnet to tourists. If it were not for the cars one could be walking in Tudor England. Modern facilities include three pubs, a garage and filling station, a post-office-cum general store, an estate agent, several craft shops, a newsagent housed in The Steppes which was the rectory until 1777, a voluntary assisted Church of England primary school of 1866, and the church, about which more later.

Two very popular annual fairs are held at Pembridge; the Horticultural Show is in July, and the Art Market and Craft Fair is in September. There is also a horse show, the Pitfield, and the ancient May Fair, granted by Royal Charter in the 13th century.

The village green is down by the hump-backed three-arched grey-stone bridge over the Arrow. It is a stretch of the frequently flooded meadowland adjacent to the river.

The Market Place lies just off the main road at the centre of the village. It has a venerable Market Hall of the 16th century which stands on eight carved posts. On the east side are two stones believed to have been 'nails' where bargains were struck. It used to have an upper storey but is now roofed with stone tiles. Around the Market Place are some notable buildings. These include the Market House, which has a 14th century core, and the Court House Farm. The latter has some excellent outbuildings, especially the Great Barn, and it is thought that the complex occupies the site of an Anglo-Saxon defensive position to which the fragment of moat that remains once belonged. The New

Inn we see today is 17th century; it replaced one of 1311 which in turn replaced an even earlier ale-house which burned down. It is thought that the treaty made after the Battle of Mortimer's Cross was signed here in 1461.

In Bridge Street are: Duppa's Almshouses, founded by Brian Duppa, Bishop of Winchester, probably in 1661; the 16th century Clan Arrow Cottages; and Bridge Cottage which has a 14th century hall and cruck trusses. Over the bridge is Clear Brook, a handsome 17th century house with three gables and cusped, concave-sided lozenges.

On the main road in East Street, is a fine, large early 16th century house, now a shop. Pembridge Terracotta, in East Street, sell all manner of terracotta pottery from flower pots to huge Ali Baba storage urns. They manufacture these wares themselves in a 17th century barn which they brought from elsewhere and had re-erected here. The clay they use is from Herefordshire. The Old Chapel, also in East Street, is now an arts and crafts gallery. The Greyhound Inn, is early 16th century with an overhanging first floor on carved brackets and close-set vertical framing. At the end of East Street are the Trafford Almshouses founded in the late 17th century by Alice Trafford, the vicar's wife. One of her uncles was Sir William Davenent, Poet Laureate.

The other half of the main road is called West Street and here are more fine timber-framed houses, several of which have crucks. In almost any other town in any other county in England any one of these houses would justify a paragraph. In such numbers as they are at Pembridge it is the grouping that impresses most. Time really has stood still here.

But that is not all that Pembridge has, because rising majestically amongst the gravestones in the churchyard is the famous detached, 14th century, timber-framed bell-tower. It is a striking sight. Eight massive posts support a three-stage pagoda style roof topped by a tiny spire. The main, first-stage roof rests on an octagonal stone base wall which has arrow loops. There are similar constructions in Norway and Sweden and in Essex but there is nothing like it elsewhere in this part of the world. It has a peal of five bells.

Saint Mary's stands on the site of a large Norman church. What we see today is mostly 14th century. The door has its original hinges. The holes in the planks were reputedly made by Civil War musket shot but there is something else far more intriguing. Beneath the old sanctuary knocker on the church door is a tough, leathery substance said to be the skin of a marauding Dane. These Viking marauders were viewed with great hatred and could expect to be skinned alive if taken prisoner. The leather on the old great west doors of Worcester Cathedral is said to have been tested and found to be human. (Being situated on the River Severn, Worcester fell easy prey to the Danes in their long boats.)

Saint Mary's has chancel, nave, transepts and aisles. All that remains of the preceding church are the 13th century font, and in the chancel two 13th century blocked arches and part of a pillar. The windows are striking and there is a clerestory of ten circular lights. The pulpit is Jacobean - how often they are! - likewise, the reader's desk lectern which in one panel has a dragon and a puppy. There is a wall painting in the south transept and some 14th century stained glass fragments in the west aisle windows. Amongst the monuments are: effigies of a 14th century knight and his lady; a 14th century civilian and his lady; Mrs. William Sherborne, died 1660; Mrs. Essex Sherborne, died 1668; William Sherborne, died 1671; Thomas Trafford, died 1685; and members of the Evans family.

In the rich farmland around the village are some notable houses: Broxwood Court, rebuilt from the stone of the demolished old house; the Byletts; Moorcourt which has a long avenue of elms; Weston Court, 2m SW, which has cruck trusses in a barn; and Crump Oak.

The Leen Farm, 3/4m NW of the church, is situated close to the River Arrow, near the earthwork of Rowe Ditch. It is a typical 500 acre lowland farm with a large Friesian dairy herd, and arable fields in which potatoes and cereal crops are cultivated, but here there is also an important pedigree herd of Hereford cattle used for breeding. There is a Nature Trail and wildlife includes mink, cormorants, pipistrelle bats, woodpeckers, leeches, crayfish, waterfowl and moles. The moles have built castles two to three feet high which they use for breeding. The old breast-shot waterwheel of the mill has been restored. It is called Lady Antonia and is of a design perfected by John Smeaton (1724-92) which has a 50% efficiency. The mill was used to drive static farm machinery in the great barn opposite via an underground drive-shaft. The water was taken upstream from the River Arrow by leats and sluices. The name Leen is from Leon, the Old English name for the Lugg-Arrow area which, in turn is from the Celtic lei, 'to flow', meaning 'river' or 'flood'.

At Lower Bearwood, 1.1/2m S of Pembridge, is Hay's Head where Dunkertons have their family run cider works. Bearwood itself is a scattered settlement of black and white and red brick cottages with a Methodist Church of 1864 and boarded barns.

Here are some notes on the folklore, beliefs and customs of the Pembridge area. Old Pembridge lay 1/2m or so to the north in the Shobden Marshes. A fiddle player from Eardisland played at a dance at Pembridge. When he got home he realised he had left a pair of white gloves tied with red ribbons. He returned to fetch them but the village had gone. Overnight it had sunk into the swamp. The marshes are now drained and used as pastures but there is a well here, and if you drop a stone down it you can hear it hit the steeple of the old church. This might all seem somewhat fanciful but there are often elements of truth in old tales. The Anglo-Saxons often built settlements in marshlands, using them as defences, and the very name Pembridge means 'bridge by the alders'. Perhaps the original settlement was further north but flooding forced a move to higher ground.

Mrs. E.M. Leather, the folklorist, heard two gipsy fiddle players at Pembridge Fair in 1908. They were John Lock and possibly his brother Polin, two of the nine children of Ezekiel Lock, and were known locally as the Gentlemen Locks. Subsequently Mrs. Leather and Cecil Sharp collected a set of country dance and morris tunes from John Lock. Polin used to serenade Mrs. Leather beneath the windows of her home. By 1926, however, he was crippled with rheumatism and unable to play. One of the Locks was found dead in the snow near Church Stoke, Montgomeryshire, with his fiddle by his side, and was buried with it. Vaughan Williams came on folksong collecting trips to Pembridge in the early years of the 20th century.

An old waggoner from The Haven, Pembridge, told how a local farmhand came home from work and his wife told him dinner was nearly ready. He said he was just popping out for a moment but was taken by fairies who chamged him into one of themselves. Twenty years later he walked back into his kitchen and said, "Well missis, be my broth ready?"

A lady of Pembridge died but came back as a distressed

spirit. In life her father had taken land owned by the poor of the parish and it had passed to her brother. She let it be known what had happened and he gave it back. The lady was the wife of Doctor Breton, a minister at Pembridge during the Commonwealth.

Funeral processions took a roundabout route from the deceased's home to the church and circled the churchyard 'the way of the sun' before the internment took place. This is quite probably a remnant of Celtic ritual much of which was adopted by the early Christian missionaries.

After Saint Katherine had had her revelation at Much Marcle and went on her travels seeking bells ringing without bell-ringers, she visited Pembridge in her search. She finally heard them at Leominster, which also has a detached belfry. The wooden belfry at Pembridge is said to have been built in honour of her visit. (See Leominster.)

Ghostly black dogs have been seen near Pembridge. Dogs of Hell the Welsh call them. In the 17th century a clothier of Pembridge, who frequently had garments stolen from his shop, went out with a crystal ball about midnight. He made his chant to call up the spirits and found a pure virgin boy or girl to look into the crystal whereupon the face of the thief would appear. If he tried that today I think he might well end up in Court - virgin children at midnight? "Well, you see your Honour, I'd just lost a good wool coat and......"

There used to be Lammas Lands at Pembridge. These were 'commonable' meadows similar to those that still exist at Lugwardine. (See Lugwardine.) It was a common belief in the area that to have willow in the house on May Day brought good luck and provides a defence against a curse being placed on the occupants. However, to strike an animal or a child with a withy stick (or sally twig) would cause it to cease to grow. A local cure for whooping cough was to make the child inhale the breath of a piebald horse.

PENCOMBE *3.5m WSW of Bromyard*
The name is from the Anglo-Saxon and means 'the pen, or enclosure, in the valley'. It hides in a little valley in a broad bowl ringed around by low hills, a pleasant place lost to the world and watched over by a circle of old farms: - Pencombe Hall, Steward's Hyde, Winslow, Hawkhurst, Durstone, Hegdon Hill, Stone Farm and Pencombe Cross. The settlement has some basic facilities but these have to be justified by people and that means some modern houses have arrived. The village has a post office and shop, the Wheelwright's Arms, a war memorial, a stand of firs and a tiny green.

The 19th century squires were the Arkwrights of Hampton Court and George Arkwright was rector here from 1861. Family money paid for the building of a new school, which still flourishes; a big new rectory, now an old persons' home; and a new church, rebuilt on the site of the old. Pencombe also plays host to the local Women's Institute, Brownies, a playgroup and the Young Farmers' Club. One can always escape the extravagance of this social whirl by repairing to the church.

Saint John's is of 1865 to a Norman-cum-Early English design by Thomas Nicholson. It has a 15th century font, a 17th century chest, and a brass plate to Richard Jordan. In 1832, at the age of 19, Master Jordan joined an expedition to explore the River Niger. It was led by the distinguished and experienced Richard Lander but of the 48 men who left for Africa only eight returned. Both Jordan and Lander were amongst those who perished. It is said that the rector wanted to rebuild the church in a place more central to the parish but that the spirits of the dead intervened, prevented the work, and only allowed the new church to be constructed on the old site.

In mediaeval times the lord of the manor of Pencombe was given a pair of gilt spurs on the death of every Mayor of Hereford who died during his term of office. Such a death tribute is called an heriot.

Isolated places were often thought of as being either poor or of having an inhospitable climate. The name of the village followed by "God help us" is a saying found in several Herefordshire villages. "And where do you come from?" Reply: "Pencombe, God help us." Such self-deprecatory comments would be made by country people to reinforce the townsman's often false notions of his country cousin's condition. In much the same way they would 'play the yokel' and not at all object to such taunts as "Pencombe is the place where they put the pig on the wall to watch the band go by, and thatch the river to keep the ducks dry."

Below the Old Forge at Pencombe runs the stream, a tributary of the River Lodon. At one of the springs that feeds it a small stone reservoir has been constructed. This is the Washing Pool and has stone slabs to use as washboards. It was also used as a fresh water supply before mains water came. As elsewhere in the county such spring water is still collected for use in making tea.

At Grendon Court, 1.1/4m N of the church, an outbuilding is said to have been a chapel. This might well be an ancient site because the Holywell Brook (sometimes called Holly Brook) that flows through Grendon Bishop, 2.1/2m N, is named after the Holy well at Holywell Cottage. This cottage is now used as a farm building and stands in the middle of a field. The spring was formerly tapped and the water pumped to Grendon Court.

Pencombe Hall lies 1/2m S of the church. It is Victorian Neo-Jacobean with a symmetrical front, shaped gables and a recessed porch, all nicely bedecked with wisteria. It overlooks a little wooded valley and is now a retirement home.

At Pencombe Cross there is a pink-washed house, a stand of pines and a private sports club. The road from here to Pool Head on the A417 is quite delightful; it follows a ridge with gentle pastoral views on both sides.

Just outside Pencombe Cross a sign directs one down a mile long lane to Shortwood Working Dairy Farm, Visitors can help feed the animals, which include rare breeds, collect eggs and follow a trail through woods and orchards. Between Bitterley Hyde and Westfields, 2m WSW, there are superb views over Herefordshire to the Welsh hills.

PENCOYD *5.5m WNW of Ross-on-Wye*
The name is from the Welsh pen-coed, meaning 'the end of the wood'. It is in the Domesday Book Hundred of Arkenfield where Welsh customs predominated over those of the Anglo-Saxons and the Normans. The settlement is scattered, ranging around the church amongst pools - there are seven in the immediate vicinity - and orchards to the west of the Hereford to Ross road, the A49.

The church of Saint Dennis has a nave of about 1300, a 14th century tower, and a rebuilt chancel of 1878. The font is of about 1200 and a mediaeval coffin lid has been used as a window lintel. The silverware is of 1636. Outside there is a handsome yew tree and the remains of the churchyard preaching cross. The 'H'-shaped Court is stone-built Jacobean with gabled wings. The hamlet of Netherton, 1/2m E, is really part of Pencoyd. Netherton Farm has a cruck truss and an early 17th century porch.

Above: Hereford cattle grazing near Haye on Wye.
Below: A ploughing match somewhere in Herefordshire c.1960.

PETERCHURCH 7.5m ESE of Hay-on-Wye

The name is self-explanatory, 'the church dedicated to Saint Peter'. It lies in the lush, gentle land of the Golden Valley, on the road from Hay-on-Wye to Abbeydore and Ewyas Harold. The Golden Valley takes its name from the River Dore and the Welsh ystrad-our, 'valley of the river of gold'. The gold could be the sunlight on the river, the colour of crops such as corn, or simply the golden nature of this friendly, open and fertile valley. It is best seen from the hills to the west, looking east to the mountains of Wales. It is a verdant vale with a national reputation.

Peterchurch is the social centre of the valley but despite its impressive Norman church it is a somewhat dull little place. Amongst the modern bungalows and the old stone cottages are the Nag's Head, the Broughton Arms, a post office-cum-general store, a police station housed in a flat-roofed shack, a primary school and village hall, a tall television receiver mast, a stone-built Wesleyan chapel, now a house, a red brick Baptist chapel with lancet windows, and a caravan site at Poston Mill 1/2m S. There are also fringe developments across the river at Hinton, Fine Street and Barley Knapp.

Saint Peter's Church is a large and well-preserved Norman building, but its origins go back to the 8th century when King Offa built the first stone church here. The missionaries who were based at the church included an Italian bishop from Rome. When the church was rebuilt by the Normans in 1130 the Anglo-Saxon shape and size was retained. Instead of the usual chancel arch dividing the church into two sections, there are three arches dividing it into four.

In his guide book the Reverend John C. de la Tour Davies explains that the east end, with the altar, was reserved for the clergy; the next compartment, the Solea and Presbytery, was for the Prior and those monks who were ordained clergymen; next came the Choir; and at the far west the Nave, for the lay congregation. This, apparently, was the typical layout of an Italian church of the 8th century.

The arches that make these compartments descend in height as one approaches the altar in the apse which is surmounted by a single, small Norman window. Pevsner suggests that the first and second arches supported a tower. The 'true' chancel arch is the second, the most ornately decorated. The present tower is of about 1280 and was built as a place of refuge from marauding Welshmen. It has walls 7ft thick at the base and the entrance was so high it could only be reached by a ladder. At the base is a Catholic mass sundial and there is another on the Norman south doorway, which is decorated with zig-zag. The tall spire of 1320 was taken down in 1949 and was replaced by a new 186ft fibreglass thing prefrabricated in three sections. The font is Norman and tub-shaped with rope mouldings, and in the churchyard are Douglas firs and a superb yew tree with a girth of some 30ft. There is something very humbling about these mighty and oh-so-long-lived creatures; little wonder they had such a powerful religious significance to the Celts and the Anglo-Saxons.

There are those who are of the opinion that the Norman work in the church was begun by the master mason who worked at Shobdon, but that he was lured away to Kilpeck before his work was complete. There is no suggestion, however, that his work included the painted plaster fish on the nave wall. This is a carp with a golden chain around its neck that is said to have lived in Saint Peter's Well. This is actually more closely associated with Dorstone, three miles up the valley, and the story is related in the article on Dorstone.

The churchyard of Saint Peter's is also the last resting place of Private Robert Jones who, at the age of 19, was one of 11 men awarded the Victoria Cross for their extreme bravery at the famous battle of Rorke's Drift Mission Station in 1879, when a small number of British soldiers were attacked by some 4,000 Zulus. Jones served with the 2nd Battalion 24th Foot, South Wales Borderers. He died in 1898 from a self-inflicted gun-shot wound in the garden of Crossways, Peterchurch. The coroner's verdict, which came 20 years after the event, was suicide, but it is now considered to have been an accident.

It seems amusing, and slightly unbelievable, but churches used to have a problem with stray dogs making a nuisance of themselves, and dog catchers were employed to remove them. They used specially made tongs to avoid being bitten and the dog catcher at Peterchurch had the 'use and enjoyment' of a piece of land adjoining the church called dog-acre.

Another custom here is far more ancient. The pagan tradition of carrying the coffin in funeral processions around the churchyard before internment became mutated to processing around the two chancels of Saint Peter's. When it was suggested that this pre-Christian custom be stopped there were such mutterings amongst local people that things were left as they always had been. Superstitions die hard in these borderlands.

One wonders what happened to the bridegroom who failed to pay the bellringers at his wedding, for in revenge they cursed him with bad luck by playing the peals backwards. And what about the local bell-jingle: "withy and birch, say the bells of Peterchurch". Withy is the rowan or mountain ash which, together with birch, has anciently been used as a protection from the 'evil eye' of witches and wizards. It is also widely said in Herefordshire that "the withy is the tree on which the Devil hanged his mother".

By the side of the lane leading to Blakemere Hill Wood, 1/2m ENE of the church, are Saint Peter's Wells (SO 353 388). This is quite probably an older religious site than the church itself. The stone sculpture of a head, from the mouth of which the water once issued, survives but it is now buried up to its nose in concrete, part of the tanking works done by the local water board. We have seen such insensitivity elsewhere. At one time the water flowed into a stone-lined bathing pool which was used to beneficial effect by sufferers from rheumatism. The two eye-like holes in the stone wall beyond were springs used to cure complaints of the eye. Offerings of pins were made. These springs are now closed up. There was once a changing-room-shed for the benefit of rheumatic bathers and an iron cross has been found in the wood above the wells, presumably an attempt to claim this pagan place for the Christian God.

Just down the hill from Saint Peter's Wells is Wellbrook Manor which the learned Nikolaus Pevsner says is "one of the best examples in the county of a 14th century hall-house". It is timber-framed but was later built around with stone. The service wing no longer exists but the hall and the solar remain, though the great hall has been divided with a first floor. Upstairs the trusses and their crucks and foils are all perfectly preserved. The original solar stone chimney piece and the original stone octagonal chimney stack survive and the solar roof has cusped wind braces.

Until late into the 19th century several old customs relating to Feast Days were practised in the Peterchurch area. Country people tended to ignore new Christmas, 25th

December, and celebrated Old Christmas, the 12th day after, for then "the Holy Thorn blossoms and the cattle go down on their knees at 12 o'clock in remembrance and tears pour down their cheeks".

At Easter it was usual to go to the orchards and make offerings for a good crop by burying a piece of cake and pouring cider on to it. This custom was practised in the Golden Valley long after it had ceased elsewhere in the county.

Belief in the powers of wise men and wise women was widely held. When cattle were ill in Peterchurch the farmer had to follow this ritual: he must not speak to anyone either going or coming back from seeing this wise woman; he must not ask her for assistance but mention his problem casually in conversation; the wise woman would understand and put matters right; the farmer must not offer payment or thanks but an unsolicited gift would shortly find its way to her.

On feast days blood sports were practised in the Golden Valley and at Peterchurch in particular, especially badger-baiting and cock-fighting. These took place in a meadow behind the Broughton Arms, where there was a cock-pit. In the churchyard at Saint Peter's is the grave of one John Andrews, a noted cock-fighter who died in 1799. His nickname was Captain, after his most famous and unbeaten bird, and there is an epitaph in doggerel verse inscribed on his tombstone which alludes to his sadistic pastime.

In the mid-19th century Peterchurch was a small regional centre of craft trades. These included three shoemakers and an ironworks. The disused railway track that passed through Peterchurch was the Golden Valley Railway. This was built in 1881 between Pontrilas and Dorstone and extended eight years later to Hay-on-Wye. It was not very successful; the passenger service ceased in 1941 and the line closed in 1957.

At Urishay, 1.1/2m WSW of Peterchurch, are the remains of a Norman castle. The motte is sizeable, about 52 yards in diameter, and there are traces of an outer enclosure. On the motte are the ruins of a large house of the 17th and 18th centuries. Just north of the castle moat is a Norman chapel, a plain oblong building which was used as a barn for many years.

Snodhill Castle lies 1.3/4m NW of Peterchurch. It was built in about 1080, either by Bernard de Newmarche or Hugh L'Asne (Hugh the Donkey). In the reign of Henry I it was held by Roger de Chanders and in about 1200-30 it was re-fortified with a stone keep and bailey walls. By 1355 it was ruinous. It was again re-fortified in 1403, still in Chanders' hands. It then passed to the Bruges, the de la Meres, the Nevilles, to Robert Dudley Earl of Leicester, to the Vaughans and then to William Prosser of London who built, or rebuilt, Snodhill Court. The castle was finally destroyed by bombardment from the Scottish Army in 1645. The earthworks cover some 10 acres. At the east end is a steep motte with an elongated hall-keep which has a gateway to the bailey. Sections of the stonework survive, especially of the bailey walls. Just to the south-east of the castle is Snodhill Court Farm, an almost symmetrical gabled stone house probably built in, or shortly after, 1665 when William Prosser bought the castle.

Saint Mary's Well, SO 311 392, lies 1m SW of Snodhill Castle at the foot of a steep bank below the drive to New Lodge. It is renowned for curing complaints of the eye. The water is caught in a brick tank within which is the original circular stone bowl. The well was used for medicinal purposes until at least the 1930s.

A group of undated lynchets (field terraces) runs in a north-easterly direction across a field, 1/4m WNW of the church.

In the early 17th century Rowland Vaughan constructed a system of waterworks in the Golden Valley for the purposes of irrigation and industry. The Trench Royal runs along the west bank of the River Dore from Peterchurch to Newcourt 3m to the south. It was so level that water could flow either way. Vaughan utilised all the hillside streams and the Trench Royal may well have followed the route of an early Roman road. A sawmill driven by a water-wheel was operating in this elaborate complex in 1610. This was a pioneering work, one of the first such schemes in the whole of Britain.

At the hamlet of Hinton, 1/2m ENE of Peterchurch, is the Old Bakery, a Victorian tea-room and gift shop which specialises in home-made cakes and scones. The proprietors also keep a variety of crafts and antiques for sale. Hinton, was where King Offa's missionary priests had their accommodation. The name is from Higna-tun, 'settlement of the monks'.

PETERSTOW *2.5m W of Ross-on-Wye*

The name means 'Saint Peter's religious place', and it stands astride the A49, Hereford to Ross road. It is increasingly a place of new houses inhabited by people who work outside the village. The settlement has two pubs, the Yew Tree and the Red Lion at Winter's Cross, a post office and shop, and a village hall which was formerly the Methodist chapel of 1874. The school of 1844 closed in the early 1970s and is now a dwelling. Many of the farms have been amalgamated and the surplus farmhouses sold off. The area is well known for its high quality soft fruits and orchard produce, and at Broome Farm, Kenelm Johnson and his son produce their own cider.

The common has avoided enclosure and the grazing rights are still held by local people. Older residents have fond memories of old Jimmy Link. Until 1940 he brought his small flock of sheep to graze on the common each morning, watched over them all day, and drove them home each night. In cold or bad weather he sheltered beneath a horse-chestnut tree in the centre of the common. A Gospel Bush once stood in the north-west corner of the common. It was one of the places where the Rogationtide procession stopped whilst beating the bounds of the parish. Close by is the old village well, complete with pump. It was very much still in use until 1959, when mains water was brought in.

The church of Saint Peter is a pre-Conquest foundation and most of the north wall is of the Anglo-Saxon stone-built church. It contains some unusually large blocks below a small Norman window. The chancel, chancel arch and the scissor-braced roof of the nave are 14th century; the small, battlemented tower and the font are 15th century; and in the churchyard are the remains of an old preaching cross and a 14th century coffin lid. There is a list of rectors dating from 1060; that is quite, quite remarkable.

In fields south-west of the common are patches of black, burned soil which mark the sites of Roman iron smelting furnaces. To the south of Peterstow are the big orchards of the hamlets of Wilson and Clewstone, and a mile to the south-west is Weirend, now as much on the banks of the Ross Spur A40(T) as on the River Wye. It was at Weirend that Noelle Gordon made her home for a number of years. She played the part of Meg in the long-running television soap opera called *Crossroads*. She died of cancer in 1985 at the age of 61 and is buried at Ross.

PIPE AND LYDE *2.5m N of Hereford centre*
Pipe is an old English word meaning water-pipe, or in this case probably water-course, referring to a small stream that has its source near here. Lyde is from the Anglo-Saxon hlyde meaning a 'roaring stream', a 'torrent'. This is more likely a reference to the River Lugg itself which bounds the area to the east and frequently floods.

Approaching from the north, along the busy A49, one leaves the land of many huts planted along the road by the Ministry of Defence, passes the grey sheds of an intensive chicken farm, white painted cottages, a brown hopyard and a red telephone box and arrives at Pipe and Lyde. Actually, there is a small mystery here because Pipe seems to have disappeared; everywhere that has a name is called Lyde - Upper Lyde; Lower Lyde Farm; Lower Lyde Court, which has the remains of a moated manor and a holloway indicating the site of a deserted mediaeval village; Lyde Hill, which is cut through by the Hereford to Leominster railway; Lyde Cross; and Lyde Arundel.

On the main road are the fish tanks and black plastic tunnels of the Kenchester Water Gardens. Opposite them stands the church of Saint Peter, embowered in trees. It looks new and, indeed, much of it was rebuilt by F.R. Kempson in 1874 when the broach spire was added to the 13th century tower. The chancel is also late 13th century. The rebuilt nave retains an original Norman doorway with Transitional moulding, and an early 13th century lancet. The rood beam is 15th century, a much admired piece with carved vine foliage, and in the churchyard are the remains of a 14th century preaching cross. However, the jewel in the crown of Saint Peter's is the 16th century leather chalice case, embossed with shields and fleur-de-lis, which is now kept at the town museum in Hereford. Near the old red brick vicarage, about 1/2m south beside the main road, is a boundary stone at which the sheriff and his merry javelin men met the visiting circuit judge and escorted him to Hereford. We use the word merry because the occasion tended to be, shall we say, convivial.

In a field east of the church, in the area of SO 497 439 and 400 yards W of the church, are the slight earthworks of one of the three Lydes mentioned in Domesday Book, the Lay Subsidy Roll, and the Poll Tax of 1377. A reference to a castle occurs in a Charter of about 1225-50. It was probably held for the Bishop of Hereford by a knight from the time of the Norman kings until the 14th century. Earthworks were discovered in 1976 consisting of a raised platform surrounded by a ditch on three sides with more ditches and a dried out fishpond.

The geographical centre of Herefordshire is at Pipe and Lyde. The spot is marked by a small stone monument and a few yew trees at SO 504 436. They were planted here by one William Jay and a few of his friends in 1857. These markers stand beside the Hereford to Leominster road, the busy A49, about 1.1/4m N of the Starting Gate roundabout at Holmer, at the top of a long, gentle incline on the east side of the road.

PIXLEY *3m WNW of Ledbury*
The name is from the Anglo-Saxon and means 'Peoht's glade in the forest'. It stands on the busy A417, part of the Roman road from Dymock to Dinmore, in a land of small woods and orchards. In 1066 the manor was held by Askell, the Bishop of Hereford's man. By 1086 it had passed to Humphrey de Bouville who held it directly from the king.

Things have not changed much since then; there is just the Court and a little chapel. The mid-17th century Pixley Court Farm is mainly red brick with some parts timber-framed and is not altogether handsome. However, across the yard, embowered by a close ring of mature trees and standing on a low mound, is the atmospheric little red sandstone church. So close do the trees grow it is almost as if the Green Man has claimed the place for himself.

Saint Andrew's is 13th century and the two lancet windows in the east wall of the chancel are original. It has nave and chancel in one with a Victorian bell-turret and a shingled spire. The walls lean somewhat but the surprise here is the screen that separates the chancel from the nave. It is constructed of massive, carved, dark oak timbers that form three bays with a carved cross-beam. It looks old but probably is not, unlike the large hinge on the south door which is 13th century. The stained glass probably dates from 1865 when the church was restored.

Close by Saint Andrew's is a ruined cider mill and half a mile away is a fishing pool.

Mr. Edward Thompson, who owns the 500 acre Pixley Court Farm, is a pioneer grower of the new 7ft high dwarf hop variety called First Gold. He has 30 acres under cultivation and is also chairman of a machinery company at Bromesberrow Heath which manufactures dwarf hop harvesting machines. However, his main crop at Pixley is blackcurrants, with some raspberries.

Just north of Pixley is the crossroads hamlet of Trumpet, named after the Trumpet Inn. It was here, in 1913, that Vaughan Williams collected an excellent version of the Night Visiting Song entitled 'O who is that?' Across the road is a service station. The Trumpet area is well known for its horse and tractor ploughing competitions, and also for the virtually permanent gipsy encampment in a main road lay-by.

A short way out, on the main road to Ledbury, is Mainstone Court. Just north of the moated site there is the red ashlar house of 1821. It has five bays, two storeys, and a central bay window converted to a porch with Tuscan columns. Further east again, on the road to Ledbury, are Little Verzon's Garden Centre and Coffee Shop and the Verzons Hotel, formerly a farmhouse. Of the latter we do not have fond memories, thanks to a surly landlord.

Knapp Farm lies 1/4m SE of the church. The name is from the Anglo-Saxon cnaepp, meaning 'top', usually of a hill.

Oilfield Publications Ltd., of Homend, Ledbury, is a company that publishes and distributes technical reference books, maps and electronic products on the subject of petroleum oil. They have a worldwide market and customers include manufacturers of oil supply vessels and oil exploration companies. The firm was founded in Maidenhead by David Gallimore, a native of Pixley, about 16 years ago and subsequently moved to Ledbury. His co-partner is Tony Madsen.

PONTRILAS *11m SW of Hereford*
Pontrilas lies on the Hereford to Abergavenny road, the A465(T). Pont is probably from the Welsh pant, 'a valley'. The settlement stands at an important meeting of the ways where the Golden Valley meets the the Monnow Valley and the Hereford to Abergavenny road. Here, too, the Dulas Brook joins the River Dore and here the Golden Valley Railway of 1881 joined the main line.

Ross Workhouse

He was old and broken,
No money, no hope,
and now his home was
the workhouse at Ross.
All that he had to call his own
were fading memories
and a few old songs.
"Even these are deserting
me now," he said.
"Yesterday I lost another.
It just packed up its bags
and left. Such a shame.
Those songs were my friends.
Maybe they're waiting for me
on the other side;
I do hope so."

Michael Raven
1995

In Domesday Book Pontrilas was called Elwistone. It was held by Earl Harold Godwinson but after the Norman Conquest it passed to Alfred of Marlborough, nephew of Osbern 'Pentecost' and father-in-law of Thurstan of Wigmore. The tax value of Pontrilas in 1086 was 30 shillings and three sheep. The Welsh border is 1/2m to the south and the area was defended by the castles at Ewyas Harold and Howton.

Today, Pontrilas is virtually a residential extension of Ewyas Harold. The dominant building is Pontrilas Court, which lies just off the main road. It is a striking gabled stone house of about 1630 with a gabled porch and a round-headed entrance arch. Inside there are two good plaster ceilings and outside there is a good, square, timber-framed dovecote.

The main road dominates the scene. Cars and lorries rush by through what is, in fact, a very pretty little valley with small, wood-fringed meadows beside the sparkling River Dore. Yet it is industry that lords it here. Alongside the A465 is Downey Engineering, blacksmiths and agricultural engineers, in a brick and weather-board building, and on the road to Ewyas Harold there are two small industrial estates, Westwood and Long Meadow.

But lord of lords here are the large and flourishing Pontrilas Sawmills, 1/2m NE on the A465. The company was founded in 1947 by John R. Hickman, based around the Old Mill. The New Mill was built in 1992 and is a state-of-the-art, computer-operated softwood processor with a capacity of 70,000 cubic metres a year. The company has its own drying kilns, preservation treatment plant and lorry fleet. There is a photograph in the office block reception of timber wagons in the Welsh hills on a gloomy, wet evening that is a true work of art.

On high ground, very close to the sawmills but still managing to maintain an admirable aloofness, is the little church of Saint Mary, sometimes called Kenderchurch. The early 12th century name was Lanncinitir from llancynidr, 'the church of Saint Cynidr'. It stands on a rise near the confluence of the Worm Brook with the River Dore. What with the roar of the busy main road, the clatter of the mainline railway, the squeals from the timber yard and the hum of the electric grid cables, it knows little peace these days.

Saint Mary's was much restored in 1871. It consists of nave, chancel with a Tudor waggon roof, and a Victorian bellcote. The pulpit is Jacobean, the screen is Perpendicular and the font is Norman, with zzig-zag ornament around the rim. There are two Norman, or possibly Anglo-Saxon, stone coffin lids with incised crosses, and in the churchyard is a cross with a mediaeval base. To the north-west there are views up the Golden Valley.

At Howton, 1m NE of the church, between the road and the railway, is a mound about 45 yards in diameter and about 7ft high, with traces of a ditch around the base. It could be a motte and bailey castle site.

At the beginning of the 20th century the house-keeper at Pontrilas Court was Mrs. Cummings and she related folk beliefs that she had heard from an old lady at Pontrilas called Mary Phillips. The old lady would use charms and herbs to cure all manner of minor ailments but could not cure herself. Fairies were a fact of life to her. One night she had seen dozens of them dancing, to a band playing lovely music, in the long meadows at the back of Llangua church, 1.1/4m SSW of Pontrilas. When they had finished she watched as they went tripping over the bridge and disappeared into the wood beyond.

She said that Monmouth Cap, 3/4m SSW of Pontrilas, got its name because the Duke of Monmouth raised his cap as a sign of victory after a great battle. The dead were buried in a meadow by the River Monnow, marked by a mound encircled by a path where grass never grew. Once a man mowed the meadow by moonlight in the summer to avoid the heat. He heard music and saw a group of soldiers and their ladies dancing around the mound and he ran away in terror, but his neighbours said not to be frightened, because it was just the fairies who were often seen there at midnight.

Monmouth Cap was for a long time the terminus of a horse-drawn tramway used to bring coal up from South Wales. In 1829 the tramway was extended to Hereford and a good stretch can be seen at Howton.

In the Monnow valley, to the south-east, there is a low mound in the field between the river and the road to Kentchurch. This is all that remains of a 17th-18th century water-powered iron forge.

PRESTON-ON-WYE *7.5m WNW of Hereford*
The name Preston is from the Old English (Anglo-Saxon) and means 'settlement of the priests'. The church lies on low ground close to the River Wye; the modern village stands on higher ground, 1/2m S, at Ploughfield. Ploughfield was the site of a mediaeval borough planned in 1262, but it did not grow until recent times. In 1086 Preston was a flourishing place with a mill and a sizeable population and was held by the Canons of Hereford. This explains the priests of the place name, you might think. However, the manor belonged to the clergy long before the Norman Conquest. It is almost certain that Preston was the Bolgros mentioned in the *Liber Landavensis* where there is an account of the perambulation of the bounds by Bishop Ufelwy, the suffragen bishop of Ergyng (Archenfield) at the end of the 6th century A.D. The Bishop was a disciple of Saint Dubricius. Here is that account.

"Be it well known.....that Gwrfodwr, King of Ergyng, having gained a victory in battle over the Saxon nation, and giving thanks to God and for the prayers of Ufelwy, and his clergy, granted in alms to him, and all his successors, under the refuge of St. Dubricius and St. Teilo, for ever, the land called Bolgros, on the banks of the Wye, at some distance from Mochros (Moccas), the quantity of three uncias (about 134 acres). And the land having been given as an endowment, Bishop Ufelwy, with his clergy, went round the whole on its boundary, sprinkling holy water, the holy cross with the holy relics being carried before; and in the presence of the King, with his witnesses, built a church in the middle thereof, in honour of the Holy Trinity, and Saint Paul, and of Saint Dubricius, and Saint Teilo; and he also granted the land free of all fiscal tribute, to God and to the Bishop who was present, and all his successors at Llandaff, and with all commonage in field and in woods, in water and in pastures.". (Could it be that the freeholders of Preston have a claim under this deed not to have to pay Council Tax? Until a few years ago the people of Knighton, near Newport in Shropshire, had just such a privilege not to pay the old rates.)

We avoid being unkind whenever we can but here are our travel notes on Preston as we found it; they speak for themselves. We approached from the east, from Lulham. "Nursery gardens. White polythene on the fields both as 12 inch high tunnels and as flat sheets. Around the village green at Ploughfields are the Yew Tree pub and its scruffy sheds, dour modern houses, a grey-clad farmhouse with rusty corrugated iron barns, a red brick and render Primitive Methodist Chapel of 1862, a handful of rendered cottages, a few trees and a Baptist Chapel of brick with stone dressings of 1869. Further down are a few larger houses but even they have to contend with an horrendous blue and grey garage surrounded by rusting wrecks. The village hall is the social centre. About all this place has to be proud of are the song birds and a red telephone kiosk. The church has escaped all this and gone to live down by the river." It is, of course, the other way round. The modern village of Ploughfield has moved uphill because of the ever present danger of flooding in the valley below. Most of the old village dwellings have gone but what remains is quite delightful. This is Preston proper.

The church of Saint Lawrence is large and spacious. It was much restored in 1883 by T. Nicholson (known as 'the destroyer') but retains a late Norman doorway with trumpet-scalloped capitals and zig-zag ornament in the arch; a Norman north window with roll moulding; the chancel doorway of about 1300; a 14th century chapel and a largely 14th century tower. The pulpit is Jacobean - so many are in Herefordshire - and the 16th century bench-ends are carved with daisies and pointed leaves.

The stream to the south of the church is lined with alders which were coppiced every 10 years by clog-makers who camped out whilst cutting the timber and shaping them into clogs. Preston Court is part 16th century, and Lower Bellamore is 17th century. The pool belonged to the old mill which burned down during the Second World War. There are several cruck-framed dwellings in the parish.

The River Wye was once more or less navigable, though when stone was brought down river from Capler on barges they had to be winched up the falls at Monnington, just below Bycross. Bycross is so named because there was a ferry there and the Ferry Cottage still stands. Two miles downstream, at Byford, there is a ford, still usable in summer. Hamlets adjacent to Preston include Hainstone, 1/4m W, and Bellamore, 3/4m SE.

PRESTON WYNNE *5.5m NE of Hereford*
Preston means 'settlement of the priests'; at the time of Domesday Book it was held by the Canons of Hereford. Wynne is from Dionisia la Wyn who held the manor in 1303. Wyn might be from the Welsh gwyn, meaning 'white'. We approached from the A465, turning north past a small gipsy encampment hiding in a hollow littered with scrap iron and broken pallets next to an orchard. A hedged lane crosses a tributary stream of the Lugg and wends its way to Lower Town.

The church stands dramatically isolated in a field beyond the platforms and hollows of the deserted mediaeval settlement. The owner refuses to let the remains be excavated. Good for him; let them lie in peace. The present stone-built church is not old. Holy Trinity was built in 1727, though the silver chalice and cover paten are dated at 1576. The Roman road from Ashton (near Berrington on the A49) to Ariconium (near Bromash, Ross-on-Wye) came through Preston Wynne. The lane that passes close to the east side of the church formed a part of this. Bearing in mind that the Romans often followed the lines of prehistoric trackways, this thoroughfare could be ancient indeed.

A little higher up the slope is Lower Town Farm, a charming group of friendly, brick and stone buildings set around a wood-fringed pool well stocked with skinny-legged moorhens. Even the green-painted corrugated iron sheds do not look out of place. The hop kiln stands watch over the old hop fields which are protected by tall hedges and tree windbreaks.

The lane leads on past an old orchard with proper, full size trees, to the present village called Upper Town. One hesitates to call it the new village because lording it over derelict farm buildings, suicidal chickens, holiday cottages and domestic dwellings is Court Farm complete with 14th century timbered hall. It is, alas, in a sorry state. As one sees it from the road it is the centre, rendered part that contains the roof timbers of the original building. The square, timber-framed parts to left and right are of the 17th century. The higher right cross wing is inhabited but the rest of the building is in a state of collapse. English Heritage and the local council want it repaired and restored but are only able to offer the owner token grants. The problem is that the cost would be far greater than the market value of the restored building. The 14th century remains include a cruck-truss with a collar beam, arched braces and a spere-truss with spere posts.

To the east, near the post office and guest house, is the ground of the Cross Keys Cricket Club. The local pub, the Frenchman's Inn, has been demolished and the shop and the school have ceased trading. The natives, however, are very friendly; not so the land to the east. Deep roadside drainage ditches indicate the wetness of the pastures. This is Preston Marsh. Many of the little cottages of the poor people who once scraped a meagre living here have been much extended and turned into desirable residences, but there is still a feeling of the forlorn hereabouts. Onwards, past the village hall, housed in a surprisingly large corrugated shack, and we reach our starting point, the Hereford-Bromyard road.

Preston Wynne is a backwater with a distinctly mediaeval feel to it. If you are travelling the Hereford to Bromyard road and are not in too great a hurry this little diversion is to be recommended.

Incidentally, there is a slight possibility that the famous Jenkins, a man with powers beyond the normal, and who lived somewhere between Hereford and Bromyard, was a farmer from Preston Wynne. Jenkins is not his real name; it is an alias invented by the folklore collector Ella Mary Leather who apparently knew his real identity but chose not to disclose it. Tales of Jenkins' exploits are legion. One is recounted in the Almeley article in this book. Indeed, it is because this tale in particular is sometimes attributed to 'a farmer from Preston Wynne' that the connection with Jenkins and the settlement has been made.

PUDLESTON *4.25m E of Leominster*
The name is from the Old English and could mean either 'the hill of the mouse-hawk', or 'Pyttel's Hill'. It lies amongst the small hills and woods between Leominster and Bromyard and is most easily approached off the A44 at Docklow. It is beautiful, friendly country, its gentle pastures well watered by numerous little streams, the kind of landscape one sees illustrated in children's stories. Pudleston is a scattered hamlet with a few red brick cottages, a village hall (the old school of 1874), and a church.

Saint Peter's is built of small red sandstone 'bricks' and has a big slated-stone roof. For company it has yews and a fine cedar tree. The church tower could be Anglo-Saxon with its long and short quoins, a distinct batter (slope) to the walls and the appearance of the windows from inside. What is more, the nave has a Norman window which, from its spread, seems to have been constructed without consideration for a tower being erected above, meaning that the tower seems to be a later addition. It might be early 13th century but the mystery remains. Above the tower is a shingled spire. The west doorway is also Norman and has typical zig-zag decoration in the arch. The chancel has two lancet windows of the 13th century. The east window is of 1875; the nave was re-built in 1813 and the aisles were added in 1851. The stained glass in the aisle was designed by A.W.N. Pugin and paid for by Mr. Chadwick of Pudleston Court.

Pudleston Court has a beautiful setting amongst woods in quiet, serene country. The east gates are impressive, flanked by sandstone lodges garnished with turrets and battlements. The fortress feeling is maintained by electronic devices and high, well maintained security fencing. The house is a vaguely mock-Tudor irregular building of 1846 and is also castellated. The stone was delivered from a local quarry by a temporary railway. During the Second World War it was a convalescent hospital for R.A.F. personnel and until recently it was a boarding school for boys. In the grounds there are two ancient oak trees called Adam and Eve.

The Old Rectory stands just north of the church. It is Georgian and has five bays, two storeys, a pedimented doorway and was for many years the home of Esmond Bulmer the present chairman of the famous cider company. (He now lives at Poston House, Vowchurch.) The Bulmers farm their extensive estate and are the only local landowners to employ full-time agriculture labour.

Ford Abbey, 1m SSW of the church, is a timber-framed house with a two-storey porch, a moat, an orchard and a stream. The house was built about 1500 and about 1600 the south wing and part of the east wing were re-built. In the 17th century the south wing was extended to the west. However, there is no trace of the chapel or any local tradition of it. The moat is 30 yards square and is now dry. The track of the disused railway from Leominster to Bromyard passes a little to the south.

Rosedale, 1.1/4m N of the church, is a hamlet set around a square of little lanes, with woods and a wildfowl pool. Golder Field is 3/4m NNE of the church. Golder is from the Anglo-Saxon golde-ora, 'the slope where marigolds grew'. Today the fields of gold are rape-seed; the agriculture of the area is mixed arable and cattle and sheep grazing.

Herefordshire is noted for its equable climate but in these hills the winters can be cold. Snowdrifts of up to 20ft occur in the narrow lanes and in 1963 the parish was cut off from the outside world for six weeks.

PUTLEY *4m W of Ledbury*

The name is Anglo-Saxon and can mean either 'the wood of the kite', or less excitingly 'Putta's clearing in the wood'. We are not claiming any connection but a cleric called Putta is thought to have been the first Bishop of Hereford in 676 A.D. At that time the county of Herefordshire did not exist; the unit of administration was the diocese. The Old English leah can mean either 'a wood' or 'a clearing in a wood', but either the geographical situation or the other elements in the name often give a good indication as to which applies.

Putley is somewhat lost in the lanes south of the Hereford to Leominster road, the A438. It is a most attractive area, and the old houses and half-timbered cottages hide amongst woods and orchards well watered by numerous small streams. Much of Putley lies on the eastern flank of the famous Woolhope Dome, a limestone highland noted for its varied natural beauty. Such desirability is reflected in the high house prices of the parish and the number of 'incomers' who work elsewhere. Although still numerous the orchards are in decline and hopyards are vanishing fast. Soft fruits such as blackcurrants are grown, and there is some experimentation with vines. However, agriculture is predominantly arable and animal fattening for slaughter.

Excavations in 1954 revealed the remains of a Roman villa in the grounds of Putley Court, south of the present house and east of the Putley Rectory. Two open drains running north-south, about 12 yards apart, were revealed in which were found flue tiles, daub, and 3rd and 4th century pottery.

Putley Court as we see it today dates from 1712. It is a brick house of five bays and two and a half storeys with quoins, a segmented pedimented doorway, a parapet and a hipped roof with a lantern. In the rear garden is a summerhouse with four Tuscan columns and a pediment. From 1872 to 1922 the owner of the Court and the Putley estate was John Riley, a much loved local squire who kept Longhorn Cattle and Tamworth pigs and was an authority on the growing and marketing of soft fruits. The village hall at Putley Green was given to the village by his children in 1927. It is a well-used venue famous for the Putley Ceilidhs (ceilidh is pronounced kaylee). These are country dance nights held at the beginning of each month, from Harvest Supper in November to All Fools in April. Attached to the hall is the post office-cum-general store; the shopkeeper is also the hall caretaker, a very neat arrangement.

When the Norman church at Putley was being restored in 1876 a quantity of Roman remains including pottery was found near the north wall. The architect of the new church was Thomas Blashill. A gloomier interior we have never seen; but its location in a wooded hollow by a pond and an old yew tree is quite delightful. Fragments of Norman stonework were used to block one of the three 13th century doorways. Also 13th century are the handsome piscina and a cusped lancet window. The chancel is decorated with elaborate pictures in wood, alabaster and mosaic and the stalls have tall traceried canopies lit by skylights in the chancel roof. The pulpit and screen have Jacobean panels made from the old Squire's Pew. The tower bell is 15th century, the porch 16th century. In the churchyard there is a well-worn preaching cross, complete with head which has Christ being crucified, the Virgin Mother and two saints.

The Brainge, 1/3m NNE of the church, is a most attractive brick-built house of 1703. It has a five-bay front, quoins, pedimented doorway, hipped roof, and an early 19th century Doric-columned porch on the three-bay side. The windows have sham lintels of red and black brick. Old Castle, 1/2m NE of the church, is a house of about 1700 that has been added to and altered in this century. It has five bays, two storeys, a hipped roof and wooden cross windows. Newtons, 1/4m SSW of the church, has a cruck barn and The Lacons, 300 yards NW of the church, is of cruck construction.

Putley Mill, 200 yards E of the church, is now a Heritage Centre with limited camping and caravanning facilities. The fabric of the mill has been renovated and the upper floor is now used as a venue for music concerts. The setting is quite delightful. Stone steps lead up to the mill pond from where there are views over the wooded village.

Putley Mill is presently owned by Annie Jones. She is the widow of Dave Jones (1940-91). He was a singer, a musician, a dancer and an impresario but above all he was a collector of local folk traditions. He not only collected songs, morris dances, mumming plays and ancient customs, but re-established them in the community where they are now firmly rooted. Sadly, he was cut down by a

Lilac Tree

I'm sure as sure can be
That my lilac tree
Is watching me
Looking at her
Admiringly,
And feeling proud
When I say out loud
"I love you lilac tree."

News at One

It was on the *News at One*:
They have to cull the wild deer
Because they eat too much;
They have to shoot the wild geese
Because they breed too much.

So what about me?
And what about you?
What about all of our
Gluttonous crew?

"Don't worry," said God,
With a courteous nod
In the direction of Satan,
Who raises a hoof
Whilst remaining aloof:
"Our terrorist friends,
I dare say,
Will not in Old Ireland delay,
And out in Beirut
There is still rotten fruit;
I expect a consignment today.

Border Lord

He lived in castles strong with stone,
All dressed in rich attire,
In gold and green and ruby red,
And won my heart's desire.

In sunset mist enshrouded,
In valleys full of blood,
He calls his hirelings homeward,
To dine in that dark wood.

I see him now when rested,
The wine his soul has stirred,
And beg my liege's pardon,
As I betray my word.

I see that hated Frenchman,
His hand upon her breast,
And she her eyes disdaining,
This wild man from the West.

I plunged my dagger ever deep,
Laughed at her wails of woe,
The sigh that sails mountains,
That wolves and Welshmen know.

And now that I am hunted,
And death my only fate,
I'll cry no more for Ceinwen,
And all her fine estate.

Robin Hood

I can see you, Robin Hood,
peeping around that tree,
calling me to join your merry band.
I'm sorry, but I have things to do,
places to go, and people to see.
I'd love to come,
but I've a race to run.

I can see you, Robin Hood,
hiding behind that holly,
girt in green, beckoning me
with promises of freedom.
I can hear your hunting horn
hallowing through the groves,
and curling down the river.

To you I will confess,
my spirit is subdued,
I need to be renewed,
Hold on, my friend,
I'm on my way,
not today, of course,
but tomorrow,
probably .....
perhaps .....

But Robin was gone,
to the wild woods he'd run,
and after him followed
a raggle-taggle bunch
of men far braver than me.
No-one looked back,
and I skulked home
for my tea.

Michael Raven 1996

brain tumour and taken from us in his prime. It was Dave Jones who formed the Putley Old Wonder Not for Joes morris side in 1987. Their costume and dances are based on descriptions obtained from Bill Scarrett of Pershore, in Worcestershire. It was Dave Jones who collected the Cradley Mumming Play from Albert Philpotts which is printed in full in Roy Palmer's *The Folklore of Hereford and Worcester*, and it was Dave Jones who, in 1975, revived the custom of Burning the Bush on New Year's Day. Amongst the songs he collected are some previously unrecorded pieces such as Rainbow Hill and I Loves My Sarah. Probably his best known monument is the Bromyard Folk Festival which he established in 1967 and which still flourishes as one of the major festivals in the whole of England.

For The Wonder, 1m SW of Putley church, see Much Marcle. Woolhope Cockshoot, 1m WSW of Putley church, is a crossroads hamlet on the steep slopes of the Woolhope Dome. The name is probably from cock-shut, a funnel-shaped net permanently set up to catch birds. To the north of Putley are Putley Common and Durlow Common, both with a handful of squatters cottages. Aylton, to the east, has its own article. Both Aylton and Putley participate in the Big Apple festivals which were begun in 1989.

QUERENTUNE
The site of this Domesday Book place is not known but is probably in the area of Bradley Cottage, 2m S of Presteigne, in OS grid square 32 61. The name might be from either cweorn, 'a milestone', or Quenen, 'a woman or a queen'. In 1086 it was wasteland covered by a wild wood "in which this Osbern goes hunting and he has from them what he can catch. Nothing else." Querentune and the other 10 adjacent places were probably devastated by Gruffydd ap Llywelyn in 1052 during the invasion recorded in the *Anglo-Saxon Chronicle*.

RICHARDS CASTLE *4.5m SSW of Ludlow*
The Richard after whom the settlement was named was Richard le Scrob. He was a Norman nobleman who had settled here and built himself a substantial motte and bailey castle before the Conquest of England by Duke William. It has been suggested, but with no corroborative evidence, that Shrewsbury - originally called Scrobbesbyrig - was named after him. Not long after the Conquest the land on which now stands the town of Ludlow was given to Richard's son, Osbern Fitz Richard, and was held from him by Roger de Lacy. It was at this time that Ludlow Castle was being built in stone and the new town laid out.

The remains of the castle at Richards Castle are on a wooded slope, 1m NW of the modern village. The approach road runs uphill and at the top, as it veers right, is the Old Village green on the left. There are two cottages, one in stone and one in half-timber. A path leads to the church, and the great moat and the motte of the castle are revealed. There are far ranging southerly views from here and it is an evocative place. Tall pine trees now stand sentry with their feet in a tangle of briars, ground ivy, nettles and grass. Beneath this ground cover is a great deal of fallen masonry.

The mound itself was long thought to be just that - an earthen base for the original wooden fort. However, excavation has revealed that in the early 12th century a great octagonal tower of stone, 50ft in diameter and with walls 20ft thick, was built on top of the mound. As this tower collapsed the material from the upper parts surrounded the base to first floor level and the whole appeared to be part of the motte. The original mound was 35ft high; as we see it today it is 55ft above the original ground level. In the early 13th century the curtain wall and a residential tower to the E were added. There is evidence to show that in addition to the defences of the castle there was a town wall that encircled the whole of the top of the hill so that the church and the settlement were also afforded protection.

The town, for it was a borough, was not insignificant. By 1340 there were 103 burgages (housing plots) and it had a weekly market and an annual fair.

Richards Castle is of great interest because it is quite possibly the earliest true castle in Britain, and was certainly only one of three pre-Conquest castles in the country. The Celts, the Romans and the Anglo-Saxons fortified settlements, not private houses. Indeed, the local Anglo-Saxon nobility complained bitterly to the king (Edward the Confessor) about Richard le Scrob's castle and tried to have it dismantled. But the king was pro-Norman and allowed the fortress to stand. By 1540, when Leland visited the area, the castle was no longer lived in and was beginning to become ruinous.

The large and impressive stone-built church of Saint Bartholomew stands 100 yards E of the castle. The Norman church, probably built by Richard Fitz Scrob in the 11 century, consisted of a nave and a chancel. The present north wall of the nave is original Norman and has two round-headed windows; the rest of the building is 14th century, except the 15th century west window and the later east window. Although now a redundant church Saint Bartholomew's is well maintained and open to the public. Inside there are box pews and the canopied Salwey family pew. There is a tangible atmosphere here, almost monastic, and very mediaeval. The roof stands high, supported by thick, bare walls, some of which lie at odd angles. As one approaches the church a bricked up door and window can be seen below the chancel. These belong to Saint Anthony's Bower, a crypt that was possibly once a hermit's cell. Beyond the chancel is the detached bell tower, square and strong like a castle keep and, indeed, it was designed as a part of the village defences. There are three bells beneath the pyramid roof. The church was abandoned in 1892.

Richards Castle is known for its Bone (or Boney) Well. The name is misleading, for it is really a section of a stream rather than a spring or a well that is referred to. This is situated about 100 yards W of the castle at Ordnance Survey map reference SO 480 702. It is most easily approached along the dirt track that leads through the farm of the old 16th century manor house now called Green Farm (which is on the road between the modern Richards Castle village and the church). At the bottom of the hill the track crosses a stream in a wooded dingle. This is the Boney Well. The ground is marshy and there are signs of springs in the slopes to the right. A water pump 'ram' lies in a pit covered by corrugated iron, and a brick spring cap can be seen nearby. The well gets its name from the fact that at times of heavy rain numerous spiny bones accumulate here, washed out of rocks laid down in a Silurian sea. In a strata of rocks called the Upper Ludlow beds there is a thin layer of fish bones. In former times they were believed to be either frogs' legs or the bones of wrens who came here to die.

The modern, main road village of Richards Castle is, in fact, not so very modern. There are several black and white houses which must be at least of the 17th century, and many cottages of the local yellow stone. There is a handsome pub, The Castle, a red brick Methodist church, a crescent of council houses, a modern estate, and a village hall; but the post office, shop and school are with us no more. The settlement lies on a slope surrounded by fields laid mainly to pasture.

Between the main road and the castle there are several good houses, notably the Court House. This is where parish matters were discussed and decided. The black and white part is the original building; the north wing of stone was added in 1620-30 but was subsequently shortened and rebuilt at the west end. In the garden there is a handsome dovecote. This is at least 14th century and has nearly 1,000 nesting holes in its circular, 3ft to 4ft thick walls. At the north-west corner of the house there is a 17th century cider mill.

RISBURY 4m SE of Leominster
The name is from the Old English hris - burg, 'the fort in brushwood'. When the Anglo-Saxons used burg in a place name it almost always refers to a prehistoric fortress, not one of their own. The village lies 1/2m E of Risbury Camp, a large Iron-Age hill fort. This is situated on a long promontory skirted by the Holly Brook and covers some 28 acres. The actual enclosure is only 8.1/2 acres. The rest is occupied by the defensive earth ramparts and ditches, three lines to the west and four lines on the east, with possibly two main entrances. The interior of the fortress has been planted with fruit trees in modern times.

In the steep-sided valley adjoining the fort to the south is an old water-mill and a Georgian mill house. They are delightfully situated, set behind a lawn and a wood-fringed pool. It was about six o'clock in the evening when we visited. My goodness, watch your back. City workers hurtle down the narrow lanes desperate to get to their cottages in the country. We have noticed this outlandish behaviour at this time of the day wherever we have been.

The village lies 1/2m E of the hill fort, around a crossroads. It has cottages of brick, stone and timber-framing, some modern houses and bungalows, a post office, a pub, an equestrian centre and a red brick Methodist church with dressed lancet windows. The countryside around is mostly ploughland and pasture with the occasional hopyard, and is part of the serene landscape that stretches from Leominster to Bromyard, a land of little hills and numerous streams. Turn off the A44 at almost any point, north or south, and the traveller is unlikely to be disappointed.

For a description of the cross-country route of a disused section of the Roman road to the west of Risbury Camp see the article on Humber.

RODD 1m SE of Presteigne
The name is from the Old English rod 'a clearing'. It lies in the valley of the Hindwell Brook, 1/4m S of the Welsh border on the Kington road, the B4355. The embankments that run parallel to the road are part of the disused railway line to Kington.

There are some good, old houses in the area. Rodd Court is a stone house of about 1625 with a later brick front facade, gables, mullioned and transomed wood frame windows, three storeys, a full height porch, and some good ceilings. Just to the north is Little Rodd, a mediaeval cruck-framed house. The cruck is not visible from outside. Upper Nash Farm, 1m W by the woods and cliffs of Nash Scar, is a timber-framed house with a mediaeval centre and a 16th century addition which has a gable and a moulded beam supporting the first floor.

Little Brampton, 1.1/2m SW down the valley from Rodd, is a delightfully irregular, gabled, timber-framed house of the 16th century. Highland, 1.1/4m SE on the lower slopes of wooded Wapley Hill, has a mediaeval cruck truss in the east wing.

ROSS-ON-WYE 9m SSE of Hereford
The name is from rhos, Welsh for 'hill' or 'promontory', and it does, indeed, stand on a hill. It earns its living as a regional market, shopping, service and tourist centre. As such it had one of the Union Workhouses which were operating into the 1920s. The Ross Workhouse has a small but important footnote in folkloric history because it was here that Cecil Sharp collected some 45 songs from the inmates. Many of these are particularly good versions. The Workhouse became a mental hospital and was demolished in 1995. From its ashes is arising the new Dean's Hill Hospital.

Ross was an Anglo-Saxon settlement and took over from the Roman iron-working town of Ariconium, centred on Bromash 3m E. The town probably developed originally because of its position opposite a ford across the River Wye. After the Conquest the Normans built a castle at Wilton (see Bridstow), on the opposite bank, to guard this crossing and command the waterway.

By the 16th century there was a wooden bridge, which may have been at the end of Wye Street, where the ferry terminated at a later date. After an overloaded ferry overturned, with between 30 and 40 people drowned, a stone bridge was constructed at Wilton in 1599. This handsome and robust edifice has survived to this day, albeit having been widened and strengthened over the years. It has six round arches and substantial cutwaters. During the Civil War one of the spans was dismantled as a defensive measure but reinstated after the hostilities.

In 1016 Ross was acquired by the Bishop of Hereford and it is believed that his church was built near the town end of Brampton Street. In about 1120 the market was established and in about 1150 it became a borough. By 1285 there were 105 families living here. The Bishop's Palace stood on the site now occupied by the Royal Hotel and when the foundations of the hotel were being excavated a small dungeon was found. The town prospered in the Middle Ages but suffered terribly from the plague of 1637. The Plague Cross in the churchyard stands near the plague pit and commemorates the 316 lives lost.

Ross has had numerous small industries - nailmaking, leather-working, shoemaking, brewing, iron founding, corn milling, glove-making, wool stapling, basket-making, flax dressing and rope-making. The Rope Walk still exists as a path between Wye Street and the play area near the Ross Rowing Club. In modern times farm machinery and plastic mouldings, amongst other things, are manufactured in the industrial estate around the disused railway station. Now that the railway has gone - it came in 1855 and departed in the 1960s - Ross is once more akin to the coaching town it was in the 18th and 19th centuries. Today, though, those in a hurry can use the fast new A40, opened in 1960, which by-passes the town and robs the Wye Valley of much of its former tranquility; it is not traffic so much as speed that generates noise.

Ross, seen over the river, is a much admired prospect, a view that owes a great deal to John Kyrle (1637-1724) the Man of Ross, immortalised by Alexander Pope. Kyrle was born at Dymock, in Gloucestershire, a man of considerable wealth who lived modestly, had a cheerful disposition, gave generously to the poor and infirm, was sought for social advice and took pleasure in doing good works. When he died the entire population of Ross attended his funeral. He brought a proper water supply to the town, donated a library, repaired the causeway to Wilton Bridge, restored the soaring 14th century church spire that dominates the view of the town and planned the public garden of 1700 called the Prospect. The south part of this remains. It has a handsome gate with Corinthian pilasters and a pediment. The view to the west is admirable, despite the motorway and its 350ft long bridge.

In the 1830s a new road was cut beneath the red cliffs and in 1837 the Royal Hotel was opened. The town was now in the height of its Victorian tourism boom and the hotel was built in Continental picturesque with white stucco, barge-boarded gables and prominent chimney stacks. At the same time the area was made mediaeval Gothic with sandstone walls, arrow-slits, bay windows on corbels carved in the rock face, and a prominent round tower with lancet windows. The whole effect is of ancient town walls and done well enough to deceive the unknowing.

The tourist trade that had inspired these works had commenced in 1745 when the Reverend John Egerton arranged boat trips for his friends and relatives down the lower River Wye. In 1760 a basket maker, James Evans, hired boats on a commercial basis and the Wye Tour proper was born. The fame of its beauties and grandeur soon spread and in 1782 William Gilpin wrote his influential *Observations on the River Wye*. This was followed by Charles Heath's *Excursion Down the Wye* of 1799. By 1827 eight boats a day were leaving Ross. It cost 1.1/2 guineas to go to Monmouth and 3 guineas for the two-day trip to Chepstow.

Customers included William Wordsworth, Thomas Gray, Thomas Cobbett, Lord Nelson and Lady Hamilton, George IV and Princess Mary of Teck (later Queen Mary). Charles Dickens (1812-70) was a regular visitor to Ross because his manager, George Dolby, lived here at Ashfield Lodge. On one visit he took what many travellers say is 'the prettiest walk in England', the 11 miles from Ross to Monmouth down the Wye Valley. In 1867 he met his friend and biographer, John Forster, at the Royal Hotel and finally decided to accept the lucrative but exhausting reading tour of America that began his rapid decline into ill-health and led to his death in 1870. In 1902 the stern wheel steamship *Wilton Castle* was launched at Ross. She was built to carry 100 passengers at 8 knots on pleasure cruises, but was laid up in 1912 for lack of customers.

The extension of the railway to Monmouth in 1855 provided a much cheaper way to see the Wye Valley and contributed to the decline in the river-borne trade. Since the Second World War the Wye has become too silted-up to take large tourist vessels. Now there are only short trips to Symonds Yat.

The centre of the town is on high ground at the junction of Broad Street, Gloucester Road, Walford Road and High Street. At the crossroads is the small, triangular Market Place, in the centre of which is the red sandstone Market Hall of 1660-74. It is open on the ground floor and the first floor hall is supported on columns and arches, six to each side with twin gables and a clock turret. On one gable is a medallion of Charles II paid for by John Kyrle. Two fresh produce markets are held each week. The Market Place runs down the steep hill and becomes Broad Street in which there used to be a central row of timber-framed houses known as Under-Hell.

Facing the Market Hall is John Kyrle's house, a large, three-storeyed, black and white former inn with close-set uprights. The ground floor has plate-glass shop windows; upstairs are the offices of the *Ross Gazette*, and we will take this opportunity to publicly thank the General Manager, Kevin Minton, for the courteous assistance he offered us in the course of our enquiries. In the garden at the back of the house is a rather nice summerhouse of about 1700 in red sandstone which has a lancet window topped by a steep gable on each side of the entrance. A winding path with three grotto arches leads to the summerhouse. This is one of the earliest picturesque garden landscapes in England, despite its small, town house scale. At the foot of the three steps leading from the door of the summerhouse is a crude swan mosaic made of horses' teeth. The teeth were collected by local people and brought to John Kyrle. They are said to be from horses killed in a cavalry battle at Witton Bridge during the Civil War. Incidentally, it was a member of the Kyrle Society, Octavia Hill, who was a prime mover in the formation of the National Trust.

Notable buildings near the Royal Hotel include: the British and Foreign School of 1837, which has four storeys and a pedimented gable; and nearby is a small Gothic sandstone house with four-headed windows; the Vaga House, Late Georgian with giant pilasters and Tuscan porch and canted bay windows; the Man of Ross, which has a Dutch gable and is possibly 17th century; and the Castle Vaults, neo-Tudor of 1838.

The mediaevalisation continues into Edde Cross Street where the Valley Hotel has a polygonal tower and the Merton Hotel has a sham, ruined summerhouse. In Saint Mary's Street is Palace Pound, late 17th century with quoins. In Church Street are the Rudhall Almshouses founded in 1575 by William Rudhall, of red sandstone, with gables and little mullioned windows. In High Street is the King's Head, an early building with a 19th century facade (not uncommon in market towns), and the Saracen's Head, black and white, with close-set uprights and carved beams. In Copse Street are the Webbe's Almshouses, founded in 1717 as a Bluecoat School, but reconstructed in 1798 of brick with seven broad bays and Tuscan-columned doorway. Here, too, is a candle-maker, about which more later. In New Street is the former, square, red sandstone Lock-Up which has lancet windows and pyramid roof. At the bottom of the hill Broad Street becomes Brookend Street. Here, by the stream, is the watermill, the old industrial heart of Ross. Here, too, is the early 18th century Railway Hotel with its quoins and hipped roof, and the Friends' Meeting House of 1804.

And so to the parish church. Saint Mary's is set high above the town in a most spacious and attractive churchyard well stocked with a wide range of handsome trees, not just broody yews. We were struck by three things; the splendid views over the river from the Beacon-brazier, the large number of very old people buried in the graveyard - (the air must be good here) - and the towering 10ft high walls of the vicarage, a former incumbent's tribute in stone to the Goddess of Privacy. The oldest part of the church is the south arcade, with its circular columns and double-chamfered arches. Most of the rest was rebuilt in the 13th and 14th centuries and zealously re-built and restored again in 1734 and 1862.

It is a lofty, spacious church and well stocked with monuments to local worthies. Here lie: William Rudhall, Attorney-General to Henry VIII, died 1530 and wife, in alabaster effigy; William Rudhall, died 1609; Nathaniel Hill, died 1632; John Rudhall, died 1636; Colonel Rudhall, died 1651, in statue; Elizabeth Markey, died 1681; G. Abrahall, died 1729, in the Markye Chapel; John Kyrle, died 1724, this monument erected 1776, with portrait

Top: Ross on Wye, the classic prospect over the river.
Middle left: the A40 between Ross and Monmouth.
Middle centre: Harry Diamond, Victorian minstrel buried at Ross.
Middle right: Noele Gordon, 'Meg' of *Crossroads*, lived at Weirend, near Ross.
Opposite: Dennis Potter, TV playwright, lived and died in Ross.

head; John Partridge, died 1810; and Thomas Westfalling, died 1887, white marble bust.

A curious and charming feature is the ivy-trailing plant which climbs the east window of the north aisle. This grows out of the stumps of elm trees which formerly grew within the church. These were planted by John Kyrle, either deliberately inside the walls or by offshoots coming through the foundations from a churchyard tree. The stained glass east window has four 15th century figures: Saint Ethelbert, Saint Thomas of Cantilupe, Saint Ann and The Virgin, and Saint Joachim. These were brought here when the Bishop of Hereford's house at Stretton Sugwas was demolished.

In the graveyard lie the mortal remains of Harry Diamond (died 1907). He was a popular entertainer of some renown, a minstrel singer who accompanied himself on the banjo. In the Summer he played at seaside resorts; in the Winter he returned to Ross, his adopted home, where he taught his instrument and performed at musical evenings. He died penniless and his marble tombstone, which features a banjo with a broken string, was paid for by public subscription. An entertainer of more recent times was Dennis Potter, the highly regarded television playwright whose last two works were the related *Karaoke* and *Cold Lazarus*. Potter lived at Ross for many years and died here in June, 1994. Also buried here is the actress Noelle Gordon, star of the long-running television soap opera called *Crossroads*. Her home was at nearby Weirend.

The Italianate, grey brick Baptist Chapel in Broad Street is of 1861 by G.C. Haddon. Horn Green Church, 1.1/2m SW, was dedicated in mediaeval times as The Paraclete, but what we see today is of 1906 by G.F. Bodley. It has an unusual range of tall, octagonal piers along the centre, effectively making two naves.

Ross is a picturesque town that owes much of its present prosperity to the tourist trade connected to the delights of the Wyre Forest and the River Wye. It has all the usual facilities of a regional centre - banks, solicitors, a Chinese take-away, (have one of these and you really are a town), numerous small shops including a book store, three schools, a cattle market now banished north of the Ross Spur near Netherton, a swimming pool and sports centre, a library, and a theatre, The Phoenix, owned and run by the enterprising Ross Operatic and Dramatic Society, Palace Pound. The Larruperz Centre in Grammar School Close has a variety of meeting rooms and a concert hall for hire by the public. (The Larruperz were a group of young drinking men who sang and collected for charity.)

Ross even has an internationally acclaimed candlemaker, and not many towns have one of those. Colin Hughes learned his trade in Germany and Austria but then developed a process for engraving extremely fine detail which, despite his patent, has been copied by large German and Japanese manufacturers. His crowded little workshop hides away in a narrow back street, off the Gloucester Old Road.

Some curiosities, customs and legends. Richard Atkins, a native of Ross, went as a Protestant missionary to Rome. For his audacity he was tortured and burned alive in front of Saint Peter's. Mrs. E.M. Leather reports that in the early 1900s when a boy was drowned in the river at Ross it was remarked that his brothers would now be careful to keep away from the bank. An old man hearing this said: "Let 'em go, let 'em go, no one else'll be drowned this year, the river has had its due".

Keele, in his *Romance of the History of England,* recounts the legend of the Spectre's Voyage. The stretch of the River Wye between Ross and Hereford was haunted by a woman in a small boat. She would sail "from Hereford to Northbrigg, a little village then distant about three miles from the city, of which not even the site is now discernible". She landed on the eastern shore, a little beyond the village, and made the most fearful lamentations. Then she sailed off and vanished at a point where the current ran strong, about half a mile from Hereford. The spectre only appeared after eight o'clock in the evening. To meet it proved fatal so boatmen refused to venture on to the river after that hour.

The shoemakers of Ross had a holiday on 25th October, Cobblers' Day, and a local rhyme was

"The 25th of October,
Cursed be the cobbler
That goes to bed sober."

The name Cob's Cross at Ross is thought to be a corruption of Corpus Christi Cross, after a pageant that was performed there. Capel Tump, presumably the Iron-Age hill fort with a cut-rock entrance in Chase Wood, 1m S of the town centre, was the scene of festivities in Whitsun week. These celebrations were often debauched in the extreme and so were kept away from all but those who chose to go.

In 1305 a party of sixteen men felled and took away trees from the wood in Ross Foreign owned by the Bishop. They were denounced by name in the six local parish churches and ordered to do penance by walking once around the church at Ross on Sunday, dressed only in their shirts, and once around the Market Place on market day. They also to return the trees. The two ringleaders had to do double penance.

Alton Court, 1/2m SE of Ross, is a handsome though much restored, 16th century timber-framed house with close-set uprights and herringbone bracing. In the 17th century a young gardener called Roger Mortimer once worked here. To tell his story we cannot do better than quote from Roy Palmer.

"Roger Mortimer fell in love with his employer's second daughter, the beautiful Clara Markey. She reciprocated, but they were fully aware of the social gulf between them and therefore kept their feelings secret. To their dismay the time came when Clara's father told her that he arranged for her to marry a young man from the well-to-do Rudhall family. (Monuments to both Markeys and Rudhalls can still be seen in Ross Church).

Mortimer was so distraught that an old woman called Nancy Carter was accused of bewitching him. Straws in the shape of a cross were strewn after her and pins plunged into her in attempts to lift the imagined spell. (Drawing a witch's blood was thought to remove her powers). Then Mortimer's hat was discovered lodged against the central pier of Wilton Bridge, and searchers found his body upstream, near The Acres.

The body was carried to the Welsh Old Harp Inn, Alton Street and Jack 'the Scrape' Clements, who lived in Walford Road, was hired as sin eater. A quart of beer and sixpence were passed over the corpse to him, and he stated: 'I take all the consequences and so I has all the beer'. After sunset the body was taken up the road and buried without ceremony other than the driving of a stake through the heart, so as 'to be sure he would not walk, and bite people in their beds'. That was how Corpse Cross (now Copse Cross) acquired its name, though Mrs. Leather suggests it is a corruption of Corpus Christi Cross. (The bodies of those who had committed suicide were buried there in similar fashion until 1823, when the law ended the practice).

Clara's marriage was due only a few days after the burial. At the Church when the parson enquired whether she would take Rudhall as her husband she uttered a scream, then fainted. She was taken home unconscious, but half an hour later she was found wandering in a daze, seeking where Mortimer had been buried at the crossroads on Alton Road. Her family led her home, but every time she could escape their vigilance, she would slip away to pace slowly up and down the lane leading to Corpse Cross. Eventually she was given her head, and made her lonely walk for decades until she herself died. The lane is still called Old Maid's Walk".

Ross had a long tradition of Morris dancing and, until Dave Jones found one from Cradley, the Ross Mumming Play was the only one collected in the county. This was given to Mrs. E.M. Leather by William Powell at Ross in 1908.

The new year festivities in recent years have become quite notorious. In 1991 arrests were made and policemen injured. In 1992 some 1,500 people congregated at the Market Hall. On New Year's Day there is a walk and fun run from Court Farm, via Hole-in-the-Wall to the Anchor Inn at Ross.

It was a belief held locally that it was bad luck to borrow fire during the 12 days of Christmas, but you could buy it for the price of a pin. On the 12th day it was the custom to light 12 fires. One was larger than the others and was used for 'burning the witch'.

Here is an abbreviated version of the King of the Cats story told by an old lady of 90 years who was living at Ross in 1882. The same story has been collected in Denmark.

A hunter returned home late after losing his way in the fog. After his supper he sat with his friend before a roaring fire with their dogs and the house cat at their feet. "I had an adventure today", said the hunter, "I was lost in the forest and then I saw a light. I followed it hoping to get help but it disappeared so I climbed a big oak tree the better to look for it. I looked down and there it was, beneath my feet, in the hollow of the tree. It was like a church. I heard singing and saw a coffin surrounded by torches. You won't believe me, but the coffin and the torches were carried by cats and on the coffin was a crown and sceptre". At that the house cat jumped up and shrieked with excitement, "By Jove old Peter's dead, now I'm King of the Cats", and with that he rushed up the chimney and was never seen again.

The story of King Herla, another tale with a local connection, is recounted by the Herefordshire scholar, Walter Map, in his 12th century *De Nugis Curialium* (Courtiers' Tales). Here is an outline of the story.

An ancient British king called Herla was visited on his wedding day by a pygmy king with horned feet riding on a goat. The pygmy invited Herla to his own wedding in 12 months' time and the king accepted. On the appointed day the pygmy led King Herla and his entourage into a cave richly bedecked and lit with lamps. The wedding ceremony over, King Herla was given a small bloodhound with the warning that no-one should dismount from their horse until the dog leapt from the king's arms of its own accord. After travelling for some time Herla met a shepherd and asked for news of his Queen. The shepherd could barely understand the King's speech. "The only queen I know of by that name", he said, "was the wife of a British king called Herla who mysteriously vanished 200 years ago, a year after his marriage". As they had only been away for three days this greatly disturbed some of King Herla's men and they dismounted to question the shepherd further, whereupon they immediately turned to dust. Herla and the remainder of his entourage rode off but the dog never did jump out of the king's arms and they only ceased their wanderings when they tried to cross the River Wye in Herefordshire and were drowned in the first year of the reign of King Henry II (1154). Their deaths were witnessed by a number of Welshmen which probably means that the location was in Arkenfield, somewhere between Hereford and Whitchurch, near Ross.

ROWLSTONE *12m SW of Hereford*
It is most easily approached off the Hereford to Abergavenny road, the A465, at Pontrilas. The name is from Hroaldr's - tun. The first element is an Old Norse personal name; the second is Old English for 'a fence', but in place names can mean many things from 'homestead' to 'town'. Without further information we usually fall back on 'settlement' which covers all the possibilities.

Rowlstone stands on high ground above the valley of the Cwm Brook, 1.1/2m WSW of Pontrilas, in the territory called Arkenfield. It is a small hamlet with a handful of dwellings, the church and a castle mound. The flat-topped mound lies just west of Court Farm. It is about 40 yards in diameter at the base and rises to about 15 feet above the bottom of the ditch. The ivy-clad, stone-built Court Farm itself is a four-bay, two-storey house. It looks ordinary enough with its low-arched, Georgian-Victorian windows but the left side has 11th century stonework, the centre is 13th century with walls 3ft thick and the right side is mid-17th century. It is a BSE free dairy farm - the farmer does not buy cattle in and never has.

In the churchyard of Saint Peter's there are yews, an ancient oak and a preaching cross on a mediaeval base. The tower and the barrel roof of the chancel are 16th century, the porch is Victorian, and in the east end there are some 15th century Perpendicular windows. The rest is Norman, and in the south doorway and the chancel arch is some of the very best sculpture by the Herefordshire School of Carvers. Nothing is known of these men though there seems to be a presumption that they were local Celtic/Anglo-Saxon craftsmen and that their master-designer had knowledge of Continental emblems and design ranging from Scandinavia to Spain.

The tympanum of the south doorway depicts Christ in Majesty, seated, knees apart and feet close together, his right hand raised in blessing and four angels flying around him holding the halo which encircles him as an oval frame. The semi-circle of the tympanum is bordered by a band of cable ornament and the arches of the doorway are elaborately carved with a variety of figures and designs.

The decoration of the doorway shafts is no less marvellously worked and includes carvings of cocks and a pagan Green Man with foliage emanating from his mouth. Birds feature on the other masterpiece, the capitals of the chancel arch. Some say they are cocks, others that they are doves. No matter, the design and execution are of the highest order. There is also an angel and a bishop, depicted once the right way up and repeated upside down. The font is also Norman. The tympanum, by the way, is almost identical to the badly worn work at Shobden and just goes to show what a treasure was lost there.

The long, 15th century wrought-iron candelabra brackets in the chancel are some of the rarest pieces in the whole of England. There are two, 4ft 7ins in length, each with five spikes for five candles and each decorated with six pairs of birds, one set with tails up, the other with tails down. Until the early years of the 20th century a Welsh Bible was preserved at the church. Welsh was for long the native language of the area. Rowlstone is one of several places mentioned by Mrs. E.M. Leather in 1912 as having a Holy Thorn, a bush grown from the Glastonbury Thorn planted by Joseph of Arimathea.

In the country around there are some old farms with old names: Wigga, 3/4m NW, probably from the Anglo-Saxon personal name; Pen-y-worlod, 1/2m WSW; and Vro, 3/4m SE, could be from Vra, the Old Scandinavian meaning 'remote valley' or 'isolated place', which well describes its location. What, with the Old Norse Hroaldr of Rowlstone, it seems there might have been a Viking settlement hereabouts.

SAINT DEVEREAUX *7m SW of Hereford*

It is not marked on the Ordnance Survey map, but is situated 1/2m E of Wormbridge (on the A465), where the easternmost lane that leads to Kilpeck crosses the main line railway. There is little more here than the church which is dedicated to the Celtic saint, Dubricius, one of four Herefordshiere churches to bear his name. For something more on Saint Dubricius, or Dyfrig to give him his Welsh name, see the article on Madley.

Devereaux could be a corruption of one of several Welsh words such as duwiol meaning 'godly'; dwyreiniol 'easterly'; and most plausibly dwr-ial, 'fertile upland watered by a stream'.

The settlement lies in the broad valley of the Worm Brook, which is surrounded by land that exceeds 600ft above sea level in places. The church has a tower of about 1200 at the bottom and of about 1300 in Decorated style above; a nave of about 1280 with two tomb recesses and Early English windows; a chancel with early Perpendicular three-light east window of about 1400; an Elizabethan cup of 1576 amongst the silver; and monuments to Thomas Goode, died 1664 and Ann Goode, died 1668.

At Didley Court Farm, 3/4m NE of the church, are the earthworks of a Norman motte and bailey castle. The motte is 26 yards in diameter and rises to 17ft above the bottom of the ditch, but the bailey is almost ploughed out. Crizeley, 3/4m N of the church, is a hamlet surrounded by woodland, an Anglo-Saxon leah if ever there was one.

SAINT MARGARET'S *10.5m WSW of Hereford*

This tiny hamlet lies on high ground in the wooded hills west of the Golden Valley and is most easily approached from Abbey Dore and Bacton. Saint Margaret's Church is a small, simple, mediaeval building with a Norman chancel arch and a weather-boarded bell-turret.

Its glory is the Welsh-style rood screen of about 1520, a beautifully carved gallery-loft parapet and coving that stretches the width of the church, and is supported on two elaborately decorated posts. "One of the wonders of Herefordshire", says Nikolaus Pevsner, and indeed it is exquisite; so light and delicate it seems to float on the lace-like beams that carry most of the foliage and fleur-de-lis decoration; the bosses have the heads of men and lions and other motifs. In former days it was used by musicians and singers during services. With the rekindling of interest in West Gallery music by such groups as Vital Spark of Malvern it will no doubt be occasionally put to its traditional use once again. The communion rail is Jacobean, the font cover 14th century, and there is a modern stained glass window of Saint Margaret in blue robes holding a model of the church in her hand.

Outside the church, against the north wall, the game of fives used to be played and the hinges that held the shutters to protect the east window can still be seen. The churchyard is rich in wild flowers and grasses which are mown each year by hand-scythe and are of interest to botanists and gardeners alike. Amongst the gravestones is one to Harriet Powell, a midwife who died in 1910. She attended 526 births and never lost a mother. In 1989 the church received the gift of 50 kneelers hand-worked with embroidery depicting events in the lives of the 100 or so parishioners. Saint Margaret's Day is the 20th July which, incidentally, is the occasion of the annual fair at Ross-on-Wye. The traditional bell jingle associated with Saint Margaret's is: "Turnips and carrots, say the bells of St. Margot's". The former Sun Inn stands next to the church but is now a private dwelling.

A circular Bronze Age burial mound lies 600 yards NE of the church. It is about 50ft in diameter, stands 10ft high and might have been used as a motte. A long, mounded burial chamber of Neolithic age, is located in Park Wood, 1/3m SSE of the church at SO 356 334. Also within the parish a fine example of a Neolithic Greenstone prestige axe has been found. Greenstone comes from the Penzance area. Prestige axes were not practical implements - they shatter when used - but were highly polished symbols of wealth and power. A similar Greenstone axe was found at Elton. Another, made from stone from Great Langdale, Cumbria, has been found at Almeley; and one from Gwynedd stone has been found in Weobley.

White House Farm, 1.1/4m NNW, although in the parish of Saint Margaret's, is much closer to Turnastone. The house and the pagan custom of Corn Showing connected with it are described in the article on Turnastone.

Middle Maescoed, 1m E of Saint Margaret's, is part of an extensive area of partially enclosed land that stretches down to Lower Maescoed, 2m S, and Upper Maescoed, 1m N. Small squatter cottages predominate in these lands that once belonged to the lordship of Bergavenny, now Abergavenny.

SAINT WEONARD'S *6.5m W of Ross-on-Wye*

It lies on the Hereford to Monmouth road, the A466, in the old Celtic territory of Arkenfield and within four miles of the Welsh border. Saint Weonard's is a small, nucleated village with a post office-cum-general store which was formerly the Treago Arms; a new school of 1976 which replaces the old one of 1846; a village hall of 1981; and the thing that makes these facilities a commercially viable proposition, a modern housing estate. When the Treago Arms lost its licence the villagers expressed their feelings by burning down the barns of nearby Pen-y-Gate. We know how they felt. The village pub is as socially important as the parish church. Mind you, I'm glad they weren't my barns. All this happened well before mains water arrived in 1952, followed by electricity in 1958.

The church of Saint Weonard is a dedication unique in England. This is not surprising because he was a Welsh saint, more properly known as Gwainarth. In the church he is depicted in stained glass as an ancient man with a book in one hand and an axe in the other. This glass is not old but is a copy of one that was in place at least from the 17th century. The axe is explained by some as indicating that he was a hermit who earned his living as a woodcutter, by others that he was decapitated by the invading Anglo-Saxons. Much of the church is 16th century Perpendicular

Top: Stoke Edith, hop-pickers being taken from the station to the farm.
Middle left: Ralph Vaughan Williams (1872-1958) was active as a folksong collector in Herefordshire.
Middle right: Tupsley, Whitehouse Farm, 1913.
Opposite: Rowlestone, Romanesque capital of the chancel arch of the church of Saint Peter.

but the doorway is 13th century flanked by windows of the same age; the chancel is modern but the vine carved cornice of the screen is of about 1550. The porch is 19th century. Of woodwork there is a Jacobean pulpit, box pews, and a 13th century 'dug out' chest. There are some re-used 15th and 16th century stained glass fragments and a monument to Robert Minors Gouge, died 1765.

In the middle of the village is a mound, a tump. This has been the traditional venue for village fetes, feasts and morris dancing since time immemorial. Legend has it that Saint Weonard was buried beneath the mound, either in a golden coffin or on top of a golden chest full of gold, the lid of which was inscribed: "Where this stood, is another twice as good, But where that is no man knows." The tump was excavated by archaeologists and they found two Bronze Age cremation burials. It is thought there are other burials here that have not yet been investigated. The mound is about 25 yards in diameter at the top, 45 yards at the base and rises to 14ft. The Normans used it as the foundation of a castle motte, hence its present shape. Traces of the ditch can be seen on the east side.

Another mark of prehistoric man is the standing stone near the crossroads south of the village on the A466, at SO 497 235. It is a low pillar of red sandstone lying north-south, 3ft high with cup marks on the east side. The story goes that a man stole a sheep and was carrying it home strapped to his shoulder. He rested against the stone, the sheep slipped and trapped his neck against it. He was found dead the next day but the sheep was unharmed. At another local crossroads a pig with a saddle on its back appears at midnight.

Treago Castle lies 1/2m SW of the church. It stands on a shelf commanded by rising ground to the west, and is encircled by a moat. There are mentions of the castle in the late 13th century and it has the form of a 14th century fortress. However, the earliest fabric we see today is of the late 15th century. It was, indeed, built in about 1480 by Richard Mynors, a wealthy administrator in South Wales. He was Sheriff of Herefordshire in 1500. The Mynor family have owned the estate from the 14th century to the present day. The castle is square with a central courtyard and has towers at each of the four corners. Over the years the building has been much altered. The sash windows are 18th century; the Tudor style windows are of 1840, except for the original by the south-east tower which was used as a model. The staircase and the plaster ceiling of the room west of the hall are of about 1670. In the 18th century the north wall was raised and probably at that time the courtyard was roofed over, the cross loops inserted and the south-east tower made taller with an overhanging extension. The main entrance is by a three-storey porch on the north side. The castle is very picturesque and is set amidst attractive gardens within its own park.

Just north of Treago castle is the ancient Tithe Barn, and 1/2m SSE is Old Furnace which stands beside a tributary stream of the Llantywaun Brook. This was the site of a 16th to 17th century water-powered ironworks. South of Old Furnace are homesteads with strong names: Velindra, Trippenkennett, and Hongar, probably from angr, Old English for 'grazing land'. Saint Weonard's lies in a landscape of small hills and valleys. The main road runs against the grain and is something of a switchback. Sandyway, 1m N, is a stone hamlet with low field hedges sheltering in a little valley. Old Hendre, 1.1/2m N, has a 'fish pond centre' and a red brick Nonconformist Chapel; and Hill Gate is a hamlet of stone and cream-painted brick dwellings with an orchard.

Llancloudy, 2m S, is a stone and render hamlet with a Methodist Chapel which stands at the foot of a long incline, a slog for cyclists, which is topped by a transmitter and National Grid cables.

The A466 is an altogether more civilised way to get from Hereford to Monmouth than the A49/A40 via Ross. For almost all its length it provides picturesque vistas and runs through unspoilt villages and hamlets. It is, indeed, something of a time warp.

There was a mediaeval glassworks at Glasshouse Farm (SO 474 230), near Garway.

SARNESFIELD *9m SW of Leominster*
It lies on the A4112, the Hereford to Hay road, 1.1/2m WSW of Weobley. The name is from the Welsh, sarn, meaning 'road'; and the Anglo-Saxon felde, meaning 'open land'. Remarkably, this early name is still descriptive of the area which is ringed by deciduous woods. There are sheep grazing, lovely, gentle views to the south, and at the crossroads is the 11-bay, two-storey asbestos roofed red brick warehouse of Nick's Timber Supplies. Elsewhere there are a few scattered farms and cottages, the Court and the church.

Saint Mary's has Norman work in the nave arcade and nave aisle, and a Norman nave window that now looks into the tower. The tower is of about 1300. It has a batter (a slope) to the walls at the base, and some 1,100 nesting holes for doves. Church towers are very rarely used for animal husbandry in England. The 14th century chapel has fragments of some good 14th and 15th century stained glass. The 14th century nave roof is very handsome with its tie beams and pointed-trefoiled wind braces. The timbered porch is also 14th century and there is a 14th century coffin lid with a floral cross to Isabel de Sarnesfield.

In the graveyard, by the porch, is the simple stone tombchest of John Abel, the carpenter and constructor of majestic timber-framed buildings of note who died in 1674 aged 97. He was a master craftsman of his age yet, ironically, he gained the title King's Carpenter for making hand operated gunpowder mills at Hereford for the Royalists during the Civil War. He designed his own simple tomb and on it are depicted the tools of his trade, miniature figures of himself and his two wives, an hourglass, and a poetic inscription commencing: "This craggy stone a covering is for an architect's bed". But best of all visit Saint Mary's on a Spring day. You need go no further than the roadside gate. There she stands, floating in a sea of wild flowers and meadow grasses, serene and sheltered by the tall trees around her. John Abel chose well.

Hell Moat, nearly 1m NW of the church, encompasses an irregular island with inner banks in the woods of Sarnesfield Coppice. The Batch, 1/2m NW of the church, derives its name from the Middle English bache, meaning 'valley of a stream'. In the woods north of the church there are three pools; someone likes their fishing. Little Sarnesfield, at Whitehill, 1m NE of the church, has an orchard and the earthworks of a moated site are clearly visible from the road.

It was the custom in these parts that a widow should lay a place at mealtimes for her departed husband and should do for the rest of her life.

SELLACK *3m NW of Ross-on-Wye*
In about 1150 it was Lann Suluc, 'Sulac's church'. Sulac is a pet name (a hypocoristic form, in etymological jargon) of Suliau who was also known by another pet name, Tysilio, formed by adding the prefix ty, meaning 'thy'.

Suliau was a Celtic saint who followed his cousin as head of the monastery at Saint Asaph's.

The settlement stands on the River Wye opposite King's Capel, where the river makes a great meandering loop. The ferry was replaced by a 190ft single span suspension bridge in 1895. The towers on each side are twin tapered iron columns linked by an iron brace. The suspension cables are steel, fixed to concrete anchorages, and light steel rods support a timber deck. It is one of only two suspension bridges across the River Wye; the other is at Foy, 2.1/2m E of Sellack. "They are", said a man from the County Council, "our pride and joy." Nice to hear a smidgen of passion from normally dour civil servants.

At Sellack, Hentland and King's Capel, pax or peace cakes are given to the congregation after the morning service of Palm Sunday. The cakes have degenerated into wafers stamped with a Paschal Lamb and the words 'Peace and Good Neighbourhood', a phrase that is inscribed on many church bells in Herefordshire. In former times a glass of beer was included in the offering. It was quite probably an old custom, but in 1570 Lady Scudamore made a bequest that financed its continuance, and possibly its inception.

Two hundred yards south of the bridge-head is the church of Saint Tysilio, a dedication unique in England, but once again not surprising because he was a Welsh saint in an area which was traditionally Welsh. The Victorian transept separates a 14th century aisle and chapel and there is an original Norman arch in the arcade. The four-light east window is Perpendicular; the stained glass is of 1630, but utilizes 15th and 16th century fragments. The woodwork of the doors to the nave and the chancel, the west gallery, the panelling of the east wall and altar rails, the reading desk and canopied pulpit, are all 17th century. There are noteworthy monuments to: Helip Fox, died 1678; William Powell, died 1680; and Thomas Symonds, died 1760. In the churchyard there is a gravestone with an embossed hand pointing upwards and the one word epitaph GONE.

Caradoc Court stands on high ground about 1/4m S of the church. It is a large, imposing house, partly 16th century black and white and partly stone of about 1620, with mullioned and transomed windows. It has subsequently been much altered and the front has Victorian gables, a porch and a bay window. The bay at the rear is original, of about 1480. Inside there is some good panelling and some 17th century wall painting which include landscapes. Baysham, 1/2m E of Sellack church, is a somewhat larger hamlet and Sellack Marsh, 1/2m SE of Baysham, is clustered around a crossroads close to the Wye. At Backney Bridge, Sellack Marsh, there is a council maintained Picnic Site close to the River Wye. Upper and Lower Grove Common, 1m SSW of Sellack church, stand adjacent to some of the large orchards which are a feature of this region. One always starts to think of Druids when one sees the name Grove in close proximity to a church of ancient Celtic foundation.

SHOBDON *6m WNW of Leominster*
The name is from the Anglo-Saxon Sceobba's - dun, meaning 'Sceobba's down (pasture on a slope)', though dun can also mean a hill or even a mountain. It lies on the Ludlow to Presteigne road on the long, lower slopes of Shobdon Hill. To the north, on the upper slopes of the hill, is an extensive area of woodland; to the south are the old wetlands of Shobdon Marshes, drained by the Pinsley Brook.

At the time of Domesday Shobdon was held by Ralph Mortimer; it was a well populated manor then and has remained so to this day. It has a black and white pub, the Bateman Arms, a post office-cum-general store, a shop, a hairdresser's, a car showroom and a garage and the people get regular visits from the butcher, the baker and the mobile library. The Gothic, gabled school is to a design by E.B. Lamb. There is a cider press and mill on the village green and at Hanbury Green they have one of the best developments of traditional style modern houses we have seen in the county. There is also a council estate. The inhabitants even have a golf course. This is attached to the Pearl Lake caravan park which stands beside a large, wood-fringed pool on the western boundary of the village. There are eight other pools and ponds on the slope just above the settlement, part of a post-glacial landscape that becomes more evident to the west.

In 1940 a war-time aerodrome was constructed on the edge of the marshes. The ground proved to be too unstable for use by heavy bombers and only one runway was completed. This was used by No. 5 RAF Gliding School which trained personnel for the Normandy and Arnhem landings. Today it is probably busier than it was during the war. Here one can participate in flying, parachuting, gliding, microlighting and paragliding (see the article on Capel-y-ffin). There is a small caravan park and around the perimeter there are several light industries nicely camouflaged by orchards and broadleaved woodland.

The church of Saint John the Evangelist lies 1/2m N of the village, close to the Norman castle and what is left of the Court House. We approached this old village centre from Easthampton, a hamlet of substantial stone houses and stone walls. A half-mile-long avenue leads through meadows and a large field used for growing soft fruit. But what is this? You are greeted by the grim asbestos-roofed shacks of the Sun Valley Hatchery where chickens and turkeys begin their short lives. Around the corner, out of sight, is a large modern building with a brick facade.

The Norman church was consecrated by Robert de Bethune, Bishop of Hereford between 1131 and 1148. About 1140 a priory was founded here by Oliver de Merlimond, chief steward to Hugh Mortimer, lord of Wigmore castle. The priory moved to Aymestrey, then returned to Shobdon and finally settled at Wigmore. The venerable Norman church was dismantled by the dis-Honourable Richard Bateman who lived at Shobdon Court from 1752 to 1756. He was a friend of the connoisseur, Horace Walpole, 4th Earl of Oxford (1717-1797), who influenced him greatly in matters of aesthetic taste. The result was that Bateman's replacement church is of the style known as Strawberry Hill Gothic. Inside there is frothy white and blue stucco cavorting with ogee arches, a squire's pew with a fireplace and a servants' pew without. It retains the old, stumpy 13th century stone tower but the re-built nave, chancel and transepts are of ashlar, with battlements. The furnishings are of the rebuilding; only the font was saved from the Norman church. Notable monuments include a tablet to Anne Chaplin of 1697, and a portrait medallion on an obelisk to John, the last Viscount Bateman, who died in 1802. The building as a whole is pleasant enough but has no gravitas.

Bateman's big house was demolished in 1933 and the outbuildings were used as a chicken hatchery. In 1957 Colonel Uvedale Corbett bought the 700-acre estate and the red brick Georgian servants' quarters were converted into a new, more modest house. Other survivors are the stables, the octagonal dovecote, the gate piers and iron gates. In a hollow to the west is the site of the estate gas works and further west again on a hill is a game larder. The latter faces north and its walls have hooks at varying heights on which to hang carcasses.

North of the church, at the end of a lawned ride, are Shobdon Arches. This was designed as an eye-catcher to be seen from the Court. It incorporates the best bits from the old Norman church - the chancel arch and the two doorways and their tympana - which were given battlements, pinnacles and a gable. The original sculptured decorations of the Norman work was of the highest order and of national importance. It was made by the same craftsmen who worked at Kilpeck. The two tympana represent the Harrowing of Hell and Christ in Majesty. Fortunately, an almost exact replica of the latter exists at Rowlstone and in 1852 the ensemble was captured on lithographs by G.R. Lewis. Today the Shobdon sculptures are so degraded by exposure to the weather that they are almost unrecognisable, thanks to Mr. Bateman.

Near the church, but hidden amongst the big factory sheds of Sun Valley, are the earthworks of an early Norman castle. The motte has a flat top about 50 yards in diameter and rises to 12ft above the ground. The ditch has traces of a bank but is filled in on the north and east sides. There is another, post-mediaeval mound 1/4m S of the church alongside the drive that leads to the village. It is roughly circular, about 21 yards in diameter at the base, and rises to about 11ft above the ground. Excavations have not proved conclusive about its origin. There are several pools alongside this southerly drive and one is especially beautiful. It has been planted around with a variety of trees and bushes and a little, green, single-arched metal bridge acts as a focus. Alas, the present owners, the Corbetts, satisfy their blood lust by breeding and then shooting pheasants. Killing for pleasure is quite simply a pervsion. I put this to one of the Corbetts. His justification was that many people were employed in the trade, and that their livlihoods depended on its continuance. Well, in that case....

The Corbett family were prime movers in the founding of the Sun Valley Poultry group and although they sold their 50% share in 1983 they still have breeding sheds on Shobdon Aerodrome and at Easthampton that supply Sun Valley. The family has an estate of 1,200 acres, 850 of which are farmed. Arable, potatoes and fruit are the main crops.

Did you know that if you feed a rabbit with two pounds weight of scoff it will reward you with one pound of meat? This is exceptionally efficient and beats cattle hands down. Interested? Then contact Michael Griffin at Winforton Commercial Rabbits, Birch House, near Birches Garage, Shobdon. He supplies television companies with rabbits for films and advertisements, pet breeders with thoroughbreds, and Third World countries with commercial food breeding stock and the necessary equipment. Things have come a long way since the Normans introduced these delightful little creatures to England. The company's own farm is in Powys, about 4 miles from Presteigne. The reader will have gathered by now that your author deplores killing animals for pleasure. But he has to allow that animals bred for food, that would not otherwise have lived at all, have, in effect, had something for nothing. As long as they are treated with kindness and consideration and die a quick and painless death, it would be difficult to deny them that taste of life however short. It is the cruelty that is the problem - the chickens couped up in cages in sheds, and the veal calves confined all their lives in tiny crates. How can dairy farmers sell their calves to people who do this? The truth is their like did it themselves before it was made illegal in England.

The Cobbler's Mound stands behind the war memorial on the eastern approach of the village. The story goes that the Devil had heard what a wonderful church they had at Shobdon and came out with a shovelful of earth with which to bury it. However, he got lost and asked the way from a travelling cobbler. The cobbler said he was trying to find it too and had worn out the sackful of shoes he was carrying in his search. Disgusted, the Devil dumped his spadeful of earth and went home. As it happens, cobblers lived in a nearby cottage for many generations, reported a correspondent of the *Hereford Times* in 1906.

For the tale of Old Pembridge disappearing into Shobdon Marsh see the article on Pembridge. The spring-fed Lady Pool which stands over the sunken church is just south of the airfield at SO 403 603. Drop a stone in it and you will hear it strike the steeple, so they say. The pre-Christian custom of Burning the Bush on New Year's Day was practised at Shobdon. The old bush, a globe of hawthorn, was burned in a wheatfield and as it burned a new one was made and singed in the fire of the old. Cider was then poured over the new bush. At the point where the boundaries of the parishes of Shobdon, Kingsland, Lucton and Aymestrey meet there is a Gospel Oak, so named because a gospel reading was made there during the ceremony of Beating the Bounds - walking the parish boundary - held at Rogationtide.

The hamlets of Uphampton and Ledicott are within the parish. At Ledicott there is a good Georgian house of five bays and two storeys which has a one-bay pediment and a hipped roof.

SOLLERS HOPE *7.5m SE of Hereford*
At the time of the Norman Conquest it was simply Hope, meaning 'settlement in the valley' and was held by Hagen, an old Scandinavian personal name. By 1086 it was part of the estates of Ansfrid de Cormeilles and was a manor more wealthy than most with its own mill. By 1242 the local lord was Walter de Solar, son of James de Solar, hence the Sollers of the place name. The daughter of John de Solers married into the family that was later to beget Dick Whittington, Lord Mayor of London. The settlement hides away in a little wooded valley in the southern limestone hills of the Woolhope Dome. All that is there is a farmhouse, a barn and a church but a splendid little group they make. Access is down a track through fields.

The stone-built church is dedicated to Saint Michael, often an indication that an Anglo-Saxon church stood on the same site. It has nave, chancel and bell-turret with a spire, and is mostly 14th century Decorated, with a Perpendicular east window and Perpendicular windows in the nave. (The Perpendicular style covers a period of nearly 200 years from about 1350 to about 1550.) The pulpit is 17th century and there are some fragments of mediaeval glass in several windows. The font is 13th century, and there is an incised slab, or coffin lid, commemorating a knight of about 1225, probably one of the de Solars. In the churchyard there is a mediaeval cross that was repaired and made into a war memorial by the Victorians.

Court Farm stands just to the north-east of the church. It is a 16th century timber-framed house of character with two gables, a projecting first floor, close-set uprights and two chimneys, one of which is especially handsome. It is crow-stepped, surmounted by panels and shafts with star-shaped tops. In the garden of Court Farm is an area about

Top: Stretton Grandison.
Above: Whitney on Wye, the bridge.
Right: Elizabeth Barrett Browning (1806-1861), born Hope End, near Wellington Heath, Ledbury. From posthumous bust by W.W. Story.

36 yards in diameter which contains a flat-topped mound rising a few feet above the ditch. The ditch has an outer bank that surrounds it. This could be the site of either an early Norman castle or a mediaeval manor house.

The surrounding settlements have some good names: Lower and Upper Buckenhill, Peartree Green, Falcon, Rattle Hill and Foxhalls.

STANFORD BISHOP *2.5m SE of Bromyard*
Stanford means 'stoney ford and the manor once belonged to the Bishop of Hereford. In Domesday Book it was simply called Stanford and it is often so called today. William the Conqueror gave the tithe of the manor to Saint Mary's of Cormeilles, one of his family's foundations in Normandy.

Most of the village lies along the main road, the B4220, between Bromyard and Acton Green. Here is the inn, the village hall, the old rectory and Stanford Court. Stanford Court is a good 18th century farmhouse. In the outbuildings, and now a part of a hop-kiln complex, is the mediaeval solar (the first floor living room) of the old house with its 14th century timbered roof. Standing in a field at the south end of the village is the stone-built Rhumney Barn. It was founded as a school for girls by Phineas Jackson, the vicar, in 1731, but was rebuilt with assistance from the National Society in 1826. Altogether, there are only just over 40 dwellings in the whole parish. Six of them are 17th or 18th century farmhouses. The agriculture of the area is mixed - pasture, hops, orchards, soft fruits and arable crops. The countryside is undulating and there are numbers of small copses.

The church of Saint James lies 1/2m W of the main road, just south of The Hawkins. It stands alone with only trees to share the long views. There is an ancient yew but its even more venerable brother was cut down by the Victorians because it had become a refuge for tramps, of whom as many as ten would be sleeping there on occasion. The Norman parts of the church are: the south doorway; the north doorway; the nave north window; the chancel south window; some tower windows and the imposts that support the nave tower-arch. The tower and some of its windows are early 13th century Early English. The east part of the chancel is late 13th century and the porch is 14th century. The whole was restored by the Victorians. The pulpit is Jacobean and the door has original mediaeval hinges.

Some writers in the past have been very excited about a mediaeval armchair kept at the church. It has posts with boards slotted into them and wooden peg hinges of a kind also used in Roman times. The story of its discovery by one James Johnston and his belief that it was used by Saint Augustin in 603 A.D., when he met with the Celtic Bishops at an unidentified place in the Marches, is very interesting, but is now thought to be implausible. Credence was given to the story because the chair was held for a time by the Canterbury Museum. It is now back in the church and is still an old and interesting piece of furniture in its own right.

Wofferwood Common lies 1/2m SE of the pub with a typical cluster of squatter cottages and an orchard. Wofferwood can be explained as 'the wood of the wolves', or, more prosaically, 'Wulfere's wood'.

The track of the dismantled railway from Bromyard to Worcester crosses the main road just north of Stanford Bishop.

STAPLETON *1m NE of Presteigne*
The meaning of the name is not clear but is thought to be 'settlement with a steeple', though there is not a church here now. It lies on the lower slopes of a hill south of Hell Peak in the valley of the River Lugg. The Normans shaped the contours of a natural hill to make a mound and traces of the motte and bailey castle still exist. At the time of Domesday the manor was held by Osbern Fitz-Richard and the earthworks may date from that period. It later passed to the de Says and the castle is first mentioned in 1207. From the de Says the manor went to the Mortimers, and in 1304 to the Stapletons who garrisoned it against Owain Glyndwr in 1403. At some time prior to this it had been fortified with stone.

In the early 17th century a large 'H' plan house was built on the mound partly re-using old materials. It was 'defaced' in 1645 by the Royalists. Later it went to the Harleys who repaired it but now it lies in a severely ruinous state. The castle site has many legends of chivalry, kidnap, revenge, murder and hauntings associated with it. Near the ruins are some very old cottages of the 13th and 14th centuries, such as Canter's Cottage which has three cruck trusses inside.

Most of the settlement dwellings lie 1/2m S along the road to the River Lugg. This is crossed by a rubble-stone bridge with three segmented arches and cutwaters, and probably dates from the 17th century. The Lugg has five weirs in a one mile stretch as it passes between Presteigne and Stapleton and, incidentally, forms the border between Herefordshire and Radnorshire. (Radnorshire is in Cymru, not Wales; Wales is from the Anglo-Saxon walh meaning 'bloody foreigner' and is a term of abuse.) Weirs were made to keep the waters deep, either for fishing or to lift the level to feed mill leats or for both. The water meadows here are wide and lush. A good variety of social and commercial facilities are available at Presteigne just over the river in Powys - sorry, I mean Radnorshire.

STAUNTON-ON-ARROW *5m ENE of Kington*
The name means 'settlement on stony ground near the River Arrow'. Most of the village lies on high ground well above the broad, lush meadows of the wriggling River Arrow. In 1066 the manor was held by Edric, said to be Wild Edric the Anglo-Saxon warrior rebel whose escapades have entered the realm of legend. (See the article on Burrington for more on Edric.)

We approached the settlement from the north-west to be welcomed by the handsome Old Court, a black and white house of about 1600. It was originally two buildings and the cider press was working until recently. Opposite are two orchards: one is traditional with trees, recognisable as such, and sheep grazing the lawns between; the other is one of those modern things with bushes arranged in rows.

The village centre is most attractive, though windy, and in the winter it can be cold. Here are the stone school and schoolhouse, the post office, the modern village hall, the vicarage, a red telephone kiosk, a stone and black and white building that looks as though it was once an inn, and the church.

Saint Peter's stands on raised ground and the tower with its turret is a landmark for many miles around. The churchyard is walled about and appears to be on an ancient site. However, the substantial building we see today was designed and constructed by the architect Thomas Nicholson in 1856. It is of grey stone with sandy coloured trimmings and inside it has transept chapels but no aisle.

The remains of an early Norman motte and bailey lie just to the south-west of the church. The motte has a flat top about 21 yards in diameter and rises to about 28ft above the ground. The ditch has gone and the mound is overgrown.

There are a number of other mounds near Mowley Woods which were once thought to be prehistoric burial places. However, they are actually moraines deposited by the last retreating ice-sheet.

There were several mills and tan houses on the river and a complex system of leats can be seen. The main mill and millhouse still stand with a water channel running around the side of the hill. They now constitute a desirable residence. The road leads down to the river and the four-arch stone bridge. The vistas are wide and the land remarkably flat - good water-meadow country.

The Roman route from Mortimers Cross to Clyro (near Hay-on-Wye) crossed the Arrow by means of a ford where the bridge now stands. Some years ago a figure of Mercury, the Roman god of merchants and commerce, was found here. However, the local vicar was a keen collector of historical objects and there is an element of doubt as to the source of the sculpture. The Court of Noke stands beside the river, close to the bridge. It is an early 18th century, red brick mansion of seven bays and two storeys with a hipped roof, a pediment and a columned porch also with a pediment. Inside there is a good staircase; outside, to the left, is an extensive range of red brick outbuildings. There is evidence of water-works here also. In Spring the paddock in front of the house has a splendid show of daffodils.

Wapley Hill Camp stands on a high hill 2m NW of Staunton-on-Arrow. It is a strong, multi-vallate fortress, roughly triangular in shape, with a splendid 100 yards long southern entrance passage. The fort covers about 25 acres and utilises a steep north-western scarp. In the centre of the enclosure is a well that has never been known to run dry. It has been suggested that this shaft is not really a water well but a ritual shaft, a link with the spirits of the underworld. Wapley is one of several sites on which Caractacus, the last leader of the British, in the 1st century A.D., might have made his final stand against the Romans. He concluded his days living in Rome on a pension from Claudius. Not the most heroic of ends. Owain Glyndwr, the last leader of the Welsh, did things with more style. He simply disappeared into glorious legend leaving us all guessing as to his fate. Wapley Hill now has a car park and a three-mile way-marked trail.

Staunton Park and the hamlet of Staunton Green lie nearly 1m NW of Staunton church. In the park there are two of the many small glacial lakes that dot the countryside between here and Shobdon to the east. An avenue leads from Staunton Park and joins up with the Forestry Commission tracks on Wapley Hill that lead to the Iron-Age camp. The Rowe Ditch passes Staunton, 1/2m to the east, and a good section adjoins the lane between Court of Noke and the crossroads at Milton Cross. (See Marston for more on this Anglo-Saxon earthwork.)

STAUNTON-ON-WYE *9m WNW of Hereford*

It lies just off the Roman road from Hereford to Hay-on-Wye and a good mile to the north of the River Wye. The mediaeval name was Standon, meaning 'stony hill'. The village has a post-office-cum general store; a pub, the rendered New Inn where the playing of boules is a popular pastime; a green-painted tin shack for a church hall, a war memorial, modern bungalows and a handful of timber-framed houses, urban orchards, a scraggy cattle farm that has given birth to a litter of black sheds, and some mundane concrete-block council houses. Nevertheless, it is a cheerful place. This is largely due to the presence of children, a scarce commodity in many rural places these days because most are bussed off to distant schools.

Staunton-on-Wye was fortunate in having one George Jervis who left money in his will of 1792 to be spent on helping the parishes of Staunton, Bredwardine and Letton. Somewhat belatedly, an Act of Parliament allowed for the administration of the charity, and a social services complex was constructed at Staunton. This consists of a school, almshouses for six men and six women, a medical officer's house, and a quarter-master clerk's house. Part of the school is now a youth hostel and the children sport gaily in red tops and black bottoms.

Along the main street, towards the eastern end of the village, there are three generations of the 'big house', Lower House Farm. The 17th century model stands on the north side of the road facing its replacement of 1963. A short distance along is the original hall house which had a living room two storeys high and was open to the roof. Attached to this is a byre, a cattle shed, with an internal door giving direct communication to both parts. It was, in fact, a superior longhouse. Subsequently, a first floor has been inserted in the hall and additions made to the house, but, the direct communication to the byre was used into this century.

The church of Saint Mary has what is probably an 11th century pier and capital, once part of a two-bay, north-side arcade; two 12th century Norman doorways; and a 13th century tower with a substantial pyramid roof. The chancel was rebuilt in the 18th century and altered again by the Victorians. The panelling beneath the tower is Jacobean (1603-1625) and the six medallions with heads in profile are of about 1530. The font and three coffin lids are 13th century. In the churchyard there is a much worn stone effigy of a 14th century lady under a five-leafed canopy.

During the Commonwealth Roger Breinton was deprived of his living as vicar of Staunton and Credenhill for being "active and incendious against Parliament". He was one of 49 Anglican parish and cathedral clergy to be replaced by Independant preachers. Others were dismissed for drinking and loose living.

The brick-built, cream-painted Portway Inn stands on the main road, near the Portway Hotel, and the Maddle Brook. There are orchards and nursery fields covered in sheets of hideous black polythene. One day someone will enter such a field for a modern sculpture exhibition and stand a good chance of winning. The name Portway usually denotes a pre-Roman road.

There is record of the 'how to find lost keys' custom being enacted at the Portway in the 19th century. Lost keys are actually not lost; they have been taken by mischievous fairies, or brownies. Members of the household sit in a semi-circle around the fire and a cake is placed on the hearth as an offering. Everyone sits silently with eyes closed and the keys will be flung forcibly against the wall at the back of the party.

Other Staunton customs include a balm to alleviate the pain of teething in young children: take the hair from the cross-marking on the back of a donkey, plait it into a necklace and hang it around the child's neck. Similarly, the Rector was often asked by parents if they could have the baptism water to use as a cure for minor ailments. On the 5th of January 1878 the Reverend Kilvert made a note in his famous diary of the words of "old James Meredith" at Staunton-on-Wye. "I was watching then on Old Christmas Eve (12th Night) and at 12 o'clock the oxen that were standing knelt down on their knees and those that were lying rose to their knees and there they stayed kneeling and moaning, the tears running down their faces."

Two dead end lanes lead north of Staunton into the wetlands of Letton Lake, which periodically flooded over a huge area. No roads cross it even now. One lane leads to Little London and the other, called Duck Street, leads to World's End. Along them are squatters' cottages, the homes of poor people who eked out a living on this marshy common lane and worked as seasonal labourers at local farms. Humble their homes were but of character they had plenty. Over the years they have grown and display a wide variety of local building materials. It is ironic that such areas are now in favour with the well-to-do middle classes

STOKE EDITH *5.5 E of Hereford*
The name means 'the religious place of Queen Edith'. She held the manor in 1066. It was a flourishing settlement which in 1086 had two priests and a mill. Stoke Edith stands on the Hereford to Ledbury road, the A438, in the broad valley of the River Frome at the foot of the northern slope of the picturesque Woolhope Dome. It is friendly, lived-in country, full of hopyards, orchards, green pastures, fertile fields and big skies.

Queen Edith chose well. She was the daughter of King Edgar the Peaceable who reigned from 959 to 975. Incidentally, it was at this time that our country was first called England. At the age of 15 Edith was Abbess of Wilton, near Salisbury; she died aged 23 and was subsequently canonised.

At the entrance to the Old Vicarage, and below the church is a bank from which issues a spring. This is Saint Edith's Well, an ancient healing well. The water issues into a square font and flows into a large, brick-lined bathing pool. The entrance to this cave is arched over with brick and stone but has been blocked by a wrought-iron gate, the work of Lady Emily Foley whom, it would appear, had little regard for tradition or the moral rights of others. Legend has it that Saint Edith was carrying water up the hill to mix the mortar to build the first church here when, becoming exhausted, she knelt and prayed for divine assistance and the spring burst forth.

There is little sense of a village at Stoke Edith even though it has a church, the Old Vicarage, estate offices, roadside lodges and a handful of cottages.

The church of Saint Mary stands 1/4m S of the main road. It is quite Classical and somewhat refined for a country place. The tower is of 14th century stone with angle buttresses and lancet windows topped by a thin recessed spire. The rest of the church was rebuilt between 1740-42 in Georgian brick with a hipped roof. The nave has two front doorways, one at each end, surmounted by round windows and in between are three round-headed windows. Inside there are giant Tuscan columns and a small, marble font-bowl on a blue and gold coloured wrought-iron stand. The original pews and the three-decker pulpit have survived and among the fragments of stained glass is one of a lute player. The east window glass is of 1846 by W. Warrington.

Amongst the monuments are memorials to: a 15th century lady in alabaster effigy with dogs at her feet; Paul Foley, Speaker at the House of Commons 1690-1694, died 1699; Edward Foley, died 1806; and tablets to Henry Wolstenholme, died 1738 and his wife died 1749.

There is a local tradition that if you walk around the church seven times and peep through the keyhole you will see the Devil. If you asked someone locally "where did you get that from" the retort would be, "where the Devil got the Friar from", meaning "mind your own business". Near the church are yew trees galore and an abandoned black and white cottage.

Stoke Edith Park House was rebuilt in the last few years of the 17th century by the Thomas Foley of Worcester who bought the estate in 1670. But his splendid mansion was burned out in 1927, partially rebuilt in 1936, and finally demolished in 1957. The cause of the fire was related to accidental misuse of the central heating system by a new butler. It was a slow burning fire that began in the wood panelling but the fire brigade were severely handicapped because all the local ponds were frozen.

The house was left as a shell and the priceless murals and ceilings painted by Sir James Thornhill were totally destroyed. It is thought that Francis Brett Young based his novel *White-ladies* on the fire at Stoke Edith. They say that lightning never strikes twice but the Foleys' other great house, the spectacular Great Witley Court, also burned down, though the ruins still stand and are a tourist attraction.

Humphrey Repton landscaped the grounds of Stoke Edith in 1792 and the family still have his Red Book. This shows the Foleys' great house in its original setting, and then, by turning on a half page overlay, one can see how it would look when his scheme was completed. Repton was an excellent water colour artist and we were delighted to have been given a viewing of what is a little masterpiece in its own right.

The stables of the big house remain and the walls of the Victorian walled garden still stand though it is now disused and very overgrown. On the road are two lodges. The West Lodge is brick-built with Tuscan columns and a copper dome. The East Lodge has a pediment over the centre bay and one-bay lower wings.

A member of the family now lives at the Old Rectory, or Stoke Edith House as it has been re-named. This was built in about 1740 and is most handsome and beautifully maintained. It is constructed of brick and has five bays, two storeys, a hipped roof and a doorway with decorated corbels.

For a few years the Old Rectory was run as the Stoke Edith House Hotel, and in December 1969 Andrew Lloyd Webber, the composer, and Tim Rice, the lyricist, booked in. They hired a piano and here they wrote the greater part of *Jesus Christ, Superstar*. The record became a best-seller and was followed by the international rock opera stage show and film. Between writing and composing they went for long walks in the surrounding countryside and watched Tom and Jerry on television.

A little lane runs up the hill, past the church, through holly hedges to a group of old stone cottages that stand beside a ridged field grazed by sheep. Flowers, charm, and lovely views are the order of the day up here. In 1912 Mrs. E.M. Leather wrote that a Holy Thorn was growing at Stoke Edith. A Holy Thorn is a bush grown from a cutting taken from the Glastonbury Thorn that rooted from the stave of Joseph of Arimathea

The Foley family of Stoke Edith are now firmly established as members of the landed aristocracy of Herefordshire. Their forebears, however, came from Dudley in the West Midlands where Richard Foley (1580-1657) was born, though he later moved to Stourbridge and is buried at Oldswinford church. Richard was an iron-master but the immense fortune he accumulated was based on metal-slitting. This was a slow, labour-intensive process.

Top: Tyberton, the church of Saint Mary.
Middle left: Treago Castle, Saint Weonard's after a drawing by Mike Salter.
Middle right: Symond's Yat, the chain ferry.
Opposite: Whitchurch, church of Saint Dubricius.

Thin slats and wires were cut by hand from sheet iron and then fashioned into the hundreds of different kinds of nails required for a multitude of different purposes. But it was the initial process of slitting that restricted production.

In 1627 Richard Foley set up a mechanical slitting mill at Kinver, in south Staffordshire. His technology was not new. A similar mill had been established in Kent 28 years earlier, but Foley was a man of enterprise and within a few years had built the foundations of an iron-working empire that earned a vast fortune for his family. This enabled them to buy estates in Worcestershire and Herefordshire, and to buy their way into Parliament. (They were not the only ones to do this. In those days if you did not, an opponent certainly would.) Today the Foleys' Stoke Edith estate runs to 4,500 acres and they have large holdings in Kentucky and West Virginia.

There is a romantic story relating to Richard Foley's early days which has elements of truth but we do not know quite how much. The earliest known source is a work of 1812 by the poet S.T. Coleridge. In brief, this relates how Richard Foley went to Sweden, masquerading as an itinerant fiddle player, and succeeded in stealing the secrets of their iron-slitting machine. There is, indeed, documentary evidence amongst the Foley papers held at the Hereford Record Office that Richard did go to Uppsala. Here are some doggerel verses I dashed off a few years ago and about which I am not too embarrassed to present to the public at large.

FOLEY THE FIDDLER

I'm Foley the fiddler, to Uppsala I came,
To search for my fortune, and so make my name.
Through storms on the sea, and the northern wind's cold,
I scraped and I scratched with my good English bow.

I played them long dances and circles and reels
And haunting slow aires paid for many a meal,
But when the sun shone on the frost and the snow,
I skulked around corners, their secrets I stole.

And so back in England fine fortunes I made
With a mill and cold rollers that to the world gave
Such numbers of nails that the people did sing
In praise of young Foley and his slitting machine.

And now that I'm dead, and long gone to my grave,
I hope that my sons will be dashing young blades,
And fashion in friendship and good English iron
The sword and the gun, the true voice of the lion.

But fairest of all, and by every degree,
Are the nails that once hung a man to a tree,
And held up his cabin, and shod his fine horse,
In peace there is plenty; in war but remorse.

This tale has already entered tradition and at least one variant has developed in which Richard has a cow seized for non-payment of rent, disappears for three years to Holland, plays the flute, acts as a harmless fool and returns with the slitting mill secret.

To conclude on a more prosaic note: the Great Western Railway line between Hereford and Ledbury was opened in 1856. It was allowed to pass through Stoke Edith estate on condition that members of the Foley family could stop any train on demand at Stoke Edith station. This concession existed until the station was demolished in 1962 as part of Dr. Beeching's rationalisation of the railways.

(See Tarrington, the estate village of the Foley family.)

STOKE LACY *4m SW of Bromyard*
It lies in the valley of the River Lodon on the Bromyard to Hereford road, the A465. The Anglo-Saxon name was simply stoc, meaning 'a place', but often 'a religious place'. Roger de Lacy was the tenant-in-chief in 1086.

Stoke Lacy is a pleasant, main road village mostly of Victorian red brick dwellings with some 15th century farmhouses. On the river is a derelict old mill which was grinding corn until it closed in the 1940s. Nearby, along a track, is a cottage with a true cottage garden full of herbs, shrubs and flowers tended for 50 years now by Madge Hooper. There is also a plant nursery here, which is open to the public on Saturdays from May to September.

Close to the main road, amongst mature trees, stands the church of Saint Peter and Saint Paul. It retains its Norman chancel arch on scalloped capitals but was rebuilt in 1863 by F.R. Kempson in Early English style. Poor old Kempson comes in for a drubbing from both Nikolaus Pevsner, who hates the rock-faced masonry with smooth dressings of the tower and the profile of the spire, and from Arthur Mee, who is so rarely disparaging, but here throws kindness to the winds and snarls at the "great round stone pulpit which, like the piscina, is a mass of over-elaborate carving". That, coming from Arthur Mee, is like a judge handing out the death sentence. The church has three pre-Reformation bells which sing:

"Hang Tom Potter, and kill old Gun,
Smith o' the wood is dead and gone".

The Morgan family is from Stoke Lacy and the Morgan who made the once well-known three-wheeler motor cars was born here. George Morgan was rector of the church for over 50 years. South of the main road, at Lower Hopton, there is a circular homestead moat.

The village facilities lie up the hill to the east at Stoke Cross. The school of 1876 closed in the 1960s and is now the village hall. There is a post office-cum-general store, the Plough Inn, a group of council houses, and Symonds' Cider Works. Symonds began business in 1727 and until recently it was a family run concern. We passed through the village late one Summer's evening to see men playing football on the forecourt of the cider shop as two lost sheep trotted down the road. The light was fading fast; so was the traffic. I hope those dusk-dwellers survived the night.

Just north of Stoke Cross, adjacent to the lane that leads to Tuthill Farm, is a moated mound that could be either an early Norman castle or a mediaeval moated site. The slope of the hill has been artificially steepened and a ditch about 3ft has been cut, which drops into a stream at the north end. The top of the mound is flat and the sides are steep. The name Tuthill might very well be from toot, or twt, meaning 'a small mound'. Stoke Lane lies 1/2m NE of Stoke Cross on the lane to Munderfield. The landscape around Stoke Lacy is one of little hills with pastures for sheep and cattle, orchards, hopyards and arable fields for cereals.

STOKE PRIOR *2m SE of Leominster*
It lies 1/2m E of the confluence of the River Arrow and the River Lugg and has been by-passed by a modern stretch of the A49. It is now a place you have to look for, no doubt to the satisfaction of the residents. The name

means 'the religious place belonging to the priory at Leominster'.

In 1485 Henry Richmond was on his way to the Battle of Bosworth where he won his famous victory against Richard III and was crowned Henry VII. He had passed through Pembridge and Eardisland and crossed the River Arrow near Stoke Prior. Here he recalled an old prophecy that promised victory in a national strife to him who should 'shoot the arrow first'. Henry interpreted this to mean the crossing of the River Arrow and so encouraged his men with this favourable portent.

In the 19th century the village was a flourishing settlement with a full compliment of craftsmen and traders. Today it is something of a dormitory town but the new houses do support a pub, a shop, a school, a football side and a team of ten bell-ringers.

The Norman church of Saint Luke was demolished in 1863 and replaced with a substantial building in the Decorated style by George Colley. The embattled tower has five bells, one of which is dated at 1460 and was cast at Worcester. The font and stoup are 14th century and the hammerbeam roof 17th century. The stained glass of the east window is a memorial to Thomas Bryan, a Victorian M.P. for Leominster; and the oldest tombstone in the churchyard is that of Elizabeth Howl, died 1331. The path leading to the porch is lined with umbrella-shaped trees. Ordinary elms have been crowned with wych elm grafts to make an almost rainproof tunnel. The graft joints can be seen quite clearly once one is aware of them.

The Priory stands about 300 yards ENE of the church. It is a 14th century stone house with two blocked windows and is thought to have been used by a cell of monks. Leading from the north of the building is Paradise Walk. The Great House has a west end cross-wing and the south gable has tooth-edged decoration to the bargeboards. South-east of the house is a dovecote with 470 nesting holes, probably of the 17th century.

Bury Farm was charged with the payment of the Trug Corn to the vicar of Leominster for conducting services at the chapels of ease at Stoke Prior and Docklow. When they acquired their own priests the Trug Corn was paid to them. A trug is one twelfth of one horse-wagon load. It is said that this custom is unique in England.

At Humber and Risbury a 16th century three-field system has been identified from later plans of enclosed strips. This work has been published by H.L.Gray in his book *English Field Systems*, 1959.

The track of the disused Leominster to Bromyard railway passes the southern outskirts of the village and is fringed with orchards

Just over 1/2m E of the church Roman coins, pottery, skeletons and the remains of a hypocaust were found during construction of the railway in 1881. For more details of this see the article on Humber. In 1891, at Slough Farm, a hoard of seven silver vessels was found in a rabbit hole. It is thought they might have been hidden during the Civil War when Sir William Waller took Leominster in 1643 and left a garrison under the command of Colonel John Birch. The silver was declared treasure trove and went to the Victoria and Albert Museum. The discoverers were awarded £25 each. The curiously named Wheelbarrow Castle lies 1/2m NNW of the church.

STORRIDGE *7m SW of Worcester*
But for the grace of God it would have been in Worcestershire, and if my small dealings with the bureaucracy of that county's principal town are anything to go by the people of Storridge do not know just how lucky they are. The settlement lies on the Hereford to Worcester road, the A4103, on the northern foothills of the mighty Malverns and is virtually surrounded by broadleaved woods. It is one of those places that lies annoyingly on the edge of the Ordnance Survey map. You need Landranger-150 for Storridge. The name is probably from the Old English stan - hryg, meaning 'stony ridge'.

The church of Saint John the Evangelist was built in 1856 by Frederick Preedy of Worcester in late 13th century style. The tower is topped by a broach spire and the stained glass of the east window is also by Preedy.

At Crumpton Oaks Farm, just off the main road east of Storridge, the Knight family make traditional cider on the premises. The locally grown apples have a different flavour from those used in the west of the county and they produce a range of dry, medium and sweet ciders. It is the proportion of tanin to acid that determines the character.

STRETFORD *3.5m WSW of Leominster*
The name is from the Old English straet-ford, meaning 'ford on the Roman road', in this case the western branch of Watling Street that ran from Wroxeter to Kenchester to Caerleon. The actual ford is 1/2m SSE of the hamlet, where the road, the A4110, crosses the Stretford Brook, a tributary of the River Arrow. The road was paved and considerable stretches of the original surface must lie under the modern highways. Stretford gave its name to the Domesday Book Hundred of Stretford and the Moot Court met here. There is little more at Stretford than an orchard, the Court and the church surrounded by ploughland and pasture.

The church of Saint Peter is almost square with a timber bell-turret. Inside it is divided into four parts: a Norman nave and chancel, and an aisle and chancel chapel of about 1230. The effect is that there are two naves and two chancels running parallel to each other. This is a remarkable and very rare arrangement. Today the work of 1230 is used as the actual nave and chancel. The roof was added in about 1530 and unifies the whole; it has one tie-beam, stretching the whole width, the rest being arched braces to collar beams with cusped wind braces. The font is Norman; the pulpit Jacobean; the two screens are early 16th century; the shrine is late mediaeval and rests on a 13th century coffin lid; the pillar piscina is Norman; and the two pairs of knights and their ladies are mid-14th century.

Half a mile south of Stretford is a lane that runs from the main road to Ivington in the east. Along this are the hamlets of: Dorstone, which has some black and white and a brick-built farm; Hyde Ash, which has some small squatter-type cottages, orchards and drained marshland; Knoake's Court; and Cold Harbour, where there are pastures and a couple of painted stone cottages.

This is as good a place as any to quote John Aubrey's 17th century account of sin eating as practised in Herefordshire. Aubrey owned estates at Stretford and Burleston. "In the County of Hereford it was an old Custome at Funeralls to have poor people who were to take upon them all the sinnes of the party deceased. One of them I remember lived in a cottage on Rosse highway. He was a long, leane, ugly, lamentable poor raskel. The Manner was that when the Corps was brought out of the house and layd on the Bierre, a Loafe of bread was brought out and delivered to the Sinne-eater over the corpse, as also a Mazer-bowle of maple full of beer, which he was to drink up, and sixpence in money, in consideration whereof he took upon him ipso facto (by the same token) all the Sinnes of the

Defunct, and freed him or her from walking after they were dead......" He goes on to say that the custom continued even in Puritan times at Dinedor and Hereford but by the mid-17th century it had largely died out. As late as 1912 the healing well dedicated to St. Cosmas and St. Damian was being used to cure weak eyes by local people. It probably stood beside the path from Stretford Court to the Stretford Brook.

STRETTON GRANDISON *8m ENE of Hereford*

Stretton is from straet, Old English meaning 'Roman road'. The settlement stands on the Roman road that runs from Hope-under-Dinsmore to Dymock and was also connected to Kenchester by another Roman road. In 1303 the manor was held by William de Grande Sono, which later became Grandison. The family held court at their castle in Ashperton, 1.1/2m SSE of Stretton.

Stretton Grandison is a most attractive village in the fertile valley of the River Frome, but is spoiled by the main road which has a double kink making is particularly dangerous. There are no facilities such as a pub or a post office.

In 1842 Roman remains were found near Stretton Grandison during the construction of an aquaduct carrying the Hereford to Gloucester Canal over the River Frome. The site is about 600 yards south of the church and just west of the A417 at SO 633 434. The finds included remains of buildings, bracelets, a steelyard and a lamp with figures of a boy and a leaping dog. They probably mark the northern extent of the minor roadside settlement of Epocessa, the nucleus of which was at Canon Frome, 1.1/4m SE of Stretton Grandison.

At the western end of the village is Town End Farm. It has a good, big barn with its old woven wattle panels intact. These were never meant to be covered in daub; they keep out the worst of the weather yet allow ventilation. The farmhouse itself was built of red brick in about 1700. It has two low storeys with projecting wings, a hipped roof, and a central pediment.

The church is prominently positioned on high ground, its tall thin spire rising above the trees, and its entrance guarded by a delightful black and white thatched cottage. Saint Lawrence's has some Norman work in one corner of the chancel but was rebuilt in the 14th century in the Decorated style. There is an Easter Sepulchre in the chancel north wall; the porch is 17th century; the hexagonal font is 14th century but over restored; and the wall painting of a lady in a red robe over the south doorway is 14th century. There are monuments to John Taylor, died 1676; Sir Edward Hopton, died 1668, with an actual piece of armour, a sleeve and gauntlet laid before it; and William Jauncey, died 1797. More recent members of the Hopton family are commemorated in the clock of 1912 and a Flanders Cross.

The Old Vicarage is now a home for the elderly and the former school has been converted into flats for the elderly. The 'big house' is Homend, 1/2m E of the church. (Hom means 'flat land by a stream.) One can drive through its park along a lane that runs to the hamlet of Upper Egleton. The present house is early 19th century. It has five bays. The centre three have two and a half storeys, the others two-storeys, all with arched ground floor windows. The side windows are flanked by Corinthian pilasters. Today the mansion is in multiple occupation, having been converted to flats. There are more dwellings in the old cowsheds, stables and other outbuildings. At Upper Egleton is Moor Court Farm, an attractive 15th century timber-framed dwelling with red brick infill and a cluster of tall chimneys. To the left of the house there is a pair of square hop kilns with pyramid roofs which are still used for drying the hops grown on this livestock farm. Bed and breakfast can also be obtained here.

Saint Catherine's Well, a healing spring, is in Homend Park beside the footpath to Lower Egleton, 1m NW of Homend House. Here Saint Katherine rested on her travels in search of bells that rang unaided by man. The spring burst forth to refresh her. Her travels concluded at Ledbury. Man does seem to have a desire to worship many gods. The early Christian saints are the equivalent of the numerous Celtic and Roman spirits and, indeed, still are deeply revered. New House, 3/4m ENE of the church, is of about 1600 and was visited by the traveller Celia Fiennes. It has a moat and stands close to the line of electric pylons that sweeps majestically down the Frome Valley, singing in the wind to the hop fields and orchards.

Green Lane, 1m N of Stretton Grandison on the A4103, is a red brick hamlet. Lower Egleton, a little further east, has a scatter of black and white, red brick and stone dwellings and the estate office of Leighton Court, a roadside farm with large barns.

STRETTON SUGWAS *3m WNW of Hereford*

The Domesday name was Sucwessen, from the Old English sucga, 'a hedge-sparrow', and waesse, 'a swamp'. Later, Stretton was added, referring to the Roman road that ran from Kenchester (Magnis) to the minor fort and settlement at Canon Frome/Stretton Grandison. East of Stretton Sugwas there is a four-mile, dead straight stretch of this road.

The settlement stands at a crossroads. It is a residential hamlet flanked by the large nursery fields of Swainshill Garden Centre to the east, and the pale green sheds of an R.A.F. stores complex to the west. (The R.A.F. camp is soon to be the new home of the 22nd S.A.S. Regiment.) There is a pub, The Travellers' Rest, a bridge, some A.R.C. sand and gravel pits, the Court and the church.

The church lies 1/2m SW of the pub near the Hereford to Hay-on-Wye road, the A438. The Norman church stood further to the north. It was dismantled and a new one built on the present site by the architect Cheiake between 1877-80. He re-used the timbers for the black and white tower, the mediaeval windows, and three Norman doorways. Above one of the doorways is a perfect and well-preserved tympanum of about 1150, executed by the Herefordshire School of Carvers whose work is of international standing. It depicts Samson sitting astride a lion and forcing open its jaws. The lion stands on a rope moulding supported by two primitive heads. The design is simple and bold, yet graceful and immensely satisfying. There is another work of art in the church, a slab monument to Richard Grevelhey and his wife, died 1473. The slab has a beautifully worked, incised, black-line portrait of the couple, he in a fur-trimmed gown and she with a butterfly head-piece and a little dog hiding in the folds of her dress. There are 15th century heraldic tiles in the vestry, the font is mid-14th century, and the altar table is Jacobean.

Stretton Court lies 3/4m NE of the church. It is a late Georgian brick house with two good overmantels, one dated at 1598. Close by is the little mediaeval bridge with one pointed arch that carries the road to Credenhill over a stream. Between the bridge and Stretton Court Farm, which stands beside Stretton Court, is the site of the deserted mediaeval village of Stretton Sugwas. A plan of 1757 shows 11 dwellings to the west of Stretton Court

Above:
Druids in an oak-grove, from an English steel engraving, circa 1900.
Opposite:
Goodrich, the Queen Stone, at Huntsham, an enigmatic Bronze-Age monolith thought by some to have been used in human ritual sacrifice.

Farm. Today, only the earthworks remain in a very stony field. Nearby there are two ponds with traces of ground water-works. The foundations of the old church can be discerned in the grounds of Stretton Court. This is just one of about 200 deserted mediaeval village sites in Herefordshire.

Sugwas Court lies 3/4m SSW of the church ensconced in a wood surrounded by orchards. The present brick-built house is of about 1800 and has five bays, two storeys and wide, segment-headed windows. It stands on the foundations of one of the Bishop of Hereford's palaces, but of this only one doorway and a few stones remain in the stables. They were probably a part of the old chapel.

The low, domed, wooded hill to the north-west, beyond the R.A.F. camp, is Credenhill, the Iron-Age capital of Herefordshire. (See the article on Credenhill.)

SUTTON SAINT NICHOLAS 3.5m NNE of Hereford

"Sutton Wall and Kenchester Hill
Are able to buy London, were it to sell."
(W.C. Hazlitt, *English Proverbs*.)

Although never spoken of as being an especially wealthy or influential settlement, Sutton has quietly been taking care of itself very nicely, thank you. A small reminder is the fact that endowments to aid the poor are still being distributed from the legacies of five local families - the Walwyns, the Freenes, the Lingens, the Unetts and the Aldridges. The name in Domesday Book is simply Sutune, from the Anglo-Saxon sup-tun, meaning 'southern settlement'. In 1086 it was held by Nigel the Doctor. By 1242 there were two Suttons and to differentiate them they were called Sutton Saint Nicholas and Sutton Saint Michael. In recent times the two parishes were combined and they are, to all intents and purposes, one settlement again. It is called after Sutton Saint Nicholas because that is much the larger of the two. Saint Michael is only a hamlet.

The settlement lies in the wide, watery valley of the River Lugg, a river notorious for its tendency to flood. It is a mixed residential area with some black and white cottages, a good Georgian farmhouse with a cider mill and stone weather-boarded barns, mature Victorian detached houses and 20th century estates. These are serviced by the Golden Cross Inn, a county primary school, a post office, shop and a daily bus service to Hereford where many of Sutton's inhabitants work.

Sutton Walls is an Iron-Age hill fort 1/2m NW of the village. It stands on a ridge, the single rampart following the contour of the hill protecting an elongated oval enclosure of about 26 acres. The earth walls are preserved except on the east side but much of the interior has been badly disturbed by quarrying, and by it being used as a dump for toxic waste materials. It was occupied over an extended period. The earliest settlement preceded the earthworks and was probably protected by a timber stockade. The earth for the ramparts was obtained from the external ditch and from inside by digging hollows. In the hollows huts were erected and can be dated by finds of Iron Age B-type pottery. About A.D.25 the walls were heightened by the Belgic Celts. (For an excellent description of these people and their life-style see *A History of Herefordshire* by J. & M. West.) The Roman invasion is marked by finds of large numbers of skeletons, some of which had been decapitated, indicating a massacre. It is likely that the fort was slighted and it then fell into decay. There was still some occupation, however, and in the 2nd century a substantial building with a stone floor was erected, and a stone-built drying kiln may also belong to this period. The interior of the fort was then used as arable land well into the 4th century. That is where the archaeology ends and where oral history and legend take over

In 794, Ethelbert, King of East Anglia, came to the palace of King Offa of Mercia with the intention of marrying Offa's daughter, Alfrida. The palace was probably at Sutton Walls or could have been on the site of the Old Vicarage at Morden, 3/4m NW of Sutton Walls. Here Ethelbert was murdered on the orders of King Offa who had been influenced by his wife, Queen Quenrida (or Kenfrith as she is sometimes called). Some say he was decapitated, others that that a cloth was placed over a chair and that he fell to his death in the pit below. Old maps show a King's Cellar. Poor Alfrida became a hermit in the marshes of Crowland, Lincolnshire and Ethelbert was buried at Morden. His remains were later transferred to Hereford Cathedral, which is dedicated to him, and where miracles were wrought, but his tomb was destroyed by marauding Danes in 1050. For more on Saint Ethelbert, as he later became, see the articles on Morden and Hereford. For a full account of the legend see *The Folk-Lore of Herefordshire* by E.M. Leather pp 216-19.

As has already been mentioned, at the time of the Norman Conquest there were two separate manors at Sutton. That now called Saint Michael is thought to be the one that had a church and a mill and was held by Spirtes, the priest, a wealthy cleric who also had estates in the West Country. One always has to bear in mind when naming mediaeval landowners that as often as not they did not live in or even visit many of their manors, and that they were purely sources of income. Even worse, most bishops were absent from their Sees, for as long as 20 years on occasion. Bishops were more political appointments than religious.

But to return to Saint Michael's. It is nicely positioned with long views over the water meadows to the Welsh hills. The dedication is typically Anglo-Saxon but the church we see today is Norman and mediaeval. It is small with a nave and chancel and a bell-turret topped by a pyramid roof. Norman are the chancel east and north windows; the chancel arch, though that has been remodelled, and the round font with its lion feet. The second font is mid-17th century, in the shape of a small classical urn, and is extremely rare. The other windows are early 14th century and there is a big, rustic, tablet monument of 1654 to Elizabeth Cotton. There is a mass dial by a window. Adjoining Saint Michael's and immediately south-west and opposite Freen's Court, at SO 526 458, is the site of a deserted mediaeval village. The traces of the house platforms and holloways are very slight, but it is one of only two such Herefordshire sites which have been scheduled as Ancient Monuments. Freen's Court is a timber-framed house of the 15th century which has traces of its former moat. (For something on Sir Harry Lingen of Sutton Saint Michael see Amberley.)

The church of Saint Nicholas probably has Norman stones in the nave but of what we see today the chancel is 13th century; the arch mouldings, the transepts, the porch and the piscinas with ballflower decoration in the nave and the chancel are 14th century; the two-decker pulpit is Jacobean - aren't they all?

Wergin's Stone lies 1m S of the village. It is an undated monolith. The upstanding stone is coarse and unworked, about 5ft high, and sits in a roughly round base with a tooled-out, cup-shaped depression about 4" deep. A possible history is that the upstanding part is a prehistoric monolith later fitted to a base and then used as a place to make ceremonial offerings or cash payments, the coins being deposited in the cup. It might well have served as a boundary marker also.

The Wergin stone is quite probably one of the stones mentioned by Silas Taylor who wrote, in about 1650, that there were several stones set in the meadow "to direct a passage when the waters cover the meadows to a bridge called the Worgen over Lugg to Sutton". That does not, of course, preclude other or earlier uses. According to Daniel Defoe, who visited Herefordshire in the 1720s, the stones were moved 240 paces for no apparent reason by persons unknown. When they were returned to their former position nine yoke of oxen were needed to haul just one of them. This mystery led to them being called the Devil's Stone.

It stands near to the road and is clearly visible from it as the highway is literally that - it is on an embankment to lift the road above the water meadows which are regularly flooded, despite the low earth embankments that parallel the meandering River Lugg. It is a lovely river, though, with sand and pebble beaches fringed by pollarded willows and lush alluvium rich meadows grazed by cows and sheep. My dogs spent a happy half hour splashing about by Wergin's Bridge one hot Summer afternoon. I must admit we trespassed on the eastern side; but for those who wish to be street legal there is a footpath crossing the meadows to the west.

TARRINGTON *6.5m E of Hereford*

The name was Tatintune in Domesday Book, meaning 'Tata's settlement'. It must always be remembered that the Domesday names were written by Norman-French clerks who wrote what they heard phonetically. This can lead to some peculiarities of nomenclature but in truth is actually very reliable. Were they to return now they would spell London, Lundun, and Cholmondeley would be Chumley, as we say it. After all English is supposed to be a phonetic language, and it is surely more relevant and interesting to know what the local people call a place than what a learned scribe thinks it ought to be called. In Domesday Book the common suffix 'ton', from the Old English 'tun', is written 'tune'; this is presumably how it was pronounced then - as 'tewn' or 'toon', like the Scots do today.

Tarrington is very much the estate village of the Foley family of Stoke Edith, one mile to the west along the A438. It has a post office cum-general-store, a doctor's surgery, black and white and red brick cottages, rendered Council semi-detached houses and the Glass Pig. That name is objectionable. It was, and should still be, the Foley Arms. It is a friendly, Late Georgian red brick house with three bays, two storeys, a one-bay pediment and a porch with Tuscan columns. The settlement lies on the southern edge of the broad Frome valley, an area renowned for its fertility and equable climate. Hopyards, orchards, arable fields and pastures make a merry patchwork of colour in the Spring.

The church of Saint Philip and Saint James has stood watch over these lusty acres since Norman times. Much of the Norman work has been preserved in the nave and chancel by the restorers and the apse foundations have been left exposed after excavation. The tower is 16th century Perpendicular, as is the east of the chancel which has some 14th-15th century stained glass fragments. In an early 14th century tomb recess is the effigy of a lady of about 1360 decorated with dog-tooth and ballflower ornaments. In the churchyard are the steps, base and stump of a preaching cross. On the cul-de-sac approach lane to the church there is a charming thatched stone cottage called Columbine.

In 1644 the Royalist vicar of Tarrington, John Praulph was challenged by a troop of Massey's horse who asked him who he was for to which he replied "For God and the King", whereupon one of the horsemen shot him through the head. This happened near Saint Edith's Well, Stoke Edith.

Legend has it that if you walk around the churchyard seven times saying the Lord's Prayer backwards and then look through the keyhole of the church door, you will see the Devil. Mind you, anyone who can say the Lord's Prayer backwards is probably related to the Devil anyway.

A local rhyme runs:

> "Lusty Tarrington, lively Stoke,
> Beggars at Weston, thieves at Woolhope."

Landlordly greed reared its rapacious head during the early 19th century Parliamentary enclosures of the 12 open fields at Tarrington. Permission was given to enclose the scattered holdings so that land could be improved. Edward Foley received 168 out of the 450 acres enclosed. Smallholders and tenants always came off badly in these divisions.

At the level crossing, 1/2m NNW of Tarrington, is a little industrial enclosure in the grounds of Sparchall Farm. There is a substantial corn mill with Price's Perry painted on the side wall. Adjacent to it on the left is a curious, four-bay, two and a half storey, red brick, chapel-like building with round headed windows, blue brick dressings and one-storey wings right and left. There were once railway sidings here.

Tarrington Court (SO 617 405) lies about 300 yards SW of the church on the lane to the squatter community on Tarrington Common. It is a late 16th century house with fragmentary remains of a moat that enclosed about one acre. Foley Cottage, 1m SSE at Alder's End, has ancient cruck trusses in the east and west walls. Little Tarrington lies 1/2m NE of the church on the north side of the main road. Here there is a large, man-made fishing pool being planted around with trees, a pretty black and white cottage, a black and white farm, red brick houses, a hopyard, and gipsy caravans tucked up against the railway embankment. At Free Town, 1/2m N, there are orchards, a pedigree herd of Hereford cattle, and part of a moat. Back on the main road between Eastwood and Trumpet there is a fair-sized roadside gipsy encampment. There used to be a famous oak tree at Eastwood. Arthur Mee reports that when it blew down about 800 pounds of honey was found in its hollow branches.

TEDSTONE DELAMERE *3.5m NE of Bromyard*

The Domesday Book name is simply Tedesthorne, meaning 'Teodec's thorn-bush', perhaps meaning his homestead near a thorn-bush. By 1200 it was held by Thomas and Jordan de la Mare, hence Delamere. The settlement lies east of the Bromyard to Great Witley road, the B4203, in the lovely country of the Sapey Brook valley. It is a hamlet of scattered cottages centred on the Court and the church. The Court turns its red brick back to the road and is outshone by the handsome stone barns and hop kilns of its farm and the tall conifers and evergreen bushes of its enclosed garden. Follow the lane south a few yards; the view over the woods in the valley to the gentle hills beyond have delighted the eye of many an artist. The church lies on a slope in the middle of a field with only two horses for company. It was not always so. The grassed-over house platforms and holloways of the deserted mediaeval village can be seen quite clearly between the Court and the church. And that was probably the problem. In the 18th and 19th centuries it was not uncommon for local lords to remove cottage homes if they spoiled the view. The front of the Court faces south-east, over the site of the old village. It has four bays, with a canted bay to the right, and has been rendered grey.

The church of Saint James has a nave, a chancel and a timber bell-turret with a spire. The nave is Norman and has thick walls that could be partly Anglo-Saxon, two tufa Norman windows and an arch in the wall that could be part of an Anglo-Saxon doorway. The quoins are tufa also. The font is Norman; the screen is mediaeval; the hour-glass in the porch is of about 1700; the east window glass is by Hardman of 1857; and the 14th century cross has a head of 1629. The original head is by the west gate and has the Crucifixion on one side and the Virgin and Child on the other.

On the west lane from Hill Cross to Pixhill, is Saint Agnes' Well. (SO 692 587.) This is very overgrown but in Victorian times a clear-cut path led to the well and a stone wall. At one end of the wall is a cross which is still visible. Water for baptisms used to be collected here and carried to the church. It is quite likely that the baptisms were originally carried out at the well itself.

From the late 16th century through the 17th century a will had to be 'proved' by providing a list of all the deceased's possessions in the smallest detail. Many hundreds of these inventories still exist and are held at the Record Office in Harold Street, Hereford. Details of that belonging to Roger Conynge, a wealthy farmer at Tedstone Delamere who died in 1592, are given in of *A History of Herefordshire* by John and Margaret West. It is interesting to note that a quarter of his total wealth was in money loaned out. There were no banks in those days and loans were arranged privately between individuals.

At Pixhill, 1/4m SSE of the church, the Belville family have a deer farm. The animals are slaughtered for venison. They also have pigeon shoots here.

The Sapey Brook runs through its delightful wooded valley 1/4m E of the church. In the bed of the brook there are whirlholes a few inches in diameter caused by hard stones being swirled around, eroding the softer bed rock. But there is another explanation. Many years ago a young girl had her mare and colt stolen. She and her father's servants followed their tracks until they came to the stream and there they ended. The girl prayed for divine assistance, then walked downstream and found hoof prints in the solid rock. She and her party followed these and were led to a beautiful place in the valley called Witchery Hole, though to some it is another romantic spot called Hoar-stone. There they found the robber and recovered the mare and her colt. Apparently, local people in this century thought there was more than half a truth to this tale.

From Tedstone Delamere we headed south "past a rendered Gothic-y lodge, the orchards and woods of Pixhill, sheep and mistletoe, super views, steeply downhill and even better views into mysterious valleys, to Bentley Wood Common, a proper common with bracken and scrub woodland, past a house called The Sconce, to a strange brick and stone lodge with steep steps by the Sapey Brook"; but we were now at Whitbourne.

TEDSTONE WAFER *3.5m NNE of Bromyard*
Tedstone Wafer is a main road hamlet on the Bromyard to Great Witley road. With regard to the name: Tedstone is as in Tedstone Delamere; Wafer is from Robert de Wafre, the holder of the manor in 1242.

The settlement stands at a staggered crossroads. The main road is a ridge road with streams flowing west on one side and east on the other. Such highways are always ancient. At Tedstone Wafer there are a few cottages, council houses and detached dwellings, sheep in the pastures, holly in the hedges, peacocks in the lane to Tedstone Delamere, and churches ancient and modern.

The old Norman church of Saint Mary stands in ruins with only the west wall and part of the north wall left standing to a height of about 6ft. The masonry includes some fine-grained tufa. The new church was built nearby in 1873 to a design by E. Haycock. It is built of brick and has nave and chancel in one, a porch and a chapel, a bell-cote and a tall roof of red and blue tiles. The two broken halves of the mediaeval churchyard cross are in niches in the graveyard wall.

An excavation report on the deserted village site at Tedstone Wafer "showed a number of mediaeval buildings, interpreted as the remains of a nucleated settlement that was deserted, on pottery evidence, in the 13th or 14th century". There were also traces of a mediaeval street and ridge and furrow in the fields. This would have been the site of the Domesday manor held by Roger de Lacy, just one of his numerous manors in the county. High Lane, 1m N of the church, is named after High Lane House, a dour stone dwelling with three wide bays, a canted bay and a hipped roof. Most of the other roadside dwellings are red brick. There is a pub, the Gate Hangs Well, a service station and a Primitive Methodist church of 1862, built of brick with round-headed windows. South of High Lane is ploughland and pasture with small, squatter-type cottages hard on the highway.

About half way between High Lane and Tedstone Wafer, west of the road by Coppice House, is the site of a small Roman fort (SO 676 602). Crop marks photographed from the air indicate a rectangular Roman fortlet, about 85 x 65yds, which encloses an area of about one acre. Excavations revealed two filled-in ditches about 10ft wide and 5ft deep, probably of the late 2nd century. Stone metalling in a farm gateway line up with the paved track and ford running north and slightly west of the fort at Tedstone Wafer. These indicate the north-south Roman road from Kenchester to Droitwich. Elsewhere it has been traced on aerial photographs, and from field and farm names.

THORNBURY *3.5m NW of Bromyard*
The name is from the Anglo-Saxon and means either 'the fort where thorns grow' or 'the fort protected by a thorn hedge'. The Anglo-Saxon byrig, or bury, almost always refers to an earlier fort, not one of their own defensive positions. In this case the early Iron-Age fortress of Wall Hills lies 1/2m E of Thornbury. It stands on a flat-topped hill some 760ft above sea level and covers about 23 acres. The single rampart rises to between 35ft and 40ft above the bottom of the ditch and there are four entrances. The structure is impressive and the views far ranging over this land of little hills, hopyards, pastures and orchards.

In 1066 the Anglo-Saxon, Siward, held the manor of Thornbury. By 1086 it had passed to Alfred of Spain, his only holding in Herefordshire. His Norman name was Alfred de Hispan. This is a play on words for he came from Epaignes in the Department of Eure in France, not Spain.

Hop-picking in the Bromyard area, probably inter-World War.

He also had estates in Dorset, Devon, Somerset, Wiltshire and Gloucestershire. Like so many places in Herefordshire Thornbury is a parish with scattered homesteads rather than a nucleated village.

The church of Saint Anne has a Norman nave with a Norman window on the north side and a Norman doorway with zig-zag in the arch. The tub-shaped font is also Norman. The tower, the re-set south doorway, and the remains of the south arcade are 13th century. The chancel was rebuilt in 1865 by F.R. Kempson but retains four 13th century lancets. The bier and the vestry table are 17th century.

The hop-picking area around Bromyard was invaded by heathens from the Black Country each autumn. They came from industrial slums and things were no better, if not worse, on the farms where they lived in primitive wooden huts. Local vicars went evangelising and brought not a few lost souls to the bosom of the Church of England's God. In September 1901, for example, five children of hop-picking parents were baptised at Thornbury.

The Lady Well, an ancient healing spring, is situated beside the footpath that leads east from the church at SO 626 596. It has been tanked but there is a small reservoir. The well is said to have been the source of water for the Wall Hills fort. Legend has it that there was a tunnel from the yew that stands by the well to a pair of yews that formerly stood on the western edge of the camp.

The Park Pale is an earthwork that surrounds Park Farm, 3/4m W of the church. A rampart and ditch encloses an area of about 97 acres and was probably raised to defend land under cultivation from forest animals - deer, for example, can decimate young plants. It has not been dated. Wooding Farm, 1/4m WSW of the church, has one remaining roof truss of the 14th century open hall. This consists of arched braces and a collar. For Netherwood, the birthplace of the Earl of Essex, which lies 1m NW of the church, see the article on Collingwood.

THRUXTON *5.5m SW of Hereford*
The mediaeval name was Turcleston, meaning 'Terkil's homestead', and it is most easily approached off the Hereford to Abergavenny road at Tram Inn. In 1066 it was held by Robert, son of Wymarc, but by 1086 it had passed to Durand of Pitres, Sheriff of Gloucester.

Thruxton is a small hamlet on the edge of a large area of old common land. Between here and Allensmore, 2m NE, there are Arkstone Common, at Hungerstone, Cobhall Common and Winnal Common. All have scattered roadside squatter cottages. The Herefordshire Commotion started in this area; see the article on Allensmore.

The church of Saint Bartholomew is 14th century Decorated, except for the early Perpendicular east window. The octagonal font is of 1677 and in the chancel is a fine, early 14th century stained glass Crucifixion scene. About 100 yards west of the church there is a large, round mound that has a diameter of about 125ft and is surrounded by a ditch with an outside bank. It is thought to be a Bronze-Age round barrow that was later used as a defensive position by the Normans. The mound is said to have been investigated in the 19th century and that a chamber constructed of undressed stones was found.

Ancient customs linger long in country places. At Thruxton, on the eve of May Day, people used to put trays of moss outside the door at night for the fairies to dance on. To cure a child's rupture one splits an ash tree and passes the patient through it nine times. This must be done in total silence. The tree is then bound up with withies and the cure is complete. A similar transference cure for whooping cough was practised at Thruxton and nearby Kingston. It is detailed in the article on Kingston.

TILLINGTON *4m NW of Hereford*
The name is from the Anglo-Saxon and means 'the settlement of Tylli's people'. It lies on the old road from Hereford to Weobley at the point where it is crossed by the Roman road that connected Kenchester to Watling Street. It is a spread-about village with outlying clusters of dwellings at Tillington Common, 1m NW, and Crowmoor, 1/2m S. There is a pub, The Bell, but there were two more. The Bird in Hand is now a garage and The Live and Let Live is now a shop. The Nonconformist chapel is of 1857. The impressive Burghill School was built in 1875 with stone quarried from Badnage Wood, which adjoins Tillington Common. It is now a private house. East of the village crossroads are orchards and beyond these is Tillington Court which has been sub-divided to form three dwellings. The estate is now owned by the Co-operative Wholesale Society who have large soft fruit farms here.

There is a local story about a badger-baiting friar who lived in West Hide Wood and how he got taken by the Devil. West Hide Wood is 1/2m S of Westhide which is 5.1/2m ENE of Hereford. This is how Mrs. E.M. Leather told it in 1912. "The Friar was a jovial fellow, a lover of sport and money. Badger-baiting was much in vogue in the county just then, and when one day he succeeded in trapping a badger in the wood, he put his quarry in a bag, and, throwing it over his shoulder started to walk to the Bell Inn, at Tillington. Here he hoped to get a good price for his capture. But soon the bag began to get heavier, and a voice said 'Mamma calls'. The Friar heard, but it did not occur to him that the voice would come from inside the bag. Again he heard 'Dadda calls', this time from the bag unmistakably, and the burden became heavier. So he put it down in astonishment, and opened it to see what was happening, when out came the 'old un' himself. The Devil seized the Friar and took him away; he was never seen again."

TITLEY *3m NE of Kington*
The name is probably from the Anglo-Saxon Titta's-leah, 'Titta's glade or clearing in the wood'. In 1066 it belonged to Earl Harold (Godwinson) King of England. By 1086 it had passed to Osbern son of Richard and was waste, though there was a hedged enclosure there in a little wood. The settlement sprawls along the road between Kington and Presteigne, the B4355, which passes through an attractive landscape of undulating pastures, woods and glacial pools. Old drovers roads traverse the parish. They were used by men driving cattle and sheep from Wales to the English markets, and who avoided the ordinary public highways wherever possible.

Remarkably, it was once possible to travel from the station at Titley to London without changing trains; the line closed in the 1960s. The school of 1826 closed in 1962 and the shop followed suit. However, they do still have a post office, a village hall, the stone-built Stagg Inn and a church. There is a cluster of old houses and weather-boarded barns on top of the hill, by the Court, but most of the village is down in the valley, 1/2m N. Mature Georgian and Victorian villas such as Boddington's House (the old vicarage) have been invaded by 20th century bungalows, though they mingle well enough. It is a leafy place with a war memorial and an ancient healing well called The Spout. The spring bubbles up into a pool in the churchyard and in 1864 it was piped to a drinking fountain by the church gate at the expense of Lady Elizabeth Hastings. The tap is set into a blank stone arch and there is a drinking cup on a chain.

The church of Saint Peter is the fifth on the site since the Norman Conquest. The first disappeared at the time of the Black Death; nothing is known of the second; the third was burned down by Owain Glyndwr in the early 15th century; the fourth fell into disrepair; and the fifth, the one we see today, was built in 1868 by the architect E. Haycock, Junior. His church is of grey stone with yellow stone dressings and has a collection of silver plate ranging in date from 1569 to 1733.

In the churchyard is the newly restored grave of Lazar Meszaros, the Hungarian national hero. He led his country's army against the Austrians and won its freedom. However, in 1849 the Russians invaded and Meszaros escaped to the United States of America. He died in 1858 whilst visiting the house of Lady Langdale at Eywood. Her daughter had married his friend, Count Teleki. Meszaros was buried in Lady Langdale's plot. The Hungarian government has made repeated attempts to have the General's remains taken back to Hungary. However, that government has been communist influenced since the second Russian invasion of 1956 and exiled Hungarians have successfully objected to his removal. The grave of Lazar Meszaros is now a shrine and receives pilgrims from all over the world.

The first Norman church at Titley was the chapel of a cell of the reformed Benedictine abbey of Tiron in La Beaune in France. They were here from 1120 to 1391. There were only four cells of this Order of Tiron in England, the other three were in Hampshire. Their chapel to St. Tirella was on the north side of the church site and the priory was about 100 yards WSW of the church. All that remains of the priory are a 14th century holy water stoup, now privately owned, and probably some timbers in the newly restored timber-framed house behind the churchyard.

Titley Court was bought by the Greenly family in 1861. Ownership of the house gave them the advowson, the right to recommend a member of the Anglican clergy for a vacant benefice. The Greenlys had previously been the tenant farmers of the estate. Now, to show their new stature, they remodelled the house. By 1885 it had a new facade, but retained much of the old fabric including a good, late 17th century ceiling and some Jacobean woodwork. It is a friendly looking place, protected by evergreens and standing in its own mediaeval deer park.

Eywood, 3/4m SW of the church, is approached from a lane just north of the Court. It is beautifully situated amidst large pools and small woods in a hilly landscape. Eywood Mansion was built in the late 17th century for the Honourable Edward Harley and later became the principal residence of Edward Harley, fifth Earl of Oxford, Earl of Mortimer and Baron of Wigmore, and Auditor of the Imprest to Queen Anne. (See the article on Brampton Bryan for something on the Harley family.) William Wordsworth (1770-1850) and Percy Bysshe Shelley (1792-1822) were both visitors to Eywood in its heyday. The estate was sold in 1954, the mansion was demolished and the service buildings converted to private dwellings. The Eywood lakes adjoin the main road at Flintsham, 1m SW of the church.

On the other side of the road, behind a Victorian black and white cottage, are the kennels and the abattoir of the Radnorshire and West Herefordshire Hunt. They have been here since 1895, much to the distress of the local foxes and badgers. I am totally against blood sports. Killing for pleasure is perverse. Perhaps worst of all is the universal practice of blocking up the entrances to badger setts to stop foxes taking refuge in them. Whole families of badgers are suffocated to death because the hunt helpers use old cans and stones instead of straw and wire mesh. It is more than whispered that our future king, Prince Charles, rides with the Herefordshire hunts. Local people will tell you that he often stays at Captain Dunne's Gatley Park estate, at Leinthall Earls, 8m NE of Titley.

Early man has left his mark at Titley. Middle Stone-Age implements have been found in the parish and flints, scrapers and tools have been found in the vicinity of a ploughed out ringwork, or disc barrow, at Oatcroft Farm (SO 311 603). There was another Bronze-Age barrow at Priory Leasowe, but this has also been ploughed out. A third Bronze-Age barrow is still upstanding at Flintsham, 1m SW of the church. It stands just south of the road at SO 324 587 and measures about 21ft in diameter and 2ft in height. It is slightly dished at the top (which often means it has been plundered, usually by the Victorians) and is surrounded by a ditch 6ft wide. Close by is a section of the 8th century Offa's Dyke.

Shawl is a main road hamlet, 3/4m S of the church, and from here a lane leads south to Titley Mill on the River Arrow. The Forge, 1m SE of the church, is an interesting looking hamlet with a scatter of squatter-type cottages near the site of the old railway bridge over the Arrow. There are several weirs on the river hereabouts.

Cabal Tump lies 1/2m SSW of The Forge at Strangeworth Farm, close to the junction of the disused railways from Kington to Presteigne and Kington to Leominster. It has been suggested that the mound and its surrounding ditch is the site of an early, square-shaped castle which probably had no stonework. It was partly excavated prior to 1875. In 1931 a trench was cut immediately to the south-east of the mound and 'wasters' of mediaeval pottery were found, indicating the site of a kiln. There are low banks and ditches in the vicinity but these are probably field or paddock boundaries of a later date. It seems that the earthworks were raised as a 12th century castle and were later used as a mediaeval moated homestead. The name Cabal is from the Old English meaning 'a rounded hill'.

Another lane leads from the main road north of the church, past the stone cottages and farms of Mowley, to Horseway Head, a small settlement of bungalows, brick semis and a timber-framed farm. Here the track of the disused railway from Kington to Presteigne passes through embankments to the south and cuttings to the north. It is quite exposed and windy yet this is the home of Horseway Herb Gardens who sell directly to the public.

TRETIRE *5m W of Ross-on-Wye*
The mediaeval Welsh name was Rhythir, from rhyd - hir, meaning 'long ford'. The 'T' is from association with Tre, 'homestead'. It stands at a minor crossroads on the road from Owen's Cross to Abergavenny, the B4521, and at the confluence of The Gamber and a tributary stream.

The church of Saint Mary was rebuilt in 1856 in the style of 1300 and has nave, chancel and a narrow, five-sided, stone bell-turret. Inside there is a 13th century coffin lid and outside is the base of a mediaeval churchyard cross with a Victorian shaft and head. The church bells are said to chime "Pigs in the mire, say the bells of Tretire". The stone-built rectory is of about 1700. In the garden there is a Norm arch and the old, 15th century, font.

The site of Tretire Castle lies just to the south-east of the church. It belonged to Fulk Fitzwarine in the 13th century and the earthworks consisted of a roughly rectangular mound about 70 x 55 yards. It was probably a fortified house rather than a stone castle. Today there is nothing to see; it has been ploughed out. Chapel Tump, 1m ESE of Tretire, near Owen's Cross at SO 539 243, was probably a ring motte but the site has been badly damaged by ploughing and housing development. It was probably oval in shape and covered 3/4 of an acre. There are traces of a bank on the north-west and south-east sides and the interior rises to about 8ft above the ditch.

Twelfth Night celebrations were quite elaborate and were still celebrated throughout the county late into the 19th century. Here is the classic description which appeared in 1791 in the *Gentleman's Magazine*: "In Herefordshire, at the approach of the evening, the farmers and their friends and servants meet together, and about six o'clock walk out to a field where wheat is growing. In the highest part of the ground, twelve small fires, and one large one, are lighted up. The attendants, headed by the master of the family, pledge the company in old cider, which circulates freely on these occasions. A circle is formed round the large fire, when a general shout and hallooing takes place, which you hear answered from all the adjacent villages and fields. Sometimes fifty or sixty of these fires can be seen all at once. This being finished, the company return home, where the good housewife and her maids are preparing a good supper. A large cake is always provided, with a hole in the middle.

After supper, the company all attend the bailiff (or head of oxen) to the wainhouse, where the following particulars are observed: The master, at the head of his friends, fills the cup (generally of strong ale), and stands opposite the first or finest of the oxen. He then pledges him in a curious toast: the company follow his example, with all the other oxen, and addressing each by his name. This being finished, the large cake is produced, and, with much ceremony, put on the horn of the first ox, through the hole above mentioned. The ox is then tickled, to make him toss his head: if he throws the cake behind, then it is the mistress's perquisite; if before (in what is termed the boosy), the bailiff himself claims the prize. The company then return to the house, the doors of which they find locked, nor will they be opened till some joyous songs are sung. On their gaining admittance, a scene of mirth and jollity ensues, which lasts the greatest part of the night."

At Tretire oxen were not worked for any of the twelve days. Here, if the cake was thrown forward, it belonged to the head oxen man, if backward it went to the labourers.

TUPSLEY *1.25m E of Hereford*

It is now an eastern suburb of Hereford centred on the road to Ledbury, the A438. At the time of Domesday Book it was Topeslage, from the Old English meaning 'pasture for rams'. Tup is still a commonly used word for a male sheep.

The old inn, the Cock of Tupsley, kept a strong shire-type horse to go to the assistance of carriers and coaches unable to make it up the steep incline of the Aylestone Hill. The coach driver would sound a bugle, and the 'Cock' would be despatched.

The settlement grew rapidly after the opening of the Great Western Railway station at the bottom of Aylestone Hill in 1855. Ten years later it broke away from the parish of Hampton Bishop and was given its own church. The gradient of the hill was greatly reduced in the 1930s and the area was developed with semi-detached houses proliferating.

Tupsley Court, a substantial timber-framed mansion, and the old inn were demolished and a new public house was built in their place. Even now it is a little strange to see such wide open lawned spaces around the new Cock of Tupsley. We have imbibed there on a couple of occasions amidst old photographs of long-dead horses.

The steep entrance to Ledbury Road used to lead to the Hampton Park Brick and Tile Works which ceased production at the time of the First World War. A little of the wilderness that it became remains though there are playing fields here now. There is a school, Bishop's School, opened in 1958 and a shopping centre with 15 or more retail units.

The deserted mediaeval village of Tupsley lies 1/2m E of the fringes of the modern village, by the water meadows of the alluvial plain of the Wye-Lugg confluence. The area suffered badly from flooding and no doubt the village moved for that reason. The modern flood protection wall of earth that defends nearby Hampton Bishop actually extends beyond the Tupsley site. The scheduled area covers 21.1/2 acres north of the former Isolation Hospital, around SO 544 398, but it has not yet been excavated.

TURNASTONE *9.5m WSW of Hereford*

The name is not properly understood but is probably from the Old English and means 'thorn or thicket by the stone'. The folk have another explanation that also includes nearby Vowchurch. One of two quarrelling sisters said to the other: "I vow I will build my church before you turn a stone of yours." The churches of the two hamlets face each other about a 1/4m apart over the River Dore in the Golden Valley.

The small church of Saint Mary Magdalene at Turnastone has thick, Norman nave walls, a chancel and a bell turret with a pyramid roof. The south doorway is Norman; the nave windows are early 13th century; the wagon roof is Tudor; and the bell-turret and pulpit are Jacobean. There are notable monuments to Thomas Aparri, died 1522, and wife, whose portraits are engraved on a slab together with a satyr playing the bagpipes; and Mrs. Traunter, died 1685, shortly after her wedding at the age of 18.

In 1410 the Bishop of Hereford made a famous declaration forbidding the worship of a well and a stone at Turnastone. The stone has disappeared, though its obvious religious significance to the community confirms that the second element of the place name is indeed 'stone', and not a corruption of 'ton'. The well was probably the Ladywell, about 600 yards SSW of the church, at, SO 350 362. This has been tanked for domestic use and is no longer visible, but the overflow still runs past the roadside.

Near the sharp, right-angle bend at Turnastone is a green, white and black enamel sign advertising the Raleigh All Steel Bicycle. Such signs are collectors' items these days. It is attached to the wall of a house which is also a petrol filling station. The pumps are hidden behind the garden wall. Quaint.

The Whitehouse, 3/4m SW of the church, is 'L'-shaped. One wing is gabled with mullioned and transomed windows of the 17th century; the other is of stone with three bays, a parapet and pointed windows. The fireplaces come from a dismantled east wing. Cothill Camp, 1.1/4m W of the church, and 600 yards NW of Cothill Farm at SO 338 364, is possibly the site of a prehistoric burial mound, later used by the Normans for a motte and bailey castle that was abandoned in the 14th century. The mound is

Top Left: Madley, Earth Satellite aerial dish.
Top right: Bronze-Age Beaker vessel from one of the Olchon Valley cist tombs. See Llanveynoe.
Opposite: A Hereford bull.
Below: Wigmore Castle, once the caput of the mediaeval Mortimers, from an engraving by Samuel Buck of 1732.

surrounded by a ditch and has been damaged by the removal of field soil. Chanstone Court stands below the deciduous Chanstone Wood, a good 1/2m south-east of Turnastone. The name means 'Cheney's manor by the stone'. Cheney is a family name taken from a French place name. What did happen to this sacred stone?

At the White House, 3/4m SW of the church, the ancient custom of corn showing was practised, a relic of a pre-Christian fertility ritual. It was described to Mrs. E.M. Leather thus: "It was the custom at Lulham, in the parish of Madley, and also at the White House, Saint Margaret's for the bailiff to proceed on the afternoon of Easter Sunday to a wheat field on the farm. Plum cake was provided, and cider in wooden bottles, and consumed by the families of the workmen, and any neighbours who chose to attend. A small piece of cake was buried in the nearest part of the field, and then, a little cider being poured on it, they wished the master a good crop."

TWYFORD 3m S of Hereford

We approached the hamlet from the south, off the road that joins Aconbury to the A49. The lane descends into a shallow valley with sheep pastures to Twyford Farm, a stone, red brick and render dwelling. The narrow, wooded lane wends its way down over an old ford, now bridged over, to a second ford, also bridged over. The name Twyford actually means 'two fords'. Twyford Brook Farmhouse, a black and white house with a low, one-storey, right-hand wing and a boarded barn, stands beside the lower ford and guards the entrance to Twyford Common. This has a scatter of lanes with spaced out, mostly rendered, squatter cottages and smallholdings, many of which have been extended and modernised beyond all recognition. It is a charming, hidden place, with small buttercup meadows, well-wooded hedgerows and the murmur of contented sheep. The concrete structure on the top of Ridge Hill, which forms the eastern flank of the valley, is part of a water reservoir. On the main lane there is a tiny Nonconformist chapel, constructed of unusually large red bricks laid in Flemish Bond, with headers and stretchers alternating. At a later date a cheap, modern house was attached to it that is now unoccupied. There are a number of rusty, red corrugated-iron barns in the area. These are acceptable in a rural environment; not so their gleaming super-galvanised younger brothers.

TYBERTON 8m W of Hereford

The name is not understood but could be 'the settlement of Tyber', or a similar personal name. It lies on the Madley to Bredwardine road, the B4352. To the west is the long ridge that separates the Golden Valley from the broad plain of the River Wye. It is a Domesday village and there is still a mediaeval atmosphere here, despite the derelict, ivy-clad, corrugated-iron barns. The land is flat and there are three pools close to the road making a pleasing group with a few cottages and several substantial farmhouses. These include a five-bay, red brick Georgian dwelling and the very handsome Lower House Farm, which is red brick and half-timbered with four gables and a stone-slate roof. It is very quiet here; the only the music to break the silence is the hum of a distant tractor and the quacking of ducks.

The church of Saint Mary stands embowered in the grounds of Tyberton Court. This, from all accounts, was a "magnificent" mansion of 1728 designed by John Wood of Bath but now, alas, it is no more. The old Norman church was also demolished and only the Late Norman south doorway was retained in the new, red brick church of 1721. Brick was fashionable at that time. The tower has arched windows but those of the nave and chancel were made into lancets in 1879. The font, lectern, Royal Arms, box pews, pulpit and communion rail are remarkable for being all of the period and preserved almost complete. Best of all is the carved panelling behind the altar, which was designed by John Wood, and executed by a master craftsman. The reredos is Italian. There are numerous monuments to members of the Brydges family dating from William Brydges, died 1668 to Francis W.T. Brydges, died 1793. The family lived at Tyberton Court. The Duke of Chandos was a Brydges. In the churchyard there is a well preserved, complete 14th century preaching cross with a Crucifix on one side and the Madonna on the other.

Shenmore, 1.1/4m SE, is another watery place with three pools which shelters below the steep, wooded ridge of Barrett's Hill. The name is from the Anglo-Saxon, scene - mor, 'beautiful moor', or scene-mere, 'beautiful mere'. Our word scenic, meaning 'beautiful landscape', comes from the Anglo-Saxon scene.

The numerous small pools and meres of the Wye valley hereabouts are glacial in origin. In 1912 there was a Holy Thorn, a cutting from the Glastonbury Thorn, growing at Tyberton.

ULLINGSWICK 4.5m SW of Bromsgrove

The name is from the Anglo-Saxon and means 'the dairy farm of Willa's people', though wic can also mean many things from homestead to town to a street. At the time of Domesday Book the manor was held by 'a man at arms', that is a knight, in the service of the Bishop of Hereford. With six hides he had a good-sized holding; a hide was about 120 acres. The old village centre lies in pleasant, undulating country at the end of a dead-end lane. Huddled together in a hollow are the Upper and Lower Courts and the church, which seems not to have a dedication.

As an aside may one ask: why are Anglican churches always dedicated to almost everyone but God himself? Why are there so very few Holy Fathers, God Almightys, Heavenly Fathers Lords of All, or such like? Certainly there are none in Herefordshire. The answer is probably that we are pantheonic at heart and saints, sons, mothers and disciples are substitutes for the spirits of rivers, trees, stones and springs. So, at Ullingswick we have a House of God, a name not easily bettered.

The nave is Norman and there are two Norman windows in the north wall. The chancel was rebuilt and lengthened in the 13th century and has the typical Herefordshire window of three lights under one arch. The stained glass Virgin and Child is 15th century; the other chancel windows have Victorian neo-13th century glass. The font is genuine 13th century; the 13th century coffin lid with a foliated cross was re-used in 1699 as a memorial to I.P; John Hill, died 1591, is painted on stone with his wife and three children kneeling and two babies in shrouds. In recent times a vestry was added using material brought from the ruined church at Avenbury, 1m S of Bromyard - ecclesiastical quarrying, forsooth. The rectory was rebuilt in the 19th century.

The aforementioned John Hill's family lived at Lower Court, a half-timbered farmhouse just down the lane from the church. Inside there is a good Jacobean overmantle with stucco decoration of fleur-de-lis and pomegranates. Upper Court, which stands next to the church, is built of stone and is 16th to 17th century. The cone of a hop kiln competes with the church bellcote, but hops are no longer grown in the parish. However, there are orchards of cider apples and perry pears. Along the lanes are half-timbered and stone cottages and farmhouses, many of which are listed. The Three Crowns pub, 1/4m SE of the church, has a stone gable and a half-timbered front. It is a free house and resides in a tranquil position.

The greater part of the modern village now lies in Upper Town, 3/4m SW of the church. Modern bungalows mingle with older properties such as The Steppes, a fine 17th century, timber-framed farmhouse that is now a private hotel. Near the main road, the A417, is The Camp, a collection of Nissen huts built to house Land Army girls during the Second World War, which later became a home to Italian prisoners of war. The village has virtually no service facilities. The school, the shop and the village hall have closed down and the people have to travel to Burley Gate, 1.1/2m S. The depopulation of the old village was largely due to the 19th century enclosures. The tithe map of 1839 shows 290 acres of open cultivation in Bebury Field, Broomhill Field and Wood Field. By 1902 these strip cultivated fields had been enclosed and the old curved boundaries had given way to the surveyors' straight lines. The land is now mostly to pasture with no trace of the old ridge and furrow ploughland. Labour intensive smallholdings have given way to limited companies and the old farming families are gone; their only memorial is the collection of gravestones now moved to the wall of the churchyard.

The famous wizard called Jenkins lived somewhere between Hereford and Bromyard, and amongst the deeds attributed to him was that he made many old women go lame in Ullingswick; why we don't know. On another occasion he foretold the return of a stolen tablecloth to an Ullingswick laundress, nothing in itself but just one of a multitude of small events which indicate that he had some considerable power, whether psychological or demoniacal is open to question. There was a strong tradition of wassailing at Ullingswick.

Another old custom, the Hop-pickers' Feast, was celebrated in the parish. At the end of the season a King and a Queen were chosen, each cross-dressed, as we would say today. They and the Pole-Puller carried poles of the last hops, which were taken from the field to the homestead where they were carefully dried and hung in the kitchen. The occasion was one of much mirth and merriment. This ceremony was performed at many places during the 19th century, including Hatfield and Blakemere.

UPPER SAPEY *5.5m NNE of Bromyard*
It lies in the shallow valley of the Sapey Brook where the stream crosses the Bromyard to Stanford on Teme road, the B4203. This was part of the route taken by many of the farmers to Mamble Colliery, near Stourport-on-Severn, to get charks of coal for the hop drying kilns. A description given by the son of Inett Homes of Bosbury of the last journey he made in 1910 is printed in *A Pocketful of Hops*. The waggoners stopped at the stone-built Baiting House Inn, Upper Sapey, for their bait (refreshment). On the outward journey they were ambushed twice by robbers intent on stealing their provisions. Only having a dog saved them. Highway robberies were very common, even as late as 1910, it seems. In 1810 there were 144 acres of hops in the parish of Upper Sapey; in 1925 there were none, and there are still none.

There are places on the banks of the Sapey Brook where travertine, a light-coloured porous, calcareous rock can be seen being deposited around small springs in the river cliffs. This tufa, as it is often called, was much prized by the Normans for dressed stonework.

The church at Upper Sapey has a Norman nave and chancel, and a tower of 1859 which has a pyramid roof and a spire. The very fine Norman chancel arch was moved to become the tower arch and is decorated with zig-zag and rare rows of pointed arches. The font is 13th century, four plain benches are 16th century, and the altar table is Jacobean. The mid-19th century pulpit is largely the work of a local carpenter, John Kitchen.

Today there is much new, red brick housing at Upper Sapey and it now boasts the Sapey Golf Club, which will, no doubt, attract more new, red brick housing.

UPTON BISHOP *3.5m NE of Ross-on-Wye*
The Domesday Book name is simply Uptune, meaning 'higher settlement'. It belonged to the Bishop of Hereford and the suffix Bishop was later added to differentiate it from the many other Uptons in England.

The village lies in a valley in hill country and is really now one settlement with Upton Crews and Crow Hill, which adjoin it on higher ground to the west, from where there are splendid views to the Brecon Beacons, the Malverns, the Cotswolds and the Forest of Dean. The school of 1845 closed in 1972, and in recent times the shop, the post office, the butcher and baker have also met their demise, a farrier, the Moody Cow pub, a vintage car restorer, a parish room and a Baptist chapel of 1860. Have survived. At the Wobage Farm Pottery they also have craftsmen wood carvers, furniture-makers and jewellers. Most of these facilities and services are at Crow Hill. There have been changes in the local agriculture too. Wheat and barley continue to be grown but the hopyards and orchards have been replaced by arable crops such as peas, parsley and sugar-beet.

The church of Saint John the Baptist has a tower, nave, chancel and south aisle. Of Norman work it has a blocked north doorway and a south arcade of three bays with fat pillars with carved creatures. The chancel was re-built in the 13th century; the aisle is of the 14th century; the grey stone tower was completed in the 15th century; and the 14th century porch has a 16th century barrel roof. There are four piscinas; the pulpit is Jacobean; most of the stained glass is Victorian; and in the south aisle is the 14th century effigy of an unknown civilian. Oldest of all in the church is part of a Roman tombstone. This is built into the wall of the chancel and consists of the head and shoulders of a man with his right hand raised set beneath an arch, and alongside, beneath another arch, is a fragment of his left hand. The Reverend Francis Havergal was vicar at the church from 1874 to his death in 1890. He was a cultivated man, an historian, scholar, musician, and philanthropist. His sister was the hymn writer Frances Ridley Havergal who lived at the village for a short time.

Within the parish there are dwellings and farms of stone, brick, render and timber-framing and barns of stone and weather-boarding. Notable houses include: Upton Court, 3/4m NE of the church, a 14th century, stone-built house with later additions. Most of the tie-beams, collar beams and other timbers of the original roof have been preserved. It also has a 17th century brewhouse. Many farms made their own beer and cider well into the 19th century. An allowance of weak beer was often a part of a man's wages. Felhampton, just over 1/2m from the church, is a most handsome timber-framed house with gables, close-spaced uprights and diagonal strutting. Tedgewood, 3/4m E, is an early 16th century, timber-framed house near Queenswood. The South Herefordshire Golf and Country Club is at Twin Lakes, Upton Bishop, and adjoins Lynder's Wood. In the early 1800s the parish workhouse was built at The Crews, as the locals call Upton Crew.

As late as 1849 a witch was persecuted at Upton Bishop. Hannah Goode lived in a cottage on Hill Top. One day a crowd gathered round with the intention of making her 'ride the stang', a public humiliation ceremony. The stang was an ash pole decorated with a ram's skull and garlands of nettles. She came to the door, refused to co-operate and so the crowd stoned her before dispersing. Later, she successfully took some of the mob to court and they were duly fined.

The boundary of the broad acres of Queenswood is only one mile from Upton Bishop, but the main reception area is near Kempley Green, 2m NE, and amost double that by road. There are picnic benches, grassy glades and a large car park. Most of the trees are conifers - Douglas fir, larches, and Norwegian spruce. In the centre of the wood there is a small lake frequented by wildfowl. One of the delights of Spring in Queenswood and the adjoining Dymock Wood and Hay Wood is the blossoming of the gean, the wild cherry. The wood is much prized by the furniture industry for the ease with which it can be worked and for its warm, green-gold colour.

VOWCHURCH *9.5m WSW of Hereford*

The name is from the Old English meaning 'multicoloured church'. It lies in the lovely Golden Valley at a gap in the eastern hill-ridge followed by the road to Kingstone, the B4348. The church and a few dwellings stand close to the bridge over the River Dore. The Old Vicarage is early 16th century with close-set uprights, always a sign of quality because oak was more expensive and durable than the wattle infill. The left gable has herringbone strutting.

The church of Saint Bartholomew has Norman walls, a Norman window in the nave, and a Norman font. The bell-turret is of about 1522. Most of the rest is mid-14th century. The chancel window has the typical Herefordshire east window of three lights within one arch. The roof was re-fashioned in or about 1613 by the highly regarded master-craftsman John Abel. It has tie-beams, queenposts and collar beams but the unusual feature is the manner of their support. They rest, not on the walls, but on a veritable forest of oak posts that reach straight to the ground, as though the builder felt he could not trust the ancient walls. Some of the original 14th century roof timbers were re-used, in particular those in the chancel. There is some good 17th century furniture and a rare Jacobean beech-wood Communion Cup with engraved birds. A mediaeval altar stone with consecration crosses now serves as a window sill and there is a monument to Sir Edward Boughton, died 1794.

Poston Lodge, now called Poston House, stands 1m N of the church in woods at the top of a little valley with superb views to the south-east. It was built in 1780 as a shooting lodge and originally comprised an elegant domed, circular room with an entrance hall and Tuscan-columned portico with a wood pediment. The architect was Sir William Chambers and his client was Sir Edward Boughton. The original structure survives but it later acquired two Victorian wings. It is, nevertheless, an eminently desirable property and is now the home of Esmond Bulmer, Chairman of the famous cider company and grandson of the founder.

Vowchurch Common lies on the steep slopes 1/2m NE of the church, and has attracted a goodly scatter of squatter-built cottages. They. too, have some glorious views over the Golden Valley to the Black Mountains. On the east side of the common at SO 369 377, there is a spring called the Heavenly Well, said to cure all ills.

The Vowchurch area was popular with early man. Neolithic flint arrow-heads and a Bronze-Age axe-head have been found in the parish and there are two uninvestigated tumps less than 1/2m SSE of the church, one on each side of the river. There is another, oval mound, 1.1/4m ENE of the church, which measures about 60 yards by 52 yards.

An Iron-Age hill fort stands on a promontory, 3/4m NNW of the church and about 200 yards SSW of Poston Lodge. It was excavated and researched in the 1930s and its building history was revealed. The first fortress dates from the 1st century B.C. and had a single rampart and outer ditch. It was dated from pottery sherds founds at hut sites close to the ramparts. The outside ditch became silted up and huts were built over it. Then, in the middle of the 1st century A.D., with the Roman invasion, the fort area was extended and a second rampart and ditch constructed with a stone-faced wall at the entrance. The huts of this period were of stone and had clay floors. Work on the third phase was probably carried out at the time of Frontinus's campaign in the Welsh Marches. A third rampart and ditch were raised between the first and second earthworks and the entrance was moved to the east end. The fort continued to be occupied into the Romano-British period as evidenced by finds of coarse, wheel-turned pottery.

Note: Monnington Straddel, marked on the Ordnance Survey map simply as Monnington Court, is 1.1/4m ENE of the church at Vowchurch and has its own article.

WACTON *2.75m NW of Bromyard*

The hamlet lies at the end of a dead-end lane off the Bromyard to Leominster road, 1m NNE of Bredenbury, and stands on high ground between two tributary streams of the River Frome. This is sparsely-populated hill country, renowned as a hop growing area. But, though the parish of Wacton had 100 acres of hops in 1810, by 1910 and ever since there have been none.

The Court house and a couple of cottages stand watch over a woebegone little group: the embankments and cuttings of the dismantled Bromyard to Leominster railway; the ruins of the church, pulled down in 1881; the doleful oval tump of an early Norman motte and bailey castle, which is about 26 yards in diameter at its widest point and rises to 12ft above the former ditch; and the site of a deserted mediaeval village where much pottery has been found after ploughing.

We like these places, full of melancholy spirits in deserted landscapes where the imagination takes over. The name Wacton is from the Anglo-Saxon Wacca's-tun.

WALFORD, near Leintwardine *1.5m SW of Leintwardine*

The name was Welleford in 1242, from the Old English waelle -ford, meaning 'ford over the river'. This place name shows the importance of going back to early name forms. If all one had was Walford it could be explained as meaning wealh-ford, 'the ford of the Welsh', as it is in Walford near Ross-on-Wye. Walford lies on the Leintwardine to Knighton road, the B4113, and is watered by a tributary stream of the River Teme. We entered from the east to be greeted by pine trees, the grey stone Walford Lodge, stone-built cottages and barns with weather-board cladding. Walford House is built of grey stone but has an

Pembridge Castle, Welsh Newton.

Above: General Sir Peter de Billiere, retired Director of the SAS, lives at Aston Crews near Weston under Penyard.

Vowchurch Herefordshire

horrendous red brick extension to the front. The Primitive Methodist chapel of 1866 has stone quoins and dressings and gets its feet wet in the stream that runs alongside, as do the pollarded trees in this flat, alluvial plain.

A quarter of a mile on, to the west of the chapel, one passes a round barrow (SO 386 723) on the south side of the road. The mound is 56ft in diameter and 3ft high, and a Roman urn was found beneath it in the 18th century.

However, we have now passed the village which lies south of the chapel. Inside the Court House there are the remains of a Jacobean plaster frieze with lozenge panels - one of which is inhabited by a forever-landlocked mermaid - and two capitals, one of the 12th century and one of the 13th century, probably looted from Wigmore Abbey, 1.1/2m SE.

Walford Castle lies 270 yards south of the crossroads, in a field near the road, at SO 391 724. All that remains is the motte of a Norman castle, about 30 yards in diameter and 10ft high above the ditch. There is a causeway on the south-west side. It did not have a bailey.

WALFORD, near Ross-on-Wye *2m S of Ross-on-Wye*
The name is from the Old English wealh-ford ,'ford of the Welsh'. In 1086 it was one of the extensive estates held by the Church of Hereford.

Walford is a long village. It straggles down the B4234 (turnpiked in 1791) for 1.1/2m, from Coughton in the north to Kerne Bridge in the south. The dominant landmark is Goodrich Castle, dramatically perched on its rocky red cliff to the west, but that has its own article.

Approaching from the south one passes a large timber yard and sawmill, the cream rendered Mill Race pub, a service station, Victorian and modern houses, the Memorial Hall, church, war memorial, stone barns and stone walls, Walford Court with an animal pound opposite, and the school with a well done brick extension. Walford lies in the flat valley of the Wye and the country around is mostly laid to pasture. It is not the most exciting place in the world, but there are things of interest hereabouts.

The church is dedicated to Saint Michael and All Angels, a dedication that often denotes a pre-Conquest site. Parts of the nave are Norman; the rest is mostly of the 13th century. The north chapel was paid for by the mediaeval lords of the manor, the de Walford family. Elsewhere there are monuments to William Adams, died 1681; Edmund Yerne, died 1707; and John Stratford, died 1738.

Close to the church is Walford Court, which lies adjacent to the track of the disused railway that ran from Ross to Monmouth. Just 50 yards NE of the church is the site of an irregular-shaped Roman military camp. In the last century a hoard of some 18,000 Roman coins dated A.D. 290-360 was unearthed here.

Half a mile to the north-east is Old Hill Court, a handsome timber-framed house of the 16th century. Just to the west is the approach avenue of the large, symmetrical, brick mansion of Hill Court. This was built in 1698-1700 and the one-bay wings were added in 1732. Inside there is a good hall and staircase; outside are impressive gate piers and gates (the iron work is of 1933), and an octagonal dovecote topped by a lantern. The gardens are a feature and the attached retail Garden Centre is open daily.

One mile north-east of the church is The Cedars, a good, Late-Georgian house of four bays with a two bay pediment and four Doric porch columns. Upper Wythall, meaning 'willow slope', lies 1/2m ENE of the church. It does, indeed, lie on the lower slopes of Bull's Hill and can be seen from the main road. It is a striking black and white house with several irregular gables and has been tastefully restored in recent times. Higher up the hill is another timber-framed house. Opposite this is a rare black poplar tree. Carry on further and one enters a large area of rough, wooded, common-like hill country laced with rough tracks and dotted with 17th and 18th century miners' cottages. It stretches from Howle Hill and Deep Dean, near Caughton in the north, to the banks of the Wye at Drybrook, in the south, west to Ley's Hill and east to Kiln Green and The Dam.

The rocks here are different from elsewhere in Herefordshire; they are blue-grey carboniferous limestones that contain deposits of coal, iron and lead. There are signs - slag and patches of black burned earth. - of Roman age iron smelting on some hilltops

In later times iron working was centred on Bishopswood, a little to the south. It began in earnest in 1590 with the Earl of Essex. Blast furnaces were built by the Foley family (ironmasters from the Black Country) in the reign of Charles II.

By 1801 the works were in the possession of the Partridge brothers, John and William, who also had holdings in the Forest of Dean and in South Wales. They did not smelt iron ore here. They had forges in which crude pig iron (full of impurities which made it very coarse and brittle) was heated and beaten with great hammers to refine it into more useful wrought iron. The fuel they used was charcoal. Although coal was available it did not burn hot enough. The charcoal was made by burning local trees and the flat terraces made by the charcoal burners can still be found - beneath the grass the earth is black.

The forges were powered by water-wheels and therefore were always situated either on rivers or in the valleys of streams, where the water could be dammed to give a controlled flow.

Coal was mined but only used for domestic heating and firing hop kilns. The seams outcropped here and when the easily reached deposits had been removed the land reverted to woodland or rough pasture. The coal and iron were transported down the Wye from the Bishopswood Wharf, now known as Pebbley Beach. However, the river could only be used in the Spring and Autumn because in winter it was often a raging torrent and in summer it had impassable shallows. Packhorses were the only alternative then.

The church of All Saints at Bishopswood was paid for by John Partridge, designed by John Plowman, Junior, and built in 1845. This essentially simple church, with its half-machiolated bellcote, is constructed of stone and stands in woodland facing the Wye. Adjacent is the school of 1850, also paid for by John Partridge. It is now a private house. The Bishopswood estate was dispersed in 1949.

The handsome Kerne Bridge was built in 1834 to a design by B.D. Jones. The name means 'the bridge by the mill', from the Old English cwyrn, 'quern', a millstone. On the west bank are the remains of the now much redeveloped Flanesford Priory. Just south of the bridge, opposite the pub, is a County Council Picnic Site, complete with car parking and bench tables. There is also a shop and a post office nearby. At Great Howle, 1.1/2m E of Walford church, there is is a prehistoric hill fort, a rectangular enclosure with earth walls nearly 10ft high.

To conclude, a little pot pourri. Roger Whittaker, the mellow-voiced singer, lives at The Cleaves on the back road from Walford to Ross. At Kiln Green, 1m ESE of Walford church at SO 601 196, is an isolated pub called New Buildings. Beside the door is an enamelled sign advertising Golden Hop Pale Ale brewed by the Alton Court Brewery in Station Street, Ross-on-Wye, which existed from 1846 to 1956. If living life in the fast lane is not exhilerating enough for you why not try a bit of slow-moving aerial terror and take a balloon trip over the Wye Gorge. Ross Balloons of Springfield, Walford will oblige.

WALTERSTONE *7m NNE of Abergavenny*
It lies lost in the Welsh borders and is most easily approached from Pandy on the Abergavenny to Hereford road, the A465. The name in 1249 was Walterestun, meaning 'Walter's manor'; Walter de Lacy held the manor soon after the Norman Conquest.

Walterstone stands on a hillside overlooking the River Monnow which here forms the border with Wales. The distinctive hill to the south-west is Sugar Loaf Hill above Abergavenny. The farms of the parish are scattered evenly over the hills in the distinctive Welsh pattern that arose from 'gavelkind', the traditional Celtic inheritance system, whereby a man's property was divided equally between his sons and not passed on intact to the eldest as in England. Many of the farmhouses in the parish have old cores often not apparent externally. For example: Court Farm, 350 yards SE of the church, has an internal mediaeval cruck truss forming a pointed arch; Upper Goytre, 3/4m E, has a room with moulded beams of about 1590; and Allt-y-Ynys, 1m SSW, has a plaster ceiling of about 1600. The church of Saint Mary has nave and chancel of about 1400 with a large Victorian bellcote. The doorway is Tudor; the font is 13th century; the chest is 17th century, as is a piece of stained glass in the chancel with heraldic emblems and foliage; in the churchyard is a cross with the shaft intact and pine trees for company.

One hundred yards west of the church are the earthworks of a Norman motte and bailey castle. The motte has a diameter of about 50 yards at the base and rises to about 50ft above the ditch. The bailey is kidney-shaped and still discernible to the east and south-east, mostly bounded by a scarp, with the remains of a rampart to the south. A circular mound, 300 yards SW of the church, might be a Bronze-Age burial place. The barrow is about 21ft in diameter and something over 2ft in height. Walterstone Camp is a circular Iron-Age hill fort situated on a spur, 1/2m E of the church. It occupies a site of about 4.1/2 acres and has entrances to the south-west and the north-east. Small forts are often quite old. It has three impressive ramparts covered with woodland, and in the enclosure is a mysterious, neglected garden. It covers several acres and amongst the trees and shrubs copper beech, bamboo, tulip tree, magnolia, acacia and azalea. The garden is now wild and overgrown.

Beyond the north-eastern ramparts are a series of rectangular mounds and ditches possibly related to the chapel known to have existed in the area. The nearby farm is called The Grove, and one cannot but speculate that this may have been the site of an early Celtic religious centre.

Here is a little mystery. In the 18th century a Roman settlement was discovered in the area and a mosaic pavement was removed. Not only has the mosaic disappeared but there is now no record of the site itself.

A modified form of the ancient custom of sin-eating lingered into the 20th century at Walterstone. Before a funeral the mourners drank port wine and ate biscuits in the presence of the corpse to transfer the sins of the deceased and so let it rest in peace. If this were not done the sinful spirit would return in a distressed state. An old man at Walterstone told Mrs. E.M. Leather: "No murderer can sail the sea, for the ship will sink. That's the auld sayin' but I dunna believe it myself." A local cure for a ruptured child was to split a young ash tree into two halves, pass the child through it, thus transferring the problem to the tree, and then bind whole again with nine nut tree withies.

The custom of riding the stang was practised into the 20th century at Walterstone. This was a public disgrace ceremony that involved burning the effigy of a person who had behaved in a socially unacceptable way, especially by being unfaithful to a marriage partner. In ancient times it would have been the person who was burned alive, not their effigy. The Druids still cast their shadow over this land.

Allt-y-rynys, 1m SSW of Walterstone, is a handsome, mellow, stone house with 15th century parts but re-made in the early 18th century. It is beautifully positioned below the hill, at the confluence of the River Monnow and the Honddu, and was once the home of the great-uncle of Lord Burleigh, Treasurer to Queen Elizabeth I.

WELLINGTON *5m NNW of Hereford*
In 1038 the name was Weolintun, which is thought to be derived from weo-leah, meaning 'the temple clearing'; but it could also mean 'Weola's clearing', Weola being a personal name. The Anglo-Saxon weoh, meaning 'holy', is thought by some to be the root of the river name Wye. We doubt it; most river names are pre-Celtic.

In Hereford Cathedral library there is an ancient Latin version of the Gospels on the back of which is a note written in Anglo-Saxon in the reign of King Canute (1017-1035). This is a very rare written record of a decision made by an Anglo-Saxon Shire-mote, a meeting of the Bishop, the Sheriff and the noblemen (thanes) of the county, at which disputes were settled. To cut a long story short, a man complained to the Court that his mother would not give him land he thought rightfully his. This land lay at Wellington and Eardisley. The mother was questioned. She said she had no land that pertained to her son and she was very angry with him. The Court bore witness that she wished all her property, money and clothes to go to a female relative who was married to Thurcyl the White. Thurcyl then went straight to Hereford and made a note of this decision in the Gospel Book.

He did this as a precaution because records of Mote Court decisions were not taken as a matter of course. The Court met at Aegelnoth's Stone, which is now lost but used to stand at the top of Aylestone Hill in Hereford. The name Aylestone is thought to be derived from Aegelnoth's Stone.

Domesday Book records that a Thurcil held the manor of Walinstone in 1066. It was a flourishing and well-populated place with two mills, holdings of salt at Droitwich, a priest, a reeve, a smith and four radknights (civilian riding men who carried messages and did escort duties).

Wellington is a substantial village. It stands on the Wellington Brook and adjoins the A49, yet is easily missed as one hurries by on the busy main road. It stretches for a mile to the west, and though there has been some new development it retains its ancient charm. Along the main street there are houses of mellow red brick and timber-framing of all ages, an early 18th century octagonal dovecote, a barn with wattle infill, and a post office-cum-general store. Out on the main road, at Wellington Marsh, by the numerous sheds of the Army Ordnance Depot, are the village policeman's house and the Old Comrade Inn. At the junction with the A49 is Bridge House, formerly the Bridge Inn, a large, Early-Georgian building of eight bays with segment-headed windows and angle pilasters that is now derelict. The blacksmith's shop used to stand opposite Bridge House but this was dismantled, when the main road was widened, and rebuilt at the Avoncroft Museum, near Bromsgrove.

Adjacent to the forge site are the Almshouses founded by Sir Herbert Perrott in 1682, but rebuilt in 1887, Queen Victoria's Jubilee year. Still in the main street, Bridge Farm is a substantial black and white building with sturdy, square framing and a good range of brick and timber-framed outbuildings, bounded by the stream and an orchard. The east wing houses the first floor solar of about 1400. This, the main living room, has the original, massive, arched, brace truss and a large stone fireplace; the decorated plaster ceiling is of about 1600. The west wing has thinner framing and was built in the 17th century to house a hop kiln.

The church of Saint Margaret has an unusual Norman tower, a mixture of rubble and dressed stone with broad buttresses pierced by deep windows. Also Norman are the north and south doorways and a south window in the nave. The chancel is 13th century Early English and has a very fine piscina; the aisle is 15th century Perpendicular, with octagonal piers in the arcade, and a good roof of quatrefoiled wind-braces. The pulpit is Jacobean and there is a notable monument to Sir Herbert Perrott, died 1683. In the churchyard, which is raised 5ft above road level, there is a 14th century cross with its original 12ft, five-sided shaft. Adjacent to the churchyard is the Old Parsonage which has a 14th century core. In 1636 a new vicarage was built, now called the Old Vicarage.

Wellington Court is a handsome, square, brick house accessed from a lane by the ford. This was a home of the Tomkins family who played a major part in the development of the Hereford cattle breed. At the west end of the main street a lane leads north, over the Wellington Brook, past some late timber-framed houses with skinny timbers, to Woonton. In the big broadleaved wood to the north there used to be lime kilns. The woods stretch westwards to Lawton Hope, one of the places where Owain Glyndwr is reputed to have died.

East of the wood on the A49, nearly 1.1/2m NNE of the church, is Burghope. Burghope Court is a 17th century haunted house. Samuel Goodere, a sea captain, was concerned that his elder brother, John, was going to disinherit him so he had him murdered on board his ship. Samuel was found out and hanged at Bristol in April 1741. A sad little tale.

Auberrow, 1/2m off the main street of Wellington, is an outlying hamlet. Berrow is from the Anglo-Saxon meaning 'a hill' or 'a mound'. The prefix would be from a personal name. At Wellington Quarry, 3/4m E of the village at SO 508 480, the remains of an Iron-Age lowland farm settlement were discovered, one of only two so far located in Herefordshire. (The other is at Kenchester.) In 1988 a new gravel pit was opened on the border of the parishes of Wellington and Morden, 1.1/2m E, and the remains of a Roman villa were discovered. It is said that the first cuckoo of Spring in Herefordshire is heard at Wellington.

WELLINGTON HEATH *1.1/2m N of Ledbury*

The name is from the Anglo-Saxon and probably means 'the temple clearing on the heath'. It lies around a steep-sided valley amongst orchards and woods in the foothills of the Malverns. There are a few older houses but this is very much a leafy suburb of Ledbury. There is a pub, a memorial hall, a wind pump, and a few small 18th century black and white dwellings, but most of the houses are of the 20th century. Christ Church was built in 1951 using parts from the previous church of 1840.

Notable houses in the parish include Peg's Farm, 1/2m NW of the church. This is a substantial, 14th century, timber-framed dwelling in which the well-preserved roof timbers of the open hall have been exposed to reveal the original roof-trusses, the spere truss, and foiled openings above the collar beams. The spere truss is not altogether common in Herefordshire. It stands on two posts placed far enough away from the walls to allow doors to be placed in the spaces at ground level with a screen between them. At Peg's Farm the horizontal division of the hall, to make a ground floor and a first floor was done early, in the 16th century, and the floor joists are heavily moulded beams. In the 17th century a parlour wing was added with thinner framing than the main house.

Woodhouse Farm, 1.1/2m WNW, has a mediaeval cruck truss of the original open hall. Burton's Farm, 3/4m SW, has close-set vertical framing of the early 16th century, and square framing of the 17th century. Prior's Court, 1m WNW, is a large red brick house.

At Frith Farm, 3/4m SSE of the church, numerous Neolithic flint flakes and artefacts have been found scattered over a wide area. These include fragments of polished axes, used for tree-felling, and leaf-shaped arrow heads.

Staplow, 1.1/4m WNW of the church, is a pleasant main road hamlet on the B4214, Ledbury to Bromyard road. The name means the 'prehistoric burial mound with a pillar (or a post)'. It stands on a low hill and there is a good Victorian house, a stand of Scots firs, brick and render and black and white cottages, the Oak Inn, and hopyards and orchards.

Hope End, 3/4m NE of the church, is a beautifully situated house at the end of a lovely, hidden valley surrounded by woodland. The land was held by Roger and Juliana de Hope in the 13th century. A Queen Anne house was here when Edward Moulton-Barrett arrived in 1809. He was a Jamaican sugar plantation owner who had received a legacy and who set about spending some of it on a new house. This was fancifully decorated with Moorish motifs - minarets, cupolas, ogee caps and the like. The Queen Anne house was converted to stables and similarly attired. In the 1870s Mr. Moulton's Moorish house was demolished, but the stables were retained. A new Victorian house was built on the hill to the left of the entrance drive by the walled garden. That burned down in 1910 and the ruins are now amongst the trees. The present house was fashioned out of the stables and is now run as a hotel by Patricia Hegarty, the author of *An English Flavour*, subtitled Recipes from an English Country Garden. The Queen Anne house to the left front of the hotel is of the 20th century. The old stone and stucco courtyard gate pillars, the patio with a fountain, the old stables and the new Queen Anne house make a charming and quaint ensemble in a setting that would be hard to better.

It was in this delightful spot that Elizabeth Barrett-Browning (the daughter of Edward Moulton-Barrett) had some of the happiest days of her life and she often wrote and alluded to this place in poems such as *The Deserted Garden* and *The Lost Bower*. Then came the riding accident, at 15 years of age, which made her an invalid for the rest of her life. This was followed by the death of her mother and the family's move to London, to Wimpole Street, followed by the drowning of her brother at Torquay and, the harsh, though well-meaning treatment she

Roman fort, Buckton
near Brampton Bryan. The photograph is an aerial view of the site of a Roman border fortress at SO 390 733. The outline of the foundations is shown in a field of ripening corn. The original fort had an earth and turf rampart but this was subsequently strengthened with stone walls and gatehouses. The drawing is a reconstruction of the east gatehouse. The interior buildings were of timber and were serviced by a symmetrical grid of roads. About 140 A.D. the fort was dismantled and the stone was taken away, presumably to be used elsewhere. Some may have been used to construct the 2nd century bath-house at Leominster, the stone of which shows signs of having been used previously.
(After S.C. Stanford, *The Archaeology of the Welsh Marches*, 1980. Photograph: W.A. Baker.)

received from her father. Finally, she found happiness with Robert Browning in Italy where she died in 1861. Today she is better known for her tragic story than her poetry - a final twist of the knife.

At Burton's Farm, and stretching north, is a surviving section of the short-lived Gloucester to Hereford Canal, completed in 1845.

WELSH BICKNOR *4 SSW of Ross-on-Wye*

The name means 'Bica's ridge'. There is also an English Bicknor, 1.1/2m SSW in Gloucestershire. The River Wye makes a great meandering loop, part of the famous gorge south of Ross, and Welsh Bicknor is effectively on an inland peninsula and only approachable down a lane from Goodrich, though there is a bridge linking a quarry to the works across the river in Gloucestershire.

The church of Saint Margaret is down by the river and reached by a steep path. It was built in 1859 by T.H. Rushforth and paid for by the vicar, Stephen Allaway. The style is mixed Norman and Early English, and the materials and workmanship are of a high order. The south arcade, for example, has a rich alabaster capital carved with heads of the Four Evangelists, and the pulpit, font and reading desk are carved out of expensive Caen limestone. All that was kept from the preceding church were two mediaeval bells and the superb late-13th century effigy of a lady. She wears a barbe-and-coif head-dress and her dress has tight sleeves under a draped gown with angels at her pillow and a little dog at her feet. This is believed to be Margaret Montacute, the wife of Sir John, whose father had arrested Roger Mortimer, the first Earl of March. Mortimer had eyes on the throne, and was therefore a great threat to the boy king, Edward III.

Courtfield, about 600 yards ESE of the church, is magnificently situated on a wooded bluff overlooking the river. It was the home of the local squires, the Vaughan family, for some 300 years. In the 19th century Colonel Francis Vaughan and his wife Louisa had 13 children; six of them became priests and four became nuns. Herbert, one of their sons, became Cardinal Vaughan and it was he who founded the Mill Hill Fathers who now occupy the house and train young men for missionary work. The present building dates mostly from 1805. Its mediaeval predecessor was home to Henry V as a child. When he became king he gave his old nurse, Joanna Waring, a £20 annuity. The future hero of Agincourt's house is gone but he would doubtless recognise the park where he played. It was Henry's father, King Henry IV, who had battled with the Welsh leader, Owain Glyndwr, for 10 years in these border lands.

WELSH NEWTON *3m N of Monmouth*

It stands on the scenic hill road from Monmouth to Hereford, the A466, less than a mile from the Welsh border and firmly in the extensive Norman Hundred of Arkenfield, where Welsh customs were allowed to prevail in the Middle Ages. The name means 'new town', but new in Anglo-Saxon times when almost everyone in this area was Welsh.

It is an attractive little settlement that consists of a some new stone cottages, a couple of bungalows, a strange farmhouse with one-bay extensions to each side, a group of tall specimen trees, a small transport yard, a war memorial, and the parish church of Saint Mary. It lies on the Mally Brook which has cut a steep-sided gorge through the wooded Buckholt Hill before heading south to join the River Wye. Buckholt is from the Old English boc-holt, meaning 'beechwood'. Dotted alongside the road, crammed in between the highway and the stream, are little stone cottages, and just short of the border with Gwent is Saint John's church, a chapel-like stone building.

On high ground, a mile to the south-west, is Welsh Newton Common with clusters of old squatters' cottages on dead-end lanes and a lot more people than the main road village, enough in fact to have supported a chapel and a post office. Out on its own dead-end lane is St. Wulstan's Farm. South of the common is Callow Hill. Callow is from calu meaning 'bald headed', 'bare hill'.

The village church of Saint Mary is in the old village by the main road. It has nave and chancel in one and a small stone spire, all of the 13th century. The stone rood screen between the nave and the chancel is decorated with ball-flower, octagonal shafts and moulded arches. It is of the early 14th century, a very early date for a rood screen of stone. At the same time a Decorated dormer window was inserted to light it. The barrel roof is 16th century; the font is Norman; and the stone seat in the chancel is 13th century, another quite rare piece.

Saint Mary's had a chantry founded in 1547. (Essentially, a chantry was a sum of money invested to pay for a priest to sing or pray for the soul of the founder.) This must have been one of the last, if not the last, chantry to be founded in England because the king was already planning to confiscate all chantry funds as belonging to children of Popery.

The church has two bells and the jingle they are said to chime is: "Erfen, cawl, Erfen, Turnip, turnip soup". The soil on these hills is not of the best. In the churchyard is a mediaeval cross with a modern shaft and a tomb-slab with the inscription: I.K. Dyed the 22 August Anno Do 1679. This marks the grave of the Catholic priest, John Kemble, who was executed in 1679. Kemble stayed at Pembridge Castle where he was chaplain to the Catholic Scudamores. From here he sallied forth to minister to recusants (Catholics who refused to attend Church of England services) around the country. In 1678 the Bishop of Hereford ordered his arrest and Kemble was taken to Hereford gaol. He was charged with saying mass at Pembridge Castle, found guilty, sentenced to death, and was duly hanged on Widemarsh Common, Hereford. He was 80 years old. One of his hands was cut off after his execution by a follower and is now contained in a reliquary at Saint Francis Xavier's church in Hereford. Kemble was beatified in 1926 and canonised in 1970 by Pope Paul IV.

Pembridge Castle, 1m NW of Welsh Newton, is a well preserved picture-book castle, the kind of place you see in a Robin Hood film. It lies on high ground, on a slope, surrounded by a dry moat with curtain walls and towers protecting an internal rectangular courtyard. If one stands in front of the castle, the west (left) tower is the Norman tower-keep of about 1200. Adjoining it, centre-front behind the curtain wall of about 1280, are the 17th century kitchen and parlour. Next, at the east (right) corner, is the massive gatehouse of about 1280 with its portcullis and two semi-circular towers. The most easterly (right) of these has been much restored. If one now moves up the slope (right) one can see over the central, easterly curtain wall into the courtyard. This was not possible originally but the walling was damaged during the Civil War and has been restored at a much lower level - see the original height on the right. In the rear east corner is a round turret. In the rear west corner is another round turret and against it is the charming 16th century chapel. Beneath the chapel is an early mediaeval tunnel-vaulted undercroft. South of the chapel is the 17th century house, still used as such.

It is called Pembridge Castle because the earliest holders were from the village of that name in northern Herefordshire. Ralph de Pembridge, who died in 1219, may well have built the earliest parts of the castle. By 1387 it had passed to the Mortimers and then follows a litany of owners: Hopton, Baynham, Pye, then by Massey and Scudamore (successively as conquerors during the Civil War), Kemble (a relative of the martyred John Kemble), Scudamore, Townley and Bailey. By then it had been neglected but in the early 20th century it was heavily restored for use as a private residence and it remains as such today.

The castle does not advertise itself from the approach road. It comes as a surprise to the traveller - indeed it could easily be missed - and can only be seen over a five-bar gate.

If you have approached Pembridge Castle from the south, from Welsh Newton, continue to head northwards and you will be rewarded with the scenic delights of the Monnow Valley, a lovely, soft, romantic vale with the Welsh hill jagged on the horizon. The road from Welsh Newton, via Pembridge Castle, Broad Oak and Garway to Great Corras and Kentchurch is one of the unsung treasures of Herefordshire. But do not tell anyone; keep it to yourself. We first travelled this road on a June evening with a silver-grey storm light to the west, a time when the dragons of Wales cross the border to feed on careless English maidens.

WEOBLEY *7.5m SW of Leominster*

Weobley is pronounced Webbley. The name is from the Old English Weobba's-leah. Leah can mean either 'a wood', or 'a glade in a wood', usually a natural glade, not a man-made clearing. It is one of the few settlements in Herefordshire whose name is known to people outside the area. "It is", I once heard an American say, "one of the great little black and white towns of England", and he had probably seen more of England than most Englishmen. Almost every kind of timber beam, brace, truss, collar, post, panel and stud can be found in Weobley's 13th to 16th century houses. However, it is their grouping that is important; it is the ensemble that impresses.

On our first visit chance brought us to the Old Corner House, at the bottom of Broad Street. This is a cosy 14th century hall house with a cross-wing at the north end. The hall was originally open to the roof but had a first-floor horizontal division inserted during the 16th century. The house is presently occupied by Bob Kilvert, an artist with an international reputation. He specialises in water colours and collages and runs a range of holiday-tuition courses with assistance from Neil Meacher, Jean Grieve and Sandra Children. His guests stay at either the Old Corner House itself or at one of three other equally charming houses, also in Broad Street: The Gables, a mediaeval hall house with two cross-wings; the 16th century Tudor cottage with a Georgian front bedecked with climbing greenery and flowers, and Mellington House, a 15th century dwelling with an imposing Georgian four-bay facade, hipped roof and dormers. Bob Kilvert's wife, Julia, is a cook, print-maker and singer and runs the coffee shop-cum-display gallery on the ground floor which is open to the public daily. Opposite the Old Corner House is that fast-disappearing rural amenity, a family run garage with kerbside petrol pumps. Far from trying to close down such rare establishments the Council ought to be putting conservation orders on them. They are not only quaint and redolent of another, more leisurely age, they are convenient.

We must now launch into something of a list of notable buildings in the town. The Red Lion, at the bottom of Broad Street, has a 14th century cross-wing with square framing and arched braces in the gable. Behind it is a 13th century cruck cottage, one of the very oldest buildings in the town. Both houses feature in the famous picture postcard view of Weobley. West of the Red Lion is the Tudor House which is actually a 14th century hall house.

Broad Street used to have a central row of houses but these were destroyed by fire in 1943. They have been replaced by Council maintained gardens and a bus shelter. The Mansion House has a footnote in social history because in the 16th century 33 children were born to James Tonkins and his two wives. They were all born in the same room and all survived. On the western side of Broad Street is a 15th century house, now a shop, of the Wealden type, i.e. the central hall range has coving to bring its roof in line with the projecting wings.

The only other Wealden houses in Herefordshire are two that lie just around the corner and are now part of the Unicorn Hotel in High Street. Chamber Walk, also in High Street, is 14th century with square framing and an original mullioned window. In Hereford Street is The Throne, a house of about 1600, and the Old Grammar School, built just after 1658, which has a symmetrical front, a central porch with carved balusters, and pendants on the window sills. Finally, the Manor House in Bell Street is superb, and the Dairy Farm in Kington Road has big cruck trusses.

The church of Saint Peter and Saint Paul stands at the north end of the village adjacent to open country. It has a tall, 14th century tower with a tall, slender spire which is a landmark for many miles around and which provides the focal point of the famous picture postcard view of Weobley. It is the only spire in the county to be supported by little flying buttresses connected to pinnacles rising from the tower. The south doorway is Norman with zig-zag decoration and the chancel and the south transept are late 13th century. Of the early 14th century are the five-bay arcades with octagonal piers and ballflower, the north transept, the clerestory, the image recess south of the chancel arch. the octagonal font, parts of the stone pulpit, and the screen. In the tracery of a north window are some fine 15th century figures of little angels.

In more recent times a 20th century window was dedicated to the memory of the folklorist Ella Mary Leather. Hugo Bissop of Norton Canon, died about 1430, is commemorated by a 13th century coffin lid with a finely executed foliated cross, and Sir William Deveraux, died about 1430, lies here in alabaster effigy. Also in alabaster are Dame Alice Crutwell and Sir John Marbury, died 1437.

Here, too, is a grandiose white marble statue of Colonel John Birch, the redoubtable Bristol trader-cum-Cromwellian soldier, who lived in Weobley after the Restoration, and who was a Member of Parliament for the town from 1679 to his death in 1691. His monument caused resentment amongst the townspeople for its size, its position near the altar, and the arrogant inscription. It had to be protected by railings and on the orders of the Bishop of Hereford the inscription was removed. Later, when it was reinstated the Colonel's birth date was given incorrectly; it was 1615, not 1626.

To the north-east of the church a low earth bank can be seen. This was part of the town's early defences. Weobley Castle lies on a level site, 1/4m S of the church, uphill at the other end of the village. All that we have today is a ringwork with an oval bailey, about 80 yards by 68 yards wide to the north, and a strong outer bank to the south, the whole being surrounded by moats. The ringwork has been badly eroded but the eastern part probably survives to its original height. However, this is but a shadow of the substantial, stone-built fortress detailed in a plan of 1655 made by Silas Taylor. There were six round towers joined by curtain walls with a gateway, and within there was a rectangular keep with round corner towers. The keep was probably 13th century.

The first timber castle on the site was probably built by Walter de Lacy shortly after the Norman Conquest. Walter came from Lassy, in the Department of Calvados, France. His wife was Ermelina and by her he had a son, Roger, who inherited his father's estates when he died in 1085, the year before Domesday Book. Roger held the extensive 'fief with land' at Ewyas Lacy (now Longtown), and in Herefordshire as a whole he had 75 manors, but his principal seat was at Weobley. He played an important part in defending the frontier against the Welsh. In 1088 and 1094 he rebelled against William Rufus and was banished. His lands were given to his brother, Hugh, and later formed the Honour of Weobley. Roger went back to Normandy where he attained high office under Duke Robert and died some time after 1106.

But to return to Weobley Castle. In 1138 King Stephen captured it and in 1208 the castle was used as a base by William de Braose during his rebellion against King John. It was from here that he marched out to burn Leominster. Then it went to Walter de Lacy by marriage in 1200. He was the Sheriff of Herefordshire from 1216 to 1223 and as such was all powerful in the county. It was almost certainly he who raised the stone walls and towers to defend the castle from the Welsh. Subsequently, it passed to the Verdons and then to the Deveraux family who were to become Earls of Essex in the reign of Elizabeth I. The last Earl died in 1646 and the castle went by marriage to the Dukes of Somerset, and then to the Thynne family.

Weobley was important enough in the late-13th century to be entitled to have two Members of Parliament. The burgesses were disenfranchised in 1307, apparently because they refused to pay their M.P.'s expenses of two shillings a day - a lot of money at the time. The right was reinstated in 1628 and there were some hard fought elections amongst several of the county's big landowners. However, by 1754 Weobley's two parliamentary seats were virtually the property of the Marquises of Bath, the Thynne family of Wiltshire. As lords of the manor they had bought up the majority of the town's burgage tenements, only the tenants of which had the right to vote. Weobley was now one of the 72 'rotten boroughs' of England. You did not vote against the wishes of your landlord if you wanted to keep the roof over your head. What is more, whereas a handful of burgesses in Weobley had two members, Manchester and other large industrial towns had none at all.

In 1832 the Third Reform Bill was passed and the 'pocket boroughs' were abolished. Now that their rented-out houses no longer bought parliamentary seats the Thynnes demolished at least 40 of them, presumably to avoid maintenance costs; some were prize specimens as old illustrations demonstrate.

Many of the Weobley town papers are now at Longleat, the Thynnes' principal seat. Their house at Weobley was Garnstone Castle, a neo-Gothic mansion built for them by John Nash in 1807. The house and park stood on the southern outskirts of the town adjacent to the Norman castle. It replaced the house that Colonel Birch had bought in 1661 and lived in after the Restoration of Charles II, Incidentally, the old Cromwellian rogue became a staunch Royalist. He could have taught any sea captain a thing or two about sailing with the wind. Then came the infamous 1950s when England lost so many of its wonderful country houses. In 1959 Garnstone Castle was pulled down. The landscaped park with its specimen trees remains, but of the big house all that remains, are some stone and weather-boarded barns, and ruined, ivy-clad service buildings. Today the estate is owned by Major Philip Verdin of The Butt House, Canon Pyon, 4m ESE, a major local landowner.

The wealth of Weobley lay in its flourishing market and two fairs and as a regional service centre; there used to be many more shops than there are now. It prospered from the mediaeval wool trade, and the area was known for its fine fleeces throughout Europe. In the 17th and 18th centuries there were well-established weaving and glove-making industries which peaked during the early 19th cent-ury, when the wars with Napoleon curtailed imports from France. Of some consequence, too, was nailmaking and the town's brewery trade was famous - Weobley ale was much admired in Wales. The magnificent old Market Hall reflected this long-term wealth, but alas it has been pulled down.

A local saying is "Poor Weobley, proud people, Low church, high steeple." Though rich in mediaeval times and always economically sound enough, nevertheless, Weobley in the second half of the 19th century and the early 20th century was 'very quiet', as they say. Indeed, that is why so many old houses have survived. Had the wealth of the industrial revolution been theirs they would have been replaced by fashionable Victorian town houses and villas. In relative terms the people of Weobley were poor, as, indeed, was most of Herefordshire.

By Herefordshire standards Weobley is still a small town. It has several shops, including a butcher's, a hardware shop, a general store, a tea shop, a post office, Jean's Fashions, and a newsagent. It also has three pubs, two restaurants, a doctor, a dentist, a village hall, playing fields, and a small industrial estate. Nicholas Farah Rhodes restores old timber-framed buildings, and an agricultural machinery dealer has taken over the gaunt Victorian mill. There are two estates of modern houses, two schools, a Methodist chapel and a Roman Catholic church. The latter is Saint Thomas of Hereford. It was built in 1834 and is constructed of stone with pointed, two-light windows. The attached brick-built priest's house is taller and has three bays and two storeys. The Weobley Rural District Council offices are located in the Old Workhouse, a Georgian-style red brick building of about 1836.

In Back Lane there is a small local museum. In a field off the lane the local history group excavated a kiln (SO 401 515) of the 14th to 15th centuries, the earliest known mediaeval kiln site in the county.

The Ley stands 3/4m SW of the church. Many consider it to be the finest timber-framed house in Herefordshire. The oak timbers have been left untreated to gleam silver-grey as nature intended; it has gables galore, in the wings, over the windows and over the porch, which is set off-centre to the mediaeval hall. The house is 'H'-shaped and was built for James Brydges in 1589. Early in the 19th century a paper was found in the roof which granted safe conduct to a member of the family during the Civil War. Another outlying farm, Throne Farm, 1/2m NE of the church, has a Civil War association, for it was here that

Top left:
Weobley, Broad Street.
Top right:
Ella Mary Leather, author of
The Folk-Lore of Herefordshire.
Middle left:
Weobley, monument of Colonel John
Birch in church of Saint Peter and Saint Paul.
Middle right:
Weobley, the Unicorn Hotel.
Opposite:
Wormbridge, landscape.

Charles Stuart (Charles I) had supper and stayed the night after the Battle of Naseby in 1645. (Or was it at The Throne? a house in the town; sources differ.)

Little Sarnesfield, 1m W of the church, just off the main road, has a hall and two cross-wings probably of the 14th century. In the south wing are two of the original trusses, one with a tie beam, the other with a collar beam and arched braces. Beside the entrance lane there are the earthworks of a moated site, clearly visible from the main road. Whitehill, 1/4m NE of Little Sarnesfield, comprises a petrol filling station, a couple of cottages, and a small industrial estate, close by the Newbridge Brook. Fenhampton, 1.1/4m SW of the church, is a gabled Jacobean house. The name means 'dwellers by the fen'. At Weobley Marsh and Ledgemoor, 1m SE of the church, there are a few scattered squatters' cottages. The Marsh was locally known for its witches and diviners, about which more is said later.

In 1912 Mrs. Ella Mary Leather (nee Smith of Dilwyn, born 1874, died 1928) published her monumental book *The Folk-Lore of Herefordshire*. This was the result of many years assiduous collecting by Mrs. Leather and a handful of helpers. After her marriage, in 1893, this independently-minded, middle-class, Victorian lady gladly consorted with gypsies, farm labourers and hop-pickers in search of anything to do with the traditional stories, customs, songs and superstitions of Herefordshire. It is one of the most important works of its kind and has an international reputation. She sought out Cecil Sharp and Vaughan Williams, the leading folksong collectors of her day, and introduced them to the singers she had found. Between 1909 and 1922 they saved several hundred songs for posterity. What is more, many of these were of the very highest quality, matched perhaps by versions from other parts of the country, but not exceeded. Some of the carols are truly divine.

Living at Weobley Mrs. Leather naturally collected extensively in this area. One of her most fertile hunting grounds was The Homme, which stands on high ground 1m NE of Weobley, near Dilwyn. The original timber-framed manor house stood in the wood adjacent to the farmyard but was later replaced by the square, red brick Georgian house with two and a half storeys, three bays and a pyramid roof that we see today. To the left there is a substantial extension, and opposite are a good, red brick barn and an interesting granary-cum-stable block of about 1900, complete with a square hop kiln with a pyramid roof. The Homme is a 300-acre mixed arable sheep and cattle fattening farm with a 12-acre hopyard, and is one of the many estates owned by Major Philip Verdin.

The tenant farmer is John Pudge, a gentle, mild-mannered man with several equally likeable dogs. It was his grandfather, also John Pudge, who hired seasonal labour, which included gipsy families such as the Smiths and the Whattons, to bring in the Autumn hop harvest. It was largely from these travellers that Mrs. Leather collected and recorded many of the fine carols so admired by Vaughan Williams.

These songs are not of gipsy making; they are English traditional pieces that have survived amongst these wanderers. Their descendants still live in Herefordshire but the old songs are no longer of interest to them. Country and Western is now more to their taste. There used to be a gipsy camp 2m E on the A4110 but council officials closed it in 1995. They also dug ditches in the grass verges at a nearby crossroads (SO 442 551) to stop them using this traditional stopping place. It should be remembered that most caravan-dwelling gipsy families only travel in a relatively small area. Herefordshire Romanies rarely leave the county and have been here for many generations.

Both Herefordshire and Shropshire have their own council paid Gipsy Liaison Officers and unpaid Travellers' Support Groups. As guardians of lawful and moral rights the latter are by far the most effective. Indeed, most of their battles in the past have been with the council. The official Herefordshire Gipsy Count conducted by Pat Weale in January 1996 recorded 108 families with an average of about four members per family. Of these, 42 families lived on unauthorized roadside sites, 24 were camped on private sites, and 42 were on authorized Local Authority sites. Plus, of course, the 'ones that got away'. In the Autumn these numbers can double with 'foreigners' coming in for the seasonal work available on the fruit farms and in the hopyards. Labour is still needed in hopyards, it is just far less intensive than it used to be.

Here is a selection of the customs and superstitions Mrs Leather found in the town and the countryside around.

Relics of moon worship were common in the county. Pig killing and gardening operations were regulated by changes in the moon. At Weobley it was believed that nettles beaten with a stick on the day of the first full moon in May would not grow again. Flowers and herbs not only had medicinal properties but were often symbolic of human emotions and used for divination. Relics of this include the old man at Weobley who grew Sweet William and Fair Margaret, one to each side of his front door, so that lovers separated in life could grow and be joined in death.

It is a sign of rain when jackdaws flutter and caw around Weobley church spire. If bees are not told of the death of their owner, they will quickly die themselves, or cause another human to die. They must not be bought or sold or even given away. The bond with their owner is for life.

Dunwood Farm, 1m E of Weobley, used to be haunted by the ghost of Old Gregg. He was poisoned by his family who gave him stewed toad for supper. A farmer at Field's End, Weobley, committed suicide and came back as a calf at nearby Garnstone Park. The farmhouse was also haunted by a spirit that kept ripping the bedclothes off the bed. It was laid by a priest who lured it into a snuff box and then buried it in the pool in Garnstone Park.

In 1669 a farm rented by Elizabeth Bridges at Burton, 1.1/2m S of Weobley, was haunted by a veritable demon who overturned furniture, ruined food, knocked on doors, caused cows to die, a sow to do a dance of death, and many other mischiefs. A valiant Welshman called John Jones volunteered to stand guard one night to catch the culprit. There was a knock on the door, he opened it, and a multitude of cats rushed into his room screeching like banshees. The Welshman dropped his sword, his candle went out, his mastiff howled in terror, and they both fled the house for a half a mile before looking behind them.

To summon up the Devil all one has to do is walk slowly round the preaching cross in the churchyard seven times at midnight saying the Lord's Prayer backwards without making a mistake. Witches have no power over anyone who rides a broomstick so young boys at Weobley rode them like Hobby-horses, and taunted Old Charlotte, a Weobley witch, who could only shake her fists at them in frustration.

A nurse from Weobley Marsh would tell young women that if they were tidy about the house they would get assistance in their chores from a fairy, who would come at night when they were asleep. At Weobley Marsh they also believed that witches flew at night in the form of bats. There was also a diviner at the Marsh called Betty who was known to Mrs. Leather personally. Amongst other things she could make the receivers of lost or stolen property return the goods to their rightful owners. In many cases the mere fact that the loss had been reported to a diviner made its return quite likely because of belief in their powers to curse the dishonest.

A love charm used at Weobley was used by girls who wished to know the person they would marry. She had to walk around the church at midnight on Saint John's Eve without stopping and chant the following rhyme over and over:

"Hemp seed I sow,
Hemp seed I hoe,
Let him that's my true love,
Come after me and mow."

Her future husband then appeared in a vision.

Other customs practised at Weobley, such as those of Twelfth Night and Riding the Stang, were similar to those of other places in the county and are described elsewhere. Likewise, many of the generally held beliefs and ceremonies which Mrs. Leather does not give specific examples or locations of would have been held at Weobley.

WESTHIDE *5.5m ENE of Hereford*

The name means 'the western hide'. A hide in Herefordshire in 1086 was about 120 acres. In 1066 Westhide belonged to Queen Edith; by the time of Domesday Book it had passed to Ralph de Tosny III, also called Ralph de Conches. His chief seat was in Flamstead, Hertfordshire.

Westhide is one of the most unspoilt little villages in the county and the atmosphere here is positively mediaeval. The land is fertile and there are many sturdy, half-timbered yeoman-farmers' houses in the countryside around. The settlement is somewhat off the beaten track between Withington and Ocle Pychard.

We entered from the west past a raggledy farm with rotting corrugated iron, mud on the road, old barns stuffed with hay, black and white cottages, dwellings of stone and red brick and arrived at Westhide Court. The access lane to the Court is bordered by a delightful stone and red brick wall overhung with evergreen shrubs and ivy. The Court is most handsome. It is built of ashlar stone with a five-bay front flanked by projecting one-bay wings. The style is Georgian and it has hipped roofs, mullioned and transomed windows, and a stone porch with a parapet. It was in the process of being renovated when we called and jolly music blared, out much to the discomfort of the specimen trees in the garden. A lone horsewoman paraded down the lane, her head turned towards the church.

The tower of Saint Bartholomew's was raised in the 12th century, the same century that Ralph de Tosny died (1102). It is short, stocky and strongly built of grey stone with slit windows and a pyramid roof. Inside, the early, pointed arch to the nave has responds with trumpet-scallop capitals. The chancel and the north side of the nave were rebuilt in 1867, but the chancel arch and its two side windows and two corbels with carved heads are 14th century. Also 14th century are the nave roof and arcade, and the south aisle with its trefoiled piscina and carved corbel heads.

On the aisle walls is some mediaeval scroll work painted in red, and in the chancel are some early stained glass fragments, and a 15th century tile with the emblems of Saint Peter and Saint Paul. In the aisle recess is the effigy of a curly-headed, early 14th century civilian holding his heart in his hand. Nearby is a fragmentary 16th century Elizabethan slab with two effigies, and an alabaster slab with the engraved figures of Richard Monyngton, died 1524, and wife. He is in full armour with a dog at his feet, she in a girdled gown, and below them 16 children, eight boys and eight girls. The font is 13th century, likewise a coffin lid set in the modern porch. Next to the church is the Victorian, red brick former school dressed with stone and blue brick.

At Kymin, 1/2m N, the wooded bed of the old Hereford to Gloucester canal can be seen quite clearly. Westhide Wood, 1/2m S, is a large broadleaved wood, once the home of a badger-baiting friar. For this see the article on Tillington.

WESTON BEGGARD *4.5m ENE of Hereford*

It lies close to the river in the lush lowlands of the fertile valley of the Frome, an agricultural paradise of rich pastures, ploughlands, orchards and large hopyards with tall wind-break hedges. The name means 'settlement to the west belonging to Beggard', a family name probably derived from the Old French begard, used of a religious sect.

The hamlet has its own approach lane that runs between Bartestree on the A438 and Shucknall on the A4103. In 1066 it was simply called Westune and was held by Gunfrid. In 1086 it had a population of 17 families, a priest and a mill and was part of the extensive estates held by Roger de Lacy. Today the church has for company a clutch of white-capped hop kilns (oasthouses), a stand of cypresses and a couple of black and white dwellings, one of which is thought to have been the vicarage.

Saint John the Baptist has a Norman doorway of about 1200 decorated with a chamfered roll and a head on each side, and a pointed Norman chancel arch with carved capitals. Most of the church, including the tower, is 14th century, but was restored by T. Nicholson in 1881 who renewed all the windows in the style of about 1300. In the chancel there is an "uncommonly sumptuous" tomb recess. It has foliage and shields, and an ogee-headed arch of the early 1300s, amongst the lavish decoration of the canopy. Another tomb recess with ballflower of the same date faces it.

Of the 13th century there is a coped stone by the porch and a fragment of a coffin lid in a window sill. In the churchyard are the steps, base and broken shaft of the mediaeval preaching cross. A sundial of 1649 has been affixed to the base. The stream runs alongside the road and the sheep-grazed orchard opposite the church, but the ambience is greatly disturbed by the nasty-shedded, machine-noisy farm next door and its litter of derelict 20th century buildings.

In 1688 a yew tree was planted in the churchyard in celebration of the overthrow of James II. The king wanted to rule with absolute power and to restore the Roman Catholic religion. In 1688 he issued his own Second Declaration of Indulgence, suspending all penal laws against Nonconformists and Roman Catholics, and ordered the clergy to read it at divine services. The Anglican clergy in general disobeyed and seven bishops were tried for seditious libel but were acquitted. James was friendless and fearing for his life fled to France. The following year, 1689, both Houses of Parliament met in convention and selected William (son of Mary, daughter of Charles I) to be king. Thus commenced the reign of William III and Mary from 1689 to 1702.

Hill End, 600 yards WNW of the church, is a farmhouse that has a striking 17th century stone-built wing with mullioned and transomed windows and a timber-framed block. It is now the nucleus of a development of bijou dwellings in the brick and stone outbuildings. The hop kilns with conical caps survive.

Pigeon House Farm, 1/2m NE, is brick-built Georgian with seven bays and a pedimented gable and, as one might imagine from its name, has an 18th century brick-built dovecote. Close by is a group of four pairs of semi-detached, red brick council houses.

At Shucknall Court, 3/4m N, near the bridge over the main line railway, is a moated site. Remains of the moat are just visible at the south-west corner of the former enclosure. A little to the north, by the side of the Hereford to Worcester road at Shucknall is The Spout, a spring which used to be the main source of water for the inhabitants of the squatter cottages on the wooded slopes of Shucknall Hill.

The road that leads from The Spout to the chapel was built by the cottagers themselves. Today, The Spout is mostly used by travelling families, though some locals take it for tea and wine-making. Higher up the hill, in Westhide Wood, there lived a badger-baiting friar. For this see the article on Tillington. In 1609 a team of twelve morris dancers performed on Widemarsh Moor, Hereford. Their ages totalled 1,200 years. One of their 'whifflers', a crowd marshal, was Thomas Andros, aged 108, of Weston Beggard. He was a subsidy man, a man of substance liable to pay money to the king for special needs.

WESTON-UNDER-PENYARD *2m ESE of Ross*
'The settlement to the west under Penyard Hill'. The wooded Penyard Hill lies just south of the village, an outlier of the Wyre Forest. The name is from the Welsh pen-ardd, meaning 'high hill'. In 1066 the manor was held by Gunnar, an Old Danish personal name, but by 1086 it had passed to Durand de Pitres, Constable of Gloucester Castle and Sheriff of Gloucestershire.

The settlement stands on the busy Ross to Gloucester road, the A40(T). It has one small, modern estate but is a mature place which, for all its small size, has several notable houses. Facilities are few. The post office-cum-general store closed recently and all there is now is the Weston Cross Inn, a telephone box and the church.

Saint Lawrence's has an impressive Late-Norman arcade of four arches on circular piers and carved heads of animals amongst the decoration. The north doorway is also probably Norman and has a man being devoured by a beast. The tower is 14th century Decorated, with a Perpendicular west window, and the chancel is 13th century Early English. Most of the windows and the chancel arch were either heavily restored or renewed during the restoration by G.E. Street in 1867. The timber porch is of about 1400, and the scissor-braced nave roof is of about 1350. Amongst the memorials is a brass plate engraved with a picture of Walter Nourse, died 1601, kneeling at prayer. His family lived at Lower Weston, now called Weston Hall, from the 16th to the 18th centuries. A window and the clock tower commemorate Edward Hawkshaw, died 1912, and his wife. The traditional bell jingle of the church is:
"Stick a goose and dress un
Say the bells of Wessun."

T.D. Fosbroke, in his *Ariconensia* (1821), describes 'the beating of the bounds' of the parishes of Ross and Weston. This commenced at the stool of an oak, which grew over a spring in the bottom of a little meadow called Flaxbridge in Penyard. This spring, he says, was venerated of old. The oak was a gospel oak, where a passage of the scriptures was read on the perambulation, and the well is most attractively located on the south side of Penyard Park at SO 621 220. From Frogmore all you have to do is follow the line of the overhead electric grid cable.

Weston Hall stands guard over the village's western approach behind its early 18th century wrought-iron gates. It is an early 16th century Jacobean house, built of red sandstone with canted bays in the gables, a gabled porch and mullioned windows. The Wye is a Late Georgian house of five bays and two storeys, which has a Greek Doric porch and two canted bay windows. It looks a bit Continental with its shutters and yellow painted extensions. It became a hotel but since 1985 has housed the Leadership Trust. This is a management training company. They run five-and-a-half day residential courses, and have clients from all over the world. Paul Winter is their Chief Executive. If ever they need a guest speaker they have Sir John Harvey Jones of the television series *The Troubleshooter* fame, living at Rudhall House, just over a mile to the north-east. (See Brampton Abbotts.)

The Weston Cross public house is stone-built with Gothic, pointed-arch windows and is dated by a plaque at 1760. The Elizabethan Weston House is much admired, likewise the Queen Anne House on the Bromash road. Adjacent to the latter, and the embankment of the disused Ross to Gloucester railway of 1840, is an old dwelling thought once to have been a chapel. A little further on is Saint Mary's, a cruck cottage reputedly once used as a House of Correction for Cistercian monks, probably attached to Flaxley Abbey. Close to Saint Mary's is a spring which flows into a horse trough, which was also once the principal well of the settlement.

The Old Rectory, 1/2m NE of the church, is a handsome, symmetrical, late 17th century William and Mary house of stone with seven bays, two storeys, 10 bedrooms, hipped roof with dormers, and a doorway with Tuscan pilasters and a pediment surmounted by a panel with an open book sculpture. It is said to have been constructed from stone quarried from Penyard Castle. In 1972 the house was put up for sale by the Diocesan Board and was purchased for £67,000 by Marc Feld, better known as Marc Bolan the rock music superstar, who died in a car crash in 1977. Your author met the 'electric warrior' once, at the BBC Pebble Mill television studios, when we appeared in a show together. Off-stage he was a very pleasant, ordinary little fellow. Nearly 20 years later his records still sell well and he is something of a cult figure. He never actually lived at the Old Rectory and sold it after three years.

Hunsdon Manor Hotel is stone-built with two prominent cedar trees and was formerly called Sandiford. Street House, 1/4m N of the church, is a stone-built dwelling of 1711 with five bays, two storeys, wooden cross windows and an arched hood over the door. It was owned by the Merrick family who also owned Bollitree Castle.

Bollitree Castle, 3/4m NNE, is a late 17th century house of red stone with five bays, two storeys, a hipped roof, gabled dormers and a duck pond. However, in about 1770 the timber-framed outbuildings were made wildly Gothic with battlements, corner turrets, ogee arches and quatrefoils. Some of the material is mediaeval, brought here from Penyard Castle and from a church at Bristol.

Penyard Castle lies on a steep slope, 1m SW of the church at SO 618 226. It is first mentioned in 1338 when it

Lines on Gatley Park

And here I saw the Inglorious Prince
point to the sky, and heard his son to cry:
"Please, let me kill that lovely bird."
And the prince's heart did jump with joy,
that he had bred so gallant a boy.
"Of course, my son, and when you're done
to the Round House we'll repair
to see the day go down, 'Tis Heaven there.
We'll watch the skyline turn to blood,
we'll watch the sun burn down the wood.
How wonderful to be alive,
so go ahead my bonny son,
and when the noble deed is done
we'll prepare tomorrow's fun.
Look! see those eyes so shining bright,
in the trees, in the evening light -
just a little to your right?
That be Mr. Reynardine,
and he's as good as mine."

Michael Raven
1996

was owned by the Talbot family who may have had a house here in the reign of Henry II (1154-1189). On the death of Gilbert Talbot, 7th Earl of Shrewsbury, in 1627 it went to his daughter Elizabeth, Countess of Kent. By the 19th century it was owned by the Partridge family. In the late 17th century a farmhouse was built on part of the site and in 1691 there is mention of "the demolished castle of Penyard". There is little left to see today, far less than was examined by the Royal Commission on Historic Monuments in the 1930s. The farmhouse has collapsed and undergrowth is obscuring the four-bay vaulted undercroft. All that is left of the castle above ground are a two-light, 14th century window re-set in the gable of the house, a fragment of walling west of the house, and traces of ditches a little further west. It is likely that the castle was used as a hunting lodge as the park was created out of the Forest of Dean.

At Ask Barn near Bollitree Castle, there are fields called Kill Dane Meadow, Kill Dane Field, and Kill Dane Orchard. Human bones are said to have been found in the area. It is quite possible that these names relate to the events of 1002 when King Ethelred ordered that all the Danes in England be killed. This, the Massacre of Saint Brice's Day, was in retaliation for Danish and Norwegian attacks on England. One of those slaughtered was Gunhild, the sister of Sweyn, King of the Danes. He returned to England to gain revenge and in the succeeding years ravaged the whole of the country. In 1013 Ethelred fled to Normandy and Sweyn was proclaimed king. Sweyn died in 1014 and Ethelred was restored to the throne. He was succeeded by his son, Edmund Ironside, who was murdered seven months later. The Witon then chose Canute, son of Sweyn, to be king of all England. Bloody times.

At the main-road hamlet of Ryeford, 3/4m SE of Weston, is Hownhall, built in 1914 to a design by Sir Patrick Abercrombie, and the Baptist Chapel of 1731. The chapel is a striking building of red and grey stone with arched windows, giant pilasters, a frieze and a pediment. In the grounds of Ryeford Villa is its unassuming forerunner of 1661.

Of other outlying hamlets Kingstone, 1m N, has a preaching cross; Pontshill, 1m SSE, has a solitary grave in the grounds of New House Farm which was once part of a Quaker settlement of about 1800; Dancing Green, 1.1/2m S, has a tradition of dancing round the maypole and outdoor meetings; and Kettle Bottom, hidden from public roads and approached over a ford, is probably named after the Reverend Kettle who lived hereabouts.

Bromash, 1m NE of Weston-under-Penyard, is at the eastern centre of a large Celtic-Roman industrial ironworking complex that covers some 250 acres to the north and south of the Bromash-Bollitree road. This is the probable site of the Roman town of Ariconium, one of only two places in Herefordshire mentioned in the *Antonine Itinerary*. The other was Magnis (Kenchester). Excavations are far from complete and the history and development of this extensive site is by no means fully understood. There do not appear to have been any city walls but foundations of Roman buildings have been found, including those of a probable granary, a tessellated pavement that indicates a sizeable villa, and two rectangular buildings, one of which has a hypocaust system. Other finds include many shards of Samian ware, Rhenish ware and imitation Samian ware, Roman coins from the 1st century to the 4th, pins, rings, objects in bronze and Celtic-British gold and silver coins including some Cunobelin.

Most interesting, though, are the large quantities of iron slag scattered over the area and the six furnaces, clay pits and working hollows found about 220 yards north of the Bromash-Bollitree road. It seems likely that this was an Iron-Age industrial site, occupied by the Romans, who built a posting station and a large villa-farm with ancilliary buildings and continued to use the site for industrial purposes. Ariconium was linked to Ashton in the north (near Leominster) and to Chepstow in the south by a paved 8ft wide Roman road. This ran through the Forest of Dean to Lydney, where it joins the A48 (another Roman road) to Chepstow on the Severn estuary. It is only partly used by modern highways but is traceble by green lanes and field boudaries.

To conclude, we must take a trip down the lane between Ryeford and Coughton which passes along one of the most charming valleys in Herefordshire. It is a hidden domain, a secret place guarded by friendly wooded hills and is thought to have been used by the Roman road that linked Ariconium (Bromash area) with Blestium (Monmouth). On leaving the main road at Ryeford one passes an orchard and a fortress-like, stone-built farm, and ignores the turn to Pontshill and Dancing Green. The valley view appears almost immediately. Scattered cottages in buttercup meadows bask in the sun and the large, irregular sandstone hulk of Parkfields comes into view. This is a Late Georgian house of five bays with two-bay sides which have one-storey bow windows. It was in the process of being extended when we visited.

A sharp kink in the road brings the traveller to Bin Mills. This is a delightful little place and one can even bring oneself to ignore the big, modern, grey factory shed and the even worse close-board fencing which seems to have escaped from a suburban garden and found its way to more peaceful pastures. The old mill complex consists of a terrace of stone cottages, stables, mill-house and the mill itself, which has round-headed windows and a small industrial chimney. The leat, pond and water-wheel have survived and it really is a most charming spot. Not surprisingly many of the buildings have been converted to holiday cottages. The big, modern shed houses the processing plant of Dayla Soft Drinks (Western) Ltd. There was a mill on the site from at least the 14th century and in 1638 Walter Lloyd was making paper here. In 1830 it became a corn mill. However, its history goes back to Roman times when it was probably the site of Villa Milliaris, 'the villa of the mile-stone'.

The lane continues westwards through the lovely hills of Penyard Park, and the cultivation of the lower slopes of the hills becomes apparent. The rich soil of this sheltered valley is well suited to the growing of vegetables. The fields belong to Cobney Farms, a very modern company concern based at Coleraine Farm. All is efficient and it flourishes. The high stacks of wooden crates so neatly arranged are used to transport the produce of the farm which amounts annually to 18,000 tons of potatoes, 6,000 tons of onions and 12,000 tons of carrots. Most of this is put into cold storage before despatch. They also have a Chicken Site; sounds ominous.

The owners of the farm live at Cobney Park, a substantial, stone-built, Georgian house of three broad bays and two and a half storeys. It was built in 1830 to replace the previous black and white building that was destroyed by fire. The only blemish on the idyllic landscape in which it is set are the two lines of electricity pylons that stamp their steel boots down the valley as they march from Gloucester to Coughton and points north.

At the hamlet of Coughton are the kennels of the Ross

Harriers where 21 couples of hounds, Old English Harriers, are kept for hunting hares. The hunt was founded in 1820 and operates from October to March, meeting on Tuesdays and Fridays. The huntsmen follow on horses and their colours are a green coat with a yellow collar. We spoke to the kennelman, Mark Reynolds. He said they catch 20 hares in a season if they are lucky and bemoaned the fact that hares were not very common in south Herefordshire these days, too many being taken by birds of prey, foxes, and lampers with lurchers. Hares do not go to ground and so do not need to be dug out. Mr. Reynolds thought that foxhunters were very wrong to dig out foxes gone to earth, that it is an ignoble and cruel practice. He puts down his hounds at between 9 and 12 years of age and buries them. Foxhunters either feed their dogs back to the pack or dispose of the carcases in offal bins. As a hunter Mr. Reynolds has a heart of gold. I had a chat with a hare shortly after and told him all this, but he didn't seem impressed.

WHITBOURNE *4.5m ENE of Bromyard*

The name probably means 'white stream'. The village lies on a tributary stream of the River Teme in the northwestern corner of the county and is most easily approached off the Bromyard to Worcester road, the A44, at Meadow Green. It lies in a land of pastures, wooded hills and orchards. The village is a pretty place, unspoilt and quite delightful, with the willows by the stream, the Court, church and cottages making a charming ensemble. Brian Hatton, the Hereford painter, was no stranger to these parts.

The doorway of Saint John the Baptist is Late Norman with trumpet-scallop in the capitals and zig-zag in the arch; and there is Norman masonry in the walls. The tower is 14th century and has diagonal buttresses; the chancel has 13th century lancets and a 15th century Perpendicular east window; the south nave wall is 13th century; the north aisle is of 1866; and the font is Norman. During the Victorian restoration the walls were scraped and the monuments moved to beneath the tower, including that to Bellingham Freeman, died 1689. The timber-framed lych gate is mediaeval.

A curiosity kept at the church is a piece of an elaborately worked red velvet mediaeval cope. This quite probably belonged to one of the bishops of Hereford, who had a manor house on the oval site now occupied by Whitbourne Court. It was this Bishop's house that came into the possession of the Cromwellian commander, Colonel John Birch, and which he re-fortified as a country retreat. In 1665 he was arrested here and imprisoned at Hereford Gaol, suspected of having Royalist sympathies. The Court still has some mediaeval fabric and much of the moat, which has traces of an inner defensive bank on the northeast side.

Bishop Francis Godwin was buried at the church in 1633. He was the author of *The Man in the Moon*, a very early science-fiction story in which he manages to reach the moon and finds a kind of paradise. If the people found evil qualities in their young they were banished to earth. They must have had some bad broods in recent years, methinks.

The Old Rectory stands beside the church. It is of mellow Georgian red brick and has three bays, a hipped roof, an arched doorway and Venetian windows. Nearby there are two charming black and white cottages, and one of which has Tudor chimney stacks.

Meadow Green, 1/4m WSW of the church, has rendered concrete council houses, a post office-cum-general store (how important these places are), modest red brick houses, a stone-built school which stands opposite the village hall, Saint John the Baptist's church also of stone, the Live and Let Live pub, a remarkable stone lodge in Greek-gone-wrong, and out on the A44 the rendered Wheatsheaf.

The lodge stands at the entrance drive to Whitbourne Hall which lies 1.1/4m W of the church at Whitbourne. It stnds in wooded grounds by a lake in the valley of the Sapey Brook. It was built in 1862, probably by the architect E.W. Elmslie (1819-89) and uses features copied from the Erechtheum. It has a grand pedimented portico of six Ionic columns, a central hall with pillars supporting a gallery, and a staircase designed to impress. Whitbourne Hall was built for Edward Bickerton Evans (1819-93), whose family owned the Hill Evans Vinegar works in Worcester, which was founded in 1830. They later diversified into British wine and their factory was the largest in the world. Edward was a great traveller. Altogether, he owned 2,586 acres and was listed in *The Great Landowners of Great Britain and Ireland*.

Elsewhere in the parish there are cottages and farmhouses with mediaeval cruck-trusses such as Lower Poswick, Bradburne's Farm, Fincher's Farm, and the Ring of Bells.

Whitbourne was once a major hop growing area. Hops were an established crop in the parish by 1649 and in 1807 Whitbourne had 400 acres under cultivation, the highest in the county with the exception of Bromyard. In the last few days of August 1905 some 1,000 seasonal labourers disembarked at Knightwick railway station, 1m S of Whitbourne. However, by 1975 the acreage of hops had dwindled to 10 and now they only survive at Poplands Farm. At Huntlands, 3/4m SW of Whitbourne, there is a rare relic: a brick creosote tank with an arched fire opening and a chimney stack. Creosote was used to preserve the hop poles. The house itself is of cruck-framed timber construction.

Just south of Huntlands is Gaines, and its little lake. Old Gaines is 16th century timber-framed. New Gaines is an 11-bay, 18th and 19th century brick house with an early Gothic Revival room of some quality, Adam-style stucco decoration, and a domed, oval stairwell.. Hamish Park, 1m SW of Gaines, is also of brick. Today, brick is mundane, but in the 17th and 18th centuries it was most fashionable and prestigious.

WHITCHURCH *5m SW of Ross-on-Wye*

The name 'white church' usually means a church made of light-coloured stone. It now stands on, and is divided by, the motorway-like A40(T) on the tourist route to the scenic splendours of the lower Wye valley. Whitchurch is well catered for in the way of facilities, with a variety of pubs, shops, guest houses and restaurants, a memorial hall, post office, bakery and a fire station. Opposite the post office is the Old Mill and near the square is the Crown Inn, a former coaching hostelry. Next to that are three houses that were fashioned out of the old lunatic asylum. Near the school of 1981 is the Wye Valley Visitors' Centre which has tea rooms, gardens, the World of Butterflies and craft workshops. A bridge connects these to the Jubilee Park of 1977 which has a maze, amusement arcades, an exotic bird park (with tame parrots that will sit on your shoulder) and a wharf from which river boat trips depart. On the outskirts of the village is Mill Valley Golf Club.

Down by the river, and casting a quizzical eye over all

this 20th century frippery, is the church founded by the Celtic saint, Dubricius, in the 5th century. Most of what we see today is 14th century Decorated, though a round, moulded 13th century column has been built into the south wall. The single-framed nave and chancel roofs are also 14th century. The north aisle is of 1860 and the font is Norman. (For something on St. Dubricius see the article on Madley and the index for other references.) In the churchyard there is a rare tulip tree. The Gwillim family, who have a tomb vault in the church, lived at the Old Court, now a hotel. It stands 1/4m W, a large 'E'-shaped stone house of the 16th to the 17th century with mullioned windows.

King Arthur's Cave, 1.1/4m SSW of Whitchurch, was investigated thoroughly in the 1870s and the 1920s. It is a natural cave with two entrances and two chambers in the Carboniferous limestone of the Wye gorge some 300ft above the river. The cave has been occupied from at least the New Stone Age (Neolithic), 8,000-10,000 years ago, after the last Ice Age. The bones of many animals have been found - mammoth, giant deer, horse, bison, cave lion, hyena, woolly rhinoceros - and flints and artefacts from every age from Neolithic to Roman. King Arthur's Cave is on an organised nature trail from the Biblins Youth Adventure Centre, 3/4m SSE, which also takes in a nearby rock-shelter called Merlin's Cave that may have been used as a camp site in Stone Age times. A good summary of the finds made at different levels is given in *The Archaeology of the Welsh Marches* by S.C. Stanford, 1980. There is also a Neolithic cromlech, a burial chamber, in the area.

Little Doward Camp, 1.1/4m SSW of Whitchurch, is near King Arthur's Cave. It is an Iron-Age Silurian hill fort with four entrances that was extended in the 5th century B.C. It has double ramparts from 6ft to 8ft high, enclosing about 19 acres with a steep fall on each side. A further area of two and a half acres, defended by a single rampart, adjoins the main fort. In the same area, but hidden by undergrowth, are the remains of five Bronze-Age burial mounds, some square and some round.

On the boundary of the parishes of Whitchurch and Ganarew, 1.1/2m SW, a Roman mosaic and Roman coins were discovered in the 19th century but have disappeared into private ownership. At Crocker's Ash, slag from Roman iron smelting furnaces has been found. In the 18th century one of the six Lower Wye Valley iron smelting blast furnaces was located at Whitchurch. The iron-ore came from the Wyre Forest but the smelting works spread out to sites with water power and supplies of charcoal. The other furnaces located on tributary streams of the Wye were at Bishop's Wood, Redwood; Lydbrook; Saint Weonard's; and Tintern.. Most of these were owned by the Foley family. The earliest commercially successful blast furnace in the area was that at Lydbrook, built in 1608 by the Earl of Pembroke.

The name Doward is from the Old Welsh dou-garth, meaning two hills. Little Doward has been mentioned. Great Doward, 1/2m S of Whitchurch, has a large number of squatter cottages and Victorian modern villas. Symond's Yat is the name for the gorge between Great Doward to the west and Huntsman's Hill to the east. The name is from yat, meaning 'a gate, or a gap' and the owner in the 1600s was Robert Symonds, High Sheriff of Herefordshire. By the river at Symond's Yat West is the Paddocks Hotel, formerly the Ferrie Inn. A ferry is still operated here by a rope-controlled boat, and there is another near the Wye Rapids Hotel. At the top of Great Doward is the Herefordshire Rural Heritage Museum which has one of the largest collections of farm machinery, vintage tractors, horse drawn wagons and rural bygones in Britain.

Just downstream of the Biblins, nearly 2m S of Whitchurch at SO 549 144, there is a rope bridge across the River Wye. The ropes are actually strong steel hawsers and the bridge is made a little more stable by the addition of a steel mesh lining to the base and sides. Nevertheless, for most people it is a bit of an adventure to cross it, especially if the river is in flood. A little further downstream there are dramatic, precipitous, limestone cliffs several hundred feet high. Above them is the outcrop called the Seven Sisters. Many claim that the view from the top of the gorge at the Seven Sisters is the best on the whole of the Wye. Mind you, it is not for the fainthearted, and children and dogs should be kept well clear; it is wonderful but dizzy-making and dangerous. Peregrine falcons returned to nest at Symonds Yat in 1982 after an absence of many years. R.S.P.B. officers with powerful telescopes provide a viewing service to the public between April 1st and August 31st. These birds of prey are very rare in Britain with only 1,100 known breeding pairs. (For more on this area in general see the articles on Ross-on-Wye, Walford, Goodrich and Ganarew.)

WHITNEY-ON-WYE *4m NE of Hay-on-Wye*

The name is from the Old English and means either 'white island', or 'Hwita's island'; this refers to the island in the River Wye, 1/4m SE of the church. The settlement stands on the old drovers' road from Hay to Hereford, the A438, which here runs very close to the Wye. In recent times it was straightened and now cuts the village in half. Whitney was also on the track of the disused railway from Hay to Kington, which followed the route of the old horse-tub tramway. The embankments and a tram-wharf (siding) can still be seen. The railway crossed the river a good half mile west of the village and the massive stone abutments still stand. They had to be strong because the Wye hereabouts can be wicked. When it rains in Wales it becomes a dangerous, raging torrent. Little wonder that early man made offerings to the river gods. Whitney once had a Norman castle, but that was washed away and is now only visible as a sandspit, just south of Whitney Old Court at SO 272 465. Likewise much of the church was destroyed in the floods of 1735, and the rectory with it. Most of the later dwellings have been built on higher ground to the north.

Between Whitney and Clifford there used to be three stone toll bridges but they fell victim to the river and now there is just one, a replacement built in 1802. It has stone abutments with a timber-framed carriageway, timber piers and timber cutwaters. The piers were renewed recently with Green Heart from the Far East. There is a 50 pence toll charge, the weight limit is 7.5 tonnes and the speed limit 5 m.p.h. In the last century a witch used to be tollkeeper here. One day a farmer drove over and refused to pay, so with a single look she stopped his horses in their tracks. Not until he paid could they move. On the main road there is a picnic area and a garage. You can also buy lamb creeps, those little trucks that are stuffed full of hay.

Timber from Whitney Wood is processed at the roadside sawmill. There also used to be a quarry and a pottery in the wood. The pots had a distinctive honey-coloured glaze and shards are frequently found. Canoeists and anglers are no strangers to the river banks at Whitney, though both must exercise care. East of the bridge is the Victorian red brick and black and white Boat Inn, a service station-cum-

Top: Wigmore Abbey at Adforton.
Bottom: Wigmore, main street and church of Saint James.

general store, a handful of substantial mature dwellings, and the church.

When Saint Peter and Saint Paul's was rebuilt in 1740 much of the old fabric was re-used. It has a nave, a chancel and a battlemented tower with a pyramid roof. Inside there is a west gallery with a staircase, formerly used by singers and musicians. The Norman font has a 14th century pedestal and the Norman priests' doorway forms part of a peace shrine. There is a tablet monument to Thomas Williams, died 1698, and a window of 1908 was given in memory of Major Frederick Mapleton Dew. Another window is dedicated to the rector, Henry Dew, a collector of antiquities who acquired many of the good timber furnishings of the church.

The rebuilt rectory of 1740 is now called Wardour House; that was superseded by a new rectory of 1846, now called West Hills. Saint Peter's Well, a healing spring, issues from a pipe in a stone wall in the field north-east of the church at SO 267 476.

The large, five-bay, stone-built, neo-Tudor house on high ground 300 yards north of the church is Whitney Court, built in 1898-1902, by T.H. & A.M. Watson of London, for the Hope family, who replaced the Dews as lords of the manor and who still reside here. Most of the local farmers are tenants of the estate and many of the stone cottages were built for estate workers. Opposite the red brick estate pump house is the former school, and beyond that is a gated track that led down to the station. Beyond the railway track is the Whitney Court estate electricity power house with a tall chimney stack.

Allan Lewis, the son of a carpenter and a lady's maid, of Wyeside Cottage, Whitney-on-Wye, won the Victoria Cross for acts of valour in September 1918 at Ronsoy in France. He single-handedly captured two enemy machine guns but three days later was killed after rushing his men through a German barrage.

Stowe, 1m W along the main road, is really one large farm: a brick house, a few labourers' cottages and numerous grey-black sheds. Millhalf is a hamlet on a stream, 3/4m NE of the church.

WIGMORE *8m SW Ludlow*

The name could mean several things: 'big wood' from the Welsh gwig mawr; or 'Wicga's moor', or 'Wicga's mere', from the Old English. We favour the latter because from high ground it is quite clear that Wigmore lies on the shore of a bowl, the Vale of Wigmore. This was formed during the Ice Age when the former southern valley of the River Teme was blocked by terminal moraine from a tongue of the Wye glacial valley. A lake formed as the ice melted and the shoreline can be seen to this day. The Teme finally wore down a gorge through the Silurian limestone (named by the geologist, Sir Roderick Murchison,) and escaped to the east by Downton. The boggy ground of the old lake would easily have flooded during times of heavy rainfall until drained by later farmers. Incidentally, this wet moorland was enclosed by an Act of Parliament in 1772. This was early as Parliamentary enclosures go but late compared to those made by mediaeval lords elsewhere.

It is quite possible that Wigmore is the Wigingamore of the *Anglo-Saxon Chronicle*, where King Edward had a castle in 921 that repelled an attack by marauding Danes. In Domesday Book Wigmore is in Hazletree Hundred and was in the possession of Ralph de Mortimer who "holds a castle. Earl William built it on waste land which is called Merestun, which Gunfrid held before 1066.....the Borough which is here pays £7." Wigmore held this borough status for 800 years but was never represented in Parliament.

The earthworks of the Domesday Book castle, built by William FitzOsbern, Earl of Hereford, stand just to the west of the church. On this small motte was a timber keep and the early borough streets lay within the protective bailey. It was this castle that Ralph de Mortimer took possession of in 1075; the much larger, more famous, castle came later.

Today, the approach to the village from the east is not auspicious. Bungalows and council houses have submerged the stone-built Bury Court and suburbia continues almost to the village centre. At the junction with the main road, the A4110, is a striking 17th century house of red brick on stone foundations. There are several sheds in the main street. The most surprising is that which houses the post office-cum-general store. It can only be described as a large Nissen hut with a mock black and white facade. One day it will be listed as a curiosity. The Courthouse of about 1840 is now occupied by a cash-and-carry carpet dealer; and the three Nonconformist chapels have been converted - one to a garage and the others to houses. There are two modern schools, two old pubs - the Stone Compass Hotel and Ye Olde Oak Inn - a craft pottery, a village hall and a small industrial estate. Wigmore Hall is at the south end of the village, a handsome black and white house of the 16th century with a gabled porch. On the edge of the village is a range of three former 15th century cottages called Gotherment, which were later converted to a farmhouse and are now run as a bed and breakfast guest house. The name is from the Old Scandinavian meaning 'the place of the goats'.

The church of Saint James dominates the village from high ground north-east of the centre. It has an early Norman nave with herringbone masonry, visible outside in the north wall, and a blocked window that can be seen from inside. The south aisle and its arcade of octagonal piers and chamfered arches is of about 1300. The chancel is late 13th century Decorated. Only one bay and traces of a second of the 15th century north aisle remain. The fat tower is 14th century. In 1864 the church was restored by Bodley. The nave roof is 14th century and that of the chancel is 15th century. The early 16th century, ten-sided pulpit, which has seven linen-fold panels, and the choir, with poppy-head ornament, are arranged so that they could face a central altar, in the democratic manner of the Puritans.

But the romance of Wigmore is its mediaeval castle. It lies on a ridge, isolated, detached from the village, 1/4m NW of the church. It is a crumbled castle, an overgrown ruin, not a tourist trap all tarted up with plaques and wax figures and cream teas. This once handsome edifice was probably begun in the early 12th century and by 1191 it had a stone shell keep. However, most of what we see today is of the rebuilding by Roger Mortimer IV in the early 14th century. It was laid siege to several times and fell more than once. The Mortimers were people to be reckoned with, these Norman knights in shining armour. Their power lay in the fact that the Welsh had the temerity to persistently attempt to recover their stolen lands by force of arms. To keep their power these men from out of the mighty, gleaming white castle of Wigmore carefully cultivated their enemies.

This was political stuff. More than one Welsh maraud was but a bluff. to make the king in London glad that in those distant hills he had Mortimers to quell the swell of mountain men from out of the wild west. If only he could see their most outrageous glee as Englishmen with golden locks sang songs with wiry Welshmen, and danced with girls as dark as midnight, in fields full of flowers in secret camps well hidden in the hills of Powys.

For nearly 400 years the Mortimers held sway in the middle Marches (they also had extensive holdings in Ireland) until the male line became extinct with the death of Edmund Mortimer in 1425. In that year Wigmore Castle and the Earldom of March passed to Richard, Duke of York, a great grandson of Edward III and the son of the heiress, Anne Mortimer. His son was victorious at the Battle of Mortimer's Cross (less than 4m S of Wigmore), and in 1461 he seized the throne as Edward IV. Ludlow had now eclipsed Wigmore but the castle was lived in until 1642 when the Harley family dismantled much of it to prevent it being used by the Royalists in the Civil War.

The basic design of the castle is straightforward. A small upper ward, on a high mound, is protected by a large tower ward to the south-east. Within this is a slightly elevated, flat-surfaced, middle ward. The walls and towers that defended these wards are now in ruins but they are very substantial ruins indeed. They are at their most impressive when viewed from near the stream to the west. To the north-west and the south-east the outer defences are further protected by a deep ditch, the natural slope of the hill being sufficient on the other two sides.

To this great border fortress came powerful people accompanied by retinues of knights and servants. This was an important place, the base of one of the most powerful families in England. Visitors to the castle included Llewellyn, Prince of Wales, Queen Isabella, Edward I and Edward III. The King's Council met here and colourful tournaments were held in the jousting field, probably the large enclosure that ran north-east of the castle and across the main road, but which can only be distinguished today by crop marks photographed from the air.

In 1995 English Heritage started the work of making Wigmore Castle safe for visits by the public. One million pounds has been allocated, but the buildings are not to be restored and the debris is not to be excavated; the intention is to keep it as a romantic ruin, and that is just how it should be. (For more on the castle see *The Castles of Herefordshire and Worcestershire* by Mike Salter.) Wigmore Abbey is situated 1.1/2m N of Wigmore village, at Adforton.

Herefordshire has long been favoured with the presence of gypsies, both true Romanies and travellers from the Emerald Isle. I know there are those who shun their company but in Herefordshire we have a debt of gratitude for they preserved numbers of songs, carols and traditions which would otherwise have died. In 1970 a gipsy funeral was held at Wigmore. It was done in style, with flowers in profusion arranged symbolically to represent the Gates of Heaven, open to welcome the deceased, and a chair with a broken leg to remind one that he would no longer be seated at the table on this earth. The ceremony was concluded by a bare-fist boxing match, but was interrupted because the crowd blocked 'the pavement', as the top of the old market place is called, and disrupted the traffic.

Note: brief histories of the Mortimer family are given in Arthur Mee's *Herefordshire*, pp 198-200 and in J. & M. West's *A History of Herefordshire*, pp 48-52.

WILLERSLEY 6m S of Kington
It lies on the Hereford to Clyro and Hay-on-Wye road, the A438, on a tributary stream of the Wye, and only 1/2m from the river itself. In Domesday Book it was one manor with Winforton, one mile to the west, and it is so small that things should not have changed. All there is here are flat pastures, a few scattered cottages, a stone bridge, a farm with a big collection of round-topped, grey sheds and a yew tree standing in the middle of the turning circle before the tiny church of Saint Mary Magdalene, which has now been converted to a dwelling. There was probably more here in 1086 when Ralph de Tosny held it. The farm is Willersley Court and is a hall house with gabled solar and buttery wings of at least the 16th century. It was given a brick facade in Georgian times. The church had nave and chancel in one with a Victorian bell-turret. The Norman doorway has a lintel with what can only be described as haphazard carved motifs of zig-zags, rosettes and squares. In the north wall of the nave are the last vestiges of a Norman window. Willersley is, as they say, a wayside place.

The Holm, 1/2m SSE, lies at the end of an access track close to the River Wye. The name is from the Old Scandinavian holmr, meaning 'island', and there is, indeed, an island in the river, 1/2m SW, opposite Turner's Boat, on the south bank. This was presumably the site of a ferry.

WINFORTON 5m NE of Hay-on-Wye
In Domesday Book it is Widferdestune, from the Old English 'Winfrip's homestead, or settlement'. It lies on the A438 Hay to Hereford road, in the wide valley of the Wye. It is a place of some character, despite the mundane council houses, and has some good black and white such as Old House Farm, with its close-set verticals, and Cross Farm, which has an exposed cruck-truss. There are stone walls, a stone farm with good timber-framed barns, and the rendered Sun Inn. It was a settlement of yeoman farmers, once the heart and soul of the nation.

Opposite the remains of the mediaeval preaching cross on the main road is the old parish hall. This was formerly the malthouse of the Winforton House estate. During the Second World War pictures from the National Gallery were stored here. Winforton House itself is Georgian.

It is thought that the parish church of Saint Michael stands on the site of a 9th century church. To the south there was a hermitage on an island in the River Wye, established by Saint Cynidr. Only scant ruins remain and as the river has changed course it is now only an island at times of flood. Saint Michael's has a mediaeval tower, with a 16th century timber-framed belfry and a pyramid roof. The nave has a doorway with 13th century roll moulding, but most of the building was heavily restored by the Victorians. The roofs of the nave and chancel are 14th century, the pulpit is 17th century, the communion rail is of 1701, and the organ case is 18th century.

Winforton Court is a good looking 'E'-shaped, black and white house with diagonal bracing forming lozenges in the left gable, and stands beside the main road. Traces of a recusant Catholic chapel have been found in the attic. The Winforton open fields, cultivated in strips in the mediaeval manner, were not enclosed by Acts of Parliament and subdivided into one-owner fields until 1779. A track leads south from Winforton Court and then becomes a footpath that leads to the site of an old ford across the Wye to Clock Mills on the far bank. The steep, dark, wooded hill that looms to the east of Clock Mills is Merbach Hill. The name means 'hill by the marsh in the river valley'.

About 200 yards north of the Sun Inn is Winforton Common, where there are a few old squatters' cottages and some modern bungalows. Several of the bungalows were used as laboratories by Professor Merton, who worked with Barnes Wallace testing the prototypes of the 'bouncing bomb', used to destroy German dams during the Second World War.

WITHINGTON *4m NE of Hereford*
The name is from the Old English and means 'homestead amongst the willows'. The manor was held by the Canons of Hereford, both before and after the Norman Conquest. In 1086 it was a flourishing community with a mill. The nuns of Hereford also had a holding here, probably at Nunnington.

We turned off the Hereford to Worcester road, the A4103, to look for a local shop and found one, Norman's. Some local shop! It is a superstore housed in a big, grey shed. So, provisioned beyond all expectation, man and dogs were watered and well fed and ready for anything that the natives of Withington could throw at us. In 1987 they numbered 1,053, a veritable battalion. Near the store there is a factory that manufactures timber-framed houses, but it is for ceramic tiles that the village is famous.

Encaustic tiles - that is, tiles with inlaid clays of different colours like marquetry in wood - have been manufactured here since 1848 and have been installed in Windsor Castle and in many churches and cathedrals. In 1857 Withington tiles were used in the restoration of Hereford Cathedral. Today, though, only mass-produced, glazed wall tiles are made here.

Agriculture is still a major industry in the parish but many of the small farms have been absorbed by large, company-run estates. There are two engineering companies, one a specialist in agricultural machinery, and a blacksmith's shop.

The natives live in a variety of dwellings from modern estate semis to yeoman farmhouses, Victorian villas and thatched cottages. Social facilities include a post office, a garage, a modern red brick school of 1984 with a low pitched roof, a stone-built Baptist chapel of 1821 with a hipped roof, and the parish church.

Saint Peter's stands at the north end of the village. It has Norman masonry and two plain Norman doors, though the north door is now blocked. The nave is long, the windows are of various styles and the chancel is new. It is the 14th century tower and its tall, graceful, octagonal, recessed spire that catch the eye. Inside, the tower arch is equally good. In the place of a chancel arch there is a 15th century oak screen with eight, traceried one-light bays. The stained glass is by Ward & Hughes of 1892. In the churchyard are the steps of a churchyard cross of about 1400.

The area called White Stone, 1/2m S of the church on the main road, takes its name from a 5ft high wayside cross, re-used in 1700 as a direction marker, pointing to Hereford, Worcester, Ledbury and Leominster.

Withington Court lies 150 yards SE of the church, on the lane to Westhide. From the road it looks so neat; the fences, the orchard, the avenue of trees, even the sheep look newly groomed. The drive leads to some gaunt farm buildings with a tall industrial chimney, a development of attractive stone cottages with pantile roofs, and the old Court. Withington Court is a stone-built, ivy-clad house with an irregular five-bay, two-storey front, a columned pedimented porch, a slate roof, an orangery to the right and inside is a 16th century hall and 14th century panelling. The whole complex lies on a north-facing slope. The poet John Phillips (1676-1709) lived at Withington Court. His most famous work is *Cyder* and he has a memorial in Poets' Corner, Westminster Abbey.

Half a mile to the east is Dodmarsh, a dinky little enclave of cottages old and new, half-timbered and of brick, all huddled together amongst well-wooded gardens and an orchard, the domain of a Hereford bull. A little further east, on the south side of the road, is a most charming little thatched, black and white squatter's cottage. Old Mother Hubbard must surely have lived in a place like this; their kind are as worthy of a Grade I listing as any grand country house.

Withington Marsh lies 3/4m NW of Withington on the Hereford to Bromyard road, the A465, at the point where two streams join forces before flowing south towards the River Lugg. The aspect it presents to the main road is not of the highest order. The glum looking Cross Keys has a petrol filling station, a Country Furniture store, a plant nursery, and a tea room for company. Elsewhere there is a chapel, a post office, and cottages ancient and modern.

Nunnington, 3/4m SSW of Withington Marsh, is a main road hamlet. At the bottom of Nunnington Pitch there was a hopyard in which hops were picked by hand for the last time in Herefordshire. The yard belonged to the estate of the Eau Withington Court, 1m SSW of Withington Marsh. This is a 17th century house with a more recent five-bay front. At the back it is timber-framed with a rear facing gable. Inside there is a good staircase; outside, to the west, is a small building dated 1682.

Thing Hill Grange, 1/2m N of Withington Marsh, is a 14th century timber-framed hall-house, complete with a roof spere truss and buttery and solar wings. The spere truss is supported by two posts that reach down to ground floor level, a few feet from the walls, to allow doors from the hall to the service area to be fitted. It is rare for these to survive, and even here one has been cut off at the bottom. One door has an ogee head. The solar wing also has its original roof.

Thing Hill Grange has its own entrance drive, but 1/2m NE along the main road is the entrance to another drive. It is guarded by a delightful, fairy-tale, lodge; a romantic delight in rusticated grey stone with red stone dressings and little round towers with conical roofs, pyramid roofs, dormers and decorated chimneys. The drive leads uphill to a windswept knoll. Here there once stood a magnificent Victorian country house built in the same style as the lodge. It was called Thing Hill Mansion but was taken down and transported to be rebuilt "in London or New York". All that remains is a stand of lonesome pines and a little, round, derelict brick shed with a conical roof built into the hillside. There are first class views over the surrounding countryside. The drive makes a right-angled turn and leads on to Thing Hill Farm, and the Thing Hill dog kennels which are attached to a red brick house with yellow brick dressings.

Between Thing Hill in the north and Nunnington in the south there are some 140 acres of tree nurseries. A Withington resident is the niece of Eric Savill who created the Savill Garden, at Windsor Great Park. Some trees planted there came from these nurseries.

Mrs. E.M. Leather collected two old beliefs held at Withington: that a cure for whooping cough is to tie berries around the neck; and that if a maid kneading bread rubs her doughy hand over a young boy's face he will never grow whiskers. She also relates how a Withington man, an owner of a brick kiln, had a barrow of coal stolen one night. He went to the well-known local wizard, or seer, called Jenkins who told him not to worry, that it would be restored. By the time he got home it had been returned. There are so many simple little stories of this kind about Jenkins that it is impossible not to believe that he had some powers, even if only psychological. It seems

Top: Pembridge, Saint Mary's and detached bell-tower.
Middle left: "Lady" taunts a young Hereford bull, 1986.
Middle right: Pensioners at 'the hamlet', Stoke Edith, 1915. The forlorn lady is Ann Mellin.
Above: Cloddock Mill with Hatterall Hill behind.
Opposite: The Wye Rapids Hotel, Symonds Yat.

that Mrs. Leather, the folklorist, knew him personally but she never gave his real name or address. He is believed to have lived somewhere north of the Hereford to Bromyard road.

WOLFERLOW *4.5m NNW of Bromyard*

The early mediaeval name was Ulferlav which means 'Wulfhere's burial mound'. At the time of Domesday Book it was held by Roger de Lacy, though Ralph de Mortimer also had a small part of the manor. It is most easily approached from Three Gates on the Bromyard to Stanford Bridge road, the B4203, but the access lane is gated to control livestock.

The church and the Court stand alone on a hillside with isolated farms dotted in the countryside around: Poswick Farm, Upper House Farm, Heath Farm and Forty Acre Farm. Park Farm, 1.1/2m N of the church, stands in Wolferlow Park - a mediaeval hunting park?

The church of Saint Andrew was mostly rebuilt by the Victorians in 1863 and 1890-94, but the entrance arch and tympanum, the chancel arch and another walled-up doorway with a band of saltire crosses are all Norman. The bell-turret has mediaeval timbers and supports a brooch spire. In the chancel there is a handsome, late-13th century effigy of a lady, though the stylized parallel folds of her dress are more typical of the 12th century. She has a dog at her feet and two angels at her head. Court Farm stands a little to the east of the church. It is timber-framed and has a gable with prestigious close-set verticals. The garden is walled to keep out livestock and rabbits and to protect plants from the wind. The oasthouse is disused; in 1815 there were 60 acres of hops under cultivation in the parish; in 1935 there were none.

In 1858 a survey showed that there were tanners working at Wolferlow. At that time most rural villages in Herefordshire had four times the population they have today. The lane continues westward to an escarpment, from which there are good views over Stoke Bliss, Sweet Green, Pie Corner and Bank Street in Worcestershire.

WOOLHOPE *6.5m ESE of Hereford*

The name is from the Anglo-Saxon Wulfgifu-hop. Hop means 'valley' and Wulfgifu, or Wulviva, together with her sister, Lady Godiva, gave the manor to Hereford Cathedral in the 11th century before the Norman Conquest. Woolhope lies at the centre of the lovely and varied landscape of the uplands of the Woolhope Dome, a Silurian limestone island in an Old Red Sandstone sea.

We approached the village from Mordiford. This is 'easy to get lost in' country, but that is part of its charm. It is a secret, hidden place in which every turn and twist of the lane brings some unexpected vista. It really is beautiful up here - and only 10 minutes from Hereford. What is more, there are numerous commons on the Dome - Tarrington Common, Checkley Common, Common Hill at Fownhope, Broadmoor Common, Putley Common and Durlow Common - where one has the right to roam at will.

The alternating exposures of limestone and shales on the Dome, and the gentle slopes and steep scarps, are home to a wide variety of flora and fauna. The area has long attracted geologists and naturalists and in 1851 the country's world famous Woolhope Naturalists' Field Club was founded. Their published *Transactions* are a collection of diverse studies on almost anything to do with the natural history and archaeology of Herefordshire, and their standards of research and scholarship are of the very highest. At the time of writing their membership is some 800, which includes universities and other learned institutions.

Woolhope is an agricultural community with some 16 farms engaged in dairy, beef and arable farming. The village has cottages of stone and brick, and is noted for the number of its stone boundary walls. In recent times there has been some very tasteful new development, especially the row of terraced houses at the Old Forge. Modern bungalows are tucked away along the drive to Wessington Court, a 19th century, ivy-clad Gothic mansion in wooded grounds. It is built of brick with stone dressings and has eight bays and four gables, and has been converted to provide four flats. The village has a pub, the Crown Inn, a telephone kiosk, a parish hall and playing fields but the shop, the school and the post office are no more. The small population and its comparative isolation meant that Woolhope did not get mains electricity until 1959, mains water until 1970 and mains sewerage until 1979.

The church of Saint George is approached down a line of limes. Of the Norman building there is a window in the chancel and a massive arch in the north arcade. The south arcade is Victorian but most of the rest, including the diagonally buttressed tower, is of about 1300. There is an early 14th century effigy under a canopy with ballflower ornament, and hanging on the wall are engraved coffin lids: one is of a 14th century man, the other a 13th century woman. Lady Godiva and her sister Wulviva are depicted in the modern memorial window to the lawyer Arthur Stollard.

The Butcher's Arms public house, 1/4m E of the church, is a 14th century building that was formerly a block of three cottages. One later became a butcher's shop and another a cider house. The 35 acres of Broadmoor Common, 3/4m NW of the church, were designated a nature reserve in 1986 in the care of the County Council. It has the obligatory scatter of squatter cottages amongst the bracken and scrub woodland. Adjoining it to the west are the broad acres of Haugh Wood, in the capable hands of the National Trust who have laid out organised forest walks. Haugh is from the Old English haga, meaning 'an enclosure', in this case of woodland. Terrace Hall, 1m out of Woolhope on the Fownhope road, is a black and white farmhouse, now the home of the sculptor Walenty Pytel. Other old houses in the parish include Buckenhill (1592), Croose, Yare, Bent Orchard and Sapness.

WORMBRIDGE *7.5m SW of Hereford*

The name means 'the bridge over the Worm Brook'. Worm is from the Welsh gwrm, meaning 'dark'. Wormbridge lies on the Hereford to Abergavenny road which crosses the stream between Howton Grove Farm and the church. There are some unspectacular but delightful countryside views hereabouts: gently undulating pastures and arable fields with mature trees in the hedgerows and little wooded hills in the distance. It is a friendly landscape in which nothing nasty could happen - until you hear the cry of the hounds, the huntsman's horn, the bark of a shotgun, or the chink of a spade as a farmer digs out badgers to sell to thugs in Manchester. These poor creatures cannot seek sanctuary anywhere, but in the 15th century if you were a human felon in Wormbridge you most certainly could.

The reason for this was that in mediaeval times the church, manor and 200 acres of land at Wormbridge were owned by the Dinmore Commandery of Knights Hospitallers of Saint John of Jerusalem. This order achieved a privileged position and one of the rights granted to them was that of sanctuary. Any felon who took refuge in a house owned by them could claim protection from arrest by any officer of the King of England. In 1485 a burglar, William Bongham of Garway, took refuge in one of the Hospitaller's Wormbridge houses and was arrested there by Roger Bodenham, the Sheriff of Herefordshire. He pleaded guilty but the Hospitallers claimed their ancient privilege in court and William Bongham was returned to the protection of their house. What happened subsequently we do not know. After the Dissolution of the Monasteries the Wormbridge manor was sold and through marriage came to the Clive family of the village of Clive in Shropshire. Their mansion stood opposite the church but all that has survived is a part of the laundry; this is now used as the village school.

The church and the Court stand close together beside the main road with tall trees to shelter them. Behind the gabled brick facade of the Court lurks a Jacobean timber-framed house which contains a hall with two cross-wings. One wing is now part of the farm buildings. Inside there is a good overmantel with pilasters and caryatids (draped females used as pillars); outside there is an 18th century brick dovecote.

The church of Saint Peter, formerly Saint Dubricius, has a 13th century tower, topped by a brooch spire, and a Norman nave doorway of about 1200. The chancel, the spire and much of the rest is of the restoration of 1851-9. The five woodwork panels came from Newnham Paddox in Leicestershire and in origin are English, Dutch and Italian. Amongst the stained glass are some good, early 15th century figures. Notable monuments include two marble panels with portrait busts to Lady Catharine Clive, died 1882, and Charles Clive, died 1883.

Trelough, 1/2m NE of the church, is an early 18th century brick house of five bays with a hipped roof which has a stand of wind-break trees and a telephone box for company. Opposite the house a track leads off to Wormbridge Common, 1/2m N of the church. On the fringes of the Big Wood are a few small, brick-built squatter cottages, charming structures and delightfully situated. On the main road is a sign declaiming that the land to the north belongs to the Whitfield estate. Whitfield is 1.1/2m NNW of the church.

There is a well preserved section of the Hereford to Abergavenny tramway 300 yards SE of the church, at SO 430 312. It was built at the beginning of the 19th century to carry coal from South Wales via the Newport to Brecon Canal. The tubs were linked to form trains which were hauled by horses. It had its heyday in the 1840s but the railway came and superseded it. (See the Appendices.)

Near the derelict Withington Cottage, 1/2m S of Wormbridge, at SO 428 300, there is a large, ruined stone building. This housed a horse gin, a central shaft attached to gears and belts. which was turned by a team of five horses. From the early 19th century it was used for powering threshing machinery but fell into disuse when steam engines were introduced.

WORMSLEY *7m NW of Hereford*

The name means either 'Wrym's glade in the wood' or, 'the glade of the snakes'. Wormsley lies in the lovely wooded hills that stretch north-east from Hereford to Weobley. The traveller from the south is first greeted by a few stone cottages and the modern, timber-clad premises of the Herefordshire Golf Club at Raven's Causeway. The club moved here in 1931, and the course was once part of the Foxley estate. From the road there are long, beautiful, windswept views over most attractive country.

The church lies just off the main road, amidst upland pastures and arable land, with a few cottages clustered about it. There are two larger farmhouses in the hamlet, both built in 1555: Upper House Farm, which is now a private dwelling, and Court House Farm, to which now belongs most of the land at Wormsley. In the woods and hills of the parish there are small mounds. These are the remains of primitive dwellings, many of which were quite literally mud huts. They had to be maintained by white-washing the exterior to keep out the rain. Such houses were roofed with thatch or even turf. Once abandoned they simply melted back into the ground. We came across similar mounds in South Shropshire. In the borders this construction has ceased to be used but in the South-West such cottages are lived in to this day.

Saint Mary's was made redundant in 1972 but is beautifully maintained by the local people. It has a Norman nave with two Norman doorways. One has a tympanum decorated with squares and lozenges; the other is now blocked. The windows are mostly 13th century. The chancel has been rebuilt but retains its 13th century arch. The font is 13th century and the pulpit is Jacobean. In the churchyard are the table tombs of Richard Payne Knight and his brother, Thomas Andrew Knight, grandsons of Richard Knight of Madeley, the Shropshire-based ironmaster who made a fortune and which they spent far more wisely than most.

Richard (1750-?) became a Classical scholar and a collector of fine art. It was he who built the fairy-tale, Gothic, castle-mansion at their 10,000 acre estate at Downton, close to their ironworks at Bringewood, and he who enhanced the natural, wild grandeur of its landscape. Richard bequeathed his art collection to the British Museum. His brother, Thomas (1759-1836) was a dis-tinguished naturalist who did important work on the propagation and development of fruits and vegetables.

In mediaeval times the church was visited once a month by the monks of Wormsley Priory who held mass here for their estate workers. The priory's fishpool is fed by the Sap Well, a spring whose waters were used for curing abcesses. This is located just to the east of the church at SO 427 478, below Court House Farm. The water channels that led to the pool can still be seen. Wormsley Priory was founded in about 1216 for Augustinian Canons. It lay in a valley, 1/2m NE of the church, just to the east of Wormsley Grange. As well as their living quarters the monks had a chapel and a water-mill.

Wormsley Grange, commanding and grim-faced, is an Early-Georgian stone-built mansion with five bays and two and a half storeys, and Victorian bay windows. In the outbuildings are several oasthouses, somewhat unusually constructed of stone; most hop kilns are built of brick. The landscaping and planting of the estate was probably the work of the Payne brothers, both of whom were born at Wormsley Grange.

The main road leads north-west from Wormsley, downhill, past conifers, to the small, red lowland fields of Ledgemoor, 1.1/2m NW of Wormsley. The hamlet has a gipsy-ish feel to it: small stone and brick cottages and farmhouses, a tin shack, a small stone building with mullioned windows, a boarded-up Primitive Methodist chapel, sheep and children on bicycles. To the north Ledgemoor adjoins Weobley Marsh. (See Weobley.)

YARKHILL *6m ENE of Hereford*

It lies in the lusty acres of the fertile Frome valley in the domain of the Foleys of Stoke Edith. The name in 811 was

Geardcylle, from the Anglo-Saxon geard - cylen, meaning 'enclosure with a kiln'. In 1066 it was held by Arkell, a knight of King Harold, and there was a mill in the manor. The Roman road from Kenchester to Stretton Grandison (1.3/4m NE) passes through Yarkhill. It follows modern roads from Stretton Sugwas, loses them between Withington and Newton, and continues through fields to Yarkhill.

We approached the settlement from the west. The land is very flat and the river all but invisible because it lies 4ft below ground level, like a drainage ditch. One passes arable fields, Cleveland House of substantial red brick with blue crosses, a hopyard with a Toxic Wilt No Entry sign, sheep and horses, and arrives at the hamlet, a pleasing, tranquil little place at a kink on the lane.

The Vicarage is of 1855, red brick with black, square lozenges (diapers). Next to the door are all that remains of the Norman work of the church, two capitals with trumpet scallops. The church of Saint John the Baptist is essentially of the 13th century, but was much restored in 1862. The tower is also 13th century with a top stage probably of 1466. The dark stone font with its fluted bowl is Norman; the font beneath the tower is 13th century; and the third, fluted font, is probably 17th century. In the churchyard there is an ancient yew, and inset above the entrance door is the head of the mediaeval preaching cross. In the porch itself there is a mediaeval holy water basin, a stoup.

South of the church, on the other side of the road, is a substantial, more or less rectangular, moated site. The ditch is quite broad and well filled with water. The island inside is very overgrown and the timber bridge connecting it to the outside world gave up the ghost long ago. In the adjoining field to the north-east there are traces of a ditch with a right-angled bend. The moat site is probably of the mediaeval manor house.

On the way to the hamlet of Covender, 1/2, NE, is a concrete bridge of 1911 that crosses the steep, deep and dangerous channel that imprisons the River Frome. The old school, 3/4m NW by the Hereford to Worcester road, is Victorian Gothic of 1865 and has a circular window with good glass designed by Casolani. It is now used as the village hall. The old schoolhouse has a lime tree and close by is the site of the village blacksmith's shop. There is a well-known skew bridge over the Hereford to Gloucester Canal, 1m NNE of the church, but for something on this see Monkhide.

YARPOLE *4m NNW of Leominster*
The mediaeval name was Garepolla, from the Anglo-Saxon gear-pol, meaning 'pool formed by a dam for catching fish'. A mile to the north-west there are several pools in Fishpool Valley, a lovely, wooded place accessible from the entrance drive to Croft Castle, now a National Trust property. The same stream that feeds the pools passes through the village, which hides away from the main roads.

Yarpole is a substantial little place with two shops, a post office, the Bell Inn, a village hall, some good 17th century black and white dwellings and a small estate of modern houses. The Manor House has a quaint stone gatehouse which has been used as a lock-up, a secret Quaker Meeting House and, most recently, a bakehouse.

The church of Saint Leonard is noted for its detached tower, one of seven in Herefordshire. It is thought to be 13th century and has two stages: stone in the lower part, with a weather-boarded bell-house above, and a shingled pyramid roof and a spire. Inside, the four huge support pillars stand free from the wall and are strengthened by scissor-bracing.

The church itself is also of about 1300 but was much restored by Sir G.G. Scott in 1864. He also rebuilt the chancel and added the north aisle at the same time. The original mediaeval crown post roof was retained and the octagonal font is Norman. The locals will tell you that the chime of the bells says: "Red fire and charcoal, Say the bells of Yarpole". That had a special significance to farmers of the parish in 1968-9, when the carcases of cattle suffering from foot and mouth disease were burnt on Bircher Common, 1m NE of the village. The fires burned into the night, casting a doleful glow on the horizon. Shades of B.S.E.

Bircher Common extends to 335 acres and is in the care of the National Trust. There is a variety of terrain from pasture to scrub and bracken to the delights of Oaker Coppice, a conifer plantation but leavened with beech and oak and ringed with Scots pine. On the lower slopes of the common is a lightly-wooded area where rights to remove material for roadstone are exercised in small quarries. Birds of prey, herons and snakes are no strangers at Bircher, and man lives up here with them. There is a considerable squatter community and many make full use of their rights to graze horses, sheep, chickens and pigs. Yes, pigs roam free, taking advantage of the right of pannage, but they are in decline. Beware the Common on Bank Holidays. The place becomes a car park full of noisy children and lager-toting townies. On the main road is the crossroads hamlet of Bircher itself. Note the gatehouse on the east side of the road. It has a carving of a human head in an arched recess, all made from one stone. It is at least Norman and could well be Anglo-Saxon.

(For more on this area see the articles on Bircher and Croft.)

YATTON *5m NE of Ross-on-Wye*
In 1066 it was held by an Anglo-Saxon thane, a man who was mounted and armed and who paid for his land by doing military service for his overlord. In rank he came between a freeman and an hereditary aristocrat and he did not pay taxes to the king. The name of Yatton in Domesday Book is Getune, from the Anglo-Saxon geat-tun, meaning 'settlement, or homestead, in the pass'. There is no nucleated village or hamlet at Yatton but it does have two churches.

The old Norman church lies in a hollow beside Chapel Farm, 1m E of How Caple and 1/4m N of Yatton Wood. The church is a typically simple, early Norman building with nave and chancel in one; the timbered belfry was added in the 16th century. The doorway has zig-zag ornament and a Tree of Life in the tympanum. This is the work of the Herefordshire School of Carvers, though the craftsmanship is not of the same order of excellence that they demonstrated elsewhere in the county. Inside is the original piscina and font. The chapel has been disused for many, many years but is in good order and was recently re-roofed.

The new church is situated 1/4m E of the old, though it is 3/4m by road. All Saints was built in 1841 to a cruciform design by William Roberts and has nave, transepts and chancel. The rib-vaulted stone apse was added in 1903. The 15th century screen and the 17th century altar table were brought here from the old chapel. On the walls are two 16th century, Continental carved wood panels, one depicting Christ before Pilate and the other the Resurrection.

Top: Leominster, Brierley Court, has Europe's largest hopyards, owned by Whitbread and Company p.l..c.
Middle left: Leominster, Broadward Hall, 'stately Georgian'.
Middle right: Kingfisher on the River Lugg.
Opposite: Leominster, Eaton Hall bridge, over the River Lugg.
Drawings by S Demaus

There is no settlement by the new church; cottages and farms such as Welsh Court, and the 16th century Dean's Place, are scattered around the lanes every 200 yards or so.

Yatton is now in the parish of Much Marcle and the last burial here was in 1978. It is hard to believe that there was once a shop, a post office, a school and a pub at Yatton. It has not so much become deserted as disappeared. Although Yatton is close to the River Wye all the streams drain several miles eastward to the River Leadon.

YAZOR 7.5m NW of Hereford
The mediaeval name was Iaglsoure, from the Welsh personal name Iago, and the Old English ofer, 'a slope'. It lies on the Hereford to Kington road and culturally is a part of Mansell Lacy and the Foxley estate. The last Anglo-Saxon holder of the manor was a thane of Algar, Earl of East Anglia from 1051. A thane was an armed, mounted knight who held his land in exchange for military service. Algar was the son of Leofric and the famous Lady Godiva. He was twice outlawed but on each occasion won back his title and estates with the assistance of Gruffydd ap Llewelyn of Gwynedd and Powys. Earl Algar died in 1062, four years before the Norman Conquest. Today, Yazor consists of a cottage and a redundant church on one side of the main road, and a large farm, a former school, and a ruined church on the other.

The old church of Saint John the Baptist lies in a field behind the Court. Only the transept has a roof; its windows are of about 1300. The arcade is Perpendicular with octagonal piers. Much of the ruins, including the tower, are ivy-clad. An ancient, hollow yew tree with a girth of some 27ft soldiers on manfully.

The new church of Saint Mary was built in 1843 to a design by George Rowe for the Price family. It is all but hidden from the main road by pines and oaks. The plan is cruciform; the style is Early English; the entrance porch is in the base of the tower; the font is 15th century, from the old church; the stained glass in the chancel lancet windows is highly regarded; and there are several monuments to the family of Sir Ulvedale Price (1747-1829), the leading proponent of English Picturesque landscaping. In the churchyard we saw a lone pheasant in search of sanctuary from the gun-happy Davenports, the present owners of the Foxley estate. (See Mansell Lacy.) The main road school was built in 1869 but closed when the Church of England built a new one at Mansell Lacy in 1889.

In the 17th century there was an established tradition of morris dancing at Yazor; today it is unlikely that the settlement could raise the eight men necessary to form a team.

Yarsop, a farming hamlet, a good 1/2m NNE of the church, lies hidden in a lovely, secluded, wooded valley. Here there are several murky pools from which the Yazor Brook emerges and passes through Mansell Lacy and Credenhill on its way to Hereford.

APPENDICES

THE LOWER LUGG VALLEY
This article was taken from *Six Walks Exploring the Landscape History of the Lower Lugg Valley*, a most excellent little book that we can heartily recommend. The author is Anthea Brian of Bodenham Hall, Bodenham, HR1 3JT, and it was published in 1993. Profits from the sale of the book go to the Herefordshire Nature Trust. We offer our most sincere thanks to Anthea Brian for granting us permission to reprint these background notes to the walks.

Introduction
The Lugg is Herefordshire's neglected river. Attention has always focussed on the River Wye with its spectacular scenery glorified by the picturesque movement. But the Lugg is even more Herefordshire's own river. Its catchment covers half the area of the county and for over three-quarters of its length it flows within the county. In contrast the Wye is shared with many other counties and less than a half of its length lies within Herefordshire. The wide, serene valley of the Lower Lugg has contributed greatly in the past to the wealth of the county.

Early History of the valley
The width and importance of the Lugg valley stems chiefly from the fact that the Lugg was formerly the larger of Herefordshire's two main rivers, the Wye being its smaller tributary. At the end of the Ice Age the River Teme, swollen with water from the melting ice, joined the Lugg to form one mighty river flowing down the centre of what was to become Herefordshire and carving out the great wide valley that we see today. Later moraines blocked the outlet of the Teme and forced it to flow east to join the Severn leaving the wide valley, underlain by sheets of gravel, to be occupied by the now much smaller Lugg on its own.

As vegetation returned following the end of the Ice Age and the retreat of the ice around 8,000 BC the damp valley floor would have become covered by alder woodland. When man settled in the area he began to clear this flat, fertile land by the river together with the gentler slopes of the valley. But where the valley sides were steep and difficult of access woodland was left and remnants of this are still present today and can be seen from the Walks. The higher parts of the cleared land were converted to arable. The flat river side areas of the floodplain became grassland which would have been managed at first as pasture grazed by flocks of sheep and cattle. In these early days the flocks came from many settlements, some situated far from the river, and all grazed together on the riverside pastures. This practice is known as intercommoning and there is evidence that it dates back to the Bronze Age (c.1700-650 BC). Intercommoning continued up to the 19th century on the Sutton meadows where, in addition to the local people, parishes like Preston Wynne, Felton and Little Cowarne, situated well away from the Lugg, all had grazing rights at that time. Still to this very day farms in Lugwardine, Hampton Bishop, Tupsley and Holmer retain their ancient rights to graze their animals in common on the Lugg Meadows close to Hereford.

It is thought that the settlements intercommoning on the riverside grasslands would, in Bronze Age and Iron Age (c. 650 BC-50 AD) times, have all been part of a single territorial unit much larger than a present day parish and in the lower Lugg valley the Iron Age hillfort of Sutton Walls was probably the centre of one such territorry.

In these early days the floodplain grasslands were managed as pasture rather than hay meadow. To make hay some grass cutting instrument is required. The Romans (c.50-400 AD) certainly had scythes but it is not known how much earlier the practice of hay making first began. It must however have been well established in the Saxon period (c. 400-1070 AD) because by Norman times nearly all settlements had their own meadows. These were considered of greater value than arable and they were all carefully recorded in Domesday Book in 1086. The meadows in the Lower Lugg Valley were much the largest in the county at that time.

By early mediaeval times (c. 1070-1350 AD) the open field system of agriculture was widespread over the country. This system was especially associated with the Midlands but existed over most of Herefordshire in some form and was very well established in the Lugg Valley. Under this system each settlement, consisting of houses with enclosed paddocks around them, was surrounded by the land farmed in common by the inhabitants. This land was typically made up of four elements:
1) open arable fields where corn and other crops were grown,
2) woodland which provided building timber, stakes, firewood, etc.,
3) pasture and rough grazing all the year round on the manorial waste,
4) common meadows where the hay needed to feed the plough oxen and other stock through the winter was grown. Meadow land was still valued more highly than arable,

Figure 1 (not given here) shows how these four elements were probably situated in one of the Townships of Bodenham. The organisation of these different areas was controlled by the manorial court in such a way that the settlement was virtually self-sufficient.

The system broke down gradually over the course of time as manorial courts lost their power and in most places the change from communal to private ownership of land was completed by an Enclosure Act in the 17th-19th centuries.

Surviving evidence of all the four elements of the open field system will be pointed out on the Walks but the emphasis is on the Meadows. This is for three reasons:
1) ancient meadows were especially well developed in the Lugg valley and it still possible to see their outlines,
2) documentary evidence of their use is particularly good for the area,
3) one of the meadows complete with its flowers still survives more or less in its mediaeval form. This meadow, Lugg Meadow near Hereford, is the largest and in most ways the best example of a mediaeval common meadow now left in the whole of Britain.

The Meadows

The management of these early hay meadows held in common by people of a settlement is of great interest. The inhabitants held strips, often called doles, in the common hay meadow on which they were entitled to cut hay for their own use. These strips were a permanent feature of the meadow with bounds marked out by stones (dole stones) but every year each person held different strips and lots were cast before mowing began to determine who had which strips for that year. When the hay had been cut and carried and the grass had had a chance to grow again the animals of the settlement were allowed into the meadow to graze the aftermath. This usually took place on Lammas day (August 1st). The animals remained in the meadow until winter or sometimes on until Candlemas (Feb. 2nd) when the meadow was 'shut up' again for the hay to grow.

Individual common meadows acquired different names derived from different aspects of the system. Sometimes they were called Lammas Meadow, sometimes Lot or Dole Meadow. Sometimes they were called after the settlement viz. Bowley Common Meadow, Hampton or Moreton Meadow, but most often they were called after the river by which they lay and so several of the Lugg valley settlements had their own Lugg Meadow. What is known as 'Lugg Meadow' today, situated near to Hereford, was just one of the many 'Lugg Meadows' in the valley - in the days when people did not move far from home this would not have caused confusion. Finally, some meadows acquired individual names such as The Wergins, Walney Meadow and Mitley. Whatever the name given to the meadow the system of management was the same.

Not all the meadows were held in common. The Lord of the Manor, in addition to holding strips in the common meadows had a private meadow of his own. Some of these former demesne meadows can be identified and will be pointed out on the Walks.

These common or Lammas meadows, once so widespread in the country, have nearly all gone now. Gradually the manorial system broke down and individuals began to enclose their strips in the meadows with permanent fences without being fined by the manorial court. Then, by exchanging strips with neighbours individuals acquired larger blocks of the enclosed land. Finally what was left of the common meadow was usually divided up into private ownership as the result of an Enclosure Act. This happened in Marden and Sutton in 1808. For some unknown reason the Lugg Meadows near Hereford were never enclosed and so became registered as common land under the 1963 Commons Act. But the commoners could of course only register rights for half the year, from Lammas to Candlemas. The other half of the year the land is in private ownership, held in strips with all owners growing their own crop of hay but unable to fence their strips because of the commoners rights for the rest of the year. Commonland of this type only operates on 15 other meadows in the whole country.

Common meadows are or were mostly situated beside a river or stream. They may flood regularly in winter and the silt deposited by the retreating waters fertilises the soil and builds up a level surface. In many cases underlying gravel ensures good drainage so that the meadows never become water-logged. In addition to having the river on one side nearly all the meadows are bordered on the other side by a stream, in Herefordshire often called a rhea. Some of these - Sutton Rhea, Lugg Rhea and the old Ea, - will be pointed out on the Walks. These side streams or rheas lie just where the flat meadow ends and the hillslope begins and often run for a mile or more before at last entering the river, thus making each meadow almost an island. This watery boundary to the meadow would have acted as a barrier keeping cattle out of the meadow during the hay growing season and inside it for the rest of the year and it is most probable that these rheas were made deliberately by diverting the lower courses of side streams. If this was so then the rheas are as old as the common meadows themselves and an integral part of the system. The rheas also help to drain the meadows after floods. As a later development it only needed a simple weir to be built across the river to enable the system to be used to flood a meadow thus deliberately changing a natural floodplain meadow into a man-engineered water-meadow at will. Some land owners achieved the same result even more easily by putting flood gates in the arches of the bridges. Places where meadows were formerly 'drowned' in this way will be noted on the Walks.

The Bridges

The Lugg has a very fine set of bridges. When Leland travelled through Herefordshire in the 15th century he recorded eight stone bridges on the Lugg from Leominster down to the confluence. In contrast there were only two bridges on the Wye in the whole county. Three of Leland's bridges on the Lugg remain, four have been rebuilt and only one has really gone. (It seems possible that he missed bridges at Bodenham, Marden and Moreton.) Many of these old bridges were altered in the 18th century for the benefit of navigation and the alterations are themselves of interest. Only two of the bridges have been rebuilt in recent years and are unattractive, concrete structures. There are now 16 bridges, excluding the railway bridges, between Leominster and the confluence. All have an interesting history and are focal points of interest on the Walks.

The Mills

Today there are no working mills on the Lower Lugg and only two places where some of the mill buildings still stand, Tidnor and Lugg Bridge. Domesday Book records at least five mills for settlements beside the Lower Lugg and these were the most valuable mills in the whole county. Their high value indicates large size and this presumably resulted partly from the large amount of corn grown in the fertile Lugg valley, as indicated by the high number of plough teams recorded in Domesday Book, and partly because the Lugg provided a good and constant source of power.

By the end of the 17th century the number of mills had risen to ten but only a few years later there was only one. It might seem that some natural disaster had swept the mills away but that was not the case. The disaster was man-made. The mills were destroyed as the result of an Act of Parliament passed in 1695 which set up Trustees with wide-ranging powers to promote the Navigation of the Wye and Lugg by buying up all the mills standing on the two rivers with their associated, obstructing weirs and destroying them. Many people objected at the time complaining that local inhabitants would be unable to get their corn ground and that fords would become impassable. Others said that, with the weirs down, the rivers would flow so fast in some places and cause such shoals and shallows in others that navigation would become harder instead of easier. No notice was taken of these complaints but in the event the objectors were proved right and this was publicly admitted in a second Act passed in 1727 which now urged Trustees to persuade riparian land owners to build new mills and weirs. But it was too late. By then other arrangements for grinding corn had been made and only one new mill was built following the 1727 Act. This was the mill still standing at Lugg Bridge (see Walk 3). Although the mills and their weirs were destroyed and a lot of the materials that had gone into their make-up had probably been carried away some of the broken down stonework collapsed into the river forming a short length of stony bed in parts of the river where normally the bed is made up of silt. The stones themselves can only be seen when the river is very low but their presence can be inferred when in July the water crowfoot is in flower for this plant grows only where the bed of the river is stony and so is a useful indicator of the presence of some former man-made structure.

An even more reliable guide to the positions of these old mills comes from a Survey made in 1697 when the Trustees asked for a "competent person" to go up the river inspecting all the obstructions, finding the owners and values of all the mills and recommending how the obstructions could be made navigable. The Survey survives and it is almost certain that it was made by a Mr. Daniel Denell who, at about that time, was employed by Exeter City Council as engineer in charge of major, pioneering works on the Exeter Canal. A lot of the information given in this booklet has been derived from this Survey.

The Navigation

Although the 1695 Act had ended in disaster another attempt to improve navigation on the Lugg was made around 1750 which seems to have been initiated by Leominster Borough. As a result of this phase of activity a much more sensible approach was adopted which involved building a number of locks. There is documentary evidence for nine locks and remains of some of these and of a possible three others are still visible in the river under certain conditions.

Information about the cargoes carried is very scanty but they probably consisted mainly of timber, cider, malt, hops, wool, corn and oak bark for tanning, the latter was a major export from Chepstow from about 1850. The most famous cargo was the Leominster Priory bells which were taken down the Lugg and Wye to Chepstow to be recast in 1756 and returned by the same route. Warehouses for the storage of goods awaiting shipment or collection were built on the Wye and Walk 4 goes past the site of such a warehouse beside the Lugg. However, this Navigation was never very successful and with the building first of a canal and then of a railway to serve Leominster it went gradually out of use.

LOST VILLAGES

There are 30 settlements listed in Domesday Book that lie within the modern county boundary but which no longer exist. For eight of these we have later names, given in parenthesis, and four have approximate locations (from wood and field names). These are given by the Ordnance Survey grid reference numbers. The remaining 22 have not been traced in any way, though it is possible that some may exist as modern settlements under a different name.

Alac
Alcamestune
Bageburge (Bagburrow) 74 45
Beltrou
Bertune Barton (in Hereford) 49 39
Burcestanestune
Bernoldune (Bernaldeston)
Chipelai (Cuple)
Chetestor
Curdeslege
Edwardestune
Elnodestune
Hanlie (Hanley's End) 69 46
Lege
Luncombe
Mateurdin
Midevrde (Middlewood in Winforton) 30 45
Merestone / Merestun
Pene Gecdoc
Querentune
Stane
Stanway 40 70
Tumbelawe
Turlestune
Wadetune
Wapleford
Westelet
Winetune
Westvode (Westwood)
Wluetone

GLOUCESTER TO HEREFORD CANAL

The Gloucester to Hereford Canal was begun in 1793. The length from Gloucester to Ledbury was designed by Hugh Henshall, brother-in-law to the great James Brindley, and reached Ledbury in 1798.

The price of coal immediately dropped from 24 shillings a ton to 13 shillings and 6 pence. However, shortage of water only allowed it to be used for a few months of the year.

It was not until 1839 that the Ledbury to Hereford section was begun. This was designed and overseen by the engineer Stephen Ballard. It reached Canon Frome and Ashperton in 1842 and arrived at Hereford in 1845.

The canal was finally sold to the Great Western Railway. It closed in 1880 and after 1877 the stretches not used for the railway itself were auctioned off in small lots. Except for the Manchester Ship Canal of 1894 this was the last main line canal to be constructed in Britain.

The track of the canal can be seen in several places between Ledbury and Hereford. It roughly follows the line of the A438, but between one and two miles to the north of the road. The deep, gloomy cuttings at each end of the 400 yard Ashperton Tunnel, the embankments over the Frome and Lugg valleys and the tunnel under Aylestone Hill at Hereford are especially prominent.

HEREFORD CATTLE

All Herefords, even cross-breeds, are distinguished by having a white face. The predominant body colours are red and white.

Today, 50% of the beef bulls bred in Britain are Herefords and 40% of dairy cows are cross bred with a Hereford bull. In recent years medical concern has been expressed at the high fat content in Hereford beef. Nevertheless, Herefords are still the most numerous meat breed in the world.

The reasons for its popularity are its docility, its ability to forage, to breed profusely, produce calves easily, and its hardiness - it can survive outdoors in almost any climate.

The breed developed in Herefordshire as both a beef and a ploughing ox, probably the result of cross breeding the ancient, large Welsh white and smaller Celtic-Roman red. They were a very varied group in both size and colouring and not until the 18th century did a recognised breed develop. Probably the most influential breeder was Benjamin Tomkins who began work in 1738 at his Court House farm, Canon Pyon. He suppressed the work oxen characteristics and developed a beef animal. His son took Black Hall farm in 1769 and continued to refine the breed.

The first herd book was begun in 1846. Herefords were first exported in to America 1817, and to Australia in 1825. Today there are 1,200 registered breeders and some 5,000,000 pedigree Herefords worldwide.

Note: The natural Hereford has horns. In America, in 1900, Warren Gammon developed the polled, or hornless, breed by using naturally hornless animals. In England a polled strain was developed by using a Galloway bull. This breed was established in 1955. Despite this flagrant flouting of the rules of pedigree these animals have been entered in the British Herd Book. The pure bred Hereford is now in serious danger of becoming extinct.

TOPOGRAPHY AND GEOLOGY

Herefordshire is saucer-shaped with a diameter of about 30 miles. The high land of the perimeter dips to a central lowland with the City of Hereford at its centre. However, the lowland is not flat. Except for the flood plains of its rivers the land is undulating with a few pronounced hills and ridges, almost all of which are wooded.

The Wye is the largest river in the County. It enters from the west, wriggles around Hereford, and leaves to the south through the dramatic gorge of Symonds Yat. Most of the county's other major rivers - the Arrow, the Lugg, the Frome and the Dore drain into the Wye. The Teme and the Leadon drain eastwards into the Severn.

Four-fifths of Herefordshire is Devonian Old Red Sandstone, red rocks that have weathered to fine-textured red earths. Silurian limestone outcrops in the north-west and the south-east and also form the famous Woolhope Dome, six miles east of Hereford. The Malvern Hills to the extreme east consist of ancient pre-Cambrian gneissic rocks, forced up through the much younger limestones. To the south are small areas of Carboniferous rocks that contain iron and lead ores.

Stone for building has been quarried in all parts of the county. Iron was mined and smelted in Celtic times to the 18th century in the area south of Ross-on-Wye. Today the only mineral working is at Leinthall Earls in the north-west, where limestone is quarried, and near Hereford and Leominster where sand and gravel is extracted.

THE ENGLISH OAK

The English Oak is the commonest of all broad-leaved trees in both England and Europe. There are two prime species: the pendunculate oak, which has stalked acorns and stalkless leaves; and the sessile (or durmast) oak, which has stalkless acorns and leaves with stalks. In practice there are numerous hybrids. Both species adopt a different shape depending on their proximity to each other. If they are close, in a dense wood, they grow tall with a straight trunk and a cluster of upwardly pointing branches (stag-headed); if they are well spaced they adopt a rounded shape with heavy curved boughs. In mediaeval times woods were deliberately thinned and the growth bud nipped out to encourage the development of massive curved boughs because these curved timbers were required for both the construction of ships and the trusses of buildings. Those old, parkland-like groups of 12 oaks to the acre were not natural at all, but carefully managed.

Most oaks live for between 300 and 500 years, but in mediaeval times they were felled at about 200 years and produced about 75 tons of timber. Today they are commercially cut at less than 100 years and produce half the weight. In nature most broadleaved trees, including the oak, are killed by the weight of their own branches. These put a great strain on the bole of the tree which cracks, allowing frost to freeze the sapwood and water and disease spores to get into the heartwood which then rots. A carefully pollarded and tended oak tree can live for over 1,000 years.

Commercially it is only the heartwood of an oak that has any real value. This is soaked in tannin and is extremely durable - Hearts of Oak became a symbolic phrase to describe courageous Englishmen. The sapwood, about 20% of the tree, is normally discarded.

From the bark of the oak tannin was extracted for the preservation of hides; and from the oak apple (a spongy ball caused by the gall wasp laying her eggs in a shoot) ink was made by mixing the gall with iron filings.

The tallest oak in England is at Whitfield House, Hereford, and measures 135 feet. The largest oak in England is at Croft Castle and measures 42 feet 6 inches at the bole.

The oldest oak in Herefordshire and possibly England, is one of the Old Grey Men of Moccas which could be 2,000 years of age.

SOME SOCIAL FACILITIES

Tourist Information Centres
Bromyard, Rowberry Street
Hay-on-Wye, The Car Park
Hereford, Saint Owen Street
Kington, Mill Street
Ledbury, Church Lane
Leominster, Corn Square
Ross-on-Wye, Broad Street

Libraries
Bromyard, Church Street
Hay-on-Wye, Chancery Lane
Hereford, Broad Street
Kington, Bridge Street
Ledbury, The Homend
Leintwardine, Trippleton Lane
Leominster, Buttercross
Ross-on-Wye, Cantilupe Road
Tenbury Wells, Teme Street
Weobley, Back Lane

Newspapers and Radio Stations
Hereford Times, Holmer Road, Hereford, 01432 274413
Hereford Journal, 43 Broad Street, Hereford, 01432 355353
Hereford Admag, 3 East Street, Hereford, 01432 353444
Ledbury Reporter and Malvern Gazette, 11a High Street, Ledbury, 01531 633233
Ludlow, Leominster and Tenbury Wells Advertiser, 2, Upper Galdeford, Ludlow, 01584 872183
Ross Gazette Limited, 35 High Street, Ross, 01989 562007
BBC Hereford and Worcester, Broad Street, Hereford, 01432 355 252
Radio Wyvern, 18 Broad Street, Hereford, 01432 343400
Hereford Hospital Radio, County Hospital, Union Walk, Hereford, 01432 343400

Market Days
EC means Early Closing
Bromyard: Thursday, EC Tuesday
Hereford: Wednesday, main livestock, no EC
Kington: Tuesday, Thursday, EC Wednesday
Ledbury: Wednesday livestock, EC Wednesday
Leominster: Friday, EC Thursday
Ross-on-Wye: Thursday, Saturday, livestock Friday, EC Wednesday

Swimming Pools
Hereford Leisure Pool, Saint Martin's Avenue
Ledbury Swimming Pool, Lawnside Road
Leominster Swimming Baths, Caswell Terrace
Ross-on-Wye Swimming Pool, Red Meadow Road
Tenbury & District Swimming Pool, Palmer's Meadow

Cinemas and Night Clubs
Cannon Cinemas, Commercial Road, Hereford
Regal Cinema, Riverside Mews, Tenbury Wells
The Entertainer, Widemarsh Street, Hereford
Euphoria Nightclub, South Street, Leominster
Marilyn's Nightclub, Commercial Road, Hereford
Mavericks' Nightclub, Gaol Street, Hereford
Norma Jean's, West Street, Hereford

Golf Courses
Bodenham, Brockington Golf Club
Burghill, Burghill Golf Club, Tillington Road
Hay-on-Wye, Summerhill Golf Course
Hereford, Belmont Lodge and Golf Club, Belmont
Kington, Kington Golf Club, Bradnor Hill
Leominster, Grove Golf Centre, Fordbridge
Ross on Wye Golf Club, Gorseley
Tenbury Wells, Cadmore Golf Club, St. Michaels
Upper Sappey, on the B4203 near Tenbury
Upton Bishop, South Herefordshire Golf and Country Club, Twin Lakes
Weobley, Herefordshire Golf Club, Wormsley
Whitchurch, Hill Valley Golf and Country Club

DEER PARKS
Moccas, fallow deer
Kentchurch, fallow deer
Eastnor, red deer
(Dinmore, escaped fallow deer in Queenswood)
Ganarew, Wyastone Leys

A NOTE ON CIDER

Cider was being made in Herefordshire in pre-Roman times. The original cider apple was a wild fruit, small and very bitter, though over the years 265 varieties have been developed. They have fetching names such as Slack My Girdle, Handsome Maud's, Skrymen's Fancy, Bloody Turk, Sheep's Nose, White Norman, Brown Snout, Foxwhelp, Knotted Kernal, Frequin, and Kingstone Black (one of the few apples that produce a good cider without being blended). Many of these are lost but some rare ones are being re-cultivated by the Dunkerton Cider Company.

In rural areas cider was often drunk instead of water, which was not always pure. Indeed, it was common practice for farmers to give their workers an allowance of cider as part of their wages. Production increased during the 18th century, dipped during the Napoleonic Wars, but flourished again in the mid-19th century when the canal (1845) and the railway (1855) came to Hereford. Cider could then be economically transported around the country.

In 1887 Percy Bulmer started up in business as a cider maker. By 1891 his factory covered eight acres and in 1897 the famous Woodpecker brand was introduced. Today, Bulmer is the largest cider maker in the world. One thousand tons of apples can be processed in a day and the gigantic Strongbow tank can hold 1.6 million gallons, making it the largest alcoholic drink container in the world. earth. This, and other great, steel cider storage tanks dominate the western skyline of Hereford. Between them they can hold 15 million gallons. The Bulmers' highly mechanised production method consists of wash-ing; milling, to extract the juice; settling; fermentation with yeast in oak vats, a process that takes between four and 12 weeks; and finally storage, when the cider can mature.

Cider apples grow well in Herefordshire because it has mild Springs, warm Summers and a good rainfall. Today there are 8,000 acres under cultivation. The species are propagated by grafting and budding on to other root stocks. Older orchards have full grown trees;whereas recent varieties are more like bushes, designed for machine picking. Harvesting begins in mid-September and may

Above: Hereford in the early 17th century. The norman motte and bailey castle has been strengthened in stone and the town walls still stand strong. This is a photograph of a model on display at th Old House Museum.
Opposite: Hereford: a trow being pulled manually upstream by a team of six bow-hauliers to the wharves at Hereford. From a contemporary etching of 1778. Note that the cathedral still has two towers; the western tower collapsed a few years later, in 1786.
Below: Hereford, the elegant Saint Peter's Square in the early 19th century. The new Shire Hall with its Greek Doric columns was built between 1817 and 1819 by Sir Robert Smirke.

continue up to Christmas. The apples are kept for about four weeks to mellow before being milled. The average bush-tree produces 1.1/3 cwt. of fruit which converts to about 10 gallons of cider.

Traditionally, the apples were processed on the farm and many hundreds of the small, old, stone mills can be seen lying derelict around the county. The apples were placed into the circular channel and crushed by the large, vertical millstone attached to a central post and pushed around by a horse. The resulting mash was then folded into layers in a coarse horse-hair cloth and pressed in a separate horizontal press. (Note: the mills, or mashers, are often incorrectly called presses.) The juice was collected and put into an oak barrel. As the cider fermented it frothed and had to be constantly topped up or it went sour. Fermentation took about six weeks. The barrel was then sealed with a bung and the cider left to mature for eight weeks.

A curiosity is the Cider Bible, so called because Wycliffe translated 'strong drink' as 'cider'. A copy of this Bible is kept in the chained library at Hereford Cathedral.

Some Herefordshire Cider Producers
H.P. Bulmer, Plough Lane, Hereford, off the Brecon Road
Dunkerton's Cider Company, on a minor road 1.1/2m S of Pembridge, at Hay's Head, Luntley
Lyne Downe Farm, on A449 near Much Marcle, near Ledbury
Symonds Cider, on A465 at Stoke Lacy.
H. Weston & Sons Ltd., Much Marcle, near Ledbury
Cider Museum & King Offa Distillery, Pomona Place, Hereford.
Great Oak Cider, Great Oak, Almeley
Knight's Cider, Crumpton Oaks Farm, Storridge, just off A4103

There are an increasing number of small farmers who make cider on their own premises and who offer it for sale locally. For those interested in making their own cider the Worcestershire College of Agriculture at Hindlip has a course entitled Basic Cider Making for the Small Producer

HUNTING IN HEREFORDSHIRE
There are eight foxhunts that operate in the county: North Herefordshire, Ledbury, Ledbury North, Clifton on Teme, South Herefordshire, Radnor and West Hereford, Cotswold Vale, and Golden Valley. The Ross Harriers at Caughley hunt hares. Little wonder that Herefordshire soil is so red.

A NOTE ON COMMON LAND
A Common is land owned by the Lord of the Manor, or his successor, over which the local inhabitants have rights in common with the owner and each other. These rights vary in kind and detail from one place to another but usually include one or more of the following: 1) the right to use pasture for cattle and sheep, and sometimes other animals and birds, 2) to turn out pigs to forage, pannage, 3) to take wood, for fires or repair buildings, or bracken for animal bedding, estovers, 4) to take sand and gravel or building stone, 5) to take fish, piscary.

The Anglo-Saxon common lands were once very extensive and a vital part of the rural economy. However, over the years they have been whittled away: in the 12th century by the avarice of the new Norman landlords, and in the 16th and 18th centuries by Parliamentary Acts of Enclosure. The result is that most of what is left is what was unwanted - steep hill pasture, heath, moor and bog - often in remote places. Paradoxically these are just the areas that are now held in high esteem by walkers and seekers of solitude.

The law relating to Commons is a tangle, but all have one of six kinds of legal status. On Regulated Commons (regulated by a local authority), National Trust Commons and Act of Parliament Commons the public at large has the right to roam; but on Private Commons, Section Nine Commons (owner not known) and Commons in Trust (usually conservation areas) only the owner and the local commoners have right of access. However, as Commons cannot be fenced about and most are crossed by public footpaths the public is usually allowed on sufferance. Remember though, that all Commons are owned by somebody and that many Commoners still depend upon them for at least a part of their livelihood.

In Herefordshire there are 197 Commons on the Register held at the Department of the Land Agent in Bath Street, Hereford. Together with some border areas registered by adjacent authorities there are nearly 6,500 acres of Common land in the county.

Village Greens are not classed as Commons. They have similar origins but are primarily for leisure use by the villagers and are not used for agriculture. There are 42 registered Village Greens in Herefordshire.

AN AFFAIR OF DISHONOUR
In the February 18th, 1996 edition of the *Sunday Times* there appeared an article by Russell Miller on how Brigadier Peter de la Billiere, Director of the SAS, caused a virtual mutiny among his men by ordering them to go on a suicide mission code-named Operation Mikado during the Falklands War of 1982. The objective was to destroy three Exocet missiles at Rio Grande on Tierra del Fuego, southern Argentina. The problem was that there was very poor intelligence on the enemy's defences; they did not even know where the missiles were stored. What is more, because of the long distances involved, there was no real hope of escape even if the object was achieved.

Senior N.C.Os, men with years of experience and tried and tested on numerous engagements, agreed the plan was a madcap scheme, an impossible mission. But de la Billiere was adamant. He wanted action for the regiment, he wanted a feather in his cap and was quite literally running around London seeking commissions. The leading N.C.O., a staff sergeant called 'Jakey' and the most highly regarded man in the entire regiment, did the unthinkable; he sought 'permission to withdraw'. To be blunt, he refused to go.

De la Billiere, who was now more a politician than a soldier, was furious. To save face he turned on the young officer in charge of the 65 men of B Squadron, Major John Moss, and quite unfairly accused him of having generated what he called "this luke-warm attitude". Luke-warm! The men were about to mutiny! So, he sacked the young officer. To be removed from his command during a war just about finishes a soldier's career. In his autobiography, *Looking for Trouble*, de la Billiere gives an account of the affair which is grossly misleading. Now that many of the men involved have left the army the truth is emerging.

Incidentally, the raid was aborted at the last moment because news came in that a previously unknown radar station had been located. De la Billiere's plan would, indeed, have been suicidal. The N.C.O.s were right; their Director was wrong, though he still will not admit it.

But what about the scapegoat, the disgraced young officer? He had little option but to leave the army and is now employed by a security firm in London. The Brigadier went on to become General Sir Peter de la Billiere and he now lives in a rather nice Georgian house in the village of Aston Crews, four miles east of Ross-on-Wye.

SIR THOMAS CLAVOWE
Sir Thomas Clanvowe was a knight of Welsh descent who held the manors of Ocle Pychard, Cusop, Hergest and Yazor from the Mortimer, Earl of March. He was a soldier and a poet who consorted with kings and was a leading intellectual of his day. Amongst his friends was Geoffrey Chaucer. Clanvowe, together with Edmund Mortimer (uncle to the 11-year old Edmund Mortimer, Earl of March), was captured by Owain Glyndwr's forces at the Battle of Pilleth in 1402. His marcher lands were destroyed by the Welsh and in recompense he received an annuity for life from King Henry IV. In middle age Clanvowe adopted the 'heretical' Christian beliefs of John Wyclif and became a Lollard.

OWAIN GLYNDWR'S LAST DAYS
What happened to Owain Glyndwr? His rebellions against King Henry IV had failed and in 1412 he simply vanished from history. The mystery has led to speculation and various stories will be found elsewhere in this book. Most of the theories have the old warrior seeing out his last days being comforted by one of his daughters, three of whom had married English aristocrats and lived in Herefordshire.

To avoid confusion here is a listing of Glyndwr's children by his wife, Margaret Hanmer, herself the daughter of an English border lord, whom he married in 1383. They had six sons, all of whom, but one, died before Glyndwr disappeared, and five daughters. (Don't tell Margaret but there were also several illegitimate children about whom virtually nothing is known.) Glyndwr's daughters were:
Isabel, married Adam of Iorwerth, but nothing is known about her except that she was probably the eldest.
Catherine, married Edward Mortimer in 1402, but she probably died before Glyndwr disappeared.
Alice, married Sir John Scudamore after 1403. Scudamore held both Kentchurch and Monnington Stradel (near Vowchurch).
Margaret, married Roger (or Richard) of Monnington.
Janet, married Sir John Croft, possibly in 1412, but there is no record of the date.

The late Geoffrey Hodges, in his book *Owain Glyndwr* (1995), favours the idea that Glyndwr spent his last years with Alice and died on Lawton Hope Hill on a journey to visit his other Herefordshire-based daughters.

In 1413 Henry IV died. The new king, Henry V, offered the Welsh rebels a pardon but Glyndwr never took up the offer. There would have been terms attached, pride would take a tumble, his followers would feel betrayed, and could the king be trusted? These were treacherous and callous times. One of Henry V's first actions was to persecute the comparatively harmless Lollards. He had Lord Cobham (Sir John Oldcastle) hung in chains and burned to death, and he was killed for a philosophy; Glyndwr had slaughtered Englishmen, and Herefordshire men in particular. Remember Pilleth, and New Radnor? In battle he was a butcher and often killed wantonly and beyond all need. He could have expected little mercy had he been captured and anyone sheltering him would have to be prepared to pay the ultimate price. And would Glyndwr be selfish enough to endanger the lives of his daughters?

Yet, there were those who would not care a jot, namely those many hundreds of his ardent admirers in Wales. Here were men who would have gladly died for him, who would have been proud beyond measure to have helped him in his hour of need. Look to the Berwyn Mountains, whence he came, to wilderness places of safety amongst loyal friends. Why risk hiding in Herefordshire surrounded by people whose fathers and sons you had slaughtered? Servants and farm workers would betray you in no time at all. If you must seek the house of a blood relative, look for Isabel and her Welsh husband, or one of his illegitimate children, or the connections of his brother Tudur, or those of his brothers-in-law who fought with him in the early days of his rebellion.

The fact remains, all we really know is that Owain Glyndwr disappeared in 1412. For a national hero that was a pretty smart move. We all love a good mystery. He was not called 'the old fox' for nothing. Furthermore, all his six sons died childless, so there are no direct heirs, no descendants to do anything that might tarnish the legend.

Finally, Glyndwr had another very good reason for not surrendering to Henry V; his loyalty to Richard II. Richard had been deposed by Henry IV in 1399, and had almost certainly been murdered in 1400 at Pontefract Castle, where he had been held prisoner. However, it was widely believed at the time that he had escaped and was living in Scotland. Glyndwr was, in effect, waiting for his old master to claim back the throne and reward his faithful servant, and Wales, with grace and favour.

ROY PALMER, A BRIEF BIOGRAPHY
Although he has the misfortune to live just over the border, at Greenway near Dymock in Glocetershire, Roy Palmer is very much an adopted son of Herefordshire. He has walked much of the county and is an expert on its folklore.

In the *Oxford Book of Traditional Verse* the editor, the late Frederick Woods, described Roy Palmer as "that prince of traditional researchers", and there are few practising folk musicians and journalists who would disagree with this opinion.

Roy is also a singer and a writer but, first and foremost, he is a folk scholar. In modern times these have been few and far between. A. L. Lloyd and Ewan McColl, for example, both thought of themselves more as part of the tradition rather than students of it. In consequence, one is never quite sure what was of the people and what was of their own making.

Roy Palmer, by way of contrast, is a meticulous researcher. He tells us as it was, not how he thinks it ought to have been. His books of songs and folklore are models of their kind with sources fully credited, background notes provided and any editorial dabblings duly documented.

What is more, he is a gentle man who is both receptive of the views of others and generous with his time to fellow researchers. These are not qualities found in abundance amongst academics. In many respects he reminds me of Hamish Henderson, the poet and Head of Scottish Studies at Edinburgh University, kindly scholars both.

Roy Palmer was born in 1932 at Markfield in Leicestershire, of parents native to that county. He was introduced to traditional music by the headmistress of his village school at Newtown Linford.

The village itself left a lasting impression. In those days it was a sleepy place, with a main street lined with thatched cottages and working farms. Nearby was Bradgate Park, with its tales of Lady Jane Grey and how the massive oaks had been pollarded as a gesture of mourning when she was beheaded.

In 1943 Roy went to the grammar School at Coalville

where, despite a reputation for being something of a buffoon and mischief-maker, he won a State Scholarship and was accepted at Manchester University. Here he completed an honours degree course in French, married Pat, his school sweetheart, and then went on to get an M.A. by a thesis on Victor Hugo's *Les Miserables*. He completed his National Service at Catterick and then took a teachers' training course back in Manchester. During his studies in that town 'of cotton twists and twills' he wrote poetry, which was published in anthologies, and took part in public readings, one of them on the same bill as the celebrated John Heath-Stubbs. His musical interests included jazz and he attended classical concerts by the Halle Orchestra, but he was increasingly attracted to traditional music. Major influences were radio programmes such as *Ballads and Blues*, and Peter Kennedy's *As I Roved Out*, and the radio ballads of Charles Parker, especially the *Ballad of John Axon* (1958).

Roy's first teaching post was at Calder High, a comprehensive school at Mytholmroyd in the West Riding of Yorkshire. He and his wife were allocated a council house above Heptonstall, a thousand feet up, close to the Pennine Way. "During the long, windy and television-less evenings of our first Winter there," he said, "Pat taught me to read music and play the treble recorder. I then set about teaching my pupils traditional French Songs as a treat at the end of lessons. That led to learning English Songs and I even bought a guitar by mail order."

At Calder High the senior boys gave performances of the local pace-egg play each Easter, and the power of the words and style of the performers stimulated his interest in traditional arts.

Roy then produced his first book, an anthology of the writings of *French Travellers in England*, published by Hutchinson in 1960, followed by editions of two French plays. By now he had moved to Hemsworth Grammar School, arriving just after Geoffrey Boycott had left, and in 1963 he became head of modern languages at Shenley Court Comprehensive in Birmingham. He was now a father twice over with a third on the way.

In Birmingham he found a flourishing folk scene, centred on Ian Campbell's club held at the Digbeth Civic Hall. Roy became a resident singer at The Partisan, a club with left-wing sympathies, and was a founder member of the Birmingham and Midland Folk Centre, a group led by Charles Parker. The Centre's objectives were to seek out both the oral and printed songs of the area and to study traditional performance techniques. They put on concerts, ran the Grey Cock Folk Club and organized seminars.

Roy's academic skills were put to good use in research projects. "In retrospect", he said "it seems to have been all very earnest and at times constricting but it provided a sound basis for my future work". He began to contribute articles and reviews to newspapers and periodicals, and started to edit collections of songs, initially for use in schools.

In 1972 he became headmaster of the Dame Elizabeth Cadbury School at Bournville and in 1974 Penguin published his *A Touch on the Times*. This collection of songs of social change, illustrated with evocative old photographs, received critical acclaim in the national press and Roy's reputation as a researcher was established, not just in the folk arena but in the outside world. Then came *The Folklore of Warwickshire* (1976), which was the first book that he wrote rather than edited.

He appeared on local and national television and radio, lectured, wrote scripts for schools and was involved in making several L. P. records.

In 1983 the opportunity to take early retirement arose and after 27 years as a teacher he left the profession to take up his career as a folklorist full time. Four years later he moved to the Gloucestershire-Herefordshire border where he and Pat still live.

"I didn't become a poet", he reflects somewhat ruefully, "but I've had intense gratification from my writing and from the people I've met and the places I've visited".

To conclude: I was talking just the other day to a man whom I supply with C.D.s and music books, a man who has a long-established mail order business and who runs stalls at folk festivals up and down the country. "I'll take anything by Roy Palmer", he said; "I can't get enough of his stuff. No sooner is it in than it goes out."

Michael Raven

LIST OF BOOKS BY ROY PALMER
French Travellers in England, 1600-1900. Editor. (Hutchinson, 1960)
Marie Tudor, by Victor Hugo. Editor. (Hutchinson, 1961)
Henri III et sa Cour, by Alexander Dumas. Editor. (Hutchinson, 1962)
Room for Company, Folksongs and Ballads. Editor. Cambridge University Press, 1971)
Songs of the Midlands, Editor, with Pamela Bishop and Katherine Thomson (E.P. Publishing, 1972)
The Painful Plough, A Portrait of the Agricultural Labourer in the Nineteenth Century, from Songs and Ballads and Contemporary Accounts. Editor. *(CUP, 1972)*
The Valiant Sailor, Sea Songs and Ballads and Prose Passages illustrating Life on the Lower Deck in Nelson's Navy. Editor. (CUP, 1973)
Love is Pleasing, Songs of Courtship and Marriage (CUP. 1974)
Poverty Knock, A Picture of Industrial Life in the Nineteenth Century, through Songs, Ballads and Contemporary Accounts. Editor. (CUP, 1976)
The Folklore of Warwickshire (Batsford, 1976; reprinted by Llanerch, 1994)
The Rigs of the Fair, Popular Sports and Pastimes in the Nineteenth Century through Songs, Ballads and Contemporary Accounts. Editor with John Raven. (CUP, 1976)
The Rambling Soldier, Life in the Lower Ranks, 1750-1900. Editor. (Penguin, 1977; reprinted by Alan Sutton, Gloucester, 1985)
Feasts and Seasons, 4 vols. Editor with Anthony Adams and Robert Leach. (Blackie, Glasgow, 1977-8)
Strike the Bell, Transport by road, Canal, Rail and Sea in the Nineteenth Century through Songs, Ballads and Contemporary Accounts. Editor. (CUP, 1978)
A Ballad History of England from 1588 to the Present Day. Editor. (Batesford, 1979)
Folk Music in School. Editor with Robert Leach (CUP, 1978)
Everyman's Book of English Country Songs, Editor. (Dent, 1979; reprinted as *English Country Songbook*, Omnibus Press, 1986)
Birmingham Ballads. Editor. (Birmingham Education Dept., 1979)
Everyman's Book of British Ballads, Editor. (Dent, 1980)
Manchester Ballads, Editor with Harry Boardman. (Manchester Education Dept., 1983)
Folk Songs collected by Ralph Vaughan Williams, Editor. (Dent, 1983)

George Dunn, The Minstrel of Quarry Bank, Reminiscences and Songs, Editor. (Dudley Leisure and Amenity Services, 1984)
The Folklore of Leicestershire and Rutland, Editor. (Sycamore Press, Wymondham, 1985)
A Checklist of Manuscript Songs and Tunes collected from Oral Tradition by Frank Kidson. (English Folk Dance and Song Society and Mitchell Library, Glasgow, 1986)
The Oxford Book of Sea Songs, Editor. (CUP), 1986; paperback, 1988)
The Sound of History, Songs and Social Comment. (CUP), 1988; reprinted Pimlico, 1996)
What a Lovely War, British Soldiers' Songs from the Boer War to the Present Day. Editor. (Michael Joseph, 1990)
Britain's Living Folklore. (David and Charles, Newton Abbot, 1991; reprinted Llanerch, 1995)
The Folklore of Hereford and Worcester. (Logaston Press, Almeley, 1992)
The Folklore of Gloucestershire. (West Country Books, Tiverton, 1994)
Ripest Apples, An Anthology of Verse, Prose and Song. Editor. (Big Apple, Putley, 1996)
Let Us Be Merry, Christmas Songs and Carols from Gloucestershire. Editor. (Green Branch Press, Lechlade, 1996)
A Gazetteer of Warwickshire Folklore. (King's England Press, Barnsley, 1997)
Secret River, An exploration of the Leadon Valley. (Green Branch Press, Lechlade, 1997)

THE BORDER LORDS
The Normans had little difficulty in conquering the Welsh initially because they were weak and divided after the deaths of their two great pre-Conquest leaders, Gruffydd ap Rhydderch of Dehuebarth (died 1055), and Gruffydd ap Llewellyn (died 1063). However, maintaining control was another matter. Trevor Rowley writes:

"William the Conqueror devised a scheme by which the Marches were administered as semi-autonomous earldoms based on the Saxon towns of Chester, Shrewsbury and Hereford. Within this framework the land was divided between the Marcher lords - in all some 153 separate lordships were created, functioning almost as little kingdoms, which, technically at least, did not revert to their mother counties until the Act of Union (1536). Recent research indicates that the units chosen for their lordships were pre-Norman, and coincided with the *comniotes,* the social and territorial cells of the Welsh kingdoms. Within each lordship one or more castles were built, and these castles formed the nuclei on which the border boroughs were subsequently created.

The parts of Wales conquered by the Normans came to be known collectively as 'The Welsh Marches' *(Marchia Wallia)* to distinguish them from the unconquered parts, which were known collectively either as 'Wales' *(Wallia)* or 'Wales proper' *(pura Wallia).* The distinction between Wales and the Marches was not simply geographical, it was also legal and constitutional; 'Wales proper' lived under what was then conventionally called 'the law of Howel', i.e. the indigenous Welsh law, while 'the March of Wales' lived under what were called 'the customs of the March', under which the Norman Marcher barons were allowed a considerable degree of autonomy, and the rest of England was strictly under royal control.

There was therefore a real distinction between Normanised England and the Normanised March of Wales. The lords of the Welsh March were allowed to exercise extensive judicial powers in return for conquering the March. These lords had jurisdiction over all civil and criminal cases, high and low, with the exception of crimes of high treason. They established their own courts to try these offences and subsequently they executed sentences and collected fines. They possessed all of the royal perquisites - salvage, treasure-trove, plunder and royal fish. They could establish forests and forest law, declare and wage war, establish boroughs, and grant extensive charters of liberties. They also had unique rights of unlicensed castle-building and of waging what was conventionally called 'private war'. The Marcher lord was thus established in the position of a petty king, exercising both royal and lordship rights. In this respect, a lord of the March of Wales differed from a lord of an estate in England, for the latter enjoyed none of the royal privileges but held his lordship as a direct grant from the king.

The Marcher lord took responsibility for the defence of his own lordship, and though he regarded the king as his sovereign, the king had little right to interfere in the lordship except on the lord's death, when he had right of entry to conduct an inquiry as to the legal heir and to arrange for the succession. He could not, however, normally interfere with the succession, which usually passed from eldest son to eldest son, by the custom known as primogeniture; in the absence of male heirs, the lordship was divided equally among the daughters. If, however, the lord abandoned his territory, or if he were found guilty of treason or felony, the king could then confiscate the estates.

The three great territories based on Chester, Shrewsbury and Hereford were to be defended by castles both internally and, where possible, west-wards into Wales. Hugh d'Avranches (made Earl of Chester in 1070) was based in the north with a forward defence under his cousin Robert against the Welsh at Rhuddlan. In the centre Roger de Montgomery, Earl of Shrewsbury, built an outpost on the Welsh side of Offa's Dyke in the region of Montgomery. In the south the Normans, headed by the Conqueror's friend William Fitz Osbern, Earl of Hereford, defended the Wye basin with castles at Wigmore, Clifford and Ewyas Harold, and following an invasion of Gwent, established the lordship of Striguil around Chepstow. By the time the Earl of Hereford returned to Normandy in 1070 he had pacified his section of the Border and had completed the organization of the Marches from Ludlow to Chepstow. William Fitz Osbern was killed in Flanders the following year leaving as his legacy a chain of Norman strong points on the Welsh border, as well as a number of infant boroughs which he had created in order to centralise Norman political control. The franchises and laws of his boroughs, such as Hereford, were based on the laws of Breteuil in Normandy and these served as a model for a considerable number of newly created towns in the rest of England and Wales. William Fitz Osbern was a powerful and ruthless man, typical of the eleventh-century Norman Marcher barons. The historian Ordericus Vitalis (baptised at Atcham in 1075) dismissed them thus: 'Puffed up with pride they gave no heed to the reasonable complaints of (the king's) English subjects and distained to wave them in the balance of equity. They shielded their men at arms who most outrageously robbed the people and ravished the women ...'

Time places a shield between us and the worst excesses of the Norman lords, but even at this distance they are not men to romanticise." But it is hard not to do so. These were, after all, brave and adventurous men, quite literally knights in shining armour and a long way from home.

HEREFORD, A RIVER PORT

Cargo-carrying boats of a modest size could travel up the River Wye from Bristol to Monmouth without too much difficulty, but the passage to Hereford was beset with problems - shoals and shallows in Summer, and fast-flowing floods in Winter.

Nevertheless, attempts were made to navigate the Wye and for a short period were reasonably successful. The way was shown by the Sandys family of Ombersley Court in the mid-17th century but their locks and weirs were not very substantial and required a lot of maintenance.

New works were constructed in the early-18th century with local government assistance, and from about 1750 to 1850 there was a reasonable trade on the river.

At Hereford there were three wharves. The main coal wharfe was on the south bank, adjoining the bridge to the east. Of this some warehouses remain. Opposite them, on the north bank, was another wharf which had The Old Bell Inn, the boatmen's 'local'. The third, the Corporation Wharf, was also on the north bank, adjacent to the castle mound. Here the buildings have been demolished but part of the stone facing of the quay and an overgrown slipway remain.

There was also a small ship-building industry at Hereford. There were two main yards, one upstream of the bridge and the other downstream, on the Bishop's Meadows.

Most of the boats used on the Wye were flat-bottomed trows, and their basic cargoes were bulky - coal, grain, cider kegs, wood and a tannin bark. When travelling downstream the current carried them, but to come upstream required either the use of sails when there was a breeze or, more reliably, the use of men. A team of five or six men could pull a boat carrying 20 tons. These bow-hauliers, as they were called, were a rough, tough lot.

With the coming of the tramway, the canal and finally the railway the river became uneconomic and the trade ceased.

GOVILON TO HEREFORD TRAMWAY

The tramway from the Brecknock Canal at Govilon, via Monmouth Cap (near Pontrilas), to the Hereford terminus at the Wye bridge was completed in 1829. It was designed to carry coal from South Wales to Hereford.

The track consisted of stone blocks which supported cast iron sleepers on which were laid plate rails. The L-shaped plates were 4 feet long and 4 inches wide, and had a vertical internal flange 3 inches high which guided the plain, unflanged 12 inch wheels. It was a single track with passing places. The trams were open iron carts, each of which could carry one ton of coal. A train of 12 trams could be pulled by one horse, though more were needed on steep inclines.

The Hereford terminus buildings were on the south bank of the Wye but were demolished when the new Greyfriars Bridge was constructed in 1966. However, the embankments that carried the track can be seen in the meadows upstream of the bridge. The tramway was bought by the Newport, Abergavenny and Hereford Railway in 1845 and closed in 1853. Much of the route taken by the main-line railway followed the old tramway.

Tram Inn is a hamlet on the Much Dewchurch to Winnal road which developed around the Tram Inn, once the terminus of the tramway before it was extended to Hereford. The main-line railway still runs through Tram Inn, over a level crossing and past a signal box, but the hostelry itself lies empty and gloomy, and even the sign was missing when we visited. Along the road to the east are the glass-houses of Allensmore Nurseries with a grumpy notice saying Trade Only. Further on again is a scatter of cottages, a red brick house with a stone barn and a 'set-aside' field full of weeds. This is Kilver Noll.

STAGECOACHES AND RAILWAYS

Until the end of the 18th century the only means of public transport was the mule train for goods and the cumbersome stage-wagon, which carried both goods and passengers.

By 1774 there was a stagecoach service from Hereford to London; the journey took 36 hours. By the 1830s, the heyday of coach travel, London could reached in about 17 hours, Bristol in 4 hours, Shrewsbury in 6 hours, and Liverpool in 11 hours. With the improvement in the roads, paid for by tolls at the turnpikes, the average speed was 10 miles per hour.

The teams of four horses were changed about every 10 miles and many of the coaching inns with stables can still be seen spaced out at that interval along the main routes. The coaches and their attendants were colourfully attired and competition was fierce. However, by the 1860s the days of the stagecoach were all but done and railways were in the ascendant.

The first steam locomotive line linked Ludlow to Barr's Court Station and the Gloucester Canal wharves at Hereford in 1853. This was followed by the line to Newport (Gwent) via Abergavenny in 1854, the line to Gloucester via Ross in 1855, to Worcester via Ledbury in 1861, and to Brecon via Hay in 1864.

There were three stations at Hereford - Moorfields, Barton and Barr's Court - but only the latter survived as a passenger station into the 20th century. The Gloucester and Brecon lines closed in the early 1960s.

CAPEL-Y-FFIN *7m SSE of Hay-on-Wye*

This article is not really about the village of Capel-y-finn; it is about the mountain road from Hay-on-Wye in the north to Llanyhangel Crucorney in the south. Furthermore, this 15 mile journey is entirely in Wales. We include it because for most of the way the route only trespasses over the border by about a mile, and provides access to three places popular with Herefordshire people: Hay Bluff and the Black Mountains, the Youth Hostel and pony trekking farms of Capel-y-ffin, and the monastery at Llanthony, not to mention the dramatic and beautiful valley these places of pilgrimage lie within.

Take the Brecon road out of Hay and just west of the town centre turn south into Forest Road, signposted Capel-y-ffin. The road passes through a bit of bungalow-land and then becomes 'single track with passing places' as it climbs steadily up the lower slopes of the Black Mountains. From now on sheep become omnipresent. New Forest is a three-bay, two-storey, stone-built farm with a hipped roof and a range of low-roofed outbuildings in most charming, wooded country with black and white cows in the lower pastures. It is a friendly landscape. Just past the farm fork right, cross the cattle grid and note the grit bins; it must be treacherous on these inclines in the Winter. Some little lawn-like laybys provide a perfect stopping place to water your dogs in the babbling brook that chatters over grey stones in the shade of some tall conifers. In Spring the hawthorne bushes which dot the hillsides are resplendant in their garb of green leaves and cream blossoms. In many places it is only they who have survived the munchings of the multitudinous sheep and the hostile winds of Winter.

Suddenly the sheltered valley gives way to the closely-cropped lawns of upland pastures and heather-bracken moors, a place of huge skies and long vistas. Prehistoric man found this place as uplifting as we do today. Many of his marks have vanished, and some remain to be discovered, but one of his burial cairns has survived, called Twyn y Beddau. This lies beside the road, and less than a mile further south there is a stone circle. This now marks a recognized parking area, a place to gaze westwards over the limitless ranges of the Black Mountains to the west.

Immediately behind one, to the east, are the dramatic heights of Hay Bluff and the Herefordshire Black Mountain ridge that marks the border with Wales. The hills here are alive not so much to the sound of music as with the swish of nylon canopies. On Summer days paragliders leap to uncertain fates: beginners from the lower slopes of Hay Bluff and old hands from the summit. Tough little mountain ponies and wiry sheep look on bemused.

I spoke to Dave Hopkins, also tough and wiry, with powerful bronzed legs and an easy smile. He is the Chief Flying Instructor of the Paraglide International Flying School, which is based at Shobdon Aerodrome (telephone 01568 708075). Mr. Hopkins is a good man. I can say that with some confidence because he has two border-collie crosses that would follow him to hell and back. In fact, they already do, almost every day. As their master leaps off the Hay Bluff shelf into the deep valley of the Digedi Brook, off they go desperate to be there when this friend of theirs, who can turn himself into bird, finally lands. To streams, bogs and rocks they pay no heed. Heads held skywards, they race on regardless. Mind you, their idea of hell is not quite the same as we, oh so frail, humans. Ziggy, the 'oldster' of the pair is more than faithful; she is useful. When helmets go walk-about on a hillside, she dashes off to retrieve them. When a piece of forgotten equipment is needed she will collect it and race up almost vertical slopes in seconds, whereas a man would take an age and be totally exhausted in the process. Nea is young and has a lot to learn, but she will be a beauty.

Modern paragliders are usually of an elliptical wing shape and are designed for soaring flight. They fold small enough to fit into a back pack and are relatively cheap. However, by its nature, paragliding is an inherently dangerous sport and competent, professional training is essential. The Shobdon school has a range of courses from a one-day taster at £65 to a 10-day Club Pilot at £390. Accommodation is provided in on-site caravans and a camping ground, or at local inns and hotels at extra cost. The school also organizes canoeing, climbing and abseiling, mountain walking, mountain biking and pony trekking. They have some 20 flying sites in the Welsh borders and also go on expeditions to Turkey, India, the Pyrenees and the Himalayas.

On leaving the parking area take the left fork into the hills. As one enters Gospel Pass, Lord Hereford's Knob juts out to your right, a dark green bluff cut through with steep little rivulet ravines. Just beyond the summit of the pass, there is another parking place with good views down the lovely valley of the Afon Honddu. We will follow this river all the way down to its confluence with the Monnow at All-y-frynys, a mile north of Pandy.

The road descends, past the side valley of Parc Bach with its dense, dark green conifer plantation, over a cattle grid, past wooded hedgerows, sheep fences and low stone walls lying all-a-tumble, past the King George VI Memorial Youth Hostel and into the tiny village of Capel-y-ffin ('chapel on the boundary'). The settlement stands at the confluence of the Nant Bach and the Afon Honddu. There are more ponies than people. They belong to the Grange Pony Trekking Centre. The simple, stone-built and white and red rectangular church of Saint Mary is ringed around with eight venerable yews. This is an ancient, prehistoric religious site if ever there was one. The present church is thought to have been built in 1762. It has rectangular windows, a porch of 1817 and a bellcote with a pyramid roof, which has stone-tiles like the main roof.

Inside there is a gallery along the west and east walls approached by stone steps. The octagonal font is probably mediaeval, the pulpit is of 1780, the settles of 1783 and the altar rails probably of the same period. Note the stained glass of the north window; it is, in fact, decorated with coloured paper.

Close by, on the other side of the Afon Honddu, is a rendered Baptish chapel, formerly the village school. By the barn on the road we communed with a young jackdaw. This bold little bird crunched digestive biscuits out of my hand without a care for the presence of two Rottweiler crosses and at least three farm dogs. They were in equal disdain of the bird. The farmer's wife, however, was not impressed by this act of avian bravery. All she could see was a threat to weak lambs in the next Spring. "If you like it so much, why don't you take it with you," she said.

On the side lane that leads up the valley of the Nant Bach is The Monastery. This was founded in 1869 by the Reverend Joseph Leicester Lyne (1837-1908) as an Anglican Benedictine monastery, which he named Llanthony Tertia. He adopted the name Father Ignatius and was ordained at his monastery in 1898. Francis Kilvert met him and wrote in his diary that this cowled monk dressed in Benedictine black was "a man of gentle simple kind manners with a fine brow and saintly face".

After his death the property passed to Caldey Island Priory and in 1924 to the sculptor and type-face designer, Eric Gill, and his community of artists, writers and craftsmen. The Gill family are still resident there. The Cloister dates from 1870 and the church from 1872. It was inspired by, and is partly a small-scale copy of, the mediaeval monastery at Llanthony, about which more later. The style is Romanesque-Early English Transitional and the design was by Charles Buckeridge (died 1873). The church collapsed in about 1920, when the vaults gave way, and it is now a tall, grey ruinous skeleton. The German reredos was taken to Saint Aaron, near Newport, Gwent. In the 1920s the cloisters were enclosed by the construction of a private chapel. On the beams are some inscriptions by Eric Gill, and there is a gravestone inscribed by him in 1907. In the refectory is a mural of the Crucifixion in Byzantine style, by David Jones, of about 1930, and a humorous wall painting by D. Tegetmeier of 1934. The premises were later used as a Youth Hostel but are now part of a private house.

Close by is the white-painted, Virginia-creepered Grange Pony Trekking Centre, and I thank Mr. David Griffiths for the information he gave me.

The Vision, 3/4m SW of Capel-y-ffin at SO 265 310, was the setting of *On the Black Hill* by Bruce Chatwin (1940-1989), first published in 1982. This popular and hightly evocative novel was later made into a feature film. I remember being very touched on hearing of Bruce Chatwin's death. It was so sad to see such a talended and likeable person cut down in his prime.

The road continues south, past a derelict stone cottage, and is now closely hedged. A sign directs one down a side lane to Travelog Trekking. There are some seven pony trekking establishments in the valley; this, and bed and breakfast, are important supplements of the local economy. There are about 90 smallholdings in the parish, with a total resident population of only 170, and many of these are in neighbouring valleys. The average farm has about 100 acres. Nearly all have sheep and most have some cattle also. Turnips and rape are grown in rotation on the best land, and some of the better quality meadows are ploughed and re-seeded periodically. Dogs are essential for herding on the valley slopes. Dol Alice is a typical valley farm, built of pink stone and standing in buttercup-strewn water-meadows.

The traveller now crosses the dark waters of the Honddu on a stone bridge and passes the white-rendered Half Moon Hotel. The ruined farm buildings opposite herald the Priory at Llanthony. Follow the signs to The Priory Hotel and The Abbey Hotel; they are one and the same. As you pass through the yard of the Court, the priory church, now the parish church, is on the right. There is a good car park with informative display boards. Entrance to the ruins is free and a guide book can be purchased in the bar of the hotel which occupies the vaulted cellar of the former prior's quarters.

Local tradition has it that Saint David, the patron saint of Wales, built a cell or a hermitage here in the 6th century. The name Llanthony is a corruption of Llan-Ddewi-nant-Honddu, which means 'the church of Saint David by the Honddu Brook'. Over the years the cell was deserted and became ruinous. Then, in the reign of William Rufus (son of William the Conqueror), William de Lacy, a Norman knight, lost his way during a hunting expedition. In this wilderness of forest and marsh he stumbled upon the ruined chapel of Saint David. He was overcome with religious fervous and dedicated the rest of his life to contemplation and the rebuilding of the chapel. It is said that he never removed his armour as penance for past sins. Word of William's work reached the court of Henry I and inspired Ernisius, chaplain to Queen Matilda, to join the knight in his wild Welsh valley. They attracted followers and built the first priory church, which was dedicated to John the Baptist and consecrated by the Bishops of Hereford and Llandaff. The Marcher lord, Hugh de Lacy gave money and land to support the community. In the early 12th century, Archbishop Anselm of Canterbury persuaded William and Ernisius to regularize their affairs and align themselves with an established order, They chose to be Augustinians (Black Friars), and Ernisius became the first prior. By 1121 there were 40 canons, all ordained priests. who were not confined to contemplation as were lay brothers.

The buildings we see today were bugun in 1175, at the expense of Hugh de Lacy, and completed in 1230. In brief, they consist of a cruciform church with arcades and a central tower, adjoined to the south by a cloister surrounded by the Chantry, the Refectory and the Prior's Quarters. During the Welsh rebellions of Owain Glyndwyr, in the early 15th century, the canons had trouble collecting their rents and the monastery fell into a decline from which it never recovered. The end came in 1538 with Henry VIII's acts of dissolution and it became ruined. Subsequently, the chapel (not the priory church) and the infirmary became the parish church.

The estate passed through several hands until it was purchased by the poet, Walter Savage Landor, of Bath in 1807. He was a man with a mission. He planted large numbers of beautiful trees - beech, chestnut, larch, cedar and oak - built bridges, improved roads and for his troubles was faced with tenants who refused to pay their rents. Furthermore, it is said that when he attempted to build himself a house, they took down at night all that had been raised in the day. Poor Landor withdrew and went to live in Italy.

The Prior's Quarters became an inn, the Traveller's Rest, now the Abbey Hotel. The ruins of the priory are presently in the care of Cadw, the official guardian of Welsh National Monuments.

The monastery was built in the Transitional period, between the Norman Romanesque (round-headed windows) and the Early English (pointed windows). The work was not fully completed when Gerald of Wales, accompanied by the Archbishop of Canterbury, visited during a journey around Wales to collect funds for the Third Crusade. In his account of their visit to Llanthony Gerald wrote: "Those mountain heights abound with horses and wild game, those woods are richly stocked with pigs, the shady groves with goats, the pasture-lands with sheep...."

In 1792 Turner visited Llanthony and in 1744 he painted a highly romantic picture of the ruins, altering the perspective, removing buildings, making hills higher and raising river beds. It is now at the Tate Gallery in London.

As one heads south the valley has a softer, more gentle countenance. On the eastern side it rises to the Hatteral Ridge where there are fine stretches of heather moorland. The dwarf shrub growth of the heather and whinberry provide an upland habitat favoured by raven and merlin, close to their southern range. The Hatteral Ridge has long been managed as a grouse moor and supports a large population of red grouse. The heather is burned to produce a patchwork of different growth forms and ages to provide good and shelter for both young and adult grouse.

At the end of Hatterall Hill is The Darren, a rocky cliff face with slopes of scree below. The cliffs were caused by the Old Red Sandstone rock strata slipping over wet, clayey layers. A little further south the church at Cwymyoy lies drunkenly, its back almost broken by movement of the scree on which it is built. It must be somewhat worrying to be the owner of one of the substantial houses of the village. Beside the valley road, south of the pony trekking station at Neuadd, there are breeding pens for several species of game birds, including pheasant, partridge and grouse.

All along the western side of the valley are dense conifer woods that stretch the four miles from Llantony to Stanton. Stanton - now there's a nice English name - is a hamlet of cottages old and new which has the Queen's Head Inn, a stone-built hostelry with Real Ales, camping in a meadow beside the tree-fringed river, and pony trekking,

As one approaches the railway bridge an aroma of fish prevails. This emanates from the Crucorney Trout Farm. It seems to be the fashion to make these places as ugly as possible and here we have a dedicated follower. It is grim, noisy and factory-like with concrete tanks, poles, wire netting, gushing fountains, old plastic barrels, cheap sheds and machines that suck up fish and fire them out of a gun barrel into containers. Mind you they are not daft at Crucorney. At 50p a time you can buy food from their shop and feed their fish for them

The farm has been here for about 12 years and they produce 160 tons of trout per annum, about half a million fish, which are sold to supermarkets. The fish are killed by electrocution in a holding tank, several thousand at a time. Some are processed here; others go elsewhere.

Our journey is now all but done. The valley lane joins

the Hereford to Abergavenny road at Crucorney (Llanvihangel Crucorney on the map). The Afon Honddu used to head south from here and joined the River Usk at Abergaveeny, but after the last Ice-Age a moraine blocked the valley and it now flows northwards to join the Monnow at Alt-y-rynys, one mile north of Pandy.

ANGLO-SAXON REMAINS

Most of the county's place names are of Anglo-Saxon (400-1066 AD) origin but for a people who have given us the greater part of both our language and our culture they have left surprisingly few visible physical remains. One feels that ther must be unacknowledged Anglo-Saxon fabric in some timber-framed buildings, especially cruck-framed dwellings, hall houses and barns. Field sytems also seem to be under-researched. Here is a list of Anlo-Saxon remains mentioned in this book, though there is an element of doubt about some of them. Offa's Dyke is clearly marked on Ordnance Survey maps so only the page numbers of references to it in the gazetteer are given here.

(Note that the Index includes similar lists of mentions for the Romans, and Bronze-Age and Stone man and for castles, moated houses and other subjects.)

Acton Beauchamp 9th century carving, 9
Bircher, carved head, 223
Bishop's Frome, mound, 22
Bromyard, masonry in church, 33
Buckenhill, piscina, 18
Burghill, lynchets, 36
Clodock, inscription, 40
Cradley, frieze, 42
Eardisland, look out mounds, 54
Edvin Loach, church masonry, 56
Hereford, Mote Court note, 202
Kenderchurch, coffin lids, 87
Kilpeck, church masonry, 88
Little Cowarne, church masonry, 122
Llanveynoe, funeral stones, 126
Marston, Rowe Dyke (Ditch), 138
Munsley, herringbone masonry and inscription, 153
Ocle Pychard, fort, 154
Pembridge, fort and moat, 157; Dane skin and note on marsh defences, 158
Perrystone, earthwork, 62, 63
Peterchurch, church design, *128*, 160; lynchets, 162
Peterstow, church masonry, 162
Staunton-on-Arrow, Rowe Dyke (Ditch), 182
Tedstone Delamere, church masonry, 191

BITS AND BOBS

Here are some mislaid notes and information that came to hand too late to be included in the gazetteer.

Hereford's Secret Tunnel

The monastery of the Black Friars was originally within the Hereford City walls but differences arose between the monks and the Cathedral, and Bishop Cantilupe had the monks removed. The building of a new monastery commenced on the present site in 1322. Edward III and his son, the Black Prince, attended the the consecration. Because the new building was beyond the protection of the city walls an escape tunnel was constructed that led from the monastery, under the walls, into the town. This is not a folk myth. In 1941 the lawn north of the monastery collapsed and an R.A.F. man from Credenhill descended into the pit and followed a partially collapsed tunnel for about 139 yards befor he came to a blockage. Also, the floor of the cellar in a house (now demolished) in Conningsby Street subsided and and required several lorry loads of rubble to fill it in. This house lay in a direct line with the monastery and the city walls.

Hereford's Power Station

In 1980 one of the first Combined Heat and Power electricity power stations in Britain was opened by the M.E.B. in Plough Lane, Moorfields, Hereford. It has three tall chimneys which are a local landmark.

Power is generated by two SEMP Pielstick diesel engines, each capable of producing 10,000 horsepower and each driving a 7.5 million watts generator.

By recovering heat from the exahust gasses and cooling system the power efficiency ratio is double that of a traditional power station. Hot water and steam are fed directly to H.P. Bulmer, Sun Valley Poultry and other local firms..

If there was a breakdown in the National Grid Hereford would be self-suffient in electrical power.

Weston Beggard Blacksmiths

In the outbuildings of Shucknall Court at Weston Beggard is a small industrial estate of half-a-dozen tradesmen - joiners, mechanics and the like. Amongst them are the smiths of Cadwallender Forge. They make latches, hinges and similar small wrought iron-work for retail sale, but also undertake private commissions for any beaten-iron goods - curtain rails are very popular at the moment, apparantly. One of their number is a farrier.

The Biblins, Whitchurch

The Biblins Adventure Centre is located in the Wye Gorge, 2m S of Whitchurch at SO 549 145. It is a log cabin with dormitories, cooking facilities, toilets and a telephone, and is hired out to parties of up to 36 young people at a charge of £230 for a weekend in the Summer.

Female S.A.S.

"They're not trained killers but they are trained to kill." Thus spake a former Director of the S.A.S. with a nice line in army logic.

In September 1996 it was officially disclosed that the S.A.S. has women amongst its numbers. They are entitled to wear the winged dagger cap badge but are primarily used in urban surveillance and intelligence gathering. They are based at Hereford but operate in trouble spots all over the world.

Most of these ladies are recruited from the 14th Independent Intelligence Company which was formed to operate in Ulster. They have the same firearms training as the men and undergo similar physical and mental training.

In reality, however, their role in not normally altogether glamorous. In the words of a former S.A.S. trooper: "They help us blend in. You can sit in places that the terrorists use regularly, pretending to be a courting couple. Some of the girls are real lookers, but we make them eat more so that they put on weight. You don't want to be walking round with a stunner so every terrorist is watching her instead of you watching them." Two books by former S.A.S. women are to be published in 1997.

Note. Andrew Kain, the author of the *S.A.S. Security Handbook* (Heinemann 1996), is an ex-S.A.S. counter-terrorist instructor who lives in Hereford. In 1991 he founded a security company called Andrew Kain Enterprises (AKE) with offices at Mortimer House, Holmer, Hereford. His company employs ex-S.A.S. men.

Above: A street plan of Hereford.
Opposite: Bye Street Gate, Hereford, from a painting by Thomas Hearne of 1794. Bye Street is now called Commercial Road.

Stained Glass

Are you a stained glass person?
Are you coloured through and through?
Is what I see really you?
Or are you painted, as some glass is,
A superficial frothy fizz?

I am a Rabbit

I am a rabbit and I am dying.
The young man who shot me
is laughing,
And the lady beside him said:
"Well done."
These moments are my last
And I am very frightened.
With my eyes
I ask the young man:
"Why?"
But he does not hear me.

Brinsop Court

Madelaine she once lived here,
Those ruby lips of yesteryear
That scorched a thousand silver screens
Around the world with siren screams,
And tears of joy and pretend grief.
That paid for stones to be renewed
Beneath the hills of Creden.
The trees now mourn in Autumn,
And shed a golden leaf,
And beg forgiveness
From a maid who sold emotion cheap.
Yes, my dear,
Many a heart in deep disdain
Silently you've slain.
Though you are gone,
Life still goes on.
Those tears that drop
From withered leaves,
The sun that sparkles
On the sheaves,
Know full well,
But your secrets will not tell.

Come You to Kilpeck

Come you to Kilpeck,
I'll meet you by the door,
By the Ringerike Dragons
We'll laugh there and more,
Shake hands with the ages
And when sleep it comes.
We'll race to the sun.
So come you to Kilpeck,
I beg you dear one.

Dark Invader

I have a dark invader,
I have a thing in black,
Meet him on the way, my friend,
And there's no going back.
He cannot stand a stranger,
And be you thin or fat,
There is no denying that
You will see the night descend,
For this devil has no friend,
But me.

Cidery Wine

"Don't wake him," I said,
"Let him lie on his bed
Of daisies and cidery wine;
Tomorrow is so long a time."

Rhododendron

Rhododendron, rhododendron,
You loose Victorian lady
Who escaped
From the house on the hill,
And now lives it up
With the wild woods
Deep in the valley below.
Bright without you are,
But dark within;
Slow to smile you are,
But quick to sin.

Michael Raven

INDEX

A

Abbeydore, 8, *11*,
Abbey Hotel, Llanthony, 237
  90, Grey Valley *115*, 153
Abel, John, 8, 103, 108, 176
Abercrombie, Sir Patrick, 213
Abergavenny, 135
Abona, river name, 16
Abrahall, George, 62, 171, John (of Eton), 62
Acle, the Holy Land, 154
Aconbury, 8, 197; Hill, 92, 122
Acre, 48
Acres, The, Ross, 173
Acton Beauchamp, 9
Acton Cross, 9
Acton Green, 9
Adam and Eve, oak trees, 167
Adam of Iorwerth, 232
Adam of Orleton, 157
Adam, Robert, 141
Adams, William, 201
Adbaston, 107
Adders, superstition, Birley, 21
Addyman, Tom, 34, 143
Adforton, 9, 216, 218
Aegelnoth's Stone, 202
Aegheard, 54
Aelpelmund, 16
Aepelgifu, 16
Aescbeorg, 13
Aethelhelm, 138
Africa, 159
Agincourt, 67, 110
Ailey, 98, 99
Albert, Paul and Christine d', 14
Albion House Hotel, 95
Albion mower, 132
Alderbury, Salop, 42
Alder's End, Tarrington, 190
Aldridge family, 189
Alford's Ferry, 62
Alfred of Marlborough, 147, 165
Alfred of Spain, 191
Alfrida, daughter of King Offa, 189
Algar, Earl of East Anglia, 225
Ali, 98
Allaway, Stephen, 205
Allensmore, 10, 235
Allt-y-rynys, 202, 238
Alma, The, 112
Almeley, 10, 55, Wootton, 10
Almshouses in Hereford, 70, 75
Alnoth, 36
Alretune, 155
Altborough, 80
Alton Court, Ross, 173
Alton Court Brewery, 202
Amberley, 12; Court, 137
America, 124, 228

American General Hospital, 123rd, at Mansell Lacy, 135
American Football, 78
Amhurst College, Massachusetts, 46
Amstell Pond, 9
An Affair of Dishonour, 231
An English Flavour, 203
Analytical Inquiry into the Principles of Taste, Knight, 52
Anchor, The, Ross, 174
Ancient Camp Inn, Eaton Bishop, 56
Andere, Mary, 12
Andrews, John, 162
Andros, Thomas, 211
Angel House, Kingsland, 91
Angel Inn, Grosmont, 134
Angel Inn, Kingsland, 91
Anglo-Saxon: for a list of visible physical remains see the Appendices.
Anglo-Saxon Chronicle, 169, 217
Anne, Queen, 45
Anselm, Archbishop of Canterbury, 237
Anthills, Wyson, 30
Anthony's Bower, Saint, 169
Antonine Itinerary, 13, 213
Ansfrid de Cormeilles, 179
Aparr, Thomas, 195
Apocalypse, 110
Apostolic Church, Leominster, 110
Apostles (house), 55, 94
Apostles, The, Elgar, 79
'Apple Orchard', Hoarwithy, 80
Apples, names of, 229
Aramstone, 91
A.R.C. quarry, Stretton Sugwas 187
Archaeology of the Welsh Marches, Stanford, 204, 215
Archenfield, hamlet, 12
Archenfield (also Arkenfield), territory, 13, 124, 125, 127, 159, 174, 175, 205
Archer-Shepherd, Rev. E.M., 16
Archer's Ford, 111
Arcop, 55
Ariconensia, Fosbroke, 211
Ariconium, 101, 167, 213
Ark, The, Dewsall, 45
Arkell, 223
Arketel, 124
Arkstone Court, 94; Common, 193
Arkwright family, 107, 99, 160; John, 67, 83; Henry, 67; R. 67; Rev.George, 159; Sir Richard, 99; Sir John, 99; Lady Stephanie, 99
Armstrong, Major, 32
Army Ordnance Depot, 203
Arngrim, 124
Arnhem, 178
Arrow, River, 29, 54, 86, 95, 96, 98, 107, 110, 228, 138, 157, 185, 186, 194
Arrow Fisheries, 29
Arrow Green, 54, 143
Arrow Mill, 54
Arthur, King, 130, 134, 149
Arthurian Links with Herefordshire, Andere, 12
Arthur's Cave, Whitchurch, 215
Arthur's Stone, 52
Arts and Crafts Movement, 33
Ashfield Lodge, Ross, 171
Ask Barn, 213
Askell, 163
Ashmoor, Kingswood, 95
Ashperton, 13, 187, 228
Ashton, 14, 213
Aspretonia, 13
Asshe Farm, Bridstow, 29
Astenofre, 55
Astley family, 32; Capt. Phillip, 32
Aston, 14
Aston Crews, 102, 199, 232
Aston, near Eyton, 60
Aston Ingham, 14
Atcham, 233
Athelstan, King, 13
Athelstan's Hill, 122
Atkins, Richard, martyr, 173
Atkinson, William, 135
Auberrow, 203
Aubrey, John, 186
Aubrey's Almshouses, 70, 75
Audley, Mrs., 125
Audley, Sir Nicholas, 103
Audley, Staffordshire, 103
Augustine, Saint 102; his chair, 181
Augustinian order at: Aconbury, 8; Adforton, 9; Goodrich, 66; Limebrook, 111; Llanthony, 237; Wormsley, 222
Australia, cattle export to, 228
Avenbury, 16, *31*; 197
Avoncroft Museum, 203
Avranches, Hugh d', 235; Robert d', 235
Axe and Cleaver, 147
Aylestone Hill, 195, 202, 228
Ayton, 16, 169
Aymestry, 16, 37, 112, 131, 178

B

Babylon Farm, 14
Bacca, 17
Bach Camp, 66
Bacho, The, 134
Backbury Hill Camp, 50
Backney Bridge, 178
Bacton, 8, 17
Bacqueville, Rouen, 55

Badela, 18
Badger-baiting: Peterchurch, 162; Tillington, 193; Wormbridge, 221
Badnage, Brinsop, 32
Badnage Wood, Tillington, 192
Bad Squire, The, Kingsley, 15
Bage, The, 40
Bageburge, 18
Bagburrow, 18
Bagley Head, 46
Bailey family, Pembridge Castle, 206
Bailey, Sir Joseph, 123
Baiting House, 198
Baker, Michael, 106, 147
Baker, Sir Henry W., 142
Baker, W.A. 204
Ballad of John Axon, 233
Ballads and Blues, 233
Balance Inn, 133
Ballard, Stephen, 14, 41, 142, 228
Ballingham, 82, 134
Ballsgate Cottage, 112
Bank Street, 221
Bannerman, John, 63
Baptist Chapels, Fownhope, 62; Garway, 64; Lyonshall, 133; Ross, 173; Weston-u-Penyard, 213; Withington, 219
Bardsey Island, 134
Baret, Philip, 24
Bark Cottage, Fownhope, 62
Barking and Dagenham Outdoor Centre, Cusop, 45
Barley Knapp, 161
Barneby family, 32; John, 32
Barneby, W.H., 26
Baron's War, 55, 86
Barre, Sir John, 38; Eden, 38
Barrett, Edward Moulton, 103, 203
Barrett's Hill, 197
Barrow Mill, Cradley, 42
Barr's Court Station, 74, 235
Bartestree, 18, 130
Barton, Colwall, 67; Court, 41
Barton station, 235
Basker's Gate, 60
Baskerville family: of Eardisley, 55, 96; Sir Ralph de, 55; Robert, 55; Walter de, 94; family of Bredwardine, 28
Basket weaving, 67
Batch, The, Sarnesfield, 177
Bateman Arms, Shobdon, 178
Bateman, Richard, 178; John, last Viscount, 178
Bathurst, James and Hon. Sarah, 55
Battle Bridge, Leominster, 108
Baysham, 178
B.B.C.: transmitters, Orleton, 157; Pebble Mill studios, 211
Beacon Country House Hotel, 96

Beacon Hill, 100
Beadles, police, 29
Bear-baiting, 98
Bearswood Common, 42
Bearwood, 158
Beating the Bounds, 211; see Rogationtide
Beattie, Lt. Commander Stephen, V.C., 134
Beauchamp, Robert, 54; Lord, 131; bones of, 56
Beavon's Hill, 112
Bebury Field, 198
Beccius, 138
Becket, Thomas a, 50, 87; chapel at Leominster, 108
Beeching, Dr., 185
Beer, Simon, 71
Beggar's Ash, 104
Beirut, 168
Belgic Celts, 189
Bellamour, 165
Bell, John, 68
Bell, Orchard House, 103
Bells: Bosbury, Celtic, 24; Marden, Celtic, and legend of, 137; Peterchurch, played backwards, 161 (numerous other mentions not listed here)
Bell, The, Tillington, 193
Belmont, 18
Beltane, 151
Belville family, 191
Benbow Pond, 38
Bender tents, 59
Benedict, Saint, 20; Order of (Black Monks): Belmont, 20; Capel-y-ffin, 236; Ewyas Harold, 58; Hereford, 238; Kilpeck, 88; Leominster, 108; Monkland, 143; Ocle Pychard, 155; Titley, 194
Benfield House, Bredwardine, 26
Bennett, Vice Admiral Thomas, 79
Bentley Wood Common, 191
Bent Orchard, 221
Bearnwynn, 36
Beortweald, 18
Bergavenny, (Abergavenny) 175
Berkeley Castle, 150
Bernard de Newmarche, 162
Bernando, caravan site, 122
Berne, John, 24
Bernithian Court, 125
Berrington, 141; Green, 102; Hall, 20, 23, 59; a type of barn, 90
Berrington, John, 22; Lady, ghost of, 153
Bertha, Queen, 50
Berwyn Mountains, 232
Best, John, 131
Betty, a diviner, 210

Bible, Authorised Version, 79
Biblins Youth Adventure Centre, Whitchurch, 215, 138, note on, 238
Bick, David, 142
Bicton, 60
Bidney Farm, Dilwyn, 46
Big Apple Festival, 16, 169
Big Million, 67
Big Wood, Wormbridge, 222
Billiere, General Sir Peter de, 102, *200*, 231
Bin Mills, 213
Birch, Col. John, 16, 64, 186, 206, *208*, 214
Bircher, 20; Common, 20, 44, *114*, 157, 223
Birches Garage, Shobon, 179
Birley, 21
Birmingham, 59, 63; Dogs Home 40; University, 52
Bishop's Frome, 21
Bishop's Meadows, Hereford, 235
Bishop's School, Tupsley, 195
Bishopstone, 21
Bishopswood, 22; wharf, 201
Bissop, Hugo, 206
Bitterley Hide, 159
Black Country, 122, 193, 201
Black Darren, 126
Black Death, 58, 133, 194
Black Dog of Hergest, 55, 96
Blackfriars, Hereford, 70, 75
Blackhall, King's Pyon, 92
Blacklands, 13
Blackmoor Farm, Kingstone, 94
Black Mountains, 40, 42, 49, 126, 127, 129, 199, 236
Black Poplar, English, 110, 201
Black Prince, 238
Black Swan, 149
Black Vaughan, 95, 96
Black and White Trail, 54, 94
Blakemere, 22; Hill, 68; Wood, 161
Blaney family, 99
Blashill, Thomas, 166
Bleathwood Manor, 123
Bleddyn, King, 37
Blessed Hill, Orcop, 155
Blessed Katherine of Audley, 103
Blestium (Monmouth), 213
Blewhenstone, 127
Blomfield, Sir, Reginald, 59, 135
Bloody Acre, 37
Blore, Edward, 66
Blount, Martha, 155
Blozabella, 98
Blue Bee Sewing Service, 137
Bluecoat Schools: Hereford, 74; Ross, 171
Boarfields, 91
Boat Inn, Whitney-on-Wye, 215

Bodcott Farm, Dorstone, 52
Boddington's House, Titley, 193
Bodenham, *11,* 22, 122, 137, Bank, 151 Hall, 225; Moor, 22
Bodenham family, 46, 129; Sheriff Roger, 222
Bodley, G.F., 37, 99, 125, 173
Bohun family, 86
Boiling corpses, 38
Bolan, Marc, 211
Bollingham, 24
Bollitree Castle, 211
Bolstone, 24, 106
Bolton, Broxwood, 34
Bone, or Boney Well, 169
Bonfiglio, 21
Bongham, William, 222
Booth Hall Hotel, 75
Booth, Capt. Rudhall, 28
Boot Inn, 157
Border Lord, poem, 168
Boresford Farm, Lingen, 112
Borough English, 67
Bosbury, *19,* 24, 48, 138, 198
Boscobel, Salop, 46
Boston, Lincs., 147
Bosworth, Battle of, 186
Botterell Farm, Bredwardine, 28
Boughton, Sir Edward, 199
Boulcott family, 147
Bouncing bomb, Winforton, 219
Bounds, The, Much Marcle, 151
Bourene family, 147
Bouville, Humphrey de, 163
Bow Bridge, Downton, 52
Bowburnet, Aston, 16
Bower Farm, Holme Lacy, 82
Bow-hauliers, 235
Bowley Common Meadow, 226
Bowley Town, 84
Bowne, Daniel, 109
Box Bush, Ashperton, 13
Boxing, 62
Boy Bishop, 72
Boycott, Geoffrey, 232
Bradburne's Farm, 214
Bradford, Yorks., 32
Bradgate Park, Leics., 232
Bradley Cottage, 169
Bradlow Hill, 102
Bradney, Sarah, 102
Bradnor Hill, 95
Brainge, The, 166
Brampton,
Brampton Abbotts, 25
Brampton Bryan, *19,* 25, 111, 112
Brandon Camp, 10
Brantone, Brian de, 25
Braose family, 86
Bravinium 107
Brazenose College, 122

Brecknock Canal, 235
Brecon, 235
Brecon to Hay to Eardisley to Kington Tramway, 38, 55, 95
Bredenbury, 26
Bredwardine, 26, 55, 98, *114*
Bredwardine, John de, 28
Breinton, 28
Breinton, Roger, 182
Brent-Dyer, Eleanor, M., 79
Bretlege, 29
Breton, Dr., 159
Brian, Anthea, 225
Brickendon, Francis, 46
Bricge, 28
Brick House, Adforton, 9
Brickhouse Farm, 58
Brick-kiln and black cat tale, Bosbury, 25
Bride Well, Hereford, 75
Bridge Cottage, Pembridge, 158
Bridge Court, Kingstone, 94
Bridge Farm, Wellington, 203
Bridge Inn, Kentchurch, 87
Bridge Inn, Wellington, 203
Bridges, Elizabeth, 209
Bridge Sollars, 28; bridge, *31*
Bridgenorth furnace, 36
Bridstow, 28
Brierley, 29, 59, 108, 110, *224*
Brilliana, Lady, 25, *31*
Brilley, 29
Brimfield, 30, 123; Hill, 124
Brimpsfield, Glos., 103
Bringewood: Forge, 52, 112; Hall, 52
Bringsty Common, 30
Brinkley Hill, 33
Brinsop, 30; Court, *23,* 32, *113*
Brinsop Court, poem, 240
Bristol, 203, 211, 235
British Empire Medal, 125
British and Foreign School, Ross, 171
British Lion, King's Caple, 91
British Rail, 103
Britley, 111, 112
Brito, Richard de, 50, 86
Brixton, London, 33
Broad Ditch, Cusop, 45
Broadfield Court, Bodenham, 22
Broadmoor Common, Woolhope, 221
Broad Oak, 63
Broadward Hall, 110, *223*
Brobury, 26, 32
Brocheberie, 32
Brockett, Lord, 99
Brock Hall, 66
Brockhampton by Bromyard, *31,* 32
Brockhampton by Ross, *27, 33*
Brockington Grange, 26

Brockmanton, 66
Bromash, 13, 102, 170, 213; Hundred, 112
Bromsberrow Heath, 50, 163
Bromley, 80; Court, 80
Bromyard, 33, *53,* 103, 122; Downs, 33; Folk Festival, 33, *116,* 169; hop-picking, *192*
Bromyard-Leominster Railway, 26, 48, 181
Bronsil Casle, *26,* 55, 131
Bron Horse Fair, 25
Bronze-Age sites and remains:
  Abbeydore, barrow, 8
  Adforton, bowl-barrow, 10
  Aymestry, cist tomb, 17
  Brinsop, cist tomb, 32
  Buckton, two round barrows, 34
  Colwall, on Midsummer Hill, round barrows, 41; palstave, 56;
  Dorstone, standing stone, 52; Arthur's Stone, 49
  Dulas, burial mound, Twyn-y-beddau, 54
  Eardisley, ring ditch, Camp Earthwork, 55
  Eaton Bishop, axe, 56
  Garanew, King Arthur's Cave and burial mounds, 63
  Goodrich, Queenstone at Huntsham, 66, *187*
  Hay Bluff, Twyn-y-beddau, burial cairn and stone circle, 236
  Hereford, dagger, 70
  Kinsham, three barrows and two standing stones at Coombe, 99
  Knill, five standing stones just west of, in Wales, 100
  Linton, flint working floor, 112
  Llangarron, burial mound, 125
  Llanveynoe, cairn and stone circle, 127
  Lugg valley agriculture, 225
  Madley, five burial mounds, 134
  Michaelchurch Escley, standing stone and three burial mounds, 139
  Much Marcle, palstave, 151
  Olchon valley (near Longtown), two cist tombs, 127; beaker from, *195*
  Saint Margaret's, mound, 175
  Sutton Saint Nicholas, Wergin's Stone, 189
  Saint Weonard's, standing stone and two cremation burials, 177
  Titley, three barrows, 194
  Thruxton, round barrow, 193
  Turnastone, mound, 195
  Vowchurch, axe-head and possible burial mounds, 199

Walterstone, barrow, 202
Whitchurch, King Arthur's Cave and five burial mounds in vicinity, 215
Yatton, barrow, 106
Brook Bridge, 91
Brook Farm, Little Marcle, 124
Brook House, Kimbolton, 90
Brookhouse, King's Pyon, 92
Broome Farm, 162
Broomhill Field, Ullingswick, 198
Broom's Green, 50
Broomy Bank, 79
Broomy Hill, 78
Broughton Arms, Peterchurch, 161
Brown, Capability, 20, 23, 52, 141
Browning, Robert, 205; Elizabeth Barrett, 99, 103, *180*, 203
Brown, Rev. Thomas, 20
Broxash Hundred, 122
Broxwood, 34; Court, 158
Bruge family, 162
Bruneshope, 30
Bryant, map, 153
Bryan, Thomas, M.P., 186
Brychan, King of Brecon, 134
Brydges family, 28; Sir John, 28; William, 197; Francis, 197; Duke of Chandos, 45, 197; James, 45, 207
Brynmelin, Cusop, 45
Brynca, 30
Bryngwyn, 149, 155; dower house to, 127
Bryni, 28
Brynlegh, 29
B.S.E., 174
Bucca, 34
Buck Inn, Woonton, 12
Buck, Samuel, 195
Buckenhill, 34, 58, 181; house, 221; Farm at Ballingham, 18
Buckeridge, Charles, 236
Buckholt Hill, 205
Buckingham Palace, 87
Buckland, Lower, 48
Bucknall Court, Birley, 21
Buckton, 34; Roman fort, *204*
Bufton family, 147
Bulkeley, Lydia, 32
Bulla, 24, 36
Bull-baiting, Kington, 98
Bullinghope, Superior, 36, 130; Inferior, 36
Bull's Head, Crasswall, 49
Bull's Hill, 201
Bulmer plc, H.P., 78, 149, 154, 229, 238; Esmond, 167, 199; Percy, 229; Railway Centre, 68, 74
Bunch of Carrots, 67
Bunn's Lane Farm, 154

Burcott Farm, 82
Burghill, 36, 84; murder at the Court, 36
Burghope, 203
Burgos, seige of, 55
Burleston, 186
Burleygate, 147, 154, 155, 198
Burley, Sir John, 71
Bulingjobb, 95, 98
Burne-Jones, 33
Burning the Bread, 60
Burning the Bush: Birley and Shobdon, 21; Kington, 98; Putley, 169; Shobdon, 179
Burning cattle, 223
Burnt Hengoed, 86
Burrington, 36
Burton, Weobley, 209
Burton Court, 54
Burton Court, Linton, 122
Burton's Farm, Wellington Heath, 203, 205
Burton Hill, 153
Burton House, Kington, 95
Burton-on-Trent, 29
Bury Court, Wigmore, 217
Bury Farm, Luston, 133
Bury Farm, Stoke Prior, 186
Bury Hill, Bromash, 13
Bush Bank, 92
Bushel Measure, 33
Bush Inn, 92
Butcher's Arms, 221
Butcher's Row, 103
Butler, Samuel, 150
Butt house, King's Pyon, 92, 207
Bycross, 139, 166
Byford, 37, 166
Byletts, 158
Byron, Lord, 99, 100
Byton, 37, 99; Common, 99

C

Cabal Tump, Titley, 194
Cadbury factory, Hope-u-Dinmore, 83
Cadw, 237
Cadwallender Forge, 238
Caen, Normandy, 18; limestone, 205
Caerleon, 87
Cae Thomas Well, 127
Cage Brook, 56
Calder High School, 232
Caldey Island, 236
Californian Redwoods, 83
Callow, 37
Callow Hill, Welsh Newton, 205
Calver Hill, 154
Calvinistic Methodist Chapel, Clifford, 40

Cambrensis, Geraldus, 28, 237
Camp, The, Much Dewchurch, 149
Camp, The, Ullingswick, 198
Campbell, Ian, 232
Campbeltown, HMS, 134
Camden, 87
Camp Wood, Abbeydore, 8;
Camp Wood, Michaelchurch Escley, 139
Camp Wood, Upper Lyde, 17
Canals:
  Exeter Canal, 227
  Hereford to Ledbury to Gloucester, Canal, 14, 41, 71, 82, 103, 142, 152, 154, 186, 204, 209, 226; note on, 228; *Hereford to Gloucester Canal,* Bick, 142;
  Leominster to Stourport Canal, 30, 59, 90, 108, 123, 157;
  Manchester Ship Canal, 228;
  Newport to Brecon Canal, 66
Candelabra, rare wrought-iron, 174
Candle-maker, Ross, 171, 173
Canon Frome, 37, 187, 228
Canterbury Museum, 181
Canter's Cottage, 181
Cantelupe, Bishop Thomas, 44, 71, 238
Canute, King, 202, 213
Capel Tump, Ross, 173
Capel-y-ffin, 235-7
Capler, 166; Camp, 62; Cottages 33; Hill, 33
Caple Feast, 91
Caple Grange, 84
Capriole Crafts, 108
Captain, fighting cock, 162
Caractacus, 182
Caradoc Court, 177
Caradoc ap Gruffydd, 135
Caravan Club of Great Britain, 154
Carboniferous rocks, 228
Car boot sale, Callow, 37
Cardiff, Archdiocese of, 131
Cardiff family, 123
Carey, 18
Carlsberg-Tetley, 29
Carlesse, John, 78
Carp, record size, 125
Carpender, Margaret, 50
Carpenter, R.C., 20
Carroll, Madelaine, filmstar, 32
Carrots Fishery, 67
Carter, Nancy, witch, 173
Carwardine, Thomas, 90
Casolini, 223
Castles. (m&b) = motte and bailey only; (s) = stone-built. Many stone-built castles also have a motte and bailey(s).
  Abbeydore, (m&b)?, 8

Almeley, (m&b), 10
Ashperton, (s),13
Aston, (m&b), 14; (s), 16
Bacton, Newcourt, (m&b), 17
Bredwardine, (m&b), possibly two
Breinton Camp, fortified dwelling, 28
Bridstow, (s), 28
Brilley, (m&b), 30
Bronsil, (s), 55
Buckton, (m&b), 36
Castle Frome, (m&b), 38
Clifford, (s), 38
  Old Castle, (m&b), 40;
Clodock, The Mound, 40
Colwall, The Citadel, tower mound, 41
Combe (near Kinsham), mound, 99
Cusop, (m&b), 45; Mouse Castle, (m&b), 45
Didley Court, (m&b), 175
Dilwyn, (m&b), 46
Dorstone, (m&b), 50, 52
Downton, (m&b), 52
Eastnor, (s), 49
Eccleswall, (s), 122
Edvin Loach, (ring work?)56
Ewyas Harold, (m&b), 58
Foy, (s), 62
Goodrich, (s), 64, *65*, 122
Hampton Court, (s), 67
Hereford, (m&b), 70,75
Hergest, Castle Twts, (m&b), 96
Huntington, Turret Castle, (m&b), 86; Hell Wood, (m&b), 86; Huntingon Castle, (s), 86
Howton, Pontrilas, (m&b), 87, 165
Kentchurch, (s), 87; (m&b), 88
Kilpeck, (s), 88
King's Caple, The Tump, (m&b), 91
Kingsland, (m&b), 91
King's Pyon, (mound), 92
Kingswood, (m&b), 94
Kington, (m&b), 95
Kinnersley, (s), 98
Knill, five (m&b) just to the west, in Wales, 100
Laysters, (m&b), 100
Lingen, (mound), 111
Longtown, (s), 65, *129*,
Llancillo, (s), 124
Llanrothal, Tregate Farm, (s), 126
Lyde, Upper, Camp Wood, (m&b), 17
Lyonshall, (s), 133
Michaelchurch Escley, (m&b), 139
Moccas, (s), 141
Monnington Straddel, (m&b), 43
Much Marcle, Mortimer's Castle, 150

Much Dewchurch, The Camp, 149
Mynydd-y-bridd, (m&b), 52, 153; Nant-y-bar, (m&b), 153
Ocle Pychard, Castleton, (m&b)?, 154
Orcop, (m&b), 155
Owen's Cross, Chapel Tump, (ring motte), 195
Richard's Castle, (s), 169
Rowlestone, (m&b), 174
Peterchurch, Urishay, (m&b), 161; Snodshill, (s), 161
Saint Weonard's, Treago, (s), 177; (mound), 177
Shobdon, (m&b), 179
Sollers Hopse, (mound), 181
Stapleton, (s), 181
Staunton-on-Arrow, (m&b), 18
Stoke Lacy, Tuthill, 185
Thruxton, (mound), 193
Titley, Cabal Tump, (square mound), 194
Tretire, (site of fortified house), 95
Turnastone, Cothill Camp, (m&b), 195
Vowchurch, Chanstone (moated mound), 199; also unexplained mound on west bank of river
Wacton, (m&b), 199
Walford, near Leintwardine, mound), 201
Walterstone, (m&b), 202
Weobley, (s), 207
Weston-u-Penyard, (s), 211,212
Whitney-on-Wye, (site of) 215
Wigmore, (m&b), 217; (s), 217
Castle End, The Lea, 102
Castle Farm, Madley, crock of gold, 135
Castle Frome, 38; font, *39*
Castle Frome (house), Allensmore, 10
Castle measuring cord, 137
Castle Pool Hotel, 75
Castle Tavern, London, 62
Castleton, Ocle Pychard, 154
Castle Vaults, Ross, 171
Castles of Herefordshire, The, Shoesmith, 12
Castles of Herefordshire and Worcestershire, The, Salter, 218
Caterham car, 141
Cathy Come Home, Sandford, 68
Catley Southfield, 25
Cat's Back, 126, 127, 130
Cat's Eyes, 48
Cats, killed by gamekeepers, 52, 142
Catterick, 233
Cattern's Stone, 104
Causeway Farm, Hereford, 75

Cavendish, Thomas, 36
Cawley, Frederick, M.P., 20; Lord, 20
CD (compact disc) manufacture, 63
Cedars, The, Bullinghope, 36
Cedars, The, Walford, Ross, 201
Cefn Hill, Craswall, 42
Ceina, Saint, 87
Ceinwen, 87, 168
Celtic bronze bells, Marden, 137; Bosbury, 24
Celtic Endless Knot sculpture, 22
Celtic harp maker, Letton, 111
Celtic-Iron-Age names, 67
Celtic Roman cattle, 227
Cena, 86
Centre of Herefordshire, 163
Chadwick, Mr., 167
Chained Library, Hereford, 71
Chained Swan, 95
Chalet books, 79
Chambers, Sir William, 199
Chanders, Roger de, 162
Chanders, Duke of, 45
Chanders Anthem, Handel, 45
Changeling farmer, Pembridge, 158
Chanstone Court, 197
Chapel Farm, Yatton, 223
Chaplin, Ann, 177
CHAR, 78
Chardstock, Dorset, 68
Charity Farm, 126
Charles I, 92, 209
Charles II, 46, 79, 110, 143, 171, 207
Charlotte, witch of Weobley, 209
Charlton, Bishop, 75
Chaston Syndicate, 83
Chatwin, Bruce, 45, 236
Chaucer, Geoffrey,
Cheaton Brook, 67
Cheers, H.A., 74
Checkley, 146
Chelsea Pensioners, 25
Cheese manufacture, 142
Cheese family, 133
Cheney Court, Bishop's Frome, 21
Cheney family, 197
Chepstow, 79, 108, 171, 213, 227
Chequers Inn, *105,* 108
Cherry Hill, 62
Cheshire, 103
Chester, 234
Chesterfield, 10th Earl, *81;* Lord, 90
Chesterman family, 140
Chick, W., 59, 122
Chickward, 94
Childe, Harold, Byron, 99
Children, George, 12
Children, Sandra, 206
Chingtune, 95
Chitty, L.F., 34

Chocolate crumb, 83
'Chair of Saint Augustine', 181
Cholstrey Court, 110
Christie, Agatha, 41
Christ in Majesty, 174
Christ of Trades, 139
Christ's College, Cambridge, 42
Church Farm, Mathon, 138
Churchill Gardens, Hereford, 24, 64, 79; Museum, 74
Church Stoke, Mont. 158
Chute, Dame Margaret, 137; Anne, 137
Cider Annie, 147
Cider, article on, 229; Bible, 231; brandy, 74; ceremony, 54; manufacturers, 230
Cidery Wine, poem, 240
Cinders, Laysters, 100
Cinemas, 229
Cirencester, 134
Cistercian, order of, 8; house of correction, 211
Cist tombs, see Bronze-Age
Citadel, The, 41
Civil War:
  Aconbury, 8
  Aylton, 16
  Bridstow, 28
  Brampton Bryan, 25
  Canon Frome, 37
  Goodrich, 64
  Holme Lacy, 82
  Hereford, 70
  Ledbury, 103
  Lingen, 112
  Lucton, 131
  Mordiford, 143
  Much Marcle, 150
  Pembridge, 158
  Ross-on-Wye, 169, 171
  Snodhill, 162
  Stapleton, 181
  Stoke Prior, 186
  Tarrington, 190
  Wigmore, 218
  Weobley, 207
Clan Arrow Cottages, 158
Clanvowe, Sir Thomas, 154, 232
Clare, Gilbert de, 56
Clare, Saint, 84
Clarissa, Lady, 59
Clark, Hester, 110
Classic Jaguars, 110
Clayton, John, 74
Clear Brook, Pembridge, 158
Cleaver, The, 147
Cleaves, The, Walford, 201
Cleongar, 38, *47*
Clements, Jack, sin-eater, 173
Clerkenwell, 48

Clerk, Lord James Beau, 79
Clewstone, 162
Cliff, The, 123
Clifford, 38
Clifford family, 38; Roger de, 9; Jane, 38; Lord, 55;
Clifford's Mesne, 14
Cimber's Oak, 106
Cimbing Jack Common, 106
Clinker, C.R., 95
Clisset, Philip, 24
Clive family, 220; Lady Catherine and Charles, 221
Clock Mill, Bredwardine, 26
Clock Mills, 38, 218
Clodock, *39*, 40, 130 138; Mill, *220*
Clodwyn, King, 40
Clog-makers, Preston-on-Wye, 166
Clore, Sir Charles, 45
Cloth of Gold, Field of the, 48
Cloud Nine Tearooms, 41
Clover, mowing, *131*
Clun, River, 107
Clun, Workhouse, 142
Clyde Petroleum, 40
Cldowg, Prince and Saint, 40
Clynnog, Camarthenshire, 126
Clyro, 26
Coach travel, 235
Coal mining, Walford, Ross, 201
Coalville, Leics., 232
Coates, Clarice, 100; Joseph, 59
Cobbler's Day custom, 173
Cobbler's Mound, Shobdon, 179
Cobhall, Allensmore, 10; Common, 193
Cobham, Lord, 232
Cobnash, 91
Cobney Farms and Park, 213
Cock-fighting: Craswall, 42; Kington, 98; Peterchurch, 162
Cock Gate, 44
Cock at Tupsley, 195
Cocks family, 55; Joseph (d.1778), 55; Charles, Lord Somers (d.1855), 55
Cockshot Hill, 138
Cockyard, 94, *121*
Coda, 40
Coddington, 40
Coffin creases superstition, 24
Cofield, Ms., 42
Cogwell Brook, 90
Cola, 40
Cold Blows the Wind, 142
Cold Harbour, 186
Cold Lazarus, Potter, 173
Cold Nose Farm, Dewsall, 45
Coleraine Farm, 213
Coleridge, S.T., 185

Coles family, 68
Cole's Hill, 99
Colewelle, 40
Colley, George, 186
Collington, 40
Cologne, 42
Colonel, The racehorse, 106
Colstaffe riding, Cradley, 42
Coltsfoot Gallery, 68
Colwall, 40, *43, 121*; Stone, 41
Comberton Farm, 157
Come You to Kilpeck, poem, 240
Common Land, article on, 230
Commons on Woolhope Dome, 221
Commonwealth, 159; clergy dismissed, 13
Compass Hotel, 217
Conches, Normandy. 142
Conches, Ralph de, 210
Coningsby family, 75; Lord, 67; Sir Thomas, 74
Coningsby Hospital, 70
Congregational Chapel, Hengoed, 86
Constantia, of Lingen, 147
Conygra, Cusop, 45
Conynge, Richard, 191
Coombe (Cwm) Hill, Aston Ingham, 14
Coombe near Byton, Farm, Moor, and Bronze Age monuments, 37
Cook's Folly, Wharton, 60
Co-operative Wholesale Society, 36
Copeland, Rev., William, 9
Coppet Hill Common, 64
Coppice House, Tedstone Wafer, 191
Corbet family, 179. 224; Col. Uvedale, 178
Cork, Ireland, 33
Cormeilles, Abbey of Saint Mary, 112, 180; Ansfrid de, 12
Corn Dollies, Eye, 59; Mordiford, 145
Cornewall Arms, Clodock, 40, 129
Cornewall family, 20, 26; Eleanor, 44; Sir Richard, 59; Edward, 141; Sir George, 141; Sir William, 141
Corn Exchange, Leominster, 108
Corn Showing, Lulham, 135
Cornwallis, Lord, 108
Corpse (Corpus Christi)) Cross, 173
Cosmos, Saint, 188
Costelin, 147
Cothill Farm and Camp, 195
Cotswolds, 52
Cottager's Comfort, 142
Cotterell, Sir Richard, 135
Cottingham, Lewis, 88
Cotton industry, 108
Coughton, 201; valley road, 213
Countess of Huntigdon's Connexion, 87

Counting rhyme, 92
Country dance tunes, 158
Country Furniture, 219
County Asylum, 36
County Gaol, 75
County Rangers, 83
Court Farm, Preston Wynne, 166
Court Farm, Rowlestone, 174
Court Farm, Sollers Hope, 179
Court Farm, Walterstone, 202
Courtfield, Welsh Bicknor, 205
Courtfield Estate, 66
Courthouse, The, Wigmore, 217
Court House, Allensmore, 10
Court House, Canon Pyon, 228
Court House, Longtown, 129
Court House Richard's Castle, 170
Court House Farm, Pembridge, 157
Court Mills, factory, 50
Court of Noke, 182
Covender, 223
Covenhope Valley, 147
Cowarne Court, 147
Cow's Hill, 99
Cows posing, 58
Coxall, 59; Knoll, 25, 34
Crac o' Hill, 90
Cradley, 42, 78; Brook, 41, 42, 138; witch, 42; Mumming play, 169
Crafta Webb, 26
Crampton Hill, Cradley, 42
Cranston, James, 108, 129
Cranstown, B., 84
Craswall, 42, *48*, 126
Cream of the Well, 34, 36
Creda, King, 24
Credenhill, 30, 42, *43*, 70, 80, 238
Creoda, 42
Creosote tank, Whitbourne, 214
Cressewell, 42
Cress Well, Bodenham, *10*, 22
Crewe to Newport railway, 71
Crews Hill, 102
Crizeley, 175
Crocker's Ash, 63, 215
Croft, 44, 133; oak grove, *47*; Croft Oak, 44
Croft Ambrey, 106
Croft Castle, 131, 223, 228
Croft family, 44; Bernard de, 44; Richard and wife Eleanor, 44; Sir John, married Janet Glyndwr, 232; Sir Jasper, 131; Sir Herbert, M.P., 131
Cromwell, Oliver, 25
Crooked Well, 98
Croose, Woolhope, 221
Cross End, Moccas, 141
Cross Farm, Winforton, 217
Coss Keys, Withington Marsh, 219; cricket club, 166

Crossroads, 163, 171, 173
Cross Ledge Farm, Dorstone, 52
Cross of the Tree, 112
Crossway, How Caple, 84
Crossway, Kingswood, 94
Crossways, Peterchurch, 161
Crown and Anchor, Lugwardine, 131
Crow Hill, 112, 198
Crowmoor, 193
Crown Inn, Bosbury, 24; Whitchurch, 214; Woolhope, 221
Crown, The Lea, 102
Crumpler, Alan, musician, 108
Crump Oak, 158
Crumpton Oaks, 186
Crutwell, Dame Alice, 206
Cuckoo, first, at Orleton, 157
Cummings, Mrs., 165
Cunobelin, 213
Cupid's Inn, 87
Cursneh Hill, 110
Curzon Herrick family, Eardisley, 55
Curzon, H., 111
Cusop, 44, 55, 232
Cwm, The, Lanrothal, 126
Cwm Annwn, 97
Cwm Brook, 174
Cwmbran, 63
Cwmma, The, 30
C.W.S., 193
Cwm Farms, Longtown, 129
Cwymyoy, 236
Cyder, Phillips, 219
Cynebald, 90
Cynheard, 98
Cynehelm, 99
Cynidr, Saint, 87, 165, 218
Cyprus, 48

D

Dabinetts, apples, 123
Daily Prayers for Those who have to Work Hard, Baker, 142
Dairy Farm, Weobley, 206
Dale family, 59; nursery, 59
Dalgetty Produce, Castle Frome, 38
Dam, The, Walford near Ross, 201
Dame Elizabeth Cadbury School, 60, 233
Dancing Green, 83, 213
Dandelion Dead, 32
Danes, 70; at Leominster, 107; skin at Pembridge, 158; on River Severn, 158; at Wigmore, 217
Daniel, Amisia, 42
Daniel, prophecies of, 110
Dansey family, 123; Sybil, 123
Dark Invader, poem, 240
Darkley, 99
Darren, The, Llanthony, 237

Daubney, John, 66
Daunsey family, 32
Davenent, Sir, William, 158
Davenport family, 135, 154; Charles, 154
Davies, A.J., 84
Davies, Bertie, 46
Davies family, of Wigmore, 44
Davies, Gareth, 102
Davies, John Scarlett, 110
Davies, Rev. John C. de la Tour, 161
Dawber, Sir Guy, 26
Dayla Soft Drinks, 213
Dead Man's Hand cure, 155
Dearmod, 50
Decangi, 42
Deep Dean, 201
Deepwood, Downton, 52
Deer Farm, at Tedstone Delamere, 191
Deerfold, 52, 112
Deer leap, at Moccas, 141
Deer Parks, 229
Deer farming, research on, 60
Defoe, Daniel, 190
Deheubarth, 135, 234
Delabere family, 45
Delamere family, 123
Delaney, Peter, 29, 160, *115*
Demaus, 224
Denco, 78
Denell, Daniel, water engineer, 227
De Nugis Curialium, 174
Deormund, 50
Deorsige, 50
Deserted Garden, The, Barrett-Browning, *203*
Deserted Mediaeval Villages. (Some 200 have been located altogether.)
  Berrington Hall, 23
  Bishopstone (two), 21, 22
  Brinsop, 32
  Dilwyn, 46
  Kilpeck, 88
  Kimbolton, 90
  Little Dilwyn, 46
  Lower Bullingham, 130
  Leinthall Starkes, 106
  Pipe Lyde, 163
  Quebb, 55
  Stretton Sugwas, 187
  Sutton Saint Nicholas, 189
  Tedstone Delamere, 191
  Tupsley, 195
Deveraux Court, Bodenham, 22
Deveraux family of Bodenham, Viscounts of Hereford, 22; owned Lyonshall Castle, 133; of Weobley, 206, 207; Sir William, 205; Robert, Earl of Essex, born Netherwood, 40

Deveraux Wootton, 99; ghost story, 153
Devil, The, Birley, 21
Devil charm, Tarrington, 190
Devil's Garden, The, Kington, 98
Devil Stone, Combe, 99
Devil's Triple Six, 64
Devil Summons ritual, 108
Devil's Wood, 149
Devil's Wood, Orcop, 155
Devonian Old Red Sandstone, 228
Dew, Maj. Frederick Mapleton and Rev. Henry, 217
Dewi, 45
Dewi (David), in church names, 123, 149
Dewsall, 45
Diamond, Harry, *172*, 173
Dikens, Charles, 171
Diderot, 100
Didley Court Farm, 175
Digbeth Civic Hall, 233
Digedi Brook, 236
Dilwyn, 45, *51*, 94, 209
Dinedor, 46; Cross, 46; Hill, *51*
Dingwood Park, 50
Dinmore (Manor), 46; deer, 83; *120*
Dionisia la Wyn, 166
Dippersmoor Manor, 90
Dishley Court, 110
Dobyns, Mrs., and Catherine, 56
Docklow, 48, 166
Docwra, Sir Thomas, 48
Dodmarsh, 219
Doenitz, Admiral, 74
Dog Inn, Ewyas Harold, 59
Dogs of Hell, 159
Dol Alice, 237
Dolby, George, 171
Dole Meadow, 226
Dolyhir, 38, 95, 98
Domesday Book spelling, 190
Dominican order, founded by Saint Dominic (c.1170-1221), 75
'Donkey Man', at The Lea 102
Donkeys at Eaton Bishop, 56
Donnington, 48
Dore, River, 8, 52, 94, 161, 165, 195
Dormington, 50
Dorstone, 50, 161, 162; Arthur's Stone, *49*
Dorstone, near Streford, 186
Dovaston, Rod, 60
Doward, Great and Little, 215
Downes, H., blacksmith, 22, *120*
Downes, Margery de, 21
Downey Engineering, 165
Downton, 36, 52, 106, 107; Castle, *38;* on the Rock, 52; estate, 142
Dowty Seals, 78
Doyle, Sir Arthur Conan, 55, 96

Dragon of Mordiford, 145
Drago son Poyntz, 138, 153
Dream of Fair Women, Tennyson, 38
D.R.G. Plastics, 78
Droitwich, 146, 149; salt road, 103
Dropwort, 131
Drovers, at Kington, 95; road at Titley, 193; road at Whiney-on-Wye, 215; Rhydspence, 30
Drowned villages: Dorstone, 52; Pembridge, 158
Druids, 125; in oak grove, *188*
Drum, The, 84
Drumlins, Lucton, 131
Drybridge House, Hereford, 75
Drybrook, 201
Dual, knightly, 58
Duck decoy pond, 60
Duck Street, 183
Dudley, 183
Dudley, Robert, Earl of Leicester, 162
Duffryn, Cusop, 45
Duke of York, inn, Laysters, 100
Dulas, 54
Dulas Brook, 44, 54, 58, 59, 153, 163
Dunkerton's Cider, 46. 158, 229
Dunna, 48
Dunre, 46
Dunne family, 17; Capt. Thomas 106
Dunseal Farm, Abbeydore, 8
Dunwood Farm, 209
Duppa, Bishop Brian, 158
Durand of Pitres, Sheriff of Gloucester, 193
Durlow Common, 169, 221
Durham Cathedral, 98
Dutton House, Leominster, 108
Dwarf hops, 163
Dwyes Welle, 45
Dyfrig, see Saint Dubricius
Dying curse, power of, 154
Dyke House Farm, 50
Dymock, Glos., 124, 163, 170, 187, 232; Wood, 199
Dyslexic School, 137

E

Ealdfrip, 9
Eardisland, *53*, 54, 78, 95, 158
Eardisley, 54, 95; font, *49*; Wootton House, 55
Earth Satellite Station, Madley, 134
Earthworks, unexplained, Kington, 94
East Angles, 79, 137
East Anglia, 110
Easter Folk Fair, Ledbury, 104

Easthampton, 178, 179
Eastnor, *49*, 55, *57*, 104, *118, 119*
Easton Court, Little Hereford, 123
Easton, Middleton, 139
Eastwood, oak tree, 190
Eaton Bishop, 56
Eaton, bridge, 108; Hill, 110; Hall, 110, *224*
Eau Withington Court, 219
Ebenezer Methodist Chapel 129
Ebroicus, Stephen d', 133
Eccles Green, 154
Eccleswall Castle, 122
Edefen family, 58; Matil de, 58
Edgar, King, 183
Edith, Queen, 133, 183, 209
Edmund Ironside, 213
Edna the Inebriate Woman, Sandford, 68
Edric, 21
Edric, the Wild, 37, 181
Edvin Loach, 56
Edvin (Edwyn) Ralph, 56
Edward I, 54, 71, 95, 108, 218
Edward II, 104, 150, 157
Edward III, 137, 205, 218, 238
Edward IV, 44, 92, 218
Edward the Confessor, 58, 70, 92, 95, 112, 122
Edward ap Meredith, 141
Edwin, 36
Egelton, (Egleton?) 78
Egerton, Rev. John, 171
Egerton, Sir Thomas, 29
Egleton, 187
Elmslie, E.W., 214
Eleanor, Queen, 38
Elecrtricity pylon, rent of 146
Electric power at Hereford, 238
Elgar, Edward William, 36, 76, 79
Elizabeth I, 17, 40, 58, 71, 108
Elizabeth II, 71
Elizabeth, Countess of Kent, 213
Ella, 58
Ellis, Cough Willaims, 54
Elmehurst, John, 112
Elms Green, Brierley, 29
Elton, 58
Empty place custom, 177
Encaustic tiles, 131, 219
Endless Knot sculpture, 22
Endrin, poison used by gamekeepers, 106, 147
English Field Systems, Gray, 186
English Foy, 62
England's Gate, 22
English Heritage, 143, 218
English Nature, 60
English Oak, article on, 228
English Picturesque, 34
English Proverbs, Hazlitt, 189

Enmore Field, 60
Epaignes, Dept, Eure, France, 191
Ercing, 13
Erechtheum, 214
Erging, 13
Erlslen, 54
Ernisius, 237
Esbec, 58
Escley, 129; Brook, 138
Essex, 158
Essex Arms, 83
Essex, Earl of, 40, 201
Ethelbert, King, 137, 189
Ethelred, King, 213
Ethelbert's: Camp, 50; Almshouses; 70, 75; Well, 75
Eton College organ, 22
Eton Episcopi, 56
Etune, 56
Eurddil, 134
Eure, Sampson, 106
European Aviation Works, 104
Evangelical Free Church, 82
Evans family, Pembridge, 158
Evans, Edward Bickerton, 214
Evans, Frances Isabella, 135
Evans, James. 171
Evans, Thomas, 146
Everlasting Mercy, The, 104
Evesbatch, 58
Evil Eye, 127, 138
Ewyas, 126
Ewyas Harold, 58, 147, 165
Ewyas Lacy (Longtown), 207, 129
Ewyas, Vale of, 45
Exeter, City Council and Canal, 227
Exocet Missiles, 231
Experimental Husbandry, 60
Eye, 59
Eye of Amr, 149
Eye Well, Bromyard, 33
Eyton, 29, 59, *115*, 133
Eywood, 100, 194

F

Faerie Queen, The, Spenser, 82
Fair Oaks, Hereford, 70
Fairfield, Adforton, 9
Fairies: Cusop Dingle, 45; Kington, 98; Longtown, 129; Orcop, 149, 155
Faith, Adam, 134
Falcon, 181
Falcon Hotel, Bromyard, 33
Falklands War, 231
Fallow deer, 55
Fanshaw, Admiral, 50
Far Barn, Mocktree, 142
Far East, 60
Farm, The, Evesbatch, 58

Farm-brewed beer and cider, 198
Fawley, 60, *61;* Cross, 60
Feathers Hotel, Ledbury, 103
Feld, Marc, 211
Fell family, 151; Doctor Fell, 151
Felton, 60, 225
Fencote station, 68
Fenhampton, 209
Ferguson, Mr. Holcombe, 91
Fernhill, Brilley, 30
Ferrie Inn, Symonds Yat, 215
Ferry Cottage, Bycross, 166
Ferry Lane, Fownhope, 62
Fiddler's Elbow, Mocktree, 141
Fido, William, 90
Field's End, Weobley, 209
Field's Place, Dilwyn, 46
Fiennes, Celia, 187
Fife and tabor, 78
Fincher's Farm, 214
Fine Furniture, 133
Finch, John, bell founder, 154
Fir Tree, pub, 146
First Gold, 163
Fish with golden chain, 52
Fishing custom, 80
William Fitz Osbern, see Osbern
Fishpool Valley, 44, 223
Fitzponz family, 50
Fitzwarin, Fulk, 194
Five Ashes, 100, 139
Fives court, Craswall, 42
Five Bridges, 18
Five Jars, The, 149
Fine Street, 90, 161
Flamstead, Herts., 210
Flanders, 234
Flanesford Priory, 66, 201
Flaxbridge, spring, 211
Flaxley Abbey, 211
Flaxman, John, 91
Flea circus, 102
Flight into Egypt, French painting, 138
Flights Farm, 104
Flintgham, 194
Flintshire, 126
Flowers of the Meadows, 134
Flynn, Errol, 40
Foal Show, 91
Foliat, Hugh, 103
Foley Arms, 190
Foley Cottage, 190
Foley family, 201, 222; Wye valley ironworks, 215; Richard 183, 185; Thomas, 183; Lady Emily, 183; Paul, M.P., 183; Edward, 183
Foley the Fidler, poem, 185
Folk Festival, Bromyard, 33
Folk Ley, 111
Folk Museum, Leominster, 108

Folk-Lore of Herfordshire, Leather, 45
Folklore of Hereford and Worcester, Palmer, 12, 62, 169, 189, 208
Folklore of the Northern Counties, 45
Folklore of Warwickshire, The, Henderson, 233
Folly, The, Leinthall Earls, 106
Font, cynlindrical, 14; Italian, 102
Forbury Chapel, 108
Ford, 60, *121*
Ford Abbey, 167
Forest of Dean, 83, 102, 201, 213
Forfeit Song, Marden, 137
Forge, The, Titley, 194
Forge House Gallery, 30
Forty Acre Farm, 221
Fosbroke, T.D., 211
Foster, Mrs., 90
Foster, Thomas, 147
Fouleshurst family, 28
Foulgar, Emma, 16
Fountain, The, 155
Four Seasons Products, 44
Fownhope, 62; hovels, *61*; tympanum, *128*; River Wye at, *61*
Fownhope Motors, 62
Fox, Edmund, 147
Fox, Freddie, 91
Fox, G.E. 55
Fox, Helip, 178
Fox Hill, 38
Fox Inn, Leinthall Starkes, 107
Foxes Dingle, Craswall, 42
Foxhalls, 181
Foxley, 135, 144, 154, 222, 225
Foy, 62
Fragrant Garden, 79
France, 55, 59
Francis I, King of France, 48
Framington, 137
Franklin, effigy, 150
Franklin family, 123
Franklin, Benjamin, 100
'Free of fiscal tribute', Preston, 165
Freeman, Barry, 59
Freene family, 189
Freen's Court, 189
Freer, Sarah, 22
Freetown, Ashperton, 14;
Freetown, Tarrington, 190
French Travellers in England, 232
Frene (de Fresnes) family, 141; Richard, 141
Frith Farm, 203
Frogmore, 211
Frome Manor, Evesbatch, 58
Frome. River, 13, 18, 33, 37, 56, 146, 151, 157, 183, 187, 199, 210, 222, 223, 228

Fromes Hill, 38
Frontinus, Governor, 10, 199
Funerals: procession belief, 98; superstition at Pembridge, 159, and Peterchurch, 161; monuments at Llanveynoe, 126, *127*

G

Gaer Cop, 70
Gaines, and Old Gaines, 214
Gallimore, David, 163
Galloway bull, 228; sheep, 58
Gallows Knapp, 88
Gamaches, Normandy, 135
Gamage Farm, 151
Gamber Brook, 127, 138, 149, 194
Gamber Head, 149
Game Laws, 100
Gammon, Warren, 228,
Ganarew, 63; Sellarsbrook House, 119
Garbett, Anne, 100
Gardiner, Isabella, 9
Gardiner, N., 134
Garn, The, Longtown, 130
Garnon's Hill, 135, 154, *119*
Garnon's Park, 135
Garnon, Peter, 134
Garnstone Castle, 207
Garnstone Park, 209
Garnon Brook, 155
Garrick, David, 79
Garrold, Richard, 14
Garston, family, 145
Garway, 63, 88, 126; Common, 64; Hill, 155
Garway's Cruel Feast, 64
Gate Hangs Well, 191
Gatley Farms, 106
Gatley Long Coppice, 107
Gatley Park, 106, 147, 212
Gatsford, 25
Gauset, 157
Gavelkind, Celtic equal inheritance custom, 202, 127, 130
Gean, wild cherry, Queenswood, 199
Gebons, Thomas, 9
Gedda, 56
Gelpack Excelsior, 79
George IV, 171; Memorial Youth Hostel, Capel-y-ffin, 236
Gentleman's Magazine, 8, 195
Geoffrey of Monmouth, 134
Gerald (Geraldus) of Wales (Cambrensis), 28, 237
Gethin, John, 91
Getty, John Paul, 71
Getune, 223
Ghosts:
  Avenbury, haunted church, 16
  Bromyard, hidden gold, 34
  Callow, phantom house and ghost of Callow Farm, 37
  Deveraux Wootton, Lady Berrington, 153
  Aylton, Emma Foulgar, 16
  Goodrich, Charles Clifford, 64
  Hereford Cathedral, 72
  Kenchester, Roman soldiers and Thomas a Becket, 87
  Longtown, hurdle-maker, 129
  Lyonshall (two), 133
  Middleton-on-the-Hill, 138
  Much Dewchurch, cat, and struggling men, 149
  Much Marcle, (three), 150
  Ocle Pychard, in pool, 154
  Orleton, piano player, 157
  Weobley, Old Grgg, 209; demon cats, 209; calf man, 209;
  Welsh border, Wild Edric, 37
Ghost Stories of M.R. James, 149
Gibbons, Grinling, 82, 87
Gibetting, Longtown, 129
Giffard, Sir John, 103
Gill, Eric, 29, 236
Gillow Manor, 70
Gilpin, William, 171
Gilwern, stream, 95
Gisborne family, 112
Gipsies, note on, 209;
  Bron Horse Fair, 25; Dormington, burning caravan, 50; Wigmore, funeral, 218; Pixley, roadside camp, 163; Weobley, The Homme, gipsy singers, 209; Peter Delaney, 29, *115;* Gentlemen Locks, fiddle players, 158; Jeremy Sandford of Hatfield Court, and *Songs from the Roadside,* 68; gipsies at the Swan Inn, Huntington, 86; at Little Tarrington, 190; at Monkland, 142; at Shucknall, for water, 211; Gipsy Count, 209; gipsy music, 68, Travellers' Support Group, Brinsop Common, 32
Glacial lakes, Kinsham, 99, Vale of Wigmore, 217
Glacial landscapes: Shobdon, 178; Staunton-on-Arrow, 182, Tyberton, 197
Gladstry, 86; Brook, 86
Glasshouse Farm, Garway, 177
Glass-making, 177
Glass Pig (Foley Arms), 190
Glastonbury Thorn, 121; see also Holy Thorn
Gleichan, Lady Feadora, 150
Glen Olchon, 127
Glibes, The, 139
Gloucester, 213, 235; gaol, 36
Gloucester, Earl of, 56
Gloucester to Hereford Canal, note on, 228
Gloucester Priory, 147
Gloucestershire, 89
Glove-making, Cradley, 42
Glyndwr (Glendower), Owain: *Owain Glyndwr,* book, 12; 37, 38, 44, 48, 50, 63, 68, 86, 87, 88, 108, 143, 153, 181, 182, 203, 205, 237; his last days, article on, 232; *Ode to Owain Glyndwr,* poem, 148; Glyndwr's Great Seal, *148;* his children listed, 232; Tudur, his brother, 232
Godiva, Lady, 221
God of the Three Ways, 138
Godric, 64, 135
Goswin, Bishop Francis, 214
Godwinson, Earl Harold, 108
Godwin's tile works, 18
Godwin, William, 131
Goff, Edward, 86
Goggin, The, 106
Gold spurs custom, Mordiford, 145
Gold treasure, Longtown, 130; legend of, Saint Weonard's, 177
Golden Cockeral Press, 59
Golden Cross Inn, 189
Golden Cross, 143
Golden Hop Pole Ale, 202
Golder Field, 167
Golden Valley, 8, 58, 67, 68, 143, 161, 162, 175, 195, 199; railway, 50, 68, 162, 163
Golden Well, Dorstone, 52
Gold mine, Hope Mansell, 83
Golf courses, list of, 229
Gomme, Sir Lawrence, 110
Good Bros., timber merchants, 147
Goode, Hannah, 199
Goode, Thomas and Anne, 175
Goodere, Capt. Samuel, 203
Goodrich, 64, 205; castle, 64, *65,* 121, 201; Queen's Stone, *188*
Goodships, Munderfield, 151
Goodwin, Meg, 78
Goose Pool, 10
Garden Marquees, 29
Gordon, Noelle, 162, *172*
Gore, Jack, 134
Gorges, Ferdinando, 59
Gorseley Common, 14. 112
Gospel Bush, Peterstow, 162
Gospel Oak, Shobdon, 179; Lucton, 131
Gospel Pass, 45, 236
Gospel Yew, Bosbury, 25
Gotherment, 217
Gouge, Robert Minors, 177
Gould, Rev. Baring, 126

Gouldstone, Roger, 50
Gourlay, Malcolm, 40
Govilon to Hereford Tramway, 235
Grafton, 66
Grandison, Lady, wife of Sir Peter, 150
Grandison, William de, 13; Katherine and Edward II, 13; John, Bishop of Exeter, 13; family 13
Grandmont, order of, Crasswall, 42
Grand National, 106
Grange Farm, Abbeydore, 8
Grange House School, Marston, 137
Grange Pony-Trekking Centre, 236
Grantsfield, 90
Grant, H.L., 186
Gray, Thomas, 171
Great Barn, Pembridge, 157
Great Corrs Farm, 88
Great Doward, 63, 215
Great Fire of London, 122
Great Goytre, 124
Great Heath, 100
Great House, Dilwyn, 46
Great House, The, Stoke Prior, 186
Great Howle, 201
Great Landowners of Great Britain and Ireland, The, 214
Great Oak Cider Company, 12
Great Penllan, 86
Great Turnant, 126
Great West Field, Kingland, 91, 146
Great Witley Court, 183
Green Dragon Hotel, 75
Green Farm, 169
Green Grize, 80
Green Heart wood, 215
Green Man, King's Pyon, 92; Ledbury, 104; Much Marcle, 150; Rowlestone, 174
Green Man Inn, Fownhope, 62
Greenly family, 194
Greenstone 175
Gregory family, 84
Gregory, Sir William, 84
Grendon Bishop, 66
Grendon Court, 159
Grendon Green, 66
Grendene, 66
Greswolde-Williams family, 26
Gravelhey, Richard and wife, 186
Greyfriars Bridge, 70, 235
Grey, Lady Jane, 110, 232
Grey, Lord, of Wilton, 29
Grey, Roger de, 28
Grey Valley, 94
Greyhound Inn, Pembridge, 158
Grieve, Jean, 206
Griffin, Michael, 179
Griffith Farm, Burleygate, 155
Grifiths, David, 236

Griffiths' Garage, Leintwardine, 107
Griffiths, John, 63
Griffiths, Robert, 36
Grimbald Pauncefot and wife Constantia, 147
Peter Cripwell & Associates, 143
Gritton of Garway, 64
Grosmont, Yorks., 42
Grove House, Bromsberrow Heath, 50,
Grove, The, Llangrove, 125
Grove, The, Langarren, 125
Grove, Upper and Lower, 178
Grove, The, Walterstone, 202
Gravenor's Bridge, 139
Gruffydd ap Llewelyn, 108, 169
Gruffydd ap Mareddudd, 135
Grumar, Richard, 10
Guinndo, 40
Gun dogs, poisoned at Leinthall Earls, 107
Gunfrid, 210
Gunnar, 211
Guoruoe, 64
Gurney's Oak, 33
Guthlac's Priory, Saint, 144
Guy's Hospital, London, 45
Gwent, Dr. John, 88
Gwillim family, 215
Gwillin, John, 129
Gworlodith, 153
G.W.R., 133, 146, 185, 228, 195
Gwrfodwr, King, 165
Gwyllyn, William, 125
Gwynne, Nell, *68,* 74, 79

H

Habbington family, 32
Haddon, G.C., 54, 173
Haffield, 50
Hagen, 179
Hagley, 18
Hague, The, 40
Haig, Major, 149
Haines, George H., 55
Hainstone, 166
Hakluyt, Richard, 59, 110; Sir Leonard, 59
Hakluyt's Voyages, 110
Half Moon Hotel, Llanthony, 236
Half Moon, Mordiford, 145
Hall Court, Rushall, 151
Ham Green, Mathon, 138
Hamilton, Lady, 171
Hamish Park, 214
Hamlet, Prince of Denmark, 153
Hamnish Clifford, 66
Hampton Court, 67; deer, 83; blacksmith of estate, 22
Hampton Bishop, 57, 67, 195, 225

Hampton Meadow, 67, 225
Hampton Park Brick and Tile Works, 195
Hampton Wafre Farm, Docklow, 48
Handel, G.F., composer, 45, 141
Hansom, C.F., 34
Handkerchief trees, 83
Hanmer, Margaret, 232
Hanbury Green, 178
Harding, Gilbert, *77, 79*
Hardman, stained glass designer, 191
Harwicke, 38, 67
Hardwicke, Thomas, 75
Hare and witch, Longtown, 129
Hare hunting, Clodock, 40
Harewood, 48, 68
Harewood End, 68, 138; Inn and Park, 138
Harford, John, 24
Harleian Manuscripts, 25
Harley family, 95, 112, 218; at Bosbury, 24; at Kinsham, 99; Robert, came to Brampton Bryan in 1309, 25; Robert, First Earl of Oxford, 25; Hon. Edward, 5th Earl, 194; Sir Edward, 25; Thomas, 20; Thomas, M.P., 59; Thomas, (died 1738), 99
Harley's Mountain, 112
Harley Street, London, 25
Harold Godwinson, Earl of Hereford and King of Englnd, 86, *128,* 133, 147, 165
Harris, George, 90
Harrowing of Hell, 54
Hastings, Lady Elizabeth, 194
Hatfield, 68; 'charmer', 121
Hatterall Hill, 40; Ridge, 237
Hatton, Brian, 76, *77,* 79, 214; Hatton Gallery, Hereford, 74
Haugh Wood, Woolhope, 145, 221
Haven, The, Hardwicke, 68
Haven, The, Pembridge, 158
Havergal, Rev. Francis and sister Francis Ridley, 198
Havisham, Miss, 112
Hawkersland, Cross, 137
Hawkhurst, Pencombe, 159
Hawkins, Lady Margaret, 95; John, pirate, 95
Hawkshaw, Edward, 210
Hay-on-Wye, 42, 50, 68, 79, 162, 235
Hay to Kington tramway, 214
Hay Bluff, 45, 236
Hay's Head, 46, 158
Haycock, E., 191
Haycock, E., (Junior), 194
Haye Park Wood, 106
Hayes Farm, Laysters, 100
Haywood, 68; Forest, 10

Hay Wood, Upton Bishop, 199
Hay Wood, Linton, 122
Hazel, Farm, Ledbury, 104
Hazlitt, W.C., 189
Headland, Bagley Head, 46
Heart burial, 38
Hearne, Thomas, 235
Hearts of Oak Society, 62
Heath Farm, Wolferlow, 221
Heaving, Ledbury, 104
Headley, Bishop, 20
Hegarty, Patricia, 203
Helyon, Walter de, 136
Hell in Herefordshire, poem, 15
Hell Moat, 177
Hell Peak, 181
Hell Wood, 86
Hellens, 104, 150, Hemhill, 131
Hemsworth, G.S., 233
Henderson, folklorist, 45
Henderson, Hamish, 232
Hengoed, 86
Henning, Martin and Kate, 98
Hennor House, 66
Henry I, 55, 76, 108, 161, 237
Henry II, 38
Henry III, 55, 71, 129
Henry IV, 133, *148,* 204, 232
Henry V, 59, 110, 205, 232
Henry, VI, 55
Henry VII, 186
Henry VIII, 48, 108, 171, 237
Henshall, Hugh, 228
Hentland, 68, 80, 133
Hepworth, James, 58
Heptonstall, 233
Hereford's Knob, Lord, 45
Hereford, *69,* 70-80, 145, 157,163, 234, *239;* a river port, 235, *230;* S.A.S. camp, 79, 80, *121;* secret tunnel, 238; street plan, *239;* Bishop of, 170, 173, 189, 194, 205, 206; Castle, 70, 75, *230;* Cathedral, 71, 149, 153, 137, 202, *119, 230, 73;* Bishop's Cloister, Chapter House, College of Vicars Choral, Bishop's Palace, Boy Bishop, and Cathedral ghosts, 72; precinct, 71; stone for, 33; tiles for, 219; Canons of, 165, 166,
Hereford Bull Inn, Bristow, 29
Hereford cattle, article on, 228; photo. of Hereford bull, 196; mentions of cattle at:
  Bagley Head, 46
  Hay-on-Wye, *159*
  Huntington (near Hereford), 84
  Kimbolton, 'Anxiety IV, and American Herefords, 90
  King's Pyon, 92
  Llandinabo, 124
  Lugwardine, 131
  Marden, 137
  Moccas, 139
  Monkland, 142
  Norton Canon, 154
  Tarrington (Freetown), 190
  Wellington, 203
Hereford Charters, 71
Hereford College of Agriculture, 82
Hereford Galvanizers, 78
Hereford family, 145; James, 145
Hereford Jazz Club, 76
Hereford, Lord, 67
Hereford Free Library, 149
Hereford, public and other notable buildings listed, 74, 75
Hereford Races, 77
Hereford Times, 75, 76, 179
Herefordshire Beacon, *35,* 41
Herefordshire Commotion, 10
Herefordshire Community Health Trust, 20
Herefordshire County Record Office, 74, 184
Herefordshire, Buildings of England, Pevsner, 71
Herefordshire, King's England, Mee, 218
Herefordshire Nature Trust, 106, 225
Herefordshire Rural Heritage Museum, 73, 215
Herefordshire School of Carving, examples at:
  Castle Frome, 38
  Brinsop, 30
  Eardisley, 55
  Fownhope, 62, 128
  Kilpeck, 88, *93*
  Orleton, 157
  Rowlestone, 174
  Shobdon, 179
  Bridge Sollars, 28
  Stretton Sugwas, 187
  Yatton, 223
Herefordshire Travellers' Support Group, 32
Herefordshire Village Book, 10, 102
Herefordshire Waterworks Museum, at Broomy Hill, Hereford, 74
Herbs, monastic, 9
Hergest, 232; Court, 98; Croft, 96; Pool, 96; Ridge, 95; *Hergest Ridge,* 96
Herl, Sir Andrew, 10
Herla, King, tale of, 174
Herewold, Bishop, 138
Hetfelde, 68
Heyns, Rev. Richard, 10
Hicks Farm, Lingen, 112
Hickman, John R., 165
Hide, (120 acres in Herefordshire) see Monkhide, 142
Higgins, Mrs., 154
Higgin's Well, 122
Higginson, Edward, 32
High Collis, 106
High Lane House, 191
High Town, Hereford, 70
High Vinnals, 16, 58
Highland, Rodd, 170
Highway robbery, 198
Hill, The, King's Pyon, 92
Hill Cross, Tedstone Delamere,191
Hill of Eaton, 62
Hill End, Weston Beggard, 211
Hill Evans Vinegar, Worcester, 214
Hill Farm, Castle Frome, 38
Hill Farm, Laysters, 100
Hill farm, Much Dewchurch, 149
Hill Fort House, 56
Hill Gate, 177
Hill House, Bosbury, 24
Hill, John, 197
Hill, Nathaniel, 171
Hill, Octavia, 171
Himalayas, 236
Hindwell Brook, 96, 99, 100, 170
Hinton, 16, 162
Hir, John, 96
History of Herefordshire, Duncombe, 9
A History of Herefordshire, 188, 190, West, 217
History of Kington, Parry, 95
Hitler, Adolph, 99
Hitrees, Plant Nursery, 60
Hoarstone, 191
Hoarwithy, 80, 90, 123, *114*
Hodges, Geoffrey, 12
Hogg's Mount, 70
Hole-in-the-Wall, 62, 174
Holemere, 82
Holgate Farm, 91
Holland, 185
Holland, Henry, 20
Hollin, Peter, 22
Hollington Farm, Ballingham, 18
Hollins, Murray, 46
Holly Brook, Risbury, 84, 170
Holme, The, 134
Holm, The, Willersley, 217
Holme Lacy, 78, 82, 87; bridge, 62; House, *80*
Holme Marsh, 133, 134
Holmer, 67, 78, 82, 163, 225
Holy Land, 48, 50
Holy Sepulchre, 64
Holy Thorn trees at:
  Acton Beauchamp, 9
  How Caple, Hugh's Well, 83
  King's Thorn, 92, 122
  Orcop, 155

Peterchurch, 162
Rowlestone, 175
Stoke Edith, 183
Tyberton, 197
Holy Wells and important springs:
   Aconbury, St. Anne's Well and
     Lady Well (St. Catherine's), 8
   Acton Beauchamp, Roaring Water,
     9
   Bacton Manor spring, 17
   Bodenham, Cross Well, 22
   Bolstone, Monk's Well, 24
   Bosbury, Job's Well, 24
   Bromyard, Eye Well, 33
   Brampton Bryan, 25
   Clodock, St. Clodock's Well, 40
   Colwall, 40; Prime's Well, 41;
     Waum's Well, 41
   Craswall, Cress Well, 42;
     The Pot Well, 42
   Dinedor, 46
   Dinedor Cross, 46
   Dinmore, 48
   Dorstone, Golden Well, 52
   Ewyas Harold, St. Martin's Well,
     59
   Hereford, Bride Well, 75;
     Ethelbert's Well, 75
   Kenchester, 87
   Kington, Holy Well, 98;
     Crooked Well, 98
   Llanveynoe, Cae Thomas Well,
     127
   Longtown, St. Martin's Well, 130
   Lower Eggleton, St. Katherine's
     Well, 187
   Luston, Holywell, 133
   Marden, inside the church, 137
   Moccas, Depple Well, 141
   Mordiford, The Spout, 145
   Much Dewchurch, Eye of Amr,
     149
   Pencombe, 159
   Peterchurch, St. Peter's Well, 161
   Pencombe, Washing Pool, 159
   Richard's Castle, 169
   Shobdon, Lady Pool, 179
   Shucknall, The Spout, 211
   Snodhill, St. Mary's Well, 162
   Stoke Edith, St. Edith's Well, 183
   Stretford, St. Cosmos and St.
     Damian's Well, 187
   Tedstone Delamere,
     St. Augustine's Well, 191
   Titley, The Spout, 192
   Thornbury, Lady Well, 193
   Turnastone, Lady Well, 195
   Weston-u-Penyard, Flaxbridge,
     211
   Whitney -on-Wye, St. Peter's
     Well, 217

Holybush Hill, Malverns, 56
Holywell Brook, 159
Holyewll Dingle, 55
Homend, Stretton Grandison, 187
Homes, Inett, 198
Homme, The Weobley, 209
Homme House, Much Marcle, 150
Honddu, Afon, 201, 236
Honey lake Brook, 86
Honeymoor Common, 56
Hongar, 177
Hooper Madge, 185
Hooper, William, 131
Hops, drawing, 11; references to
  hops at: Acton Beauchamp, 9;
  Bosbury, 24; Brierley Court, 29;
  Bromyard, 34; Castle Frome, 38;
  Edwin Ralph, 56; Much Cowarne,
  147; Preston Wynne, 166; Wacton,
  199; Weston Beggard, 210;
  Whitbourne, 124
Hop-pickers' Feast, 68,
  description at Blakemere, 22,
  Ullingwick, 198; hop-picking,
  Bromyard area, *192;*
  Hop-picking song, 29, 60
Hope End, 41, 178, 203
Hope Farm, Bircher, 20
Hope Mansell, 83
Hope, Roger and Juliana de, 203
Hope-u-Dinmore, 67, 83,
Hopkins, Sir Anthony, 70
Hopkins, Dave, paraglider, 236
Hopton Arms, Ashperton, 13
Hopton family, of Canon Frome, 37,
  187; Michael, 37; Sir Edward, 187;
  Major, 103
Hop Pole Inn, Bromyard, 33
Horse and Jockey, Colwall, 41
Horse gin, Wormbridge, 221
Horseway Head, herb garden, 194
Horticultural Society, 58
Hoskins, Mr., 72
Hotel Cottage, Downton, 52
Houghton, Charles, 36
Houlder, C., 52
Hound of the Baskervilles, Doyle, 96
Hound of Hell, 96; Llanveynoe, 127
How Caple, 84
Howel, Law of, 233
Howl, Elizabeth, 85
Howle Hill, 201
Hownhall, 213
Howorth, Jane, 82
Howton, 87
Howton Grove Farm, 221
Hroaldr, 174
Hudibras, 151
Huaggal, J.W., 124
Hugh L'Asne (the Donkey), 62, 162
Hughes, Colin, candle-maker, 173

Hughes, Robert, 123
Hugo, Victor, 233
Hulland, Capt., 147
Hulme, William, 25
Human scrifice, Much Dewchurch,
  149
Humane slaughter, 100
Humber, 84; Brook, 84
Humber Marsh, Nature Reserve, 84
Humphrey de Boulville, 163
Hundred, The, 14
Hungary, 194
Hungerstone, 10, 193
Huns, 42
Hunsdon Manor Hotel, formerly
  Sandiford, 211
Hunt, Rev. C.G., 153
Hunt, John, 78
Hunthouse Cottage, 130
Huntingdon, Lady, 87
Hunting foxes, list of hunts in the
  county, 230; hunting hares at
  Longtown, 129, and Weston-u-
  Penyard, 213, 214
Huntington (near Hereford), 84
Huntington (near Kington), 86, 95;
  Fair, 86
Huntlands, Whitbourne, 213;
Huntsham Court, 66;
  Farm Park (rare breeds), 66
Hurstley, 98
Hurstway Common, 55; Forest, 54
Huskisson, G.H., 41
Hutchison family, Kimbolton, 90;
Rev. Thomas, 90
Hutchinson, Mr., 32
Hutchinson, publishers, 233
Hwita, 215
Hyde Ash, 186
Hymn of Sacrifice, 99
Hymns Ancient and Modern, 142

I

I am a Rabbit, poem, 240
Ice-Age landscape of Lugg Valley,
  225; glacial landscape, at Shobdon,
  179, at Lucton, 132; Vale of
  Wigmore, 107, 217
Ignatius, Father, 236
I Love My Sarah, 169
Inco-Alloys, 78, 82
'In Common', 131
Independent Chapel, Broxwood, 34
Independent Intelligence Company,
  14th, 238
India, 236
Ingham, Richard, 14
Inglestone, 62
In Spite of All, Lyall, 24
Instone Court, 157

Inter-Commoning, 225
Iranian Embassy, 80
Ireland, 107, 168
Iron-Age fort-cum-settlements:
  Note that many hill-fort sites were previously occupied by Stone-Age and Bronze-Age peoples.
  Aconbury Camp, 8
  Adforton, Camp Brandon, 10
  Aymestry, fort, 17
  Brilley, Twyn Camp, 30
  Broadward Hall (Salop), 110
  Brobury, The Scar, 32
  Buckton, Coxall Knoll Camp, also a settlement, 34
  Burghill, fort site, 36
  Colwall, Herefordshire Beacon, *35*, 41, Midsummer Hill Camp, 41, 56
  Credenhill, fort, 42
  Croft Ambrey, fort, 44
  Cusop, Mouse Castle, fort, 45
  Dinedor Camp, 46
  Dinmore Camp, fort, 83
  Docklow, Uphampton Camp, 48
  Dormington, Backbury Hill, (Ethelbert's) Camp, 50
  Donnington, Wall Hills Camp, 50
  Dorstone Hill, fort, 52
  Downton Camp, 54
  Eaton Bishop, fort, 56
  Fownhope, Capler Hill Camp, 62
  Great Howle, fort, 201
  Grendon Bishop, Westington Camp, 66
  Hamnish Clifford, Bach Camp, 66
  Hentland, Gaer Cop, fort, 70
  Ivington Camp, 86
  Kenchester, lowland settlement, 87
  Kimbolton, Bach Camp, 90
  Ledbury, Wall Hills, 102, 104
  Michaelchurch Escley, defensive post 139
  Monnington Straddel, Timberline Hill, 143
  Much Marcle, Oldbury Camp, 151
  Risbury Camp, 84, 170
  Ross, Capel Tump, 173
  Staunton -on-Arrow, 182
  Sutton Saint Nicholas, Sutton Walls, 189
  Thornbury, Wall Hills, 191
  Vowchurch, near Poston Lodge, 199
  Walterstone Camp, 202
  Wellington, lowland settlement, 203
  Whitchurch, King Arthur's Cave and Little Doward fort, 215
Iron mining, Walford near Ross, 201
Iron grave slabs, Brilley, 29;
  Burrington, 36
Iron-working:
  For Celtic and Roman iron-working see Bromash, 214, and Crockers Ash, Whitchurch, 215; a note on 16th-18th forges, 201; iron working in Wye Valley, 215; list of sites in the county:
  Downton (Bringewood Forge), 52
  Llancillo, 124
  Linton-by-Ross, 112
  Pontrilas, 165
  Ross, 170
  Tidnor, 131
  Walford, near Ross, 201
  Saint Weonards (Old Furnace), 177
  Whitchurch, 215
Isabella, Queen, 150, 218
Isabel, Glendower, 232
Isles, Doug, apiarist and festival organizer, 33, 116
Isolation Hospital, Tupsley, 195
Italy, 59, 205
Italian Romanesque, 80
Iunopi, 124
Ivington, 29, 86, 108; Green, 86; Ivingtonbury, 86; Camp, 86

J

Jack, G.H., 74
Jack of Kent, 88
Jack with a Lantern, 98
Jackdaw, omen, 209
Jackson Almshouses, Bromyard, 33
Jackson, Jeremiah, 64
Jackson, Phineas, 181
Jackson, Rev. E., 104
Jackson, Rev. John, 104
Jakarta, 40
'Jakey', 231
James I, 149
James II, 210
James family, 67
James, M.R., 149
Japanese Maples, 83
Jarvis, George, 26
Jauncey, William, 187
Javelin men, 163
Jean's Fashions, 207
Jenkins, wizard, 12, 34, 166, 198, 218
Jerusalem, 64, 71
Jervis, George, 182
Jesuit Missionary Centre, 126
Jeus Christ, Superstar, 183
Job's Well, Bosbury, 24
Jockey Morris Men, 116
John, Augustus, 26
John, King, 71

Johnson, Alan, 12
Johnson, of Birkenhead, 74
Johnson, Kenelm, 162
Johnson's of Kingsland, 106
Johnston, James, 180
Jones, Alfred Price, and wife Harriet, 142
Jones, Dave, 33, 42, 78, 104, *155*, 166; wife Annie, 33, 116, 166
Jones, David, 236
Jones, Sir John Harvey, 25, 211
Jones, Gwyn, 96
Jones, Robert, 94
Jones, Robert, V.C., 161
Jones, Thomas, 96
Jordan, Alexander, 22
Jordan, Fred, *121*
Jordan, Richard, 159
Joseph of Arimathea, 154, 183
Jubilee Drive, Malverns, 41
Jubilee Park, Whitchurch, 214
Judas Iscariot, 104

K

Kain, Andrew, 238; Andrew Kain Enterprises, security company, 238
Katherine, (Catherine) of Audley, 'Saint', 103, 150, 159
Katherine, Saint, of Alexandria, 103; Hospital at Ledbury, 103
Keck, Anthony, 131, 141
Keene, Kathleen, 54
Kemble family of Pembridge, 206; Saint John, *73*, 205
Kemble, Stephen, actor, 98; Roger, 79
Kempe, C.E., 29, 41, 124, 150
Kempe and Tower, 66
Kempen, van, 67
Kempley Green, 198
Kempson, F.R., 21, 28, 36, 66, 74, 95, 122, 131, 163, 185, 193
Kenderchurch, 87, 165
Kennel Wood, 98
Kenning's Hospital, 70
Kenny family, 150
Kent, 185
Kent, John, 87; Jack of, 87
Kenchester (Magnis), 70, *85*, 86, 187, 203
Kenchester Water Gardens, 163
Kentchurch, 64, 82, 87
Kentucky, 185
Kerne Bridge, 201
Kerry Almshouses, Hereford, 75
Kerry Arms, Hereford, 72
Kerry's Gate, 8
Kettle Bottom, 213
Kettle, Rev., 213
Kidley, John, 62

Kilforge House, Ballingham, 18
Kill Dane, field name, Bolitree, 213
Kiln Green, 201
Kilpeck, 88, 88, *89, 93,* 161
Kilreague Farm, 125
Kilver Noll, 235
Kilvert, Bob, and wife Julia, 206
Kilvert, Rev. Francis, 26, *27,* 32, 98, 141, 182, 236
Kimbolton, 90
King of the Cats, folk tale, 174
King Arthur's Cave, 63
'King of the Black Market', 59
King of the Fairies, Kenchester, 87
King family, 37
King George V, engine, 68, 74
King George Playing Fields, 79
King Stephen's Chair, 71
King's Caple, 60, 90, 178
King's Carpenter, The, see John Abel
King's Cellar, 189
King's Council, at Wigmore, 218
King's England: Herefordshire, 25
King's Head, Ross, 171
King's Mills, 145
King's Pitts Wood, 8
King's Pyon, 92
King's Thorn, 92, 122
King's Wood, Bullinghope, 36
Kingsland, 91, 131, 145
Kingsley, Charles, 15
Kingsthorne, 18
Kingstone, 92
Kingstone Black, 123
Kingstone, Weston-u-Penyard, 213
Kington, 38, 94, 95, 193
Kington to Eardisley and Brecon Tramway, 133
Kington to Presteigne Railway, 194
Kingswood, 94
Kingswood House, Kington, 94
Kinnersley, *97,* 98, *119*
Kinsham, 99; Dingle, 99
Kintley Farm. Brilley, 30
Kinton, 107
Kinver, 185
Kipper Knowle, 48
Kitchen, John, 198
Knapp Farm, 162
Knapp, The, Eyton, 60
Knapp, The, Ledbury, 104
Knapton Green, Birley, 21
Knight family, 44; Richard of Madeley, 36, 52, 222; Richard Payne, 52, 222; Thomas Andrew, 58, 222
Knight family, cider makers, 186
Knight, W.H., 146
Knighton, near Newport, Salop. 164
Knightshill, 103
Knights Hospitaller, see Saint John of Jerusalem, order of
Knights Templar, 64, 75
Knightwick, 214
Knell, Raven, 45
Knill family, 100
Knill, 10
Knoak's Court, Ivington, 85
Knoak's Court, near Sretford, 186
Kuala Lumpur, 80
Kymin, 155, 210
Kynaston Chapel, 151
Kyrle Chapel, 150
Kyrle family, 60; Sir John, 150; Sir John and wife, *143;* John, the Man of Ross, 170, 171

L

Labinsky, Count Numa, 63
Lacy (Laci), de, of Lassy, France, 38, 133, note on, 207; Walter, 42, 129, 133, 202, 207; his wife, Emelina, 207; his son, Roger, 10, 26, 82, 142, 147, 154, 169, 141, 135, 185, 207, 221, Roger's brother, Hugh, 207; Hugh, 237; William, 237; Gilbert, 129
Lace, John, 78
Lacons, The, Putley, 167
Laddin, 124
'Lady' and Hereford bull, *219*
Ladylift, 154
Lady Meadow Farm, 133
Lady Pool, Shobdon, 179
Lady Well, Thornbury, 193
Lady Well, Turnastone, 195
Lamb, E.B., 178
Lambert, Sarah, 41
Lame beast charm, 100
Lammas Lands, Lugwardine, 131
Lammas Lands, Pembridge, 159
Lammas Meadow, 226
Lamping, Mocktree, 142
Lancashire, 76
Land, meaning in place names, 107
Land Army, 198
Lander, Richard, explorer, 159
Landor, Walter Savage, 237
Lane End, 83
Lanehead Farm, 56
Langan, Jack, 62
Langdale, Lady, 194
Langland, William, 42, 104
Langlands Farm, 104
Langstone Court, 125
La Tene Celts, 86
Larport, 133, 146
Larruperz Centre, 173
Lassy, Calvados, France, 207
Lawns, The, Hampton Bishop, 67
Lawrence, Mrs., Agnes, 125
Lawton Hope, 203; Hill, 48
Laysters, 100, 124, 139
Laystone Bridge, 137
Laugh Lady Well, 25
Lea, The, Kimbolton, 90
Lea, The, near Ross, 102
Lea Bailey Hill, 83
Leabbrink, 62
Leadership Trust, 211
Leadon, River, 24, 50, 102, 153, 228; Valley, 234
Lea Line, 102
Leather chalice case, Pipe & Lyde, 163
Leather, E.M., 25, 33, 45, 122, 127, 154, 158, 155, 166, 173, 174, 175, 183, 189, 202, 206, *207,* 209, 210, 219
Lechmere family, 62
Lechmere's Lay, 62
Lectune, 111
Ledbury, 67, *97, 101,* 102, 163, 203,
Ledbury Hunt, 103; kennels, 50
Ledbury to Gloucester Canal, 103, 228
Ledbury to Worcester railway, 71, 235
Leddon, River, 122
Ledgemoor, 209, 222
Lee, Lennox Bertram, 84; Peter, 84;
Lee-Milne, James, 32
Leen Farm, Pembridge, 158
Legge family, 112
Leighton Court, 187
Leinthall Earles, 104
Leinthall Common, 44
Leinthall Starkes, 106
Leintwardine, *97,* 107, 141
Leland, John, 70, 110, 111, 168, 226
'Lemster ore', 108
Lene district, 91, 142
Lent, stream, 104
Lenthal, Sir Rowland, 67
Leofgeat, 21
Leofric and Godiva, 225
Leominster, 40, 86, 94, *105,* 107, *118,* 151, 186, *224*
Leominster to Bromyard railway, 68, 84, 167, 186, 199
Leominster to Kington and Radnor railway, 91, 138
Leominster to Stourport canal, 30, 59, 90, 108, 123, 157
Leon, territory, 133
Leslie, Earl of Leven, 143
Les Miserables, Hugo, 233
Lethaby, W.R., 27, 33
Letton (near Brampton Bryan), 111
Letton (near Staunton-on-Wye), 110
Letton Lake, 99, 110, 183
Leviot, William, 99

Lewis, Alan, V.C., 217
Lewis, Rev. T.T., 17
Lewstone, 63
Ley, The, Weobley, 207
Ley's Hill, 201
Liber Landavensis, 165
Libraries, county, 229
Lilac Tree, poem, 168
Lilando, 124
Limebroke, 111, 137; Priory, 124
Limestone:
   quarries at Dolyhir and Burlingjob, 98; at Leinthall Earls, 106; disused with kilns at Mocktree, 141; likewise at Croft, 44; Aymestry beds, 17; burning at Fownhope, 62
Lime mortar, 34, 143
Linden Manor, Colwall, 40
Line Farm, Orleton, 157
Lines on Gatley Park, poem, 212
Lingen, 111
Lingen family, 12, 111, 189; Ralph 111; Constantia, 111, 147; Sir John, 111, 147; Sir Henry (Harry), 12, 64, 189; *Harry Lingen's Fancy,* 12
Lingen's Hospital, 75
Link, Jimmy, 162
Linton, 102
Linton-by-Ross, 112
Lion Hotel, Leintwardine, *97,* 107
Little Birch, 92, 122
Little Black Hill, 127
Little Brampton, 170
Little Cobhall, 10
Little Corras, 64; Farm, 68
Little Cowarne, 122; grazing rights, 225
Little Dewchurch, 80, 123
Little Dilwyn, 46
Little Doward, 63, 215
Little Gorseley, 14, 112
Little Hereford, 123
Little Logaston, 12
Little London, 183
Little Malvern Priory, 41
Little Marcle, 124
Little Merthyr, 30
Little Million, 67
Little Musgrove and Lady Barnard, 124
Little Penllan, 86
Little Rodd, 170
Little Sarnesfield, 209
Little Southend Farm, 137
Little Tarrington, 190
Little Verzons Garden Centre, 163
Live and Let Live, Bringsty, 30
Live and Let Live, Whitbourne, 214
Liverpool, 107, 235

Lives of the Welsh Saints, Gould, 126
Llanbister, 96
Llancillo, 124
Llancloudy, 177
Llandaff, 134, 138, 165
Llandinabo, 124
Llandovery, 103
Llanfrother, 80, 124
Llanhedry, 30
Llangarren (Llangarron), 78, 124, 125
Llangrove, 125
Llangua, 165
Llanrothal, 125
Llantony Priory, 45; Abbey, 130; Canons of, 37
Llantywaum Brook, 177
Llanveynoe, 126, 128, *196*
Llanwarne, 124, 127
Llanwathan, Cusop, 45
Llanwonnog, 127
Llan-y-coed, 12
Llanyhangel Crucrney, 235, 238, trout farm, 237
Llewellyn, Gruffydd ap, 70, 225, 234
Llewellyn, Prince of Wales, 218
Lloyd, A.L., 232
Lloyd family, Quaker bankers, 90
Lock family, John, his brother Polin and their father, Ezekiel, 158
Lock' Hill, Castle Frome, 38
Lockup, The, Bridstow, 28
Lock-up, The, Ross, 171
Lodon, River, 142, 147, 159, 185
Lodge Farm, Letton, 111
Logaston, 12; Logaston Press, 12
Lollards, 12, 111, 126, 232
London, 100, 130, 237; coach travel, 235; Aberystwyth coach road, 200
Longhorn cattle, 166
Longhouse, building type, 40, 54, 182, 126
Long Grove, 125
Longleat, 207
Long Leinthall, 107
Long Meadow, industrial estate, 155
Long Range Desert Groups, 80
Longtown, 8, *65*, 126, 129, 130, 133; 'Harriers', 130
Longworth, 131; Mill, 131; Hall, 18
Looking for Trouble, Billiere, 103, 231
Lord Hereford's Knob, 236
Lord's Wood, Garanew, 63
Lord Lieutenant of Hereford and Worcester, Capt. Dunne, 107, 147
Lost keys, how to find, 182
Lost Bower, The, Browning, 203
Lost Hearts, James, 149
Lost Villages, list of, 227

Love charm from Weobley, 210
Low Countries, 98
Lowe The, Eyton, 60
Lower Bearwood, 158
Lower Broxwood, 34
Lower Bullingham, 36, 130, 147
Lower Burton, 46
Lower Court, Kinsham, 100
Lower Easton, 139
Lower Hardwicke, 46
Lower House Farm, Michaelchurch Escley, 138
Lower House, Orleton, 155
Lower House Farm, Tyberton, 197
Lower House Farm, Staunton-on-Wye, 182
Lower Eaton, 56
Lower Farm, longhouse, Burrington, 36
Lower Hopton, Stoke Lacy, 185
Lower House, Hampton Bishop, 67
Lower Kinsham, 37
Lower Lugg Valley, article on, 225
Lower Lyde, 163
Lower Lye, 112
Lower Maescoed, 175
Lower Stockton, 90
Lower Town, Preston Wynne, 165
Lower Upton, 124
Lower Vinetree Farm, 21
Lower Walton Farm, 21
Lower Welson, 55
Lower Weston, 211
Lower Wither Farm, 139
Ludlow, 157, 169, 235
Ludlow to Leominster railway, 157
Lucton, 130; Mill, 147
Lugg, River, 37, 59, 60, 67, 91, 99, 107, 110, 111, 112, *117*, 130, 131, 135, 137, 142, 143, *144,* 145, 146, 147, 163, 166, 181, 185, 189, 195, 225, 228
Lugg Navigation, 108, 110, 145, 225, 227
Lugg Meadows, 225
Lugwardine, 131, 225, *132,* 78
Lulham, 135, 197
Luntley Court, 46
Luston, 133
Lutley family, 32
Lyall, Edna, 24
Lydiatts, Farm, 133
Lynder's Wood, 199
Lye, 99, 112
Lye Court, Birley, 21
Lyne, Rev, Joseph Leicester, 236
Lyne Down, 151
Lynhales, 133
Lyonshall, 95, 133
Lyre, Normandy, 155
Lyston Court, 127

Lyvers Ocle, 155

M

Maredudd ap Owain ab Edwin, 135
Mabel, friend of Katherine of Audley, and Mabel Furlong, Ledbury, 104
Mabinogeon, 96
McBride, Gwen, 149
McColl, Ewan, 232,
McDonald's Chicken Nuggets, 78
McLean, Col. J.F., 125
MacMillan Guide to, Britain's Nature Reserves, 141
McNamara and Clayton, 34
McSwiney, Terence, 33
Maddle Brook, 182
Madley, 78, 134, *136*; hop-bagger, 47; aerial dish, *196*
Maerdy Farm, 124
Maescoed, 175
Magena, 24
Maghene, Bryan de, 24
Magnis, 42, 70, *85,* 86, 213
Magnosetum, 24, 135
Mahollan Bridge, 98
Maidenhead, 163
Main Ditch, Orleton, 157
Mais, John, 78
Malaya, 80
Mallet Man, 110, 157
Malsters Inn (The Stars), 155
Malvern, *35,* 38, 90, 55, 138, 203; Hills, 186, 228; Water, 41
Malveshille, 21
Mamble Collieries, 30, 108, 198
Man in the Moon, The, Godwin, 214
Man of Ross, 170
Mancell's Ferry, 62
Manchester, 84, 207, 221; Ship Canal, 228; University, 232
Manders, Peter, artist, 76; see also illustration credits
Mando, John, 78
Manna, 143
Manor House, Weobley, 206
Manorial Earthworks (or castle), Ashton, 14
Mansell family, 83
Mansell Gamage, 135
Mansell, Lacy, 135, *144,* 225
Mansion House, Weobley, 206
Map, Walter, 12th cent. scholar, 174
Maples and Birches, National Collection, 96
Mappa Mundi, 12, 71
Marblestone charm, 34
March, Earl of, 104
Marcher Lords, article on, 234
Marches Archaeology, 12

Marchia Wallia, 234
Marden, 135, 226
Mare, Thomas and Jordan de la, 190
Margaret Roper School, 78
Marian Fathers, 130
Marian Sykes, Bridstow, 28
Markey, Clara, 173; Elizabeth, 171
Markfield, Leics, 232
Market days, 229
Market House, Leominster, 108
Marlas, 88
Marlbrook, 60
Marlow, 107
'Marquis, The', Lower Bullingham, 130
Marsden, Tony, 163
Marsh, The, house at Eyton, 59
Marsh Court, Bridge Sollars, 28
Marsh defences, Eardisland, 54
Marsh Hall, Orleton,, 157
Marsh House, Moreton-on-Lugg, 146
Marston, 137
Martin, W.E., 18, 24
Martindale, Maurice, 55
Martin's Castle, 40
Martin's Croft, 56
Mary Knoll Valley, 138
Mary Tudor, 150
Masefield, John, E., 102, 104
Mason's Arms, Ailey, 99
Massacre of Saint Brice's Day, 213
Massey family, 206; Colonel, 103, 190
Masters, Robert, 36
Merryhill Farm, Grafton, 66
Merton, Professor, 218
Messina, de, 21
Meszaros, Lazar, 194
Metheurum, 138
Metropolitan Museum, New York, 82
Mezotint, The, James, 149
Michaelchurch, Escley, 138
Michaelchurch on Arrow, 30
Michalmas Fayre, 133
Miceltune, 139
Michelin, apple, 123
Middle Blackhill Farm, Craswall, 42
Middle Hill, Birley, 21
Middle Maes-Coed, 153
Middleton on-the-Hill, 78, 123, 139
Middleton House, Dilwyn, 46
Midland Folk Cente, 233
Mid Summer Camp, 41
Mid Summer Hill, 56
Miffin, Mr., 12
Milbourne, Sir John, 36
Mihalf, 217
Milk Marketing Board 58
Mill Farm, Fownhope, 62

Mill Hill Fathers, 205
Mill Race, pub, 201
Mill Valley Golf Club, 214
Miller, Russell, 231
Milton Cross, 182
Ministry of Agriculture, 60
Ministry of Defence, 163
Minn's Close, Abbeydore, 8
Minton, Kevin, 171
Mirabeau, 100
Mistletoe, 90
Mistletoe Oak, 112
Mitley Meadow, 226
Moated houses:
   Ashperton, Freetown, 14
   Bishopstone Court, 21
   Bodenham, Moat House, 22
   Bolstone, The Moors, 24
   Bredwardine, Old Court Mound, 28
   Brinsop, two sites, 32
   Castle Frome, New Birchend, 38
   Collington, Martin's Castle, 40
   Dilwyn, Field's Place, 46
   Eardisley, Lemore Farm, 55
   Edvin Ralph, 58
   Ivington, Upper Wintercott, 86
   Kinsham, Lower Court, 98
   Little Dilwyn, 46
   Lower Hopton, 185
   Lugwardine, Old Court, 131; Old Longworth Hall, 131
   Lyonshall, The Yeld, 133
   Mansell Lacy, Court House, 135
   Mathon, Ham Green, 138
   Moerton on Lugg, 146
   Much Cowarne, Pauncefoot Court, 147
   Much Marcle, Bryngwyn, 149
   Nunsland, 154
   Ocle Pychard, Ocle Court, 154
   Orcop, Moat Farm, 155
   Pudleston, Ford Abbey, 167
   Quatsford, 153
   Rushall, Hall Court, 151
   Sarnesfield, Hell Moat, 177
     Whiethill, 177
   Shucknall Court, 211
   Sollars Hope, 181
   Stoke Lacy, Tutley, 185
   Tarrington Court, 190
   Titley, Cabal Tump, 194
   Whitbourne Court, 214
Moccas, 134, 139, 143, 165, 228; Court, 26; deer park, *140*
Mocktree, 141
Mally Brook, 205
Monastery, The, 236
Monkhall Court, Dewsall, 45
Monkhide, 142
Monkland, 142

Monk's Coert, Eardisland, 54
Monk's Well, 24
Monmouth, 63, 125, 171, 214, 235
Monmouthshire, 88
Monmouth Cap, 165
Monmouth, Duke of, 165
Monington, Margaret, 143
Monnington Roger (or Richard), married Margaret Glyndwr, 143, 232
Monnington-on-Wye, 68, 135, 138, 139, 143; Falls, 166
Monnington Straddel, 87, 143
Monnow, River, 13, 42, 64, 87, 88, 124, 125, 127, 129, 130, 163, 202, 206,
Monnow Valley Shooting School, 88
Mont Blanc, 67
Montacute, Sir John and wife Margaret, 205
Montgomery, Roger de, 234
Monyngton, Richard, of Westhide, 210
Moody Cow, 198
Moon worship, relics of, 209
Moor, The Hereford, 75
Moor Abbey, 139
Moor Court Farm, Upper Egleton, 187
Moorend, Ashperton, 13, 14
Moor Mansion, Cusop, 45
Moor Meadows, Bridstow, 29
Moor Park, 84
Moorcourt, Pembridge, 158
Moorfields, Hereford, 238; station, 235
Moorhampton, 154
Moors, 147
Mop, Ledbury, 104
Marbury, Sir John, 206
Marden, 78, 79, 135, 203, 226
Mordiford, 143, *144*; Sufton, *113*
Mordred, 149
Moreton, near Eye, 59
Moreton Jeffries, 146
Moreton-on-Lugg, *140*, 146; Meadow, 226
Morgan Brothers, Almeley, 12
Morgan family of Morgan cars, 185; Rev. George, 185
Morgan, Lady, 99
Morimund, 8
Mormons, 38
Morris dancing at:
  Avenbury, 16
  Brimfield, 30
  Bromyard, *116*
  Cradley, and mumming play, 42
  Dilwyn, 46
  Hereford, 76, 77
  Ledbury, 104

A GUIDE TO HEREFORDSHIRE

Much Marcle, 151
Putley, 169
Ross, and mumming play, 174
Yazor, 225
Sides mentioned:
  Jockey Morris Men, (from Birmingham), *116*
  Leominster Morris Men, 151
  Old Wonder Not for Joes, 169
  Saddleworth Morris Men, *116*
  Silurian Border Morris Men, (from Colwall), 41, 104,
Morris, William, 33
Mortimer family, 36, 38, 44, 52, 91, 111, 150, 157, 181, 206, 217, 218; Blanche, 150; Earl Mortimer at Eywood, 194; Edward, 108; Edward, died 1425; Edward, married Catherine Glyndwr, 232; Earl of March, 232; Edmund, uncle to Earl of March, 232; Hugh, 9, 178; Ralph de, 9, 21, 178, 217, 221; Roger de, 79, 104; Roger, 173; Roger IV, 150, 217, 157; Roger, First Earl of March, 205
Mortimer Forest, 14, 138
Mortimer House, Holmer, 238
Mortimer's Castle, Much Marcle, 150
Mortimer's Cross, 87, 91, 99, 146; Battle of, 70, 158, 218
Morton, Thomas, 24
Moseley Mere, 94
Mosse, William 78
Mouse Castle, 45
Mousnatch, 91
Mowley, 194
Mowley Woods, 182
Much Birch, 130, 147
Much Cowarne, 111, 122, 147
Much Dewchurch, 149
Much Fawley, 60
Much Marcle, 104, 149, 159, 225
Muncorn, 147
Mundel 151, 153
Munderfield, 151, 184
Mundersfield Harold, 26
Munsley, 153
Munts, 86
Munstone House, 82
Murimonth, Adam de, 56
Murphy, Muriel, 33
Murray family, 48
Music recording, 63
Musica Celestis, 150
Mussegros, Eure, France, 124
Mussgros, Roger, 124
Must Mill, Kingland, 91
Mynde, The, 149
Myndydd Fyrddyn, 130
Mynors, Richard, 177

Myntdd Brydd, 52, 153
Mytholmroyd, Yorks., 233

N

Nail-making, 185
Nant Bach, 236
Nant-y-Bar, 139, 153
Napoleon, 207
Naseby, Battle of, 209
Nash Farm, Fownhope, 62
Nash, George, 12
Nash, John, 75, 87, 141, 207
Nash Scar, 170
Nashend Farm, Bosbury, 24
National Contaminated Land Register, 122
National Gallery, 218
National Trust, 44, 171
National Women's Cricket Association, 41
Nazis, 99
Nea, 236
Nelson Column, The, 75
Nelson, Lord, and Lady Hamilton, 171
Neolithic, see Stone Age
Nether Lye, 112
Netherlands, The, 40
Netherton, Brampton Abbotts, 25;
Netherton, Pencoyd, 159;
Netherton, Ross, 173
Netherwood, Collington, 40
Neuadd, 237
Neville Arms, 8
Neville family, 162
New-Age Travellers, 151
New Buidings, Walford, 201
New Court, Lugwardine, 131
New Harp Inn, 80
New House, at Bishop's Frome, 21; at Stretton Grandison, 187
New House Farm, Quaker grave, 213
New House Wood, 153
New Inn, Longtown, 129
New Inn, Pembridge, 155
New Mills, Ledbury, 102; Much Birch, 147
New Lodge, Snodhill, 162
New Radnor, 232
New Stone-Age, see Stone-Age
New Street, 134
New Weir, 87
New Weston Farm, Bredwardine, 28
Newbridge Farm Park, Little Marcle, 124
Newbridge Brook, 209
Newchurch, Logaston, 12
Newcourt Farm, 17
Newent Woods, 14
New Forest, Hay, 235

Newhouse Farm, Goodrich, 66
Newmarche, Bernard de, 162
Newnham Paddox, Leics., 222
Newport to Brecon canal, 66
News at One, poem, 168
Newspapers, local, 229
Newton, list of in county, 153
Newton, near Kinnersley, 98
Newton, near Monkhide, 142
Newton Farm, near Orcop, 155
Newton, near St. Margarets, 153
Newton, Robert, 126
Newtons, house, Putley, 167
Newton Tump, 40
Newton Linford, Leics., 232
Newtown, near Leominster, 110
Next End, 134
Nicholson and Son, 14, 18
Nicholson, Thomas, 48, 129, 137, 138, 155, 166, 181, 210
Nick's Timber Supplies, 177
Nieuport House, 10
Nigel the Doctor, 16, 189
Niger, River, 159
Night Clubs in the county, 229
Nightingale, Florence, 99
Nightjar Music, 76
Nimbus, (recording company) 63, 98
Noble, John, 106
Nordar Hall, 133
Norman, William Fitz, and son Hugh, 88
Normandy, 181, 213; landings, 178
Norman's store, Withington, 219
Norris, Ian, 60
Northbrigg, 173
North Herefordshire Hunt, 26
North Hill, Malverns, 40
North Sea Gas, 82
Northumberland, Duke of, 110
Norton Canon, 153; Wood, 98, 154; Garnon's Hill from, *119*
Nourse, Walter, 211
Norway, 158
Nun Upton, 124

O

Oak Apple Day, 46, 62
Oak bark for tannin, 62, 145, 228
Oak font, King's Pyon, 92
Oak Inn, Staplow, 203
Oak seed stand, Queen's Wood, 122
Oak trees, Moccas, 141
Oaker Coppice, 223
Oaker Wood, 60
Oaklands Small Breeds Farm, Kingswood, 94
Oaklee Farm, Eyton, 60
Obelisk, The, Cusop, 45
Observations on the River Wye, 171

Ocle Pychard, 154, 210, 231
Oddfellows, Colwall, 41
Ode to Owain Glyndwr, poem, 147
Offa, King, 63, 75, 79, 161, 162, 189
Offa's Dyke, 30, 37, 98, 100, 133, 134, 135, 154; Path, 45, 86, 96
Ogilvey, Gilbert, 50; Sir, Reginald, 50
Oh Whistle and I'll Come to You, My Lad, James, *149*
Oilfield Publications, 163
Olchon Valley, 126; Court, 126, *89;* Cottage, 126; Brook, 126, 127, 128
Old Bakery, The, Peterchurch, 162
Old Bell Inn, Hereford, 235
Oldbury Camp, 151
Old Castle, Putley, 167
Old Castle Twt, Allensmore, 10
Old Christmas, see Twelfth Night
Old Comrade Inn, 202
Old Corner House, Weobley, 206
Old Court, Bosbury, 24
Old Court, Bredwardine, 28
Old Cort Farm, Longtown, 130
Old Court Nurseries, Colwall, 41
Olde Oak Tree Inn, Ye, 217
Old Forge, Woolhope, 221
Old Furnace, St. Weonard's, 177
Old Gore, 84
Old Greg, ghost, 209
Old Hendre, 177
Old Hill Court, Walford, 201
Old House, Hereford, 74, 230
Old Lily Hall, 124
Old Longworth Hall, 131
Old Maid's Walk, Ross, 174
Old Meg, 104
Old Pembridge, legend of, 158
Old Pump House, Eardisley, 55
Old Radnor, 98
Old Rectory, Weston, 211
Old Red Sandstone, 83, 221
Old Straight Track, The, 66
Old Sufton, Mordiford, 145
Old Wonder Not for Joes, 42, 169
Oldcastle, Sir John (Lord Cobham), 12, 88, 89, 111, 126, 232
Old Field Farm, 106
Oldfield, Mike, 96
Oldswinford, 183
Oliver, Mr., 82
Ombersley, 235
Ongar Street, 112
On the Black Hill, Chatwin, 236
Opella, 78
Operation Mikado, 231
Orchard offerings, Peterchurch, 162
Orchards grubbed out, 50
Orcop, 64, *154;* Hill, 149
Ordericus Vitalis, 234
Orgys family, 147

Orleton, 155
Osbern, Earl William Fitz, 12, 40, 58, 155, 217, 234; 'Pentecost', 165; of Querentune, 169; son of Richard, 193
Oswell, A.Lloyd, 124
Our Lady of Charity and Refuge, Convent of, 18
Outdoor Education Centre, Longtown, 129
Overton, 25
Overton, Salop, 138
Owen's Cross, 194
Ox Ford, 67
Oxford, 44
Oxford, Kington, 95
Oxford Book of Traditional Verse 232
Oxford, Earls of, see Harley family
Oxwood Farm, 146

P

Paddock's Hotel, Symonds Yat, 215
Paegna, 157
Palaeolithic, see Stone-Age
Palace Pound, Ross, 171
Palmer, Canon, 55
Palmer, Roy, 12, 96, 145, 169, 173, 232
Palmer's Churn, 157
Palm Sunday, 68
Pandy, 201, 238
Pandy Inn, Dorstone, 50
Pantheon, 52
Paper Mill House, Cusop, 45
Papists, 64
Paraclete, 173
Paradise Walk, 186
Paradise Green, 137
Paragliders, 236
Parc Bach, 236
Pardon Monument, 58
Parish Registers, kept at County Record Office, 74
Park Farm, Colwall, 41
Park Farm Wolferlow, 221
Parker, Charles, 233
Parkfields, Hope Mansell, 83, 213
Parkinson, John, 99
Park Pale, Park Farm, Thornbury, 193
Parks, The, Kinnersley, 98
Parkway, 50
Park Wood, 175
Parliamentary Enclosures, Tarrington, 190
Parry, Richard, historian of Kington, 95
Parry, Blanche (ap Harry), 17
Parsonage Farm, 147

Partridge family, ironmasters, 213, John, 173; John and William, 201
Pateshill Farm, 90
Paunceford Court, 147
Paunton, 157
Pax (peace) cakes, 68, 91, 178
Payne, brothers, 222
Pearle Charity, 37
Pearle family, 45
Pearl Lake, Shobdon, 178
Peartree Green, 181
Pebbley Beach, Bishop's Wood, 201
Pedic, 88
Pedawrdine, 112
Peg's Farm, 203
Peibau, King of Erging, 134
Pembridge, 17, 95, *155,* 156, *220*
Pembridge Terracotta, 158
Pembridge Castle, 205, 200
Pembridge family and Ralph de, 206
Pembrugge, Sir Richard, 38
Pembroke, Earl of, 92, 215
Penance at Ross, 173
Pen in place names, 68
Pencombe, *117,* 121, 159, Cross, 159
Pencoyd, 159
Penda, King, 24
Penebruge, 157
Pengethley Manor Hotel, 70
Penllan, 86
Pennoxstone, 90
Penny Farthing, Aston Crews, 102
Penoyne family, 38
Penrhos Court, 133
Pentaloe Brook, 145, Mill, 62
Pentwyn Farm, 68
Penyard Castle, 211-212
Penyard Park, 83, 211, 213
Pen-y-Gate, 175
P-y-lan, 68
Pen-y-mor, 68
Pen-y-Park, 68
Pen-y-Worlod, 175
Penzance, 175; Greenstone, 58
Peoht, 163
People and Places, Lee-Milne, 32
Peregrine falcons, at Symonds Yat, 215
Perrier water family heiress, 54, 106, 142
Perrot, Sir Herbert, 203; Robert, 143
Perry, note on, 123
Perrystone Court, 62
Perrystone Hill, 149
Pershore, 169
Peterchurch, *128,* 161, 137
Pevsner, Nikolaus, 33, 38, 41, 56, 71, 124, 185, 161, 175,
Peytoe, 9
Phillips, Dick, morris dancer, 78, 139
Phillips, Elizabeth and Mary Anne, 18
Phillips House, Much Marcle, 150
Phillips, John, 219
Phillips, Mary, story-teller, 165
Philip, Prince, 106
Phillips, Robert Biddulph, M.P., 18
Phillips, Sydney, estate agency, 56
Philpotts, Albert, 169
Phoenix Theatre, Ross, 173
Pichard, Roger, 154
Pidgeon, Lady Pamela, 134
Pie Corner, 40, 221
Piers Ploughman, Langland, 42, 104
Pierrepoint, John, 130
Pigeon House Farm, 211
Pigmore Common, 46
Pig Street, 154
Pikestye, 137
Pilgrim Hotel, 147
Pilleth, Battle of, 154, 232
Pinsley Brook, 110, 178
Pinsley Park, 91
Pipe and Lyde, 163
Piper, John, 71
Pipewell Lane Hereford, 79
Pierrepoint, Albert, 36
Pistol Club, Hereford City, 46
Pitchfork tale, 112
Pitfield Show, 157
Piman, Major General, 26
Pixhill, 191
Pixley, 163
Plague Cross, Ross, 170
Plas Gwyn, Hereford, 79
Plash Farm, Dulas, 54
Platt, David, 58
Pleck Farm, cheese shop,`42
Plontenet, Alan de, 10
Plough, The, 107
Ploughfield, Preston-on-Wye, 165
Ploughing competitions, *159;* at Trumpet
Plough Inn, Little Dewchurch, 123
Plowman, John (Junior), 201
Plymouth Brethren, 62, 137
A Pocketful of Hops, 34, 122, 197
Poet's Corner, 219
Poke House Wood, 17
Polish Camp, Mansell Lacy, 135
Pollarding, note on, 118
Pomona Farm, Bartestree, 18
Pondside Cottage, Eyton, 59
Pontefract Castle, 232
Ponthendre, 129
Pontrilas, 50, 162, 163, 174; sawmills, 165
Pontshill, Weston-u-Penyard, 213
Poole, Rev. William, 80
Poolmill, Bridstow, 29
Poor Clares, 130; at Much Birch, 147
Poor Man's Wood, 149
Pope, Alexander, 155, 170
Poplar plantation, Brierley, 29
Port Madoc, 54
Portmeirion, 54
Portugal, 107
Portway, Orleton, 155
Portway, Burghill, 36
Portway, Callow, 37
Portway, Laysters, 100
Portway, Mansell Gamage, 135
Portway, Staunton-on-Wye, 182, 183
Poston Lodge, 199
Poswick Farm, 221
Poswick, Lower, 214
Potter, Dennis, *172*
Pot Well, Craswall, 42
Powell, Harriet, 175
Powell, John, 153
Powell, L,. 135
Powell, William, 174, 178
Powells, 28
Powers of Marcher lords, 234
Powys, 126
Preaching Crosses, 22
Prehistoric Sites of Herefordshire, 12
Preedy, Frederick, 186
Presteigne, Radnorshire, 37, 138, 157, 169, 179, 181, 193
'Prestige' axes, Neolithic, 174
Priory Leasowe, Titley, 194
Preston Brook, 151
Preston Marsh, 166
Preston-on-Wye, 139, 165
Preston Wynne, 166, 225
Price family, Sir Ulvedale, 225, 135
Price's Almshouses, 75
Price's Perry, 190
Prima Voce, 63
Prime's Well, Colwall, 41
Primitive Methodist Chapels at:
 Ivington, 86
 Ledgemoor, 222
 Walford, near Leintwardine, 201
 Little Birch, 122
 Lyonshall, 133
 Tedstone Wafer, 191
Prior's Court, Little Marcle, 124
Prior's Court, Wellington Heath, 203
Priory, The, Stoke Prior, 186
Priory Farm, Clifford, 40
Priory House, Kilpeck, 88
Priory Hotel, Llanthony, 237
Priory, The, motel, Skenfrith, 126
Priory Wood, Clifford, 40
(Priories are listed under the Saint of their dedication.)
Pritchard, J., 63
Pritchard, Roger, 10
Promither Mill, 80
'Prophet of Herefordshire', 122
Prospect, The, Ross, 171

Prosser, William, 130, 162
Protestant martyr, 173
Prudential Insurance, 45
Public Penance ceremony, Madley, 134
Puddlebrook, 83
Pudlestone, 100, 166
Pudge family, Much Cowarne, 147; Bishop's Frome, 21; John, of The Homme, Weobley, 209
Pugin, A.W.N., 20, 38, 55, 167
Pugin and Pugin, 18
Pugin, Welby, 18
Pulley, Sir Joseph, 56
Pulpits Farm, 123
Punch, 15
Pura Wallia, 234
Putley, 151, 156, 167; Green, 166; Mill, 167; Celidhs, 166; Dave Jones, *156*
Putnall Tunnel, 157
Putson Manor, 75
Putta, first Bishop of Hereford, 167
Putta, 166
Pwch Farm, Michaelchurch, Escley, 138
Pye, W.R., archaeologist, 52
Pye family of Much Dewchurch, 149; Walter, Attorney General, and Robert, 149
Pyon Camp Wood, 17
Pytel, Walenty, 221
Pyttel, 166
Pyrenees, 236

Q

Quakers: Allensmore, 10; Almeley, 10, 12; Bromyard, 33; Quaker's Farm, Michaelchurch Escley, 138; Weston-u-Penyard, 213, Yarpole, 223
Quarelay, 153
Quarrelly, 153
Quarry Field, Bromyard, 33
Quatsford, 153
Quebb, 24, 55
Queen's Head, Stanton, 237
Queen's Stone, 66
Queenswood, Hope-u-Dinmore, 22, 135; deer escape, 48, 67
Queen's Wood, near Ross, 122, 198, 199
Queest Moor, 24
Quenrida (Kenfrith), 79, 189
Querentune, 169
Quincy, Capt. De Quincy, 137

R

R.A.F., 44, 167, 178, 187

Rabbit breeding, 179
Racehorse memorial, 131
Raddle Bank, 100
Radio stations, local, 229
Radknight, 149
Radlow Hundred, 146
Radnorshire and West Herefordshire Hunt, kennels at Titley, 194
Rafting on the Wye, 78
Raggedstone Hill. 41
Railway Hotel, Ross, 171
Railways:
    Bromyard to Leominster, 26, 48, 181
    Golden Valley, 50, 68, 162, 163
    Hay to Kington, 215
    Hereford to Abergavenny, to Newport, 124, 235
    Hereford to Hay, 38, 98
    Hereford to Ledbury and Worcester, 235
    Hereford to Leominster, Ludlow, and Shrewsbury, 108, 146, 157, 163, 235
    Kington to Presteign, 194
    Leominster to Kington and Radnor, 68, 84, 167, 186, 199
    Ross to Gloucester, 211
    Ross to Monmouth, 201, 171
    Worcester to Bromyard, 108
Rainbow Circle, 60, 151
Rainbow Hill, 169
Raleigh bicycle sign, 195
Ralph, Earl of Hereford, 58, 70, 108,
Ramping House, Garway, 64
Rankin, Sir James, 149
Rare Breeds Survival Trust, 124
Rattle Hill, 181
Raven, birds, at Brockhampton, 32; at Llanthony, 237
Raven, Michael, 152, 148, 164, 168, 121; Jon, 233
Raven Knell, 45
Ravenham House, 154
Raven's Causeway, 222
Raven's Nest, poem, 152
Reading, monastery, 108
Rebecca Riots, 95
Red Book of Hergest, 96
Red Book, of H. Repton, 183
Red Darren, 126
Red deer, Eastnor, 55
Red Earl's Dyke, 56
Red Kite, killed at Leinthall Earls, 106
Red Lion, Peterstow, 162
Red Lion, Weobley, 206
Red Rail, 80, 190
Red Sea, 72
Redcliffe Gardens, 79
Redlake, River, 34

Redmarley, Farm, 9
Redstreak, apple, 82
Redwood, Laysters, 100
Reed family, 131; Sheriff William, 131; William (d.1634), 131
Reed, Sybil. 147
Reeves, Norman, C., 110
Reform Bill, Third, 207
Reprieve Riddle, 130
Repton, G.S., 141
Repton, Humphrey, 135, 141, 145, 183
Revell's Farm, 112
Rever, 36
Reynolds, Gerald, 63; Michael, 63
Reynolds, Mark, 213
Rheas, water channels, 226
Rhenish ware, 213
Rhine, River, 42
Rhiwallon, King, 37
Rhodes, 48
Rhododendron, poem, 240
Rhumney Barn, 181
Rhydd, The, Dewsall, 45
Rhydderch, Gruffydd ap, 234
Rhydspence, 30
Rhymney, River, 135
Rhyse, The, 138
Rhythir, 194
Ribbentrop, Herr, 99
Rice, Tim, 24, 183
Richard I, the Lion Heart, *120*
Richard II, 71, 136, 231
Richard de Brito, 50, 86
Richard, Duke of York, 218
Richard, Earl of March, 92
Richard le Scrob, 169
Richard, Osbern Fitz, 181
Richard's Castle, 169
Richardson, Brian, 32
Richmond, Henry, 186
Ridge Hill, Twyford, 80, 197
Ridgeway, Leominster, 110
Riding the Stang, 110, 197, 202
Rifle Club, King's Thorn, 92
Riggal's Motorway, 133
Riley, John, 166
Ring of Bells, 214
Ringerike dragons, Kilpeck, 88
Ringing home the dead, 154
Riparian rights on the Wye, 90
Risbury, 66, 84, 170, *117*
River sacrifice belief, Ross, 173
River trade on the Wye, 235
Robert de Bethune, Bishop, 178
Robert, Duke of Normandy, 207
Robert, William, 223
Robin Hood, 101; poem 168; Butts at King's Pyon, 92
Robinson, Gavin, 42

Rocket, 41
Rocklands, Huntsham, 66
Rock's Place Hotel, 151
Rodd, 170
Rodney, Admiral Lord and son George, 20
Roebuck Inn, Brimfield, 30
Rogationtide, Lucton, 131; Pterstow, 162; Shobdon, 179; see Beating of the Bounds
Rogers, Arnold, 134
Roman remains:
  Abbeydore, road, 8
  Aconbury, pottery, 8
  Adforton, road and settlement, 10
  Ashperton, road, 153
  Aston Ingham, coin-hoard, 14
  Aylton, road, 16
  Bartestree, road, 18
  Bin Mills, Villa Milliaris, 213
  Acton Beauchamp, road, 9
  Bishopstone, road and villa, 21
  Brampton Bryan, marching camp, 25
  Bromash (Ariconium), road, iron works and setlement, 13, 112, 213
  Buckton, two forts, 36, *204*
  Canon Frome, fort and settlement, 38
  Clifford, buckles and clip, 38; fort, 40; road at Hamnish Clifford, 66
  Donnington, kiln and pottery, 50
  Eaton Bishop, road, 56
  Hentland, road and pottery, 68
  Holmer, road, 82
  Humber, road, settlement, gold, kiln, hoard of coins, 84
  Huntsham, villa, 66
  Kenchester, (Magnis), fort, settlement, temple roads, 86, 87; pavement, aerial photograph, 85
  King's Caple, road, 90
  Kinsland, road, 91
  King's Pyon, 92
  Knill, fort, 100
  Leintwardine, Watling Street, fort and settlement (Bravonium), 107
  Little Dewchurch, pottery, 123
  Little Marcle, road, 124
  Longtown, fort, 129
  Lugwardine, civil settlement, 131
  Madley, road, 134
  Mortimer's Cross, Watling Street, 146
  Michaelchurch, altar, 138
  Peterchurch, road, 162
  Pixley, road, 163
  Preston-on-Wye, 166
  Putley, villa and pottery, 167
  Risbury, road, 170; Sutton Walls massacre, 89
  Staunton-on-Arrow, 182
  Staunton-on-Wye, road, 135
  Stretford, Watling Street, 186
  Stretton Grandison, roads, settlement (Epocessa), jewellery, 187
  Stretton Sugwas, road, 187
  Tedstone Wafer, road and fort, 191
  Tillington, road, 193
  Uphampton Camp, pottery, 48
  Upton Bishop, tomb stone, 198
  Walford near Leintwardine, urn, 201
  Walford near Ross, fort and coin hoard
  Walterstone, villa and pavement, 202
  Wellington, villa, 203
  Whitchurch, pavement, coins and iron works, 215
  Yarkhill, road, 223
Roman soldier love legend, 87
Rome, bishop from, 161
Romance of the History of England, Keele, *173*
Romilly, Sir Samuel, 100
Ronsoy, France, 217
Rood screen of exceptional quality at Saint Margaret's, 175
Rope bridge over the Wye, 215
Rorke's Drift Mission, 94, 161
Rosamund, Fair, 38
Rosedale, 167
Rosemaund Farm, 60
Ross Balloons, 202
Ross Gazette, 171
Ross Harriers, 214
Ross-on-Wye, 64, 103, 125, 170, *172*; A40 at, *172;* Foreign Forest, 173
Ross to Monmouth railway, 201
Ross to Gloucester railway, 211
Ross Workhouse, poem, 164
Rose Cottage, Lugwardine, 131
Rothal, 125
Rotherwas, 130; Chapel, 46 House, 46
Rothmore, Ireland, 83
Rotton boroughs, 207
Rough Hill Wood, 122
Round church, 64
Round House, Leinthall Earls, 107, 108
Round House, Moccas, 141
Rowden, 26
Rowe Dyke (Ditch), 137, 182
Rowe, George, 225
Rowland, Elizabeth, 26
Rowley Fields, 90
Rowley, Trevor, 124
Rowlestone, 48, 174, *176*
Royal Assurance, 147
Royal Commission on Ancient Monuments, The, 12, 130
Royal family, 106
Royal George, Lyonshall, 133
Royal Hotel, Ross, 171
R.S.P.B., 106, 215
Ruckhall Mill, 56
Rudhale, Joan, 25
Rudhall Almshouses, 171
Rudhall Brook, 102, 112, 122
Rudhall, William, 171; John, 171; Colonel, 171
Rufus, William, King, 207
Ruillic, 21
Rushall, 151
Rushforth, T.H., 205
Rushock, 98; Hill, 96, 98
Russia, 154
Russian convoys, 126
Rust, Mike, storyteller, 75
Rustin, wood treatment, 60
Ruxton, 90; Court, 125
Ryeford, 102, 213
Ryeland sheep, 108

S

Saddleworth Morris Men, 116
(Parish churches are not listed.)
Saint Albans, Duke of, 79
Saint Anne's House of Correction, 211
Saint Asaphs, 178
Saint Augustine, 102, 181
Saint Beuno, 126
Saint Ceina, 87
Saint Clare, 84
Saint Cldowg, 40
Saint Cosmos, 188
Saint Cynidr, 87, 164
Saint Damian, 188
Saint David, 58, 237
Saint Deveraux, 134, 175
Saint Dinabo, 124
Saint Dubricius (Dyfrig), 80, 66, 68, note on, 134; 139, 165, 175, 215
Saint Ethelbert, 79
  Ethelbert's Fair, 76
Saint Francis, 84
Saint George's Fair, Orleton, 157
Saint Gwainorth, 175
Saint Gwennog, 127
Saint Guthlac's Prory, 145
Saint John of Jerusalem, Order of (Knights Hospitallers), 8, 24, 46, 48; at Callow, 37; Bosbury, 24; Garway, 64; Hereford, 74; Din-

more, 46, 47; Wormbridge, 221;
   Medieval Museum, 74;
   Ambulance Association, 48
Saint John the Baptist, Priory of, 66
Saint Margaret's, 175
Saint Martin, 130
Saint Martin's well, 59
Saint Mary, Priory of, Craswall, 42
Saint Moi (Mwy), 62
Saint Nazaire, 134
Saint Peter, 52; Priory of at
   Conches, 142
Saint Stephen, 94
Saint Sulac, 177
Saint Suliau, 178
Saint Teilo, 165
Saint Tirella, 194
Saint Ursula, 42
Saint Weonard's, 175
Saint Winifrid, 126
Saint Wulstan's Farm, 205
Sabatini, Raphael and Madame, 26
Saffron's Cross, 22
Saladin, ransome, 147
Salmon, life of, 60
Saltemarshe Castle, 56
Salter, Mike, 184, 218
Salt Water Ballads, Masefield, 104
Salwey Arms, Brimfield, 30
Salwey family, 169
Sanctuary knocker, Dormington, 50;
   Pembridge, 158
Sanctuary rights, 48; at Bosbury, 24;
   at Wormbridge, 221
Sand and gravel quarries: Aymestry,
   17; Belmont, 18; Pembridge, 17;
   Stretton Sugwas, 188; Wellington,
   203
Sandford, Jeremy, 68
Sandiford, 211
Sandstone clading, Dorstone, 50
Sandys family, 235
Sandyway, 177
Sapey Brook, 104, 190, 191, 198;
   legend of hoof prints, 104, 191
Sapey Golf Club, 198
Sapness, Woolhope, 221
Sargeant, John, 150
Sarnesfield, 177
Sarnesfield, Isabella de, 177
S.A.S., see Special Air Service
Satyr, playing bagpipes, 195
Saunders, Mick, harp-maker, 111
Savil, Eric, 218
Say, de, family, 181
Scapula, 42, 44
Scar, The, Monnington, 143
Scarrett, Bill, of Pershore, 169
Sceobba, 178
Sconce, The, 191
Scotland, 232

Scott-Bowden, Mrs., 41
Scott, G.G., 9, 55, 56, 139, 222
Scottish Queen, 133
Scrobbesbyrig, 169
Scudamore family, 75, 91, 103, 204,
   205; Sir John and wife Alice, 87,
   232; Sir John (died 1571), 82; John
   (died 1571), 87; Alice, 143; William (died 1649), 18; Sir John,
   M.P., 82; Sir James, John, ambassador to France, 82; Barneby, 29;
   Barnabas, 143; Lady, 70, 178;
   Lord, 8; 2nd Viscount, 82;
   Rowland, 125; 10th Earl (sold
   Holme Lacy), *81*
Scut Mill, 135
Secke, Sarah, 108
Second Declaration of Indulgence,
   210
Secret River, (Leadon), 234
Secret Garden, Walterstone, 202
Seddon, J.P., 9, 68, 80
Sellack, 68, 90, 177; Boat, 90;
   Marsh, 178
Sellarsbrooke House, 63
S.E.M.P. Pielstick, engines, 238
Senhouse, Rev. Peter, 112
Seventh Wonder Clinic, 151
Severn River, 103, 108, 158
Seven Sisters, 215
Seward, H.H., 131
Seward, William, 45
Shadowlands, 70
Shakespeare, 60
Sharp, Cecil, 158, 209
Sharp, Jack, *77, 79*
Shaw Common, 122
Shaw, Mrs. Mary, 153
Shawl, 194
Sheep slaughter, 80
Sheep-stealer, tale, 177
Sheepskins, dance, 130
Shell Guide, Verey, 42, 45, 48
Shelley, Jane and William of
   Marden, 137
Shelley, Percy Bysshe, 100, 194
Shelwicke, 67, 82
Shenley Court Comprehensive,
   Birmingham, 232
Shenmore, 197
Shepherds and the crows tale, 129
Shepherd's Meadow, 56
Sherborne, Mrs. William Essex,
   158; William, 158
Sherlock Holmes, 96
*Shire County Guide to
   Herefordshire,* Freeman, 59
Shire Ditch, 41
Shire-Mote Court at Hereford, 202
Shobdon, 131, 174, 178, 236; Hill,
   99, 147; Marshes, 158, 178;

burning the bush, 21
Shoesmith, Ron, 12
'Shooting the Arrow', 186
Shooting Schools, 48, 88
Shortwood Working Dairy Farm,
   Pencombe, 159, 123
Showman's Guild of Great Britain,
   76
Shrewsbury, 169, 124, 235
Shrewsbury to Hereford railway, 108
Shropshire, 78, 103, 209
Shucknall, *113;* Court, 211
Sienna, 55
Silurian Border Morris Men, 41, 104
Silurian Limestone, 102, 221, 222
Silures, tribe, 214
Silver chalice of Leominster, *105,*
   108
'Silver', Hereford cow, 92
Sin-eating, stretford, 186
Sinclair, George Robertson, 79
Sir Gawain and the Green Knight, 96
Sisters of Charity, 130
Siward, 191
*Six Walks Exploring the Landscape
   History of the Lower Lugg Valley,*
   Brian, 225
Skeleton of card player, 125
Skenfrith, 126
Skew bridge, 142
Skirrid Mountain, 135
Slatch, The, Bosbury, 25
Slaughterhouse Pitch, 99
Slip Tavern, The 151
Slough Farm, silver hoard, 186
Smalman, Francis, 99
Smeaton, John, 158
Smile at Time, Sitwell, 32
Smirke, Sir Robert, 50, 55, 74
Smith family, gipsies, 209
Smith, Humphrey, 122
Smith, Miles, 79
Smith, Pountney, 54
Smith, Rev. Thomas, 66
Smoke Alley, 103
Snail Farm, Credenhill, 44
Snake's Head, 131
Snead, Richard and Margaret, 56
Sneyd's Barn, 126
Snodhill Castle, 162
Solar, James de and son Walter, 179
Solaris family, 52
Soliers, Caen, 28
Sollers Hope, 179
Somers, Earl, 55
Somerset, Dukes of, 206
*Songs and Dance Tunes of
   Herefordshire,* CD, Raven 104,
   147
Songs of the Wayside, Sandford, 68
Sonke, Johan Philpott de, 125

South Herefordshire Golf Club, 199
South Wales, 52, 63, 95, 126, 177, 201; coalfield, 66; South Wales Borderers, 161
Southampton, Lady, 87
Southend Farm, Mathon, 138
Spanish Armada, 95
Special Air Service (S.A.S.) 44, 48, 67, 77, 80, 102, *120;* note on,180; 187, 231; females. 238
Spectre's Voyage, 173
Spenser, Edmund, 82
Spere truss, note on, 203
Spinning frame, 99
Spirtes, 16, 122, 189
Spout, The, Mordiford, 145
Spout, The, spring, Shucknall, 210
Spout, The, Titley, 193
Springfield Grange, Aston Ingham, 14
Spring, Tom, 62, 79
Spurs, heriot, Pencombe, 159
Stained Glass, poem, 240
Stafford family, 86
Staffordshire and the Black Country, Raven, 96
Stagbatch, 110
Stagecoach travel, 235
Stagg Inn, Titley, 196
Staick, Eardisland, 54
Stallard-Penoyre, A.M. Broadbelt, 45
Stalls of Barchester Cathedral, The James, 149
Stanford, S.C., 215
Stampede, The, Eardisley, 55
Stanbury Bishop, 71, 181
Stanford, S.C., 204
Stanmer Rocks, 98
Stanton, 237
Stanton, William 75
Stapleton, 181
Staplow, 152, 203
Stomer Hall, 107
Stars, The, Orcop, 155
Starting Gate, 162
Station in oaktree, 146
Status Quo, 70, 76
Staunton Green, 182
Staunton -on-Arrow, 181
Staunton-on-Wye, 182
Steamboat, Breinton, 28; Belmont, 20
Stephen, King, 103, 207; and Matilda, 70
Stephenson, George, 41
Steppes, Ledbury, 103
Steppes, The, Lugwardine, 131
Steppes, The, Pembridge, 157
Steppes, The, Ullingswick, 197
Stercher, 107
Stewward's Hyde, 159

Stile Cottage, Cattery, 133
Stirling, Col. David, 80
Stocking Farm, Lucton, 131
Stockmoor Cottage, 46
Stockton, 66, 90; Bottom, 90
Stockton Bury, 90
Stockton Cross, 90
Stoke Bliss, 221
Stoke Cross, 185
Stoke Edith, 183, 190, 222; steam engine at, *176*, Hotel, 183; pensioners at, 220
Stoke Lacy, 185
Stoke Prior, 185
Stokes, Leonard, 34
Stollard, Arthur, 221
Stone-Age monuments:
  Abbeydore, Neolithic long barrow, 8
  Almeley, 'prestige axe', 12
  Archenfield, long barrow, 13
  Buckton, axe and flints, 34
  Colwall, Midsummer Hill, tumulus, 56
  Crasswall, settlement, 42
  Dorstone, Arthur's Stone, 49, 52; Cross Lodge long barrow, 52; settlement, 52
  Eardisley, The Camp, ring ditch, 55
  Elton, 'prestige axe, 58
  Fownhope, flints, 62
  Grendon Bishop, Westington Camp, flints and axe heads, 66
  King's Pyon, tumulus, 92
  Knill, 10 tumulii to the west in Wales, could be Bronze-Age, 100
  Linton, flint working floor, 112
  Much Marcle, flint factory, 151
  Saint Margaret's, long mound and axe, 175
  Titley, flints and tools, 194
  Vowchurch, flint arrowheads, 199
  Wellington Heath, Neolithic tool factory at Frith Farm, 203
  Whitchurch, King Arthur's Cave, 63, 215; arrowhead from, *49;* Merlin's Cave, 215
Stone Farm, Pencombe, 159
Stone knappers, 111
Stone, Richard, 12
Stores Brook, 152
Stony Brook, 153
Stony Cross, 124
Storridge, 42, 186
Story, W.W., 180
Stourbridge, 183
Stourport, 198; wrought iron, 108
stowe, Whiney-on-Wye, 217
Stratford, John, 201
Straw Craft Centre, 147

Strawberry Hill Gothic, 178
Street, G.E., 142, 211
Street House, 211
Streona, Edric, 37
Stretford, 66, 186
Stretford Brook, 67, 186
Stretton Grandison, 124, *180*, 187
Stretton Sugwas, 55, 84, 173, 187
Strickstenning Hall, 147
Stroud, 153
Stubbs, John Heath-, 233
Subsidy man, meaning of, 211
Sufton, 145, 146
Sugar Loaf Hill, Abergavenny, 135, 202
Sulac, Saint, 176
Sulbiu, 124
Sunday Times, 231
Sunfold, Colwall, 41
Sun Inn, Saint Margaret's, 175
Sun Inn, Winforton, 218
Sunnyside Cottage, Eastnor, 55
Sun Valley, 10, 13, 78, 178, 238
Suspension bridges at Sellack, 178, and Foy, 62
Sutton, 48
Sutton Lakes, 12
Sutton Saint Michael, 12, 188
Sutton Saint Nicholas, *117*, 189, 226
Sutton Walls, 42, 75, 137, 189, 225
Sutune, 189
Swainshill, 84; Garden Centre, 187
Swan Bed Pasture, 67
Swan of horses teeth, 171
Swan Inn, Huntington, 86
Swanstone Court, Dilwyn, 46
Swanstone Court, Birley, 21
Sweden, 158
Sweet Apple Tree Field, 90
Sweet Briar Cottage, 131
Sweep's Green, 78
Swein Earl, 108
Sweyn, King, and sister Gunhild, 213
Swimming pools, 229
Swinmore Common, 153
Swiss Cottage, 37
Swordon Quarry, 146
Symond's Cider Works, 185
Symonds, Major, 124
Symonds, Robert, High Sheriff, 215
Symonds Thomas, 178
Symonds Yat, 63, 171, 214, 215, 228; chain ferry, 184
Symons family, 149
Swythamley, Hall, 96
Sylvaticus, Edric, 37

T

Tagetmeier. D., 236
Talbot, a knight at Dilwyn, 45;

family, 122; Gilbert, 7th Earl of Shrewsbury and daughter Elizabeth, 213; Sir Richard, 66; present earl, 122
Talbot Hotel, Ledbury, 103
Tamworth pigs, 166
Tannery building, Queenswood, 83
Tarleton, Sir Banastre, 107
Tarrington, 190; Common, 190
Tata, 190
Tate Gallery, 237
Taylor, John, 187
Taylor, Capt., Silas, 147
Taylor, Silas, 190, 207
Teapot superstition, 155
Tedgewood, 198
Tedstone Delamere, 190
Tedstone Wafer, 191
Teleki, Count, 194
Teme, River, 25, 34, 52, 58, *97,* 107, 122, 127, 199, 214, 225, 228,
Temeside Inn, 123
Tempest, Sir Henry, 41
Temple Bar Inn, Ewyas Harold, 59
Temple Court, Bosbury, 24
Temple Farm, 123
Tennyson, A.L., 38
Teodec, 190
Terkil, 193
Terrace Hall, 221
Terrace, The, Kington, 95
Tesselin, 142
Thames, River, freezing, 122
Thane, Anglo-Saxon, note on, 223
Thinghill Court, 155; Grange, 219; Mansion, 219
Third Reich, 74
Thomas, Archbishop, 44,
Thomas's Day, Saint, gooding, 154
Thompson, Edward, 163
Thorn Lighting, 78
Thornbury, 191
Thornhill, Sir James, 183
Three Choirs Festival, 76
Three Counties Hotel, 75
Three Crowns, Ullingswick, 198
Three Gates, 221
Three Horse Shoes, Little Cowarne; 122, Norton Canon, 154
Throne Farm, 207
Throne, The, 206
Thruxton, 94, 193
Thrumpton Hall, Notts., 126
Thurston of Wigmore, 165
Thynne family, Marquises of Bath, 133, 207
Tidnor, 131; Mill
Tierra del Fuego, Argentina, 231
Tillington, 36, 84, 193
Timberline Hill, 143
Timber prices, 147

Tippet's Brook, Dilwyn, 46
Tiron, Abbey of, 194
Tir Bill Farm, 127
Tirrel family, 32
Tithe Barns, Dilwyn, 45
Titley, 100, 193; Junction, 133
Titta, 193
Todding Cottage, 140
Todini, Ralph de, 40
Toll bridge, Whitney-on-Wye, 215
Tomkins, Benjamin and Richard, 92; Benjamin, 228;
Tomkins, James, 78
Tompkins, Thomas, 124
Tomkyns, Ulvedall, 143
Tonkins, James, 206
Topeslage, 195
Torquay, 203
Tosny, Ralph de, 218; Ralph III, 210
Totnor, 33
Totenham Hotspur, 70*T*
Touch on the Times, A, Palmer, 233
Tourist Information Centres, 229
Towerer, The, Masefield, 104
Town End Farm, Stretton Grandison, 187
Tower Hill House, Bromyard, 33
Town in the Marches, The, Reeves, 110
Townley family, 205
Townsend, 25
Townsend Farm, Edvin Ralph, 58
Toxic Wilt, 223
Tractus Globis, Hughes, 123
Trafford, Alice and Thomas, 158
Traherne, Thomas, 44, 79
Tram Inn, Allensmore, 10, 235
Tram Inn, Eardisley, 55
Tramways:
  Kington to Eardisley to Hay to Brecon tramway, 38, 55, 95, 215;
  Govilon (Abergavenny) to Monmouth Cap to Hereford tramway, 66, 71, 165; article on, 235
Transactions of the Woolhope Naturalists' Field Club, 34, 127
Travellers' Rest, Brampton Abbotts, 25; Llanthony, 237; Monkland, 142; Stretton Sugwas, 187
Travellers' Support Groups, 209
Travelog Trekking, 237
Tre Essey, 125
Treago Arms, 175
Treago Castle, 177, *184*
Treasure Island, Stephenson, 126
Trebandy, 125
Trecoyd, 67
Tredunnock, 125
Tree of Life tapestry, 71

Trees they do Grow High, The, 83
Tregate Farm, 126
Tregorz, John, 59
Trehard and Duckham, 74
Trehumphrey, 125
Trelough, 221
Trench-Royal, 162
Trereece Mill, 125
Trerrible, 125
Tressack, 80
Tretire, 194
Treverven, 125
Treville Wood, 94
Trewaugh, 125
Trilloes Court Wood, 24
Trippen Kennet, 177
Troubleshooter, The, 25, 211
Trows, 235, bowhauliers, *230*
Trug Corn, 48, 186
Trumpet and Trumpet Inn, 163
Yuck Mill, 56
Tudor House, Weobley, 206
Tudor, Owen, 92
Tufa, sources of: Bodenham, 22; Moccas, 141; Upper Sapey, 198
Tulley family, 84
Tump, The Kingsland, 91
Tumpey Lakes, 12
Tunnel House, Ashperton, 14
Tunnel Lane, Orleton, 157
Tunnel, secret, at Hereford, 238
Tupsley, 67, 195, 225, *176*
Turkey Tump, 127
Turkey, 236
Turlestone, 149
Turnant, 126
Turnastone, 175, 195
Turner, Joseph, 237
Turner's Boat, Willersley, 218
Turning, The, Garway, 64
Turnpike riots, Ledbury, 103; Kington, 95
Turret Castle, Turvey Hall, 82
Tuthill Farm, Stoke Lacy, 185
Twelfth Night (Old Christmas) customs and beliefs:
  Aconbury, 8
  Dinedor, 46
  Ross-on-Wye, 174
  Kingthorne, 94
  Ledbury, 104
  Much Marcle (orchard wassail), 151
  Peterchurch, 162
  Staunton-on-Wye (oxen weeping), 182
  Tretire (classic description), 195
Twelve Apostles, Burghill, 36
Twin Lakes, Upton Bishop, 199
Twn Farm, 111
Twyford, 197

Twyn y Beddau, Hay Bluff, 45, 236
Twyn y beddan, Dulas, 54
Twyn Camp, Brilley, 30
Twyn y Corras, Kentchurch, 88
Tyberton, 197; church, *184*
Tyber, 197
Tylli, 193
Ty Mawr, Cloddock, 40
Ty Silio, 177

U

Ufelwy, Bishop of Ergyng, 165
Ullingswick, 197
Ulster, 238
Under Hell, Ross, 171
Underhill, 62
Underworld, entrance to, 75
Unett family, 189
Unicorn Hotel, Weobley, 206, *207*
Uion, Act of (1536), 234
Union Workhouses, 103;
  at Ross, 170
United States of America, 107, 194
Uphamton Farm, Docklow, 48
Upleadon, (Upledyn), 24, 48
Upper Bach Farm, 90
Upton Bishop, 198
Upper Breinton, 28
Upper Broxwood, 34
Upper Buckenhill, 33
Upper Bullingham, 36
Upper Chilstone, 134
Upper Coldridge, 14
Upper Colwall, 41
Upper Egleton, 187
Upper Goytre, 202
Upper Hamnish, 66
Upper House Farm, Eardisley, 55
Upper House, Middleton, 123
Upper House Farm,
  Wolferlow, 221
Upper House Farm,
  Wormsley, 222
Upper Kinsham, 99
Upper Limebrook Farm, 111
Upper Ludlow beds, 169
Upper Lyde, 163
Upper Lye, 112, 147
Upper Maescoyd, 175
Upper Marston, 138
Upper Nash Farm, 170
Upper Newton, 98
Upper Pen-y-Park, 138
Upper Sapey, 122, 198
Upper Town, Preston Wynne, 166
Upper Wintercott, 86
Upper Wyche, 41
Upper Wythall, 201
Upperton, Norton Canon, *119*, 154

Uppsala, Sweden, 185
Upton Court, 124
Upton Crews, 198
Upton on Severn Folk Festival, 151
Urban, Bishop, 134
Urishay, 162
Urishay Common, 138
Usk, River, 238
Uttoxeter, Staffs., 122

V

Vaga House, Ross, 171
Vale of Arrow Trotting Races, 95
Vale of Wigmore, 9, 14, 16, 56, 58, 107, 217
Valley Hotel, Ross, 171
Vaughan family, 96, 140, 162:
  Rowland and water-works, 67, 162; Roger of Bredwardine, 26; Roger of Kinnersley, 98; family of Welsh Bicknor, Col, Francis, his wife Louisa and their son Cardinal Herbert, 205; family of Hergest (Kington), Thomas (Black Vaughan) and his wife Ellen (the Terrible), 95, 96; Henry and wife Francis of Moccas, 141;
Vaughan, Mary, of Mordiford, 145
Vaughan, Nicholas, 16
Vaughan's Oak, 96
Vauld, The, 137
Velindra, 176
Venn's Green, 137
Verdin, Major Philip, 91, 207, 209
Verey, David, 45, 48
Vern, The, 137
Verzon's Hotel, 163
Vestey, Lady, 106
Vicars Choral, Library, 71;
  Hall of 75
Victoria and Albert Museum, 186
Victoria Cross, 94, 134, 161
Vivtoria Footbridge, 79
Victoria, Queen, 95
Vietnam, 80
View from Hereford's Past, A, 12
View from a Hill, A, 149
Vikings, 88, 175
Vilberie, apple, 123
Villa Milliaris, Binn Mills, 213
Village greens, note on, 231
Vinesend, Cradley, 42
Vineyard, The, 50
Vital Spark, 40, 175
Volca Bridge, 91, 110
Volka Chapel, 91
Volunteer Inn, Marden, 137
Vowchurch, 143, 199, *200*;
  Common, 199
Vowmine, 153

Voysey, C.F.A., 41
Vro, 175

W

Wacca, 199
Wacton, 199; font to Bredenbury, 26
Waddell, Prof. L.A., 153
Wafre, Robert de, 191
Wafre, Simon de, 48
Wainherbert, 153
Waiton, William, 78
Wales and walh, meaning of, 181
Walford, near Leintwardine, 199
Walford, near Ross, 201; Castle, 201
Walford, de, family, 201
Walk Mill, Dulas, 54
Walker, Johnny, 30
Walks and More, Alan Johnson and
  Stephen Punter, 12
Wall Hills, Ledbury, 102, 104
Wall Hills, Donnington, 50
Wall Hills, Thornbury, 191
Wallce, Barnes, 217
Wallor, Sir William, 185
Wallsopthorne, 13
Walney Meadow, 226
Walsham family, 100
Walter de Helyon, *136,* 150
Walter, 5th Baron Fitz Walter, 133
Walterstone, 202
Walwyn family, 189
Walweyn, John, 41
Walwyn, Jane, 138
Walwyn, Richard, and Thomas (died 1532), and Fulke, 149
Wapley Hill, 170, 181
Ward and Hughes, 219
Wardour House, 217
Warehouse, The, Fownhope, 62
Wargart Engineering, 37
Warham, 28
Waring, Joanna, 205
Warlow Farm, 56
Warren Farm, 14
Warrington, W., 22, 183
Wars of the Roses, 44, 70, 92, 108, 146
Washing Pool, 159
Water meadows, 131; Lugg, 225-6
Water mills at:
  Aymestry, 17,
  Bagburrow, 18
  Bin Mills, 213
  Cloddock, 40
  Pembridge, Leen Farm, 158
  Stoke Lacy, 185
Water-works at:
  Hampton Court, 67
  Kington, 96
  Peterchurch, 162

Staunton-on-Arrow, 182
Waterloo, 99
Waterloo Cottage, 91
Wathen, James, 79
Watkins, Alfred, 66, 79
Watling Street, 107, 146; also see Roman remains
Watson, F.H. and T.M., 217
Waum's Well, 41
Way End Street, 55; Sunnyside, 55 Cottage, *57*
Weale, Pat, 209
Weare, Col. Thomas, 67
Weatherley, W.J., 66
Weaver, Robert, 17
Weaver's Hospital, 70
Webb, E.H., 50
Webbe's Almshouses, 171
Webber, Andrew Lloyd, 183
Webtree, 10
Wegg-Prosser family, and F.R.,
Weir, The, Kenchester, 28, 34, 87; New Weir, 87
Weirend, 162
Wellbrook Manor, 161
Wellbrook Wood, 122
Welleford, 199
Wellington, 202; quarry, 203
Wellington, Alice, 10
Wellington Brook, 92, 202
Wellington Coppice, 68
Wellington, General, the Duke of, 55
Wellington Heath, 203
Wellington Wood, 48
Welsh Bicknor, 205
Welsh Court, 225
Welsh customs in Arkenfield, 13
Welsh Foy, 62
Welsh Newton, 200, 205; road to Kentchurch, 206
Welsh Old Harp Inn, 173
Welsh white cattle, 227
Welson, Lower, 55
Weobley, 95, 206, *208;* Marsh, 209
Weola, 202
Wergin's Stone, 189
Wern Derris, 139
Weslyan Chapel, Kingswood, 94
Wessington Court, 221
West Country, 189
West End Farm, Docklow, 48
West Foy, 62
West, Frederick, 150
West Hills, 217
West, J. and M., 189,121, 218
West Malvern, 40
West Norwood Cemetry, 62
West Virginia, 185
Westbrook, 40
Westcope, Charles, 130
Westfalling, Thomas, 173

Westfields, Huntington near Hereford, 84
Westfields, Pencombe, 159
West Field, Kingsland, 91
Westhide, 210; Westhide Wood and badger tale, 210
Westington Court, 66
Westmacott, Richard, 91
Westminster Abbey, 219
Weston Beggard, 210; blacksmiths, 238
Weston Court, 158
Weston Cross, 211
Weston Cross Inn, 211
Weston, Henry, 151
Weston's Cider, 151
Weston-u-Penyard, 200, 211
Westwood Industrial Estate, 165
Whall, Christopher, 33
Wharf, The, Lyonshall, 133
Wharh House, Monkhide, 142
Wharton Bank, 62
Wharton Court, 60
Whatton family, 209
Wheatstone, Leintwardine, 107
Wheelbarrow Castle, 110, 186
Wheelwright's Arms, Pencombe, 159
Whetstone, 96
Whirl-holes, legend, 104
Whitbourne, 147, 191, 214
Whitchurch, 134, 184, 214, 238 church, *184*
White Book of Rhydderch, 96
White Cross, 75
Whitecross, 55
White Crow belief, 129
White Hart, Aston Crews, 102
Whitehill, Sarnesfield,177
Whitehill, Weobley, 209
White House Farm, Brinsop, 32
White House, Eaton Bishop, 56
Whitehouse, Laysters, 100
White House, Ocle Pychard, 154
White House Farm, St. Margaret's, 175
Whitehouse Farm, Tupsley, 175
White House, The, Turnastone, 195, fertility rite, 197
Whiteladies, 183
White Lion, Leominster, 108
White Rocks, 64. 88; legend of, 155
White Stone, Withington, 219
White, Thurcyl, 202
Whitfield, 94, 222
Whitfield House, Hereford, 228
Whitland, Carmarthen, 83
Whitney-on-Wye, 215; toll bridge, *180*
Whitney Wood Pottery, 215
Whittaker, Roger, 201
Whittern, The, 134

Whittington, Dick, Lord Mayor of London, 179
Whitton, 107
Whooping cough cures:
  Kingstone, 94
  Almeley, 12
  Eyton, 60
  King's Pyon, 92
  Orcop, 155
  Pembridge, 159
  Withington, 219
Why Oh Wye? poem, 109
Wicton Farm, 26
Wife-selling, 75
Wicga, 217
Wigga, 175
Wiggins, Henry, 78, 82
Wigingamore, 216
Wigmore, 107, 111,177, 196, *215,* 217; Abbey, 9, 107, 201, *216*; Castle, 25, 106, 111, *196,*
Wigmore family, 131
Wigmore Street, London, 25
Wigpool Common, 83
Wigwood Manor, Hope-u-Dinmore, 83, *115*
Wilcroft, 130
Wild Edric, 37
Wild Goose Hill, 42
Willa, 197
Willersley, 55, 217
Willey Hall, 112
Willey Old Court, 112
Willis, John, 78
William I, the Conqueror, 37, 40, 70, 112, 133, 169. 217, 234; Duke William, 58
William II, 142
William III, 84; and Mary, 21
William de Grande Sono, 187
William Rufus, King, 237
Williams, Ralph Vaughan, 16, 46, 76, 104, 142, 143, 158, 163, *175, 209*
Williams, Thomas, 217
Williams, John, estate agent, 56
Willison, Richard, 134
Wilson, Peterstow, 162
Wilton, 28, 171; Bridge, 171
Wilton Castle, 171
Wilton, Salisbury, 183
Wimpole Street, London, 203
Winchester, 157, 122
Windle Park, 68
Windmill, Blakemere, 22
Windmill Hill, 146
Window Tax, 110
Windsor, Barbara, 70
Windsor Castle, 219
Windsor Great Park, 219
Winforton, 218

Winforton Commercial Rabbits, 179
Winfrip, 218
Winnal, 10, 235; Common, 193
Windmill Hill, 142
Winney, Thomas, 78
Winsley House, 83
Winslow, 158
Winter, Paul, 211
Winter, Thomas, 79
Winter's Cross, 162
Winton, Misses de, 36
Wise man ritual, 162
Wishlade, Benjamin, 95
Wisteston Court, 137
Witch-burning, 83
Witchcraft, King's Pyon, 92
Witchery Hole, 191
Witches at Llangarren, 125
Witches' Tump, 149
Withington, 122, 210, 219; Marsh, 219
Withington Cottage, Wormbridge, 221
Witsetts, 84
Wobage Farm Pottery, 148
Wofferwood Common, 181
Wolferlow, 221; Park, 221
Wolferton Junction, 30
Wolsey, Cardinal, 41
Wolstenholme, Henry, 182
Wonder, The, 151, 169
Wood Field, Ullingswick, 198
Wood, John, 197
Wood, Susan, 99
Wood Sutton, 100
Wood Street, Allensmore, 10
Woodbrook, Kingswood, 94
Woodcroft Farm, 21
Wooden effigy, 150
Woodhampton Wood, 112
Woodhouse, Byton, 37
Woodhouse Farm, Leinthall Earls, 106
Woodhouse Farm, Wellington Heath, 203
Woodhouse, Elinore and Mary, 36 106
Woodhouse, Eliza, 91
Woodhouse, Francis, 145
Wooding Farm, 193
Woodlands, The, 149
Woodland Trust, 45
Woodmanton, 98
Woodpecker cider, 229
Woodruff, Wilford, 38
Woods, Frederick, 232
Woodsend, Ashperton, 13
Woohope, 146, 151, 221; Cockshoot, 169; Dome, 50, *114,* 143, 145, 167, 169, 179, 183, 221, 227
Woolhope Naturalist' Field Club, 17, 66, 67, 74, 220
Woonton, 12, 100
Woonton Ash, 134
Wootton, Oxon., 26
Worcester, 42, 62, 76, 157, 183, 186; bell foundry, 154, 186; cathedral, 158
Worcestershire, 76, 185; Beacon, 40
Wordsworth, William, 22, 30, 90, 100, 171, 194, 104
Working Horse Centre, 98
Working Lunch, 134
World of Butterflies, Whitchurch, 214
World's End, 99, 183
World Service, B.B.C., 153
Worm Brook, 12, 149, 165, 175, 221
Wormbridge, 48, 175, *208,* 221
Wormelow Hundred, 127
Wormelow Tump, 127, 149
Wormington, Tommy, 45
Wormsley, Priory and Grange, 222
Wren's graveyard, 169
Wrigglebrook, 147
Wulfere, 181
Wulphere, 221
Wulviva, 221
Wye, The, house, 211
Wye, River, 26, 28, 32, 33, 37, 38, 40, 46, *51,* 56, 60, 61, 62, 63, 64, *65,* 67, 70, 71, *73,* 75, 80, 82, 84, 86, 90, 130, 139, 141, 143, 145, 165, 171, 173, 178, 195, 201, 205, 214, 215, 218, 225, 228, 235; rafting (C.H.A.R.), 78; fishing, 79, 80, 90; Navigation, 201, 235; S.A.S. exercise on, *77*; suicides in, 130
Wye Rapids Hotel, 215, *220*
Wye Valley, 63, 138; Visitors' Centre, 214; Walk, 84
Wye Fruit Farm Ltd., 104
Wye Inn, 130
Wyastone Leys, 63
Wyatville, Sir Jeffrey, 67
Wyatt, T.H., 26
Wych Elm grafts, Stoke Prior, 186
Wycherley, Malcolm, 41
Wycliffe, John, 12, 231
Wylde, The, 106
Wymarc, Robert son of, 193
Wynd's Point, 41
Wyre Forest, 173, 211, 215
Wyson Common, 30
Wythall, Upper, 201
Wyvern (dragon), 145

Y

Y Crwys, Goodrich, 66
Yapp, Sir Arthur Keysall, 157
Yare, Woolhope, 221
Yarkhill, 222
Yarpole, 223
Yatt, 153
Yatton, 106, 223; Court, 17; Wood, 62
Yazor, 22, 55, 225, 232; Brook, 84, 86
Yeld, Ellen, 142
Yeld, The, 133
Yerne, Edmund, 201
Yew trees, ancient at Dinmore Manor, 48; Much Marcle, 149
Yew Tree Cottage, Dilwyn, 46
Yew Tree Inn, Peterstow, 162
Yew Tree Inn, Preston-on-Wye, 165
Y.M.C.A., 157
Ynr, King of Gwent, 126
Yorkist emblems, 147
Young, Francis Brett, 183
Yule Log, 94

Z

Ziggy, 236
Zulu Wars, 94

A GUIDE TO HEREFORDSHIRE

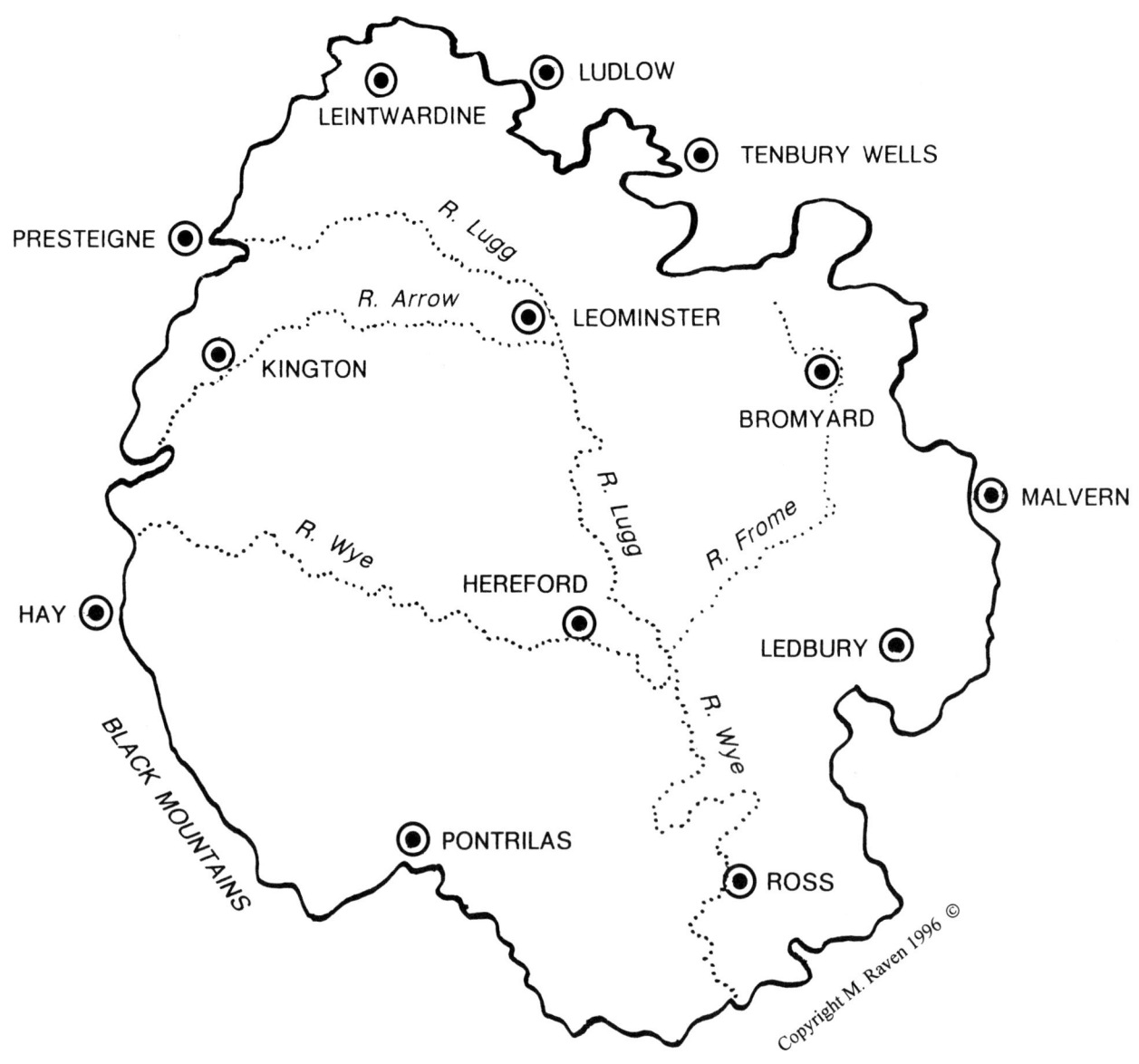

Map of Herefordshire showing the principal settlements of the county and its borders which are used as reference points in the gazetteeer.

MICHAEL RAVEN - LIST OF RECORDINGS

1966	*Black Country Three*, EP, Wolverhampton Folksong Club
	Black Country Three, LP, Transatlantic TRA 140
	Guitar Magic, Transatlantic, LP, TRA XTRA 1046
1968	*Songs of the Black Country and the West Midlands*, Broadside, LP, BRO 100
1970	*Lass from the Low Country*, Roman Head, LP, RH 021
1971	*Kate of Coalbrookdale*, Argo (Decca), LP, ZFB 29
1972	*Death and the Lady*, Folk Heritage, LP, FHR 047
1973	*Gipsy, A Variety of Guitar Music*, Cambrian, LP, SCLP 610
1974	*The Jolly Machine*, Folk Heritage, LP, FHR
	Hymn to Che Guevara, Folk Heritage, LP, FHR 054
	A Shropshire Lad, Penrhyn Castle and Stoke recordings, cassette
1977	*A Miscellany of Guitar Music*, Broadside, LP, BRO 124
1980	*Reynardine Tapes*, cassette
	Che Guevara, Big Bear, single, BB 31
	The Dutch Connection, inc. Munich Record recordings of 1976, cassette
	Folk Heritage Recordings, cassette
	Untitled Collection of Folksongs, cassette
1982	*Popular Songs for Guitar*, Books 1 and 2, cassette
	Popular Tunes for Guitar, Books 1 and 2, cassette
	A Variety of Guitar Music 2 / A Chant of Falsity, cassette
1983	*English Folk Guitar 2*, cassette
	Popular Music for Guitar, cassette
1984	*A Variety of Guitar Music 3*, cassette
	English Folk Guitar 3, cassette
1990	*Music for Guitar 1*, original pieces, cassette
	Music for Guitar 2 ..
	Music for Guitar 3 ..
	Music for Guitar 4 ..
	English Aires and Dances ..
1991	*Michael Raven : Guitar Music 1*, cassette
	Michael Raven : Guitar Music 2 ..
	Michael Raven : Guitar Music 3 ..
	Michael Raven : Guitar Music 4 ..
1992	*Soulton Hall*, solo guitar music, cassette
	Delbury Dervish ..
	Lucy's Frolic ..
	Wizard Beguildy ..
	Silent Field ..
	Star of Belle Isle ..
	Songs and Solos, CD
1994	*A Shropshire Lad*, Penrhyn Castle and Ashley recordings, CD
1995	*Recital* (English Folk Guitar 4), CD
	Flowers of Picardy, CD
	Retrospective, solo guitar, includes An English Collection, CD
	Taming the Dragon's Strings, solo guitar and poetry, CD
	Reynardine Tapes, 1980 recordings plus new duo material, CD
	Welsh Guitar, recorded 1994, CD
1996	*Songs and Dances of Herefordshire*, CD

Except where otherwise stated all recordings were
published by Michael Raven.
Appearances on compilation samplers produced by Broadside,
Transatlantic (Castle Recordings), and Folk Heritage have not
been included.

Of the 48 titles listed four involve partial duplication of old recordings on to CD.